Recent Social Trends in West Germany 1960-1990

Comparative Charting of Social Change
Series Editor: Simon Langlois

Wolfgang Glatzer, Karl Otto Hondrich
Heinz-Herbert Noll, Karin Stiehr, Barbara Wörndl

Recent Social Trends in West Germany 1960–1990

Campus Verlag · Frankfurt am Main
McGill-Queen's University Press
Montreal & Kingston · London · Buffalo

Canadian Cataloguing in Publication Data
Main entry under title:
Recent Social Trends in West Germany
1960–1990
(Comparative charting of social change,
ISSN 1183–1952)

Prepared for the International Research Group on the
Comparative Charting of Social Change in Industrial
Societies.
Includes index.
ISBN 0-7735-0909-7

1. Germany (West)–Social conditions. I. Glatzer,
Wolfgang II. International Research Group on the
Comparative Charting of Social Change in Advanced Industrial Societies. III. Series.

HN445.5.R33 1992 943.087 C92-090284-7

Die Deutsche Bibliothek - CIP-Einheitsaufnahme

Recent social trends in West Germany: 1960 - 1990 / Wolfgang
Glatzer ... - Frankfurt am Main : Campus Verlag ; Montreal ;
Kingston ; London ; Buffalo : McGill-Queen's Univ. Press,
1992
(Comparative charting of social change)
ISBN 3-593-34402-5 (Campus Verlag)
ISBN 0-7735-0909-7 (McGill-Queen's Univ. Press)
NE: Glatzer, Wolfgang

Published simultaneously in Canada and the United States
by McGill-Queen's University Press
Legal deposit third quarter 1992
Bibliothèque nationale du Québec
Printed in Germany

Contents

Acknowledgements

This volume is part of an international comparative enterprise which presents relevant sociological information about social change in different industrialized societies in a relatively standardized manner. The 78 social trends in this volume concern West Germany. The approach was developed by the International Group for Comparative Charting of Social Change. The preface written by Theodore Caplow for the first volume of this series (which follows these acknowledgements) describes the history of the group, its composition, and the purposes and criteria of the collective effort.

The research work was carried out at the Johann Wolfgang Goethe-Universität, Frankfurt am Main, mainly within the Fachbereich Gesellschaftswissenschaften. In addition to Wolfgang Glatzer and Karl Otto Hondrich, the German research team comprised Karin Stiehr and Barbara Wörndl for the first phase of the work. Renate Hornung-Draus and Heinz-Herbert Noll, who is the director of the Social Indicators Department of ZUMA at Mannheim, later joined the group. These were the principal authors of the 78 trends. For a number of trends we invited specialists and we gained as authors Johann Behrens, Mathias Bös, Bernhard Engel, Claudia Koch-Arzberger, Jürgen Kohl, Heiner Meulemann, Jakob Schissler, Jürgen Schumacher, and Karin Seibel.

In the editing stage much of the voluminous work was performed by Mathias Bös, assisted by Jürgen Beule and our secretary, Usch Büchner. Translation assistance was provided by Kenda Willey, Birgit Ghaznavi, and Käthe Roth. We wish to express our gratitude to these persons and institutions who provided us with data and with advice. We are grateful to the many people involved in this project, especially our colleagues from France, Québec, the United States, Spain, and Greece. Without their commitment and stimulation, this project would not have been realized. We also extend our thanks to the Werner Reimers Stiftung, which generously allowed usto hold meetings in its institution on two occasions.

These trend reports are a first step toward international comparisons. The International Group for Comparative Charting of Social Change will continue its work by adding trend reports from other societies, as well as substantial comparative studies.

Wolfgang Glatzer and Karl Otto Hondrich

Preface

Recent Social Trends in West Germany 1960–1990 is the next volume in a series. Similar volumes describing recent social trends in France, the United States, and Quebec are already published or will be published later this year, and other countries, beginning with Spain, will be covered in subsequent years.

These national profiles of social change all have the same format. Each consists of 78 trend reports grouped under 17 main topics, and the sequence of reports – from 0.1, "Demographic Trends," to 17.5 Trends in "National Identity" – is identical for each profile.

The object of this exercise is to provide appropriate data bases for cross-national comparison of recent social trends. That work is well underway. A collection of papers comparing trends in the family, in the workplace, in social movements, in conflict resolution, and in value systems will be published in the same series in the near future.

The collective author of the series goes by the mellifluous name of the International Research Group on the Comparative Charting of Social Change. It is an entirely voluntary organization that evolved out of an informal collaborative relationship established in the 1970s between a group investigating social change in French communities called the Observation de Changement Social and a concurrent American effort known as the Middletown III project. The first formal work session of the Comparative Charting Group convened in Paris in May of 1987. Subsequent work sessions were held at Bad Homburg in May of 1988, in Quebec City in December of 1988, in Charlottesville in May of 1989, in Nice in December of 1989, in Madrid in July of 1990, in Bad Homburg in December of 1990, and at the Greek island of Siros in June of 1991. The scholarly yield of the project has increased with each session.

The Comparative Charting Group is divided into national teams. It includes historians, political scientists, and economists, although the majority are sociologists. The team coordinators are Henri Mendras for France, Wolfgang Glatzer and Karl Otto Hondrich for West Germany, Simon Langlois for Quebec, Theodore Caplow for the United States, Sebastian del Campo for Spain, and Constantin Tsoucalas for Greece. Applications from several other national teams are pending. For the purposes of this project, Quebec is treated as a national society.

The participation of individual scholars in the national teams, and of the national teams in the international group, is entirely voluntary. Simon Langlois and the Institut Québécois pour Recherche sur la Culture provide the project with a highly efficient secretariat, but there is no executive authority at all. Each national team is responsible for its own funding and internal operations. Work is assigned and deadlines are set by consensus at the semi-annual work sessions. This loose organization has worked so exceedingly well that we are tempted to propose it as a model for other international projects of social research.

The general purposes of this collective effort are to prepare a comprehensive, numerically grounded description of recent social trends in advanced industrial societies; to identify similarities and differences among these national societies with respect to ongoing social trends; to subject these similarities and differences to comparative analysis; to develop a nontraditional model of social change to accommodate these data; and to establish benchmarks for future tracking of social trends.

The data module of this project is a trend report. Each trend report covers one of the 78 numbered topics in the List of Trends and Indicators developed by the Comparative Charting Group in a revision of the classification originally proposed by Louis Dirn. Most trend reports present and interpret multiple trends related to the designated topic. A trend report has four sections: an abstract of findings, an explanatory text, a collection of statistical tables or charts, and a bibliography of sources.

The trends described in these reports are empirical and quantitative. They are based on time series of good quality, quality being measured by explicit criteria. To be used in a trend report, a series must consist of empirical enumerations or measurements, must refer to an entire national society or to a representative sample of it, must cover a period of least ten years and end no earlier than 1983, must include data for three or more points or intervals of time recorded contemporaneously, must be amenable to independent verification, and must be replicable in the same national society and in other national societies.

The factual emphasis is fundamental. No trend is included that is not known with practical certainty, and no directionality is asserted without empirical data. Often, we have located studies of these tendencies by other scholars and used them to challenge or buttress our own interpretations. At all times, these empirical predilections keep alive the happy possibility that what we find may surprise us. And indeed it often has.

Our preference for relatively hard data restricts most of the trend reports to recent decades, since many interesting statistical series do not go back very far or lose reliability as they recede to earlier years. There are some happy exceptions; in demography and macro-economics, for example, we have an abundance of good data from the nineteenth century and some from the eighteenth. But the work has progressed, it has become increasingly clear that a sharp focus on the period 1960 – 1990 is appropriate as well as expedient. For reasons that may vary somewhat from country to country, an astonishing number of social trends show a point of inflection close to 1960, and the thirty-year period following 1960 has seemed to exhibit exceptional coherence.

It should be emphasized that the tendencies documented in these national profiles are not merely interpretations of the quantitative series. They reflect an underlying sense of social theory and of social reality that goes far beyond the raw data. The themes we have chosen, our methods of examining the available indicators, our decisions about selective emphasis among the evidence at hand, and our estimation of the significance or insignificance of observed trends constitute an intellectual structure derived from diverse national and disciplinary perspectives.

The present volume is intended primarily as a reference manual. It is meant to be consulted on particular points. Few readers will want to read it straight through, although this can be done and has been found enjoyable. What we present here is source material for the analysis and understanding of recent social change in one country, gathered for our own purpose of cross-national comparison but potentially useful for many other purposes.

The publication of these national profiles marks the beginning, rather than the end, of the intellectual enterprise for which the Comparative Charting Group was formed. Our aim is to construct a better model of social change in the modern world than has heretofore been available.

When we met in Paris in 1987 to establish permanent connections among the ongoing investigations of social change that had occupied us in our respective countries during the previous decade, we were aware that although our separate studies had attracted a fair amount of scholarly and popular attention, they had not advanced our understanding of contemporary industrial societies as much as they should have, for want of a comparative perspective. Without systematic international comparisons, it is impossible to determine whether the trends we discover in a particular national society are local accidents or features of a larger system.

We were specifically interested in the late twentieth century, the major industrial countries, and the social structure and institutional patterns that characterize the behaviour of large populations, especially those associated with the family, work, leisure, religion, education, government, politics, and voluntary associations. As we compared our separate bodies of work, we had the impression of being surrounded by the bits and pieces of a new theoretical model waiting to be assembled, a model that does not require social change to resemble scientific-technological progress, that takes the future to be open rather than pre-ordained, and that acknowledges the mixture of objective and subjective elements in social reality.

The construction of national profiles in comparable form was a preliminary task that had to be done in order to prepare for the construction of such a model. But in preparing these trend reports, we learned a great deal we had not previously known about the condition of industrial societies in the late twentieth century. We trust that our readers will find them equally instructive.

Theodore Caplow

Introduction

The objective of this study is to identify main trends of social and cultural change in West Germany. "Trends" are not primarily described in statistical terms but are rather understood as ongoing developments of special dimensions in the social process. They differ in respect to direction, speed, intensity, or simultaneity. Trends are a construction from the social research process based on empirical evidence and theoretical knowledge; they are judgements including data, social indicators, interpretations, and theory.

An approach such as this one is often confronted with questions concerning the theory behind and the reliability of the data. We are not aiming at developing theories, but we do exploit existing theories insofar as they give information about ongoing trends in this society. As well, we do not rely strictly on statistical data; we think that in most cases soft data are better than no data, and that data both stimulate and control speculation in theorizing.

As already described, this approach developed from cooperation of some research groups with similar interests but different traditions: In the beginning there were Henry Mendras and his Louis Dirn group in France, Ted Caplow and his Middletown Study group in the United States, and Wolfgang Glatzer and Karl Otto Hondrich with their working group on social change at the University of Frankfurt. Since the early 1970s Wolfgang Glatzer has worked in the context of the social-indicators movement. In 1974, the first edition of the *Sociological Almanac* was published – a handbook of social data and indicators for West Germany (Ballerstedt & Glatzer, 1975). Later, the research group *Microanalytical Foundations of Society* published an empirical investigation, *Lebensbedingungen in der Bundesrepublik* (Zapf, 1977) and extended this approach in *Quality of Life in the FRG* (Glatzer & Zapf, 1984). In 1987, a *German Social Report* subtitled *Living Conditions and Subjective Well-being* 1978 – 1984 was published (Zapf, 1987). On the other hand, Karl Otto Hondrich investigated social change from the perspective of social differentiation (Hondrich, 1982) in politics, work, and the family, with particular emphasis on stability and change of needs and values (Hondrich & Vollmer, 1983). Heinz-Herbert Noll, director of the Social Indicators Department of ZUMA, Mannheim, also collaborated in the above mentioned research on living conditions and the quality of life and contributed reports on social change in the labour market and working conditions.

When we began, Germany consisted of two states, the Federal Republic of Germany (FRG) in the West, and the German Democratic Republic (GDR) in the East. In 1991, as a result of the collapse of the state socialism in Eastern Europe and the disintegration of the Iron Curtain, the German states were unified. The Eastern part lost its political and economic institutions and became affiliated to the West. As a consequence, the Federal Republic of Germany was enlarged from 11 to 16 Bundesländer; its population grew from 61 to 79 million.

This unique historical event accounts for a special characteristic of this book: in contrast to the other volumes of this series, it covers the story of the society associated with a state, the "old" Bundesrepublik, almost from its beginning to its end. Officially, the FRG was founded in 1949. Most of the trends reported in this volume go back to this date. (In this respect, the book often fulfils more than its title promises).

Many of the social trends of the last four decades are common to West European and North American industrial societies. Among them are a great increase in per-capita consumption of consumer goods, but also in recent decades an increase of relative poverty; a spectacular improvement in machinery and equipment used both in industry and in private households; a decrease in time spent on formal employment and an increase of leisure activities and household production; a massive shift from blue-collar to white-collar employment; dissolution of old class loyalties and individualization of life styles; a vast expansion of secondary and higher education; a legitimation of unmarried, consensual unions; relaxation of long-established taboos against promiscuity and homosexuality; institutionalization of new taboos such as those against violence in the family, discrimination against women, racism, environmental damage, and so on; the institutionalization of social movements such as feminism and environmentalism; and a decline in political extremism.

Some of the trends common to most industrial societies are more pronounced in West Germany than elsewhere, for instance, the priority given to economic goals such as increasing productivity and reducing inflation. In some other trends, like the movement of married women with dependent children into the labour force, West Germany has lagged somewhat.

Finally, there are some fields of social change in which the "old" FRG had developed pecularities with respect to other industrial societies, but also with respect to prewar Germany. They are attributable to the three-fold shock that Germany suffered as a consequence of National Socialist crimes and the war: first, the destruction not only of military and economic resources, but also of collective moral integrity; second, the separation of the country into two parts, and the loss of eastern territories being incorporated into Poland and the Soviet Union; third, the occupation by the Allied forces.

As a result of those shocks, West Germany gained new institutions which, ironically, turned out not to weaken but to strengthen the country economically and politically. Among those were the "social market economy" (Soziale Marktwirtschaft), the welfare state, parliamentary democracy with strong federal elements, a confederated labour union (Einheitsgewerkschaft) and co-determination (Mitbestimmung). The latter was destined to change German heavy industry by giving unions a voice in managerial decisions, in the plants as well as on the board. It developed into a distinctive German style of industrial relations and conflict resolution. In addition to its traditionally high level of formal preparation, German labour acquired responsibility and influence that enabled it to escape from the class society more easily than labour elsewhere.

Besides the institutionalization of industrial conflict, there developed, in the 1960s and 1970s, a political culture in which social movements developed unconventional forms of political action. Strangely, this trend did not weaken, but strengthened the legitimacy of the parliamentary system. As compared with the disruptive effects of political conflicts in the past, the utilization of the integrative functions of industrial and political conflict was an innovation in German collective experience.

This was accompanied by other innovations in the value system: the fading away of nationalism, militarism, power politics, authoritarianism, utopian idealism, and a corresponding rise of Euro-cosmopolitism, pacifism, economic liberalism, permissiveness, and pragmatism. In light of the past, this marks a more dramatic change in German collective identity than in the identity of any other industrial societies – with, perhaps, the exception of Japan.

These shifts in West German value priorities did not appear abruptly and immediately after the war. There was a "value push" toward post-materialism in the 1960s and 1970s, under the impact of new technologies, increasing wealth, and the gradual transformation of social structures. Nevertheless, the learning entailed by these developments was prepared and intensified by the breakdown and discrediting of old social structures and collective self-images. Germany experienced "learning by failure" – paralleled only in the case of Japan. However, as West Germany became a success story, East Germany, in the grip of the Soviet imperium, continued to exist in relative deprivation and came to another climactic failure in 1990. By now it has become evident that state socialism, far from representing an alternative and perhaps superior form of modernization, had the unintended effect of keeping societies backward.

To West Germans, looking at East Germany at the moment of unexpected unification was like looking in a mirror and seeing one's own image of 20 or 30 years before. The same grimy decayed houses, vegetable gardens, badly paved narrow roads, outmoded technology, smoky air and bad smells, proletarian clothing and mentality, antagonistic class consciousness, working-class authoritarianism, the xenophobic prejudice of an ethnically homogeneous and relatively closed population. These were things and mentalities that adults in West Germany had almost forgotten. All of a sudden, West Germans became aware how far they had progressed during the past three decades toward a prosperous, technologically developed, ecologically minded, pluralistic, permissive, open society which had incorporated, without serious problems, five million people from other cultures.

This confrontation made for a strange shift in the West German self-image. The same intellectuals who had criticized their country for the postwar "restoration" of old capitalistic structures now discovered that its liberal, democratic, and cosmopolitan character had to be protected in the unification process. Where collective identity is concerned, much depends on the comparisons one makes or that are forced upon one!

As Mark Twain said, we should beware of making predictions, particularly those about the future. Concerning unified Germany, some foretold a resurrection of a powerful nation-state and the resurgence of older, illiberal attitudes which, to a certain degree, had survived in the GDR. Those apprehensions have to be taken seriously. Like it or not, the FRG will become more powerful not only because it has become larger, but also because its postwar period of imposed (and enjoyed!) powerlessness has ended. On the other hand, the increase in power is incorporated into, and restricted by, new supranational institutions, particularly the European Community and NATO.

The possibility that modern structures and mentalities in West Germany will be eroded and compromised by more backward ones in the East seems to be contradicted by the undeniable dominance of the West and the attractiveness of Western life styles to the East. There is nothing in the East to resist those two forces. Even those particular institutions which were considered exemplary in the GDR, such as health measures, system of kindergartens, liberal abortion laws etc. tend to be adapted to "less progressive" Western standards. Strains and tensions will be felt, but "Westernization" of the larger Germany seems irresistible.

Karl Otto Hondrich and Wolfgang Glatzer

References

Ballerstedt, Eike, and Wolfgang Glatzer
1975 *Soziologischer Almanach.* Frankfurt/New York: Campus.

Glatzer, Wolfgang, and Wolfgang Zapf, eds.
1984 *Lebensqualität in der Bundesrepublik Deutschland.* Frankfurt/New York: Campus.

Hondrich, Karl Otto, ed.
1982 *Soziale Differenzierung. Langzeitanalysen zum Wandel von Politik, Arbeit und Familie.* Frankfurt/New York: Campus.

Hondrich, Karl Otto, and Randolph Vollmer, eds.
1983 *Bedürfnisse. Stabilität und Wandel.* Opladen: Westdeutscher Verlag.

Zapf, Wolfgang ed.
1977 *Lebensbedingungen in der Bundesrepublik.* Frankfurt/New York: Campus.

Zapf, Wolfgang, ed.
1987 *German Social Report.* Social Indicators Research, No. 1, Vol. 19.

0. Context

0.1 Demographic Trends

The number of residents of the Federal Republic of Germany underwent a marked increase in the first two decades of its existence and has changed only slightly since then. The birth-rate deficit, setting in as of 1972, has up to now been compensated for by immigration of foreign workers. The age-structure pattern within the German population has led to prognoses of a "superannuation" of society.

In 1949, 49.2 million people lived in the Federal Republic of Germany. The population had grown to 61.2 million by 1987, with a peak of over 62 million in 1974 (see table 1).

Two factors are important for analysis of population development: the numerical relation of births to deaths and that of immigration to emigration. The population growth between 1949 and 1961 was equally the result of birth and immigration surplusses, and between 1961 and 1968 it was largely (by two-thirds) the result of birth surplusses. Since 1972, however, more people have been dying than have been born in the Federal Republic. The minor, unsteady population growth over the past 20 years is therefore due to considerable immigration rates (Korte, 1983).

This briefly sketched macro-pattern has had various repercussions in the demographic, social, economic, and political arenas. The numerical strength of each generation presents an influential factor for the next century. Other determinants are marriage and generative behaviour, child mortality, crisis situations, and migration behaviour. The respectively significant contexts will be illustrated here using characteristic phases in West German history.

The Postwar Period

According to official statistical data, as many as 6 million more people were living here in 1949 as were living in an area of corresponding size in 1939 (this in spite of millions of war victims).

> The increase . . . was almost exclusively due to immigrant displaced persons and refugees. They came from the region east of the Oder and Neisse [rivers], and also from regions of southeastern and eastern Europe traditionally settled by people of German descent. In addition, about 250,000 of the 8 million forced labourers at the end of the war (2 million prisoners of war, 6 million civilians) did not or could not return to their home countries. (Korte, 1983, p. 14)

In 1946, 20.8 million men and 25.7 million women were living in the four occupied zones. The surplus of women was reduced by the return of prisoners of war, but an approximate balance in gender ratio came about only over a long period of time: while the proportion of women in 1955 was considerably higher in all age groups except among those under 20 years old, by 1985 there was a noticeable surplus of women only among those over 65 years old (Statistisches Bundesamt, 1987a).

From the Founding of the Federal Republic to the Mid-1960s

Birth surplusses, to different degrees, were the rule in these years. At the beginning of the 1950s, the birth rate, at about 15 live births per 1,000 persons, lay below that of the immediate postwar period (see figure 1). Due to the dearth of young men as a result of the war, fewer marriages were entered into and the marriage age was relatively high. On the other hand, the mortality rate (number of deaths per 1,000 persons) was especially low. It was 10.5 in 1950, a rate that was never reached again in the Federal Republic (see table 2). The low mortality rate of the 1950s can be explained by that fact that many people had not reached their normal life expectancy in the preceding years, but had died during the war.

Not until the mid-1950s, after the postwar misery had faded, did a clear increase in the birth rate take place, reaching a peak in 1963 at 18.3 children per 1,000 persons (figure 1). This development stands in conjunction with a growing number of marriages as children born during the high-birth-rate years 1934 to 1939 came of marriageable age, and with a declining average marriage age, particularly among women. As the mortality rate increased only gradually, a surplus of births continued up to the mid-1960s.

The migration balance in these years – apart from the period during the Korean War, when many left the country for fear of a third world war – was consistently positive. Three-and-a-half million people came from the German

Democratic Republic alone, a stream of refugees that ended abruptly in 1961, after the erection of the Berlin Wall and the subsequent closure of the entire border with the German Democratic Republic. This period saw the beginning of a phase of immigration of foreign workers (called *Gastarbeiter*, meaning guest workers) – first Italian, then Spaniards, Greeks, and, since 1968, Turks. In 1966, 1.3 million foreign workers lived in the Federal Republic, most with temporary job contracts. Since the majority of them were comparatively young and had not yet sent for their families, they influenced the migration statistics without having much effect on the birth and mortality statistics. The economic-boom years witnessed the most immigration; the recession years, the least. There was a positive migration balance totalling over 1 million from 1962 to 1966, but the recession of 1967 showed a migration deficit of more than 200,000 persons. With the rise in unemployment, the number of foreign workers was reduced by over 300,000 (Korte, 1983).

From the Mid-1960s to 1990

Lasting changes in generative behaviour have taken place in the past two decades. First, the children born during the low-birth-rate years of the war and the postwar period came of marriage age, so the number of marriages dwindled continuously up to the early 1980s and the average marriage age started increasing. The turning point in the fertility trend, known as the "baby bust" of 1964, led to a mortality surplus, starting in 1972, which was detrimental to natural population growth (see figure 2). Though those born in the strong "baby boom" years have meanwhile reached marriage age and have slowed the downward slide, they have not turned this trend around. Since 1980, the number of live births has been stable at an average of about 10 per 1,000 persons.

Immigration by foreign workers is therefore the reason for the fairly constant population size. After the recession of 1967 to 1974, their numbers bounced back from 1.9 million to 4.1 million, then, as new economic difficulties arose and new hiring from abroad was prohibited, receded temporarily. In 1982, as a result of family members coming to the Federal Republic and the strong influx of asylum-seekers, the number of immigrants reached a peak of nearly 4.7 million. The slightly declining tendencies of 1983 and 1984 – the result of a now-defunct law offering financial incentives to foreigners returning to their home countries, and of the tightening of rules for granting asylum – have been compensated for by more family members joining foreign workers in the Federal Republic and by more applications for asylum. Since 1980, foreign citizens have comprised more than 7% of the population; in 1961, this proportion was only 1.2% (see table 3, figure 3). Interest in naturalization remains slight.

The birth surplus among foreigners in West Germany has compensated somewhat for the overall deficit, although even here decreasing tendencies caused by adjustment and adaptation can be distinguished. In 1974, every sixth child born in West Germany was of foreign descent; currently this proportion has dropped to every eleventh child (Statistisches Bundesamt, 1987a).

Prognoses Regarding Population Development

The declining birth numbers have concerned scientists and politicians for several years. The "baby boom" was at first seen as a turning point universal to all industrialized nations, but is now comprehended as a deviation from the century-old declining fertility trend (figure 1). Warnings about the negative consequences of this trend for the social-security system, economic growth, health care, and the educational system are closely associated with allusions to the threat of a superannuated society.

The changes become especially clear in a long-term perspective. In 1925, children under 15 years of age comprised 25% of the total population, but only 15% in 1985. In contrast, the over-65-years age group has grown from 6% to 15%. In 1925, the number of children under 15 was four times that of people over 65; it was only twice as high in 1955, and was down to an equal proportion by 1985 (Statistisches Bundesamt, 1987b).

Graphic representation of the age structure as a pyramid had lost validity by 1930. The fertility lapses during both world wars and the world depression left notches that give it the form of a wind-blown weather vane. If a continuation of the decrease in mortality (for increases in average life expectancy, see table 4) and of the 1984 birth incidence are presumed, barely 55 million Germans will be living in the Federal Republic in the year 2000. A population of 43 million can be projected for 2030, of whom 38% will be older than 59 years of age (Statistisches Bundesamt, 1987a; see figure 4). These predictions are made independently of migration movements of foreigners, which are heavily influenced by political and economic factors and are difficult to foresee.

Karin Stiehr

References

Abelshauser, Werner
1987 *Die langen fünfziger Jahre. Wirtschaft und Gesellschaft der Bundesrepublik Deutschland 1949-1966*. Düsseldorf: Schwann.

Bade, Klaus J.
1983 *Vom Auswanderungsland zum Einwanderungsland? Deutschland 1880-1980*. Berlin: Colloquium.

Köllmann, Wolfgang
1983 "Die Bevölkerungsentwicklung der Bundesrepublik." In Werner Conze, and M. Rainer Lepsius, eds., *Sozialgeschichte der Bundesrepublik Deutschland. Beiträge zum Kontinuitätsproblem*. Stuttgart: Klett-Cotta.

Korte, Hermann
1983 "Bevölkerungsstruktur und -entwicklung." In Wolfgang Benz, ed., *Die Bundesrepublik Deutschland*. Vol. 2. Frankfurt am Main: Fischer.

Schmid, Josef
1984 *Bevölkerungsveränderungen in der Bundesrepublik Deutschland. Eine Revolution auf leisen Sohlen*. Stuttgart/Berlin/Köln/Mainz: Kohlhammer.

Statistisches Bundesamt, ed.
1987a *Datenreport 1987*. Bonn: Bundeszentrale für politische Bildung.

–, ed.
1987b *Von den zwanziger zu den achtziger Jahren. Ein Vergleich der Lebensverhältnisse der Menschen*. Wiesbaden/Mainz: Kohlhammer.

–, ed.
1988 *Statistisches Jahrbuch 1988 für die Bundesrepublik Deutschland*. Stuttgart/Mainz: Kohlhammer.

Table 1
Population development

Year	Population	
	1,000	per km[2]
1946[1]	46,190	186
1950	49,989	203
1955	52,382	211
1960	55,433	223
1965	59,619	236
1970	60,651	244
1975	61,829	249
1980	61,566	248
1985	61,024	245
1987	61,170	-

1. Including persons in prisoner-of-war, civilian-retainment, and refugee camps, with the exception of Hamburg, Bremen, Saarland, and West Berlin, excluding foreigners in IRO (International Refugee Organization) camps.

Source: Statistisches Bundesamt, 1988, p. 50.

Table 2
Marriages, births, and deaths

Year	Per 1,000 persons				Per 1,000 live births	
	Marriages	Live Births	Deaths[1]	Surplus of births (+) deaths (-)	Out-of-wedlock live births	Infant deaths in first year of life
1950	10.7	16.2	10.5	+5.7	97.3	55.3
1955	8.8	15.7	11.1	+4.5	78.6	41.9
1960	9.4	17.4	11.6	+5.9	63.3	33.8
1965	8.3	17.7	11.5	+6.2	46.9	23.8
1970	7.3	13.4	12.1	+1.3	54.6	23.4
1975	6.3	9.7	12.1	-2.4	61.2	19.7
1980	5.9	10.1	11.6	-1.5	75.6	12.7
1985	6.0	9.6	11.5	-1.9	94.0	8.9
1987[2]	6.3	10.5	11.2	-0.7	97.1	8.3

1. Excluding still births, belatedly certified war deaths, and court-issued death certifications.
2. Provisional result.

Source: Statistisches Bundesamt, 1988, p. 72.

Table 3
Foreigners in the Federal Republic of Germany since 1961

Date	Numbers in 1,000	Proportion of population in %
6.6.1961	686.2	1.2
30.9.1967	1,806.7	3.0
27.5.1970	2,600.6	4.3
30.9.1972	3,526.6	5.7
30.9.1974	4,127.4	6.7
30.9.1976	3,948.3	6.4
30.9.1978	3,981.1	6.5
30.9.1980	4,453.3	7.2
30.9.1981	4,629.7	7.5
30.9.1982	4,666.9	7.6
30.9.1983	4,534.9	7.4
30.9.1984	4,363.6	7.1
31.12.1985	4,378.9	7.2
31.12.1986	4,512.7	7.4

Source: Statistisches Bundesamt, 1987b, p. 49.

Table 4
Average life expectancy (years)

Age	1924/26[1]		1957/58		1983/85	
	Male	Female	Male	Female	Male	Female
0[2]	56	59	66	71	71	78
20	47	48	50	54	53	59
50	22	23	23	26	25	30
60	15	16	16	18	17	21
70	9	9	9	11	10	13
80	5	5	5	6	6	7
90	3	3	3	3	4	4

1. German Imperial Kingdom.
2. At time of birth.

Source: Statistisches Bundesamt, 1987a, p. 10.

Figure 1
Live births per 1,000 persons

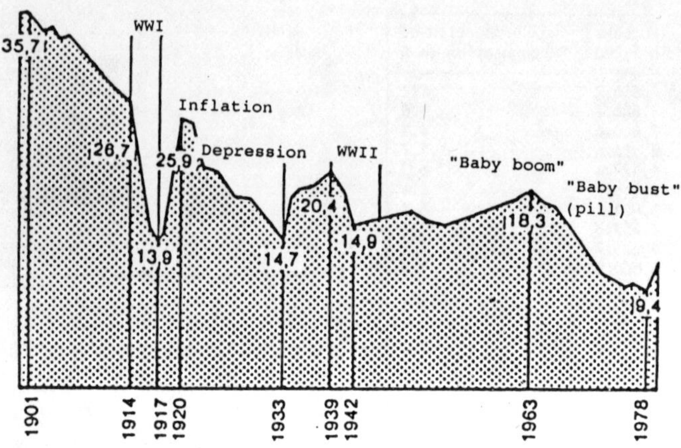

Source: Schmid, 1984, p. 25.

Figure 2
Deaths and live births since 1960 per 1,000

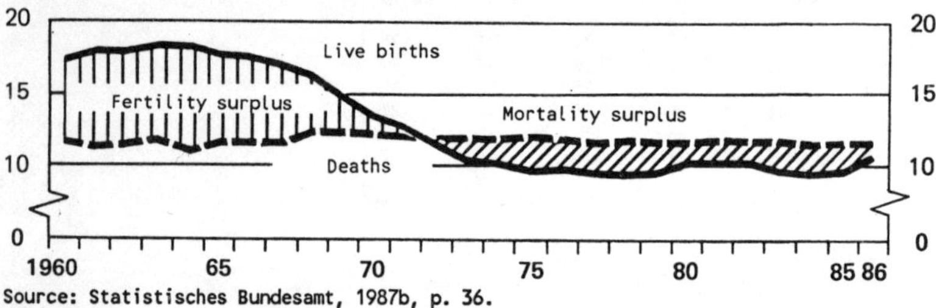

Source: Statistisches Bundesamt, 1987b, p. 36.

Figure 3
Immigration and emigration by foreigners (in 1,000)

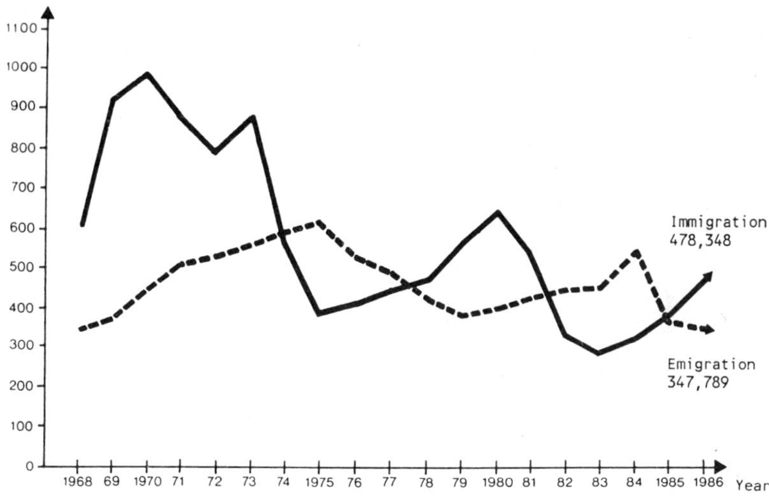

Source: Statistisches Bundesamt, 1987b, p. 50.

Figure 4
Age structure of the population

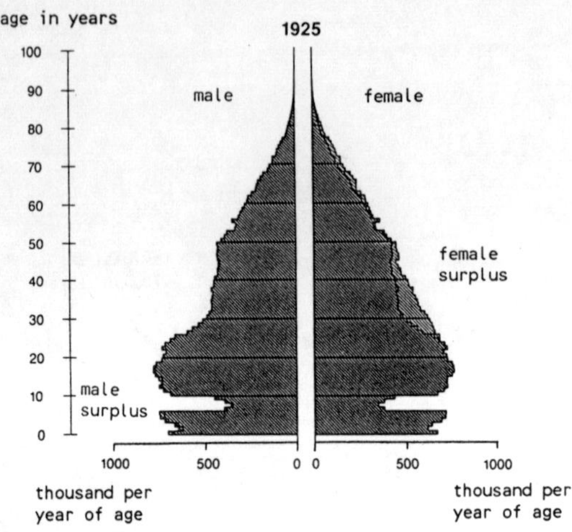

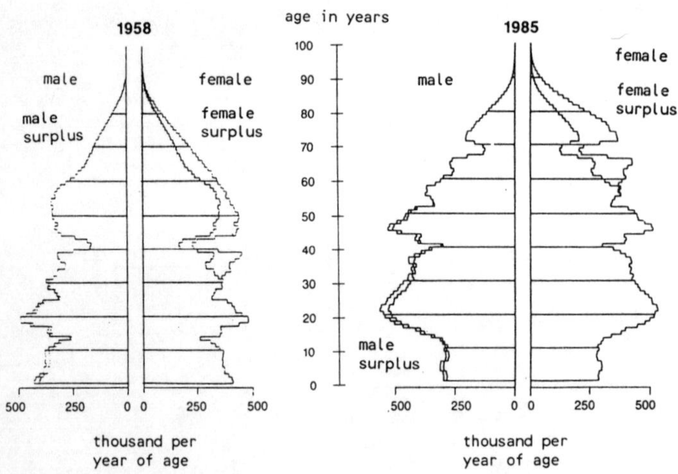

Source: Statistisches Bundesamt, 1987a, p. 11; 1987b, p. 53.

Figure 4
Age structure of the population

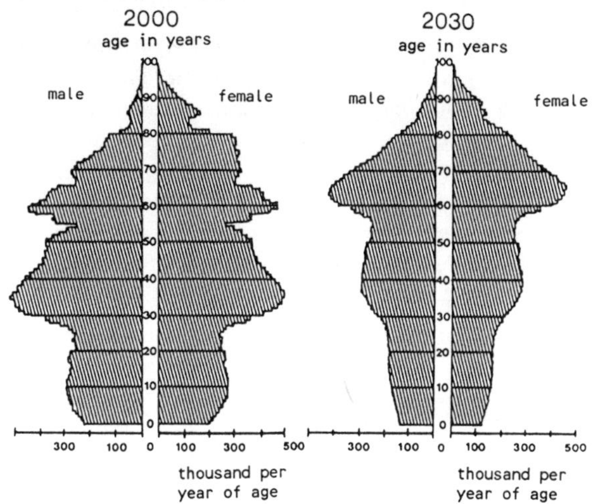

Source: Statistisches Bundesamt, 1987a, p. 11; 1987b, p. 53.

0.2 Macro-economic Trends

The economy has grown more slowly since the 1950s. The consumer-price and retail-price indices have been rising faster than has the wholesale-price index. Net investments increased until 1980, but have been decreasing since. The saving rate of German households has been stable at a high level since the 1960s. The long-term trend of increasing public expenditures is caused by expansion of the social-security system. The public deficit increased until 1980 and has been decreasing since, while the public debt has been growing continually. The net direct investment position evolved from negative to positive values after 1980. Export has always played a very important role for the German economy.

GNP, GNP per Capita, Productivity

The economy has been growing more slowly since the 1950s. Real GNP in constant (1980) DM was nearly five times as high in 1987 as it was in 1950. However, GNP growth rates show a secular trend of decline: in the 1950s, the average annual growth rate of GNP (in constant 1980 DM) was 7.5%, in the 1960s 4.5%, and in the 1970s 2.7% (see tables 1 and 14). In the 1980s, the projected average annual growth rate should be slightly below 2%. The very high levels of economic growth in the 1950s must, of course, be considered against the background of an economy completely devastated by World War II, and of massive immigration in the late 1950s from areas that had formerly belonged to the German Reich and had come under Soviet control after the war.

Over the shorter term, the growth of the German economy has been accelerating again since 1981, the year in which a growth rate of -1% was recorded (in constant 1980 DM). The growth rate was 3.4% in 1988, it was expected to be around 3% again in 1989. However, this recent upward movement has not been sufficient to reverse the secular trend of declining growth rates.

GNP per capita (in constant 1980 DM) increased 3.7 times since 1950 (from 7,417 DM to 27,104 DM, see table 15); the increase per capita has thus been considerably lower than has the increase in total GNP. GDP at 1980 prices has grown more slowly in Germany than in the United States and Canada (see table 2); GDP per capita, in current U.S. dollars, moved from third place in 1970 (behind the United States and Canada) to first place in 1987 (see table 3). However, these figures must be interpreted with great caution, because variations in exchange rates can distort the results. Productivity increase per employed person (tables 1 and 4) shows a secular trend of decline from an annual average of 6.7% in the 1950s to 1.1% in 1987. However, productivity per hour worked, which had increased at a lower rate than productivity per employed person until 1982, has had a higher growth rate than the latter since 1983 (table 1). This reversal is largely due to the reduction of working time per employed person in the Federal Republic.

Wholesale Prices and Retail Prices

The consumer-price and retail-price indices have been rising faster than the wholesale-price index. The wholesale-prices index (1980=100) grew from 55.2 in 1960 to 117.5 in 1985, then dropped to 108.8 (1986), approximately 105 (1987) and 107 (1988) (see table 5). The rate of increase in retail prices was slightly above that in wholesale prices: the index (1980=100) grew from 54.2 in 1960 to 117.5 in 1985, dropped very slightly in 1986 (117.3), and has been on the increase since then, to 117.8 in 1987 and to 118.5 in 1988 (see table 6).

The increase in the consumer-price index has been considerably higher than that in the above price indicators (1980=100), from 49.7 in 1962 to 120.7 in 1986, 121 in 1987, and 122.4 in 1988. In 1989, inflation was expected to accelerate and reach a level of 3%. Table 6 shows that households living on old-age pensions or social welfare are the worst off, as their cost of living has increased most rapidly.

Net Investment

While the volume of gross investment increased continually, net investments reached a peak in 1980 and decreased considerably in the following years. It was not until 1988 that net investments again reached the 1980 level. Because of the excellent economic situation, they have been rising considerably since then. Correspondingly, net investment as a proportion of gross investment decreased from 69.2% in 1960 to 31.1% in 1985, and rose again to 40% in 1989. Gross investment as a proportion of GNP showed a secular trend toward decline, which may reverse itself in the 1990s (see table 16).

Saving Rate

The saving rate of German households has been stable at a high level since the 1960s. Since 1960, German households have saved roughly 12% of their disposable income. Indeed, the development of the welfare state, with its social-security system, has not altered their saving habits (see table 7). Thus total household financial assets increased from 25 billion DM in 1950 to 2.36 trillion DM in 1987. The average annual capital income per household was 4,000 DM in 1987.

Public Expenditures

The long-term trend toward increasing public expenditures is caused by expansion of the social-security system. Public expenditures, excluding social security, increased from 95.3 billion DM in 1961 to 649 billion DM in 1987 (current DM). Public expenditure as a proportion of GNP increased by only about three points, from 28.8% to 32.1%, over the same period. The situation looks very different, though, when social-security systems are included in public expenditures: in this case, total public-sector disbursements grew from 34.2% of GNP in 1961 to 46.8% in 1987, with a peak of 49.8% in 1982 (see table 8).

Public Deficit

The public deficit increased until 1980 and has been decreasing since, but the public debt has been growing continually. The public deficit (including federal, state, and municipal deficits) was very low until 1970, amounting to 9.8 billion DM, or 18.6% of GNP. It rose sharply after the first oil crisis, reaching 64 billion DM, or 24.9% of GNP, in 1975. Subsequent changes in public policy and the upward economic trend reversed this development at the beginning of the 1980s. Since 1984, the deficit has stabilized at between 40 and 50 billion DM.

Deficit as a proportion of GNP and deficit per capita have both increased continually. The same is true for the public debt, which amounted to 848.5 billion DM in 1987 (see table 9).

German households are not heavily indebted. A 1983 study shows that average debt per household (excluding mortgage debts) was 1,756 DM, while average financial assets per household amounted to 23,250 DM (Euler, 1985).

German enterprises, on the other hand, have become increasingly indebted: capital resources (equity plus reserves) as a proportion of corporate assets decreased from around 30% in the mid-1960s to 18.5% in 1982 (see table 10). However, important structural differences according to sector and size of firms must be taken into account (see table 11).

Investment Position

The net direct investment position has evolved from negative to positive values since 1980. German investment abroad increased from 43.5 million DM in 1976 to 134 million DM in 1986. Over the same period, foreign investment in Germany increased from 63.5 million DM to 95.3 million DM. Germany's net investment position shifted from -20 million DM in 1976 to +38.7 million DM (see table 12). In 1986, the United States was by far the most important country for German investors (28.2% of German investment abroad) followed by France (8.1%), the Netherlands (7.7%), and Switzerland (7.5%).

Export

Export has always played a very important role for the German economy. Valued at constant 1980 prices, German exports grew from 50.1 billion DM in 1955 to 463.4 billion DM in 1987 (see table 13), while imports grew from 35.6 billion DM in 1955 to 418.9 billion DM in 1987. The trade balance was positive as early as 1955, and has remained so (see table 13). German exports as a proportion of world exports increased from 3% in 1955 to roughly 12% in 1987, overtaking even the United States' share in world exports.

Renate Hornung-Draus

References

Ballerstedt, Eike, and Wolfgang Glatzer
1979 *Soziologischer Almanach*. Frankfurt am Main/New York: Campus.

Bundesverband der Deutschen Industrie
1984 *Die Eigenkapitalausstattung der deutschen Wirtschaft*. Köln.

Deutsche Bundesbank
1983 *Jahresabschlüsse der Unternehmen in der Bundesrepublik Deutschland 1965 bis 1981*. Sonderdruck no. 5.

–
1988 *Geschäftsbericht für das Jahr 1988*.

Euler, Manfred
1985 "Das Geldvermögen privater Haushalte Ende 1983." *Wirtschaft und Statistik*, no. 5.

Institut der deutschen Wirtschaft
1988a "Auslandsorientierung der deutschen Wirtschaft." *IW-Trends*, no. 2.

–
1988b *Mehr als nur mehr; zur Diskussion über das Wirtschaftswachstum*. Köln: Deutscher Instituts-Verlag.

–
1989a *International economic indicators 1989*. Köln: Deutscher Instituts-Verlag.

–
1989b *Zahlen zur wirtschaftlichen Entwicklung der Bundesrepublik Deutschland 1989*. Köln: Deutscher Instituts-Verlag.

Statistisches Bundesamt, ed.
1987 *Datenreport 1987*. Bonn: Bundeszentrale für politische Bildung.

–, ed.
1988 *Statistisches Jahrbuch 1988*. Stuttgart/Mainz: Kohlhammer.

Table 1
National accounts (in billion DM)

Year	Current DM					Gross National Product in constant (1980) DM
	GDP at market prices	Gross National Product	Deductions	Indirect taxes minus subventions	National Income	
1950[1]	96.7	98.1	8.3	12.8	76.9	353.6
1960	302.7	303.0	23.6	39.3	240.1	731.7
1970	675.3	675.7	68.0	77.3	530.4	1,134.0
1975	1,026.9	1,029.4	115.9	109.9	803.6	1,258.0
1980	1,478.9	1,485.2	173.7	162.9	1,148.6	1,485.2
1981	1,540.9	1,545.1	188.6	169.2	1,187.3	1,485.3
1982	1,597.9	1,597.1	201.1	172.5	1,223.5	1,471.0
1983	1,674.8	1,679.3	211.4	182.7	1,285.1	1,497.8
1984[2]	1,755.8	1,769.9	222.0	190.0	1,357.9	1,548.1
1985[2]	1,831.9	1,845.6	231.8	192.5	1,421.3	1,579.6
1986[2]	1,937.0	1,948.8	240.2	195.2	1,513.4	1,618.4
1987[2]	2,012.0	2,023.2	249.7	202.1	1,571.4	1,645.6

Year	Growth rates (in %) of			
	Gross National Product		Productivity	
	Current DM	Constant (1980) DM	A[3]	B[4]
1951-60	11.9	7.5	6.7	6.2
1961-70	8.4	4.5	4.3	5.3
1971-80	8.2	2.7	2.8	3.9
1981-85[2]	4.4	1.3	1.8	2.4
1980	6.3	1.5	0.3	1.2
1981	4.0	0.0	0.9	1.9
1982	3.4	-1.0	1.1	0.6
1983	5.1	1.8	3.0	3.4
1984[2]	5.3	3.3	2.7	3.1
1985[2]	4.3	2.0	1.4	2.8
1986[2]	5.6	2.5	1.6	2.3
1987[2]	3.8	1.7	1.1	1.7

1. Data up to 1960 do not include the Saarland and West Berlin.
2. Provisional results.
3. Growth rate of Gross Domestic Product in constant (1980) DM per employed person.
4. Growth rate of Gross Domestic Product in constant (1980) DM per work hour.

Source: Institut der deutschen Wirtschaft, 1989b.

Table 2
Growth rates of gross domestic product at 1980 prices (in %)

Country	1971/75	1976/80	1982	1983	1984	1985	1986	1987
West Germany	+2.1	+3.3	-0.6	+1.5	+2.8	+2.1	+2.6	+1.7
France	+4.0	+3.2	+2.5	+0.7	+1.3	+1.7	+2.1	+2.5
Spain	+5.7	+1.8	+1.2	+1.8	+1.8	+2.3	+3.3	+5.2
United States	+2.3	+3.2	-2.5	+3.9	+7.2	+3.5	+3.0	+2.9
Canada	+5.2	+3.9	-3.2	+3.2	+6.3	+4.2	+3.3	+4.0

Source: Institut der deutschen Wirtschaft, 1989a.

Table 3
Gross Domestic Product per capita

Country	1970	1975	1980	1985	1986	1987
West Germany	3,042	6,751	13,216	10,197	14,603	18,297
France	2,824	6,543	12,335	9,466	13,123	15,818
Spain	1,086	2,952	5,668	4,268	5,905	7,417
United States	4,922	7,334	11,804	16,548	17,324	18,196
Canada	3,960	7,358	10,934	13,729	14,174	16,041

Source: Institut der deutschen Wirtschaft, 1989a.

Table 4
Productivity: Annual growth rates of real GDP per employed person (in %)

Country	1976/80	1981/85	1986	1987
West Germany	2.9	1.8	1.3	1.2
France	2.5	1.9	1.9	2.3
Spain	3.6	3.0	1.4	2.0
United States	0.3	1.3	1.3	0.3
Canada	1.1	1.7	0.3	1.1

Percentage change, annual average, or year to year.

Source: OECD; EC, national sources; IW calculations, cited in Institut der deutschen Wirtschaft, 1989a.

Table 5
Index of wholesale and retail prices (1980 = 100)

Year	Wholesale prices	Retail prices
1950	48.1	-
1960	54.2	55.2
1970	63.4	59.7
1980	100.0	100.0
1985	117.5	117.5
1986	117.3	108.8

Source: Statistisches Bundesamt, 1987.

Table 6
Index of the cost of living (1980 = 100)

Year	4-person households, higher income	4-person households, middle income	2-person households, retirement or welfare	Living cost of a child	Average cost per households
1962	50.0	50.5	48.7	47.2	49.7
1970	60.8	61.7	61.3	58.7	61.0
1980	100.0	100.0	100.0	100.0	100.0
1982	112.2	112.0	112.1	111.0	111.9
1984	118.7	118.4	118.7	117.0	118.4
1985	121.5	120.9	121.1	118.5	121.0
1986	121.4	120.7	121.4	118.9	120.7

Source: Statistisches Bundesamt, 1987.

Table 7
Income and savings of households

Year	In billion DM			Savings rate[2] in %
	Disposable income[1]	Consumption expenditure	Savings	
1960	188.0	171.8	16.1	8.6
1965	293.4	257.6	35.8	12.2
1970	428.0	368.9	59.1	13.8
1971	473.4	409.4	63.9	13.5
1972	528.2	452.1	76.1	14.4
1973	575.2	495.4	79.8	13.9
1974	624.8	533.7	91.0	14.6
1975	689.4	585.5	103.9	15.1
1976	730.3	633.5	96.8	13.3
1977	775.4	680.9	94.4	12.2
1978	824.8	725.3	99.5	12.1
1979	892.0	779.3	112.8	12.6
1980	957.9	834.0	122.9	12.8
1981	1,016.9	879.2	137.7	13.5
1982	1,052.4	918.1	134.4	12.8
1983	1,081.6	964.2	117.4	10.9
1984[3]	1,132.6	1,003.6	129.0	11.4
1985[3]	1,174.3	1,041.0	133.3	11.4
1986[3]	1,229.0	1,080.1	148.9	12.1
1987[3]	1,276.0	1,119.6	156.4	12.3

1. Undistributed profits of firms not included.
2. Savings as a proportion of disposable income.
3. Provisional results.

Source: Institut der deutschen Wirtschaft, 1989b.

Table 8
Public expenditures

Year	Public expenditure excluding social-security systems					Public expenditure including social-security systems	
	Federal	State	Local communities	Total[1]			
	In bill. DM	In bill. DM	In bill. DM	In bill. DM	As a % of GNP	In bill. DM	As a % of GNP
1961	48.6	37.0	23.6	95.3	28.8	113.4	34.2
1962	49.9	42.4	27.4	106.5	29.5	129.6	36.0
1963	55.2	46.0	31.5	116.3	30.4	140.4	36.7
1964	58.9	50.2	35.8	127.2	30.3	153.2	36.5
1965	65.5	54.6	39.0	139.3	30.4	170.2	37.2
1966	68.4	57.9	41.0	145.0	29.7	181.6	37.3
1967	76.5	59.8	41.0	153.8	31.2	193.6	39.2
1968	75.8	62.8	43.2	158.8	29.8	211.1	39.6
1969	81.9	67.1	48.4	174.6	29.2	233.3	39.0
1970	87.6	77.1	56.5	196.3	29.1	264.1	39.1
1971	98.4	88.7	67.4	226.5	30.1	304.3	40.5
1972	112.1	100.4	74.7	252.1	30.6	341.0	41.3
1973	122.1	114.7	83.4	280.5	30.5	386.5	42.1
1974	134.0	132.5	95.7	318.3	32.3	444.8	45.1
1975	159.0	144.6	102.0	360.5	35.0	509.1	49.5
1976	165.2	152.5	105.8	376.5	33.5	546.2	48.5
1977	172.4	161.6	107.7	395.2	33.0	582.7	48.6
1978	189.7	176.5	118.2	433.4	33.6	620.8	48.1
1979	203.4	191.8	130.4	469.9	33.7	669.8	48.0
1980	215.7	208.6	145.5	509.2	34.3	722.4	48.6
1981	233.0	216.6	152.1	541.8	35.1	766.2	49.6
1982	244.7	224.2	153.1	561.6	35.2	796.0	49.8
1983	246.8	228.3	151.7	570.1	33.9	816.4	48.6
1984[1]	251.8	234.3	154.7	583.6	33.0	849.0	48.0
1985[1]	257.1	243.9	163.6	604.0	32.7	875.9	47.5
1986[1]	261.5	253.1	171.7	627.4	32.2	910.3	46.7
1987[1]	268.5	262.0	179.0	649.0	32.1	946.6	46.8

1. Transfers between governmental institutions are considered.
2. Provisional results.

Source: Institut der deutschen Wirtschaft, 1989b.

Table 9
Public debt and public deficit

Year	1960	1970	1975	1980	1981	1982
			Public debt in billion DM			
Total[1]	52.2	125.9	256.4	468.6	545.6	614.8
Federal	22.6	47.3	108.5	232.3	273.1	309.1
States	14.7	27.8	67.0	137.8	165.2	190.6
Local commun.	11.2	40.3	74.4	95.2	102.6	109.9
			Deficit in billion DM			
Total	3.1	9.8	64.0	54.7	77.0	69.2
Federal	1.6	1.9	36.4	29.7	40.8	36.0
States	-0.2	2.0	19.7	21.9	27.4	25.4
Local commun.	1.6	3.6	8.0	4.8	7.4	7.3
			Deficit as a proportion of GNP			
Total	17.2	18.6	24.9	31.6	35.3	38.5
			Deficit per capita in DM			
Total	942	2,076	4,147	7,611	8,845	9,974

Year	1983	1984	1985	1986	1987[2]
			Public debt in billion DM		
Total[1]	671.7	717.5	760.2	801.0	848.5
Federal	341.4	367.3	392.4	415.4	440.5
States	212.0	230.6	247.4	264.4	284.5
Local commun.	112.5	113.1	113.7	114.8	117.5
			Deficit in billion DM		
Total	56.9	45.8	42.7	40.8	47.5
Federal	32.3	25.9	25.1	23.0	25.1
States	21.4	18.6	16.8	17.0	20.1
Local commun.	2.6	0.6	0.6	1.1	2.7
			Deficit as a proportion of GNP		
Total	40.0	40.5	41.2	41.1	41.9
			Deficit per capita in DM		
Total	10,936	11,729	12,458	13,117	13,871

1. Including European Recovery Program, Compensation Fund (Lastenausgleichsfonds).
2. Provisional results, partly estimates.
3. At end of year.

Source: Institut der deutschen Wirtschaft, 1989b.

Table 10
Evolution of capital resources[1] as a proportion of corporate assets (in %)

Year	Value
1965	29.8
1966	30.0
1967	31.4
1968	30.6
1969	28.4
1970	26.7
1971	25.9
1972	24.6
1973	24.0
1974	23.7
1975	23.7
1976	23.1
1977	22.9
1978	22.4
1979	21.7
1980	20.9
1980[1]	19.8
1981	18.7
1982	18.5

1. Capital resources are defined as equity plus reserves.
2. From 1980 on, data are based on a new statistical basis.

Source: Deutsche Bundesbank, 1983, Sonderdruck no.5.

Table 11
Capital resources[1] as a proportion of corporate assets according to size of firms

Annual turnover in million DM	1966	1980
0 - 1	31.7	-
1 - 10	31.5	14.8[2]
10 - 50	32.4	18.3
50 - 100	31.5	21.8
100 - 250	32.0	26.3[3]
250 -	36.7	-

1. Capital resources defined as equity plus reserves.
2. Companies with turnovers up to DM 10 million.
3. Companies with turnovers of more than DM 100 million.

Source: Deutsche Bundesbank, 1983, Sonderdruck no.5.

Table 12
Direct investment position of the Federal Republic of Germany (in million DM)

Year	German investments abroad		Foreign investment in Germany		Net investment position[1]
	Volume at end of year	Annual change	Volume at end of year	Annual change	
1976	43,508		63,531		-20,023
1977	46,790	+3,282	62,309	-1,222	-15,519
1978	52,703	+5,913	66,945	+4,636	-14,242
1979	61,157	+8,454	70,266	+3,321	-9,109
1980	74,353	+13,196	71,758	+1,492	+2,595
1981	88,429	+14,076	74,739	+2,981	+13,690
1982	95,400	+6,971	76,359	+1,620	+19,041
1983	106,573	+11,173	81,106	+4,747	+25,467
1984	125,875	+19,302	84,791	+3,685	+41,084
1985	130,512	+4,637	90,885	+6,094	+39,627
1986	134,009	+ 3,497	95,301	+4,416	+38,708

1. Including net capital export from the Federal Republic.

Source: Institut der deutschen Wirtschaft, 1989b.

Table 13
Foreign trade of the Federal Republic of Germany (in billion DM)

Year	Current DM			Constant 1980 DM	
	Imports	Exports	Trade balance	Imports	Exports
1950	11.4	8.4	-3.0	-	-
1955	24.5	25.7	1.2	35.6	50.1
1960	42.7	47.9	5.2	71.6	85.5
1965	70.4	71.7	1.2	129.1	120.5
1970	109.6	125.3	15.7	211.8	207.2
1975	184.3	221.6	37.3	246.7	258.2
1976	222.2	256.6	34.5	290.6	306.3
1977	235.2	273.6	38.4	297.2	318.5
1978	243.7	284.9	41.2	317.4	328.7
1979	292.0	314.5	22.4	341.5	344.5
1980	341.4	350.3	8.9	341.4	350.3
1981	369.2	396.9	27.7	324.4	373.4
1982	376.5	427.7	51.3	328.7	385.6
1983	390.2	432.3	42.1	341.8	384.5
1984	434.2	488.2	54.0	359.5	419.8
1985	463.8	537.2	73.4	374.4	444.6
1986	413.7	526.4	112.6	397.5	450.5
1987	409.5	527.0	117.5	418.9	463.4

Source: Institut der deutschen Wirtschaft, 1989b.

Table 14
Average annual growth rates of GNP in constant (1980) DM

Year	Average annual growth rates in %
1951-1960	7.5
1961-1970	4.5
1971-1980	2.7
1981-1985	1.3

Source: Statistisches Bundesamt, 1988.

Table 15
GNP per capita in constant (1980) DM

Year	DM
1950	7,417
1960	13,162
1970	18,697
1980	24,112
1988	27,104

Source: Institut der deutschen Wirtschaft, 1988b.

Table 16
Gross investment as a proportion of GNP in constant 1980 DM

Year	In %	Year	In %
1960	28.3	1974	22.9
1961	27.9	1975	21.0
1962	27.6	1976	22.9
1963	26.5	1977	22.3
1964	28.3	1978	22.2
1965	28.8	1979	24.0
1966	27.5	1980	23.5
1967	24.6	1981	20.8
1968	25.9	1982	19.9
1969	27.3	1983	20.7
1970	27.9	1984	20.7
1971	27.1	1985	19.9
1972	26.8	1986	20.1
1973	26.3		

Source: Statistisches Bundesamt, 1987.

0.3 Macro-technological Trends

The oil-price crisis of 1973 was the starting point for development of technologies with lower energy consumption and for efforts to increase diversification of energy sources. The number of internationally significant inventions has been increasing despite a decline in the total number of patent applications. The R&D sector is highly developed in the Federal Republic of Germany, and the proportion of private financing is high. Productivity increases have been slowing down since the 1970s. Agricultural productivity is low compared to France, Canada, and the United States.

In discussions about the international competitiveness of the German economy, the level of technological development is generally considered one of its main strong points.

Energy Consumption

Energy consumption increased sharply between 1950 and 1973 and has remained roughly stable since then. There has been a trend toward diversification of energy sources.

From 1950 to 1973, energy consumption in the Federal Republic of Germany nearly tripled: from just below 4,000 petajoules in 1950, it rose to over 11,000 petajoules in 1973 (see table 1). The first oil crisis, in 1973, had an immediate effect on energy consumption, which decreased by nearly 1,000 petajoules in 1975. This was the starting point for a period of disjunction between economic growth and energy consumption (see figure 1). However, the first period of diminishing energy consumption, which was concurrent with a roughly stable real GNP (1973 – 1975), was followed by a parallel upward movement of both indicators until 1979. From 1979 to 1982, further technological advances led to real GNP growth with decreasing energy consumption. Since then, the evolution of both indicators has again been parallel, but energy consumption remains on a much lower level than before (figure 1). We must conclude, therefore, that technological development has not been able completely to uncouple economic growth and energy consumption. It has been able, however, to lower considerably the ratio between real GNP and energy consumption. In 1970, 8.7 petajoules of energy were consumed per billion constant 1980 DM of GNP; in 1985 only 7.15 petajoules were needed to produce the same amount of GNP (table 1).

The structure of energy sources has changed considerably over the past forty years: in 1950, hard coal and brown coal comprised 88% of German energy sources, while only 4.7% was produced from oil. Since then, diversification has lessened the predominant role of coal in the production of energy: in 1985, only 30% of energy was produced from coal, while oil had become the most important source (41.1%) (see figure 2).

An international comparison of per-capita energy consumption shows that West Germany is situated between the United States and Canada, both with higher per-capita consumption, and France and the other major European countries, with lower per-capita consumption (see table 2). However, unlike the United States, West Germany had higher per-capita consumption in the 1980s than in the 1970s.

The rise in consumption of end-user energy was due mainly to development of the transportation system, to an increase in the volume of private and public transportation, and to increasing use of energy by private households (see table 3). On the other hand, energy consumption in the industrial sector diminished considerably from 1970 to 1987. This is certainly due in part to the importance of the ecological movement in German public life, which spurred strong efforts to develop less energy-intensive technologies, although the main impetus for this trend was certainly the oil crisis in 1973, as can be seen in table 3.

Inventions

The number of inventions with international significance increased in Germany, but the total number of patent applications decreased. Compared to the 1960s and early 1970s, the number of patent applications in the Federal Republic declined by one-third in the 1980s (see table 4). At the same time, the share of foreign patent applications decreased from roughly one-half up to 1975 to one-quarter in the late 1980s. The relative position of the Federal Republic, as far as national patent applications are concerned, also declined: in 1965, 12.3% of total OECD applications were made in the Federal Republic (United States, 17.5%; Japan, 15.1%), while in 1983 Germany's position was 9.3 percent (versus 13.5% in the United States and 32.7% in Japan) (see table 5). However, considering that the number and quality of patent applications depends very much on national legal systems (OECD, 1986b), these data do not seem to be very significant as far as the international technological position of West Germany is concerned. It might be more useful to consider only the number of inventions for which patent applications were filed both in West Germany (respectively in the country of reference) and in at least two other countries (Institut der deutschen Wirtschaft, 1989): according to these data, the number of internationally important inventions increased considerably between 1970 and 1980, and has declined only slightly since then; in 1986, West Germany occupied the second rank, behind the United States, but ahead of Japan. These data confirm the hypothesis that technology has been and remains one of the most important elements of Germany's international competitiveness.

Doctorates and Publications in Natural Sciences, Mathematics, and Engineering

The number of doctorates and publications in natural sciences and engineering increased considerably over the last 20 years. The increasing importance of technology is clearly reflected in the number of doctorates issued at German universities between 1973 and 1986 in the fields of mathematics, natural sciences, and engineering (doctorates in medicine are excluded because their scientific quality is generally inferior to those in other fields), which rose from 2,700 (1973) to 4,700 (1986) (see table 6). Within this period, 1984 marks the beginning of a particularly sharp rise in doctorates issued. The relative importance of doctorates in these fields as a proportion of all doctorates remained more or less stable at a rate of some 30%.

The number of publications in natural sciences, mathematics, and engineering shows a similar trend, increasing considerably up to 1980 (see table 7), decreasing by 28% in 1982, and increasing since. It is difficult to establish a long-term trend regarding their proportion among all publications; this proportion remained level at about 10% from 1960 to 1980, then fell to 8% in 1982, rose to a peak of 14.2% in 1984, and has fallen to the 10% level since (table 7). On the whole, scientific publications kept pace with the overall expansion of book publishing.

Research and Development

The Federal Republic has a highly developed R&D sector with a very high rate of private financing. The pace of research and development has increased remarkably since the 1960s. In 1969, R&D expenditures totalled roughly 1.8% of GDP, and Germany ranked fourth behind the United States, the United Kingdom, and France (see figure 3). Since 1981, the Federal Republic has matched the United States' level of R&D expenditures, 2.5% of GDP. As the R&D expenditures in the United States rose even higher in the 1980s, West Germany has been competing with Japan for second rank in R&D expenditures (see figure 3).

Surprisingly, the proportion of private financing of R&D is much higher in West Germany than in all other countries included in this study. With a ratio of private to public financing of 150:100, West Germany comes second of all important OECD countries (behind Japan), and the tendency toward private financing has been increasing since 1974. One explanation for the low level of public commitment to R&D is that the Federal Republic undertakes little research in defence technologies (OECD, 1984). Privately financed R&D is concentrated mostly on electronics, the chemical industry, and automobile production (see table 8). Thus, government R&D expenditure as a percentage of total public spending has been fluctuating at around 4%, a lower proportion than the American, French, and British governments spend.

Productivity

Productivity increased dramatically in the 1960s, but less swiftly in the 1970s and 1980s. In absolute terms, output per hour increased from 13 DM in 1960 to 37.60 DM in 1987 (see table 9). However, the dynamics of productivity increase show a clear trend toward decline. Overall productivity per work hour increased at an average annual rate of 5.5% in the late 1960s. In the 1970s, the average annual rate of increase was 4.3% (1971 – 1975) and 3.5% (1976 – 1980), and between 1981 and 1985 it was 2.3%. Estimated productivity increase was 2.0% in 1986, 1.9% in 1987, and 2.8% in 1988 (see table 10).

Productivity in the manufacturing industry, which had a higher rate of increase than overall productivity up to 1985, fell to 1.7% in 1986 and to 1.3% in 1987. This led to a deterioration in West Germany's national position as far as industrial productivity increase is concerned: from a middle-range position with annual increase rates lower than those in France but higher than those in the United States and Canada in the 1970s, the Federal Republic became the country with the lowest increase rates in 1987 (table 6).

Agricultural Productivity

Agricultural productivity increased less than in other countries. The gross value added per employed person in the primary sector (including not only agriculture, but also forestry and fisheries) quintupled between the 1960s and the 1980s (see table 11). By international standards, Germany's primary sector does not seem to be very productive: in 1970, the ratio between the proportion of gross value added produced in the primary sector and the proportion of persons employed was lower in the Federal Republic (0.4) than in France (0.5), Canada (0.55), and the United States (0.6). Moreover, from 1970 to 1986, this ratio declined in the Federal Republic, while it increased in the other countries (see table 12). This particular development in the Federal Republic is likely due to two factors: first, government policy in the Federal Republic has traditionally been oriented toward subsidies for small family-farming enterprises. Of course, these small units are less rationalized and therefore less productive than large industrial farming units. Second, the ecological movement of the 1970s had a strong impact on farmers and led to the development of more ecological farming techniques that were also more labour intensive.

Renate Hornung-Draus

References

Bretschneider, Joachim, et al.
1990 *Handbuch einkommens-, vermögens- und sozialpolitischer Daten*. Loseblattsammlung. Köln: Bachem.

Bundesminister für Bildung und Wissenschaft
1988 *Grund- und Strukturdaten 1988/89*. Bad Honnef.

Gerstenberger, W.
1988 "Entwicklung der Wettbewerbsfähigkeit der deutschen Industrie." *Ifo-Schnelldienst*, no. 7.

Institut der deutschen Wirtschaft
1988 "Standort Bundesrepublik Deutschland. Indikatoren, Analysen, Tendenzen." *IW-Trends*, no. 2.

–
1989a *International economic indicators 1989*. Köln: Deutscher Instituts-Verlag.

–
1989b *Zahlen zur wirtschaftlichen Entwicklung der Bundesrepublik Deutschland 1989*. Köln: Deutscher Instituts-Verlag.

OECD
1984 *Science and Technology Indicators no. 1: Resources devoted to R&D*.

–
1986a *Productivity in Industry, Prospects and Policies*. Paris.

–
1986b *Science and Technology Indicators no. 2: R&D, invention and competitiveness*.

–
1987a *Energy Balances of OECD-countries, 1970-1985 and Main Series from 1960*. Paris.

–
1987b *Energy Statistics, 1970-1985 and Main Series from 1960*. Paris.

Penzkofer, H., et al.
1989 "Innovation, Wachstum und Beschäftigung." *Ifo-Schnelldienst*, no. 1-2.

Ray, G.F.
1988 "The Diffusion of Innovations: An Update." *National Institute Economic Review*, no. 126. (German translation in Ifo-Schnelldienst 34/1988).

Reinhard, Michael
1988 "Wirtschaftliche und soziale Auswirkungen neuer Techniken im Grosshandel." *Ifo-Schnelldienst*, no. 15.

Statistisches Bundesamt, ed.
1987 *Datenreport 1987*. Stuttgart: Bundeszentrale für politische Bildung.

–, ed.
ann. pbl. *Statistisches Jahrbuch*. Stuttgart/Mainz: Kohlhammer.

Traeger, Uwe Chr.
1989 "Entwicklungstendenzen im Patentverhalten deutscher Erfinder und Unternehmen." *Ifo-Schnelldienst*, no. 23.

Table 1
Evolution of energy consumption and of real GNP

Year	Energy consumption (petajoule)[1]	Real GNP (billion of constant 1980 DM)
1950	3,971	353.6
1960	6,199	731.7
1970	9,870	1,134.0
1971	9,948	1,168.0
1972	10,383	1,217.0
1973	11,092	1,274.1
1974	10,723	1,276.5
1975	10,191	1,258.0
1976	10,853	1,328.2
1977	10,912	1,363.4
1978	11,401	1,407.9
1979	11,964	1,463.6
1980	11,436	1,458.2
1981	10,964	1,458.3
1982	10,596	1,471.0
1983	10,689	1,497.8
1984	11,022	1,548.1
1985	11,284	1,578.1

1. Petajoule = 10^{15} joule

Sources: Statistisches Bundesamt, 1987 p. 324; Institut der deutschen Wirtschaft, continnally actualized edition, 1989, p. 21; Bretschneider, et al.

Table 2
Consumption of commercial energy per capita (metric tons of coal equivalent)

Country	1970	1975	1980	1985
West Germany	5.2	5.3	5.8	5.7
France	3.8	3.7	4.4	4.0
Spain	1.5	2.1	2.4	2.2
United States	10.8	10.5	10.4	9.6
Canada	8.8	9.9	10.5	9.9

Source: Institut der deutschen Wirtschaft, 1989a, p. 63.

Table 3
Consumption of end-user energy

Item	Year	Total million metric tons of coal equivalent
Total	1960	145.7
	1970	230.4
	1973	253.9
	1980	256.9
	1984	245.5
	1985	252.1
	1986	257.1
	1987	256.7
Industry	1970	90.8
	1973	95.6
	1980	88.1
	1984	78.0
	1985	78.0
	1986	75.1
	1987	75.0
Households	1970	61.7
	1973	67.9
	1980	68.8
	1984	67.8
	1985	72.2
	1986	74.6
	1987	73.7
Small users[1]	1970	34.0
	1973	40.3
	1980	39.8
	1984	36.0
	1985	40.1
	1986	42.4
	1987	40.6
Transportation	1970	39.5
	1973	45.7
	1980	56.8
	1984	58.1
	1985	58.4
	1986	61.6
	1987	63.8

1. Agriculture, commerce, crafts.

Source: Institut der deutschen Wirtschaft, 1989b.

Table 4
Patent applications in the Federal Republic of Germany

Year	Total	Foreign applicants		Europe		United States		Japan	
	Number	Number	In %	Number	In %	Number	In %	Number	In %
1948/60	63,327	16,255	25.7	10,633	16.8	4,425	7.0	117	0.2
1961/65	62,049	26,659	43.0	15,422	24.9	9,620	15.0	1,042	1.7
1966/70	66,629	33,310	50.0	17,663	26.5	12,410	18.6	2,612	3.9
1971/75	64,595	33,354	51.6	16,627	25.7	11,455	17.7	4,484	6.9
1976/80	57,425	26,637	48.7	12,584	23.0	8,486	15.5	4,912	9.0
1981/85	46,871	15,113	32.2	6,316	13.5	3,614	7.7	4,616	9.8
1980	51,345	19,900	41.0	8,550	17.6	5,606	11.5	5,267	10.8
1981	49,002	16,738	35.9	7,001	15.0	4,374	9.4	4,945	10.6
1982	47,826	17,158	35.9	7,099	14.8	4,256	8.9	5,407	11.3
1983	47,103	15,445	32.8	6,779	14.4	3,825	8.1	4,380	9.3
1984	45,209	13,225	29.3	5,543	12.3	3,095	6.8	4,231	9.4
1985	45,213	12,998	28.7	5,160	11.4	2,521	5.6	4,117	9.1
1986	43,493	11,313	26.0	4,579	10.5	2,160	5.0	3,934	9.0
1987	41,848	10,233	24.5	4,185	10.0	1,758	4.2	3,583	8.6
1988	41,745	9,813	23.5	4,006	9.6	1,521	3.6	3,527	8.4

The data refer to the number of applications on the 31st of December of each year. For 1980 and 1981, not all foreign applicants could be identified by their country of origin.

Source: Institut der deutschen Wirtschaft, 1989b.

Table 5
National patent applications: country shares (OECD = 100)

Country	1965	1970	1975	1980	1983
United States	17.5	16.8	17.2	15.7	13.5
Japan	15.1	21.3	27.2	28.6	32.7
West Germany	12.3	10.8	10.2	9.8	9.3
France	8.8	7.7	6.9	6.6	6.3
U.K.	10.3	10.1	9.1	8.8	8.0
Italy	5.4	5.2	4.1	4.4	4.2
Canada	5.6	5.0	4.4	3.7	3.3
Spain	2.5	1.9	1.8	1.6	1.2
Australia	2.8	2.7	2.4	2.2	2.3
Netherlands	3.2	3.1	2.6	3.1	3.3
Turkey	0.1	0.1	0.1	0.1	-
Sweden	3.2	2.9	2.5	3.1	3.2
Belgium	3.1	2.8	2.2	2.4	2.7
Switzerland	3.4	3.2	2.9	3.1	3.1
Austria	2.2	1.9	1.7	2.3	2.5
Yugoslavia	0.4	0.5	0.6	0.5	0.3
Denmark	1.2	1.1	1.0	1.0	1.0
Norway	0.9	0.8	0.8	0.7	0.8
Greece	0.4	0.4	0.5	0.4	0.4
Finland	0.6	0.6	0.6	0.6	0.8
Portugal	0.2	0.3	0.3	0.3	0.2
New Zealand	0.6	0.6	0.6	0.5	0.5
Ireland	0.3	0.3	0.5	0.4	0.4
Iceland	0.0	0.0	0.0	0.0	0.0

Source: OECD, 1986b, p. 50.

Table 6
Doctorates in the Federal Republic of Germany

Year	Total number of doctorates	Doctorates in math. and nat. sciences		Doctorates in engineering	
	Number	Number	% of all doctors	Number	% of all doctors
1975	11,400	2,600	22.8	1,000	8.8
1977	11,400	2,800	24.5	1,000	8.8
1979	11,900	2,700	22.7	1,100	9.2
1981	12,300	2,700	21.9	1,000	8.1
1983	13,600	2,700	19.8	1,000	7.3
1984	14,100	3,000	21.3	1,200	8.5
1985	15,000	3,300	22.0	1,100	7.3
1986	15,500	3,500	22.6	1,200	7.7

Source: Bundesminister für Bildung und Wissenschaft, 1988, p. 190.

Table 7
Book production in the Federal Republic of Germany

Year	Total book production	Natural sciences, mathematics, and engineering[1]	
	Number	Number	% of total book production
1960	22,524	2,455	10.9
1970	47,096	4,982	10.6
1980	67,176	6,897	10.3
1982	61,332	4,938	8.0
1983	60,598	5,506	9.1
1984	51,733	7,354	14.2
1985	57,623	7,846	13.6
1986	63,679	7,387	11.6

1. Publications in medicine not included.

Source: Statistisches Bundesamt, 1989.

Table 8
Research and development expenditures by German firms (in billion DM)

Year	1965	1977	1979	1981	1983	1985	1986	1987	1988
Total	4.43	17.23	23.83	27.84	33.07	39.55	41.64	45.98	48.17
Energy, water, mining inds.	0.12	0.74	1.15	1.11	2.17	2.14	2.05	1.54	1.24
Total industry	4.21	16.05	22.21	26.13	30.04	36.38	38.47	43.04	45.49
- chemical	1.25	4.46	5.06	6.01	6.64	7.82	-	-	-
- machinery	0.36	1.77	3.06	3.31	3.71	4.20	4.37	4.64	4.84
- motor vehicles, transport. equipment	0.45	2.05	3.10	3.92	4.88	5.89	-	-	-
- aircraft, missiles	0.21	1.28	1.47	1.76	1.70	2.61	-	-	-
- electrical	1.14	4.46	6.02	6.79	7.78	9.99	11.10	13.01	13.63
- other industry	0.80	2.03	3.50	4.35	5.33	5.87	-	-	-
Other sectors	0.10	0.43	0.47	0.60	0.86	1.04	1.12	1.40	1.44
Total expenditure per capita of population	75.49	280.57	388.30	451.40	538.40	648.15	681.06	749.90	-
% of GNP	0.97	1.44	1.71	1.80	1.97	2.14	2.28	2.19	2.26
Personnel									
- total thousands	142	198	238	243	249	275	292	302	-
- per 10,000 employed	53	78	91	93	98	108	114	117	-

Source: Institut der deutschen Wirtschaft, 1989b.

Table 9
Gross national product and productivity in the Federal Republic of Germany

Year	Employed persons in 1,000	Work time per employed person (hours)	Work volume in million hours	Productivity per hour	GDP in constant (1980) DM
1960	26,063	2,152	56,085	13.0	728.9
1970	26,560	1,949	51,768	21.9	1,132.8
1980	26,278	1,749	45,942	32.2	1,478.9
1981	26,092	1,732	45,181	32.8	1,481.4
1982	25,651	1,739	44,594	33.0	1,471.8
1983	25,262	1,733	43,766	34.1	1,493.9
1984	25,283	1,726	43,631	35.2	1,536.0
1985	25,452	1,702	43,330	36.2	1,566.5
1986	25,702	1,691	43,460	36.9	1,603.0
1987	25,891	1,679	43,481	37.6	1,634.3
Annual rate of change in %					
1961/70	0.2	- 1.0	- 0.8	5.4	4.5
1971/80	- 0.1	- 1.1	- 1.2	3.9	2.7
1981/87	- 0.2	- 0.6	- 0.8	2.2	1.4

Source: Institut der deutschen Wirtschaft, 1989b.

Table 10
Labour costs, productivity, and prices (year to year change, in %)

Year	Labour costs per		Productivity per		Unit labour costs	GNP price index
	employed person	hour	employed person	hour		
1951/55	8.5	-	6.5	-	1.9	3.4
1956/60	7.2	-	5.0	-	2.1	2.7
1961/65	8.6	9.6	4.2	5.2	4.2	3.7
1966/70	8.5	9.7	4.3	5.5	4.0	3.7
1971/75	10.5	12.2	2.7	4.3	7.6	6.5
1976/80	6.6	7.1	3.0	3.5	3.5	4.1
1981/85	3.9	4.5	1.8	2.3	2.1	3.2
1961	10.2	11.5	3.2	4.4	6.8	4.8
1962	9.0	10.5	4.4	5.8	4.4	3.9
1963	6.1	8.3	2.5	4.6	3.5	3.2
1964	8.2	7.1	6.6	5.5	1.5	3.1
1965	9.5	10.5	4.9	5.8	4.4	3.6
1966	7.6	8.7	3.3	4.3	4.2	3.3
1967	3.3	5.5	3.2	5.4	0.1	1.4
1968	6.7	7.2	5.5	6.0	1.1	2.2
1969	9.5	10.6	5.8	6.9	3.5	4.2
1970	16.0	17.1	3.8	4.7	11.8	7.6
1971	11.6	12.9	2.3	3.5	9.1	8.0
1972	9.9	11.4	4.4	5.8	5.3	5.3
1973	12.1	14.1	4.0	5.8	7.8	6.4
1974	11.5	13.5	1.6	3.5	9.7	7.1
1975	7.2	9.2	1.3	3.2	5.8	6.0
1976	7.9	5.9	6.3	4.3	1.5	3.6
1977	6.6	8.7	3.1	5.1	3.4	3.7
1978	5.6	6.5	2.3	3.2	3.2	4.3
1979	5.9	7.1	2.7	3.9	3.1	4.0
1980	6.9	7.9	0.3	1.2	6.6	4.8
1981	5.2	6.3	0.9	1.9	4.3	4.0
1982	4.2	3.6	1.1	0.7	3.1	4.4
1983	3.8	4.0	3.1	3.4	0.7	3.3
1984	3.4	3.9	2.7	3.1	0.7	2.0
1985	3.1	4.6	1.3	2.7	1.7	2.2
1986	3.8	4.8	1.3	2.0	2.5	3.1
1987	2.9	3.8	1.2	1.9	1.7	2.0
1988	3.1	3.1	2.9	2.8	0.2	1.9

Source: Institut der deutschen Wirtschaft, 1989b.

Table 11
Gross value added into the primary sector[1]

Year	Gross value added in million DM	Employed persons[2]	GVA per employed person in million DM
1960	17,660	3,581	4.93
1970	21,780	2,262	9.62
1980	30,370	1,437	21.13
1983	32,220	1,391	23.16
1984	34,650	1,376	25.18
1985	31,920	1,360	23.47
1986	34,080	1,344	25.36
1987	29,360	1,327	22.12

1. Agriculture, forestry, and fishery.
2. Including self-employed, family members helping out, employees.

Source: Statistisches Bundesamt, 1989; Bretschneider et al, continnally actualized edition.

Table 12
Gross value added and labor force in the primary sector[1]

Country	Persons employed as % of total employment		Gross value added as a % of total Gross Value Added	
	1970	1986	1970	1986
West Germany	8.6	5.3	3.4	1.8
France	13.9	7.3	6.9	3.9
Italy	20.3	10.9	8.1	4.4
United Kingdom	3.2	2.5	2.8	1.7
Spain	26.9	16.1	11.3	6.02
Netherlands	6.2	4.9	-	4.6
Belgium	4.7	2.9	3.7	2.1
Denmark	11.5	5.9	6.3	5.3
Greece	40.8	28.5	18.2	17.12
Poland	30.0	21.7	-	8.73
Ireland	27.1	15.7	16.3	13.84
Switzerland	8.6	6.5	-	-
Sweden	8.1	4.2	4.7	3.5
Austria	14.5	7.8	6.9	3.4
United States	4.5	3.1	2.7	2.0
Japan	17.5	8.5	5.9	2.8
Canada	7.6	5.1	4.2	3.35

1. Agriculture, forestry and fishery.
2. 1985.
3. 1981.
4. 1979.
5. 1984.

Source: Institut der deutschen Wirtschaft, 1989a.

Figure 1
Evolution of gross national product and energy consumption

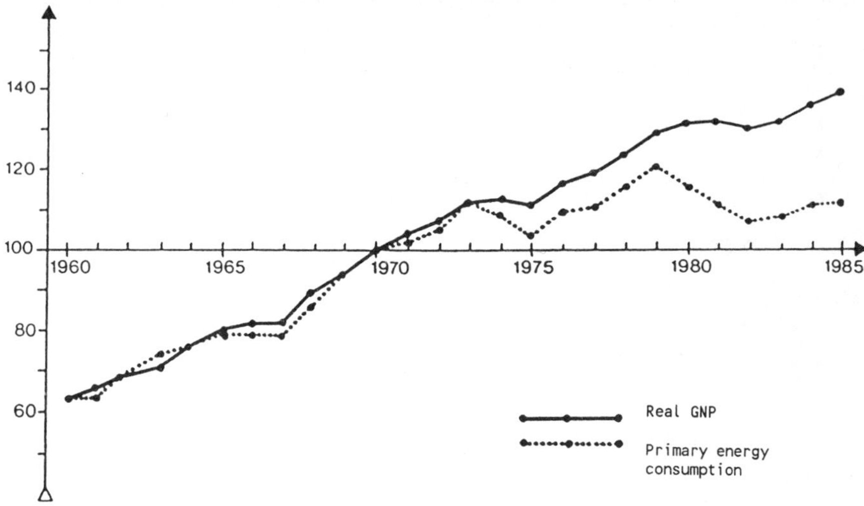

Source: Statistisches Bundesamt, 1987, p. 325.

Figure 2
Energy consumption by the sources of energy in 1950 and 1985

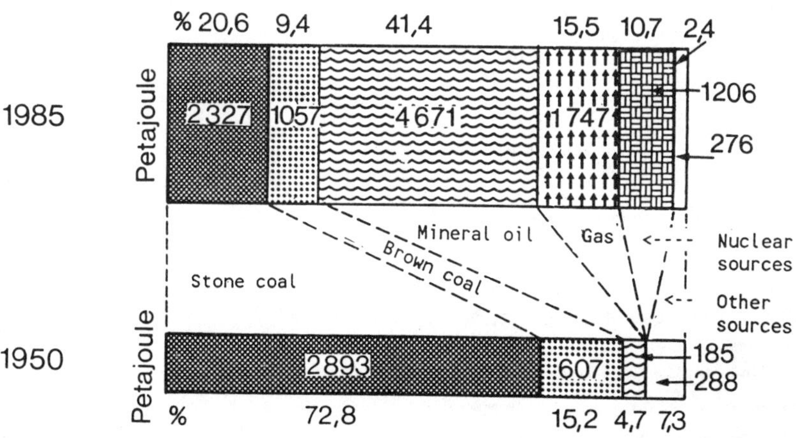

Source: Statisches Bundesamt, 1987, p. 328.

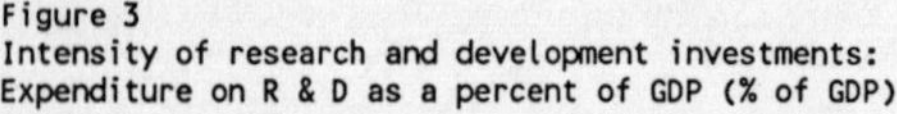

Figure 3
Intensity of research and development investments:
Expenditure on R & D as a percent of GDP (% of GDP)

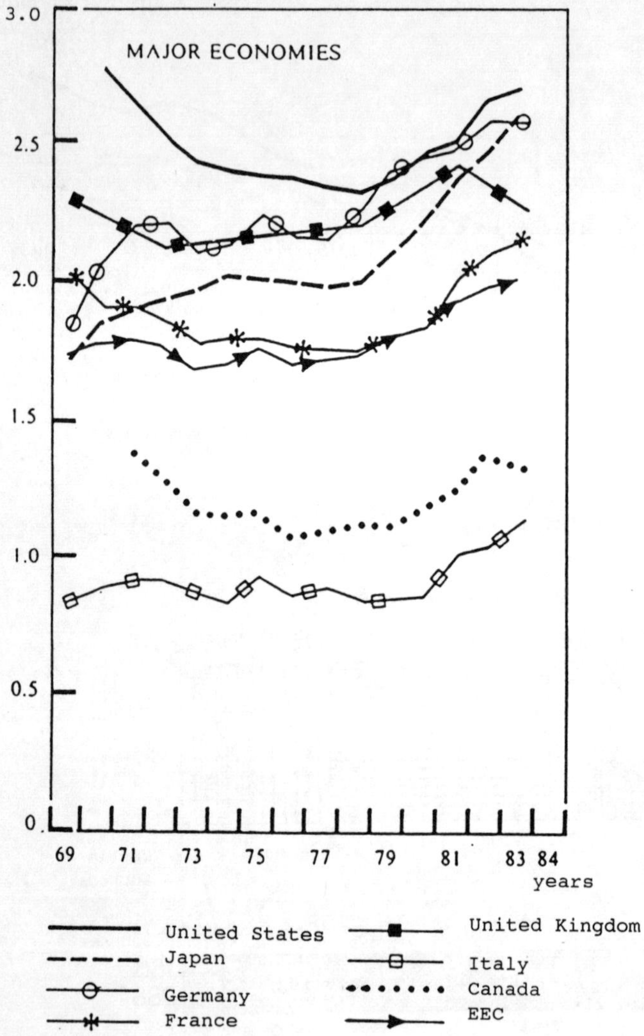

Source: OECD, 1986b, p. 20.

Figure 4
Ratio of business to public funding of gross domestic expenditure on R & D, when public funding = 100

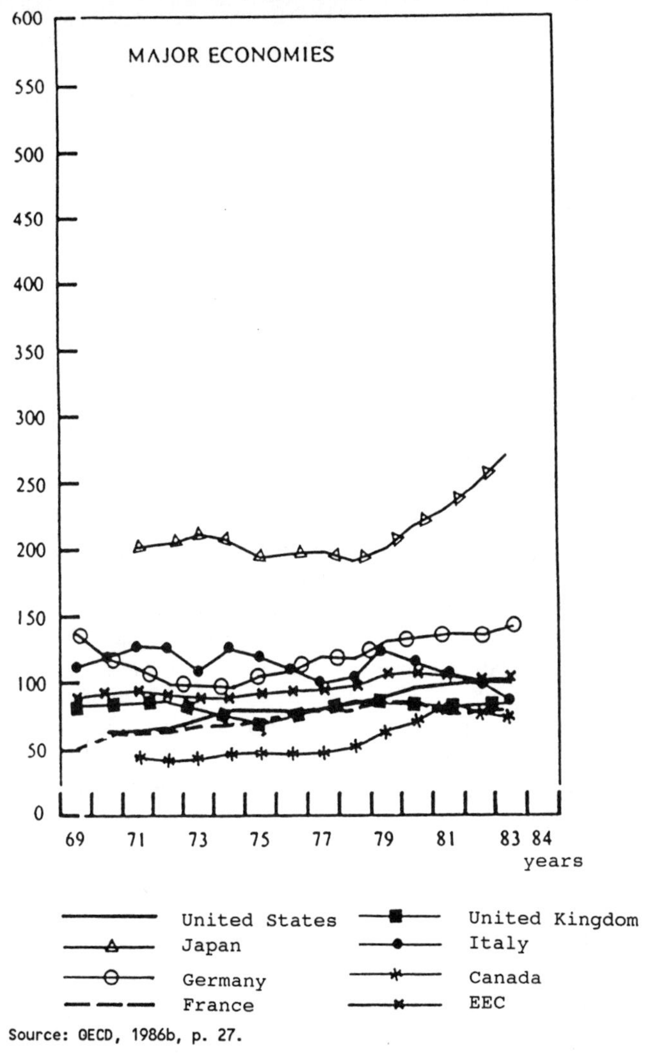

Source: OECD, 1986b, p. 27.

1. Age Groups

1.1 Youth

The increasingly long periods of time spent by young people in the educational system, as well as rising youth unemployment, have led to a lengthening of the adolescence phase. Due to job-market problems, work with no unemployment insurance for young people has gained in importance. As youths have left the parental home later over the past few years, the average age at which they establish their own families has risen.

Over the long term, extensive changes have taken place in the structure of the German population. The "age pyramid" (see 0.1, "Demographic Trends," and 3.2, "Childbearing"), deformed by two world wars and by the secular fertility decrease, has come to exhibit a clear deficit of under-25-year-olds. Whereas their share of the total population was 37.9% in 1950, it sank to 31.3% by 1986 (see table 1).

Not only has the numerical relation between the generations changed, but so has the social status of young people. In a 1962 survey, only 19.8% of 16-to-18-year-olds polled were students; in 1987, however, 59% were still in school. While the proportion of apprentices and trainees for this period dropped slightly, from 38.8% to 32.4%, the proportion of employed persons dropped drastically, from 39.7% to 4.6% (Allerbeck & Hoag, 1985).

In terms of participation in certain societal institutions and the gradual taking on of "adult" roles and responsibilities, the above-mentioned development, particularly the longer period spent in the educational system, means a lengthening of youth, with corresponding consequences for other areas, especially for place of residence, work, and starting a family.

Duration of Studies

Two factors have greatly contributed to the fact that more and more young people go through a longer period of schooling and training. One is the legislative extension of mandatory schooling to 12 years (as a rule, at least nine full academic years with a tendency toward a tenth and two to three years of vocational training), the raising of the minimum working age, the academization of career apprenticeship training, and the policy of educational opportunity for all in the 1970s. The other is the parental goal of bettering their children's job-market chances by means of more highly qualified schooling. This is expressed in increased attendance at high schools (secondary and academic high schools) as well as at career-specialized schools (Frackmann, 1985).

Results of cohort analyses show the average educational or training period increasing from 12 years for men and 10 years for women born in 1900 to 16 years for both men and women born in 1960 (see figure 1). While 16.4% of those leaving school in 1967 had not graduated from intermediate school, only 6.6% did so in 1985. The proportion of intermediate-school graduates dwindled from 54.2% to 28.9% during this period, while the percentage of secondary-school graduates grew from 20.3% to 37.6%, and that of high-school graduates from 9.1% to 26.9% (Statistisches Bundesamt, 1987a; for the history and formal structure of the West German educational system, see 8.1, "Educational System").

In the course of the educational reform of the 1970s, an obvious redistribution of on-the-job training took place in favour of educational training within the school system and at colleges. "This causes youths up to the age of 20 to be less and less confronted with the socialization conditions of companies. A change has taken place from a company- and job-related youth to a school- and learning-related adolescence" (Blossfeld & Nuthmann, 1988, p. 33).

Precarious Employment

Entry into the job market by those born in the high-fertility years from the mid-1970s to the mid-1980s at a time of economic decline led to employment problems for youths, the likes of which had not been witnessed since the early 1950s. Youth unemployment and increasing difficulties with finding a long-term job after apprenticeship still characterize the situation.

A growth in work without umemployment insurance for youth, not expressed in employment statistics, has been observed by social workers involved in youth work. Unemployment alternates with short-term, and sometimes multiple, jobs that are temporary and paid in such a way as to prevent any claims to the advantages of social insurance. These tendencies cannot be confirmed by data; only isolated survey results regarding partial fields are available.

In a representative 1984 poll, 20.3% of those under 20 years of age and 13.9 percent of 21-to-25-year-olds admitted to having a "side job." This percentage is significantly higher than that of older respondents. A remarkably high percentage

(27.1%) of those still in school or career training also described themselves as "moonlighters" (Merz & Wolff, 1986).

In 1987, 19% of 16-to-24-year-old employed persons were under a fixed-term employment contract, with the proportion of young men (26%) more than double that of young women. Among these women, however, there was a far higher share of short-term contracts of under six months (Forsa, 1987).

"Denesting" and Starting a Family

According to estimates and results of cohort analyses, the age at which youths leave home is dropping: While as many as 22.3% of men and 19.1% of women born between 1929 and 1931 still lived in the parental home at the age of 29, the proportion of men born 20 years later was 15.1%, and that of women was down to 6.7% (Mayer & Wagner, 1985; Ott, 1984). On the other hand, microcensus data from 1972, 1977, and 1982 showed that the share of the 20-to-24-year-old and 25-to-29-year-old men and women living with their parents had increased (Schwarz, cited in Mayer & Wagner, 1985; for 16-to-18-year-olds, see table 3).

Motives for young people's leaving home are employment or marriage. In a 1980 poll, 43.9 percent of the men and 61.8 percent of the women questioned gave marriage as the reason for leaving home (Ott, 1984); it must be taken into account that the average marriage age of men and women has been, after a downswing up until the late 1960s, continually climbing (see table 2). The rate of leaving home also rises when the first child either is on the way or has been born; starting in 1970, mothers have tended to be older at the birth of their first child (see 3.2, "Childbearing").

Politicial Participation

The opportunity for youths to participate in politics has improved over the past 40 years, partly because of the reduction of the voting age from 21 to 18 years. Along with the change away from the lack of involvement that marked political culture in the 1950s, youthful attitudes toward the possibility of exerting political influence have also changed. In a 1950 open poll, 44% of 18-to-21-year-old men and 40% of women of the same age could conceive of the individual having influence on politics. Two-thirds referred to participation by voting, and some saw influence as dependent upon the status and willpower of the individual. The fundamentally different result of a 1982 poll can only partially be traced to the presentation of a list of political activities: 81% of those polled considered voting to be an effective political measure. Majorities of approximately two-thirds advocated participation in citizens' initiatives and self-help groups, involvement in labour unions or workers' or personnel councils, signing petitions, and joining and working in a political party (Fischer, 1985).

Young people had more and better opportunities to exert political influence in the 1980s. The major difference lies in a shift away from comprehension of politics as formally structured and institution-oriented, and toward a political culture characterized by a broader spectrum of spheres of activity, including that of microsocial relations.

Karin Stiehr

References

Allerbeck, Klaus, and Wendy J. Hoag
1985 *Jugend ohne Zukunft? Einstellungen, Umwelt, Lebensperspektiven.* München: Piper.

Bertram, Hans
1987 *Jugend heute. Die Einstellungen der Jugend zu Familie, Beruf und Gesellschaft.* München: Beck.

Blossfeld, Hans-Peter, and Reinhard Nuthmann
1988 *Strukturelle Veränderungen der Jugendphase als Kohortenprozess.* Arbeitspapier Nr. 271 des Sonderforschungsbereich 3 der J.W. Goethe-Universität Frankfurt und Universität Mannheim. Frankfurt am Main/Mannheim.

Braun, Frank, et al.
1985 "Jugendarbeitslosigkeit - Strukturdaten und Konsequenzen." In Deutsches Jugendinstitut, ed., *Immer diese Jugend! Ein zeitgeschichtliches Mosaik. 1945 bis heute.* München: Deutsches Jugendinstitut.

Fischer, Arthur
1985 "Jugendliche und Erwachsene '85, Generationen im Vergleich." Vol. 3. In Jugendwerk der Deutschen Shell, ed., *Jugend der fünfziger Jahre - heute.* Opladen: Leske und Budrich.

Forsa, Gesellschaft für Sozialforschung und statistische
1987 Analysen mbH, *Ungeschützte und statusgeminderte Arbeitsverhältnisse. Ergebnisse einer bundesweiten Repräsentativerhebung.* Dortmund.

Frackmann, Margit
1985 *Mittendrin und voll daneben. Jugend heute.* Hamburg: VSA.

Gaiser, Wolfgang, et al.
1985 "Arbeitsmarkt - Risikoschwelle fürs Erwachsenwerden." In Deutsches Jugendinstitut, ed., *Immer diese Jugend! Ein zeitgeschichtliches Mosaik, 1945 bis heute.* München: Deutsches Jugendinstitut.

Mayer, Karl Ulrich
1985 *The Process of Leaving Home. A Comparison of Three Cohorts in West Germany.* Arbeitspapier Nr. 168 des Sonderforschungsbereich 3 der J.W. Goethe-Universität Frankfurt und Universität Mannheim. Frankfurt am Main/Mannheim.

Mayer, Karl Ulrich, and Michael Wagner
1985 *Heirat und der Auszug von Kindern aus dem elterlichen Haushalt. Ein Erklärungsmodell für die Jahrgänge 1929-31, 1939-41 und 1949-51*. Arbeitspapier Nr. 180 des Sonderforschungsbereich 3 der J.W. Goethe-Universität Frankfurt und Universität Mannheim. Frankfurt am Main/Mannheim.

Merz, Joachim, and Klaus Wolff
1986 *Eigenarbeit und Erwerbsarbeit im Haupt- und Nebenerwerb*. Arbeitspapier Nr. 191 des Sonderforschungsbereich 3 der J.W. Goethe-Universität Frankfurt und Universität Mannheim. Frankfurt am Main/Mannheim.

Ott, Notburga
1984 *Analyse der Haushaltsmobilität 1975-1980*. Arbeitspapier Nr. 157 des Sonderforschungsbereich 3 der J.W. Goethe-Universität Frankfurt und Universität Mannheim. Frankfurt am Main/Mannheim.

–
1986 "Ausscheiden erwachsener Kinder aus dem elterlichen Haushalt." In K. Zimmermann, ed., *Demographische Probleme der Haushaltsökonomie*. Bochum: Brockmeyer.

Statistisches Bundesamt, ed.
1984 *Zur Situation der Jugend in der Bundesrepublik Deutschland*. Wiesbaden.

–, ed.
1987a *Bildung im Zahlenspiegel*. Stuttgart/Mainz: Kohlhammer.

–, ed.
1987b *Datenreport 1987*. Bonn: Bundeszentrale für politische Bildung.

–, ed.
1988 *Statistisches Jahrbuch 1988 für die Bundesrepublik Deutschland*. Stuttgart/Mainz: Kohlhammer.

Table 1
Age structure of the German population

Year	Total population per 1,000	Aged from .....to .... years					
		under 15		15-18		18-21	
		1,000	%[1]	1,000	%[1]	1,000	%[1]
1950	50,798	11,849	23.3	2,266	4.5	2,153	4.2
1961	56,175	12,185	21.7	2,017	3.6	2,596	4.6
1970	60,651	14,058	23.2	2,392	3.9	2,428	4.0
1980	61,658	11,003	17.8	3,213	5.2	3,067	5.0
1986	61,066	9,070	14.9	2,606	4.3	3,111	5.1

Year	Total population per 1,000	Aged from .....to .... years			
		21-25		over 25	
		1,000	%[1]	1,000	%[1]
1950	50,798	3,000	5.9	31,530	62.1
1961	56,175	3,827	6.8	35,550	63.3
1970	60,651	3,057	5.0	38,716	63.8
1980	61,658	3,751	6.1	40,624	65.9
1986	61,066	4,297	7.0	42,982	68.7

Results from census to 1970; 1980, 1981 and 1982 results population calculation.

1. Proportion of "total population."

Source: Statistisches Bundesamt, 1984, p. 13; 1988, p. 61.

Table 2
Average marriage age in years, with family status "single" before wedding

Year	Men	Women
1950[1]	28.1	25.4
1955[1]	27.0	24.4
1960	25.9	23.7
1965	26.0	23.7
1970	25.6	23.0
1975	25.3	22.7
1980	26.1	23.4
1985	27.2	24.6
1986	27.5	24.9

1. 1950 and 1955 Fedeal Republic of Germany without the Saarland.

Source: Statistisches Bundesamt, 1988, p. 71.

Table 3
Living situation

Living with	1962	1983
Both parents	72.5	80.1
Mother and stepfather	4.1	3.3
Mother	13.3	9.6
Father and stepmother	0.9	1.3
Father	1.3	2.1
Other	7.8	3.6

Source: Allerbeck & Hoag, 1985, p. 55.

Figure 1
School and career-training time periods for German men and women

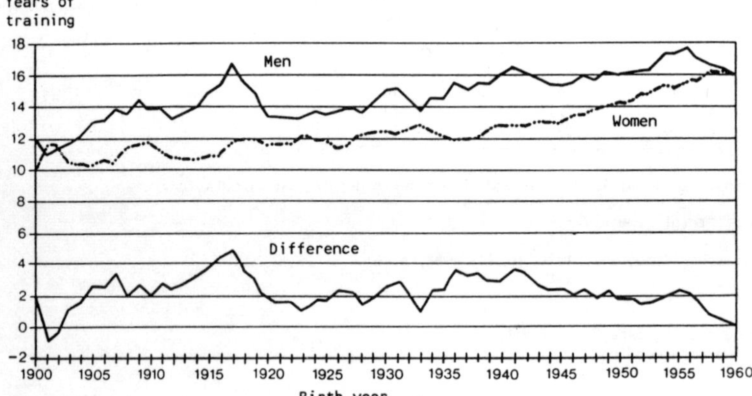

Source: Das sozio-ökonomische Panel, Welle 1 (1984), cited in Statistisches Bundesamt, 1987b, p. 394.

1.2 Elders

Higher life expectancy and earlier retirement from employment have lengthened the old-age life phase of West Germans. The increasing general affluence of society over the last few decades had a favourable effect on the income situation of old people; they are still, however, among the population groups threatened with a comparatively high risk of poverty.

Old people – defined by demographers as those over 60 to 65 years of age – comprise the fastest-growing population group in the Federal Republic, as in all highly industrialized countries. Not only does the age structure of the total population show a rising proportion of old people over time; even within the group of senior citizens, the "elderly" are clearly increasing. In 1961, 16.8% of the population was 60 years of age or over; this proportion rose to 20.5% in 1986. Within this group, the proportion of people aged 80 and over rose from 9.5% to 16.6% (see table 1). The looming "superannuation" or "geriatrization" of society has raised fears about future socio-political problems – for example, financing of social security and health care – that can be expected if the deficit in younger cohorts is not compensated for by more births and by immigration.

Life Expectancy and State of Health

A major reason for the constantly growing number of old people is the high life expectancy of those, especially women, who are already at an advanced age. The average expectancy for 60-year-old women increased by four years between 1950 and 1985, and by only one year for men of the same age (for developments in the different age cohorts, see table 2). The result was greater and greater gender imbalance with increasing age, although the respective degree of difference can vary widely among single-age cohorts. Due to war deaths in World War II, the fraction of men in the over-60 age groups is particularly low. As well, the "supermortality" of men in the birth-years after 1930 has led to a continued female surplus. In 1961, 66 men between 70 and 75 years of age per 100 women in the same age group were registered; this figure stood at only 56 in 1986; the ratio sank from 69 to 42 men per 100 women among 80- to 90-year-olds (see table 3). This means that more and more women spend their late years without a partner (see table 4). In 1982, more than half of women over 65, but scarcely one-fifth of men, were living alone.

Available findings concerning old people's state of health do not allow for any definite conclusions regarding a positive or negative development pattern (see table 5). As life expectancy has increased, there has been an overall rise in the occurrence of various old-age disorders such as blood-pressure problems, hearing and sight deficiencies, and cancer. It is said that chronic illnesses are more important in geriatric practice, since medical progress has resulted in fewer old people dying of diseases for which, however, they often remain in need of permanent treatment (Der Bundesminister für Jugend, Familie, Frauen und Gesundheit, 1986). This conclusion is not confirmed by the available data. The proportion of chronically ill persons did indeed increase by nearly 10% between 1974 and 1982. Distinct growth rates were, however, found for the ill *under* 65 years of age; old people retained the highest proportion but the most consistent level (see table 6).

Retirement Patterns

Since the mid-1960s, there has been a considerable increase – after a constant decline in the preceding years – of the granting of early retirement due to employment and/or career incapacitation (combined observation of both categories). Between 1966 and 1982, the corresponding proportions for male blue-collar workers rose from 51.9% to 55.2%, for female blue-collar workers from 49.3% to 59.7%, for male white-collar workers from 32.6% to 33.8%, and for female white-collar workers from 37.3% to 44.7% (Bretschneider et al., 1980).

The legislated age at which persons must retire has taken a clear long-term downswing. In 1889, the year Bismarck's *Invaliditäts- und Altersversicherungsgesetz* (Invalid and Old-Age Security Act) was introduced, retirement age was 70 years. In 1916, it was reduced to 65 years, a limit which remained in effect until 1973, when the flexible age limit was introduced, allowing for retirement as early as age 63. In the last few years, social plans for certain groups of workers and in certain industrial sectors (for example, the steel and mining industries), have mandated regulations for earlier retirement. Even excluding cases of early retirement due to incapacitation, to being out of work at 60 years of age, or to serious physical handicaps, there is still a drastic reduction in the number of those who retire as late as 65 years of age: in 1966, 47.5% of the male blue-collar workers did so; in 1982, only 8.2% did. Male white-collar workers have experienced a similar reduction, from 66.0% to 13.1% (Bretschneider et al., 1980).

Income

A crucial factor for development of old people's income was the widening of categories qualifying for public old-age security. When it was created, 100 years ago, the program was intended to protect mainly wage workers and low-salaried employees, comprising about 20% of the population, against old-age poverty. Just some of the groups that have since been included in the circle of social insurance – some on a mandatore, some on a voluntary basis – are work-incapacitated widows and orphans of the insured person, higher-income employees (all insured as of 1911), skilled workers (1938), farmers (1957), independent businesspersons (1972), and – most recently – artists. Public social security now covers over 90% of the population in the Federal Republic. As well, various company pension plans and a wide spectrum of private insurance schemes exist for particular groups of workers (Die Grünen und der Seniorenschutzbund "Graue Panther," 1985).

In general, old people have shared in the increasingly affluent society of the past few decades, and have at their disposal growing sums in the form of savings and real estate. In the 1970s, there was a marked increase in the level of old-age retirement pay (see table 7). In 1978, disposable income of retiree households was 1.86 times what it was in 1970, a slight advantage over worker and employee households. A lower adaptation rate has caused the pension level to stagnate in the past few years, and critics are warning of rising old-age poverty. Behind these average values are retiree households with widely varying income and capital situations. Estimates place the poverty potential of work-incapacitated older people at between 15% and 20%, with women at higher risk (Naegele, 1986; Der Bundesminister für Jugend, Familie, Frauen und Gesundheit, 1986).

The distribution structure of old-age income continues to be closely tied to distribution structures in the working world. Highly paid employment, together with a long career, leads to a high retirement income, while low income and other employment disadvantages – again applying mainly to women – have a negative effect on old-age material security (Naegele, 1986).

It can be observed that – comparable to the emergence of "youth" as a social group in the previous century – the shortened working life has brought about a new group that is gaining in social importance, the so-called *Junge Alte* or *Jungsenioren* (young senior citizens), and *Frührentner* (early retirees) (Steven & Veelken, 1985). While the "new seniors" are described as being generally more mobile, active, and self-confident than old people of past generations, early retirement does bring difficulties not solely of the financial type, since society's role patterns for this specific stage of life have not yet been sufficiently established. More recently, socio-political concepts are being developed on the federal and municipal levels which devote more attention to the resulting problems.

Karin Stiehr

References

Ballerstedt, Eike, and Wolfgang Glatzer
1979 *Soziologischer Almanach*. Frankfurt am Main/New York: Campus.

Braun, Bernard, and Hartmut Reiners
1986 "Ungleiche Verteilung gesundheitlicher Risiken und Chancen." In Hans-Werner Franz, et al., eds., *Neue alte Ungleichheiten. Bericht zur sozialen Lage der Bundesrepublik*. Opladen: Westdeutscher Verlag.

Bretschneider, Joachim, et al.
1980 *Handbuch einkommens-, vermögens- und sozialpolitischer Daten*. Loseblattsammlung. Köln: Bachem.

Bundesminister für Jugend, Familie, Frauen und Gesundheit, ed.
1986 *Vierter Familienbericht. Die Situation der älteren Menschen in der Familie*. Bonn.

Die Grünen, and Seniorenschutzbund "Graue Panther", eds.
1985 *Grundrente statt Altersarmut*. Berlin: Verlagsgesellschaft Gesundheit.

Glatzer, Wolfgang, and Maria Müller-Adnritzki
1983 "Sozioökonomie." In Wolf Oswald, et al., eds., *Gerontologie*. Stuttgart: Kohlhammer.

Hinschützer, Ursula, and Heide Momber
1982 *Basisdaten über ältere Menschen in der Statistik der Bundesrepublik Deutschland*. Berlin: Deutsches Zentrum für Altersfragen.

Naegele, Gerhard
1986 "Armut im Alter." In Hans-Werner Franz, et al., eds., *Neue alte Ungleichheiten. Bericht zur sozialen Lage der Bundesrepublik*. Opladen: Westdeutscher Verlag.

Schmid, Josef
1984 *Bevölkerungsveränderungen in der Bundesrepublik Deutschland. Eine Revolution auf leisen Sohlen*. Stuttgart/Berlin/Köln/Mainz: Kohlhammer.

Schwarz, Karl
1987 "Zur Lebenssituation alter und sehr alter Menschen in der Bundesrepbulik Deutschland." In Hans Hoffmeister, et al., eds., *Lebensbedingungen alter Menschen. Materialien zum Vierten Familienbericht*. Vol. 1. München: Juventa.

Statistisches Bundesamt, ed.
1987 *Frauen in Familie, Beruf und Gesellschaft*. Wiesbaden: Kohlhammer.

–,ed.
1988 *Statistisches Jahrbuch 1988 für die Bundesrepublik Deutschland*. Stuttgart/Mainz: Kohlhammer.

Steven, Elke, and Ludger Veelken
1986 "Junge Alte. Soziale Probleme in der Lebenssitaution einer neuen gesellschaftlichen Gruppe." In Hans-Werner Franz, et al., eds., *Neue alte Ungleichheiten. Bericht zur sozialen Lage der Bundesrepublik*. Opladen: Westdeutscher Verlag.

Table 1
Increase in number of old and very old people in the Federal Republic of Germany

Year	1,000	60 years and older		80 years and older	
		1,000	% of col.1	1,000	% of col.2
1961	56,175	9,448	16.8	897	9.5
1970	60,651	11,678	19.3	1,129	9.7
1980	61,566	11,888	19.3	1,598	13.4
1986	61,066	12,530	20.5	2,074	16.6

Source: Glatzer & Müller-Andritzki, 1983, p. 453; Statistisches Bundesamt, 1988; (author's figures).

Table 2
Life expectancy of older people

Mortality tabular periods	Average further life expectancy (in years) of person aged:						
	60	65	70	75	80	85	90
Male:							
1949/51[1]	16.20	12.84	9.84	7.28	5.24	3.72	2.66
1960/62[1]	15.49	12.36	9.60	7.20	5.24	3.76	2.69
1970/72[1]	15.31	12.06	9.35	7.17	5.36	3.92	2.81
1980/82	16.51	13.09	10.09	7.64	5.73	4.34	3.42
1984/86	17.10	13.65	10.55	7.96	5.94	4.46	3.61
Female:							
1949/51[1]	17.46	13.72	10.42	7.68	5.57	4.02	2.89
1960/62[1]	18.48	14.60	11.12	8.16	5.85	4.17	3.03
1970/72[1]	19.12	15.18	11.63	8.59	6.16	4.37	3.16
1980/82	20.82	16.77	12.99	9.67	6.98	4.95	3.62
1984/86	21.55	17.46	13.63	10.21	7.36	5.22	3.79

1. General mortality tables.

Source: Schwarz, 1987, p. 53; Statistisches Bundesamt, 1988, p. 76.

Table 3
Gender proportion among old people

Year	Men per 100 women in respective age category (in years)		
	60-65	70-75	80-90
1961	77	66	69
1970	74	61	54
1980	66	59	36
1986	69	56	42

Source: Glatzer & Müller-Andritzki, 1983, p. 453; Statistisches Bundesamt, 1988; (author's figures).

Table 4
Members of private households aged over 50 years, according to age cohort and proportion of those living alone in 1961, 1972 and 1982 (persons living alone per 100 capita)

Aged from - to under in years	Men 1961	Men 1972	Men 1982		Women 1961	Women 1972	Women 1982	
50-55	5.2	4.7	6.9		9.8	13.4	10.8	
55-60	5.6	5.7	6.7		14.9	23.2	18.3	
60-65	6.3	7.5	7.2		22.0	30.5	30.0	
65-70		9.8	9.9[1]			38.5	43.2[2]	
70-75		12.8	13.8			47.0	52.3	
75-80	10.6		18.1		32.6		59.2	
80-85		19.4	25.7	22.0		49.7	63.2	60.8
85-90			34.6				63.0	
90 and older			32.9				56.6	

1. 65 and older: 18.1
2. 65 and older: 53.1

Source: Statistisches Bundesamt (1961 census-, 1972 and 1982 microcensus results), cited in Schwarz, 1987, p. 46.

Table 5
Ill persons according to age and gender

Age cohort	Unit	1966 Men	1966 Women	1970 Men	1970 Women	1974 Men	1974 Women	1982 Men	1982 Women
Under 15	%	6.3	5.8	8.2	8.0	15.9	11.4	8.4	8.1
15-40	%	5.5	7.0	10.6	12.7	22.2	18.3	6.9	8.0
40-65	%	13.5	14.1	26.6	30.5	34.8	33.5	16.7	18.2
65 and older	%	21.3	24.5	46.5	52.0	26.9	36.6	32.8	37.3
Total (in 1,000)	N	2,629	3,657	5,324	7,540	4,054	5,542	3,945	5,411
Proportion of resident population	%	9.7	11.7	18.7	23.7	14.8	17.7	13.4	16.8

Source: Glatzer & Ballerstedt, 1979, p. 68; Statistisches Bundesamt, 1987, p. 145.

Table 6
Proportion of the chronically ill among ill persons
(in % of ill persons)

Age cohort	1974	1978	1982
Under 15	9.3	13.6	14.1
15-40	27.0	33.1	34.7
40-65	65.3	68.4	72.4
65 and older	83.5	85.0	86.7
Total	56.1	61.6	65.7

Source: Statistisches Bundesamt, Wirtschaft und Statistik (various publications), author's compilations, cited in Braun & Reiners, 1986, p. 155.

Table 7
Pension for old-age retirement in old-age security of workers and employees[1], assuming 40 years of insurance contribution

Year	Monthly pension (on 1. Jan.) DM	Pension level[2] (in %) measured according to:	
		gross work salary[3]	net work salary[3]
1957	214.10	50.9	59.3
1970	489.00	44.0	56.9
1972	548.40	43.5	57.3
1974	668.60	41.6	57.4
1976	826.00	44.8	63.3
1978	1,008.10	46.1	65.2
1980	1,095.60	44.6	63.5
1982	1,205.00	44.9	64.6
1984	1,315.50	45.3	65.2
1985	1,355.00	45.4	65.1

1. According to personal calculation base of 100% (average income).
2. Old-age pension per calendar year; taxation (1968, 1969) and reimbursement (1972) of health-insurance contribution taken into account.
3. Average gross salary of all insured persons; net salary is calculated therefrom by subtraction of average taxation (income and social taxes) of all non-self-employed persons, corresponding to national-economic total calculation.

Source: BTDrucks. 8/4327, 1980 (Materialband), p. 241, Hinschützer & Momber, 1982, p. 180; Bundesminister für Arbeit und Sozialordnung, 1986, p. 255.

2. Microsocial

2.1 Self-identification

Citizens of the Federal Republic increasingly see themselves as belonging to the middle class. Within the context of immediate personal environs, cultivation of contact with neighbours, friends, and colleagues and involvement in clubs or associations has risen: the past concentration on family relationships has thus gained a new dimension.

Each member of society develops an urge to join social groups; this process will be called self-identification in the following text. In a macrosocial context, such affiliation takes place within the dimension of class membership.

Subjective class affiliation has undergone a marked transformation over the last 30 years; this has had the most impact on the feeling of belonging to the working and middle classes. While 49% of those polled in 1955 saw themselves as belonging to the working class, this proportion had dropped by almost half (27%) by 1986. Concurrently, the fraction placing themselves in the middle class rose from 44% to 71%. Only 1% identified with the lower class or the upper class (1% each) in 1986; in 1955 these proportions had been 5% and 2%, respectively (see table 1).

One cannot speak of a homogeneous consciousness among the employed (the term "employed" includes salaried and wage workers) in the Federal Republic. Recent research infers that the majority of workers, whether skilled or master workers, are still loyal to the working class. Employees and civil servants see themselves as belonging to the middle class. Remarkably, civil servants of all three status groups have the strongest tendency to identify themselves with the upper-middle or upper classes (see table 2).

This long-term smoothing-out of subjective class affiliation has had various and quite objective reasons: while the proportion of workers among the total employed has declined by about 20% since 1950, and the proportion of independent businesspersons and family members "helping out" has dropped by as much as 50%, the proportion of civil servants and employees more than doubled (see figure

1). As early as the beginning of the 1950s, a "levelled-out middle-class society" was prognosticated. Though neither a uniform middle-class lifestyle nor uniform or consistent participation in consumption of material goods (Schelsky, 1953) can be spoken of (see 16.4, "Poverty"), it cannot be denied that "the whole pyramid of social hierarchy has changed, in favour of the middle level, into a rhombus, and – more important – has in its entirety shifted upwards. This could explain the fiction of 'ascent' and the resultant additional confusion regarding one's real class and rank" (Claessens et al., 1985, p. 298).

As regards self-identification in the microsocial field, it has been posited that, as part of a general transformation of attitudes, people are concentrating more on their individual environment – a trend that could be interpreted as a retreat into private life. Indeed, empirical long-term studies confirm that interpersonal contacts have become more frequent and closer. Interaction between family members is more intense, circles of friends and acquaintances have expanded, and incidence of visits to neighbours or colleagues and of involvement in voluntary clubs or associations has increased (see 2.2, "Kinship Networks"; 2.5, "Voluntary Associations"; 2.6, "Sociability Networks"). In 1949, 19% of West Germans complained of frequent solitude, while in 1980 only 7% did so (Piel, 1987).

Local ties have definitely strengthened among the population. In 1953 – when millions of people had just been expelled from or had fled their homes – nearly one-fourth of those polled would have preferred to move from their place of residence, while only 9% responded similarly in 1979. The proportion of those reluctant to move away rose from 70% to 83% (see table 3). The subjective reasons given are instructive: in 1953, nearly half would have missed "the countryside here"; other reasons, in order of preference, were the present house or apartment, relatives living in the neighbourhood, the circle of acquaintance, and remaining near the burial place of family members.

It is understandable that home country and family – exalted values under National Socialism, threatened by war, but fundamental in times of economic hardship and political disorientation – were the most important factors for self-identification within the immediate personal environment in the 1950s. One generation later, a different picture presents itself. Almost two-thirds of those polled claimed that they would very much miss their circle of acquaintances, and somewhat over half would miss their house or apartment. Relatives are accorded third place, and the former leading motive – the countryside – places fourth. Fifth in order of preference are neighbours, who were in seventh position, behind even the church community, in 1953. In 1979, the church community would have been missed less than, for example, club mates and neighbourhood contacts within the area or street of residence (see table 4). As identification with friends and acquaintances has grown, the countryside and gravesites have lost their importance; sociability and outside contacts have developed into dominant motives. Dwindling loyalty to the church community is the one exception, and is thus all the more remarkable.

The above-described developmental patterns of self-identification on the macro- and microsocial levels should be regarded in connection with the long-term transformation of social structures. In earlier times, relationships within the immediate personal environment were easier to grasp and more permanent; one could count on community solidarity and highly developed social control. However, the modern industrial social system has different requirements: individual mobility – in the hierarchy of the working world as well as in the geographical one – and the ability to conform to rapid changes in personal living environment. It is no coincidence that the idea of city life seemed attractive to the young generation of the 1950s, since it seemed to offer all the opportunities lacking in the closed and tightly supervised life in small towns and villages: cultural and leisure activity, places of entertainment, university, career (Korczak, 1981). Political protest and alternative movements arose in metropolitan areas in the 1960s, but in the 1970s, a rethinking of ideals set in; people looked back to the values of the smaller, closer, easier-to-comprehend community. Rural communes were founded, Buddhist-oriented sects experienced new influxes; and urban groups established their own infrastructure (organic-food stores, restaurants and pubs, educational institutions, etc.).

Rediscovery of the environment within the immediate horizon as a reaction of the "lonely crowd" (Riesman) against increasing isolation and alienation involves risks as well as opportunities. Although there has been an undeniable gain in solidarity, support, and personal interaction, some fears are being voiced that traditions specific to German history could be revived: mistrust and prejudice against out-groups, the tendency to scapegoat "strangers," the desire for "law and order." The recently observed rise in hostility toward foreigners seems to confirm this kind of development; trends toward more tolerance in wide-ranging fields contradict it (see 7.3, "Norms of Conduct").

Global endangerment of human survival, against a background of technological risk (Elias, 1987), is finding its way into public awareness. In 1970, more than half of the population was optimistic that humankind could recognize and overcome threatening situations, but the proportion of those with this opinion was down to 30% in 1984 (see table 5). Over just five years, between 1982 and 1987, attitudes toward certain values have changed dramatically in German society. More and more people believe that too little value is placed on children, marriage, family, friendship, and tenderness – that is, on aspects of the immediate social environment; wider-ranging deficits are also perceived, in terms of social justice, civil involvement in political matters, equality before the law, equal opportunity for women and other groups, and solidarity (see table 6).

These results undoubtedly show increasing consciousness of problems among the West German population. The question remains whether the growing self-identification with the more immediate social environment should necessarily be interpreted as an expression of resignation and withdrawal into private life.

Karin Stiehr

References

Ballerstedt, Eike, and Wolfang Glatzer
1979 *Soziologischer Almanach. Handbuch gesellschaftlicher Daten und Indikatoren*. Frankfurt am Main/New York: Campus.

Claessens, Dieter, Arno Klönne, and Armin Tschoepe
1985 *Sozialkunde der Bundesrepublik Deutschland. Grundlagen, Strukturen, Trends in Wirtschaft und Gesellschaft*. Reinbek: Rowohlt.

Elias, Norbert
1987 *Die Gesellschaft der Individuen*. Frankfurt am Main: Suhrkamp.

EMNID, ed.
1987 *EMNID-Information*, no. 7.

Glatzer, Wolfgang, and Wolfgang Zapf, eds.
1984 *Lebensqualität in der Bundesrepublik. Objektive Lebensbedingungen und subjektives Wohlbefinden*. Frankfurt am Main/New York: Campus.

Institut für Demoskopie Allensbach, ed.
1981 *Eine Generation später. Bundesrepublik Deutschland 1953-1979*. Allensbach.

–, ed.
1987 *Allensbacher Berichte*, no. 25.

Keupp, Heiner, and Bernd Röhrle, eds.
1987 *Soziale Netzwerke*. Frankfurt am Main/New York: Campus.

Korczak, Dieter
1981 *Rückkehr in die Gemeinschaft. Kleine Netze: Berichte über Wohnsiedlungen*. Frankfurt am Main: Fischer.

Krebs, Dagmar
1987 *Soziale Schicht und subjektive Wahrnehmung*. Unveröffentlichtes Manuskript. Mannheim.

Piel, Edgar
1987 *Im Geflecht der kleinen Netze. Vom deutschen Rückzug ins Private*. Zürich: Edition Interfrom.

Riesman, David
1958 *Die einsame Masse. Eine Untersuchung der Wandlungen des amerikanischen Charakters*. Hamburg: Rowohlt.

Schelsky, Helmut
1953 "Die Bedeutung des Schichtungsbegriffs für die Analyse der gegenwärtigen deutschen Gesellschaft." In Helmut Schelsky, *Auf der Suche nach Wirklichkeit*. Düsseldorf: Diederichs.

Statistisches Bundesamt, ed.
1987 *Datenreport 1987*. Bonn: Bundeszentrale für politische Bildung.

Table 1
Subjective class affiliation (in %)

Class affiliation	1955[1]	1976[2]	1986[3]
Upper class	2	1	1
Middle class	44	59	71
Working class	49	33	27
Lower class	5	*	1

* Category not given.

1. Janowitz, 1955.
2. Zurnabus, 1976.
3. Allbus, 1986.

Source: Ballerstedt & Glatzer, 1979, p. 251; Krebs, 1987.

Table 2
Subjective class affiliation of employed persons according to job position (in %)

Class affiliation	Working class		Middle class		Upper middle class		None of these	
	1980	1984	1980	1984	1980	1984	1980	1984
Workers								
-Qualified, unqualified	65	64	33	35	1	0	1	1
-Skilled, master workers	61	56	39	39	0	4	0	0
Employees								
-Clerical, mid-level	15	16	80	71	5	12	1	1
-Upper echelon	5	9	71	69	23	20	1	2
Civil servants								
-Clerical, mid-level	18	7	66	71	14	22	0	0
-Upper echelon	1		57		37		5	

Data base: Wohfahrtssurvey 1980 and 1984.

Source: Glatzer & Zapf, 1984, p. 103; Statistisches Bundesamt, 1987, p. 450.

Table 3
Local ties to place of residence (in %)

Wording of question: "Are you willing or unwilling to move away from here (this city, this place)?"

Item	1953	1979
Willing	24	9
Not very willing	21	25
Not at all willing	49	58
Non't know	6	8
Total	100	100

Source: Allensbacher Archiv, IfD-Umfragen 225, 1287, cited in Institut für Demoskopie Allensbach, 1981, p. 38.

Table 4
Local ties to place of residence (in %)

Wording of question: "What would you miss the most if you had to move away from your place of residence?" (presentation of list with possibility of multiple answers)

Item	1953	1979
Circle of acquaintance	36	65
Present house or apartment	42	54
Relatives living here	38	45
The countryside here	47	39
My neighbors	16	27
Graves of relatives	28	22
The street or area here	14	22
Club colleagues	8	14
I wouldn't like to work for another company	13	16
Sport colleagues	8	13
Our church or parish	17	11
My drinking buddies	4	7
Party colleagues	2	2
I'd miss nothing	12	3
Other answer	1	-
No reply	3	2
Total	289	342

Source: Allensbacher Archiv, IfD-Umfragen 225, 1287 (Halbgruppe), cited in Institut für Demoskopie Allensbach, 1981, p. 39.

Table 5
Opinions regarding the environment

Wording of question: "What do you think will happen if things continue like they are with the environment? Here is a list of opinions - which one most resembles your own view?" (presentation of list)

Item	1970	1977	1984
If things continue like this, mankind will destroy themselves and all life will be extinct.	8	11	17
Nature will be largely destroyed and it will become more threatening for humans, animals and plants to continue living under these conditions.	32	38	51
Of course it will become worse, but mankind and nature will adjust to these dangers and life will adapt.	36	37	22
I don't think it's that bad - we'll manage with these dangers.	19	12	8
Undecided	5	2	2
Total	100	100	100

Federal Republic of Germany and West Berlin, population aged 16 years and older.

Source: Allensbacher Archiv, cited in Allensbacher Berichte, 1987/no. 25, p. 3.

Table 6
Meaning of social values and norms in five-years comparsion (in%)

Wording of question: "I will now read you some concepts. Please give me your opinion in each case, if - all in all - our society attaches too much, too little, or just enough value to them."

Item	Too much value		Too little value	
	1982	1987	1982	1987
Children	8	4	43	56
Respect for marriage	7	7	47	56
Social justice	9	7	34	54
Friendship	5	5	38	51
Tenderness	6	5	34	50
Morality	11	12	42	49
Equal opportunity	7	6	35	49
Civil involvement in politics	9	10	39	45
Family	5	5	30	44
Equality before the law	4	3	33	43
Woman's equality	14	16	30	42
Solidarity	7	5	29	41
Old-age security	12	9	31	38
Religious way of life	11	11	29	37
Law and order	10	8	36	36
Sense of duty	13	13	35	34
Self-development	14	20	25	28
Happiness	15	14	21	25
Hard work	21	21	27	23
Personal freedom	21	18	18	20
Leisure time	23	26	18	19
Performance	26	28	24	18
Education (school, college)	18	15	14	18
Vacation	27	27	12	15
Money	55	62	9	7
Personal property	25	34	12	6
Higher living standard	54	58	6	5
Fashion	42	53	5	5

Source: EMNID-Informationen 1987, p. 9.

Figure 1
Employed persons according to job position

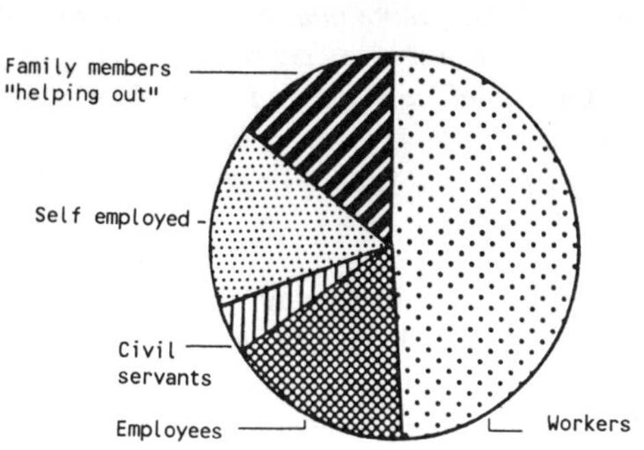

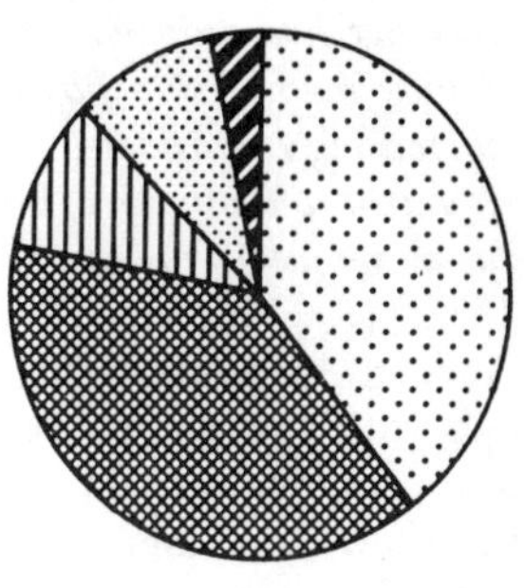

Source: Statistisches Bundesamt, 1987, p. 86.

2.2 Kinship Networks

Although the number of households in which more than two generations live together has dropped dramatically over the past few decades, the concept of family membership has been extended: third- and fourth-degree relatives are increasingly considered "family." All in all, family contact has become more frequent and intensive, but network support continues to be provided primarily by closer family members.

Until recently, empirical studies on social transformation of the family were oriented, with few exceptions, toward the "isolated nuclear family" (Parsons); therefore, non-nuclear kin relationships were often given little consideration. There are few data suitable for the direct time-series comparison necessary to a comprehensive observation of the development of kinship networks.

The requirements for family life after World War II posed serious problems: estimates recorded between 1.5 million and 2.5 million war widows, and 2.5 million badly handicapped persons. In 1948, the divorce wave reached a peak at 186 divorces per 100,000 persons, creating 80,000 so-called divorce orphans. Twenty-two percent of existent housing had been completely destroyed, and in 1950 0.6 dwellings were available per household (Vogel, 1985).

Kinship Models

An empirical survey on models of German family life in the years 1949–1951 presents the thesis of increasingly "relaxed and individualized relations in comparison with the parents' or grandparents' generation." The kinship relationship was seen as being forced out of the family and into the social sector; even parents of adult children were banished to a "kinship distance" (Wurzbacher, 1958, p. 239).

This supposition was corroborated during subsequent years by the decline in the proportion of households shared by more than two generations from 7.2% in 1955 to a mere 2.8% in 1982 (Diewald, 1984). Most of all, family size and composition had changed. The long-term increase in life expectancy contributed to an obvious extension of intergeneration kinship systems; on the other hand, a limit on collateral kin relationships was caused by the reduced birth rate, which meant a reduction in the number of siblings and cousins. While 206 children were born per 100 marriages contracted in the years 1941–1950, only 148 were per 100 marriages in the years 1970–1974. The proportion of households comprising five or more persons declined from 16.1% to 6.3% between 1950 and 1985, while the proportion of one-person households, about 50% of which currently consist of men and women over 60 years of age, grew from 19.4% to 33.6% during the same period (Statistisches Bundesamt, 1987). Remarkably, these individualization tendencies are not reflected in the subjective conception of who belongs to the family and who does not. Regardless of class affiliation and family status, distant kin – parents-in-law, uncles and aunts, nieces and nephews – were more consistently included in the family in 1979 than in 1953 (see table 1). A time comparison of the years 1969 and 1983 with regard to urban kin relationships confirms this tendency. More and more people include distant kin, such as uncles, aunts, and cousins, in the circle of relatives considered important to them personally (see table 2).

Cohabitation and Spatial Distribution

In regard to the spatial distribution of family members, a 1983 study showed a clear concentration of kin in the respondents' respective towns, and their environs, but – as expected – there was no notable number of kin residing in the household. The average journey to visit the parents was no more than an hour in two-thirds of the cases, and a similar, though less clear-cut, spatial distribution of siblings could also be observed (Lüschen, 1987). Visits between kin were more frequent in 1983 than in 1969. The average number of relatives with whom visits were exchanged at least quarterly rose from 2.3 to 5.3 in Bremen, and from 2.5 to 7.4 in Cologne (Lüschen, 1985); Christmas visits increased similarly (see table 3).

Network Support

The overall family atmosphere seems to have become more relaxed and trustful, and inclusion of distant kin is voluntary: as preferred conversation partners, sons and daughters, and third- and fourth-degree female and male relatives made considerable gains between 1953 and 1979 (see table 4). Family members were also increasingly favoured as advisors in difficult situations. When men were asked about the person in whom they confided, only 37% named their wife in 1953; in 1979 this proportion was up to 53%. Men did not enjoy such high preference as advisors: they experienced an increase of only from 42% to 44%. While sons, daughters, brothers, and sisters had a lower incidence as person confided in, they were named more frequently in 1979 than in 1953 (see table 5).

The available data do not allow for a time-period comparison for other types of network support. Close kin are still principally the persons turned to for assistance with household or garden work, or in the case of illness (see table 6). There is, however, more variation in requests made of single family members.

All surveys carried out in the past few years agree that women – in spite of two decades of continuously rising paid employment – participate to a much greater degree in the exchange of informal services within the family than do men. Babysitting is the most frequent assistance provided by grandmothers; in 1980, 23% of women between 45 and 60 years of age regularly cared for their grandchildren. With regard to housework, 39% of married women living in the same house as their mothers or mothers-in-law, and 19% of married women living near them, said that they were a great help (Deutscher Bundestag, 1986). Very old people are taken care of, for the most part, by daughters. In a recent study on the life situation of 55- to 70-year-old daughters with at least one parent alive – 45% of whom were found to be grandmothers themselves – 46% of the daughters in their sixth and seventh decade of life took care of parents in their own household (Lehr, 1985).

All in all, it can be ascertained that the "kinship distance" between the generations, which Wurzbacher called an expression of egoism, has not led to a reduction of responsibility, but rather to an emotional relationship characterized by "intimacy with distance" (Rosenmayr, 1978). The concept of family membership is no longer limited to the closest kin; where there is mutual understanding and common interests, even distant kin are increasingly being included in the exchange of family contacts.

Karin Stiehr

References

Deutscher Bundestag, ed.

1986 *Die Situation der älteren Menschen in der Familie. Vierter Familienbericht*. Bonn.

Diewald, Martin

1984 *Das "SPES-Indikatorentableau 1976".Fortschreibung bis zum Jahr 1982*. Arbeitspapier Nr. 150 des Sonderforschungsbereich 3 der J.W. Goethe-Universität Frankfurt und Universität Mannheim. Frankfurt am Main/Mannheim.

Institut für Demoskopie Allensbach, ed.

1981 *Eine Generation später. Bundesrepublik Deutschland 1953-1979*. Allensbach.

Lehr, Ursula

1985 *The Role of Women in Caring for the Elderly*. Speech at the European Science Foundation Workshop, Jerusalem, 11.-13.11.1985.

Lüschen, Günther

1988 "Familial-verwandtschaftliche Netzwerke." In Rosemarie Nave-Herz, ed., *Wandel und Kontinuität der Familie in der Bundesrepublik Deutschland*. Stuttgart: Enke.

Lüschen, Günther, et al.

1985 "Familie, Verwandtschaft und Ritual im Wandel." In Hans Franz, ed., *22. Deutscher Soziologentag 1984*. Opladen: Westdeutscher Verlag.

Neidhardt, Friedhelm
1985 *Soziale Netzwerkhilfen und Untersützungsprobleme in der Bevölkerung*. Bericht für das Bundeskanzleramt. Köln.

Rosenmayr, Leopold, ed.
1978 *Das menschliche Lebensalter*. München: Piper.

Vogel, Angela
1983 "Familie." In Wolfgang Benz, ed., *Die Bundesrepublik Deutschland*. Vol. 2: Gesellschaft. Frankfurt am Main: Fischer.

Wurzbacher, Gerhard
1958 *Leitbilder gegenwärtigen deutschen Familienlebens*. Stuttgart: Enke.

Table 1
Who counts as family? (in %)

Wording of question: "When we talk about family: who comes to mind, whobelong to your family?"

Item	Married		Single, under 30		Widowed		Workers		Clerks, civil servants[1]		Upper-echelon employ., civ.servs.	
	1953	1979	1953	1979	1953	1979	1953	1979	1953	1979	1953	1979
Children (son, daughter)	86	81	15	16	83	81	71	71	67	67	77	74
Spouse (husband, wife or companion)	96	93	15	14	35	30	72	69	65	63	85	80
Parents	19	34	78	83	13	13	26	36	27	39	29	43
Siblings	10	23	53	65	13	21	17	28	19	29	18	33
Grandchild	5	10	-	1	11	38	4	13	5	12	4	7
Parents-in-law	5	11	1	1	1	1	3	6	4	7	5	12
Children-in-law	3	5	-	2	9	24	3	8	3	7	3	5
Uncles, aunts, nephews or distant relations	1	4	3	12	4	6	1	5	3	8	3	6
Grandparents	-	5	3	17	-	3	1	7	-	5	-	4
Siblings-in-law	2	4	1	3	3	3	2	3	2	4	2	4
I'm alone and have no family	-	-	3	-	7	3	3	1	4	1	1	-
Others, and no answer	4	4	16	20	5	3	6	5	6	7	7	7
Total	231	274	188	234	184	226	209	252	205	249	234	275

1. Includes those employed in office jobs (employees, civil servants, independent businessmen, free-lancers) with following net monthly income of main breadwinner: 1953 over 400 DM, 1979 over 2,500 DM - this applying to clerks and civil servants; 1953 over 400 DM, 1979 over 2,500 DM - this applying to upper-echelon employees and civil servants.

Source: Institut für Demoskopie Allensbach, 1981, p. 31a.

Table 2
Relatives considered important by husband (male) and by wife (female) in (1969) and 1983 (in %)

Item	Bremen				Cologne			
	1969		1983		1969		1983	
	Male	Female	Male	Female	Male	Female	Male	Female
Distant relatives (uncles, aunts, cousins and kin of second or more degree)[1]	15	13	16	29	11	7	13	24
Close relatives (parents, siblings and kin of first or second degree)	47	53	40	42	52	61	51	53
Only members of own family (first degree)	35	33	32	27	33	28	22	20
No answer/absent	3	1	12	3	4	5	14	3
N = 100	158	158	115	115	123	123	108	108

1. Degree of kinship based on French civil code.

Source: Lüschen, 1987, p. 153.

Table 3
Number of relatives with whom Christmas visits of more than three days were exchanged in 1968 and 1982

Year	Bremen	Cologne
1968	3.7	4.5
1982	4.0	7.1

Source: Lüschen, 1987, p. 162.

Table 4
Preferred conversation partners (excerpt)[1] (in %)

Wording of question: "There are some with whom one likes to talk, and others with whom one would rather not have anything to do with. When you yourself think of people you like to talk to - can you tell me who it is - or don't you like to talk to anyone?" (presentation of list)

Item	Total		Men		Women	
	1953	1979	1953	1979	1953	1979
Son	24	37	23	34	24	39
Daughter	25	35	23	31	26	39
Mother	29	33	26	31	31	34
Wife	27	30	58	65	-	-
Husband	28	29	-	-	52	54
Sister	25	27	22	23	28	31
Brother	22	24	23	26	21	23
Father	19	23	21	26	18	21
Other female relative	19	28	17	25	20	30
Other male relative	17	26	19	28	14	24

1. See also Table 2, in 2.6, "Sociability Networks."

Source: Allensbacher Archiv, IfD-Umfragen 225, 1287, cited in Institut für Demoskopie Allensbach, 1981, p. 35.

Table 5
Who is closest confidante? (excerpt)[1] (in %)

Wording of question: "When you really need advice in a difficult situation: would you say you had to deal with it all alone, or do you have a person you can talk about everything with?"

Item	Total		Men		Women	
	1953	1979	1953	1979	1953	1979
Yes, there is someone I can talk about everything with	68	80	63	76	71	82
And that is:						
my wife	17	24	37	53	-	-
my husband	23	24	-	-	42	44
my mother	13	13	10	12	15	14
my son	4	8	4	6	4	10
my daughter	5	8	2	5	7	12
my father	9	8	11	11	7	7
my sister	4	6	3	4	6	8
my brother	4	5	5	5	3	5
other male relatives	3	3	3	3	2	3
other female relatives	2	2	1	2	2	3

1. See also Table 4, in 2.6, "Sociability Networks."

Source: Institut für Demoskopie Allensbach, 1981, p. 34.

Table 6
Possible assistance with some everyday problems (in %)

Helper	Apartment, garden	Cold, flu	Money problems	Intimate problems	De-pression	Important advice
Companion	54	57	16	-	53	59
Family	27	29	23	39	17	22
Relatives	3	2	2	4	2	2
Friends	8	7	2	30	17	9
Neighbours, work colleagues	7	4	0	1	1	1
Outside authority	2	1	48	5	4	1
No help	1	1	8	22	6	6

Data basis: ALLBUS 1986 (N = 2809).

Source: Statistisches Bundesamt, 1987, p. 535.

2.3 Community and Neighbourhood Types

The post-urbanization suburbanization of population and employment opportunities brought about lasting changes in the residential distribution structure of the Federal Republic. Predominantly higher- and middle-income families moved into nonmetropolitan areas surrounding cities and towns, while the inner-city area was increasingly inhabited by the poor, the elderly, foreigners, and the unemployed. Current programs for urban development and renewal aim to check this "flight from the city."

The beginning of industrialization launched a migration movement from the country into urban centres; for a long time, however, this was restricted to the natural population surplus and only rarely led to an emptying of rural areas. It was not until the postwar period that a lasting change set in. At first, this development was primarily determined by the heavy flow of displaced persons and refugees out of the eastern sections of Germany into the three western occupied zones. In a deviation from the long-term trend toward urbanization, much of the population moved into the country, since the cities had suffered particularly severe war damage and had poor amenity and supply situations. In the early 1950s, industry began to return to the old locations in cities and the surrounding areas. These companies were followed by the less locality-bound population. Small, middling, and large towns registered considerable growth rates, and the populations of rural communities dwindled. In the second half of the 1950s and the early 1960s, concurrent with the end of the stream of refugees from the east (see 0.1, "Demographic Trends"), the move into the cities slowed, communities of over 2,000 residents contributed to total population growth to an approximately equal degree, and the population decrease in rural communities was braked (Väth, 1980).

Suburbanization

The year 1970 marked a turning point in urban growth: with few exceptions, large cities have since been hit by declining numbers of residents. Migration from the city centre to surrounding nonmetropolitan ambit areas was no longer compensated for by employment-caused urban immigration. Businesses as well as populations shifted to the urban periphery. At the same time, an urbanization trend of business- and household-related service enterprises occurred in parallel with industrial suburbanization.

Retrospective observation of the evolution of residential distribution shows the importance of the creation of new political-administrative units in the course of a regional and administrative reform carried out in the late 1960s. This reform consisted of administrative incorporation of two or more small communities – usually without changing the actual living context of the residents, who as a rule continued to orient themselves according to the old local borders. Between 1968 and 1978, about two-thirds of the communities were affected by the reform, which caused the officially registered proportion of small-community residents abruptly to decline. While 26.1 out of 100 West Germans lived in communities of under 2,000 in 1954, and 20.6 per 100 did so in 1967, only 6.1 per 100 did so in 1979 and in 1986 (see table 1). Despite the formal changes caused by the reform, which have reduced the available data, there have been clear modifications in the historical "urbanization process."

A debate on the city centre – the migratory drift to ambit areas and its consequences – set in on the municipal political level in the second half of the 1970s, as the tendency toward loss of public functions within large towns became undeniable. After the reform, incorporations that could have made up for sinking resident numbers came to be the exception. As allotments by federal and state governments are based on number of residents, towns found themselves confronted for the first time with stagnating or shrinking budgets. In an attempt to check the flight from the city, measures favouring internal development of towns were implemented.

One of the causes of continuing suburbanization was the worsening quality of life in inner city areas. Available housing corresponded less and less to demand with regard to size, expense, and living environment. An additional factor was the negative consequences of concentration, such as traffic, noise, and air pollution. A distinct disparity in the price of real estate between city centres and their ambit areas also strengthened suburbanization. While only 25% of the West German population wanted to live in the country in 1950, as many as 35% did in 1980. The proportion of those preferring life in the city was halved during this period, from 27% to 14% (see table 2).

New forms of industrially standardized housing construction were developed in the course of suburbanization. From the mid-1950s to the late 1960s, housing units were erected in the urban periphery – characterized as "hanger-on settlements" (*Trabantensiedlungen*), "satellite cities" (*Satellitenstädte*), and "overflow cities" (*Entlastungsstädte*, to relieve the pressure of urban overpopulation), or "test-tube cities" (*Retortenstädte*), "sleeping quarters" (*Schlafstädte*) and "living silos" (*Wohnsilos*) (Schäfers, 1981). Large multi-unit housing projects have drawn growing criticism since the 1960s – a general trend toward living in buildings comprising only one or two dwellings (fulfillment of the dream of a one-family house) is unmistakable, even if most people still live in buildings with three or more apartments (see table 3).

Construction of insular housing quarters on the urban periphery has since been replaced by a form of suburbanization which has resulted in a restructuring of existing residential areas, small towns, and villages in the ambit areas of cities.

> In the villages, this process has often led and leads to restoration of existent old buildings, to their reappropriation 'solely' for living purposes. Through the corresponding consolidation of infrastructure in the old settlement centres, caused by the abandonment of agricultural enterprise and other factors, not only do the living habits of the new suburbanites change, but so do those of the native villagers. (Schäfers 1981, p. 251)

Infrastructure Differentials

While much political importance was placed on providing the population with housing during the first decades after World War II, priority eventually shifted to equipping the living environs with certain infrastructural accommodations – for example, schools, shops, and medical and cultural establishments. Federal laws regulating geographic planning, passed in 1965 (*Bundesraumordnungsgesetz*) and 1975 (*Bundesraumordnungsprogramm*), aimed at evening out the differences in developmental status between regions of the Federal Republic. These differences were quite considerable, particularly when seen in an urban-rural comparison. According to a 1965 survey, rural municipalities had far worse shopping conditions and traffic and transportation connections than did cities; on the other hand, urban dwellers complained more of too much traffic, noise, soot, and smoke. A 1972 study revealed the metropolitan-nonmetropolitan schism in almost every respect – cultural and sport possibilities, shopping conditions, entertainment, physicians, hospitals, lawyers, public authorities, personal-transportation connections, banks, religious institutions – with the exception of recreational facilities. Suburban areas, with their newly constructed houses, were less well equipped than cities, but usually better off than small towns and villages (Glatzer, 1980).

Since 1979, official statistics have exhibited tendentially dropping data regarding new construction of infrastructure buildings. This subject was hardly touched on by experts in the 1980s. The current political and public discussion infers that a satisfactory saturation has been achieved in certain infrastructure fields, while other problem areas – some of them new – cannot properly be dealt with due to the tight public budget.

One priority in government planning is urban renovation and development, including maintenance of old and historic parts of towns, renewal and structural improvement in inner cities, and improvement of residential areas close to inner cities (Der Bundesminister für Raumordnung, Bauwesen und Städtebau, 1985).

Inner cities and nearby residential areas are undergoing a visible transformation: dwellings are being restored and modernized, and an infrastructure catering to a distinguished taste and life style is coming into existence.

Structure of Urban Population

This development should be regarded against the background of long-term shifts in the structure of urban populations. It was mainly younger families with children and high- and middle-income earners who moved out of the metropolitan areas. Urban-core areas were increasingly inhabited by people in difficult social situations: today, 50% of all welfare recipients, 50% of all foreigners, 40% of all those over 65 years of age, and 40% of all unemployed live in cities (Schulz zur Wiesch, 1988). Recently, increased migration into city centres has been observed, with young single people and childless families of all ages the most highly represented.

Urban society is presently characterized by poor and old people, foreigners and the unemployed, the traditional working class (in subsidized housing), the old and new middle classes (with a strong tendency toward ambit areas), young urban professionals ("yuppies"), and people with "alternative" life styles – unmarried couples or groups living together in one dwelling (who prefer the inner city) (Schulz zur Wiesch, 1988).

Some authors see city life as a model for overall future development:

> In cities we see . . . the vanguard of postmodern or post-Ford society, whose contours we can as yet sketch out only very roughly: on the one hand is an individualization of life planning that must adapt to an uncertain and incalculable future . . . on the other hand is a diversification in material living comfort and financial status, leading to a reduction of the middle-income level. (Häussermann 1988, p. 89)

Karin Stiehr

References

Brunhöber, Hannelore
1985 "Wohnen." In Wolfgang Benz, ed., *Die Bundesrepublik Deutschland*. Vol. 2: Gesellschaft. Frankfurt am Main: Fischer.

Bundesminister für Raumordnung, Bauwesen und Städtebau, ed.
1985 *Wohnungspolitik und Städtebau, Raumordnung, Bauwesen. Jahresbericht 1985*. Bonn.

–, ed.
1986 *Baulandbericht 1986*. Bonn.

Claessens, Dieter, Arno Klönne, and Armin Tschoepe
1985 *Sozialkunde der Bundesrepublik Deutschland. Grundlagen, Strukturen, Trends in Wirtschaft und Gesellschaft*. Reinbek: Rowohlt.

Deutscher Bundestag, ed.
1986 *Die Situation der älteren Menschen in der Familie. Vierter Familienbericht*. Bonn.

Franz, Peter
1985 *Soziologie der räumlichen Mobilität*. Frankfurt am Main/New York: Campus.

Glatzer, Wolfgang
1980 *Wohnungsversorgung im Wohlfahrtsstaat: objektive und subjektive Indikatoren zur Wohlfahrtsentwicklung in der Bundesrepublik Deutschland*. Frankfurt am Main/New York: Campus.

Häussermann, Hartmut
1988 "Stadt und Lebensstil." In Volker Hauff, ed., *Veränderungen der Stadtgesellschaft*. Weinheim/Basel: Beltz.

Noelle-Neumann, Elisabeth, and Edgar Piel, eds.
1983 *Allensbacher Jahrbuch der Demoskopie 1978-1983*. New York/London/Paris: Saur.

Priebe, Hermann
1982 *Leben in der Stadt oder auf dem Land. Mehr Lebensqualität durch sinnvolle Raumgestaltung*. Düsseldorf/Wien: Econ.

Schäfers, Bernhard
1981 *Sozialstruktur und Wandel der Bundesrepublik Deutschland*. Stuttgart: Enke.

Schulz zur Wiesch, Jochen
1988 "Veränderungen der Stadtgesellschaft." In Volker Hauff, ed., *Stadt und Lebensstil*. Weinheim/Basel: Beltz.

Statistisches Bundesamt, ed.
1981 *Statistisches Jahrbuch 1981 für die Bundesrepublik Deutschland*. Stuttgart/Mainz: Kohlhammer.

–, ed.
1988 *Statistisches Jahrbuch 1988 für die Bundesrepublik Deutschland*. Stuttgart/Mainz: Kohlhammer.

Väth, Werner
1980 *Raumplanung. Probleme der räumlichen Entwicklung und Raumordnungspolitik in der Bundesrepublik Deutschland*. Königstein (Ts.): Hain.

Table 1
Urbanization in Germany, as of 1954 for the Federal Republic of Germany (per 100 residents in municipalities)

Item	1871	1925	1954	1963	1967	1970	1976	1979	1982	1986
Under 2,000	63.9	35.6	26.1	21.7	20.6	18.7	8.1	6.1	6.1	6.1
2,000-100,000	31.3	37.6	44.7	45.0	47.0	48.9	57.1	59.7	60.4	68.9
Over 100,000	4.8	26.8	29.2	33.3	32.4	32.4	34.8	34.2	33.5	25.1

Source: Claessens et al., 1985, p. 177; Statistisches Bundesamt, 1988, p. 66.

Table 2
Preferred living environment (in %)

Wording of question: "Where would you most like to live, if you could choose: in the country, in a small town, large town or city?"(total population)

Item	1950 June	1972 Nov.	1980 Jan.
Country	25	27	35
Small town	20	22	22
Large town	24	27	25
City	27	21	14
Undecided	4	3	4
Total	100	100	100

Source: Noelle-Neumann & Piel, 1983, p. 40.

Table 3
Inhabited dwellings in buildings with one to two apartments, and with three or more apartments, from 1968 to 1982

Item	1968[1]	1972[1]	1978[2]	1980[2]	1982[2]
Apartments in houses with three or more apartments	54.1	54.0	52.5	51.3	51.0
Apartments in houses with one or two apartments	45.9	46.0	47.5	48.7	49.0

1. Aparments in agriculture-unrelated residential housing.
2. Living quarters in residential housing.

Source: 4. Familienbericht, p. 112.

2.4 Local Autonomy

The constitutionally anchored principle of local self-administration guarantees municipalities and districts independent regulation of their local affairs. Actualization of this right is being hampered by increasing co-optation of local self-administration into federal and county administration, by growing control over municipal administrations via integrated planning processes, and by greater financial dependence of municipalities on national and county budgets.

In conformity with Germany's long federative tradition, the administrative system of the Federal Republic is highly decentralized: public administration is carried out under the auspices of states and municipalities. The right to municipal self-administration was established during the Weimar Republic, but was abolished under National Socialist rule.

After World War II, the United States took on the role of political mentor; according to U.S. constitutional history, federalist government systems were more democratic than centralized ones (Kevenhörster & Uppendahl, 1987). As a consequence of the experience with the centralist-totalitarian National Socialist system, West Germanys counties were granted a much stronger position than they had had under the Weimar constitution. The present Federal Republic of Germany is constituted as a union of 10 counties plus Berlin; as paragraph 1 of the constitution states, "The Federal Republic of Germany is a democratic and social federative state."

Besides the principle of federalism, the other core structural element for organization in government and administration is municipal self-administration. The constitution sets forth the right of the municipalities and districts to settle local community matters by legal means. There is also mandatory popular representation on the state, district, and municipal levels elected by universal, direct, free, equal, and secret vote.

Municipal responsibilities include, for example, construction and maintenance of town streets and provision of cultural and social services; districts are responsible for regional matters such as district road construction, hospitals, and so on. Municipalities are committed by law to some of their duties, and carry out the rest voluntarily. In these self-administrative matters, municipalities are subject to governmental supervision concerning legality, but not concerning usefulness or suitability, of measures. They also function as governmental administrative services (in, for example, passport and registration matters), for which they are subordinate to a superior level of the civil service.

Realization of the constitutional-legislative notion of municipal self-administration – on an administrative-organizational level, but also on a political-democratic level – was decisively influenced by the regional and administrative reforms of the 1960s to mid-1970s.

> The growing and increasingly expensive responsibilities, the demand in rural areas for equal quality of infrastructure as that in urban areas, and the necessary specialization of administrative personnel occasioned the reclassification of administrative-service units, especially of municipalities and districts. The previous classification was of a more historical origin and was not tailored to new administrative responsibilities. (Siedentopf, 1986, p. 82; see table 1)

In 1964, a territorial redistribution of administrative services reduced the number of municipalities by about two-thirds (see 2.3, "Community and Neighbourhood Types"), but at the same time achieved a common administrative framework for all of the Federal Republic, allowing for, at most, differences in nuances. To further decentralization and deconcentration, many superior administrative services passed into municipal hands. One of the requirements of municipal self-administration is local financial autonomy. Municipal budgets are made up of revenue through taxes, fees, and duties, as well as designated allotments from federal and county governments. Up to 1969, the municipalities had the entire profit-tax revenue at their disposal. Since the Municipal Fiscal Reform Law went into effect, they must turn over 40% to the Federation and the counties, and they receive in compensation 15% of the income tax paid by their local residents. While this eliminated municipal dependence upon a formerly dominant source of income, dependence upon allotments from the Federation and the states was increased (Kovenhörster & Uppendahl, 1987).

The municipalities' share of the tax revenue distributed to the various regional incorporations has not increased over the past 15 years (see table 2). Currently, structural changes in unemployment are a source of serious municipal budgetary problems (long-term and youth unemployment – see 4.1, "Unemployment"), as legislative regulation makes local and regional social-insurance authorities responsible for these costs.

The past few decades have brought marked changes in the composition of civil-service personnel. The constitution obliges the government to delegate empowerment of sovereign authority – as a rule – to civil servants under public-service and loyalty contracts. This monopoly by civil servants has, for quite some time, been curtailed by a growing number of public employees, who, like workers in public service, are employed on a steady basis under private contract and are paid according to a different system. While the number of civil servants and judges increased by about 50% between 1955 and 1985, the number of public employees doubled over this period. The changes become particularly clear in a long-term comparison: in 1927, almost two-thirds of those in public employment were civil servants, but this proportion had sunk to 46% by 1985.

In 1955, some 2.4 million people were employed full time in direct public service, and their number had grown to 3.6 million by 1985. This increase is manifested especially among those working for the Federation or for counties, and only to a small degree among those working for municipalities and districts (see table 3). The clearly dwindling proportion of those employed by municipalities in comparison to all regional incorporations (see table 4) can be understood as an indication that the regional and administrative reform's goal of rationalization and heightened efficiency of municipal administrations has been attained for the most part, in spite of the additional chores delegated to these administrations.

The idea of municipal self-administration comprises not only the organizational-legislative principle of decentralized governmental power, but also participation by citizens in administration of local affairs. Critics of the municipal reform were of the opinion that this participation was too narrowly limited to performance optimization for municipal administrations, while the political-democratic function of self-administration was relatively neglected. One result of the great reduction in number of municipalities was a 45% decrease in municipal mandates, though legal measures were supposed to compensate for this deficit. The generous geographical rearrangement of municipalities resulted in larger administrative territories, which rendered civil participation – for example, attendance at local representative meetings – more difficult. Acceptance of these new, artificial local borders as an inherent part of identification with local affairs posed a serious plausibility problem. The municipal reform strengthened the parliamentarization of municipal political processes involving decision making and public consent, which led to a reduction in independent and regional voters' associations. The preventive measures against these negative results – for example, introduction of borough and township constitutions and the furthering of direct democracy in the form of civil participation – failed to achieve the hoped-for success (Hill, 1987).

All in all, municipal self-administration was subject to opposing processes of a centralist as well as a decentralist character during the postwar period. Municipal self-administration, as opposed to the national government, is perceived as being increasingly threatened:

> Municipal self-administrations' elbowroom for action and decision making has been impinged upon under co-operative federalism by exaggerated *Verrechtlichung* [overly burdensome rules and regulations], strict authorization channels, financial intertwinement, and general centralization tendencies. Municipal sovereignty in planning, financing, organization, and personnel has been hemmed in. Municipalities and districts no longer have

a position within the overall structure of all local matters which should be the due of municipal self-administration in the politico-administrative system. (Wagner, cited in Kevenhörster & Uppendahl 1987, p. 42)

Karin Stiehr

References

Arzberger, Klaus
1979 *Bürger und Eliten in der Kommunalpolitik*. Berlin: Deutscher Gemeindeverlag.

Derlien, Hans-Ulrich, and Dyprand v. Queis
1986 *Kommunalpolitik im geplanten Wandel. Auswirkungen der Gebietsreform auf das kommunale Entscheidungssystem*. Baden-Baden: Nomos.

Ellwein, Thomas
1986 "Zur Geschichte der öffentlichen Verwaltung in Deutschland." In Landeszentrale für politische Bildung Baden-Württemberg, ed., *Verwaltung und Politik in der Bundesrepublik*. Stuttgart/Berlin/Köln/Mainz: Kohlhammer.

Hill, Hermann
1987 *Die politisch-demokratische Funktion der kommunalen Selbstverwaltung nach der Reform*. Baden-Baden: Nomos.

Hoffmann, K.-H., and J. Jacobs
1980 "Raumordnungspolitische Bestimmungsfaktoren und Auswirkungen der kommunalen Neugliederung." In Heinz Zielinsky, ed., *Lokale Politik zwischen Eigenständigkeit und staatlicher Abhängigkeit*. Königstein: Hain.

Kevenhörster, Paul, and Herbert Uppendahl
1987 *Gemeindedemokratie in Gefahr? Zentralisierung und Dezentralisierung als Herausforderung lokaler Demokratie in Japan und der Bundesrepublik Deutschland*. Baden-Baden: Nomos.

Siedentopf, Heinrich
1986 "Die öffentliche Verwaltung in der Bundesrepublik Deutschland." In Landeszentrale für politische Bildung Baden-Württemberg, ed., *Verwaltung und Politik in der Bundesrepublik*. Stuttgart/Berlin/Köln/Mainz: Kohlhammer.

Statistisches Bundesamt, ed.
1987a *Datenreport 1987*. Bonn.

–, ed.
1987b *Von den zwanziger zu den achtziger Jahren. Ein Vergleich der Lebensverhältnisse der Menschen*. Wiesbaden/Mainz: Kohlhammer.

Table 1
Administrative Units

Level	1956	1980
Federal	1 federation	1 federation
State	11 states	11 states
Regional	33 governmental regions	25 governmental regions
District	425 districts, 141 independent towns	236 districts, 88 independent towns
Community	24,444 district-subordinate communities, whereby the smallest of them in Nordrhein-Westfalen, Schleswig-Holstein, Saarland and in parts of Rheinland-Pfalz banded together into community associations	3,436 local administrative units - 2,390 district-subordinate units and 1,046 community associations with administrative authority and counting 6,135 local communities

Source: Siedentopf, 1986, p. 83.

Table 2
Tax revenues according to distribution[1] in 1974 and 1986 (in million DM)

Standards applied	1974	1986
After tax revenue distribution:		
the federation retains	119,412.5	210,584.1
the states retain	83,347.3	160,099.4
- state-independent towns (with no municipal taxes)	7,024.7	11,692.9
- other states	76,322.7	148,406.5
municipalities/community associations	32,657.9	63,832.0
common market associations	2,761.0	17,952.4
Total	238,178.8	452,467.9

1. Deviation from pre-distribution tax revenues due to time overlaps.

Source: Statistisches Bundesamt, 1987a, p. 220.

Table 3
Fully employed persons in immediate civil service (in 1,000)

Item	1927[1]	1955[2]	1985
Regional bodies	1,152	1,575	2,872
Empire/federation	167	116	313
States	460	854	1,572
Communities/comm. associations[3]	525	605	988
Imperial/federal railways	704	499	295
Imperial/federal postal service	367	334	440
Total	2,223	2,408	3,607
Including:			
civil servants and judges	1,357	1,052	1,677
employees	163	543	1,137
workers	703	813	793

1. Imperial territory.
2. West Germany excluding the Saarland, partly estimated.
3. 1927: communities with 2,000 or more residents; 1985: incl. communal special-purpose associations.

Source: Statistisches Bundesamt, 1987b, p. 73.

Table 4
Fully employed persons in civil service of regional bodies (in %)

Item	1927[1]	1955[2]	1985[3]
German Empire or Federal Republic	14.5	7.4	10.9
States/non affiliated towns	39.9	54.2	54.7
Municipalities/community assocs.	45.6	38.4	34.4

1. Imperial region.
2. Federal Republic excluding Saarland, partially estimated.
3. 1927: Communities with 2,000 or more residents. 1985: including municipal special-purpose assocs (Statistisches Bundesamt 870391).

Source: Statistisches Bundesamt, 1987b, p. 72.

2.5 Voluntary Associations

Existing associations and their members are not subject to any central registration in the Federal Republic; however, it is possible to distinguish indications of increasing activity in voluntary associations. In addition to conventional forms of associations, which are predominantly sociable in nature, groups with socio-political objectives (citizens' initiatives and self-help groups) have been gaining importance since the late 1960s.

The development of the modern affiliative association or club is closely connected with the rise of industrial society. The movement originated in the late eighteenth century, in urban areas, then spread to rural areas at the beginning of the twentieth century. For a long time, clubs and associations, because of their civil and democratic self-organization, were encumbered with the aura of political opposition; the upholding of conservative values and behaviour and the turning from political purposes to purely sociable ones gained a higher profile at the start of the twentieth century (Weber, 1910). When Hitler seized power, he immediately destroyed the proletarian associations, and later the rest of the civil associations were either dissolved or brought into line with National Socialist associations via elimination of resistance.

A revival of local associations, contributing to the integration of millions of refugees, was observed in the 1950s. In conformity with the general trend toward depoliticization of everyday life, associations limited themselves, with few exceptions, to leisure purposes; in the 1960s, sport clubs in particular enjoyed an enormous upswing (Kroll, 1987).

Poll results show that 53% of West Germans over 18 years old were members of at least one association in 1953; this proportion rose to 57% by 1979, due to increased participation by women. The proportion of women belonging to an organization remained lower than that of men: while 72% of the men in both years were in at least one association, the proportion of women in associations grew only from 36% to 45%. Gymnastics and sport clubs enjoyed the greatest rise in popularity; in 1953 a mere 12% of those polled belonged to this type of club, while 27% did in 1979 (see table 1).

The number of clubs connected with the German Sport League rose from about 30,500 to over 64,000 between 1960 and 1987, and the number of male members went from 4.3 million to 11.1 million. A disproportionate increase can be seen once again among women, whose membership rose from 1.1 million to 6.4 million. In an opposing trend, the German Singers' League lost popularity between 1960 and 1970. Since then, it has been able to register considerable membership gains, as has the German Alpine League (see table 2).

New kinds of local associations began forming toward the end of the 1960s. Neighbourhood initiatives started by singling out individual grievances within their immediate living environs. In the early 1970s, workers' initiatives in the Ruhr area tried to prevent the demolition of housing. The range of activity gradually widened, and points of reference for protest spread and overlapped to comprise extensive social criticism. Extraregional cooperation between citizens' initiatives within the framework of the new social movements (see 10.3, "Social Movements") lent them more political weight. As slight as this activity potential may be from the purely quantitative point of view, its qualitative effect should not be underestimated, as is well illustrated by the election of 'green' parties into the federal parliament and by the 'green' concepts assumed by the established parties" (Richter, 1985 p. 1).

Less spectactular but just as durable is the profusion of self-help groups that originated during the same period. Members' civil engagement differs from the traditional forms of honourary, often charitable, service. In the 1960s, self-help activities concentrated largely on the tending of children (in *Kinderläden*, a kind of autonomous kindergarten or nursery school) and help for adolescents (autonomous youth centres), a lay medical and health movement arose somewhat later, as did socio-cultural initiatives and self-help associations, such as groups for the handicapped, initiatives by the unemployed, women's houses, and homosexual groups (Braun & Röhrig, 1987).

Field-specific studies confirm the consistently high interest of the population in organized leisure activity. About half of the people questioned in a 1968/1969 survey, carried out in communities of varying size, were in some organized association. When participation in political parties and trade unions is left aside, these membership statistics are reduced by approximately 5%. Similar results were attained in a 1977 survey on sport clubs: 56% of the respondents belonged to a voluntary organization, and 37% were members of a local leisure-activity club. According to a representative poll, the Allbus (1982), 58% of West Germans were members of a voluntary association, and 53% of them belonged to leisure clubs (after membership in interest lobbies, trade unions, and political parties was left aside) (Richter, 1985). This result was corroborated by the Allbus in 1986. High growth rates in social and sport associations were registered between 1976 and 1986.

Starting in the 1950s, the integrative and identity-forming functions of club or affiliative associations are often stressed. It can be considered empirically valid that the association represents an informal, preliminary stage of local political activity. A relatively high percentage of party members belong to clubs and associations, and about every second or third club chairperson is also a member of a municipal government (Derlien & Queis, 1986; Siewert, 1984). On the other hand, the composition of local élites is not necessarily long-lasting or stable. A study on the city of Wertheim showed that identification with commercial interests, strong in the years preceding 1968, no longer existed 12 years later. The process of forming public opinion ran along more political lines than it had in 1968 (Ellwein & Zoll, 1982; Voigt, 1984).

Recently, associations have been again attracting political interest, as have self-help groups and neighbourhood networks. The different trends of structural modernization in industrialized countries (urbanization, disintegration of traditional local and professional affiliations, increases in leisure time, etc.) and changing functions of the state (for example becoming a distributor of social services and checking and controlling the economy) favour increased awareness of desires which, when not fulfilled, may lead to feelings of relative deprivation. Sociologists specializing in affiliative and club associations interpret increasing membership in voluntary associations as a possible expression of just such an awareness. Clubs and self-help groups can be perceived in this context as an alternative to bureaucracy, as a means of relieving budget woes via privatization, and as an expression of alternative life style through re-establishment of less complex contexts for action (Siewert, 1984).

Karin Stiehr

References

Bertels, Lothar
1987 *Neue Nachbarschaften*. Frankfurt am Main/New York: Campus.

Braun, Joachim, and Peter Röhrig
1987 *Praxis der Selbsthilfeförderung. Das frewillige soziale Engagement am Beispiel von vier Städten*. Frankfurt am Main/New York: Campus.

Derlien, Hans-Ulrich, and Dyprand von Queis
1986 *Kommunalpolitik im geplanten Wandel. Auswirkungen der Gebietsreform auf das kommunale Entscheidungssystem*. Baden-Baden: Nomos.

Ellwein, Thomas, and Ralf Zoll
1982 *Wertheim: Politik und Machtstruktur einer deutschen Stadt*. München: Juventa.

Kröll, Friedhelm
1987 *Vereine im Lebensalltag einer Großstadt am Beispiel Nürnberg. Eine kultursoziologische Studie*. Marburg: Verlag Arbeiterbewegung und Gesellschaftswissenschaft.

Lakemann, Ulrich
1984 *Das Aktivitätspotential privater Haushalte in der Bundesrepublik Deutschland 1950 bis 1980: Zeitliche und inhaltliche Veränderungen von Erwerbstätigkeiten, unbezahlten Arbeiten und Freizeitaktivitäten*. Studie im Auftrag des Wissenschaftszentrum Berlin. Berlin.

Noelle-Neumann, Elisabeth, and Edgar Piel, eds.
1983 *Allensbacher Jahrbuch der Demoskopie 1978-1983*. München/New York/London/Paris: Saur.

Richter, Rudolf
1985 *Soziokulturelle Dimensionen freiwilliger Vereinigungen. USA, Bundesrepublik Deutschland und Österreich im soziologischen Vergleich*. München: Minerva.

Savelsberg, Joachim
1980 *Kommunale Autonomie*. Frankfurt am Main/Main: Hagen und Herchen.

Siewert, H.-Jörg
1984 "Zur Thematisierung des Vereinswesens in der deutschen Soziologie." In O. Dann, ed., *Historische Zeitschrift*. Beiheft 9. München.

Statistisches Bundesamt, ed.
1961 *Statistisches Jahrbuch 1961 für die Bundesrepublik Deutschland*. Stuttgart/Mainz: Kohlhammer.

–, ed.
1973 *Statistisches Jahrbuch 1973 für die Bundesrepublik Deutschland*. Stuttgart/Mainz: Kohlhammer.

–, ed.
1988 *Statistisches Jahrbuch 1988 für die Bundesrepublik Deutschland*. Stuttgart/Mainz: Kohlhammer.

Voigt, Rüdiger, ed.
1984 *Handwörterbuch zur Kommunalpolitik*. Opladen: Westdeutscher Verlag.

Weber, Max
1911 "Geschäftsbericht." In *Verhandlungen des Ersten Deutschen Soziologentages vom 19.-22.10.1910 in Frankfurt/Main*. Tübingen.

Zentralarchiv für empirische Sozialforschung der
1984 Universität zu Köln /Zentrum für Umfragen, Methoden und Analysen e.V., Mannheim. *Allgemeine Bevölkerungsumfrage der Sozialwissenschaften. Allbus 1982. Codebuch mit Methodenbericht und Vergleichsdaten*. Köln.

–
1986 *Allgemeine Bevölkerungsumfrage der Sozialwissenschaften. Allbus. Codebuch*. Köln.

Table 1
Membership in associations (in %)

Item	Total		Men		Women	
	1953	1979	1953	1979	1953	1979
Members in at least one association	53	57	72	72	36	45
This association being:						
sport-/athletic club	12	27	22	37	3	19
trade union	12	11	23	19	3	5
religious or charity association	7	9	8	7	12	11
singing-/music club, church choir	6	6	13	9	3	3
other professional associations	9	5	16	9	4	2
shooting club, fireman, or hunting club	4	5	9	10	-	2
civic association, social club	4	4	7	5	2	3
womens' or mothers' association	4	4	-	-	8	6
gardening or pet-raising club	2	3	3	4	1	2
war-victims' or survivors' association	3	1	4	2	3	1
refugee association	4	1	5	1	4	1
other	7	5	9	5	5	5
Sum	75	81	119	108	48	60
Not members in any association	47	43	28	28	64	55

Source: Noelle-Neumann & Piel, 1983, p. 83.

Table 2
Development of leagues

Item	1960	1970	1987
German Sport League:			
clubs	30,486	39,201	64,251
female members	1,130,212	2,220,757	6,372,083
male members	4,289,171	6,066,198	11,148,326
German Singers' League:			
national choirs	15,851	17,366	19,073
active women	79,788	73,604	192,303
active men	462,673	369,360	397,945
German Alpine League:			
huts	-	235	296
members	-	243,066	474,956

Source: Statistisches Bundesamt, 1961, pp. 118; 1973, p. 106; 1988, pp. 382.

Table 3
Membership in Associations (multiple replies possible) (in %)

Membership	1976	1982	1986
German Confederated Trade Union	12.8	12.0	13.6
German Union of Salaried Workers	3.7	2.1	1.4
Farmers' Association	1.6	1.2	1.0
Civil-Servant Oganization	2.7	2.0	2.0
Retail- or trade association	1.8	1.5	1.3
Industrial or business association	1.0	0.8	0.2
Other professional associations	3.6	2.5	3.8
Political party	6.1	3.6	3.3
Church/religious association	5.4	4.9	6.0
Singing club	6.1	6.1	5.2
Sport club	22.1	22.4	27.1
Hobby club	4.4	4.8	5.0
Patriotic or civic association	6.8	4.4	5.6
Other social clubs	3.2	8.9	7.1
Refugee association	1.8	1.3	1.0
Welfare or war-victims' association	2.3	2.7	3.7
Youth or student association	1.8	1.1	0.4
Civic association	1.3	0.6	0.7
Other associations	10.6	10.5	12.6

Source: Allbus, 1982; Allbus, 1986.

2.6 Sociability Networks

Sociability networks have gained considerably in importance during the past few decades. Contact with friends, acquaintances, neighbours, and colleagues became more frequent, and relationships – despite the continued priority of the family in network support – have been increasingly characterized by trust and willingness to help.

In the face of a secularization process affecting all sectors of industrialized society, prognostications of rising isolation and anonymity among people, and an uprooting from traditional religion and from family and community ties were made as early as the 1950s (Riesman, 1958). The evolution of family relationships did not confirm these tendencies: aside from the high degree of involvement of family members in network support, there was an increase in contact with distant kin, in conjunction with the extension of what was understood to be family membership (see 2.2, "Kinship Networks"). The question arises as to what degree the family-kinship network has been extended to include friends and acquaintances.

Fewer people seem to be excluded from sociability networks than was the case after the war. The proportion of West Germans who often felt lonely fell from 19% to 7% between 1949 and 1980 (see table 1). The former percentage cannot be explained by external factors alone – loss of kin through the war and flight from occupied zones – and contact with other people has, all in all, improved considerably. This applies not only to family members, who were more favoured as communication partners in 1979 than in 1953, but also to people outside the family, particularly those with common interests, friends, neighbours, and colleagues (see table 2).

Social Contacts

In 1979, 82% of those polled, 14% more than in 1953, claimed to have a middling or large number of acquaintances (see table 3). A major factor in the existence of friendship relations was the individual's class identification. Empirical findings of the past 15 years show that persons with low-level education/training and income are more kin- and less friendship-oriented than are members of the upper social classes. In 1978, 64% of the working class had a "really close friend"; this figure dropped slightly to 61% in 1984. The corresponding percentages for the middle class amounted, respectively, to 78% and 76%. The proportion was the highest among the upper classes, at 85% and 88% (Diewald, 1986).

Small children (for mothers) and advanced age are considered to be other factors limiting social involvement. Women continue to have, in comparison with men, better kinship contact, but have also often intensified their friendly relations outside of the family – especially with persons with common interests, friends, neighbours and colleagues – to an even greater degree over the past few decades (table 2).

In general, the incidence of contacts with friends, acquaintances, and neighbours has increased markedly. When asked about leisure and weekend activities in 1953, 31% of West Germans replied that they visited friends and acquaintances; in 1979 this proportion had risen to 64%. The proportion visiting within their neighbourhood also doubled, from 14% to 26% (Noelle-Neumann & Piel, 1983). In 1984, 19% of those questioned met with their best friend nearly daily, 46% at least once weekly, and 27% at least once monthly (Diewald, 1986).

Network Support

Network support is still largely provided by family members, who are preferred as advisors in difficult situations. The only category that registered notable gains in this area were friends (see table 4). In nearly one-third of all cases in 1986, they were named as potential helpers in marriage or romantic problems, and as many as 17% would turn to them when suffering from depression. Neighbours, work colleagues, and distant kin played a subordinate role when it came to assistance with household or garden work, or with illness or emotional problems (Statistisches Bundesamt, 1987).

Still, relations with neighbours have become more relaxed and helpful over the long term. The proportion of those who complained about their neighbours fell from 16% in 1953 to 11% in 1979 (Institut für Demoskopie Allensbach, 1981). While only half of those polled in the former year spoke with their neighbours, three-fourths did so in 1979. More than before, neighbours take messages for each other, congratulate each other upon family celebrations, invite each other into their homes, borrow or lend things, go shopping for each other, babysit for each other, and get together toward common goals. Women maintain more contacts, but a clear increase in neighbourhood relationships among men has been registered (see table 5).

These results show that sociability networks have experienced a marked increase in importance in the past decades, and that the family-kin system has been extended to include outside friendship contacts. As with contact with distant kin (see 2.2 "Kinship Networks"), mutual liking was the basis for keeping up these contacts.

In addition to this improved integration into the immediate social environment, a new openness to the next-higher level can be observed: membership in local associations, leisure-oriented as well as socio-political, is on the rise (see 2.5,

"Voluntary Associations"), and new concepts of network support, based more on individual responsibility and self-determination, have spread in the context of the "new social movements." Forms of assistance and mutual support are more heavily oriented toward conditions within communities and regions than before, and are no longer limited solely to the family or the immediate neighbourhood; the choice of persons whom one helps, or from whom one accepts help, is considered a fundamentally free choice. A visible sign of this development is the large number of newly established self-help groups: in 1984, estimates were running at 50,000–60,000 associations, with about half a million participants (Vilmar & Runge, 1986).

The cultural pessimism of the 1950s is shown to be – as yet – unfounded in this area. "The data show clearly that there are no signs of increased anonymity or growing alienation between people. Although it is true that certain groups suffer from an appreciable deficit of contacts, the trend seems to go in a favourable direction. In this sense, much evidence points to a situation in which people, within and outside of their families, enjoy more and, presumably, more intensive contacts than in the past 30 years" (Schumacher & Vollmer, 1982, p. 334).

Karin Stiehr

References

Bertels, Lothar
1987 *Neue Nachbarschaften. Soziale Beziehungen in einer Neubausiedlung als Folge von Initiativenarbeit*. Frankfurt am Main/New York: Campus.

Diewald, Martin
1986 "Sozialkontakte und Hilfeleistungen in informellen Netzwerken." In Wolfgang Glatzer, and Regina Berger-Schmitt, eds., *Haushaltsproduktion und Netzwerkhilfe. Die alltägliche Leistungen der Haushalte und Familien*. Frankfurt am Main/New York: Campus.

Institut für Demoskopie Allensbach, ed.
1981 *Eine Generation später. Bundesrepublik 1953-1979*. Allensbach.

Keupp, Heiner, and Bernd Röhrle, eds.
1987 *Soziale Netzwerke*. Frankfurt am Main/New York: Campus.

Koch-Arzberger, Claudia
1989 *Hilfe, (r)eine Frauensache*. Vortrag beim Deutschen Frauenring Bad Vilbel am 19.01.1989.

Lüschen, Günther
1988 "Familial-verwandtschaftliche Netzwerke." In Rosemarie Nave-Herz, ed., *Wandel und Kontinuität der Familie in der Bundesrepublik Deutschland*. Stuttgart: Enke.

Noelle-Neumann, Elisabeth, and Edgar Piel, eds.
1983 *Allensbacher Jahrbuch der Demoskopie 1978-1983*. München/New York/London/Paris: Saur.

Piel, Edgar
1987 *Im Geflecht der kleinen Netze. Vom deutschen Rückzug ins Private*. Zürich: Edition Interfrom.

Riesman, David
1958 *Die einsame Masse. Eine Untersuchung der Wandlungen des amerikanischen Charakters*. Hamburg: Rowohlt.

Schumacher, Jürgen, and Randolph Vollmer
1982 "Differenzierungs- und Entdifferenzierungsprozesse im Familiensystem." In Karl-Otto Hondrich, ed., *Soziale Differenzierung*. Frankfurt am Main/New York: Campus.

Vilmar, Fritz, and Brigitte Runge
1986 *Auf dem Weg zur Selbsthilfegesellschaft?* Essen: Klartext.

Table 1
Feelings of loneliness (in %)

Wording of question: "Do you feel lonely, all alone?"

Item	1949	1973	1980
Often	19	7	7
Sometimes	26	22	24
Seldom	10	20	25
Never	45	51	44
Total	100	100	100

Federal Republic and West Berlin, population aged 16 years and older.

Source: Allensbacher Archiv, cited in Piel, 1987, p. 12.

Table 2
Preferred conversation partners (excerpt)[1] (in %)

Wording of question: "There are people one likes to talk with, and others one wants nothing to do with. When you yourself think of the people you like talking to - can you say who it is - or don't you like to talk with anyone?" (presentation of a list)

Conversation partners	Total		Men		Women	
	1953	1979	1953	1979	1953	1979
People outside of the family:						
someone with common interests	28	41	34	45	24	38
my boy-/girlfriend	24	36	27	35	22	37
neighbour	22	35	20	30	22	40
colleague	17	28	28	35	8	21
friend of the family	10	19	9	20	10	18
club comrade	8	17	15	24	2	11
childhood friend	11	16	13	16	11	16
other renters or subletters in same house	8	13	8	12	8	13
someone I agree with politically	7	12	11	17	3	8
foreman or boss	9	9	13	11	5	8
someone I can discuss religion with	9	8	10	6	9	10
pastor	8	7	7	7	7	8
business friend	7	7	12	11	3	3
someone I meet on the way to work	6	6	9	7	3	5
war-/service comrade	11	5	23	9	1	1
fellow party member	1	3	3	6	-	1

1. See also table 4, in 2.2 "Kinship Networks."

Source: Allensbacher Archiv, IfD-Umfragen 225, 1287, cited in Institut für Demoskopie Allensbach, 1981, p. 35.

Table 3
Size of circle of acquaintance (in %)

Wording of question: "Do you have many or few acquaintances?"

Acquaintance	Total		Men		Women	
	1953	1979	1953	1979	1953	1979
Many	45	43	52	46	39	39
Middling	22	39	20	37	24	41
Few	32	18	27	17	36	20
No reply	1	-	1	-	1	-
Total	100	100	100	100	100	100

Source: Allensbacher Archiv, IfD-Umfragen 225, 1287, cited in Institut für Demoskopie Allensbach, 1981, Anhang, table 14.

Table 4
Who is your confidante? (excerpt)[1] (in %)

Wording of question: "When you really need advice in a difficult situation: would you say you have to deal with it alone, or do you have someone you can discuss everything with?"

Confidante	Total		Men		Women	
	1953	1979	1953	1979	1953	1979
Yes, there is someone I can discuss everything with	68	80	63	76	71	82
Outside of the family:						
boy-/girlfriend	5	12	5	10	5	14
friend of the family	1	3	2	2	1	3
pastor	2	3	2	3	3	4
childhood friend	1	2	1	2	1	2
someone with common interests	1	2	1	2	1	2
colleague	1	2	2	2	-	1
neighbor	1	2	1	1	1	2
foreman or boss	1	1	2	1	-	1
someone I can discuss religion with	-	1	1	1	-	1
other or no reply	2	2	5	3	1	1

1. See also table 5, in 2.2 "Kinship Networks."

Source: Allensbacher Archiv, IfD-Umfragen 225, 1287, cited in Institut für Demoskopie Allensbach, 1981, p. 34.

Table 5
Relations with neighbors and other residents (in%)

Wording of question: "Do you keep up any kind of relationship with your neighbors or other renters in your house? Here is a list. Could you say what relates to your situation?" (presentation of list).

Kind of relationship	Total		Men		Women	
	1953	1979	1953	1979	1953	1979
I talk with them	51	74	50	74	51	74
Take messages for neighbors in their absence	42	60	39	58	45	63
Congratulate neighbors on birthdays, name days, communion or confirmation	44	55	43	50	45	59
Attend neighbors' funerals	55	55	56	52	55	59
Invite neighbors into my home	14	35	15	33	13	36
Loan or borrow things	22	29	21	31	22	27
Go shopping for my neighbors	22	25	19	22	25	26
Babysit for neighbors	13	19	10	15	15	22
Join up to reach a common goal	10	14	13	16	7	12
Go to church together	12	8	10	5	14	10
None of these, other or no answer	24	10	25	10	23	11
Total	309	384	301	366	315	399

Note: The question in 1953 was: "Do you have any relationship to your neighbors or other renters in your house?"

Source: Allensbacher Archiv, IfD-Umfragen 225, 1287, cited in Institut für Demoskopie Allensbach, 1981, p. 41.

3. Women

3.1 Female Roles

The role of women has undergone a fundamental change, though transformation of their position in society and behaviour toward them lag well behind the egalitarian models and expectations. Discrimination against girls in the education system has been nearly eliminated; in family division of labour, in employment and income, and in the representation of women in public life, disadvantages still exist and have been only slightly reduced.

Transformations in the role of women can be observed in the normative field, in legislation, and in subjective attitudes, but also in living conditions, pertaining to social structure and individual behaviour. It remains to be seen if and to what degree different developments have taken place in parallel, are chronologically deferred, or even run contrary to each other.

During and after World War II, women had to replace the absent men in production sectors; *Trümmerfrauen* (women who built or rebuilt bombed-out dwellings under primitive conditions immediately after the war) also reconstructed destroyed cities, performed the troublesome and difficult task of procuring groceries, and tended children under extremely hard conditions.

Nevertheless, classic concepts of the biologically caused "otherness" of women, implying their suitability for non-public life, regained prominence as early as the late 1940s. The Equal Opportunity Amendment in the constitution, with its egalitarian wording – "Men and women have equal rights. No one may be discriminated against or given preferred treatment due to gender" – was carried only due to strong public resistance against a wording that would have allowed for different treatment of women and men according to their respective "particular character." A clause was added, stating that all laws contradictory to this article were to be revised by March 31, 1953. But it was not until 1957 that marriage and family law was changed and an equal-opportunity law (*Gleichberechtigungsgesetz*) was passed, giving the father sole power of representation and decision in the case of differences of opinion between parents. This clause was rendered null and void by the Federal Constitutional Court in 1959. Nonetheless, the paradigmatic model of the housewife in marriage, anchored as it was in family law, remained untouched until the marriage and divorce law underwent reform in 1977 (Eiken, 1986).

The struggle for egalitarian wording in the equal-opportunities amendment fell upon the shoulders of active and organized women – unionists, journalists, politicians, and representatives of women's associations. Most women remained uninterested in politics and constitutional matters. In a poll carried out in March of 1949, half of the women surveyed were indifferent to the future constitution, and only one in eight women claimed to be "very interested." Six years later, in May of 1955, two-thirds of the women surveyed admitted to not knowing what was said in the constitution of the Federal Republic (Noelle & Neumann, 1956).

Women's interests were administered by associations with strongly bureaucratic structures, which – up to the mid-1960s – saw their main task as offering instruction in citizenship, and from which certain conservative puritanical characteristics never quite disappeared. In contrast to this "corporative women's movement," an autonomous women's movement sprang from the critical milieu of the student movement and gained a broad basis within the female population through the abortion debate in 1971 (see 3.5, "Reproductive Technologies"). The new women's movement analyzed through a socially critical theory the background and function of discrimination against women, and gained a foothold in politics and everyday life. Countless women's centres and self-help groups were formed in cities and rural areas; discussions about, for example, wages for housework and violence against women eventually led to political demands. Abortion trips to Holland (where abortion was legal) were organized, demonstrations and meetings took place, and a tightly organized network of women's projects, pubs, cafés, publishing houses, newspapers, music groups, and shops of all kinds was built (Vogel, 1985).

Since the beginning of the 1980s, the women's movement has been institutionalized (see 10.3, "Social Movements"), including a transformation into a "women's project movement." Simultaneously, numerous demands concerning policy and everyday life – demands which had once been perceived as radical – became a matter of consensus, at least on the normative level. Changes in behaviour and structural conditions, on the other hand, took place comparatively slowly.

Labour Division within Families

Studies on the division of labour within families largely concur that little has changed in terms of female responsibility for housework and child care. Comparisons of couples married since 1950, 1970, and 1980 showed that, for older couples, domestic work sharing was self-evidently determined by gender, while younger husbands took part in domestic activities to a slightly greater degree (see tables 1, 2, and 3). Nevertheless, only small changes in the basic gender-specific division of work were effected, for only early on in marriage was greater involvement by husbands noticeable. As soon as couples entered the "family phase," men withdrew from domestic activities, and help was primarily offered for shopping and taking care of children. An attitude favourable to equal division of domestic tasks was maintained mostly by younger couples, and full-time employed women were most likely to realize changes in role distribution. In 1985, 92% of men living with a woman claimed not to be inconvenienced by housework – because they were doing almost nothing – and this fact was usually accepted without conflict (Krüger-Oldenburg, 1986; Lebert, 1985). Women and men also agree on the question of compatibility of motherhood and career: 57% of the women and 59% of the men polled hold the view that women have the choice of *either* raising children *or* pursuing a career; realization of one goal means renunciation of the other (Institut für Demoskopie Allensbach, 1986).

Educational Differentials

Definite gains have been made in the educational situation of women. Up to the 1960s, women's upbringing was oriented toward preparation for the roles of housewife and mother, and girls were underrepresented in higher-level schools (for a description of the German school system, see 8.1, "Educational System"). The expansion of education in the 1960s proved to be a turning point: educational discrimination against girls, long taken for granted, was attenuated. The current proportion of female students at universities is approaching the 40% mark (see table 4). "Whereas in the 1960s, a distinct disparity in opportunity existed between the sexes, a nearly equal distribution of opportunities for admission to liberal-education schools has since been achieved" (Beck-Gernsheim, 1984, p. 38).

Occupational Differentials

The proportion of female apprentices has risen markedly in the course of the past few decades, but distribution according to apprenticeship and job categories still points to considerable occupational differentials. The growth in proportion of women was highest in agricultural and technical jobs, and lowest in manufacturing and service-oriented employment (see table 5).

Women's employment continues to be restricted to fewer sectors than does men's employment. Though the career spectrum for women has widened with their growing tendency to "go with the market," a considerable concentration in a small number of professions is still undeniable: in 1925, nearly 82% of all working women were found in ten occupations, and this still applied to over 70% of women in 1982 (Willms-Herget, 1985).

Developments within respective professions vary, and sometimes even run contrary to each other. In a long-term observation of structural transformations of women's occupational fields, the following tendencies became obvious: an unchanged genderorientation of traditional occupations, for example medical assistance, sewing, housekeeping; a strong genderorientation toward women in formerly "gender-integrated" professions, for example sales, administration, teaching; a relatively weak opening up of what have been exclusively men's occupations in production and in highly qualified service professions, starting in the 1960s, with no later notable increase.

Tertiarization caused some strongly gender-oriented occupations to disappear, but some "modern" occupations have become rigidly genderoriented. The expectation that the impulse to conquer traditionally male academic professions would follow from the expansion of education and the women's movement has not been confirmed by the evolution of women's presence in academic institutions.

Further feminization was noted in schools, while women are more seldom found in responsible positions in law, medical, and engineering offices. Tendencies toward a minor typization are, however, observed in some modern women's professions, for example in health care, where their proportion is lower today than it was 10 or 20 years ago. Overall, a greater degree of segregation accompanied women's increased mobilization in the labour market (Willms-Herget, 1985).

Earnings Differences

Gender-specific earnings differences become visible not so much in unequal payment for the same work, but rather in forms of structural discrimination against women. Table 6 shows that the degree of difference in earnings has changed little in the recent past. In both 1972 and 1982, there were twice as many employed women as employed men in the lowest income levels (1972: up to 800 DM; 1982: up to 1,200 DM). This also applies tendentially to the share among independent businesspersons, office employees, and blue-collar workers. Only among civil servants, for whom temporary employment plays a small role, do income structures exhibit a greater similarity between the sexes (Berger, 1986).

Wage discrimination against women in industry is largely based on the creation of *Leichtlohngruppen* ("light-wage groups") as a reaction to a federal industrial-relations court decision in 1955 requiring wage categories to be principally the same for men and women. If, however, a differentiation between light and heavy work "leads to lower payment of women, because it is they who perform the lighter or predominantly light work, then there are no legal grounds for objection" (cited in Pohl 1984, p. 79).

"Light-wage groups" included work requiring certain abilities generally considered specifically female, such as nimble-fingeredness and tolerance of monotony. This state of affairs led to the even higher disparity (up to the 1970s) between gross hourly wages for unqualified male workers, calculated according to the lowest pay level for men, and those of qualified female workers, paid according to the highest women's wage group; this disparity has since been whittled down to an average of about 8% in favour of men. While women's wages have risen from 45% to 50% to 70% to 80% of men's wages in the past century, the absolute difference between men's and women's wages has increased considerably over the period (Pohl, 1984).

Power Differences

Representation of women in influential positions of public life continues to be lower than that of men. In 1949, only 7.1% of the members of the federal parliament were women; this number dropped to 5.8% by 1972, and then rose, slowly at first, then – between 1983 and 1987 – abruptly from 9.8% to 15.4%. The Christian Democratic and Christian Social parties and the Liberal Democrats sent, as a rule, fewer women into parliament than did the Social Democrats, but even their proportion of women usually stayed well under 10% until 1983. As opposed to this, the Green Party, elected into the federal parliament for the first time in 1983 with 35.7% female representation, raised this proportion to 56.8% in 1987.

The numbers of women members of labour unions and professional associations have been on the increase since the mid-1970s. Women comprised 18.3% of members of the Deutschen Gewerkschaftsbund (DGB – German Federation of Trade Unions) in 1976; this proportion rose to 22.1% in 1985. Female office employees show the most readiness to organize. Between 1976 and 1985 their proportion in the DGB rose from 34.2% to 41.6%, and it rose from 35.3% to 41.0% in the Deutschen Angestellten-Gewerkschaft (DAG – German Union of Salaried Workers) (Statistisches Bundesamt, 1987).

In general, the data confirm that the transformation of attitudes far outreaches that of behaviour. Consciousness of the complex problem inherent to the situation of women is becoming more widespread (Schmidtchen, 1984). A poll in 1967 found that 41% of West Germans believed that women had the same professional chances as men, while only 14% thought so in 1983. Though men defended this point of view decidedly longer in time series, in 1983 63% of them, and 64% of women, said that men got preferred treatment for equal job performance.

Karin Stiehr and Jürgen Schumacher

References

Beck-Gernsheim, Elisabeth
1984 *Vom Geburtenrückgang zur Neuen Mütterlichkeit. Über private und politische Interessen am Kind*. Frankfurt: Suhrkamp.

Berger, Peter
1986 *Entstrukturierte Klassengesellschaft? Klassenbildung und Strukturen sozialer Ungleichheit im historischen Wandel*. Opladen: Westdeutscher Verlag.

Blossfeld, Hans-Peter
1987 *Bildungsverläufe im historischen Wandel. Eine Längsschnittanalyse über die Veränderung der Bildungsbeteiligung im Lebenslauf dreier Geburtskohorten*. Arbeitspapier Nr. 225 des Sonderforschungsbereich 3 an der J.W. Goethe-Universität Frankfurt und Universität Mannheim. Frankfurt/Mannheim.

Bundesminister für Bildung und Wissenschaft, ed.
1987 *Grund- und Strukturdaten 1987/88*. Bonn.

Claessens, Dieter, Arno Klönne, and Armin Tschoepe
1985 *Sozialkunde der Bundesrepublik Deutschland. Grundlagen, Strukturen, Trends in Wirtschaft und Gesellschaft*. Reinbek: Rowohlt.

Eiken, Maria
1986 "Frauenpolitik im Nachkriegsdeutschland." In *Heiß und kalt. Die Jahre 1945-69*. Berlin: Elefanten Press.

Hausen, Karin
1976 "Die Polarisierung der 'Geschlechtscharaktere' - Eine Spiegelung der Dissoziation von Erwerbs- und Familienleben." In Werner Conze, ed., *Sozialgeschichte der Familie in der Neuzeit Europas*. Stuttgart: Klett-Cotta.

Hellmann, Ulrike, and Volker Volkholz
1985 *Mädchen in Männerberufen. Befragung von weiblichen Auszubildenden in gewerblich-technischen Berufen*. Hamburg.

Institut für Demoskopie Allensbach, ed.
1986 *Allensbacher Berichte*, no. 13.

Kommission der Europäischen Gemeinschaften, ed.
1987 *Euro-Barometer. Die öffentliche Meinung in der Europäischen Gemeinschaft*, no. 27.

Krüger-Oldenburg, Dorothea
1986 "Trends und Tendenzen in der häuslichen Arbeitsteilung unter rollentheoretischer Perspektive." In Schneider, ed., *Hauswirtschaftliche Bildung*. Baltmannsweiler.

Lebert, Ursula
1985 "Der Mann." *Brigitte*, no. 21-24.

Nave-Herz, Rosemarie
1988 "Kontinuität und Wandel von Ehe und Familie." In Rosemarie Nave-Herz, ed., *Wandel und Kontinuität der Familie in der Bundesrepublik Deutschland*. Stuttgart: Enke.

Noelle, Elisabeth, and Erich Peter Neumann
1956 *Jahrbuch der öffentlichen Meinung 1947-1955*. Allensbach: Verlag für Demoskopie.

Pohl, Sigrid
1984 *Entwicklung und Ursachen der Frauenlohndiskriminierung*. Frankfurt/Bern/New York: Lang.

Schmidtchen, Gerhard
1984 *Die Situation der Frau. Trendbeobachtungen über Rollen- und Bewußtseinsänderungen der Frauen in der Bundesrepublik Deutschland*. Berlin: Duncker und Humblot.

Statistisches Bundesamt, ed.
1987 *Frauen in Familie, Beruf und Gesellschaft*. Wiesbaden.

Vogel, Angelika
1983 "Frauen und Frauenbewegung." In Wolfgang Benz, ed., *Die Bundesrepublik Deutschland*. Vol. 2: Gesellschaft. Frankfurt: Fischer.

Willms-Herget, Angelika
1985 *Frauenarbeit: zur Integration der Frauen in den Arbeitsmarkt*. Frankfurt/New York: Campus.

Table 1
Work carried out in %, food-providing tasks (including preparation of food and subsequent related tasks) (multiple answers possible)

Marriage Gender	Year	Shopping	Preparing breakfast	Cooking	Table-clearing	Dish-washing	Garbage removal
Woman	1950	62.3	82.9	98.6	45.6	75.3	34.8
	1970	56.7	77.4	80.0	34.4	62.9	28.7
	1980	41.5	74.4	75.3	25.0	53.9	16.9
Man	1950	4.3	11.5	-	2.9	1.4	34.7
	1970	5.8	6.1	2.5	2.5	2.6	26.9
	1980	4.5	5.8	5.6	-	2.2	37.0
Both	1950	33.3	5.7	1.4	51.5	23.2	30.4
	1970	37.5	16.5	17.5	63.0	34.5	44.3
	1980	53.9	19.8	19.1	75.0	43.8	46.1

Source: Krüger-Oldenburg, 1986, p. 6.

Table 2
Work tasks in %, maintenance tasks (wardrobe and housing) (multiple answers possible)

Marriage Gender	Year	Laundry	Shoe-cleaning	Vacuuming	Dusting	Home repairs
Woman	1950	98.6	25.0	79.7	89.8	3.0
	1970	95.8	21.2	76.1	88.9	1.7
	1980	92.0	24.7	58.6	80.2	-
Man	1950	-	23.5	4.3	4.3	87.8
	1970	-	13.3	1.7	-	91.4
	1980	-	7.8	6.9	-	92.8
Both	1950	1.4	51.5	15.9	5.8	9.1
	1970	4.2	65.5	22.2	11.1	6.8
	1980	8.0	67.5	34.5	19.7	7.2

Source: Krüger-Oldenburg, 1986, p. 6.

Table 3
Work carried out in %, child-care and upbringing tasks (including retrospective polling of marriage year 1950) (multiple answers possible)

Marriage gender	Year	Playing with children	Learning	Taking to sport event	Putting to bed
Woman	1950	42.8	92.3	80.0	100.0
	1970	18.7	67.3	63.9	45.8
	1980	17.9	33.3	78.1	40.5
Man	1950	-	-	20.0	-
	1970	1.8	1.0	8.4	5.5
	1980	1.2	9.6	3.1	3.6
Both	1950	57.1	7.7	-	-
	1970	79.5	30.7	27.7	48.6
	1980	81.0	57.1	18.8	56.0

Source: Krüger-Oldenburg, 1986, p. 6.

Table 4
Proportion of girls/women in academic institutions (in %)

Year	High schools (academic)	College beginners	College students
1960	36.5	27.0	23.9
1970	41.4	28.8	25.6
1980	49.4	40.1	36.7
1986	49.7	40.2	37.9

Source: Bundesminister für Bildung und Wissenschaft, 1987, pp. 47, 134.

Table 5
Proportion of women among apprentices/on-the-job trainees

Item	1969	1975	1981	1985
Agricultural occupation	9.9	17.7	31.1	35.7
Mechanic occupation	6.7	4.7	7.3	8.9
Technical occupation	37.0	37.7	50.0	53.2
Service profession	67.0	71.7	76.0	74.9

Source: Hellmann & Volkholz, 1985, p. 26; Statistisches Bundesamt, 1987, p. 69.

Table 6
Income levels, 1972 and 1982 (in %)

Income level[1]	Men	Women	Total
1972			
Under 600	9.3	46.9	22.2
600- 800	9.6	23.3	14.3
800-1200	45.5	21.7	37.4
1200-1800	23.9	6.3	17.9
Over 1800	11.5	1.8	8.2
1982[2]			
Under 1200	13.1	54.5	28.5
1200-1800	31.3	30.4	30.9
1800-2500	32.0	10.7	24.1
2500-4000	17.2	3.7	12.2
Over 4000	6.4	0.7	4.3

1. Monthly net income in DM.
2. Including apprentices/trainees and temporarily employed, totalling 17.6% of all employed persons, 6.8% of the male employed and 36.1% of the female employed.

Source: Berger, 1986, p. 148.

3.2 Childbearing

The "baby boom" of the 1950s was succeeded by a drastic downswing in the birth rate as of 1963. Population-policy measures to counter this trend are neither very pronounced nor effective in the Federal Republic.

A central function of the family in society has always been reproduction. All Western industrialized countries are witnessing a fertility slump which goes back to the nineteenth century. Long-term observation of fertility statistics for Germany and for the Federal Republic (see figure 1) reveal severe aberrations during World War I, the world depression, World War II, and a slower but more steady descent since 1963/1964 (the years of the "baby bust"). The increase in birth rate between 1933 and 1939, caused by National Socialist motherhood propaganda, and following 1954 appear to be a deviation from a long-term trend rather than a contrary development.

The fertility increase immediately after World War II can be linked to the return of soldiers; there was also an abrupt upturn in the number of marriages, many of which had been postponed due to the war. Between 1950 and 1953, the birth rate remained almost constant, presumably because the marriage age of the partners in the "re-wedding marriages" of 1950 and 1951 was relatively high – an average of 36 years (Delille & Grohn, 1985).

A higher birth rate was again recorded between 1954 and 1964, with an increase from 69.4 to 86.8 live births per 1,000 women of child-bearing age. The boom-year children born between 1934 and 1939 had come of marriage age – that is, there were phases in which a higher number of young couples had children than would normally correspond to the life-age structure of a population with steady birth-rate development. Starting in 1964, the number of live births per 1,000 women of child-bearing age sank continuously, reaching 47.6 in 1975; it has since stabilized at around this level. Those born during the strong "baby-boom" years came of marriage age and slowed the negative birth rate trend without, however, reversing it, as had been expected. Since 1975 there has been no natural population growth, and the mortality rate is higher than the birth rate. The net reproduction rate, which ascertains to what degree members of one female generation are replaced by their daughters according to the current birth-death ratio, supports the above-mentioned birth-rate development. It has hovered between 0.600 and 0.680 since the end of the 1970s: approximately one-third fewer daughters are being born than are required to maintain the population (see table 1).

The respective modal ages of mothers at first birth follow the general trend: non-age-specific data, which proceed from a statistically even number of women per annum, show a slight decline, between 1958 (first year on record) and 1970, of from 25.61 to 24.16 years of age. From 1970 to 1986, a definite upturn to 26.71 years of age was registered by the Federal Statistics Authority, supposedly with negative consequences for the birth rate. This tendency corresponds with an almost identically continuous upswing of average marriage duration at the time of the first birth as well as of subsequent births (see table 2).

The dropping birth rate is particularly visible in the reduced number of large families. In parallel to decreasing household size, a trend which is traceable through the past 100 years (see table 4), the modal number of children per individual marriage-year is also dwindling (Nave-Herz, 1988). This development is most notable in the decision against having three or more children: the proportion of couples with two children, one child, or no children is on the increase (Huinink, 1988; see figure 2). The change in attitude toward children was expressed by sociologist Karl Bolte as being "from a blessing to a burden." An average of 2.50 children were desired in 1965, but only 1.46 were in 1980. Comparison with other nations shows that West Germans want markedly fewer children (see table 3).

A final notable development is the curvilinear pattern of illegitimate births. A remarkably high number of illegitimate children were born immediately after World War II (in 1946, 116,310; despite their absolute decline in numbers, they amounted to nearly 10% of all live births in 1950). These illegitimate children were presumably often the products of "friendships of opportunity" between German women and members of the occupying forces (who had access to groceries, cigarettes, and other consumption articles) (Delille & Grohn, 1985). The proportion of almost 10% in 1950 was about halved by the 1960s, only to rise again, despite better birth-control possibilities, and is presently near postwar levels (table 1). The age of mothers of illegitimate children has risen markedly, from around 20 years old in 1970 to 30 years old in 1980. This age increase can in part be traced back to reliability of methods of preventing unwanted pregnancy, and can also be understood as an indication of desire for children being actualized independently of marriage and family.

An amendment regarding the legal rights of illegitimate children was passed in 1970 guaranteeing them official recognition of the paternal relationship. The role of the authorities is restricted to assertion of paternity and the possible pursuit of support and inheritance claims. The unmarried mother obtains total custody, and the father is refused all rights. As more and more parents voluntarily reject marriage despite having children together, further amendments are currently under consideration.

After having been ignored for decades, the fertility-rate downswing has become a theme for population experts, who warn against its consequences for the "contract between the generations" – that is, its effects on old-age pensions, economic growth, health care, and the educational system. Thus, in the last several years, the government has rediscovered the role of "the mother," which could also provide relief for the overcrowded labour market: for example, the *Erziehungsgeld* (government allowance paid for a certain period of time after the birth of a child) is now paid not only to working women but also to housewives, and one *Erziehungsjahr* (official recognition of an additional year's social-security contribution) per child is recognized in the government pension plan.

Seen in the context of the empirical data, it is questionable if these measures will have the intended effect: the first fertility-rate decrease in Germany began 100 years ago, while non-domestic employment among married women did not noticeably increase until about 1960; the ideal conception of family size is the same for working women as for housewives (Beck-Gernsheim, 1984). The causes of the birth-rate decrease are manifold and are certainly also based on a change of values in which the notion of "self-development" has gained importance for parents as well as for children.

It is for the most part female politicians and female scientists who increasingly demand the establishment of infrastructural accommodations (for example, all-day schools) to ease the reconciliation of career and family life. Other than these measures, any active population policy – a concept freighted with the memory of National Socialism – has only conventional methods at hand: "Talking as many parents as possible into having a third child, actually buying it with generous support allowances, and/or a reduction of the generative deficit via a [purposeful] immigration policy" (Linde, 1988, p. 219). The first two methods are not emphatically carried out in the Federal Republic, and the last one does not fit with present immigration policy (see 16.1, "Immigrants").

Karin Stiehr

References

Beck-Gernsheim, Elisabeth
1984 *Vom Geburtenrückgang zur Neuen Mütterlichkeit? Über private und politische Interessen am Kind.* Frankfurt am Main: Suhrkamp.

Birg, Herwig, and Helmut Koch
1987 *Der Bevölkerungsrückgang in der Bundesrepublik Deutschland.* Frankfurt am Main/New York: Campus.

Bolte, Karl Martin
1980 "Bestimmungen der Geburtenentwicklung und Überlegungen zu einer möglichen Beeinflußbarkeit." In Schriftenreihe des Bundesministers für Jugend, Familie und Gesundheit. *Bevölkerungsentwicklung und nachwachsende Generation.* Stuttgart/Berlin/Köln/Mainz: Kohlhammer.

Claessens, Dieter, Arno Klönne, and Armin Tschoepe
1985 *Sozialkunde der Bundesrepublik Deutschland.* Reinbek: Rowohlt.

Delille, Angela, and Andrea Grohn
1985 *Blick zurück aufs Glück. Frauenleben und Familienpolitik in den 50er Jahren*. Berlin: Elefanten Press.

Deutscher Bundestag
1986 *Die Situation der älteren Menschen in der Familie. 4. Familienbericht*. Bonn.

Huinink, Johannes
1988 *Das zweite und das dritte Kind. Sind wir auf dem Weg zur Ein-Kind-Familie?* Arbeitspapier Nr. 272 des Sonderforschungsbereich 3 der J.W. Goethe-Universität Frankfurt und Universität Mannheim. Frankfurt am Main/Mannheim.

Linde, Hans
1988 *Kritische Empirie. Beiträge zur Soziologie und Bevölkerungswissenschaft 1937-1987*. Opladen: Westdeutscher Verlag.

Schmid, Josef
1984 *Bevölkerungsveränderungen in der Bundesrepublik Deutschland. Eine Revolution auf leisen Sohlen*. Stuttgart/Berlin/Köln/Mainz: Kohlhammer.

Schumacher, Jürgen
1988 "Leistungsniveau und Leistungsbereitschaft in der Familie." In Karl Otto Hondrich, and Jürgen Schumacher, eds., *Krise der Leistungsgesellschaft?* Opladen: Westdeutscher Verlag.

Statistisches Bundesamt, ed.
1987 *Datenreport 1987*. Stuttgart: Bundeszentrale für politische Bildung.

–, ed.
1988 *Statistisches Jahrbuch 1988 für die Bundesrepublik Deutschland*. Stuttgart/Mainz: Kohlhammer.

Table 1
Fertility rate

Year	Per 1,000		Out-of-wedlock live births per 1,000	Net reproduction rate
	Live births	Surplus births(+) deaths(-)		
1950	16.2	+5.7	97.3	0.929
1955	15.7	+4.5	78.6	0.938
1960	17.4	+5.9	63.3	1.096
1965	17.7	+6.2	46.9	1.174
1970	13.4	+1.3	54.6	0.946
1975	9.7	-2.4	61.2	0.679
1980	10.1	-1.5	75.6	0.679
1985	9.6	-1.9	94.0	0.603
1987	10.5	-0.7	97.1	0.639

Source: Statistisches Bundesamt, 1988, p. 70.

Table 2
Live births

Standard	Units	1965	1970	1975	1980	1985
Total live births	1,000	1,044.3	810.8	600.5	620.7	586.2
Live births per 1,000 women aged 15-44 years	Number	85.2	67.2	47.6	46.7	44.1
Average age of mother at birth of first child	Years	24.88	24.34	24.81	25.19	26.18
Average marriage duration of parents upon birth of:						
- first child		1.92	1.97	2.49	2.73	2.64
- second child		4.69	5.08	5.42	5.76	5.63
- third child		7.18	7.95	8.27	8.60	8.58
- fourth child		9.11	10.11	10.61	10.87	10.87
- fifth and further children		11.74	12.76	13.64	14.00	13.93

Source: Statistisches Bundesamt, 1987, p. 25.

Table 3
Desired average of children

Country	1965	1975	1980
West Germany	2.50	1.45	1.46
Belgium	2.61	1.73	1.68
France	2.84	1.93	1.96
Great Britain	2.83	1.81	1.93
Italy	2.55	2.19	1.66
Japan	2.14	1.91	1.72
Netherlands	3.04	1.66	1.61
Spain	2.97	2.81	2.16
Sweden	2.42	1.77	1.68
Switzerland	2.61	1.60	1.53
United States	2.93	1.80	1.90

Source: Monnier, cited in Beck-Gernsheim, 1984, p. 185.

Table 4
Household size 1925 - 1985 (in % of households)

Persons	1900	1925	1950	1985
1	7.1	6.6	19.4	33.6
2	14.7	17.7	25.3	29.8
3	17.0	22.5	23.0	17.1
4	16.8	19.7	16.2	13.2
5 and more	44.4	33.3	16.1	6.3

Source: Statistisches Bundesamt, 1987.

Figure 1
Fertility statistics for Germany and the FRG

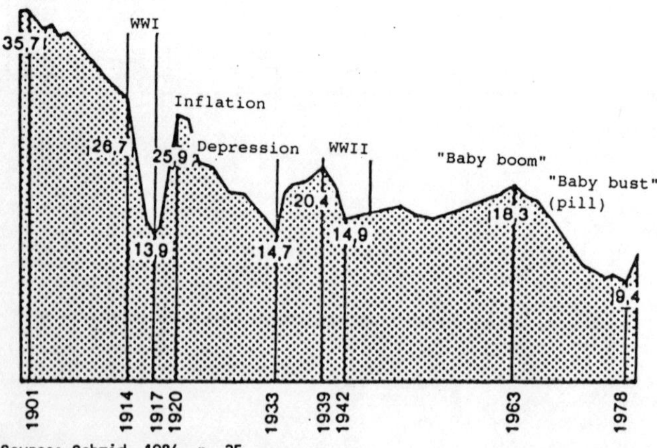

Source: Schmid, 1984, p. 25.

Figure 2
Marriges 1900 - 1975 according to final number of progeny (in %) (of 100 marriages)

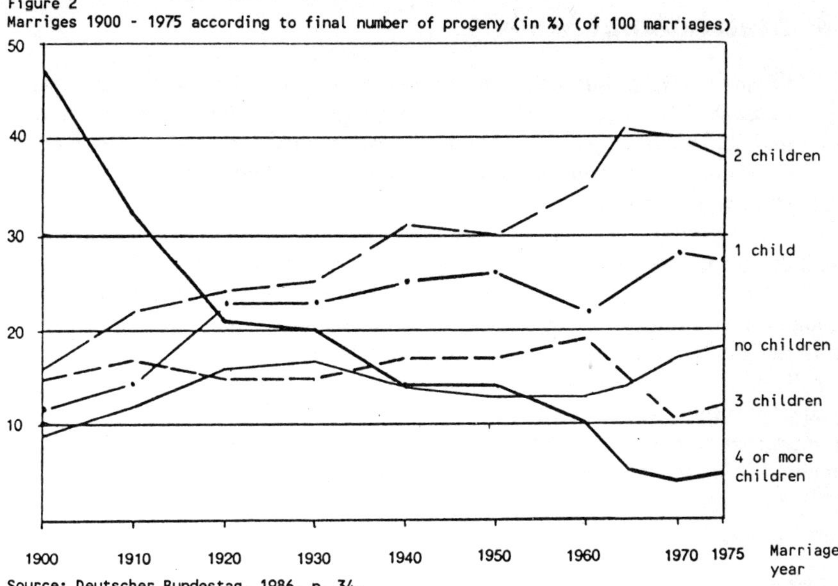

Source: Deutscher Bundestag, 1986, p. 34.

3.3 Matrimonial Models

Trends toward pluralization and liberalization can be seen in the concepts of marriage and family: there are fewer marriages and an increasing divorce rate, and non-marriage cohabitation, out-of-wedlock births, and one-parent families are on the rise. In terms of values and expectations, family and partnership still enjoy very high status.

The concepts of marriage and family have long been influenced by the bourgeois model of the woman as "spouse, housewife, mother," which became widespread (though never completely pervasive) among all social groups over the centuries. Up to the 1950s, the husband's power of decision over place and type of residence, as well as over the wife's out-of-house employment, was legally sanctioned. An equal-opportunity act (*Gleichberechtigungsgesetz*) passed in 1957, did away with these prerogatives; still, the woman's predominant responsibility for keeping house remained in force until the marriage- and family-law reform (*Eherechtsreform*) of 1977.

Marriages

These liberalization tendencies became noticeable in relations between men and women as of the mid-1960s, a time when the very institution of marriage was being increasingly questioned. The proportion of those who thought marriage necessary remained at a constant 89% between 1949 and 1963, but it fell to 64% between 1963 and 1985. Currently, one in seven persons considers marriage "outdated," and one in five is undecided (see table 1). A gender-specific comparison of answers shows that attitudinal change has been similar among women and men; the strongest tendency to be critical of marriage, however, was found among women with longer educational periods (Institut für Demoskopie Allensbach, 1989; Nave-Herz, 1988).

The tendency to marry waned correspondingly. Since the mid-1960s, the numbers of unmarried (i.e., never married) men and women of 20 to 35 years of age have climbed once again, accompanied by a corresponding reduction in the number of married people (see tables 2 and 3). In 1950, 10.7 marriages per 1,000 persons were contracted; in 1986 this proportion had fallen to only 6.1. Among every 100 men born in the years 1946–1950, 69 had married by the age of 29; among those born 10 years later, this proportion had dropped to 55. Women show a corresponding decrease from 85 to 73 first marriages per 100 (see table 4).

This development converges over time with the renewed trend toward increases in average age at marriage. The age at first marriage among men fell from 28.1 to

25.3 years between 1950 and 1975, then climbed to 27.2 years by 1985. Over the same period, the age of women at first marriage showed a corresponding decline from 25.4 to 22.7 years, and a subsequent rise to 24.6 years (Statistisches Bundesamt, 1987).

Satisfaction with marriage, partnership, family, and household is higher than it is with other spheres of life, and has declined little since the late 1970s. It is notable that women are somewhat less content with their family life than are men, which may be connected to their growing doubts about acceptance of traditional roles. The proportion of "very satisfied" women in households with small or school-age children dropped from 36% to 26% between 1978 and 1984, as did the proportion of very satisfied men, from 41% to 33% (Statistisches Bundesamt, 1985).

Despite the high overall degree of satisfaction with marriage and family, various empirical studies have shown that conflicts between marriage partners come to the point of confrontation more often nowadays than previously, or are at least perceived as conflicts. In more and more cases, conflicts lead to termination of the marriage. Excluding the high number of war-caused divorces up to the early 1950s, the divorce rate was at a relatively low level until well into the 1960s. Since then, the proportion has risen drastically: 36 out of 10,000 existing marriages ended in divorce in 1960, while 86 out of 10,000 did so in 1985 (see table 5). A short-term decline toward the end of the 1970s resulted solely from enforcement of the marriage- and family- law reforms act, which removed the principle of guilt in favour of referring to alienation of the marriage partners as grounds for divorce, and offered improvements for the economically disadvantaged spouse, usually the woman. While it was mostly men who filed for divorce during the postwar period up to 1950, it has for many years now been women who file in most cases.

The consistently high subjective evaluation of partnership and family leads to the conclusion that the growing instability of partnership relations is by no means a signal of crisis for the institution of the family, but rather that it is a result of greater individual expectations regarding the quality of family life. "The statistical rise in divorces could therefore be considered an indicator that nowadays unharmonious relationships and alienated marriages are more likely to be dissolved than in former times" (Nave-Herz, 1988, p. 85).

This assumption fits with the observation that nuptial duty and acceptance concepts are losing importance. While good-will behaviours such as sense of duty, tolerance, and patience formed the basis for marriage in the opinion of 52% of those interviewed in a non-selective poll in the mid-1960s, these values, now nearly meaningless, were named by only 8% 12 years later. In 1964 – 1965, 21% of those polled mentioned children as reasons for marriage durability, but only 9% did so in 1977 (see table 6).

Cohabitation in One-parent Families

The number of "divorce orphans" and one-parent families is steadily increasing. The proportion of families made up of children under 18 and a single family head rose from 7.7% in 1971 to 13.4% in 1986. In most cases, women head one-parent families, and it is notable that the proportion of unmarried women in this group is on the rise; it reached just under 20% in 1986. The typical single parent nowadays is female and divorced, whereas 15 years ago she was widowed. Male-headed units have become more prevalent, though their proportion dropped slightly in the 1980's. Families headed by unmarried and divorced fathers had the biggest growth rates (Fischer & Hauser, 1988).

In the Federal Republic, over 2 million women and men live in non-marriage cohabitation; their numbers tripled between 1972 and 1982 (Schenk, 1987). After World War II, so-called *Onkel-Ehen* ("uncle-marriages," or common-law marriages) were entered into, usually by older, widowed, or divorced women and men, primarily for social-security purposes (retirement income would have been combined and often reduced by the state if they had been legally married), but now almost two-thirds of unmarried cohabitating couples are under 30 years of age. The difference between prenuptial cohabitation, amounting to a kind of "trial marriage," and cohabitation perceived as an alternative to marriage should be kept in mind. In general, they are seen as ways of life that go less against the values of personal independence and self-development than do more conventional arrangements.

Non-marriage cohabitations are largely accepted and are perceived as signs of pluralization tendencies in the ways men and women cohabit. As early as 1976, 63% of West Germans saw "nothing wrong" with a man and woman living together without a marriage certificate; this percentage was up to 78% by 1986. Cohabitation outside of marriage is taken for granted by nearly all of those questioned in the age cohort under 30. Up to and including the cohort group of 45- to 60-year-olds, significantly more women than men accept it (Piel, 1987).

A 1981 study found that the majority of those polled welcomed the idea of "trial marriage," and half were for permanent cohabitation as an alternative to marriage. On the other hand, barely one-third approved of unmarried cohabitation involving a child. The relative paucity of children among unmarried cohabiting couples in the Federal Republic – as compared to Denmark and Sweden – can probably be traced to the fact that most couples end up marrying when a child is expected.

It seems to be mainly women who hope to find equality in their partnerships through the choice of unmarried cohabitation. Male dominance outside the home or female dominance within the home is rarer in these relationships than in legalized marriages, though it should be kept in mind that these relationships are usually childless (Schenk, 1987).

The motives for contracting marriage seem to have shifted since the mid-1970s. An emotional partner relationship, often in conjunction with external pressure or conditions such as the legal system and housing difficulties, used to lead to marriage. Now, the primary reason is the desire for children (Nave-Herz, 1988).

Karin Stiehr and Jürgen Schumacher

References

Claessens, Dieter, Arno Klönne, and Armin Tschoepe
1985 *Sozialkunde der Bundesrepublik Deutschland. Grundlagen, Strukturen, Trends in Wirtschaft und Gesellschaft*. Reinbek: Rowohlt.

Fischer, Ingo, and Richard Hauser
1988 *Lone-Parent Families in the Federal Republic of Germany*. Arbeitspapier Nr. 275 des Sonderforschungsbereich 3 an der J.W. Goethe-Universität Frankfurt und Universität Mannheim. Frankfurt/Mannheim.

Institut für Demoskopie Allensbach, ed.
1989 *Allensbacher Berichte*, no. 10.

Klages, Helmut
1984 *Wertorientierungen im Wandel*. Frankfurt/New York: Campus.

Linde, Hans
1988 *Kritische Empirie. Beiträge zur Soziologie und Bevölkerungswissenschaft 1937-1987*. Opladen: Leske und Budrich.

Nave-Herz, Rosemarie
1988 "Kontinuität und Wandel in der Bedeutung, in der Struktur und Stabilität von Ehe und Familie in der Bundesrepublik Deutschland." In Rosemarie Nave-Herz, ed., *Wandel und Kontinuität der Familie in der Bundesrepublik Deutschland*. Stuttgart: Enke.

Piel, Edgar
1987 *Im Geflecht der kleinen Netze. Vom deutschen Rückzug ins Private*. Zürich: Edition Interfrom.

Schenk, Herrad
1987 *Freie Liebe - Wilde Ehe. Über die allmähliche Auflösung der Ehe durch die Liebe*. München: Beck.

Schmid, Josef
1984 *Bevölkerungsveränderungen in der Bundesrepublik Deutschland. Eine Revolution auf leisen Sohlen*. Stuttgart/Berlin/Köln/Mainz: Kohlhammer.

Shorter, Edward
1977 *Die Geburt der modernen Familie*. Reinbek: Rowohlt.

Statistisches Bundesamt, ed.
1985 *Datenreport 1985*. Bonn: Bundeszentrale für politische Bildung.

–
1987 *Datenreport 1987*. Bonn: Bundeszentrale für politische Bildung.

–
1988 *Statistisches Jahrbuch 1988 für die Bundesrepublik Deutschland*. Stuttgart/Mainz: Kohlhammer.

Table 1
Attitudes toward marriage (in %)

Wording of question: "Do you think the institution of marriage is principally necessary or obselete?"

Item	1949[1]	1963	1985
Necessary	89	89	64
Obselete	4	3	14
Undecided	7	8	22
Total	100	100	100

Federal Republic and West Berlin population 16 years of age and over.

1. In 1949 adults 20 years and over were polled.

Source: Allensbacher Archiv, IfD-Umfragen 222, 256, 2098, 3032/II, 3059, 4047, 4048, 4053, cited in Piel, 1987, p. 121.

Table 2
Male population according to exemplary age cohorts and marital status

Aged from... to...	Single			Married		
	1950	1965	1985	1950	1965	1985
20-25	83.1	82.5	90.1	16.7	17.4	9.6
25-30	46.3	38.4	57.0	52.6	60.8	40.5
30-35	22.7	15.6	30.6	74.7	83.1	64.1

Source: Statistisches Bundesamt, 1967, p. 40; 1987, p. 64.

Table 3
Female population according to exemplary age cohorts and marital status

Aged from... to...	Single			Married		
	1950	1965	1985	1950	1965	1985
20-25	67.2	51.3	73.1	32.0	47.8	25.9
25-30	34.1	18.4	33.9	61.2	79.6	61.9
30-35	18.5	10.4	16.5	70.6	86.8	76.7

Source: Statistisches Bundesamt, 1967, p. 40; 1987, p. 64.

Table 4
First marriages (in %)

First marriages per 100 men born in the years ...			
Aged from...to...	1946-1950	1951-1955	1956-1960
15-24	48	43	31
15-29	69	66	55
First marriages per 100 women born in the years ...			
Aged from...to...	1946-1950	1951-1955	1956-1960
15-24	76	69	58
15-29	85	81	73

Source: F. Höpflinger, 1987, p. 57, cited in Nave-Herz, 1988, p. 63.

Table 5
Annual divorce rates since 1890 (West Germany)

Year	Divorces per 10,000 persons	Divorces per 10,000 marriages
1890	1.3	7.4
1910	2.3	15.2
1920	5.9	32.1
1940	7.1	38.1
1950	16.9	67.5
1960	8.8	35.7
1965	10.0	39.2
1970	12.6	50.9
1975	17.3	69.9
1980	15.6	61.3
1982	19.2	78.7
1985	21.0	86.1

Source: Claessens et al., 1985, p. 402; Statistisches Bundesamt, 1988, p. 78.

Table 6
Basis of marriage (in %)

Item	1964/65[1]	1977
Marriage-suitable behavior (for example dutifulness, tolerance, consideration)	52	8
Children	21	9
Togetherness, harmony	14	18
Financial security	13	9
Sympathy (love, material and spiritual understanding, loyalty, trust, comradeship)	9	16
Common interests	4	2
Religion, creed	4	1
Habit, comfort	3	3
Right choice of partner (long engagement, knowing the partner well)	1	1
Society and environs	-	5
Complicated divorce procedure	-	1
Equal rights	-	3
Institute of marriage is not resilient	-	15
Other	8	1
No answer	12	19
Total	141	111

1. Ehe und Familie, EMNID -Institut 1965, polling of 1,500 parents with at least one child 12-15 years of age in their household. Question: "In your opinion, what does the most to make a marriage permanent?" (answer at liberty); commentary March 1977.

Source: Klages, 1984, p. 120.

3.4 Women's Employment

Changes in the structure of women's employment, as well as the continuously rising proportion of working women since the early 1970s, confirm an evolution away from the once-predominant family orientation and toward a desire to combine career and family.

There are few data available on work performed by women during the immediate postwar period. According to the census of 1946, the population of the four occupied zones consisted of 44% women, 23% children, and 33% men, the majority of the latter being elderly or war-handicapped. These numbers make it clear that women by necessity replaced the absent male work force in many domains of life. The collapse of the entire econo-industrial system, the loss of the grain-producing eastern regions, and the incessant stream of refugees brought about a catastrophic shortage of food and supplies. Women were forced to deal in the black market, to make "hoarding" or "pack-rat" trips to farms, and to forage for food in woods and fields. In October of 1945, the *Kontrollrat* (Control Council) of the Allied Forces passed a "work obligation" for men from 14 to 65 years of age and for women from 15 to 50 years of age. In 1946, the military governments distributed lists of the jobs to be delegated to women – mainly construction work (Delille & Grohn, 1985). In the often completely bombed-out cities, *Trümmerfrauen* (women making the best of what rubble was lying around) had to create substitutes for destroyed housing under the most primitive of conditions.

Sociological surveys on the family and official statistics of the postwar period have shown that regular employment was not a primary concern for women, due to their general work overload and the greater attractiveness of black-market trading. Not until the currency reform of 1948 did women once again begin to turn to the employment market. The increase in absolute numbers of employed women was accompanied by an equally large increase in the number of unemployed women. There was a general population growth caused by the influx of refugees and of men returning home from the war. The proportion of employed women among the work-capable population fell from 37.3% to 31.3% between 1946 and 1950, with a very slight subsequent upturn (Delille & Grohn, 1985; Sommerkorn, 1988).

In the 1950s, the model of woman as housewife and mother dominated, and nondomestic employment activity by women met with criticism. After she married, the woman usually took on responsibility for domestic and family tasks. This social state of affairs corresponded to the legal code (valid up to July 1, 1976), whereby the woman was primarily committed to housekeeping, and the man to financial support of the family (Claessens et al., 1985). Arguments against the "double-income" family were directed solely against the income-earning wife: temporary employment in situations of economic necessity was long considered to be the only legitimate for women to have a career (Sommerkorn, 1988).

Observation of various areas of women's employment shows how the traditional family-oriented models for women have been transformed over the past few decades.

Labour-force Participation

The proportion of employed women changed only slightly between 1950 and 1980; vacillating between 30% and 33%, with no downward trend since the early 1970s. A steep increase has been recorded over the past few years, and the proportion of employed women reached its highest level of the past four decades (36.3%) in 1986 (see table 1).

Looking beyond these averages, one finds lasting changes in the structure of women's employment. Comparative examination according to age group shows that in 1950, young women between 15 and 20 years of age made up the largest group (80%) of employed women. This proportion was halved among women between 20 and 45 years of age, while many women over 65 still participated in the work force. Results for 1980 were markedly different. Extended periods dedicated to training or education caused women to enter the work force comparatively late, but a notably greater number of women between 25 and 60 years of age were employed than was the case in 1950. On the other hand, the proportion of working women over 60 years of age was considerably lower (see table 2).

Single and married women have shared equally in the growth of women's employment, but the level of participation is disproportionately higher among married women. The proportion of single women in the work force rose from 27.1% to 34.6% between 1970 and 1985, while that of married women underwent a continuous increase from 35.4% to 42.5% (see figure 1). Fewer and fewer women interrupt their careers due to marriage. The three-phase model, propagated in the 1960s and 1970s, which had the woman interrupting her career during the second family phase to take care of her children, is losing in popularity (see figure 2). There are more working mothers: the proportion of working women with children under 15 years of age, in relation to the total number of mothers with children of this age, rose from 34.6% to 41.2% between 1961 and 1986; the proportion of working women among mothers with children under six years of age went from 31.3% to 35.5% (Calame & Fiedler, 1982; Statistisches Bundesamt, 1988).

In addition, the spectrum of women's careers has undergone quite a shift over the last few decades. While over one-third of working women were "helpers-out" in or outside of the agricultural sector in 1950, mere 8% are in this category nowadays. In 1950, only around 15% of working women were engaged in clerical, administrative, or sales work; this proportion has since risen to over 40% (Willms-

Herget, 1985). This development signified more career independence and, simultaneously, a fanning out of women's employment activities throughout the career sectors.

This situation should not serve to conceal the fact that the proportion of temporarily employed women has risen drastically over the past few decades (see table 3). On the one hand, this is due to the increased number of temporary jobs offered on the market, in all employment sectors (see 4.3, "Types of Employment"). It is assumed that temporary jobs will become especially widespread in the commercial and service sectors, due to new technology and work hour-systems. On the other hand, the demand for temporary employment is widespread among working women and among women wishing to return to their interrupted careers, and far exceeds the available jobs (Institut für Arbeitsmarkt und Berufsforschung, 1984; Schumacher, 1988). However, neither the demand for temporary jobs nor the current high proportion of temporarily employed women results solely from voluntary decisions. The multiple work load of women – career, household, and family – combined with the fact that women often have only temporary jobs offered to them, frequently leaves them with no choice with regard to the extent of their employment activities. As well, the high degree of temporary employment among women erects a recruitment-pertinent background conducive to the corresponding wishes of women, in other words: a self-fullfilling desire.

Paid and Unpaid Work at Home

Another form of trying to combine employment with fulfillment of household obligations is paid work at home, a system in which persons do contracted work in their homes. The proportion of women among people engaged in this kind of employment has remained much the same since 1956 (about 90%), while their absolute numbers are currently slightly on the rise after a drastic slump between 1965 and 1975 (Bretschneider & Husmann, 1980). As new technologies are devoloped which make the switch from conventional office jobs to work at home possible, a further increase is foreseen, with particular relevance for women.

Paid work continues, as before, to represent just a small fraction of the work done by women. About half of the women between 15 and 64 years of age participate in the working world (the proportion of working women in this age group was 53.4% in 1986), while women continue to be mainly responsible for work in the field of care for and creation of individual living conditions. It must, however, be kept in mind that housework in the 1950s can hardly be compared to housework today. While observers increasingly point out that forging a harmonious family life has become the primary task, housework was formerly concerned with practical and manually strenuous labor. In the Federal Republic, households tended to have fewer electrical appliances than did those in other Western countries (for example, in 1953 only 3.5% of households had a washing machine, and 83% had one in 1983), limited storage and refrigeration capacities in the home made frequent shopping necessary, and meal preparation took a great deal of time (Delille & Grohn, 1985).

In a long-term comparison of time taken up by housework, it must be kept in mind that the respective survey methods often deviate considerably from one another; however, an overall downward trend can be distinguished. In 1952–1954, non working women spent an average of 58.1 hours per week on household and child-raising tasks; this was down to 41.7 hours in 1977. There were also declines among women with full-time and temporary employment. The greatest time saving has been registered in meal preparation, dishwashing and clearing up the kitchen, apartment-cleaning, and doing the laundry and ironing (Lakemann, 1984).

Marriage partners continue to be far from fully sharing household tasks, though a rising tendency toward "helping out" (without taking on permanent responsibility) can be observed among husbands. This tendency is greater when the wives work at full-time jobs (Müller-Wichmann, 1987).

An overall evolution can be ascertained which departs from the well-defined female family orientation of the early 1950s and proceeds in the direction of a "double orientation" – career and family. This evolution has become pervasive and culturally evident in the self-awareness of women at all levels of qualification and ability, as well as in public institutions and private enterprises. It is a fact that the proportion of employed women in the Federal Republic has been slowly but steadily rising for a long time, and that the increase in employment is not limited to certain groups of women, but has spread to include all parts of the female population – including married women and mothers of small children. This indicates that it is not just a short-term phenomenon of marginal importance.

Claudia Koch-Arzberger and Karin Stiehr

References

Bretschneider, Joachim, Jürgen Husmann, and Fritz Schnabel
1980 *Handbuch einkommens-, vermögens- und sozialpolitischer Daten*. Loseblattsammlung. Köln: Bachem.

Calame, André, and Maria Fiedler
1982 *Maßnahmen zugunsten einer besseren Vereinbarkeit von Familie und Beruf*. Berlin: Wissenschaftszentrum Berlin.

Claessens, Dieter, Arno Klönne, and Armin Tschoepe
1985 *Sozialkunde der Bundesrepublik Deutschland*. Reinbek: Rowohlt.

Delille, Angela, and Andrea Grohn
1985 *Blick zurück aufs Glück. Frauenleben und Familienpolitik in den 50er Jahren*. Berlin: Elefanten Press.

Institut für Arbeitsmarkt- und Berufsforschung der Bundesanstalt für Arbeit, ed., 1984, *Frauen und Arbeitsmarkt. Ausgewählte Aspekte der Frauenerwerbstätigkeit*. Nürnberg.

Lakemann, Ulrich
1984 *Das Aktivitätsspektrum privater Haushalte in der Bundesrepublik Deutschland 1950 bis 1980: Zeitliche und inhaltliche Veränderungen von Erwerbstätigkeiten, unbezahlte Arbeiten und Freizeitaktivitäten*. Berlin.

Müller, Petra
1985 "Neuere Daten zur Frauenerwerbstätigkeit und Erwerbslosigkeit in der BRD." In Arbeitsgruppe "Zukunft der Frauenarbeit", ed., *Dokumentation: Kongreß "Zukunft der Frauenarbeit"*. Universität Bielefeld, 4.-6.11.83. Bielefeld.

Müller-Wichmann, Christiane
1987 *Von wegen Freizeit. Argumente pro und contra 7-Stunden-Tag*. Ein Gutachten für die IG Metall. Frankfurt: Union.

Schmidtchen, Gerhard
1984 *Die Situation der Frau. Trendbeobachtungen über Rollen- und Bewußtseinsänderungen der Frauen in der Bundesrepbulik Deutschland*. Berlin: Duncker und Humblot.

Schumacher, Jürgen
1988 "Leistungsniveau und Leistungsbereitschaft in der Familie." In Karl-Otto Hondrich, et al., *Krise der Leistungsgesellschaft?* Opladen: Westdeutscher Verlag.

Sommerkorn, Ingrid
1988 "Die erwerbstätige Mutter in der Bundesrepublik: Einstellungs- und Problemveränderungen." In Rosemarie Nave-Herz, ed., *Wandel und Kontinuität der Familie in der Bundesbpulik Deutschland*. Stuttgart: Enke.

Statistisches Bundesamt, ed.
1987a *Datenreport 1987*. Bonn: Bundeszentrale für politische Bildung.

–
1987b *Frauen in Familie, Beruf und Gesellschaft*. Mainz: Kohlhammer.

–
1988 *Statistisches Jahrbuch 1988 für die Bundesrepublik Deutschland*. Stuttgart/Mainz: Kohlhammer.

Willms-Herget, Angelika
1985 *Frauenarbeit. Zur Integration der Frauen in den Arbeitsmarkt*. Frankfurt/New York: Campus.

Table 1
Employment quotas

Year	Men[1]	Women[1]	Married women[2]	15-65-year-old women[2]
1950	63.2	31.3	25.0	-
1960	63.2	33.6	32.5	47.2
1970	58.3	30.2	35.6	46.2
1980	58.4	32.6	40.6	50.2
1985	60.3	35.9	42.5	52.7
1986	60.6	36.3	42.9	53.4

1. Proportion of employed persons in total population.
2. In percentage of population of same age, gender, and family status.

Source: Statistisches Bundesamt, 1987a, p. 82; Ditto, 1988, p. 97; and additional data from same source.

Table 2
Employment of women 1950-1980
Proportion of full- or part-time employed women in following age cohorts (in %)

Item	1950	1980	Rate of change in %
15-20	78	39	-50
20-25	70	68	-3
25-30	50	60	+20
30-35	40	54	+35
35-40	36	54	+50
40-45	35	53	+51
45-50	36	51	+42
50-55	34	46	+35
55-60	29	37	+28
60-65	21	13	-38
65 and older	10	3	-70

Source: Schmidtchen, 1984, p. 12.

Table 3
Non-self-employed women according to weekly work hours - 1982

Work hours	In %
Under 21	17
21 to 39	17
40 to 41	58
42 or more	8
Development op proportion of non-independently employed women in part-time work (1 to 39 hours) in percent	
1960	14
1970	27
1982	34

Source: Institut für Arbeitsmarkt- und Berufsforschung, 1984, p. 29.

Figure 1
Employment participation by men and women 1970-1985

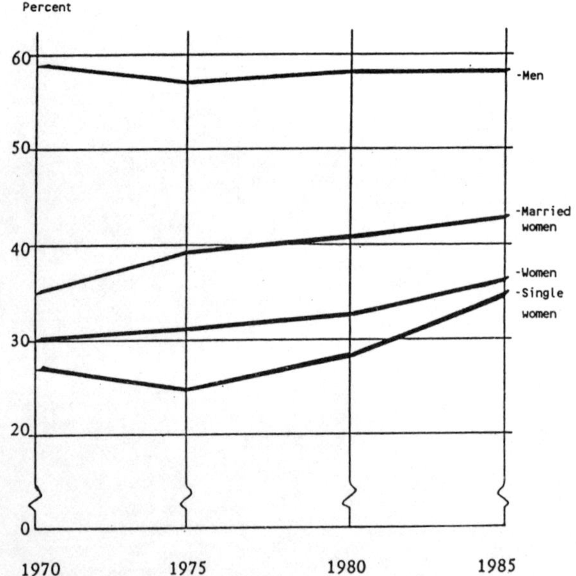

Data in percentage of employed persons in total resident population (by respective groups).

Source: Statistisches Bundesamt, 1987b.

Figure 2
Employment quotas[1] of married women according to age in years 1970 and 1981

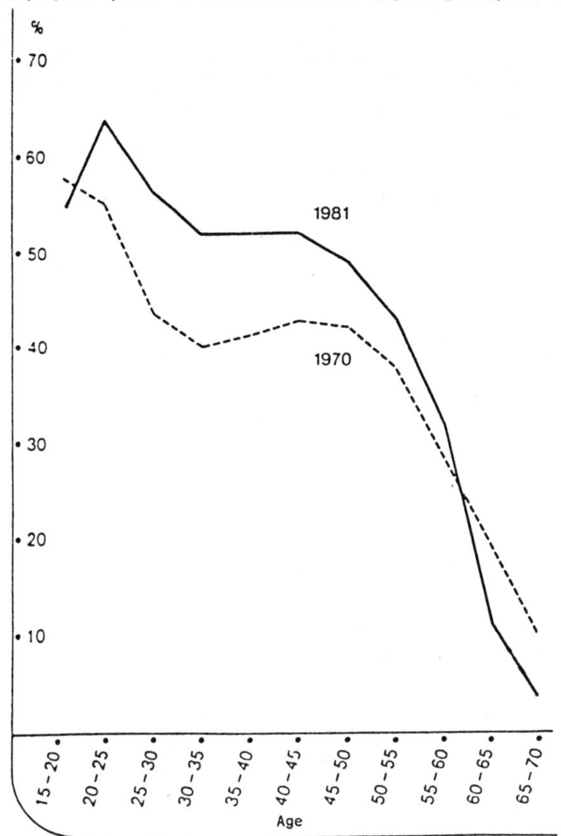

1. Proportion of employed persons (employed and unemployed) in respective resident population

Source: Institut für Arbeitsmarkt- und Berufsforschung, 1984, p. 7.

3.5 Reproductive Technologies

People have always tried to find methods of fertility control. In the more recent past, decisive, albeit controversial, progress has been made in this area with the introduction of modern contraceptive techniques and artificial insemination.

The "baby boom" of the postwar era was followed by a drastic birth-rate slump starting in 1963–1964 (the time of the "baby bust") (see 3.2, "Childbearing"). This phenomenon engendered a persistent debate over its extensive consequences for the "contract between the generations" – social security – and for economic growth. The falling birth statistics are sometimes blamed on more liberal laws regulating pregnancy termination (enacted in 1976) – wrongly blamed, as the development had set in 12 years earlier. It seems more likely that this trend correlates with the introduction of reliable contraceptive devices, especially the birth-control pill, which enable women to take a more active part in family planning. The following discussion of developments in family planning concentrates on contraceptive devices, pregnancy termination, and the modern techniques for reproductive medicine.

We know little about the contraceptive methods in the period following World War II; birth control was rarely a subject of public discussion. In the papal encyclical of 1930, the Catholic church forbade the use of contraceptive devices; the legal situation was unclear up to the 1950s, as a decree dating from 1941, making distribution of birth control punishable by law, remained valid in some parts of the Federal Republic. Nonetheless, in a 1949 study, 67% of those polled were for legalization of contraception, only 16% were against, and 17% were undecided (Friedeburg, 1953). Presumably, "home-made" contraceptive methods (coitus interruptus, condoms, etc.) were most widespread, while chemical methods, diaphragms, rhythm, and combinations of methods were less popular (Knack & Pieper, 1956).

When the Pill came on the German market, in 1961, the target group consisted mainly of married women, who were to be spared – whether for physical or social reasons – from having more children. The decision was left up to the prescribing doctor. Since then, the Pill has become a widely used contraceptive method.

According to results of a 1985 topical representative poll, 37.1% of those questioned used the Pill, followed, at a considerable distance, by those using intrauterine devices (10.3%). The use of intravaginal chemical contraception was rare (0.8%). Table 1 gives an overview of the prevalence of contraceptive methods in relation to age, family status, education, religion, number of children, and further desire for children. The authors of the study define the proportion of women using the Pill as consistent over the preceding 12 years. The proportion of users over 35 years of age is clearly lower than before, with only single women still qualifying as frequent users. More women who are committed to a religion tend to use the Pill than do uncommitted women; the latter more prevalently choose natural family planning (NFP), IUDs, diaphragms, and condoms.

The responses regarding birth-control methods practised in the past (multiple answers were permitted) indicate that use of chemical methods has dwindled ("before," 14% used them; at the time of the poll, only 0.8% did). In contrast, a trend toward NFP methods can be discerned. Though the proportion of actual users amounted to only 4%, 14% considered future use probable or very probable. "Health reasons" was by far the predominant motivation (44%), followed by a wish for "no chemicals" (23%) and "moral reasons" (3% of all polled, 6% of the Catholic women).

Non-optimal comparison with data from a study carried out in 1981 (in which only men were questioned and multiple answers were allowed) shows an increase in the use of IUDs and confirms the assumed decrease in use of chemical devices. Sterilization as a family-planning measure has enjoyed a notable upswing, a development which corresponds to the experience of gynaecologists (Döring et al., 1986).

More controversial than the debate on birth control has been that on abortion. Pregnancy terminations have always been performed in and out of the country, particularly in Great Britain and Holland, but the legal repercussions stigmatized women and doctors. Until reform of §218 in the German penal statutes only medical indication – a medicallygrounded abortion in order to save the life of the mother – was allowed, even in undeniable cases of social emergency. Thousands of people per year were convicted under this law (Claessens et al., 1985).

The abortion debate began in 1971, with a public confession in the media by women who had broken the abortion law, and crystallized in the New Women's Movement's "Action 218." The initiative was surprisingly successful: the old §218 was done away with in April, 1974, and the social-liberal coalition government passed a law allowing for legal pregnancy termination up to the third month without further stipulation. The Christian Democrats took their case against the new law to the Federal Constitutional Court, and in 1975 the Court declared the regulation unconstitutional by narrow margin. In 1976, the so-called indication model was passed by the federal parliament, leaving the decision of admissibility of pregnancy termination up to doctors, who determine in each individual case whether medical contingencies exist which unavoidably endanger the woman physically or mentally; a eugenic indication (with a deadline of 22 weeks) is permitted if there is danger of the child being born with physical or mental handicaps due to heridety or environmental causes; a criminological indication (with a deadline of 12 weeks) is given in cases of pregnancy by rape; a social indication (with a deadline of 12 weeks) is given when the birth of a child would put the woman in an economically critical situation.

The process of initiating a pregnancy termination is difficult, as several authorities must be consulted, and is emotionally stressful, as the final decision is left up to doctors. There still exists an "undetected" percentage of women who turn to illegal abortions performed by domestic (non-foreign) doctors or who choose to travel to a foreign country for the operation. The number of legal and therefore officially recorded pregnancy terminations jumped from 54,309 in 1977 to 91,064 in 1982, then returned to a lower level (see table 2).

The controversy over reform of §218 continues up to the present, caused mainly by church protests. Against a background of an increasing proportion of social indications among pregnancy terminations (from only 57.7% in 1977 to 86.8% in 1987), there are now political initiatives aimed at tightening up the law.

Poll results of recent years indicate that the population is also reacting to the problem more sensitively. While the proportion of advocates of general legalization of pregnancy termination within the first three months dwindled from 27% to 22% between 1983 and 1988, the conviction that a pregnancy termination should be permitted only in well-defined cases is gaining (see table 3). In a parallel development, only 34% of those polled – in contrast to an earlier 52% – claim that a pregnancy termination is not synonymous with killing a human being (Institut für Demoskopie Allensbach, 1988).

This change of opinion may have originated in the debate on the risks of new reproductive techniques, especially with regard to embryos, and in the argument for defence of the "dignity of mankind" and against purposeful "human production." According to present estimates, between 300,000 and 500,000 marriages in the Federal Republic are involuntarily childless. "A society that allows for postponed fulfillment of the desire for children, due to time allowed for education and due to its own social structures, must reckon with the increasing problem of involuntary childlessness" (Krebs, 1986, p. K9).

Artificial insemination of women with donated semen was practised as early as the 1950s, and by the second half of the 1970s there was a wide range of sperm banks to be found in Western industrialized countries (Brockmann & Schwerdtner, 1987). In-vitro fertilization (IVF) has also been firmly integrated into current treatment of childless couples, though the rate of success remains low – between 10% and 25%.

IVF presents the special problem that human germ cells are created which can be used for biotechnological experiments. For example, embryos can be frozen and preserved in liquid nitrogen for a practically endless period. They can be mechanically broken up for the purpose of developing mutliple progeny. Young embryos or embryonic cells of various species or breeds can be melded. The gender of the embryo can be determined. The embryo can be, in a sort of prenatal adoption, implanted in another woman; should the woman carrying the child return it to the biological parents, it is a case of "surrogate motherhood."

At present, all these possibilities lie within a juridical grey zone, which includes the problem of "double paternity" in the case of heterological insemination (i.e., semen donation by a man other than the husband), as well as that of "double maternity" (if a woman other that the wife carries out the pregnancy). The in-vitro fertilized germ cell is unprotected by criminal law up to the point of its implantation: it can be deep-frozen for future use or treatment, or be simply thrown away. In 1985, a study group, comprising members of the ministries of justice and of research and technology, was formed to work out and define a legal framework for artificial insemination, surrogate motherhood, embryo research, and human biomanipulation. There currently exists a draft for a law against which doctors' associations have protested, demanding instead the subjugation of the entire complex problem to supervision by a board of professional experts and an ethics commission.

Ethical problems were rarely discussed by the public up to the beginning of the 1980s. Things have changed, and now conflicts over artificial insemination and "test-tube babies" are often reported. It is the point of reference for nearly all moral-theological and juridical discussion of the past few years (Brockmann & Schwerdtner, 1987).

There has also been public reaction to another issue: the practice of human genetic research and consultation was established in 1945, but not until recently was the explosive power of this brand of eugenics discussed. Its early advocates (at their first international meeting in 1912) declared as their aim genetic correction to create a *Volkskörper* (a physically ideal people). Eugenics were practised with extreme consequences, in Nazi Germany through genocide, forced mass sterilization, and experiments on humans. Some German scientists and politicians are critical of certain projects ("predictive medicine") recently underway in the United States, the U.S.S.R., and Japan, which they suspect have similar eugenic purposes. The risks of modern human genetic research, according to sociologist Ulrich Beck, may lie in the very fact that the eugenics that threaten us has disposed of all trappings of a dark conspiracy and now wears the costume of healthiness and productivity (Der Spiegel, 1988). As well, the growing number of genetic tests in the course of prenatal diagnosis cause uneasiness about a burgeoning number of pregnancy terminations for eugenic reasons.

An overall look at recent decades clearly shows that fertility-control techniques have undergone a previously undreamed-of evolution and that public awareness is increasingly focused on the delicate balance between technological capability and human dignity.

Karin Stiehr

References

Bora, Alfons, and Karlhans Liebl
1986 *Einstellung zum Schwangerschaftsabbruch. Zur Bedeutung generalisierter Wertsysteme in Konfliktsituationen*. Pfaffenweiler: Centaurus.

Brockmann, Dorothea, and Heike Schwerdtner
1987 "Schlechte Menschen - Gute Gene. 50 Jahre Debatte zur Gen- und Reproduktionsforschung." In Gaby Zipfel, ed., *Reproduktionsmedizin. Die Enteignung der weiblichen Natur*. Hamburg: Konkret-Literatur-Verlag.

Claessens, Dieter, Arno Klönne, and Armin Tschoepe
1985 *Sozialkunde der Bundesrepublik Deutschland. Grundlagen, Strukturen, Trends in Wirtschaft und Gesellschaft*. Reinbek: Rowohlt.

Daele, Wolfgang van den
1985 "Auf dem Wege zur 'künstlichen Familie'. Regelungsprobleme bei In-vitro-Befruchtung und Ersatzmutterschaft." *pro familia magazin*, no. 3, 24-26.

Der Spiegel
1988 "Wettlauf zum Heiligen Gral der Biologie." *Der Spiegel*, no. 2, 154-158.

Döring, G., et al.
1986 "Ergebnisse einer repräsentativen Umfrage zum Familienplanungsverhalten in der Bundesrepublik Deutschland 1985." In *Geburtshilfe und Frauenheilkunde*, 892-897. Stuttgart/New York: Thieme.

Eser, Albin
1984 "Genetik, Gen-Ethik, Gen-Recht? Rechtspolitische Überlegungen zum Umgang mit menschlichem Erbgut." *Deutsche Gesellschaft für Chirurgie. Mitteilungen*, no. 5, Sonderdruck.

Friedeburg, Ludwig von
1953 "Die Umfrage in die Intimsphäre." In *Beiträge zur Sexualforschung 4*. Stuttgart: Enke.

Institut für Demoskopie Allensbach
1988 *Allensbacher Berichte*, no. 30.

Knack, A. V., and W. Pieper
1956 "Empfängnisverhütung als ärztliche Beratungsaufgabe." *Deutsches Ärzteblatt/Ärztliche Mitteilungen*, no. 14.

Krebs, Dieter
1986 Referat in den Verhandlungen des 56. Deutschen Juristentages. München: Beck.

Liers, Dorothee
1986 "Familienpolitik, Gen- und Reproduktionstechnologie." In DIE GRÜNEN im Bundestag, ed., *Frauen gegen Gentechnik und Reproduktionstechnik*. Dokumentation zum Kongreß vom 19.-24.4.1985 in Bonn. Köln: Kölner Volksblatt.

Linde, Hans
1988 *Kritische Empirie. Beiträge zur Soziologie und Bevölkerungswissenschaft 1937-1987*. Opladen: Leske und Budrich.

Nave-Herz, Rosemarie
1988 "Kontinuität und Wandel von Ehe und Familie." In Rosemarie Nave-Herz, ed., *Wandel und Kontinuität der Familie in der Bundesrepublik Deutschland*. Stuttgart: Enke.

Paczensky, Susanne von
1984 "Von den Gegnern lernen." In Susanne von Paczensky, and Renate Sadronitski, eds., *Die Neuen Moralisten. § 218 - Vom leichtfertigen Umgang mit einem Jahrhundertthema*. Reinbek: Rowohlt.

Pieper, Antje, and Paul Präve
1985 *Die Biotechnik*. Köln: Deutscher Instituts-Verlag.

Statistisches Bundesamt, ed.
1987 *Frauen in Familie, Beruf und Gesellschaft*. Mainz: Kohlhammer.

–, ed.
1988 *Statistisches Jahrbuch 1988 für die Bundesrepublik Deutschland*. Stuttgart/Mainz: Kohlhammer.

Table 1 (part I)
Relative incidence of use of various contraceptive methods in the Federal Republic of Germany in 1985. Various factors are exhibited that possibly influence this (percentages are given, total=1,267 women)

Item	Pill	IUD	Con-dom	NFP-method	Coitus interr.	Dia-phragma	Mini-pill	Chem. means
Age:								
15-21	43.1	3.6	5.8	1.6	3.9	1.3	2.9	0.3
22-34	44.7	12.8	6.7	6.1	3.0	3.2	0.6	1.0
35 and over	24.1	12.4	4.9	2.8	3.3	1.0	1.0	1.0
Family status:								
married	33.0	14.6	5.7	4.2	4.2	0.7	0.7	0.5
single	50.0	7.5	4.9	3.9	3.4	3.9	4.0	1.1
Schooling:								
elementary	38.6	10.8	3.8	2.6	4.3	0.2	0.5	0.4
intermediate	32.1	10.7	7.8	3.0	3.8	1.6	1.4	1.1
academic high school, college	39.6	8.9	7.2	7.2	1.5	5.7	2.4	1.2
Denomination:								
Catholic	37.4	10.3	5.2	3.8	4.0	1.0	1.2	0.8
Protestant	38.4	9.8	5.8	3.4	2.9	1.8	1.8	0.8
none	28.5	13.8	9.5	8.6	4.3	8.6	0	1.7
Number of children:								
none	41.3	6.8	5.8	3.6	3.2	3.5	1.9	1.1
1-2	35.8	14.5	5.7	4.6	3.4	0.8	0.8	0.6
3 and over	21.7	13.0	5.4	3.3	5.4	0	0	0
Further desire for children:								
yes	44.0	7.5	6.8	5.5	3.2	2.1	2.1	1.2
no	30.0	13.7	5.1	2.4	3.1	1.2	1.2	0.7
moot point	40.8	7.2	5.5	5.1	4.3	4.3	4.3	0.4
Total	37.1	10.3	5.9	3.9	3.4	2.1	1.3	0.8

Table 1 (part II)
Relative incidence of use of various contraceptive methods in the Federal Republic of Germany in 1985. Various factors are exhibited that possibly influence this (percentages are given, total=1,267 women)

Item	Mixed method	Sterilized Man	Sterilized Woman	Sterile	No contact	No contracept.	No answer
Age:							
15-21	0.9	0	0.7	1.6	13.7	4.9	15.7
22-34	2.3	0.6	2.3	2.1	0.4	1.1	13.3
35 and over	2.1	3.0	14.7	16.1	0	1.4	12.4
Family status:							
married	1.7	2.1	10.3	8.3	0	1.1	12.7
single	2.4	0.3	0.5	2.1	3.6	1.0	11.9
Schooling:							
elementary	2.2	1.6	7.7	9.9	1.6	1.3	14.4
intermediate	0.8	0.8	7.0	5.1	7.0	4.6	13.4
academic high school, college	3.7	1.2	2.1	3.3	1.5	0.6	14.3
Denomination:							
Catholic	1.7	1.0	6.3	6.9	3.6	1.5	15.4
Protestant	2.9	1.0	5.3	6.6	3.7	2.6	13.2
none	0	2.6	6.0	6.0	1.7	1.7	6.9
Number of children:							
none	2.2	0.3	1.3	4.0	6.9	3.0	15.2
1-2	1.9	2.1	8.6	7.6	0	0.6	13.1
3 and over	3.3	2.2	8.7	27.2	0	4.3	6.5
Further desire for children:							
Yes	2.6	0	0	1.8	6.4	2.5	14.4
No	2.1	2.7	12.7	12.7	0.3	1.2	11.0
Moot point	1.3	0	0	0.4	6.4	3.4	17.0
Total	1.9	1.3	6.1	6.6	3.5	2.1	13.4

Source: Doering et al., 1986, p. 893:

Table 2
Pregnancy terminations

Year	Total	According to reason for termination:					
		general medical	psychi-atric	eugenic	ethical (criminol.)	other severe emergency	unknown
1977	54,309	15,756	4,171	2,348	79	31,358	597
1978	73,548	16,872	3,686	2,731	104	49,252	903
1979	82,788	17,261	2,802	3,162	101	58,412	1,050
1980	87,702	17,655	2,444	3,053	101	63,289	1,160
1981	87,535	15,382	2,524	2,797	103	65,466	1,263
1982	91,064	15,214	2,339	2,306	74	70,000	1,131
1983	86,529	12,354	1,861	1,843	58	69,436	977
1984	86,298	10,356	1,242	1,600	93	71,904	1,103
1985	83,538	9,260	1,311	1,086	71	70,411	1,399
1986	84,274	8,312	1,244	1,113	78	72,279	1,248
1987	88,540	7,979	1,226	1,037	79	76,883	1,336

Source: Statistisches Bundesamt, 1987, p. 163; Statistisches Jahrbuch 1978, p. 373; 1988, p. 387.

Table 3
Attitudes towards pregnancy termination (in %)

Wording of question: "About pregnancy termination: Here are three opinions. Which one would you agree with?"

Item	1983	1984	1985	1987	1988
Termination of pregnancy should be principally allowed in the first three months.	27	30	29	25	22
Termination should be allowed only in certain cases, for example, when doctors recommend it, or if the social situation is difficult, or if the situation demands it.	55	50	54	56	61
Termination should be prohibited again, Par. 218 (abortion law) should be reintroduced in its old form.	11	14	11	11	12
Undecided	7	6	6	8	5
Total	100	100	100	100	100

Federal Republic and West Berlin population 16 years and older.

Source: Allensbacher Archiv, IfD-Umfragen 4030, 4045, 4065, 4097/I, 4099 I+II, cited in Allensbacher Berichte 1988/no. 30, p. 3.

4. Labour Market

4.1 Unemployment

Mass unemployment, which arose in the early 1970s, reached a maximum of almost 10% in the mid-1980s and has been shrinking since then. Women, the unskilled, and foreign workers run a particularly high risk of becoming unemployed. The increasingly long duration of periods of unemployment and the concentration of unemployment in specific groups within the labour force, which have been affected repeatedly at times when the majority is not, are indicators for structuralization of unemployment and segmentation of the labour market.

Unemployment Rates

In the history of the FRG, there have been two periods of large-scale unemployment: the postwar period up to the mid-1950s and a second period beginning with the first oil-price shock. Whereas the unemployment rate during the postwar period decreased rapidly, dropping from 11.0% to 3.7% between 1950 and 1958, the current unemployment is much more persistent and began to decline only at the end of the 1980s. The present level of unemployment was produced by two surges. Between 1970 and 1975, the unemployment rate increased from 0.7% to 4.7%; it then dropped slightly during the second half of the 1970s to reach 3.8% in 1980, and rose again sharply, to a maximum of 9.3%, in 1985 (see table 1). It became stable on that level until 1987 and then, underwent slight but steady decrease, to 7.2% in 1990.

During the 1970s and 1980s, unemployment was to a large extent due to demographic factors and changes in labour-market behaviour. Between 1970 and 1986, the proportion of the population aged 15 to 65 years increased from 64% to 70%. Statistics also show a distinct rise in the labour-force participation rate among married women (from 36% in 1970 to 43% in 1988).

In part, unemployment is also a result of structural and technological changes; however, there is no simple correlation. The reduction in jobs took place primarily in sectors with a below-average growth in productivity, whereas the number of jobs increased within sectors of the economy characterized by high-level technology and above-average growth in productivity.

The unequal distribution of unemployment can be shown by group-specific unemployment rates (see table 2). Since the beginning of the present labour-market crisis, the risk of becoming or staying unemployed has been higher for women than for men, higher for foreigners than for natives, and higher for blue-collar workers than for other employees. Middle-aged persons run a lower risk of unemployment than do younger and older people. Until 1980, the unemployment rate of part-time employees was higher than that of full-time employees. Since then, the opposite has been true.

Qualification is a major factor in risk of unemployment. The unemployment rate differs considerably between skill levels, and the differences have grown during the 1980s (see table 3). In September of 1987, the unemployment rate among unskilled workers shot up to 18.4%, while among those who had completed an apprenticeship the unemployment rate was 6.4%, among those with a university degree it was 5.7%, and among graduates from specialized technical schools it was 4.0%, compared to the general unemployment rate of 9.0%. Until 1977 the unemployment rate of people with an academic education remained below that of all other groups; since then unemployment has been lowest for the graduates from specialized technical schools and colleges.

Duration of Unemployment and Periods of Unemployment

During recent years, there has also been a trend toward increasing duration of periods of unemployment. In a cross-sectional view, the average duration of periods of unemployment increased from 6.5 months in 1977 to 13.6 months in 1988, and the proportion of the long-term unemployed (one year or more) has increased from 14% to 33% (see table 4). It should be noted, however, that the length of unemployment is overestimated on the basis of cross-sectional data from unemployment surveys because of a bias in sample selection. In 1986, the proportion of long-term unemployed totaled only 14% within a sample of people leaving the unemployment register. Nonetheless, there is a clear tendency toward an increasing duration of unemployment, which indicates the growing difficulties the unemployed have in finding jobs.

In addition to increased duration, unemployment has been distributed over a smaller number of periods of unemployment during the last decade. Data resulting from a decomposition of the unemployment rate show the number of spells of unemployment within a given period of time in relation to the labour force not including the self-employed and family workers. Between 1970 and 1975, this relationship increased from 5.5% to 20.2%. Thereafter, it decreased to 13.0% in 1979, rose again to 18.4% in 1982, and dropped to 15.5% in 1987.

As well as the increasing length of periods of unemployment, the reduction in the number of people hit by unemployment can also be interpreted as a tendency toward structuralization, if total unemployment does not at the same time decrease. It can also be shown that a limited number of persons repeatedly become jobless, whereas the majority does not experience any unemployment at all. From 1974 to 1983, labour offices registered a total of 33 million periods of unemployment but "only" 12.5 million unemployed people. On average, each unemployed person experienced 2.6 periods of unemployment (Karr, 1983). Another study concluded that the majority, amounting to two-thirds of the labour force, did not actually experience any unemployment over the preceding decade of continuous labour-market crisis, roughly half of the remaining third have suffered extensive (i.e., long-term and/or recurrent) joblessness, thus accounting for more than two-thirds of the overall unemployment burden (Büchtemann & Brasche, 1985).

Subjective Experience of Unemployment

There are only a few studies providing quantitative data regarding the subjective experience and treatment of joblessness by the unemployed. In general, it has been shown that unemployment is accompanied by a significant reduction in subjective well-being as measured by life satisfaction (see table 5). This effect is greatest if the unemployed person is the head of household or if he or she is young. The reduction in subjective well-being caused by losing a job is much less pronounced if the person is the spouse of the head of household.

In a representative sample of unemployed people, the problems of unemployment most frequently experienced as particularly stressful were financial troubles (29%) and problems related to the use of time (31%) such as boredom and the feeling that one's capacities are not being used (Brinkmann, 1984). When the results of sample surveys of 1975 and 1983 are compared, there is some evidence for at least two trends concerning the subjective experience of unemployment. In the 1980s, the fact that a person is unemployed no longer confers the same stigma as it once did. The percentage of unemployed people reporting that they are reluctant to tell friends about their joblessness declined. The more people have been hit by unemployment and the more likely it is that anyone can lose his or her job, the less frequent is the fear of negative responses in the social environment. However, the percentage of unemployed people reporting positive consequences of unemployment – for instance, being able to spend more time with one's family – has also declined. People have learned that the amount of free time unemployment offers very rarely can be used in a productive way.

Heinz-Herbert Noll

References

Brinkmann, Christian
1984 "Die individuellen Folgen langfristiger Arbeitslosigkeit." *Mitteilungen aus der Arbeitsmarkt- und Berufsforschung*, 17.

Büchtemann, Christoph, and Ulrich Brasche
1985 *Recurrent Unemployment. Longitudinal Evidence for the Federal Republic of Germany.* Arbeitspapier 1985 -3 des Arbeitskreises Sozialwissenschaftliche Arbeitsmarktforschung.

Bundesanstalt für Arbeit
ann. pbl. *Amtliche Nachrichten der Bundesanstalt für Arbeit.* Nürnberg.

Institut für Arbeitsmarkt und Berufsforschung
1988 *IAB-Zahlenfibel*. BeitrAB 101. Nürnberg.

Karr, Werner
1983 "Anmerkungen zur Arbeitslosigkeit in der nunmehr 10 Jahre dauernden Beschäftigungskrise." *Mitteilungen aus der Arbeitsmarkt- und Berufsforschung*, 16.

Krause, Peter
1987 "Lebensbedingungen und wahrgenommene Lebensqualität von Arbeitslosen." In H.-J. Krupp, U. Hanefeld, eds., *Lebenslagen im Wandel: Analysen 1987*. Frankfurt am Main/New York: Campus.

Tessaring, Manfred
1988 "Arbeitslosigkeit, Beschäftigung und Qualifikation: Ein Rück- und Ausblick." *Mitteilungen aus der Arbeitsmarkt- und Berufsforschung*, 21, 177-193.

Table 1
Number of unemployed persons and unemployment rate[1]

Year	Number of unemployed persons (in 1,000)	Unemployment rate (in %)
1950[2]	1,869	11.0
1954[2]	1,411	7.6
1958[2]	764	3.7
1962	155	0.7
1966	161	0.7
1970	149	0.7
1974	583	2.6
1975	1,074	4.7
1976	1,060	4.6
1977	1,030	4.5
1978	993	4.3
1979	876	3.8
1980	889	3.8
1981	1,272	5.5
1982	1,833	7.5
1983	2,258	9.1
1984	2,266	9.1
1985	2,304	9.3
1986	2,228	9.0
1987	2,229	8.9
1988	2,242	8.7
1989	2,038	7.9
1990	1,883	7.2

1. Annual averages.
2. Saarland not included.

Source: Bundesanstalt für Arbeit, various volumes.

Table 2
Unemployment rates - breakdown by selected socio-structural criteria[1]

Criterion	1978	1979	1980	1981	1982	1983	1984	1985	1986	1987	1988
Total	3.8	3.2	3.5	5.4	7.5	8.6	8.6	8.7	8.2	8.4	8.1
Males	2.7	2.2	2.6	4.3	6.6	7.6	7.7	7.5	6.9	7.2	7.0
Females	5.5	4.8	5.1	7.1	8.8	10.2	10.1	10.4	10.3	10.2	9.9
Foreign workers	4.6	3.9	4.8	8.5	12.3	14.2	12.8	13.5	13.5	14.7	14.3
Full-time job wanted	3.5	2.9	3.3	5.1	7.4	8.8	8.8	8.9	8.4	8.6	8.3
Salaried employees	3.1	2.6	2.7	3.7	4.9	5.9	6.1	-	-	6.0	5.9
Wage earners	4.5	3.8	4.4	7.1	10.0	11.4	11.2	-	-	11.0	10.6
Age											
under 20 years	4.4	3.1	3.5	5.9	9.1	9.7	8.4	8.9	7.6	6.7	5.8
20 to 24 years	5.8	4.5	5.1	8.5	11.5	13.3	12.9	11.5	10.5	9.9	8.5
25 to 29 years	4.8	3.9	4.4	7.0	9.8	11.3	11.4	11.1	10.5	10.2	9.5
30 to 34 years	3.4	2.9	3.4	5.6	7.4	8.6	8.7	8.9	8.7	8.9	8.8
35 to 39 years	2.6	2.1	2.3	3.3	5.8	7.2	7.3	7.7	7.8	7.9	7.4
40 to 44 years	2.8	2.1	2.3	3.6	4.9	5.7	5.4	5.4	5.0	5.5	6.1
45 to 49 years	2.6	2.2	2.4	3.7	5.2	6.1	6.4	6.1	6.2	6.2	6.0
50 to 54 years	3.2	2.8	2.9	3.9	5.2	6.0	6.4	7.3	7.6	8.3	8.2
55 to 59 years	5.6	5.7	5.5	6.6	7.8	9.6	11.4	11.7	10.9	12.2	12.7
60 to 64 years	5.3	6.5	9.1	11.9	10.7	9.4	9.5	9.2	8.1	9.6	10.8

1. Date of reference: end of September.

Source: Bundeanstalt für Arbeit, various volumes.

Table 3
Unemployment rates - breakdown by qualification[1] (in %)

Qualifications	1975	1976	1977	1978	1979	1980	1981	1982	1983	1984	1985	1986[2]	1987[2]
Unskilled	7.5	6.4	6.8	6.9	6.0	6.9	10.3	13.6	16.0	16.3	17.1	17.4	18.4
Skilled (total)	3.0	3.0	2.9	2.6	2.2	2.3	3.5	5.3	6.2	6.3	6.2	5.8	5.9
apprenticeship training	3.2	3.1	3.0	2.7	2.3	2.4	3.6	5.6	6.6	6.8	6.7	6.2	6.4
specialized technical school or college	3.3	3.4	3.2	2.4	2.1	2.1	2.9	4.4	5.0	4.7	4.5	4.0	4.0
university	1.5	1.9	2.1	1.9	1.9	2.2	3.0	3.9	4.9	5.3	5.4	5.2	5.7
Total	4.6	4.2	4.2	3.9	3.3	3.6	5.4	7.7	9.0	9.1	9.1	8.8	9.0

1. Figures refer to persons in dependent employment (civilian labour force) with same qualification. Date of reference: end of September.
2. Preliminary figures.

Source: Tessaring, 1988, p.189.

Table 4
Length of unemployment and percentage of long-term unemployed persons[1]

Year	Average length of unemployment months	Long-term unemployed[2] (in %)
1977	6.5	14.3
1978	6.7	14.7
1979	7.0	15.5
1980	6.4	12.9
1981	6.5	12.9
1982	7.6	18.0
1983	9.2	24.9
1984	10.5	28.8
1985	11.6	31.0
1986	12.5	31.9
1987	13.0	31.9
1988	13.6	32.6

1. Date of reference: end of September.
2. At least 12 months.

Source: Bundesanstalt für Arbeit, various volumes.

Table 5
Unemployment and subjective well-being

Item	General life satisfaction 1984[1]	
	Mean	Percentage dissatisfied[2]
Total		
employed	7.6	4.7
unemployed	5.8	28.6
Head of household		
employed	7.6	4.4
unemployed	5.4	30.8
Spouse		
employed	7.7	4.5
unemployed	7.0	14.3
Unmarried child[3]		
employed	7.6	4.7
unemployed	5.8	28.6

1. Satisfaction scale (0-10): 0 = completely dissatisfied 10 = completely satisfied.
2. Scores 0-4 on satisfaction scale.
3. 16 years and over, living with parent(s) in same household.

Source: Krause, 1987.

4.2 Skills and Occupational Levels

Changes in qualification and skill requirements are characterized by a continuous growth of nonmanual jobs as well as a general process of upgrading. To some extent, these are the by-products of technological change, but also of occupational and sectoral changes within the economy and a better qualified labour force.

One of the most striking changes concerning job content and skill requirements is the gradual substitution of manual by nonmanual work. Taking the ratio of blue-collar workers to white-collar employees as a simple indicator, the manual/nonmanual ratio has undergone a drastic change, from 100 blue-collar workers to 40 employees in white-collar jobs in 1950 to 100 to 131 in 1989 (see table 1). The replacement of blue-collar workers by white-collar employees occurred continuously, but underwent an exceptional acceleration in the first half of the 1970s.

According to recent studies, the limits to a further division of labour seem to have been reached, even within industrial production processes. Taylorism no longer offers the appropriate means for a further rise in productivity. Modern product designs and the current level of technology in manufacturing require a more complex definition of job tasks and a better qualified labour force. Contrary to former assumptions that technological change involves a process of dequalification, industrial sociologists recently identified a trend toward a reprofessionalization of industrial labour (Kern & Schumann, 1984).

The use of modern technologies and their impact on job content and skill requirements is not limited to industrial work contexts. Simple and highly standardized work tasks are going to be more and more reduced and substituted for all types of jobs. In a period of rapid technological and structural changes, moreover, extra-functional skills (skills which are not directly related to the specific task at hand) such as flexibility and adaptability are particularly in demand. As well, more general and social skills such as responsibility, technical intelligence, and ability to learn seem to be increasing in importance (Blaschke, 1986). There is also empirical evidence that traditional or puritanical work ethics such as diligence and punctuality are becoming less important, if not counterproductive, while communication skills such as frankness, the ability to cooperate with other people, and knowledge of foreign languages are more and more required (Schmidtchen, 1984).

Following Say's theorem that supply engenders demand, better education and qualifications in the labour force may well have contributed to the increasing skill requirements observed. Unskilled jobs have been reduced to a large extent. Between 1970 and 1985, the overall share of unskilled employees decreased from

43% to 25%; on the other hand, there was a general increase in all groups of skilled employees. The proportion of college and university graduates – the most highly qualified group of employees – rose from 7% in 1976 to 11% in 1985 (see table 2). The upgrading of professional qualifications can be observed in all sectors of the economy. The skill level is highest in the services sector, where it is higher in public services than in private-service industries. In particular, the proportion of university graduates is much higher in the public sector than in all other parts of the economy.

According to recent forecasts and projections, a continuation of current trends is to be expected. The proportion of industrial activities on a low level of qualification will be further reduced, from 25% in 1985 to 22% in 1995, and to 18% in the year 2010. On the other hand, the proportion of high-skilled jobs is expected to increase continuously, from 28% in 1985 to 39% in 2010 (see table 3).

Heinz-Herbert Noll

References

Blaschke, Dieter
1986 "Soziale Qualifikationen am Arbeitsmarkt und im Beruf." *Mitteilungen aus der Arbeitsmarkt- und Berufsforschung*, 19, 536-552.

Kern, Horst, and Michael Schumann
1984 *Das Ende der Arbeitsteilung? Rationalisierung in der industriellen Produktion*. München: Beck.

Prognos AG, Peter Hofer, et. al.
1989 *Arbeitslandschaft bis 2010 nach Umfang und Tätigkeitsprofilen*. Textband, Beiträge aus der Arbeitsmarkt- und Berufsforschung, vol. 131.1. Nürnberg.

Schmidtchen, Gerhard
1984 *Neue Technik - Neue Arbeitsmoral*. Köln: Deutscher Instituts-Verlag.

Tessaring, Manfred
1988 "Arbeitslosigkeit, Beschäftigung und Qualifikation: Ein Rück- und Ausblick." *Mitteilungen aus der Arbeitsmarkt- und Berufsforschung*, 21, 177-193.

Statistisches Bundesamt, ed.
ann. pbl. *Statistisches Jahrbuch*. Stuttgart/Mainz: Kohlhammer.

Table 1
Ratio of civil servants and white-collar employees to blue-collar workers

Year	Civil servants, white-collar employees 1,000	Blue-collar workers 1,000	Civil servants, white-collar employees per 100 blue-collar workers
1950	4,838	11,986	40,4
1960	7,488	13,251	56,5
1965	8,836	12,993	68,0
1970	9,646	12,413	77,7
1975	10,985	11,029	99,6
1980	11,957	11,052	108,2
1981	12,042	10,827	111,2
1982	12,038	10,398	115,8
1983	11,984	10,073	119,0
1984	12,074	10,018	120,5
1985	12,208	10,060	121,4
1986	12,329	10,186	121,0
1987	12,623	10,084	125,1
1988	13,886	10,419	133,3
1989	14,036	10,682	131,4

Source: Statistisches Bundesamt, various volumes; author's calculation.

Table 2
Professional qualification of the labour force by sector (in %)

Sector	No professional certificate	Completion of apprenticeship training	Master crafts-men or techni-cian diploma	College degree	Uni-versity degree
Primary Sector					
1976	73	23	3	-	-
1985	53	39	6	1	1
Secondary Sector					
1976	35	54	8	2	1
1985	26	59	9	3	2
Tertiary Sector A[1]					
1976	31	59	6	2	3
1985	23	63	7	3	4
Tertiary Sector B[2]					
1976	27	47	6	3	17
1985	21	48	7	5	18
Total					
1976	35	51	7	2	5
1985	25	56	8	4	7

1. Predominantly private sector.
2. Predominantly public sector.

Source: Tessaring, 1988; author's calculation.

Table 3
Activity by level of qualification - projection (in %)

Qualification level of activity	1982	1985	1995	2010
Low	30	27	22	18
Middle	43	45	44	43
High	27	28	34	39

Source: Prognos AG; author's calculations.

4.3 Types of Employment

In West Germany, as in other modern societies, tendencies toward a growing diversity of employment patterns can be observed. Not only is there a trend toward more flexibility and individuality in work hours, there is also an increase in atypical forms of work. Most important is the continuous growth of part-time work. Precarious employment came under increasing public scrutiny during the 1980s but still represents only a rather marginal phenomenon in the West German labour market.

The so-called standard employment relationship, which means more or less life-long permanent employment on a full-time basis, seems to have lost some of its earlier attractiveness and dominance. Part-time work and other nonstandard forms of employment, such as temporary work, agency work, and various forms of self-employment, have gained in importance. Work diversification and the appearance of atypical forms of work seems to have at least two different causes involving the supply side as well as the demand side of the labour market. First, as a consequence of economic prosperity and postmaterialistic value changes, more and more people tend to rank individual options and autonomy in use of time higher than traditional work values such as job security and career prospects. Second, the policy of deregulation of the labour market, which took place in Germany and in many other countries during the 1980s, helped to give rise to nonstandard types of work.

Part-time work is the most important and widespread form of nonstandard employment. In 1988, about 3.3 million West Germans were working part time (1 to 36 hours) weekly. Part-time employees currently comprise 14% of the total labour force.

The trend of growth in part-time employment set in as early as in the late 1950s. As available time series show, this type of employment expanded most rapidly during the 1960s and early 1970s, when the supply of part-time jobs was used primarily as an instrument of manpower mobilization. Part-time work continued to increase even during the 1980s, when the economy slowed down and the number of full-time jobs showed a marked decline. As in most other countries, part-time work has contributed considerably to recent growth in employment, accounting for roughly two-thirds of the additional jobs created during the last decade.

Part-time work involves women almost exclusively. The number and proportion of male part-timers is very low, and has remained almost constant over time. At present, one-third of the female labour force but only 2% of male employees work part time (see table 1). The proportion of part-timers within the female labour force has increased remarkably, from 9% in 1960 to 32% in 1989. More than nine out of ten part-timers are women, and 87% of them are married. The proportions of part-time workers are highest among married women with children and among women re-entering the labour market. Within these groups, part-time work has changed from a deviant to a "normal" or even prevailing type of employment. In contrast to some other countries, in Germany part-time employment is largely restricted to women in the middle and older age groups. Among unmarried women and women below the age of 30, the percentage of part-time employees barely exceeds that of male part-timers.

Part-time work has increased not only in close association with growing female labour-force participation, but also with the structural shift of the labour market to the services sector. In Germany, eight out of ten part-timers are employed either in services or in trade industries.

Part-time employment seems to correspond with the needs and work orientations of a large and growing part of the labour force. The majority of part-timers undertake this type of employment voluntarily, while the proportion of involuntary part-time workers seems to be rather small. Only 7% of female and 17% of the few male part-time employees reported that they were working part time because no full-time job was available. On the other hand, there is evidence that a considerable number of women working full time would prefer a part-time job if they could obtain one. Considering that 60% to 70% of all women re-entering the labour market are looking for part-time work, there is good reason to expect a continuation of the observed trend from full-time to part-time work, though only among women as of yet.

A labour-market phenomenon of particular interest in recent years has been that of precarious employment. Jobs can be classified as precarious if they do not provide as much protection and security as normal jobs and if they involve "serious hazards for the social and economic well-being of the worker or employee in the short, medium, and long run" (Büchtemann & Quack, 1989, p. 51). This category may include part-time work, temporary work, agency work, work at home, and even forms of self-employment, but "nonstandard employment is not necessarily associated with above-average risks and hazards" (Büchtemann & Quack, 1989, p. 51), and standard employment may have its precarious sides as well.

Quantification of precarious employment is difficult because there is no clear-cut distinction between normal and precarious employment, and they are not necessarily mutually exclusive. Part-time jobs are not necessarily less secure and of lower quality than full-time jobs, but, depending on the number of hours worked, part-time employees are sometimes not covered by protective laws and may have less access to collective fringe benefits: "'marginal' part-time workers, especially those falling below the threshold of 15 work hours per week, face discrimination and an array of disadvantages" (Büchtemann & Quack, 1989, p. 27). Part-timers working less than 20 hours per week, for example, are in general not covered by unemployment insurance. The proportion of marginal part-time employees, working fewer than 20 hours per week, increased during recent years, from 21% in 1984 to 27% of all part-time workers in 1989.

Like marginal part-time work, temporary employment also shows characteristics of precariousness. Fixed-term personnel are not only excluded from all measures of protection against job loss by definition, but also "tend to be indirectly discriminated against by all legal and collective-bargaining regulations that require a certain minimum tenure" (Büchtemann & Quack, 1989, p. 27), such as paid sick leave, paid vacation, and overtime. Detailed information concerning the proportion and composition of fixed-term contracted jobs exists only since 1984 (see table 2): there was a slight increase, from 5% to 8%, in 1986, and a constant rate of 7% since then. The finding that almost half (45%) of all new employment relationships were contracted on a fixed-term basis in 1986 (Rudolph, 1987) offers some evidence, however, that the total scope of this type of employment seems to have been considerably underestimated in cross-sectional data. There is a clear overrepresentation of temporary workers in several demographic groups and industries: part-time employees, young people at the beginning of their working life, women, and employees in the agricultural and services sectors are more likely to work on a fixed-term contracted job (see table 3) than are others.

There are also increasing numbers of agency workers and people temporarily employed in public job-creation schemes, which usually are seen as forms of precarious work as well; however, it is far from clear that the developments observed over a rather short period of time are as yet sufficient to establish a trend. The increases in precarious types of employment are rather marginal, and their total share is still relatively small. There seems to be a good chance that this phenomenon is only a temporary one, and may disappear if the demand for labour continues to increase.

Heinz-Herbert Noll

References

Brinkmann, Christian, and Hans Kohler
1989 "Teilzeitarbeit und Arbeitsvolumen." *Mitteilungen aus der Arbeitsmarkt- und Berufsforschung*, 22, 472-482.

Büchtemann, Christoph, and Sigrid Quack
1989 *'Bridges'or 'traps'? Non-Standard Forms of Employment in the Federal Republic of Germany. The Case of Part-Time and Temporary Work*. Wissenschaftszentrum Berlin für Sozialforschung, Discussion Papers FS I 89-6. Berlin.

Bundesanstalt für Arbeit
ann. pbl. *Amtliche Nachrichten der Bundesanstalt für Arbeit.* Nürberg.

FORSA - Gesellschaft für Sozialforschung und statistische Analysen mbH
1987 *Ungeschützte und statusgeminderte Arbeitsverhältnisse. Ergebnisse einer bundesweiten Repräsentativbefragung*. Dortmund.

Noll, Heinz-Herbert
1991 "Beschäftigungsstruktur im Wandel: Die Bundesrepublik im internationalen Vergleich." In W. Zapf, ed., *Die Modernisierung moderner Gesellschaften. Verhandlungen des 25. Deutschen Soziologentags in Frankfurt*. Frankfurt am Main: Campus.

Rudolph, Helmut
1987 "Befristete Beschäftigung - ein Überblick." *Mitteilungen aus der Arbeitsmarkt- und Berufsforschung*, 20, 288-304.

Statistisches Bundesamt
ann. pbl. *Stand und Entwicklung der Erwerbstätigkeit*. Fachserie 1, Reihe 4.1.1.

Table 1
Part-time employees and part-time employment rates by gender

Year	Part-time employees[1] in 1,000			Part-time employment rates in %		
	Men	Women	All	Men	Women	All
1960	200	581	781	1.5	8.6	3.9
1961	205	705	910	1.5	10.2	4.4
1962	208	835	1,043	1.5	11.9	5.0
1963	210	939	1,149	1.5	13.2	5.4
1964	212	1,068	1,280	1.5	14.8	6.0
1965	215	1,200	1,415	1.5	16.4	6.5
1966	187	1,326	1,513	1.3	18.2	7.0
1967	194	1,312	1,506	1.4	18.6	7.2
1968	195	1,381	1,576	1.4	19.4	7.5
1969	186	1,592	1,778	1.3	21.7	8.2
1970	220	1,837	2,057	1.5	24.4	9.3
1971	252	2,035	2,287	1.7	26.4	10.2
1972	249	2,200	2,449	1.7	27.9	10.9
1973	265	2,337	2,602	1.8	28.9	11.4
1974	261	2,296	2,557	1.8	28.4	11.3
1975	266	2,338	2,604	1.9	29.5	11.9
1976	279	2,325	2,604	2.0	29.3	11.9
1977	280	2,443	2,723	2.0	30.6	12.4
1978	268	2,397	2,665	1.9	29.6	12.0
1979	258	2,519	2,777	1.8	30.4	12.3
1980	203	2,463	2,666	1.4	29.0	11.6
1981	215	2,561	2,776	1.5	30.1	12.2
1982	195	2,546	2,741	1.4	30.2	12.2
1983	260	2,743	3,003	1.9	33.0	13.7
1984	286	2,606	2,892	2.1	31.1	13.1
1985	274	2,611	2,865	2.0	30.8	13.0
1986	262	2,705	2,967	1.9	31.3	13.2
1987	277	2,710	2,187	2.0	30.8	13.2
1988	335	3,002	3,337	2.3	32.0	13.9

1. Employees with an average working week of 1 to 36 hours.

Source: Brinkmann & Kohler, 1989, p. 474.

Table 2
Fixed-term contracted employment and agency work in % of employees

Year	Employees on fixed-term contracts	Registered agency workers
1984	5	0.1
1985	7	0.2
1986	8	0.3
1987	7	0.3
1988	7	0.4
1989	7	0.4

Sources: Statistisches Bundesamt, Fachserie 1, Reihe 4.1.1, various volumes;
Bundesanstalt für Arbeit, various volumes.

Table 3
Fixed-term employment

Item	1985		1988	
	1,000	%	1,000	%
All employees	1,604	7.3	1,679	7.4
German employees	1,463	7.3	1,553	7.4
Foreign employees	1,824	7.7	1,741	7.2
Age:				
under 25 years	750	19.6	784	21.0
25 to 44 years	620	5.8	682	6.0
45 to 59 years	210	3.1	194	2.7
60 years and over	24	4.7	20	3.9
Sector of the economy:				
agriculture, forestry and fishing	22	9.2	25	10.4
energy, water and mining	12	2.5	13	2.7
manufacturing	294	3.8	278	3.5
construction	66	4.2	60	3.9
trade	110	4.4	122	4.7
transport and communication	40	2.9	48	3.4
banking and insurance	27	3.3	24	2.9
services	416	9.8	484	10.6
non-profit organizations and private households	46	10.6	65	13.4
regional administrative bodies and social insurance agencies	570	22.0	561	20.5

Sources: Statistisches Bundesamt, Fachserie 1, Reihe 4.1.1.

4.4 Sectors of the Labour Force

In the FRG, the service sector of the economy is expanding. Nevertheless, the percentage of the labour force employed in services is smaller than in comparable countries.

As it did in other developed countries, a sectoral shift of the labour force toward the services sector took place in the Federal Republic of Germany which can be characterized as a process of tertiarization.

From 1950 to 1987, the proportion of persons employed in the primary sector declined from 25% to 5% (see table 1). The proportion of the labour force employed in the industrial sector increased from 43% to 49% by 1965. It remained stable until 1970, and thereafter decreased to its present level of 40%. In contrast, the percentage of the labour force employed in the tertiary sector increased continuously, from 33% in 1950 to 38% in 1960, 43% in 1970, and 55% in 1987.

The trend toward a services society becomes even more visible when we look at the functional classification of jobs. Regardless of their affiliation with economic sector, 64% of employed persons were engaged in service jobs in 1982 (Riede et al., 1987). Within the broad class of service jobs, expansion was observed primarily in the fields of business services, financial services, civil services, and educational and health services (see table 2). The increase in the services sector accounted for most of the growth in employment in recent years, and is paralleled by the increasing participation by women in the labour market and a better-educated labour force.

Compared to other countries, the services sector in the FRG is still relatively small. This lag is most notable in business services and social services, which, in contrast to, for instance, the United States, are traditionally supplied by welfare state institutions. Given the correlation between a large services sector and the strength of the internal orientation of an economy, the fairly strong external orientation of the German economy is another explanation for the observed differences (Krupp, 1986).

Heinz-Herbert Noll

References

Krupp, Hans-Jürgen
1986 "Der Strukturwandel zu den Dienstleistungen und Perspektiven der Beschäftigungsstruktur." *Mitteilungen aus der Arbeitsmarkt- und Berufsforschung*, 19, 145-158.

Müller, Walter
1983 "Wege und Grenzen der Tertiarisierung." In J. Matthes, ed., *Krise der Arbeitsgesellschaft. Verhandlungen des 21. Deutschen Soziologentages 1982*, 142-160. Frankfurt am Main.

Riede, Thomas, Andrea Schott-Winterer, and Alfred Woller
1987 *Der interne Wandel des Beschäftigungssystems der Bundesrepublik Deutschland, 1961-1982*. Arbeitspapier Nr. 223 des Sonderforschungsbereich 3 der J.W. Goethe-Universität Frankfurt und Universität Mannheim. Frankfurt am Main/Mannheim.

Sachverständigenrat zur Begutachtung der gesamtwirtschaftlichen Entwicklung
1977 *Arbeitsplätze im Wettbewerb. Jahresgutachten 1976/77*. Stuttgart/Mainz.

–
1988 *Arbeitsplätze im Wettbewerb. Jahresgutachten 1988/89*. Stuttgart/Mainz.

Table 1
Sectoral distribution of the economically active population

Year	Economically active persons (in 1.000)	Primary sector (in %)	Secondary sector (in %)	Tertiary sector (in %)
1950	19,997	24.8	42.6	32.6
1955	22,830	13.6	46.7	34.7
1960	24,792	14.4	48.2	37.4
1965	26,755	10.7	49.2	40.1
1970	26,560	8.5	48.9	42.6
1975	25,746	6.9	45.1	48.0
1980	26,278	5.5	44.1	50.4
1981	26,092	5.4	43.4	51.2
1982	25,651	5.4	42.6	52.0
1983	25,262	5.5	41.7	52.8
1984	25,283	5.4	41.3	53.3
1985	25,452	5.3	41.0	53.7
1986	25,702	5.2	40.9	53.9
1987	25,891	5.1	40.4	54.5

Saarland and Berlin not included for 1950 to 1960.

Source: Sachverständigenrat zur Begutachtung der gesamtwirtschaftlichen Entwicklung, 1977 and 1988.

Table 2
Employment in the Federal Republic of Germany 1950 - 1980 by occupational category (in %)

Occupational category	1950	1961	1970	1976	1980
Agriculture and unpaid family work	24.6	16.2	8.5	6.0	5.0
Manufacturing	37.0	37.1	36.1	32.2	32.5
Services for the manufacturing industry	9.7	14.0	16.8	18.2	18.4
Transport, trade, communication, financing	13.9	18.1	20.0	20.3	20.1
Public administration and services in the public interest	5.8	6.1	9.1	10.8	11.0
Services maintained by the welfare state	3.2	3.6	4.9	7.1	7.9
Household-related services	5.6	5.0	4.4	4.2	4.4

Source: Müller, 1983, pp. 148-152.

4.5 Computerization of Work

Computerization is taking place in many areas of working life, and is having a strong impact on the labour market. Indicators of this are rapidly growing numbers of computer installations, the increasing numbers of specialized personnel, and the fact that more and more employees are using some kind of computer-based technology at their work places.

Computerization is taking place in almost all domains of life, but particularly in the various areas of the work world. Although it started in the 1950s, it accelerated considerably during the 1980s. The rapid diffusion of computer technology is regarded as revolutionary because of its impact on the labour market, on working conditions, and on social relations in general.

Today, the numbers of computer installations are increasing rapidly, as are the numbers of people working in the computer business or using computers and computer-assisted technologies. Between 1985 and 1987 alone, the number of installed personal computers, the technology that is most frequently used within the group of "new" office technologies, leapt from 340,000 to 8,750,000. Computer-assisted technologies are also frequently used in manufacturing. The number of installed industrial robots, for instance, increased from 1,255 in 1980 to 17,700 in 1988 (see table 1). The estimated saturation limit of about 60,000 robots will not be reached before the year 2000, however (DIW, 1989).

In addition to the growing use of computer-based technologies by businesses more and more private households are equipped with home or personal computers. According to the results of a recent survey, 13% of all private households owned a personal computer in 1988. Another survey concluded that in about 40% of these households computers are used for professional purposes.

The rapid diffusion of computer-based technologies has particularly affected the labour market. The profession of computer specialist has shown the highest growth rate: 37% from 1982 to 1985, and 21% from 1985 to 1987. Between 1973 and 1987, the numbers of computer specialists nearly tripled, from 73,000 to 217,000. A manifestation of the great and growing demand for computer specialists is the fact that more and more people are interested in studying computer sciences. The number of students enrolled in computer-science courses rose from 5,000 in 1974 to 42,000 in 1987 – an eightfold increase, during a period when the total number of students did not even double (see table 2). However, the growing number of computer specialists is not the prime characteristic of the present wave of computerization; rather, it is the fact that this technology is widely used even by people who are not experts in computer sciences. More and more employees work with computers without having any special skills.

According to an estimate by the German Computer Science Association, 5% of the total labour force required professional training in information sciences in 1990, 15% required intensified training within a special domain of information technology aside from their actual professional education, and another 50% required training that enables them to use information-technology equipment.

The results of a recently replicated large-sample survey show that almost 25% of all gainfully employed person at least occasionally used program-controlled tools in their work, compared to 15% in 1979 (Troll, 1987). At present, computerization is most advanced within the finance and insurance business, where 60% of all employees now use computer facilities (see table 3).

More and more jobs are concerned mainly with information processing. On the other hand, frequent use of this technology constitutes an addition to traditional job tasks, which means that new skills have to be integrated into old professions. Computerization not only changes working conditions to a large extent and undermines the distinctions between white- and blue-collar work and between work traditionally regarded as appropriate for men and for women, it also forces the majority of the working population – estimates run at about 60% to 70% – to adapt their skills to changed requirements.

Heinz-Herbert Noll

References

Bullinger, Hans-Jörg
"Berufliche Weiterbildung - Investition in die Zukunft." In Staatsministerium Baden-Württemberg, ed., *Kongreß der Landesregierung Baden-Württemberg "Zukunftschancen eines Industrielandes - Herausforderung Weiterbildung"*, 39-48. Stuttgart.

Bundesinstitut für Berufsbildung, and Institut für Arbeitsmarkt- und Berufsforschung, eds.
1987 *Neue Technologien: Verbreitungsgrad, Qualifikation und Arbeitsbedingungen*. Beiträge zur Arbeitsmarkt- und Berufsforschung, vol. 118. Nürnberg.

DIW (Deutsches Institut für Wirtschaftsforschung)
1989 *Wochenbericht 8/1989*. Berlin.

Dostal, Werner
1986 "Informationstechnik und Informationsbereich im Kontext aktueller Prognosen." *Mitteilungen aus der Arbeitsmarkt- und Berufsforschung*, 19, 134-144.

Institut der Deutschen Wirtschaft
1990 *Zahlen zur wirtschaftlichen Entwicklung der Bundesrepublik Deutschland 1990.* Köln.

Institut für Arbeitsmarkt- und Berufsforschung
1986 *Zahlen-Fibel*. BeitrAB 101. Nürnberg.

Statistisches Bundesamt, ed.
ann. pbl. *Statistisches Jahrbuch.* Stuttgart/Mainz: Kohlhammer

Troll, Lothar
1987 "Verbreitungsgrad neuer Technologien und Veränderungen seit 1979." In Bundesinstitut für Berufsbildung, and Institut für Arbeitsmarkt - und Berufsforschung, eds., *Neue Technologien: Verbreitungsgrad, Qualifikation und Arbeitsbedingungen.* Beiträge zur Arbeitsmarkt- und Berufsforschung, vol. 118, 11-90. Nürnberg.

Table 1
Number of industrial robots installed[1]

Year	Robots (in 1,000)
1980	1,255
1981	2,301
1982	3,500
1983	4,800
1984	6,600
1985	8,800
1986	12,400
1987	14,900
1988	17,700
1989	22,395

1. Date of reference: end of year.

Source: Institut der deutschen Wirtschaft, 1990.

Table 2
Students enrolled in computer science and total number of university students

Year	Number of students enrolled in computer sciences		Total number of students	
	(in 1,000)	1980=100	(in 1,000)	1980=100
WS 74/75[1]	5.130	35.0	790.233	76.6
WS 75/76	6.398	43.7	837.079	81.2
WS 76/77	7.471	51.0	871.909	84.5
WS 77/78	8.303	56.7	905.645	87.8
WS 78/79	9.760	66.6	937.141	90.9
WS 79/80	12.120	82.7	970.284	94.1
WS 80/81	14.657	100.0	1,031.590	100.0
WS 81/82	17.686	120.7	1,121.058	108.7
WS 82/83	20.831	142.1	1,198.330	116.2
WS 83/84	26.016	177.5	1,267.263	122.9
WS 84/85	30.341	207.0	1,311.699	127.2
WS 85/86	34.215	233.4	1,336.395	129.6
WS 86/87	37.276	254.3	1,336.057	132.4
WS 87/88	41.817	285.3	1,409.042	136.6

1. WS = Wintersemester (WS 80/81 = 100.0 %).

Source: Statistisches Bundesamt, various volumes.

Table 3
Dissemination rates of program-controlled tools (in %)

Item	1979	1985
Total	15	23
Banking, insurance	-	59
Energy, wining	-	31
Public administration	-	25
Manufacturing	-	21
Trade	-	20
Transport	-	18
Services	-	17
Churches, administration	-	12
Construction	-	9
Agriculture, forestry	-	4

Source: L. Troll, 1987.

5. Labour and Management

5.1 Work Organization

Taylorism is increasingly being replaced by integrative approaches toward labour organization. Since the 1950s, there has been a high level of institutionalized worker participation at both the plant and the company level. Job enlargement has taken place in some fields, but it is not a direct consequence of technological changes. Job sharing, in the sense of compensation programs during periods of crisis, is very common; in the sense of two persons sharing one work place it is almost nonexistent. Investment in R & D and human resources has been growing and diversifying strongly. There is a net trend toward flexible work schedules, which is linked to a reduction in work hours.

Time and Motion Studies

Until the mid-1970s, the Tayloristic work structure was the leading principle of rationalization in the manufacturing industries. This was particularly so in the automotive industry, which thereby succeeded in closing the technological gap with the United States (Kern & Schumann, 1984). According to a 1972 poll by the Allensbach Institute (Kador, 1983), 5% of all blue-collar workers worked on assembly lines. Assembly lines were especially prevalent in firms employing 500 to 1,000 persons (17%) and in the metal-processing and automotive sectors, where large-scale production was the standard.

Since the late 1970s, the efficiency of excessive division of labour has been called into question, and alternative work structures such as autonomous and semi-autonomous construction groups have been developed and discussed (Arbeitskreis, 1989; Ludwig, 1986; Staudt, 1987). This development is generally considered to be the result of at least three factors. First, increasing diversification of products has reduced the areas in which large-scale production is possible or economically efficient; the trend toward smaller scales in production clearly leads to more integrated work structures (Goebel et al., 1987). Second, there has been a strong movement in favour of more humane work structures, which should be achieved by reducing the dependence of workers on machine rhythms and giving them more autonomy in their work (Goebel et al., 1987; Kador, 1983; Ludwig, 1986; Staudt, 1987). Finally, technological evolution made possible the complete automation of Tayloristic work processes. Formerly executed by blue-collar workers, these tasks are increasingly executed by industrial robots. In fact, the number of industrial robots in the Federal Republic increased from 1,255 in 1980 to 17,700 in 1988 (see table 1). This trend has been accompanied by a net diminution of the proportion of unskilled labour among the active labour force (see table 2).

Worker Participation and Self-management

In the FRG, worker participation (codetermination) is regulated by various laws, which are implemented in part at plant level (workers' councils) and in part at company level (supervisory board). The codetermination system originated in the 1920s, and was re-established and extended considerably in the 1950s. Workers' councils, representating all employees in a plant, have a series of graded rights recording codetermination of work (schedules, social services, principles of remuneration etc.), personnel matters (personnel planning, hiring and transfers of employees, hearings in cases of dismissals), and economic matters (consultation on plant alterations, codetermination of social compensation plans for the staff in case of alterations).

Codetermination at company level is regulated under one of three different systems, according to the sector and size of the firm. The most far-reaching system was introduced 1951 in the coal, iron, and steel industries (*Montan-Mitbestimmung*): the supervisory board – which elects the members of the board of directors – must be composed of an equal number of shareholders' and employers' representatives and a neutral member elected by both sides. This system applied to 29 firms in 1988, and the number is in decline (Kronenberg et al. 1989). The second system, which came into effect in 1976, applies to corporations with more than 2,000 employees and is based on an equal number of shareholders' and employees' representatives on the board, the chair (who has the deciding vote) being a representative of the shareholders. The number of firms under this system increased from 1978 (475 firms) to 1988 (500 firms) (Kronenberg, 1989). Finally, corporations with fewer than 2,000 employees are under a system according to which one-third of the supervisory board has to consist of employees' representatives.

Apart from these legally enforced codetermination systems, there exists a trend toward participatory management forms (Witte, 1982). Several firms, among them small companies not subject to the legal codetermination systems, introduced comprehensive worker-participation systems, but not all of them were successful (Frei, 1984; Frieke, 1982; Kraft, 1982).

There is no legislation in the FRG encouraging employers to introduce employee stock-ownership plans (employees could draw minor tax benefits from such schemes). Furthermore, employee stock ownership is not linked to company pension schemes. Therefore, only about 1,500 German companies offer stock ownership to their employees. These include most of the very large firms, including Siemens, Hoechst, and Daimler, which offer shares at advantageous prices, but also smaller firms, which offer other forms of equity (Hornung-Draus, 1988).

Management buy-outs rarely occur in the FRG: in 1987, there were only 20 MBOs (see table 5), although this topic is becoming increasingly popular in management literature (Batchelor, 1988; Hauschka, 1987). There have also been some isolated cases of employees taking over their nearly bankrupt firms in order to save them, but not all of these have been successful in the long run.

A special category of self-management firms emerged in the 1970s, in the context of the new social movements, to try to set up alternatives to established capitalist companies. In some cases, the initiative came from unemployed persons who founded their own cooperatives. In 1985, there were between 6,000 and 35,000 alternative economic projects (with 80,000 to 600,000 members) – depending on the precise definition of the phenomenon – and 300 to 500 initiatives by unemployed persons (Kaiser, 1985). Recent studies show that these firms have integrated fairly well into the existing socio-economic system, but at the same time they have lost a good deal of their alternative social character (Gretsch, 1986; Kreutz, 1986).

Job Enlargement

There is a clear trend toward job enlargement (Buchholz, 1989; Goebel, 1987; Kador, 1983; Sonntag, 1985; Spur et al, 1987). This cannot be perceived as a necessary consequence of the technological innovations of recent years. Many case studies show that the relationship between technological innovation and work content is very complex (Buchholz, 1989; Landau, 1988). However, the new technologies certainly facilitated the development of this phenomenon, the actual origins of which must be sought in the economic and cultural realms. Culturally, there has been growing sensitivity to working conditions and hostility toward monotonous work, which is considered inhumane. Job enlargement can thus be considered as an effort to "humanize" work (Buchholz, 1989). Economically, the trend toward flexible, small-scale production leads to job enlargement and more highly qualified personnel. At the same time, job enlargement has proved to have positive effects on workers' motivation and efficiency (Buchholz, 1989).

Job Sharing

Job sharing can refer to two different phenomena: first – as a collective action – to short-term compensation programs as an alternative to layoffs in periods of economic crisis; second – as an individual action – to the practice of two or more employees sharing one job. Job sharing as a compensation program (*Kurzarbeit* – part-time work, when hours are temporarily cut due to a slump) has been in practice since the 1950s. The state has always considered it an important instrument of labour-market policy and has paid employees partial unemployment benefits as a compensation for economically induced part-time work.

The statistics on job-sharing programs (see table 3) reflect economic cycles: the number of employees covered by these programs rose sharply during the oil-price crisis in the 1970s. The data show that recourse to them has become increasingly popular, especially among small and medium-sized firms.

The idea of job sharing, in the second sense of the term, became increasingly popular in the 1980s. However, the discussion has remained purely theoretical so far: only 17 companies and 25 public corporations are known to have split up work places for more than one person (Infratest, 1985). Still, some large firms, such as Hewlett Packard (Frankfurter Allgemeine Zeitung, 1989), make wider use of job sharing-programs: 3.1% of HP personnel at all levels practise job sharing.

One of the main obstacles to introduction of job sharing, and of part-time work in general, is the German tax and social-security system, which penalizes part-time work, especially at the middle- and upper-income levels.

Investment in R&D and Human Resourses

Private enterprises finance more than half of total R&D expenditure in the FRG (see 0.3, "Macro-technological Trends"). R&D expenditure by private firms increased from 4.4 million DM in 1965 to 48.1 million DM in 1988 (see table 4). Still, the number of people employed in R&D is comparatively low by international standards (see figure 1).

Professional training takes place mainly on the job, combined with attendance at professional school one to two days per week. The number of apprentices depends on economic and demographic factors. It reached a peak in 1985 at over 1.8 million, and has been declining since due to demographic developments. In some sectors, there is even a shortage of apprentices.

While firms' investment in professional training of youths has always been the norm in the FRG, investment in further qualification of employees is a relatively new phenomenon. At present, 92% of all firms provide further training for their employees, spending roughly 26 billion DM on these programs (Institut der deutschen Wirtschaft, 1989a; Malcher, 1988).

The idea of quality circles was imported to the FRG from the United States with a considerable time lag in the late 1970s. By 1981, only some ten German firms had introduced quality circles. Today more than 1,000 firms have gathered experience in this field (Deppe, 1985). Although there are no precise statistics available, it seems that investment in quality circles is continuing to expand (Lukie, 1988).

Flexible Schedules

Flexible working hours in the FRG date back to 1967, when the firm Messerschmidt-Boelkow-Blohm introduced a "flex-time" system for clerical jobs. Today, 14% of the active labour force works on flex-time schedules (Draus, 1989). However, this increase in flexible work hours applies only to clerical work and services. In the production sector, a strong movement toward elaborate and highly complicated systems of flexible schedules, combined with shift-work, has been generated by the reduction in individual working hours which has taken place since 1984.

Renate Hornung-Draus

References

Arbeitskreis Neue Strukturen der deutschen Automobilindustrie
1989 "Arbeitswelt Automobil." *Leistung und Lohn*, no. 210-212.

Batchelor, Charles
1988 "Where Britain leads the field (Management buy-out)." *Financial Times*, July 12, 1988.

Boeckels, L., et al.
1981 *Die Gleitzeitarbeit - Entwicklungsstand und Perspektiven in der Bundesrepublik*. Bonn: Bundesministerium für Arbeit und Sozialordnung.

Bretschneider, Joachim, et. al., eds.
n.d. *Handbuch einkommens-, vermögens- und sozialpolitischer Daten*. Loseblattsammlung. Köln: Bachem.

Buchholz, Goetz
1989 "Das geistige Potential bekommt VW gratis mitgeliefert." *Die Mitbestimmung*, no. 8, 464.

Dahrendorf, Ralf, et al., eds.
1986 *Neue Arbeits- und Tätigkeitsformen*. Dokumentation eines Kolloquiums. Luxemburg: Amt für amtliche Veröffentlichungen der Europäischen Gemeinschaft.

Deppe, Joachim
1985 *Qualitätszirkel - Ideenmanagement durch Gruppenarbeit*. Bern: Peter Lang Verlag.

Dostal, Werner
1985 "Telearbeit." *Mitteilungen aus der Arbeitsmarkt- und Berufsforschung*, no. 4, 467ff.

Draus, Renate
1989 "La flexibilité du travail." *Observations et diagnostics économiques*, no. 27.

Frankfurter Allgemeine Zeitung
1989 "Wenn sich Manager den Arbeitsplatz teilen. Job sharing bei Hewlett Packard." *Frankfurter Allgemeine Zeitung*, October 4, 1989.

Frei, Felix
1984 "Partizipative Arbeitsgestaltung und Automatisierung: Einige Fallstricke." *Zeitschrift für Arbeitswissenschaft*, no. 2, 65 ff.

Frese, Michael, et al.
1987 "Die Einführung von neuen Techniken verändert Qualifikationsanforderungen, Handlungsspielraum und Stressoren kaum." *Zeitschrift für Arbeitswissenschaft*, no. 1, 7 ff.

Fricke, Werner
1982 "Beteiligung, Mitbestimmung und Humanisierung der Arbeit." *Zeitschrift für Arbeitswissenschaft*, no. 2, 72 ff.

Goebel, Uwe, et al.
1987 *Die Zukunftsformel, Technik - Qualifikation - Kreativität*. Köln: Deutscher Instituts-Verlag.

Gretsch, Lothar
1986 "Neue Wege der Arbeitsorganisation - Erfahrungen aus Selbstverwalteten Betrieben." In: Ralf Dahrendorf et al., eds, *Neue Arbeits- und Tätigkeitsformen*. Dokumentation eines Kolloquiums. Luxemburg: Amt für amtliche Veröffentlichungen der Europäischen Gemeinschaft.

Hauschka, Christoph
1987 "Wirtschaftliche, arbeits- und gesellschaftsrechtliche Aspekte des Management buy-out." *Betriebs-Berater*, no. 32, 2169.

Hornung-Draus, Renate
1988 "Betriebliche Vermögensbeteiligung, Informationen zur empirischen Entwicklung." *Sparkasse*, no. 7, 324ff.

Hufnagel, Annette, et al.
1989 "Ausbildung und Erwerbstätigkeit, Ergebnisse des Mikrozensus 1987." *Wirtschaft und Statistik*, no. 2, 65ff.

Infratest/Wissenschaftszentrum Berlin
1985 *Flexible Arbeitszeiten*. Frankfurt am Main/New York: Campus.

Institut der deutschen Wirtschaft
1988 "Auslandsorientierung der deutschen Wirtschaft." IW-Trends, no. 2.

–
1989a "Betriebliche Weiterbildung: Die vierte Säule." *iwd*, no. 40.

–
1989b *Zahlen zur wirtschaftlichen Entwicklung der Bundesrepublik Deutschland.* Köln

Kador, Fritz-Jürgen, et. al.
1983 *Unternehmerische Personalpolitik*. Köln: Bachem.

Kaiser, Manfred
1985 "Alternativ-ökonomische Beschäftigungsexperimente - quantitative und qualitative Aspekte." *Mitteilungen aus der Arbeitsmarkt- und Berufsforschung*, no. 1, 92ff.

Kern, H., and M. Schumann
1984 *Das Ende der Arbeitsteilung?* München: Beck.

Kraft, Kornelius
1982 *Kooperation und Konflikt im Unternehmen*. Wissenschaftszentrum Berlin - International Institute of Management - Discussion papers on Industrial Policy (IIM/IP 82 - 45).

Kreutz, Henrik, et al.
1986 "Von der alternativen Bewegung zum selbstverwalteten Projekt." *Mitteilungen aus der Arbeitsmarkt- und Berufsforschung*, no. 4, 553ff.

Kronenberg, Brigitte, et al.
1989 "Mitbestimmungsunternehmen nach dem Stand vom 31.12.1988." *WSI-Mitteilungen*, no. 7.

Landau, Kurt, et al.
1988 "Zur Analyse von Anforderungsverschiebungen durch Einsatz von Industrierobotern im Automobilbau." *Zeitschrift für Arbeitswissenschaft*, no. 4, 201ff.

Ludwig, Joerg
1986 "Flexible Fertigungsorganisation am Beispiel von Fertigungsinseln." *Leistung und Lohn*, no. 177-180.

Lukie, Mario
1988 "Humanisierung der Arbeit durch Qualitätszirkel." *Zeitschrift für Arbeitswissenschaft*, no. 3, 137.

Malcher, Wilfried
1987 "Qualifizierungsoffensive: Zwischenbilanz und Perspektiven einer arbeitsmarktpolitischen Strategie." *Berufsbildung in Wissenschaft und Praxis*, no. 5.

–
1988 "Berufliche Weiterbildung: Betriebe zu Unrecht in der Kritik." *Der Arbeitgeber*, no. 6.

Niedenhoff, Horst-Udo
1979 *Praxis der betrieblichen Mitbestimmung. Die Zusammenarbeit zwischen Betriebsrat und Unternehmensleitung*. Köln: Deutscher Instituts-Verlag.

OECD
1986 *Science and Technology indicators no. 2: R&D, invention and competitiveness*.

Sonntag, Karlheinz
1985a "Erforderliche Qualifikationen beim Tätigkeitsvollzug in der flexiblen automatisierten Fertigung." *Zeitschrift für Arbeitswissenschaft*, no. 4, 193ff.

–
1985b *Neue Produktionstechniken und qualifizierte Arbeit*. Köln: Deutscher Instituts-Verlag.

Spur, G., et al.
1987 "Flexibilisierung der Produktionstechnik und Auswirkungen auf Arbeitsinhalte." *Zeitschrift für Arbeitswissenschaft*, no. 4, 207ff.

Staudt, Erich
1987 "Arbeit und neue Technik: Über ein verbessertes Verhältnis des Menschen zur Maschine." *Leistung und Lohn*, no. 195-197.

Witte, Eberhard
1982 "Klassenkampf und Gruppenkampf im Unternehmen." In *Hamburger Jahrbuch für Wirtschafts- und Gesellschaftspolitik*, 167ff.

Table 1
Industrial Robots in the Federal Republic of Germany

Year	1980	1982	1984	1985	1986	1987	1988
Total	1,255[1]	3,500	6,600	8,800	12,400	14,900	17,700
Robots handling tools	723	2,487	4,700	6,175	8,626	10,180	12,282
- coating	155	397	727	775	1,082	1,186	1,325
- welding points	339	1,331	1,894	2,548	3,152	3,413	3,717
- welding tracks	138	585	1,334	1,781	2,322	2,710	3,255
- removing burrs	5	20	22	25	52	69	76
- assembling	52	122	452	753	1,658	2,341	3,370
- other tasks	34	32	271	263	360	461	539
Robots handling work pieces	481	955	1,743	2,415	3,437	4,315	4,977
- pressing	78	70	135	173	193	222	290
- forging	24	52	75	84	113	147	188
- casting	138	120	147	174	194	218	262
- loading and unloading machines	192	193	466	805	1,156	1,427	1,565
- other tasks	49	520	920	1,179	1,781	2,301	2,672
Research	17	58	157	210	337	405	441

1. Including 34 robots for which the use is unknown.

Source: Institut der deutschen Wirtschaft, 1989b.

Table 2
Active labour force in the Federal Republic of Germany according to professional qualification (in %)

Item	1976	1987
No vocational training degree	34.3	26.1
Vocational training degree		
- apprenticeship training	52.1	56.3
- specialized secondary technical school degree	6.4	7.3
Higher education degree		
- higher technical college	2.2	3.6
- university	5.0	6.7

Source: Hufnagel et al., 1987, p. 67.

Table 3
Part-time work programs in the Federal Republic of Germany

Year	Persons covered in 1,000			Enterprises resorting to part-time work
	Total	Male	Female	
1951	93.4	41.6	51.9	2,430
1952	125.4	62.9	62.5	3,043
1953	83.1	53.7	29.3	2,330
1954	56.4	25.4	31.0	1,776
1955	24.7	10.0	14.6	868
1956	25.1	13.2	11.9	644
1957	19.3	10.7	8.6	518
1958	54.8	24.5	30.3	1,177
1959	25.9	14.3	11.5	592
1960	3.3	1.5	1.8	118
1961	3.3	1.3	2.0	95
1962	4.0	2.2	1.8	91
1963	10.9	7.0	3.9	280
1964	2.2	1.0	1.1	68
1965	1.1	0.6	0.5	32
1966	15.8	8.8	7.0	259
1967	142.7	89.3	53.4	2,323
1968	10.4	6.6	3.8	399
1969	1.3	0.7	0.6	55
1970	9.6	3.6	6.0	154
1971	86.1	52.1	33.9	622
1972	76.3	54.2	22.0	786
1973	43.7	18.1	25.6	804
1974	292.4	197.6	94.8	4,729
1975	773.3	537.7	235.7	12,548
1976	277.0	210.0	67.0	5,408
1977	231.3	181.3	50.1	3,505
1978	190.7	148.7	42.0	3,063
1979	87.6	59.2	28.4	1,924
1980	136.6	98.2	38.4	1,975
1981	346.9	239.3	107.6	7,043
1982	606.1	460.3	145.8	14,894
1983	675.1	547.8	127.3	17,246
1984	383.7	324.8	58.9	13,082
1985	234.5	197.2	37.3	13,134
1986	197.4	163.5	33.8	9,863
1987	278.0	231.2	46.8	9,058

Source: Bundesanstalt für Arbeit, ANBA; Bretschneider et al., n.d.

Table 4
R & D expenditure by private enterprises (in billion DM)

Total expenditure of firms on R & D								
1965	1977	1979	1981	1983	1985	1986	1987	1988
4.43	17.23	23.83	27.84	33.07	39.55	41.64	45.98	48.17

Source: Institut der deutschen Wirtschaft, 1988.

Table 5
Management buy-outs in Europe

Country	Estimates of total number of buy-outs to end 1967
France	200
Netherlands	175
Sweden	75
Belgium	30[1]
W. Germany	20[1]
Italy	18[2]
Switzerland	10-20[1]
Spain	10-15[2]
Norway	11
Denmark	7

1. Estimated
2. Includes buy-ins

Source: Management Buy-Outs: The Prospects in Continental Europe, a report by Centre for Management Buy-out Research, commissioned by 3 i, cited in Batchelor, Financial Times, July 12, -1988.

Figure 1
Number of researchers in relation to labour force

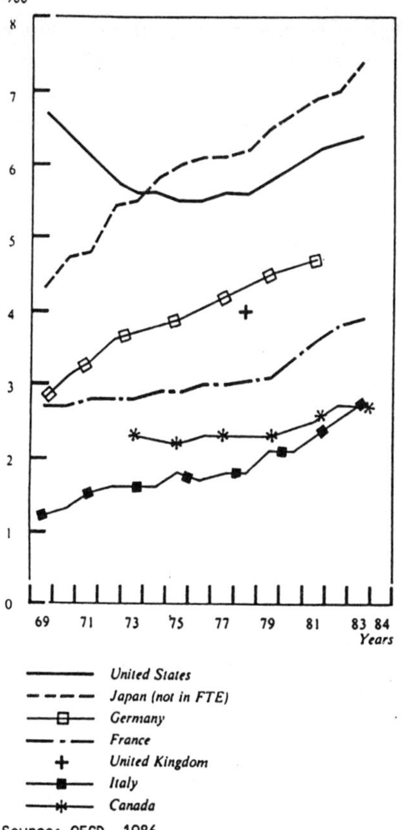

Source: OECD, 1986.

5.2 Personnel Administration

Job classification has become increasingly differentiated. In contrast to many other countries, the Federal Republic shows no significant trend toward individualization of wage and salary determination. On-the-job training is very well developed in the Federal Republic, in terms of both professional training and further training for employees. Systematic career development exists in large firms; so far, it has been focused almost entirely on male employees. Expenditures for fringe benefits have increased considerably in German companies. Grievance procedures are highly formalized.

There exists a long-term tendency toward growing differentiation of job classifications. Collective agreements on wages of blue-collar workers, for example, show that classification evolved from three categories – skilled, semi-skilled, and unskilled workers – to twelve or more wage groups. Job classification is established on the basis of several factors, including educational level, training diplomas, previous professional experience, degree of responsibility, physical and psychological strain, and working conditions (heat, cold, dust, etc.) (Adamy et al., 1985). In some fields, excessive differentiation has become counterproductive, and attempts are being made to overcome overly rigid classification structures.

Wage and Salary Determination

In contrast to many other countries, there is no significant tendency in the Federal Republic toward individualization of wages and salaries. Between 1957 and 1978, the proportion of hourly wage rates among all kinds of pay for male blue-collar workers increased from 64% to 80%, and for female blue-collar workers from 55% to 63%. During the same period, the proportion of piece rates diminished from 26% to 17% for male blue-collar workers, but by only one point – from 33% to 32% – for female blue-collar workers (Draus, 1989). These figures reflect the fact that women are overrepresented in unskilled jobs which tend to be renumerated on the basis of piece rates.

The technological evolution and ensuing changes in work organization (see 5.1, "Work Organization") have had important impacts on wage determination. In fact, they can be considered to be the most important factor leading to the relative decline of piece-rate wages (Kammer, 1989; Zander, 1986).

Profit-related pay is not at all common in the Federal Republic as a general factor in wage determination. Profit-related payments do exist – mostly in very large firms such as Hoechst and Bayer – but these are not perceived to be part of the wage, but as an extra payment "on top" of the wage. On the whole, it seems that the German system of collective wage agreements for entire sectors and regions (as opposed to agreements for individual firms, which is the usual procedure in the United States and Japan) is not conducive to the introduction of profit-related wage payments.

On-the-job Training

On-the-job training has always been the predominant form of professional training in the Federal Republic. Professional training for apprentices is described in section 5.1, "Work Organization." Recently, on-the-job training has become increasingly important in other fields of personnel administration: many firms, especially medium- and large-sized ones, have introduced "training" periods for young university graduates. Trainees usually spend one or two years in different departments and branches of the firm in order to get an overall view of its operations. There are no data regarding the number of trainees in the Federal Republic, but analysis of job offers on the labour market shows that a high proportion of positions offered for university graduates are trainee positions.

As well, on-the-job training has become an increasingly important element of further training for employees. According to a 1990 study by the Institut der deutschen Wirtschaft, further training of employees is structured as follows: 24.5% of the total volume of training hours is spent on training on the job (*Lernen am Arbeitsplatz*); 64.5% is spent on theoretical courses, most of which take place in the firm. More than 90% of further training is done during work hours. The average annual cost for further training per employee is 1,766 DM. Further training is especially important in the service, training, and information sectors, where firms spend an average of between 3,000 and 4,000 DM per employee annually. On the other hand, industrial firms' expenditures for further training are below average.

According to recent literature (*Manager Magazin* 1986, 1987a, 1987b), new forms of on-the-job training are being developed, to cope with the greater complexity of work processes (small multidisciplinary groups, quality circles, etc.).

Career Development

In 1970, executives and supervisors comprised 2.6% of all employed persons. Thus, possibilities of advancement into executive positions were rather limited. Since then, there has been a trend toward reduction of levels in hierarchies and toward more efficient management structures (see 5.3, "Sizes and Types of Enterprises"), and so it seems unlikely that advancement possibilities will have increased more recently.

Systematic career development as an instrument of personnel administration is widely practised by large companies, which recruit their top and middle management almost exclusively from within the company. With regard to methods of career development, the Federal Republic is imitating the evolution in the United States, but with a considerable time lag: assessment centres were being discussed as novelties in the late 1980s.

Career development is still focused almost exclusively on male employees. In German industry, women comprise only 2% of top management (in France, the figure is 7%, in Belgium, 8%) and 8% of middle-management positions (Hoerburger, 1988; see table 1). Very few German firms have formalized strategies for women's career development, and international data show that the Federal Republic is far behind other countries, such as France and the United States, in this respect (Hoerburger, 1988).

Fringe Benefits

German companies pay large amounts of money for employees' fringe benefits. In the industrial sector, the cost of fringe benefits, as a proportion of wages paid, increased from 35% in 1950 to 83.6% in 1988 (see table 2). In 1988, total fringe benefits were lowest in the commercial sector (69.1% of wages paid) and highest in the banking sector (100.3% of wages paid).

German statistics distinguish between two types of fringe benefits: those imposed by law and "voluntary" ones. Fringe benefits in the first category are employers' part of the social charges (50% of total contributions for old-age, health, and unemployment insurance), paid vacations, wage payments during the first six weeks of sick leave, accident insurance, and so on. Among these fringe benefits, expenditures for social charges have been the most important and most rapidly growing ones. "Voluntary" fringe benefits are granted to employees either on the basis of collective agreements (e.g., special holiday payments, "thirteenth" monthly wage, asset-forming payments) or on the basis of an offer by the individual employer (pension schemes, share options, etc.).

A recent study (EMNID & Capital, 1989) showed that fringe benefits in German companies have so far completely bypassed areas concerning family life: child-care facilities in the vicinity of work places are virtually nonexistent, and only one-third of the 500 largest companies in the Federal Republic provide some sort of fringe benefit related to the family (such as parental leave, special arrangements when children are sick, etc.). This situation corresponds fairly well with findings on role models in the Federal Republic, which are still very strongly focused on the hard-working male providing money – but no time – for his family, and the housekeeping female caring exclusively for the children – and not working.

Professional life and family life are perceived as two isolated realms, with no links to each other.

Grievance Procedures

Grievance procedures in German firms are heavily formalized. Companies with more than five employees have workers' councils (see 5.1, "Work Organization"), which possess a series of graded rights concerning work organization and personnel matters. In practice, the workers' council has a mediating role in all conflicts between employees and employers.

If the workers' council and the employer do not reach agreement on matters subject to codetermination by the workers' council, an arbitration committee with a neutral chair – usually a judge – must be appealed to. However, empirical evidence shows that the arbitration committee is very seldom appealed to – the proportion is below 1% of all decisions taken. The frequency of these appeals is proportional to the size of the enterprises (Niedenhoff, 1979). Unfortunately, there are no data available on the evolution of the number of conflicts between the workers' councils and employers.

Renate Hornung-Draus

References

Adamy, Wilhelm, et al.
1985 *Handbuch der Arbeitsbeziehungen*. Bonn: Bundeszentrale für politische Bildung.

Draus, Renate
1989 "La flexibilité du travail en Rèpublique Fédérale d'Allemagne." *Observations et diagnostics économiques*, no. 27.

EMNID, Capital
1989 "Kinderbetreuung am Arbeitsplatz ist derzeit noch die Ausnahme." *Kölner Rundschau*, August 29, 1989.

Hoerburger, Hortense
1988 "Europäerinnen in Managementpositionen". In Demmer Ch., ed., *Frauen ins Management.* Wiesbaden: Gabler

INFRATEST
1988 *Berichtssystem Weiterbildungsverhalten*, not yet published.

Institut der deutschen Wirtschaft
1989a "Kosten und Strukturen der betrieblichen Weiterbildung." Study will be published in 1990, article on press conference, *Süddeutsche Zeitung*, 5. October 1989, p. 33.

–
1989b *Zahlen zur wirtschaftlichen Entwicklung der Bundesrepublik Deutschland 1989*. Köln: Deutscher Instituts-Verlag.

Kador, Fritz-Jürgen, et al.
1983 *Unternehmerische Personalpolitik*. Köln: Bachem.

Kammer, Wilhelm
1989 "Gehört der Bereichsbewertung die Zukunft?" *Leistung und Lohn*, no. 213-215.

Manager Magazin
1986 "Drang zur Mitte - Lernstatt." *Manager Magazin*, no. 5, 284.

–
1987a "Lernen ohne Zwang und Stress - Nachwuchsschulung." *Manager Magazin*, no. 7, 166.

–
1987b "Motivationsschub an der Basis - Kleingruppenarbeit." *Manager Magazin*, no. 9, 250.

Niedenhoff, Horst-Udo
1979 *Praxis der betrieblichen Mitbestimmung*. Köln: Deutscher Instituts-Verlag.

Willenbacher, Kurt
1989 "Motivationswirkung leistungsbezogener Entgeltsysteme in Gegenwart und Zukunft." *Leistung und Lohn*, no. 216.

Zander, Ernst
1986 "Entgeltformen bei veränderten Technologien." *Personal*, no. 4, 146.

Table 1
Proportion of women in industrial companies 1978/79
(% of all employed in the relevant group)

Country	Top management	Middle management	Total
West Germany	2	8	31
France	7	9	29
Italy	2	8	26
Belgium	8	7	22

Source: EUROSTAT, Women in Europe, Hoerburger, 1988, p. 223.

Table 2
Evolution of fringe benefits as a percentage of wages paid

Sector	1966	1978	1984	1988
Industry	43.4	71.8	81.6	83.6
Banking	-	94.5	98.3	100.3
Insurance	-	84.2	94.4	96.3

Source: Institut der deutschen Wirtschaft, 1989, tables 83, 84.

5.3 Sizes and Types of Enterprises

The overall number of enterprises has increased considerably over the last 20 years. Due to the growing importance of the service sector, the proportion of small firms has risen. Job creation has taken place mainly in small companies, and at the same time the average business turnover of small companies has grown considerably. The organizational structure of companies is influenced by the growing complexity of the environment and the growing rapidity of technological change. After a period of increasing complexity of organizational structure, the most recent trend is toward a reduction in complexity.

The overall number of enterprises in the Federal Republic increased by 13% between 1970 and 1987; in the latter year, there were nearly 2.6 million firms. The number of jobs (i.e., the number of employment contracts, which is not identical to the number of employed persons, since one person may hold several contracts) increased by 11%, from 24.4 million to 27 million, during the same period.

The structure of enterprises by sector changed considerably between 1970 and 1987. The number of industrial firms diminished in both absolute and relative terms: in 1970, 19.3% of all enterprises were in the industrial sector, while in 1987 only 14% were. The same is true for enterprises in commerce, the proportion of which declined from 32% (1970) to 27.4% (1987). On the other hand, the service sector showed a marked increase in the number of enterprises with its share increasing from 25.3% to 33.3% (see table 1).

If we compare the structure of enterprises with that of employed persons, we find that industry, despite its decline in total number of enterprises, is still the sector employing the highest proportion of persons, 40%, whereas the service sector, which has the highest number of firms, employs only some 21% of the labour force (see figure 1).

Several studies confirm the hypothesis that over the last ten years, employment has been created by small companies, while very large firms suffered losses in numbers of jobs (Cramer, 1987). This evolution is linked, of course, to structural changes taking place in the economy, especially with the growth of the tertiary sector. Employment in firms with up to 20 employees increased by 13% between 1970 and 1985, while employment in firms with up to 500 employees fell by 4.2% during this period. However, employment in the small firms is generally characterized by a higher degree of precariousness (fixed-term and part-time contracts) and lower incomes than is employment in larger firms (Cramer, 1987).

Business turnover among firms has been analyzed on the basis of fiscal data gathered by Gruhler (1984). The analysis shows that the proportion of firms with low turnover decreased between 1968 (78.7%) and 1982 (73.0%), while the proportion of firms with a medium turnover increased from 20.6% to 26.3% and the proportion of firms with a very high turnover remained stable at 0.7% (see table 3).

The evolution of firms' sizes according to number of persons employed and business turnover is thus characterized by divergent trends: on the one hand, the number of persons employed tends to decrease; on the other hand, turnover per firm tends to increase.

Precise data regarding the legal structure of enterprises are available only for the year 1970. By far the largest proportion of firms were owned by one or more persons (*Einzelfirmen*), 91.14%, but these firms employed only 35.3% of all gainfully employed persons. Almost 6% of all enterprises were partnerships, but they employed 24.8% of all employed persons. The number of limited-liability and joint-stock companies was far smaller (1.8% and 0.13%, respectively), but they are typically very large firms, employing 15.3% and 17%, respectively, of the labour force (see table 2).

The absolute number of business failures increased steadily from 1960 to 1985, when it reached a peak at 18,876 failures per year. Since then, the number of business failures has decreased considerably, to 15,936 in 1988 (Institut der deutschen Wirtschaft, 1989).

The long-term evolution of numbers of self-employed persons was analyzed by the Rheinisch-Westfaelisches Institut für Wirtschaftsforschung in 1988. Between 1960 and 1981, the number of self-employed persons fell continuously not only in the agricultural sector, which diminished as a whole, but also in the secondary and tertiary sectors. The proportion of self-employed persons with respect to the total work force decreased from 12.7% in 1960 to 9.5% in 1985. One of the main reasons for the decline in the secondary and teriary sectors was found to be the deterioration in the relative income position of self-employment with respect to salaried employment.

Organizational Structure

The structure of large joint-stock companies has undergone fundamental changes. An empirical study of 50 large joint-stock companies in the West German industrial sector showed that a process of decentralization of organizational structure has taken place between 1965 and 1975. Functional structures were subdivided into product- and market-oriented structures, and one-dimensional structures were replaced by multi-dimensional ones. This trend toward increasing complexity of organizational structures was the response to the growing complexity of the environment to which enterprises were exposed (Hoffmann, 1982). Most recently firms seem to be attempting to render their organizational structures – which have become inefficient due to excessive complexity – more transparent, without abandoning the principle of decentralized organization.

Typical steps toward greater transparency are reduction in multi-dimensional structures and creation of unambiguous fields of responsibility for management (Buehner, 1989).

The organization of production processes in industry has been rationalized considerably over the last few decades. The effort to reduce costs of storage of raw materials and of products led to the concept of "just-in-time" production. According to the first empirical studies, these new concepts of production logistics have led to a clear reduction in fixed overhead costs ("Handelsblatt", 1985; Olle, 1986).

Renate Hornung-Draus

References

Bretschneider, Joachim, et al., eds.
1990 *Handbuch einkommens-, vermögens- und sozialpolitischer Daten*. Loseblattsammlung. Köln: Bachem.

Buchwald, Wolfgang, et al.
1988 "Erste Ergebnisse der Arbeitsstättenzählung 1987." *Wirtschaft und Statistik*, no. 12, 837.

Buehner, Rolf
1989 "Strategie und Organisation. Neuere Entwicklungen." *Zeitschrift Führung und Organisation*, no. 4, 223.

Cramer, Ulrich
1987 "Klein- und Mittelbetriebe: Hoffnungsträger der Beschäftigungspolitik?" *Mitteilungen aus der Arbeitsmarkt- und Berufsforschung*, no. 1, 15.

Die Zeit
1988 "Die Schwäche der Riesen." *Die Zeit*, no. 32, August 5, 1988.

Gruhler, Wolfram
1984 *Wirtschaftsfaktor Mittelstand*. Köln: Deutscher Instituts-Verlag.

Handelsblatt
1985 "Just-in-time Produktion. Herausforderung für Hersteller und ihre Zulieferer." *Handelsblatt*, June 26, 1985.

Hoffmann, Friedrich, ed.
1982 "Organisationsstrukturen und ihre Einflußfaktoren." *Zeitschrift für betriebswirtschaftliche Forschung*, Sonderheft 13/81.

Institut der deutschen Wirtschaft
1989 *Zahlen zur wirtschaftlichen Entwicklung der Bundesrepublik Deutschland 1989*. Köln: Deutscher Instituts-Verlag.

Krueger-Hemmer, Christiane, et al.
1989 "Strukturergebnisse der Arbeitsstättenzählung vom 25. Mai 1987." *Wirtschaft und Statistik*, no. 7.

Olle, Werner
1986 "Neue Dimensionen der Produktionslogistik. Die Zukunft hat schon begonnen." *WSI-Mitteilungen*, no. 4, 312.

Perich, Robert
1989 "Unternehmensorganisation im Wandel. An der Schwelle zu einem neuen Organisationsverständnis." *Zeitschrift Führung und Organisation*, no. 1, 5.

Rheinisch-Westfälisches Institut für Wirtschaftsforschung
1988 "Die Entwicklung der Zahl der Selbständigen - Nur ordentliche Gewinne machen Risiko erträglich." *Handelsblatt*, April 12, 1988.

Table 1
Number of firms in 1970 and 1987

Type of enterprise	1970		1987	
	1,000	%	1,000	%
Industry	441	19.3	360	14.0
Commerce	732	32.0	707	27.4
Services[1]	577	25.3	859	33.3
Other sectors	535	23.4	655	25.4
Total	2,285	100	2,581	100

1. Only private enterprises and liberal professions.

Source: Statistisches Bundesamt, cited in Krüger-Hemmer, 1989.

Table 2
Firms and Employees according to legal forms of companies (in %)

Legal form	Companies	Employees
Companies with owners	91.14	35.3
Partnerships	5.8	24.8
Limited liability	1.8	15.3
Joint-stock	0.13	17.0
Co-operative	0.7	1.2
Other private legal forms	0.2	0.8
Public enterprises and foundations	0.23	5.6
Total	100	100

Source: Bretschneider et al. 1990, tab. M11.

Table 3
Evolution of small, medium, and large enterprises, 1968 - 1982

Item	1968	1968	1968	1982	1982	1982	Number of enterpr.-difference between 1968-1982
	Number of enter-prises	Pro-portion %	Prop. of turnover %	Number of enter-prises	Pro-portion %	Prop. of turnover %	
Small enterprises							
a) 12,000 - 250,000 DM turnover p.a.	1,300,692	78.7	9.7				
b) 20,000 - 500,000 DM turnover p.a.				1,278,513	73.0	6.1	-22,179
Medium enterprises							
a) 250,000 - 10 mill. DM turnover p.a.	340,762	20.6	32.7				
b) 500,000 - 25 mill. DM turnover p.a.				460,774	26.3	31.3	120,012
Large enterprises							
a) over 10 mill. DM turnover p.a.	10,954	0.7	57.7				
b) over 25 mill. DM turnover p.a.				13,071	0.7	62.6	2,117
Total	1,652,408	100.0	100.0	1,752,358	100.0	100.0	+99,950

Source: Gruhler, 1984, p. 38.

Figure 1
Number of firms and employed persons according to economic sectors[1]

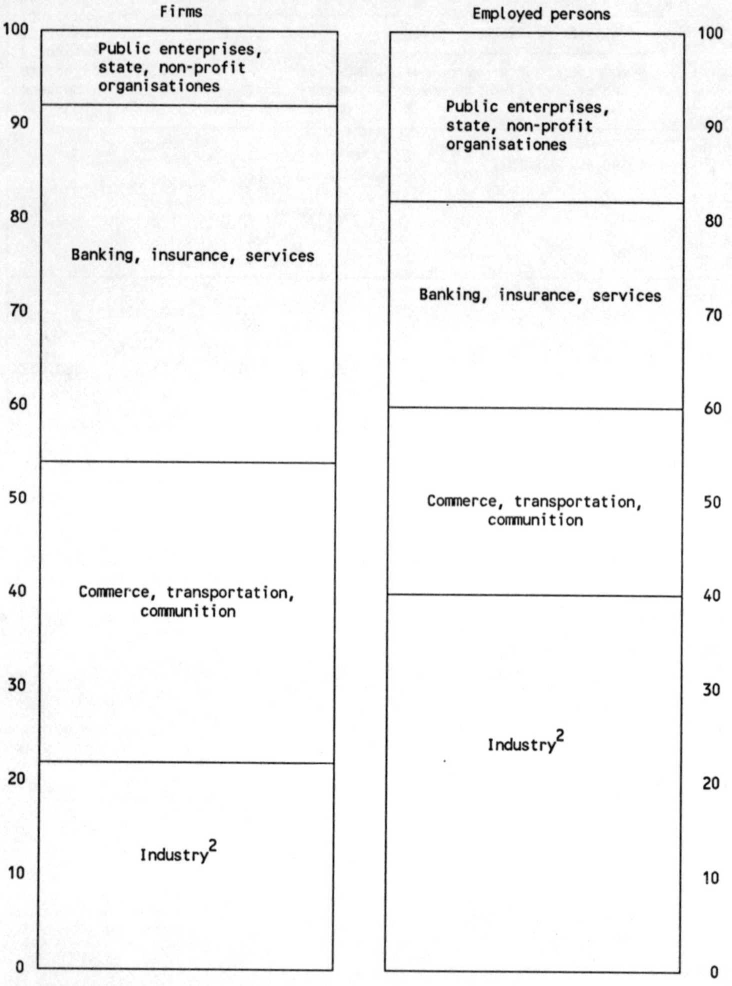

1. Provisional results.
2. Including certain firms in agriculture, forestry, fishery.

Source: Statistisches Bundesamt, cited in Buchwald, 1988, in Wirtschaft und Statistik, 1988.

6. Social Stratification

6.1 Occupational Status

After a decline during the 1970s, the economically active population is growing again. While the proportion of self-employed people and of workers has decreased, there is a considerable increase in the number of civil servants and salaried employees. There also seems to be a slight trend toward a shift from lower-level to intermediate and higher-level positions within the job hierarchy.

Population distribution in terms of labour-force participation and occupational status is of fundamental significance to the social stratification of a given society. In 1987, the economically active part of the total population (i.e., people either working or seeking employment) amounted to 46.1%, and 42.5% were actually working. Thus, more than one out of two inhabitants of the Federal Republic are not part of the labour force.

There have been changes in the labour-force participation rate since 1950. These changes, however, cannot be described in terms of a uniform trend. The overall labour-force participation rate reached a peak at 49% during the second half of the 1950s and declined to a minimum of 43% in the mid-1970s. Since then, the rate has risen again.

As the overall labour-force participation rate is influenced to a significant degree by the age structure of the population, an adjusted rate is a more valid indicator of changes in labour-force participation. The adjusted labour-force participation rate (i.e., the proportion of the population aged 15–64 that is economically active) increased from the 1950s until the mid-1960s, declined until the end of the 1970s, and has shown an upward trend since the beginning of the 1980s. In 1987, the rate was 82% for men and 54% for women.

The moderate net changes in the labour-force participation rate mask large-scale structural changes. Several factors caused a relative reduction in size of the economically active part of the population, the most important among them being the increase in number of years spent on education and training and the decline in the average age of retirement. On the other hand, the economically active part of the population increased due to the rising level of labour-force participation by women.

Distribution of the labour force by occupational status has drastically changed over the last 40 years. Between 1950 and 1987, the proportion of self-employed persons and of unpaid family workers shrank from one-third to one-tenth of all economically active persons. Currently, the proportion of self-employed persons seems to have stabilized, and self-employment – in traditional as well as new forms – regained popularity in the 1980s. The percentage of blue-collar workers in the economically active population has also declined considerably, from 49% in 1950 to 38% in 1988. This can be attributed to structural changes within economic sectors and the gradual transition from an industrial to a post-industrial society. Accordingly, the proportion of civil servants increased, particularly due to the developing welfare state and expansion of the educational system, but has been stable since the mid-1970s, while the proportion of salaried employees is still growing.

Representative data on distribution of the economically active population by position in the job hierarchy at plant level are available only for a limited number of points in time in the 1980s. According to these data, around two-thirds of all employed persons are semi-skilled or skilled workers and salaried employees who carry out jobs that consist of clearly defined tasks. About one out of six employees is in charge of more highly qualified work, comprising executive duties on the lower hierarchical level. Fewer than 10% of all employed persons work in management positions. In the short period between 1982 and 1985, the figures indicate a slight tendency toward a shift from lower-level positions to intermediate and higher-level positions.

These structural changes in the labour force are accompanied by a range of other changes which affect not only working conditions and social security but attitudes as well, and which will therefore have long-term implications for social stratification.

Heinz-Herbert Noll

References

Institut für Arbeitsmarkt- und Berufsforschung
1986 *Zahlenfibel*. Beitr. AB 101.

–
1988 *Zahlenfibel*. Beitr. AB 101.

Statitisches Bundesamt, ed.
ann. pbl. *Statistisches Jahrbuch*. Stuttgart/Mainz: Kohlhammer.

Zapf, Wolfgang
1989 "Sozialstruktur und gesellschaftlicher Wandel in der Bundesrepublik Deutschland." In W. Weidenfeld, and H. Zimmermann, *Deutschland-Handbuch*. Bonn: Bundeszentrale für politische Bildung.

Table 1
Population by labour-force participation

Year	Resident population (in 1,000)	Persons in the labour force (in 1,000)	Gainfully employed persons (in 1,000)	Labour-force participation rate[1] (in %)	Adjusted labour-force participation rate[2] (in %)
1950	47,850	21,960	20,376	45.9	68.7
1954	49,688	23,620	22,395	47.5	65.8
1960	55,433	26,518	26,247	47.8	70.3
1964	57,971	26,922	26,753	46.4	70.0
1970	60,651	26,817	26,668	44.2	69.5
1975	61,829	26,884	25,810	43.5	67.9
1980	61,566	27,217	26,328	44.2	66.7
1985	61,175	27,835	25,531	45.5	67.9
1987[3]	61,170	28,200	25,971	46.1	68.2

1. Author's computation: percentage of the resident population in the labour force (i.e., working or seeking employment).
2. Percentage of the resident population of working age (15-65 years) in the labour force.
3. Preliminary figures.

Source: Statistisches Bundesamt, various volumes.

Table 2
Gainfully employed persons by occupational status (in %)

Year	Self-employed persons	Unpaid family workers	Civil servants	Salaried employees	Workers
1950	15.9	15.5	4.2	15.8	48.6
1955	13.8	12.3	4.7	18.4	50.7
1960	12.7	10.2	5.6	23.5	48.1
1965	10.9	8.2	6.6	26.0	48.4
1970	10.1	6.5	7.3	29.3	46.9
1975	9.9	5.6	8.4	33.1	43.0
1980	8.6	3.4	8.4	37.2	42.3
1985	9.1	2.7	8.9	39.5	39.8
1987	8.9	2.4	8.7	40.7	39.2
1988	8.9	2.3	8.7	42.1	38.1

Source: Statistisches Bundesamt, various volumes.

Table 3
Persons in dependent employment by position in the job hierarchy on plant level (in %)

Position	1982	1985
Managing director, factory manager	1.8	1.8
Head of department, attorney	2.0	2.2
Area manager, proxy	1.8	2.2
Qualified employee, senior craftsman	11.7	12.2
Employee in charge of a specific area foreman	13.5	14.8
Employee in charge of clearly defined tasks, skilled manual worker	29.3	30.4
Clerical worker, unskilled manual worker	38.4	36.4
Position not reported	1.7	-

Source: Institut Arbeitsmarkt- und Berufsforschung, 1986, 1988; author's computations.

6.2 Social Mobility

In the Federal Republic of Germany, chances of intergenerational and career mobility have increased. This improvement was caused not only by structural changes in the economy but also by an expansion of educational opportunities. Although there are indications that society has become more open, social opportunities are far from being equally distributed. There is still a rather strong correlation between social status and social origin, even if educational attainment is controlled.

Intergenerational Mobility

The nature and strength of the relationship between social status and social origin provide information on how open a society is and to what extent social opportunities are equally or fairly distributed. In this respect, the following four questions seem to be particularly interesting: What proportion of sons from a particular social background remain in their fathers' status categories? What are the chances for sons from various social backgrounds to be upwardly mobile from one generation to the next? How great is the risk of downward mobility from generation to generation? Are differences in opportunities between different groups of social origin also observable among employed persons with the same level of education?

To observe changes in intergenerational mobility over time, two age cohorts have been compared: employed males born between 1931 and 1939 and between 1940 and 1948. The occupational status in 1970 in 1979, for the older and younger cohorts, respectively, are compared with the occupational status of the father when the respondent was 15 years old. The categories of occupational status were arranged in such a way that, with the exception of self-employed positions, they constitute a hierarchical order. Thus, movements between categories can be interpreted as upward and downward mobility. The analyses are restricted to employed males, since it is impossible to compare the occupational status of daughters and their fathers due to gender-specific differences in the occupational structure.

Intergenerational mobility is structurally enforced by the contraction and expansion of status categories. The occupational categories which, in the comparison of fathers and sons, contracted over time are, in particular, self-employed occupations, largely in agriculture, as well as jobs for unskilled manual workers. In addition, a decline in the number of skilled manual workers and lower-level white-collar workers becomes apparent for the younger cohort. Strong tendencies toward expansion, on the other hand, can be observed for intermediate and high-level white collar jobs and civil-service positions. These structural changes strongly affect the possibilities of status transmission as well as intergenerational upward and downward mobility.

The status-transmission rate indicates the proportion of sons remaining in their fathers' status categories. This proportion varies, according to the social background of the groups under examination, between 10% (foremen and lower-level white-collar workers) and 35% (skilled manual workers). As expected, the transmission rate decreases in the contracting status categories, but remains largely stable or even increases slightly in categories in which the proportion of persons employed is on the rise.

Social upward mobility denotes any movement into a higher status category (not including the self-employed). As can be seen in table 1, the lower the father's social status, the greater the chances of intergenerational upward mobility. This result expresses, above all, the "floor" and "ceiling" effects: he who starts at the bottom can either be upwardly mobile or keep his original status; he who starts at the top has little room left for further upward mobility. A comparison of the cohorts shows that, with the exception of the highest status group, the chances for upward mobility improved for all occupational positions. This tendency can be discerned even if upward mobility is more narrowly defined – that is, if movements only to non-adjacent categories are taken into consideration.

Accordingly, the risk of intergenerational downward social mobility decreased for the younger of the two cohorts considered here. As expected, the risk tends to be greater the higher the father's status. The risk of "social degradation," that is, downward mobility into the group of unskilled and semi-skilled manual workers, is quite low for middle-class sons.

Table 2 shows the unequal distribution of opportunities to gain access to high-status positions in white-collar or civil-service occupations: only 10% of the sons of manual workers born between 1940 and 1948 had such access, but more than 50% of the sons of higher-level civil servants or white-collar workers held a corresponding position in 1979.

As table 2 also shows, the impact of social background seems to be less if persons with similar educational degrees are considered – in this case, sons with diplomas qualifying them for college entrance (*Abitur* or *Fachhochschulreife*). However, even for persons who have similar educational degrees, the impact of social background on chances of access to higher occupational positions is weakened but not totally eradicated. Moreover, the educational degree obtained is in itself substantially determined by social background.

Regardless of educational degree, the correlation between chances of access to high-status positions and social background was the same for both cohorts. However, the chances of attaining higher-level white-collar or civil-service positions increased for members of the younger cohort because the number of corresponding positions increased. The expansion of availability of these positions benefited disproportionately those social groups which formerly had only comparatively limited chances of access to such positions, such as sons of workers and farmers. The improvement in chances for those groups can be attributed both to changes in the occupational structure and to a disproportionate increase in degrees of higher education.

Intragenerational Mobility

Intragenerational mobility denotes changes in occupational status within individuals' working life. Of special interest in this context are the chances and risks of different occupational groups to be upwardly or downwardly mobile during their occupational career.

At this point we limit ourselves to observation of the first 10 to 14 years of careers after entry into working life, and we compare two cohorts: persons who were employed for the first time between 1956 and 1960 and persons who were employed for the first time between 1965 and 1969.

The proportion of upward mobility expresses, first of all, the floor and ceiling effects: unskilled workers have the best changes of upward mobility and higher-level civil servants have the worst chances (see table 3). This pattern holds even if only movements into higher and not adjacent status categories are defined as upward mobility. The proportion of upward mobility among unskilled manual workers, however, is considerably reduced under this definition. The chances of upward mobility, as defined in this narrow sense, are by far the greatest for lower-level civil servants. Comparing the two cohorts, one can observe that the chances of upward mobility tend to improve slightly, and even significantly for particular groups.

Occupational downward mobility is less frequent in comparison to upward mobility. When interpreting the relatively low proportion of downward mobility, however, one has to take into account that the indicators used to measure intragenerational mobility cover only a part of occupational life and that the risk of occupational downward mobility might increase in later stages of the occupational career, which are not considered here.

Heinz-Herbert Noll

References

Noll, Heinz-Herbert
1987 "Social Stratification and Mobility." In *German Social Report. Social Indicators Research*, 19, 5-171.

Table 1
Intergenerational mobility: upward and downward rates of male employees, 32 - 39 years old (in %)

Item	Upward mobility				Downward mobility			
			Into non-adjacent higher categories				Into unskilled blue collar positions	
	1970[1]	1979[1]	1970	1979	1970	1979	1970	1979
Occupational status of fathers								
Farmer	*	-	-	-	-	-	24	18
Unskilled workers	76	88	44	57	-	-	-	-
Semiskilled workers	55	68	22	40	7	3	-	-
Skilled workers	37	47	30	40	17	12	17	12
Foremen, low-level civil servants	40	52	36	48	44	30	10	11
Supervisors, low-level white-collar	33	46	9	23	48	34	16	9
Salaried supervisors, middle-level white collar and civil servants	25	38	13	16	30	22	6	5
High-level white-collar, upper-level civil servants	24	25	-	-	46	36	4	1
Top white-collar, high-level civil servants	-	-	-	-	64	50	1	2
Self-employed, farmers excluded	-	-	-	-	-	-	8	4

* No indicator defined.

1. 1970: Occupational status of birth cohort 1931-1939 in 1970 in comparison with fathers' status.
1979: Occupational status of birth cohort 1940-1949 in 1979 in comparison with fathers' status.

Data base: Qualifikation und Berufsverlauf, 1979; author's calculation.

Table 2
Accessibility of high-status white-collar/civil-service positions - male employees, 31 - 39 years old (in %)

Item	All sons 1970[1]	Sons with college entrance diplomas, 1970[1]	All sons 1979[1]	Sons with college entrance diplomas, 1979[1]
Occupational status of fathers				
Farmer	4	52	18	84
Manual workers	5	63	11	74
Supervisors, low-level white-collar and civil servants	12	75	22	65
Salaried supervisors, middle-level, white-collar and civil servants	25	72	38	73
High-level white-collar, upper-level civil servants	50	82	55	75
Top white-collar, high-level civil servants	52	71	54	68
Self-employed, excluding farmers	18	60	25	55
Total	12	69	23	69
N of cases	3,979	319	3,470	542

1. 1970: Occupational status of birth cohort 1931-1939 in 1970 in comparison with fathers` status. 1979: Occupational status of birth cohort 1940-1949 in 1979 in comparison with fathers` status.

Data base: Qualifikation und Berufsverlauf, 1979; author's calculations.

Table 3
Ratios of upward and downward intragenerational mobility - male employees, 10 - 14 years after entry into working life (in %)

Item	Upward mobility				Downward mobility			
			Into non-adjacent categories				Into non-adjacent categories	
	1970[1]	1979[1]	1970	1979	1970	1979	1970	1979
Occupational status of fathers								
Unskilled workers	58	62	32	33	2	-	-	-
Semiskilled workers	25	32	10	23	1	0	-	-
Skilled workers	30	36	24	29	10	8	1	1
Foremen, low-level civil servants	27	50	25	48	10	5	1	3
Supervisors, low-grade white-collar	38	41	7	16	10	9	8	5
Salaried supervisors, middle-grade white-collar and civil servants	25	37	12	19	5	4	4	4
High-grade white-collar, upper-grade civil servants	15	23	-	-	12	7	4	2
Top white-collar, high-grade civil servants	-	-	-	-	19	5	14	3

1. 1970: Occupational status of older cohort (first employment between 1956 and 1960) in 1970 in comparison with first occupational status. 1979: Occupational status of younger cohort (first employment between 1965 and 1970) in 1979 in comparison with first occupational status.
2. No indicator defined.

Data base: Qualifikation und Berufsverlauf, 1979; author's calculations.

6.3 Economic Inequality

Although the standard of living in terms of income and wealth has improved tremendously, neither inequality of income nor inequality of wealth has been reduced considerably during the last 40 years.

Even in so-called post-industrial societies, which are supposed to be characterized by post-materialistic values, the problem of economic inequality has retained much of its significance. Income and wealth continue to be resources which – being universally convertible – determine a person's standard of living and his or her opportunities in life.

Economic inequality consists of several dimensions. We limit ourselves here to distribution of income and wealth in private households, which are of particular importance as far as social stratification is concerned.

In Germany, monthly disposable household income multiplied more than tenfold since 1950, from 357 DM to 3,705 DM in 1985 (see table 1). This enormous increase in income resulted in a historically unique improvement in the standard of living. The rate of increase was highest in the 1950s, slowed in the 1960s, and came to a standstill at the beginning of the 1980s.

In comparison, income distribution has changed much less over time. Measured by the Gini Co-efficient, the inequality in distribution of disposable household incomes has only been slightly reduced during the last 40 years. The same result is obtained when income distribution is analysed by quintile. The lowest quintile's share of total household incomes amounted to 5.4% in 1950 and to 7.4% in 1985. The highest quintile, which contains the fifth of households with the highest incomes, had a 45.2% share of total household incomes in 1950, and a 43% share in 1985. The skew of the distribution did not change over time either.

At present, it is difficult to judge whether the inequality in distribution of income has still the social meaning it had in the past, as the overall income level has increased considerably. One might argue, for example, that the rise in overall income level has resulted in a major increase in standard of living and in opportunity so that, in comparison, the remaining differences have lost significance (Beck, 1983). Bell (1976), on the other hand, claims that the evolution of rising expectations is accompanied by an evolution of rising resentments. According to his hypothesis, an amelioration of the economic situation would probably foster growing attention and sensitivity to the remaining inequalities.

A major income-inequality problem is poverty, which has not completely vanished, even in the richest Western societies, despite increases in income and a highly developed system of welfare institutions. The size of the poor population, however, depends on how poverty is defined and where the poverty line is drawn. Definitions based on institutional standards are not very suitable for international comparisons. In Germany, for example, the fact that someone's income is lower than the social-assistance benefit rate is frequently used as an indicator of poverty. Therefore, a concept which defines poverty in relative terms, as income below a certain percentage of the average income, is clearly preferable.

In 1983, 4.4% of the German population fell under the poverty line defined as 40% of the demand-oriented average per-capita household-income (see table 2). After a decrease up to the mid-1970s, the extent of poverty has since increased and once again become a topic of socio-political concern. According to recent empirical findings, unemployment is a major cause of this phenomenon (Hauser & Klein, 1985; Klein, 1986).

Along with income distribution, wealth distribution is a central dimension of economic inequality. In registering private wealth, official statistics differentiate between financial assets and tangible assets. Financial assets comprise deposits in savings accounts, life-insurance policies, savings with building societies, and securities; they do not comprise, however, deposits in current accounts and cash. Tangible assets primarily consist of productive property, land, and buildings, as well as – in the broader sense of the term – consumer durables such as jewelry, furniture, and cars. Net wealth is calculated by balancing gross wealth against debts.

In line with the rise in income level, the wealth that private households have at their disposal has grown. Wealth distribution and total net wealth have increased for all relevant types of assets over time. The most widely spread form of wealth creation is deposits in savings accounts. In 1983, 90% of all households had a savings account, compared to 60% in 1963 (see table 3). Apart from private savings accounts, life-insurance policies, which two out of three households had in 1983, are the most popular form of wealth creation, followed by land and buildings (46%), savings with building societies (40%), and securities (30%).

Each form of wealth is distributed more or less unevenly. The inequality in wealth distribution is (if productive property is not included in the analysis) most distinct as far as securities and land and buildings are concerned. The lowest concentration can be observed in deposits in savings accounts, life-insurance policies, and savings with building societies. The most marked differences can be found between households of self-employed persons and households of employees. In comparison, differences are less pronounced between occupational groups of employees. Workers' households, however, typically have less property than do households of salaried employees and civil servants. In 1983, households of self-employed persons outside the agricultural sector had average net financial assets of 36,200 DM, whereas workers' households on average had only 14,800 DM. Among households of self-employed persons, 72% had land or buildings in 1983, whereas only 50% of workers' households had such assets. Land and buildings owned by households of self-employed persons had a basic assessed value of

85,000 DM on average, a figure that is more than twice as high as that for workers' households. We should bear in mind, though, that self-employed persons normally have to make financial provisions for their old age by private means.

There is no evidence that the inequality in wealth distribution has significantly decreased over time. Although there is a lack of studies covering the entire period, so that an evaluation can be only tentative, available information indicates that the degree of concentration of wealth and the differences between the social groups under study have remained constant, or have even increased – at least for some forms of wealth.

Heinz-Herbert Noll

References

Beck, Ulrich
1983 "Jenseits von Klasse und Stand?" In R. Kreckel, ed., *Soziale Ungleichheiten*. Sonderband 2, Soziale Welt, 35-74. Göttingen: Schwartz.

Bell, Daniel
1976 *Die nachindustrielle Gesellschaft*. Frankfurt am Main/New York: Campus.

Bretschneider, Joachim, J. Husmann, and F. Schnabel
1988 *Handbuch einkommens-, vermögens- und sozialpolitischer Daten*. Köln: Bachem.

Deutsches Institut für Wirtschaftsforschung
n.d. *Wochenberichte.*

Glatzer, Wolfgang
1989 "Die materiellen Lebensbedingungen in der Bundesrepublik Deutschland." In W. Weidenfeld, and H. Zimmermann, eds., *Deutschlandhandbuch*, 276-291. Bonn: Bundeszentrale für politische Bildung.

Hauser, Richard, and Thomas Klein
1985 "Verarmung durch Arbeitslosigkeit." In S. Leibfried, and F. Tennstedt, *Politik der Armut und die Spaltung des Sozialstaats*, 213-248. Frankfurt am Main: Suhrkamp.

Hauser, Richard, and Peter Semrau
1985 *Low Income Groups and the Poor in Germany 1962 - 1983*. Unpublished paper. Frankfurt am Main.

Hornung-Draus, Renate
1989 "Das Vermögen der privaten Haushalte in der Bundesrepublik Deutschland: Bestand, Entwicklung und Verteilung." In *Jahrbücher für Nationalökonomie und Statistik*, 206/1, 18-47. Stuttgart.

Klein, Thomas
1986 *Sozialer Abstieg und Verarmung von Familien durch Arbeitslosigkeit*. Frankfurt am Main/New York: Campus.

Statistisches Bundesamt, ed.
1989 *Datenreport 1989*. Bonn: Bundeszentrale für politische Bildung.

Table 1
Disposable income of private households in the Federal Republic of Germany, 1950 to 1985

Item	1950	1960	1970	1980	1981	1985
Mean DM/Month	357	838	1,581	3,158	3,279	3,705
Gini coefficient	0.396	0.380	0.392	-	0.347	0.344
Quintiles share						
1st Quintile %	5.4	6.0	5.9	6.9	7.2	7.4
2nd-4th Quintile %	49.4	50.1	48.5	49.9	50.4	49.6
5th Quintile %	45.2	43.9	45.6	43.3	42.4	43.0

Source: Deutsches Institut für Wirtschaftsforschung - Wochenberichte.

Table 2
Number of persons in poverty and poverty ratio

Relative poverty 40 % of equivalent income[1]	1963	1969	1973	1978	1983
Number of persons (in 1,000)	3,252	1,481	881	876	1,063
Poverty ratio (in %)	5.7	2.7	1.4	1.6	2.0

1. Persons living outside institutions with incomes below 40% of the weighted average disposable income. Weighted using proportions of cost-of-living allowances according to Social Assistance Law for individual household members. German persons only; excluding institutionalized population, excluding housholds with high income.

Source: Hauser & Semrau, 1985.

Table 3
Forms of wealth of private housholds by social status of the head of household[1]

Item	Year	Total number	Percentage of households with				
		Of households (in 1,000)	Deposits in savings accounts	Life insurance policies	Savings with building societies	Securities	Land and buildings
Farmer	1962/63	1,097	63.0	37.0	11.1	5.0	-
	1969	785	88.7	66.1	31.4	14.6	96.2
	1973	620	89.4	67.9	47.4	14.0	92.3
	1983	393	92.7	77.4	60.0	28.2	92.7
Self-employed	1962/63	1,846	65.1	64.0	29.1	20.0	-
	1969	1,634	91.3	87.3	45.3	34.1	65.6
	1973	1,477	90.7	88.1	57.8	36.7	67.4
	1983	1,369	88.4	83.7	55.5	41.0	72.3
Civil servant	1962/63	1,097	71.7	53.0	23.1	15.0	-
	1969	1,241	97.3	78.8	43.7	27.7	38.6
	1973	1,352	96.4	79.6	62.4	30.1	41.4
	1983	1,527	95.8	77.2	68.2	33.9	54.0
Salaried employee	1962/63	2,632	72.6	49.0	17.0	17.0	-
	1969	3,591	95.0	80.2	33.4	30.6	34.6
	1973	4,296	96.0	80.5	48.9	35.1	37.0
	1983	5,147	93.5	74.7	54.1	36.7	48.0
Worker	1962/63	6,160	56.7	47.0	8.8	3.0	-
	1969	6,333	89.8	83.6	19.6	10.7	36.6
	1973	6,000	94.1	84.3	36.6	14.5	40.5
	1983	5,025	92.8	80.9	54.0	24.4	49.9
Not employed	1962/63	5,448	54.0	22.0	5.0	10.0	-
	1969	6,961	80.6	66.3	10.3	17.8	30.3
	1973	7,395	84.4	63.7	16.1	21.5	29.9
	1983	9,403	87.4	57.6	17.6	27.3	35.6
All households	1962/63	18,280	60.1	41.0	12.0	10.0	-
	1969	20,545	88.1	76.5	22.8	19.6	38.8
	1973	21,141	90.9	75.8	35.4	23.6	39.5
	1978	22,054	91.1	70.0	37.3	26.3	43.6
	1983	23,456	90.3	66.8	40.0	29.6	45.5

1. German households only; excluding private households inside institutions; excluding households with monthly incomes of 10,000 DM (1969), 20,000 DM (1978), 25,000 DM or more (1983).

Source: Bretschneider et. al., 1988.

6.4 Social Inequality

In terms of subjective class identification, more than half of the adult population see themselves as belonging to the middle class. Over the last 10 years there has been a weak trend toward a diminishing working-class affiliation, as well as a minor increase in middle- or upper-class affiliation.

Social inequality has many dimensions and meanings. One common way to look at it is in terms of subjective class identification. Identification with a social class indicates where people see their own position within the hierarchical structure of a society, to which social milieu they think they belong, and from which point of view they look at society and participate in social life.

In 1988, 27% of the adult population saw their own position as being in the working class, 57% as being in the middle class, and 14% as being in the upper-middle und upper classes. Only a small percentage (3%) did not identify themselves with any of these classes.

Over the ten-year period of 1978 to 1988, there was a trend toward a slightly diminishing affiliation with the working-class, as well as a minor increase in the number of people grouping themselves in the upper-middle or upper classes. By and large, however, the distribution of subjective class identification did not change.

As expected, there is a rather strong relationship between socioeconomic status and subjective class identification (see table 1). For example, two-thirds of the self-employed classify themselves as belonging to the middle class, and one-third to the upper-middle or upper class. Only 2%, however, identify with the working class. On the other hand, a majority, though not all, of those currently (employees) or formerly (pensioners) employed as blue-collar workers still consider themselves to belong to the working class.

When comparing different groups of workers, we find that the working-class identification is strongest among the unskilled. A growing percentage of workers seeing themselves as belonging to the middle class, however. In 1988, five out of ten skilled workers and foremen group themselves with middle-class people. Further analyses revealed that middle-class affiliation by blue-collar workers is not only a matter of skill, but is also more likely if workers are house-owners and are not employed in big industry.

Significant numbers of people who identify themselves with the upper-middle or upper class can be found not only among the self-employed but also among civil servants, primarily those in senior positions, higher-level salaried employees, pensioners, and students.

Heinz-Herbert Noll

References

Noll, Heinz-Herbert
1987 "Social Stratification and Mobility." In German Social Report. *Social Indicators Research 19*.

Zapf, Wolfgang, Heinz-Herbert Noll, and Roland Habich
1989 "Soziale Schichtung und soziale Lagen." In Statistisches Bundesamt, ed., *Datenreport 1989*. Bonn: Bundeszentrale für politische Bildung.

Table 1
Socioeconomic status and subjective class identification

Socioeconomic status	Total		Working class		Perceived class membership					
					Middle class		Higher middle upper class		"No" class	
	1978	1988	1978	1988	1978	1988	1978	1988	1978	1988
Self-employed, family workers	4	5	9	2	68	62	16	35	7	1
Civil servants	6	5	6	4	71	56	22	37	1	3
Upper-, high-level white-collar	7	8	10	7	71	67	19	22	1	4
Low-, middle-level white-collar	13	12	16	15	78	71	7	10	0	4
Skilled workers, foremen, supervisors	11	8	62	49	38	48	1	3	0	1
Unskilled, semiskilled workers	7	5	75	62	24	31	1	1	0	6
Pensioners-formerly blue-collar	8	7	70	62	28	36	0	1	3	1
Pensioners-formerly other	10	11	15	11	71	72	11	13	2	3
Housewives, - 59	18	18	27	30	61	54	11	15	1	1
Housewives, 60 +	8	8	43	35	47	55	8	7	2	3
Students	6	6	5	8	64	56	26	29	5	7
Apprentices	1	3	34	24	46	65	20	10	0	0
Unemployed persons	1	3	49	50	42	45	2	3	7	2
Other	1	2	17	22	77	50	6	25	0	3
Total	100	100	32	27	57	57	10	14	2	3

Database: Wohlfahrtssurveys, 1978 and 1988; author's calculation.

7. Social Relations

7.1 Conflict

Industrial conflicts in the Federal Republic of Germany are well institutionalized and are determined by the generally accepted interests of trade unions and employers' associations. Following a short phase of stronger political conflict after the World War II, the party system was formed, into which the Green Party was integrated in the 1980s. There is thus a stable system that reflects the general consensus regarding political, economic, and cultural institutions. "Classic" cultural conflicts have almost disappeared in West Germany. The women's movement was not the least of the influences that pushed the gender conflict into the public consciousness. In addition, awareness of ecological and technological risks increased, which has led to a burgeoning of conflicts concerning the dangers of modern civilization.

Industrial Conflict

In World War II, German society experienced extremely violent outgroup conflict in parallel with violent suppression of internal conflict. After the war, the country was tired of social conflict, and was not able to engage in conflicts in the face of military occupation by the allied forces, which had divided the country into zones and taken over its administration.

Industrial conflict was mitigated during the 1940s by the common cause of business and labour against plans to deconstruct and decentralize the German iron and steel industry by the winning powers. In 1947, leading managers offered a codetermination model to the newly constituted confederated trade union.

Nevertheless, trade unions had to threaten to strike before codetermination in iron and coal industry was passed as a law in 1951. This law was the only visible success in the trade unions' and Social Democrats' efforts to democratize the economy of postwar Germany. One year later, they failed in their attempt to extend "parity" codetermination from the iron and coal sector to other industries.

The short (two-day) strike could not prevent the passing, in 1952, of the *Betriebsverfassungsgesetz* (Works Constitution Act), which provided for workers' representatives comprising only one-third (instead of one-half) of the members of the supervisory boards. Under this law, at the plant level, workers' representatives in the *Betriebsrat* (workers' council) have to cooperate "peacefully" with management for the sake of the enterprise. The "workers' struggle" in Germany's "dual system" of industrial relations is restricted to the context of collective bargaining – when bargaining at the industry level fails.

This far-reaching institutionalization of industrial conflict within enterprises, as well as integration of workers' interests in a confederation of trade unions (eliminating inter-union conflict) and the definition of common interests by trade unions and employers' associations, accounts for the fact that the Federal Republic, in historical and international comparison, shows only a small amount of labour conflict. In the period before World War I (1900–1914), 10 times as many work days per year were lost by strikes and lock-outs, and between the wars almost 20 times as many were lost, as during the years 1950–1980. The average duration of strikes continously declined, from 32.2 days (German Empire) to 14.6 days (Weimar Republic), and finally to 5.8 days (Federal Republic) (see table 1).

Nevertheless, there is no clear-cut trend in the Federal Republic toward an actual diminution of workers' struggles. Strike activity was high in the 1950s, dropped considerably in the long prosperous period of the 1960s, rose again in the 1970s, and was remarkably low in the 1980s, except for 1984, when there was the most strike and lockout activity in the history of the Federal Republic (see tables 2 and 3).

Although in the 1940s and 1950s there was much programmatic engagement in political issues – for planning and democratization of the economy, for nationalization of basic industries, against remilitarization and atomic weapons – trade unions, with the exception of a two-day protest in 1952 and a one-day protest in 1955 in favour of codetermination, never called a political strike. The main reasons for strikes were wages and working conditions.

In 1969, wildcat strikes indicated employees' dissatisfaction with the results of collective bargaining, and trade-union leaders started to represent interests more aggressively. In the late 1970s, primarily in the metal and printing industries, there were numerous strikes protesting against growing rationalization, increasingly accompanied by lockouts by employers. The early 1980s were marked by conflicts over the shortening of working hours, culminating in large strikes in 1984 in the above-mentioned industries (Müller-Jentsch, 1986). Amazingly, trade unions were able to mobilize their members even in times of unemployment by arguing that fighting for the 35-hour week was synonymous with fighting for more jobs.

There are contradictory findings regarding shifting power relations in industrial conflict: on the one hand, unemployment, a tendency to deregulate work contracts, differentiation of interests, and individualization within the working class seem to weaken the position of trade unions in industrial conflict. On the other hand, despite recruitment problems, particularly in the modernized sector of the economy, there is no fragmentation of the union system and the unions exhibit remarkable stability and power, partly guaranteed by institutional means (Armingeon, 1988).

In the 1970s, trade unions tried to strengthen their position with *Schwerpunktstreiks* (exemplary strikes) in a few enterprises selected to represent a whole industry; their counterparts retaliated by locking out workers in many more enterprises, thereby exhausting the trade unions' financial resources. In the resulting conflict on the question of whether lockouts constitute a legitimate weapon in labour conflicts, the courts decided in favour of business.

In addition to collective wage conflicts on the level of whole industries and regions, there has always been, due to the character of institutionalized codetermination, widespread but mitigated conflict on working and social conditions within enterprises. It has recently been argued that decentralization of conflicts and sectoral bargaining are increasing, following the "computer revolution" and the new flexibility of plant production, which have led "to the formation of a new, independent bargaining set: the plant rationalization-protection policy" (Weinert, 1988, p. 285). Although there is a trend toward decentralization and mitigation of industrial conflict, it is not easy to quantify, nor to say whether this means a loss of significance for the unions' collective-bargaining policy.

Political Conflict

After the war and during the first decade of existence of the Federal Republic, political conflict referred to the economic and political order and to the national identity of the new state. Christian Democrats and Social Democrats, as the strongest political forces, shared consensus on elements of moderate socialism, involving nationalization of key industries and planning. The authoritarian legacy of the past was more strongly expressed by right-wing parties, which attracted around 15% of the vote, and the communist party, which garnered 5,7% of the vote in 1949. The success of the market economy in the Federal Republic and the formation of two German republics in 1949 provoked heavy conflicts in the 1950s regarding preservation of socialist elements of economic order, national reunification versus integration of the two states in the Western and Eastern bloc systems, respectively, and rearmament. The battle was lost by the Social Democrats, who, in 1959, adapted to the new situation with their *Godesberger Programm*, accepting a market economy and integration of the Federal Republic into the Western bloc. As early as 1957, extremist parties had disappeared from the federal parliament, due to illegalization, modification of electoral rules, and social and economic integration of the right- and left-wing electorate.

During the 1960s and 1970s, a three-party system was firmly established on the federal, state, and community levels. A routinization of political conflicts took place, mainly focusing on expansion of the welfare state and on national-security interests. Nevertheless, toward the end of the 1960s, the positive image of a society perfectly able to manage its distributive conflicts was shaken. The anti-authoritarian protest movement did not challenge basic democratic values, but rather asked for their implementation: against ratification of the Emergency Powers Act, against dispensing with political competition by the "big coalition" of Social Democrats and Christian Democrats (1966–1969), against concentration of media power in the Springer Publishing House, and against the war in Vietnam. In parallel to the anti-authoritarian movement, a right-wing nationalist party (NPD) got support and entered seven state parliaments between 1966 and 1969, but failed to achieve the 5% of the vote required for entrance into the federal parliament.

The 1970s were marked by a crisis in the welfare state and by growing skepticism regarding the risks and consequences of economic growth. In 1979, a new ecological party entered the political arena and, amazingly, succeeded in getting between 5% and 12% of the vote in state and federal parliaments. At the end of the 1980s, political conflict seemed to be established within a framework of two main parties (the Social Democrats and the Christian Democrats) and two small parties (the Liberals and the Greens), right-wing and left-wing extremism being "out." The ecological topics introduced by the Green Party have been taken over by the older, more established parties. The Greens, as the fourth and newest party, have brought about a revitalization of political life by introducing and institutionalizing ecological conflict not only on the federal and state levels, but particularly in community politics. The aspects of radical democracy – "grassroots democracy" and the "rotation principle" (the rotation of representatives within a single electoral period) – promoted by the new party almost got lost in the routine of parliamentary life.

Representative democracy, notwithstanding party scandals and political corruption, seems to be more firmly established than ever before in German history. There is no more value conflict about the legitimacy of basic political, economic, and cultural institutions in the Federal Republic.

Cultural conflicts

Cultural conflicts may be understood as conflicts between (or about) values and lifestyles, in contrast to distributive or interest conflicts, which always presuppose a common value orientation. Several cultural conflicts common to the German and European heritage have gradually disappeared since the founding of the Federal

Republic in 1949. First, as mentioned above, traditional ideological conflicts regarding the legitimacy of democratic and capitalist institutions have subsided; in contrast to the postwar period, there no longer seems to be an acceptable alternative to the learning and controlling functions of political and economic competition.

Second, the cleavage between Protestants and Catholics, once very pronounced in German society, lost its social importance due to postwar migration, which increased the proportion of Catholics from one-third to one-half of the Christian population, a dramatic decrease in church attendance, and a general secularization process which reduced differences between the two denominations.

Third, after the war, integration of refugees and displaced persons, amounting to almost one-third of the population, did not proceed without cultural conflict and economic tension – conflicts which were soon forgotten. As well, the integration of more than four million foreign workers between 1957 and 1973, most of them from southern Europe, was accomplished without hostility. It was only in the 1980s that the continuing de facto immigration of asylum-seekers and *Aussiedlern* (eastern Euopeans of German descent) was seen in connection with unemployment and the housing shortage, and caused anger and discussion about the Federal Republic becoming a "multicultural" society. Nevertheless, compared to the racism of the past and to xenophobic movements in other societies, the acceptance of the new ethnic diversity and the absence of manifest ethnic conflict in German society are remarkable. The German public is sensitive to, and rejects, expressions of hostility toward ethnic minorities.

On the other hand, three kinds of cultural conflict are new in the Federal Republic and have a considerable impact on social life. The first is the conflict between youth culture, as a mass phenomenon, and the rest of society. This conflict culminated in an anti-authoritarian movement in the late 1960s. Contrary to the complaints of this movement's veterans, the conflict did not fade away, but lives on in new issues: in the peace movement, and in the movements against ecological and technological risks and against the census of 1987–1988, which was felt to symbolize the dangers of an information-based society. The social basis of these conflicts is the growth of mass higher education, providing for a culture of social and humanistic ("post-material") values which differentiates it from and has gained strength with respect to the "older" culture of material values (Huber, 1988).

The second new conflict, that between the sexes – which may be considered a timeless phenomenon – has got a new cultural dimension. At first glance, it is a conflict about equal rights, and as such it is dealt with through the law (the Equal Rights Amendment in 1957, the Marriage Rights Amendments in 1957, reformed in 1977). However, it also reveals a value conflict between new and old ways of living together. Originating as a by-product of the anti-authoritarian movement and politicized in the feminist movement, its core, in the realm of private life, is the struggle between the male and the female definitions of partnership, family, and love. The character of this conflict can be seen in the changing meaning of divorce: in the postwar period, the high divorce rate arose from separation and estrangement due to the war – it did not indicate differences in respective definitions of family life. After a temporary decline, divorce rates have been rising again, revealing a basic and widening difference between the sexes as to aspirations and satisfaction with marriage: women are more dissatisfied with marriage than are men, they take the initiative for divorce, and they do not want to remarry (see 3.3, "Matrimonial Models"). The social basis for the new gender conflict is to be seen in the mass participation of women in the educational and employment systems. As well, women's increasing activities outside the home have created a specific women's culture (women's literature, women's studies, women's houses, etc.) which provide women with outside support in private conflicts.

A third type of cultural conflict appeared in the 1970s, and was institutionalized in the 1980s by the Green Party and numerous citizens' initiatives. It is the conflict of the value of economic and technological progress versus the value of a safe, healthy life within the framework of existing ecological systems. Within two decades, this conflict has led not only to large numbers of protest activities against large-scale technological projects such as nuclear power plants and airports, but also to the creation of ministries for environmental protection on the federal and state levels. A comparative study of risk consciousness between 1967 and 1987 shows that there has been a considerable increase in newspaper reports on conflicts over new technological and environmental risks (Schöneberg, 1989); furthermore, those "new" conflicts in turn stimulate conflicts over conventional risks (such as smoking and automobile traffic). Conflicts over the dangers of modern civilization, which were first expressions of a provocative youth culture, have deeply pervaded German society – to the degree that one sociological observer posits a transition from a class society to a risk society (Beck, 1986).

Conflict and Violence

A central theme of *The Process of Civilization* (Elias, 1976) states that force is eventually monopolized by government, thereby ceasing to qualify as an expression and immediate regulator of social conflict. Non-governmental force or violence loses its legitimacy in proportion to the stage of civilization. Should violence erupt in spite of this, it is then interpreted either as the failure or absence of institutionalized conflict regulation or as an indication of extreme conflict intensity. According to the Yale World Data Program using the *New York Times* Index of Conflict Events, riots (violent demonstrations or disturbances) occurred frequently between 1948 and 1952, when the institutionalization of conflict regulation was still slight, declined in number thereafter, then reached new peaks in 1968 – 1972 (a time of student revolt and anti-authoritarian movements) and 1978 – 1982 (see 10.3, "Social Movements"). Only during these periods do voilent incidents in the FRG exceed the average derived from a comparison of 15 democratic countries. The rest of the time, the Federal Republic has stayed around the middle in frequency of violent conflicts; generally, smaller countries show a lower conflict frequency (Taylor, 1983). Statistical records of the German states show a slight increase in the number of violent demonstrations, with a simultaneous decrease in proportion to the total number of demonstrations. Between 1975 and 1987, protest demonstrations clearly increased, thereby turning from an unconventional into a conventional form of conflict activity. The level of violence has dropped to a stable proportion of 4% of all recorded demonstrations (see table 4).

Karl Otto Hondrich

References

Armingeon, Klaus
1988 "Gesellschaftliche Entwicklung und ökonomischer, beschäftigungsstruktureller und politischer Wandel." *Soziale Welt*, 39, no. 4.

Beck, Ulrich
1986 *Risikogesellschaft. Auf dem Weg in eine andere Moderne*. Frankfurt am Main: Suhrkamp.

Elias, Norbert
1976 *Über den Prozeß der Zivilisation*. 2 vols. Frankfurt am Main: Suhrkamp.

Huber, Joseph
1988 "Mondraketen gegen Mütterzentren." *Die Zeit*, no. 42, 14.10.1988.

Kaase, Max
1987 *Politisch motivierte Gewaltanwendung junger Menschen in der Bundesrepublik Deutschland*. Gutachten für das Bundesministerium für Jugend, Frauen, Familie und Gesundheit. Mannheim.

Müller-Jentsch, Walther
1986 *Soziologie der industriellen Beziehungen*. Frankfurt am Main/New York: Campus.

Schöneberg, Ulrike
1989 *Risikobewußtsein im Spiegel der Presseberichterstattung. Inhaltsanalyse zweier Tageszeitungen in den Jahren 1967, 1977 und 1987*. Unveröffentl. Manuskript. Frankfurt am Main.

Taylor, Charles Lewis, and David A. Jodice
1983 *World Handbook of Political and Social Indicators*. Vol. II. New Haven/London: Yale University Press.

Weinert, Rainer
1988 "Betriebliche Rationalisierungsschutzpolitik. Ein Beitrag zur 'Dezentralisierung' kollektiv-vertraglicher Regelungen." *Soziale Welt*, 39, no. 3, 279-291.

Table 1
Labor-struggle statistics - historical comparison

Time period	Annual average		
	Strike participants (number of workers)	Strike volume (work days missed)	Average strike length (in days)
1900-1914 (German Empire)	247,200	7,970,800	32.2
1919-1932 (Weimar Republic)	948,700	13,852,100	14.6
1950-1980 (Federal Republic)	136,800	799,800	5.8

Source: Statistisches Jahrbuch für das deutsche Reich 1934, Statistisches Bundesamt, Fachserie 1, Reihe 4.3, früher: Fachserie A, Reihe 6; author's calculations, cited in Müller-Jentsch, 1986, p. 169.

Table 2
Relative strike volume in exemplary industrialized countries, 1968 - 1982

Country	Days missed per 1,000 employed persons in annual average[1]		
	1968-72	1973-77	1978-82
Italy	1,910	1,970	1,580
United States	1,530	1,100	880
Britain	996	700	1,040
France[2]	280	330	230
Japan	228	250	40
Sweden	64	20	440
West Germany	76	30	80

1. In economic sectors: mining, refining, construction, transportation.
2. Not including the strike volume of 1968, as no official numbers are available.

Source: International Labour Office, Geneva; (Depart. of), Employment Gazette, London, Jan. 1979 and March 1984, cited in Müller-Jentsch, 1986, p. 171.

Table 3
Labour-struggle statistics in West Germany 1950-1984

Yearly average	Companies concerned	Participating workers	Work days missed
In the 50's	1,023	139,734	985,385
In the 60's	226	81,662	316,310
In the 70's	595	198,278	1,164,775
Year			
1980	132	45,159	128,386
1981	297	253,334	58,398
1982	40	39,981	15,106
1983	114	94,070	40,842
1984	1,121	537,265	5,614,360

Source: Statistisches Bundesamt, Fachserie 1, Reihe 4.3, cited in Müller-Jentsch, 1986, p. 172.

Table 4
Patterns of demonstration incidence in West Germany

Year	Absolute number	% non-peaceful
1975	2,551	8.2
1976	2,956	6.5
1977	2,887	8.7
1978	2,980	7.0
1979	3,327	2.9
1980	4,471	3.2
1981	5,772	6.2
1982	5,313	4.3
1983	9,237	3.0
1984	7,453	3.1
1985	5,691	3.6
1986	7,143	3.7

Source: Kaase, 1987.

7.2 Negotiation

The Federal Republic of Germany, like all industrialized countries, has witnessed a standardization of conflict solutions. At second glance, the amount of legislative activity reputed to characterize modern German society has not increased in comparison with earlier periods; rather, negotiations are carried out in consensual agreements and court proceedings. This has affected conflict solving in social as well as industrial relations. German labour law is distinguished by several acts that oblige both sides to seek a peaceful solution. The Codetermination Act is one of the staples: "cooperative conflict arbitration," a form of bargaining secured within the framework of codetermination, appears to have staying power. The increasing decentralization of agreements and negotiations does not undermine the centralized collective trade agreements; rather, they complement each other. In fact, this kind of bargaining has expanded into the West German political system in the form of interlevel bargaining.

Social conflicts can be regulated or solved by violence, law (backed by governmental monopoly on force), dissolution of the social relationship (exit), and negotiations, in which the parties in conflict seek consensus (voice).

In industrialized countries, a general trend can be observed toward replacement of violent solutions by the above-mentioned three kinds of conflict regulation. German society is reputedly characterized by legal regulation. Nevertheless, the seeming linearity of increase in this area is misleading.

> Closer observation of the sheer number of legal provisions passed reveals that their production is not particularly high in the Federal Republic; on the contrary, there was in this respect a much higher production per annum or per legislative period during the Weimar Republic and the Nazi regime. Only when volume of publications in the *Gesetzgebungsblatt* (official publication of legal measures) is applied as a quantitative indicator does standardization activity in the Federal Republic reach or exceed that of earlier periods; that is, in comparison to the past, legal provisions are fewer but more voluminous. As observation of the Federal Republic alone shows, there has been no steady linear increase of legislation. In fact, the curve, when followed through the single legislative periods, runs quite a jagged course, with apexes in the first half of the 1960s and the middle 1970s. (Mayntz, 1987, p. 25)

The *Verrechtlichung* (regulation, or tying up of affairs in juridical and legislative measures) of social conflict is more obvious in the burgeoning number of court trials and the corresponding increase of out-of-court settlements (see 10.1,

"Dispute Settlement"). *Verrechtlichung* also tends to simplify exiting from conflict-ridden social relationships. This is particularly noticeable in the Divorce Reform of 1977, which allows for dissolution of a marriage without consent of the partner. Individual conflict solving is thus given priority over the more difficult task of consensual resolution – just as the wish to end a marriage is essentially placed ahead of the desire to preserve it.

This is not so in labour law: while voluntary resignation by the employee is subject to little restriction, dismissal by the employer has become increasingly expensive and difficult since the 1950s. Steps were taken to ease this problem in the Law for Promotion of Employment of 1985, allowing for temporary work contracts; as a result, the share of temporary employees doubled, from 4,1% in 1984 to 8,5% in 1986.

In industrial relations, the trend toward consensual agreements via negotiations is especially obvious. It is not a matter of substituting negotiations for legal regulation, but rather of doing what is already allowed for within the available legal framework. This legal framework for consensual solutions to industrial conflicts has been quite extensive from the very beginning of the Federal Republic. It constitutes a "dual system" of conflict arbitration: on the one side, the industry-wide bargaining processes and struggles between trade unions and employer associations over wages and working conditions are regulated by trade agreement law (*Tarifvertragsgesetz*). On the other side are the Codetermination Acts (*Mitbestimmungsgesetze*) of 1951 and 1976, the Workers' Council Act (*Betriebsratsgesetz* of 1952, revised in 1972), and the Federal Labour Representation Act (1974), all of which regulate labour-business conflicts by obliging both sides to seek a peaceful solution (see 10.1, "Dispute Settlement").

Though no statistics are available, there are indications that negotiations are covering more ground, thematically and quantitatively: extensive bargaining has managed necessary shut-downs and dismissals in the mining industry (since 1957) and in the steel industry (since 1966). In the course of these mediations, "social plans" and agreements for protection against industrial rationalization were worked out which have become integral parts of the standard mediation repertory for personnel threatened by dismissal.

Employee placement and training are also part of mediation within the framework of codetermination. Thus, job flexibility within firms increased (Bosch, 1988). There are employment agreements (between workers' councils and employers) on personnel placement in approximately 50% of businesses as a result of negotiations; informal agreements are even more common (Diekmann, 1985). The trend toward increases in and decentralization of mediation has been caused by technological innovations that are partially required of any business; as well, centralized regulation regarding collective trade agreements necessitate plant-level implementation programs (Weinert, 1988). Therefore, centralized and decentralized mediation usually complement rather than compete with each other.

Although there are conflicts between centralized trade-union politics and employee interests at the plant level – most recently regarding modular working hours – plant-level bargaining positions are reinforced by know-how and support from union headquarters. Therefore, it cannot be concluded that multiple, decentralized negotiations weaken the trade unions.

It appears more likely that cooperative conflict arbitration, as a particularly West German form of industrial relations, has the most staying power. "Cooperative conflict arbitration" refers to the constant mediation between management and the workers' councils on controversial points within the framework of codetermination, although this institutionalized form of bargaining often produces conflicts of its own. Cooperative conflict arbitration also means that possible conflicts between the interests of the directly concerned employees and industry-wide employee interests represented by the union headquarters are constantly being discussed and resolved.

The expansion of cooperative conflict arbitration via bargaining can also be observed in the political system of the Federal Republic. An example of such a structure is the political engagement (*Politikverflechtung*, a term coined by Fritz Scharpf) of the federal, county, and local levels. All three levels are forced to reach agreements on their contributions to the financing of common expenses (street construction, assistance to disadvantaged areas, etc.). A new and extensive field for cooperative conflict arbitration is environmental protection: ministries, government surveillance authorities, and courts negotiate with businesses concerning the acceptable degree of pollution involved in production. This results in an increase in contracts between enterprises and environment protection agencies, but also in heightened internal effectiveness of the civil service and in voluntary commitments by businesses (Beyer, 1986; Bohne, 1984). The need for formal and informal bargaining in this field is so great because definitive legal measures either are in need of reinterpretation or are entirely lacking.

Karl Otto Hondrich

References

Beyer, Wolfgang
1986 *Der öffentlich-rechtliche Vertrag. Informales Handeln der Behörden und Selbstpflichtungen Privater als Instrumente des Umweltschutzes*. Dissertation. Köln.

Bohne, Eberhard
1984 "Informales Verwaltungs- und Regierungshandeln als Instrument des Umweltschutzes." *Verwaltungs-Archiv. Zeitschrift für Verwaltungslehre, Verwaltungsrecht und Verwaltungspolitik*, 75, no. 4.

Bosch, Gerhard
1988 "Der bundesdeutsche Arbeitsmarkt im internationalen Vergleich: 'Eurosklerose' oder 'Modell Deutschland'?" *WSI-Mitteilungen*, no. 3.

Bundesministerium der Justiz
1987 *Mehr Recht durch weniger Gesetze*. Köln: Bundesanzeiger.

Diekmann, Jörn
1985 *Betriebsvereinbarungen zum Personaleinsatz*. WZB-Paper IIVG85/210. Berlin: Wissenschaftszentrum Berlin.

Mayntz, Renate
1987 "Mehr Recht durch weniger Gesetze? Gesellschaftswissenschaftliche Sicht." In Dieter Stempel, ed., *Mehr Recht durch weniger Gesetze?* Köln: Bundesanzeiger.

Rottleuthner, Hubert
1985 "Aspekte der Rechtsentwicklung in Deutschland. Ein soziologischer Vergleich deutscher Rechtskulturen." *Zeitschrift für Rechtssoziologie*, no. 6.

Scharpf, Fritz
1976 *Politikverflechtung*. Kronberg: Scriptor.

Weinert, Rainer
1988 "Betriebliche Rationalisierungsschutzpolitik." *Soziale Welt*, 39, no. 5, 279-291.

7.3 Norms of Conduct

Tolerance of different opinions and behaviour patterns has gained in importance as a value and as a pedagogic goal in West Germany. This is expressed within the family through permissiveness in parental attitudes toward children and in tolerance in the relationship between spouses. There has also been a relaxation of attitudes toward sexuality, accompanied by heightened disapproval regarding, for example, expressions of sexual violence. West German attitudes toward minorities are distinguished by more tolerance toward traditional victims of discrimination and by growing animosity toward some other groups: this can be seen as selective and calculated tolerance. The establishment of authorities and legislation protecting against libel and unauthorized circulation of personal data purportedly serves to defend privacy and self-development. Freedom of action is restricted in the name of individual rights and collective goals, as is illustrated in the setting of standards regarding punishable offences against the environment. These processes are not merely a relaxation of old norms, but the formulation of new norms.

Many behaviour patterns in everyday life, which in the past conformed to the straight and narrow, lost this standardized quality during the 1960s and 1970s. This does not mean that traditional behaviours have disappeared – it does, however, mean that alternatives have emerged and become socially acceptable. When a society permits a variety of opinions and behaviours within one and the same sphere of life, this can be comprehended as increasing tolerance. Tolerance has explicitly gained in importance as a value and a pedagogic goal in the Federal Republic: between 1967 and 1983, the percentage of those considering it essential "to respect other opinions and to be tolerant" went from 59% to 72% (see table 1). The rise in the value of tolerance would probably be even more obvious if we had access to comparable data from the 1950s, since the change in values gained strong momentum in the 1960s.

A special kind of tolerance has come about in the family resulting in the parental stance toward children known as permissiveness. Parents much more rarely demand conformity, modesty, and adherence to a religion from their children (table 1). On the contrary, not only are children's self-assertiveness and self-development tolerated, they are even encouraged. It has also become acceptable that spouses need not always share the same opinion; simultaneously, differences of opinion, especially concerning acquaintances, friends, and political questions, have multiplied (see tables 2 and 3). As family conflicts also have begun to increase (Noelle-Neumann & Piel, 1983; see also 3.3, "Matrimonial Models"), it can be said that social conflict and tolerance are two ways of dealing with growing social differences. Tolerance should not be regarded simply as a substitute for social conflict, but rather as possessing a conflict content of its own, since it is necessarily the product of repeated confrontation and discussion.

Not only within marriage, but also outside of marriage as an institution, there has been an increase in tolerant attitudes, and in permissible alternatives: marriage forfeited some of its high status during the period between 1949 and 1978 – more among women than among men (see table 4); more and more women believe that they can live quite happily and can have children without marriage (Allerbeck & Hoag, 1985). Extramarital sex was unconditionally approved of by only one in ten woman students in 1966 – but by six in ten in 1981!

Attitudes toward sexuality have undergone radical changes since the 1960s. The behaviour of women has been particulary influenced by these changes. According to studies from the years 1966 and 1981 which investigated attitudes and behaviour of woman students, female masturbatory experience increasingly resembled that of young men. Coital experience became even more frequent for women than for men of the same age cohort, a reversal attributable to all social groups (as confirmed by results of other studies). The sexually inexperienced minority questioned in the 1981 poll no longer attached particular importance to moral scruples, but rather to the fact that they had not yet found the right partner. The hypothesis that steady relationships represent a new form of sexual control was not confirmed. Only about half of those polled gave "romance" as the reason for the first coitus, a motive which had been given by over 70% of the young women in the 1966 poll. The proportion of women giving "curiosity" as a reason doubled, from 13% to 26%. Young men increasingly associated romantic love and tenderness with sexuality, and separation of "holy" love from "common" sexuality had become rarer. In contrast, women were taking liberties that were once considered male prerogatives, and the overall increase in liberal attitudes toward extramarital sex, masturbation, and homosexuality was more marked among women than among men. Manifestations of the double standard have nearly disappeared among students. Long-term comparison also generally confirms the more permissive attitudes toward homosexuality and extramarital sexual relations. It is striking that some "modern" attitudes were similarly expressed in 1949 (though there were still disparate standards for men and women at that time), but were less so in the 1960s (see table 5) (Noelle-Neumann, 1981). Liberalization of sexual attitudes has been, however, accompanied by countercurrents of restrictive norms: expressions of violence in sexuality, especially when directed against women, are more emphatically rejected than they were formerly.

Is West German society in the process of casting off its prejudices against minorities? This seems to be the case with regard to the groups traditionally victimized by such hostility: Jews, blacks, prostitutes, people suffering from cancer, and so on. According to surveys conducted in 1975 and 1981, there has been a rising tendency to accept these groups as neighbours, colleagues, even as friends.

However, animosity toward other groups has grown; especially toward committed Nazis and communists, and also toward alcoholics, children of criminals, and people from slums (see table 6). Thus, there is not an overall increase of tolerance, but rather a contemporary shifting of intolerance from certain groups to others. As Germans learn to tolerate of ethnic and religious minorities, they also learn to reject political extremism, tolerance of which has been the cause of suffering in the past. One can speak in this context of a trend toward selective and calculated tolerance.

This applies particularly to attitudes toward new immigrants – foreign workers, asylum seekers, and Russian and Polish immgrants of German descent. The first "immigration wave" of foreign workers was stopped in 1973, and did not end in hostility toward foreigners. Not until the 1980s, in the face of continued immigration by asylum seekers and eastern Europeans of German heritage, did hostility against migration of this sort once again become a subject of public debate. It is questionable if this can be taken as a indicator of growing intolerance of ethnic minorities. It is more likely a defensive attitude against continued immigration, linked with the demand that foreign workers leave the country (see figure 1). It cannot be explained as general hostility toward foreigners, but rather as fear of competition on the tight job and housing markets. According to polls conducted in November of 1988, only 22% of those questioned thought it "a good thing that many immigrants of German descent are coming into our country lately," while 61% had their doubts, and 17% were undecided. In June of the same year, 29% had thought that it was "a good thing," 59% already had their doubts, and 12% were undecided (Frankfurter Rundschau, January 16, 1989).

In West Germany, there is no ascertainable trend toward discrimination against ethnic minorites, but rather toward rejection of those who themselves discriminate against these minorities. The Federal Republic has seen the gradual development of norms conducive to protection of minorities, the breaking of which is responded to with moral and legal sanctions by the public. Nationalist parties propagating prejudice against minorities are prohibited (such as the Sozialistische Reichspartei, outlawed in 1952, and extreme rightist organizations, especially since the late 1970s). Expression of hostility toward minorities can lead to prosecution in court.

At the same time, a tendency has emerged toward more standardization of behaviour, purportedly to protect personal self-development and privacy. The *Bundesdatenschutzgesetz* (Federal Data Protection Act, 1977) and *Datenschutzbeauftragte* (Data Protection Authority) of the state and federal governments are assigned to see to the prevention not only of libel, but also of unauthorized circulation of personal data.

Expressions of violence in the private sphere are more sharply rejected than in the past: since the 1970s, violence against children and women, including marital rape and violence in pornography, has become the subject of public disapproval.

Stronger sanctions and laws against violent crime in the private sphere have been demanded by feminists, in particular. Public awareness and the resulting taboo on private violence has had the unintended consequence that this sort of violence has become more surreptitious – more hidden within the private sphere.

Conservative circles advocate more stringent action against violence in public demonstrations, against politically motivated violence in public, and against "killing the unborn" (see 3.5, "Reproductive Technologies"). Freedom of action is restricted not only in the name of protection of individual rights, but also in the name of collective goals, as is best exhibited by the example of the continuous setting of standards for environmental protection. Since 1980, punishable offenses against the environment – as defined in the *Abfallbeseitigungsgesetz* (the 1972 law regulating garbage elimination), the *Bundesemissionsschutzgesetz* (the 1972 law regulating air pollution through emission), and the *Wasserhaushaltsgesetz* (the 1976 law dealing with the state of water resources) – are considered a distinct category of crime.

The dissolution of previous codes of conduct in the family, in sexuality, and in conventional politics therefore cannot be interpreted strictly as a relaxation of social norms, but is, rather, accompanied by the creation of new norms. This process functions to contain the burgeoning number of new possibilities for action; to secure the newly permissible action alternatives by means of tolerance norms; to defend tolerance itself against violent attack; and to replace violent expression by control and sublimation of emotionality (Elias, 1976).

Karl Otto Hondrich

References

Allerbeck, Klaus, and Wendy J. Hoag
1985 *Jugend ohne Zukunft? Einstellungen, Umwelt, Lebensperspektiven*. München/Zürich: Piper.

Clement, Ulrich
1986 *Sexualität im sozialen Wandel*. Stuttgart: Enke.

Elias, Norbert
1976 *Über den Prozeß der Zivilisation*. 2 vols. Frankfurt am Main: Suhrkamp.

Koch-Arzberger, Claudia
1985 *Die schwierige Integration*. Opladen: Westdeutscher Verlag.

Noelle-Neumann, Elisabeth, ed.
1981 *The Germans. Public Opinion Polls, 1967-1980*. Westport, Conn./London: Greenwood.

Noelle-Neumann, Elisabeth, and Edgar Piel, eds.
1983 *Allensbacher Jahrbuch der Demoskopie 1978-1983*. München/New York/London/Paris: Saur.

Table 1
Pedagogic Goals (in %)

Wording of question: "We have here a list of what one should provide children with for later life, what children should learn at home. Which of these do you think are especially important?"

Item	1967 Oct.	1977 Dec.	1982 Jan.	1983 Feb.
Politeness, good behaviour	85	76	75	76
Working well and conscientiously	76	70	70	75
Thrift	75	65	66	65
Tolerance, respect of other opinions	59	64	65	72
Ability to prevail	59	68	63	68
Good judge of people, choosing right friends	53	60	61	62
Healthy way of life	58	57	58	60
Thirst for knowledge, widening one's horizons	47	49	46	49
Conformity, adaptability	61	51	45	46
Enjoyment of books	36	28	36	36
Interest in politics, understanding of politcal contexts	30	29	30	33
Modesty and discretion	37	28	27	31
Firm religious belief	39	24	25	27
Technical ability, ability to deal with modern technology	29	24	25	24
Liking for art	21	17	19	21

Source: Noelle-Neumann & Piel, 1983, p. 93.

Table 2
Tolerance of Sponse's Opinion (in %)

Wording of question: "Do you think it's necessary that men and women be of the same opinion in all matters?"

Item	Total spouses		Men		Women	
	1953	1979	1953	1979	1953	1979
Not necessary	65	78	69	79	62	78
Necessary	31	15	28	16	33	15
Undecided	4	7	3	5	5	7
Total	100	100	100	100	100	100

Source: Noelle-Neumann & Piel, 1983, p. 86.

Table 3
Parentel permissiveness (in %)

Wording of question put to parents with children between 2 and 25 years:
"Which of these describe your family?" (list)

Item	1965	1978
Now and then we have differences or even fight, but we are still a happy family.	60	66
We have a very happy family life and get along splendidly. We never fight.	24	14
We often disagree and fight. It's impossible to always share one opinion. But we all feel secure in our family.	13	16
Our family isn't very close. We all tend go go our own way.	3	4
Total	100	100

Source: Noelle-Neumann & Piel, 1983, p. 92.

Table 4
Status of marriage (in %)

Wording of question: "Do you think the institution of marriage is necessary or obselete?"

Item	Married men				Married women			
	1949	1963	1976	1978	1949	1963	1976	1978
Necessary	90	92	72	71	92	95	73	65
Obselete	3	3	9	11	3	1	8	13
Undecided	7	5	19	18	5	4	19	22
Total	100	100	100	100	100	100	100	100

Source: Noelle-Neumann & Piel, 1983, p. 88.

Table 5
Necessity of Sexual Relations (in %)

Wording of question: "In your opinion, is it possible to be happy in life without intimate (sexual) relations between a man and a woman?"
"Is such an intimate relationship essential for you to be happy in life, or could you do without it?"

Item	Persons between 20 and 30 years of age					
	Men			Women		
	1949	1963	1978	1949	1963	1978
Happy without intimate relations?						
- no	76	62	70	63	54	51
- yes	11	19	14	24	20	23
- undecided	13	19	16	13	26	26
Total	100	100	100	100	100	100
Intimate relations?						
- essential	81	67	84	56	46	65
- can do without	12	16	8	34	34	21
- undecided	7	17	8	10	20	14
Total	100	100	100	100	100	100

Source: Noelle-Neumann & Piel, 1983, p. 251.

Table 6
The Spectrum of Tolerance (in %)

Wording of question: "Here is a list of various groups of persons. Would you please pick out those who you would not want as work colleagues or neighbors?" (list)
"And which ones could easily be among your closest friends? What wouldn't bother you about it?" (list)

Item	Not as colleagues, not as neighbors		Accepted as friends	
	1975	1981	1975	1981
Committed Communists	50	63	20	13
Committed Nazis	44	63	15	10
People frequently drunk	54	58	16	16
Women earning their money as "easy women"	55	53	15	17
People with conviction records for theft	46	45	19	19
People who've spent some months in an institute for mentally ill	46	42	19	20
Foreign workers	21	26	35	36
Negroes	26	23	37	39
People who've attempted suicid	17	15	36	37
Jews	16	14	41	41
Children of criminals	14	12	32	11
People with lots of children	14	11	56	59
People who've been convicted for serious auto accidents	9	9	52	48
People living together outside of marriage	10	7	57	65
Cancer victims	11	7	49	56
People grown up in a poor part of town	6	6	56	53
People with illegitimate children	3	4	67	71
Divorcees	5	3	71	74
People grown up as illegitimate children	3	2	67	67
People grown up as orphans	2	1	76	76

Source: Noelle-Neumann & Piel, 1983, p. 79.

Figure 1
People advocating return of foreigners to their native countries

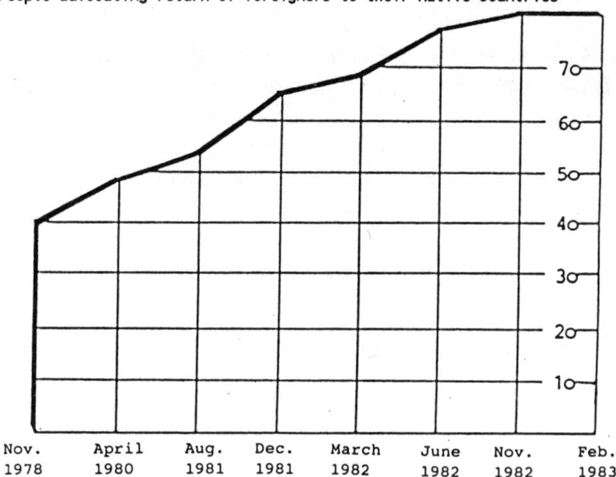

The questions were not always identical, but similar.
Data in percent.

Source: INFRATEST, INFAS, EMNID, and IPOS,
cited in Koch-Arzberger, 1985, p. 22.

7.4 Authority

Authority relations have changed radically during the last decades, particularly in the 1960s and 1970s. In the family, traditional values such as obedience and discipline gave way to liberal values. On the job, hierarchical authority, formally still existent, has lost much of its impact to functional authority, based on competence. Public and political institutions, while enjoying increasing legitimacy, are also attracting increasing criticism.

Authority in the Family

The central and primal social-authority relationship is that between parents and children. While parent-child conflicts are not necessarily conflicts of authority, they always affect parental authority. A replication study of a representative cross-section of West German youth showed that only a negligible percentage reported a bad relationship to their parents or spoke of "frequent differences of opinion" with parents. The proportion of youths dissatisfied with their relationship with their father rose from 2.9% in 1962 to 7.1% in 1983; dissatisfaction with mothers also rose, but to a smaller degree: from 1.1% to 3.2%. "Occasional differences of opinion" – conflicts of lower intensity – more than doubled between 1962 and 1983, according the adolescents questioned; in 1983 almost one-third characterized their relationship with their father this way, and almost one-fourth did so with regard to their relationship with their mother (see table 1).

Over this period, ways of raising children changed drastically: looking back upon their own upbringing, 44.9% of the adolescents in 1962 claimed to have been "strictly" or "very strictly" brought up, while in 1983 only 18.7% did so. Similarly, a trend can be seen toward granting children greater influence in family decisions (Allerbeck & Hoag 1985, p. 59). Whether more liberal child-rearing is the result of an increase in things to fight about between parents and children (e.g., widening educational disparity between generations, longer financial dependence on parents), or whether it is the greater degree of freedom which allows for, or even causes an increase in matters of dispute must remain a moot point in our particular context. Another explanation for the parallel increase in conflicts and in liberal attitudes in the family can be sought in the fact that pedagogic ideals and related demands change more quickly than does child-rearing. The number of supporters of "an upbringing which allows children a generous amount of freedom" almost tripled between 1962 and 1983 (from 9.2% to 25.6%) (Allerbeck & Hoag 1985, p. 65).

Table 2 clearly shows that the transformation from authority based on obedience and subordination to authority based on negotiations experienced a notable upswing in the 1960s: the pedagogic goal of obedience and subordination was supported by every fourth citizen between 1951 and 1967; less than a decade later (starting in 1976, up to 1983), these pedagogic values were supported by only one in ten. This concurs with the thesis that "modernization" of the value system in the Federal Republic took place gradually within one decade, approximately between 1965 and 1975 (Meulemann, 1982; Klages, 1983).

"War babies" (born around 1940) possessed the attributes of the classical bourgeois identity – diligence, obedience, tidiness, honesty, and the Protestant work ethic – and had authoritarian fathers representing the traditional understanding of role and power. Most observers ascertain fundamental changes since the 1960s, based on a long-lasting phase of economic prosperity. "Baby-boomers" enjoyed a more liberal upbringing, accompanied by diminishing respect for their elders and by previously unheard-of opportunities to express conflict and protest. On the other hand, obedience forced by threats of punishment was replaced by expectations of conformity induced by parental application of more subtle forms of power. These new forms are, by their very nature, liable to challenge and justification by negotiation.

Hence, results of opinion polls on educational objectives record a dwindling of traditional values such as politeness and good behaviour (from 85% in 1967 to 76% in 1983), thrift (from 75% to 65%), fitting in and adjusting to the order of things (from 61% to 46%), and firm beliefs and religious commitment (from 39% to 27%). This development is accompanied by increasing emphasis on "modern" values such as respect for other opinions and tolerance (from 59% in 1967 to 72% in 1983), self-assertion and tenacity (from 59% to 68%), good judgment of human nature and wise choice of friends (from 53% to 62%), and interest in politics or understanding of current events (from 30% to 33%).

With regard to authoritarianism, frequently observed in postwar Germany and characterized as sanctioning aggression and belittling the dignity of individual life, current findings confirm the increase of democratic, anti-authoritarian values in the attitudes of young West Germans within the last three decades (Lederer, 1983). An item from the Frankfurt A-scale, which was patterned after the California F-scale by Adorno et al. goes as follows: "Most young people today have it too good; it is about time that they learn strict discipline again." In 1962, 52% of the respondents agreed with this statement; 24.5% did so 20 years later.

Authority on the Job

While conflicts in the family have increased, everyday conflicts on the job seem to have declined – both with colleagues and with superiors (see table 3). This can be interpreted as a decrease in authority problems: hierarchical authority, though still existent and in fact more refined, commands less by giving orders and more via rational arguments. This type of rational or functional authority is taking over from authority based on status in a formal hierarchy: in departments of companies possessing modern technology, for example electronic-data-processing departments, the advice of the specialist is given preference over that of the boss; the opposite is true in departments with traditional technology (Schiefer, 1969; Hondrich, 1972).

In addition, there is in larger West German businesses a "double authority structure," legally anchored in the form of the Codetermination Act. Workers' councils (the members of which are elected by the employees), representatives on supervisory boards, and plant directors not only serve to check management, they also perform management functions themselves – especially in personnel and social matters – thereby gaining formal and functional authority.

Public and Political Authority

According to the cliché, Germans are *staatsgläubig*: they place their trust in government institutions and kow-tow to authority. The astounding growth in acceptance and legitimacy of the new democratic institutions in the last few decades (Baker et al., 1981; Conradt, 1980; Kaase, 1989a) could possibly be traced back to the German *Staatsgläubigkeit* and "authoritarian" character. However, the facts point to another conclusion: increased acceptance of institutions is accompanied by increasing self-confidence and a propensity toward objective criticism by citizens in the face of governmental authority. Confidence in the incorruptibility of civil servants nearly doubled between 1950 and 1978 (from 21% to 39%; see table 4). Over the same period, readiness to protest against injustice done by an administrative agency rose (from 52% to 70%) (see table 5). International comparison is quite instructive on this point: While the percentage of citizens in United States and Great Britain "who say they can do something about an unjust or harmful local regulation or national law" either declined or stayed around the same level between 1960 and 1974, it rose considerably in the Federal Republic (by 19% regarding "national law"; see table 6). As Barnes and Kaase (1979, p. 163) note, "the overall political repertory had broadened considerably by 1974, and unconventional, direct-action types of political influence had found their way into the repertory of a wider segment of the population." Even though the aggressive element of the anti-authoritarian movement of the late 1960s has disappeared and authority has re-established itself in social relationships, authority in the Federal Republic was deeply and permanently transformed in the 1970s and 1980s.

Karl Otto Hondrich

References

Allerbeck, Klaus, and Wendy J. Hoag
1985 *Jugend ohne Zukunft*. München/Zürich: Piper.

Baker, Kendall L., et al.
1981 *Germany Transformed. Political Culture and the New Politics*. Cambridge,Mass./London: Harvard University Press.

Barnes, Samuel, et al.
1979 *Political Action. Mass Participation in Five Western Countries*. Beverly Hills/London: Sage Pub.

Conradt, Davis P.
1980 "Changing German Political Culture." In Gabriel Almond, and Sidney Verba, eds., *The Civic Culture Reconsidered*. Boston/Toronto: Little, Brown and Co.

Hondrich, Karl Otto
1972 *Demokratisierung und Leistungsgesellschaft*. Stuttgart: Kohlhammer.

Jaide, Walter
1988 *Generationen eines Jahrhunderts*. Opladen: Leske und Budrich.

Kaase, Max
1989 "Mass Participation." In M. Kent Jennings, and Jan van Deth, eds., *Continuities in Political Action: A Longitudinal Study of Political Orientations in 3 Western Democracies*. Berlin: de Gruyter.

Klages, Helmut
1983 "Wertewandel: Chancen der Synthese von Pflicht- und Selbstentfaltungswerten." In *Zukunftsperspektiven gesellschaftlicher Entwicklungen*. Erstellt im Auftrag der Landesregierung von Baden-Württemberg. Stuttgart.

Lederer, Gerda
1983 *Jugend und Autorität*. Opladen: Westdeutscher Verlag.

Meulemann, Heiner
1982 *Value Change in West Germany 1950-1980: Integrating the Empirical Evidence*. Paper presented at the 10th World Congress of Sociology, August 16-21, 1982, Mexico City.

Noelle-Neumann, Elisabeth, ed.
1981 *The Germans. Public Opinion Polls, 1967-1980*. Westport,Conn./London: Greenwood.

Noelle-Neumann, Elisabeth, and Edgar Piel, eds.
1983 *Allensbacher Jahrbuch der Demoskopie 1978-1983*. München/New York/London/Paris: Saur.

Schiefer, Friedrich
1969 *Elektronische Datenverarbeitung und Angestellte. Das Eindringen der EDV in die Büroarbeit mit seinen Auswirkungen auf die Orientierung der Angestellten und die soziale Organisation des Bürobetriebes*. Meisenheim am Glan: Hain.

Table 1
Relationship to parents

Item	Mother 1962	Mother 1983	Father 1962	Father 1983
We love each other and mean the world to each other	41.2	15.3	24.4	6.2
We get along very well	46.7	57.0	51.5	52.3
There are sometimes differences of opinion	10.7	23.3	18.6	31.1
We often don't get along, with frequent differences of opinion	1.1	2.3	2.5	5.1
Our relationship is poor, with constant difficulties	-	0.9	0.4	2.0
We pay no attention to each other	0.2	0.3	2.5	3.3
Total %	100.0	100.0	100.0	100.0
N	839	1,504	753	1,456

Source: Allerbeck & Hoag, 1985, p. 60.

Table 2
Pedagogic goals (in %, multiple answers possible)

Item	1951	1967	1969	1974	1976	1979	1981	1983
Self-reliance and free will	28	37	45	53	51	44	52	49
Orderliness and industriousness	41	48	45	44	41	43	38	38
Obedience and self-subordination	25	25	19	17	10	11	8	9
Other answers	5	3	3	-	-	-	-	-
No answer	1	2	2	4	0	3	2	4

Source: EMNID-Information, no. 8/9, 1983, p. 23, cited in Jaide, 1988, p. 206.

Table 3
Advantages and disadvantages in actual job (in %)

Wording of question put to employed persons: "All careers have advantages and disadvantages. When you think of your work, which of these cards here describe your job? Please pick out what's applicable." (presentation of cards)

Positive statements	1960	1964	1973	1979	1983
Feel well at the office, get along well with colleagues	53	56	69	72	77
Can work independently, am trusted	48	56	66	65	72
Good boss, get along well with him	44	48	52	52	56
Interesting, always something new	34	41	50	51	52
Well-equipped place of work, modern and clean	26	33	39	40	43
Plenty of social benefits, the company does something for its people	21	26	28	35	35
Can earn a lot of money there	33	37	37	32	33
Negative statements	**1960**	**1964**	**1973**	**1979**	**1983**
Too much to do, too much stress	27	26	30	32	31
Too little fresh air, poorly ventilated	30	30	31	31	34
Have to stand and run around too much	26	27	28	31	30
Physically strenuous	26	23	21	23	21
Uncomfortable, cramped body position	13	12	17	20	18
Enervating, mental and emotional drain	14	15	19	19	23
Can't get ahead there, no prospects	21	18	22	19	25
No variety, always the same routine	25	24	24	19	22
Too dusty and dirty	25	21	20	18	16
Too many brown-nosers at our office	23	15	20	16	20
Too much responsibility: I get the blame if something goes wrong	14	15	19	15	20
Too noisy and loud	20	19	19	15	16
Dangerous work, risk of accidents	15	15	15	13	12
Too much exposure to the elements	15	11	12	11	10

Source: Noelle-Neumann & Piel, 1983, p. 413.

Table 4
Corruption (in %)

Wording of question: "Do you think that civil servants are, generally speaking, unimpressionable and incorruptible?"

Total population	No, not incorruptible	Yes, incorruptible	Undecided	Total
January 1950	59	21	20	100
November 1958	44	35	21	100
December 1964	29	49	22	100
October 1974	42	35	23	100
July 1978	41	39	20	100

Source: Noelle-Neumann, 1981, p. 189.

Table 5
Protest against unjust action (in %)

Wording of question: "What would you do if an administrative agency acted unjustly in a matter that concerns you? Do you think that there would be a point in protesting or not?" "How would you protest, what would you do?"

Total population	Would protest	No point in protesting	Undecided	Total
January 1950	52	37	11	100
November 1958	53	33	14	100
December 1964	51	32	17	100
November 1978	70	22	8	100

Source: Noelle-Neumann, 1981, p. 190.

Table 6
Percentage of respondents who say they can do something about an unjust or harmful local regulation or national law 1959/60 and 1974 (in %)

Local regulation: Country	1959/60		1974		1974:1959/60 differences	
	(%)	%	(%)	%		
Netherlands	(-)	-	(62)	71	(-)	-
Britain	(78)	81	(64)	74	(-14)	-7
United States	(77)	82	(71)	77	(-6)	-5
Germany	(62)	67	(67)	70	(+5)	+3
Austria	(-)	-	(43)	48	(-)	-
National war: Country	**1959/60**		**1974**		**1974:1959/60 differences**	
	(%)	%	(%)	%		
Netherlands	(-)	-	(43)	53	(-)	-
Britain	(62)	66	(57)	66	(-5)	0
United States	(75)	78	(78)	82	(+3)	+4
Germany	(38)	40	(56)	59	(+18)	+19
Austria	(-)	-	(33)	41	(-)	-

Source: Barnes & Kaase, 1979, p. 141; for 1959 and 1960: data base Almond & Verba, 1963.

7.5 Public Opinion

Participation in the electoral process has always been high. This is due to the fact that democratic experience is new and very highly appreciated. On the other hand, individualistic political interests have been developing since the late 1960s which are sometimes critical of the established electoral process. The use of surveys is burgeoning, and although their effect cannot really be quantified over the long term, they can be perceived as a parallel phenomenon to individualization and the increasing variety of life-style movements. In the long run, however, a decrease in voting participation can be expected.

Since the founding of the Federal Republic of Germany in 1949, elections and voting behaviour have played an important part in political life. For the first time, a democratic regime had the prospect of lasting a long time. The new German democracy also established its legitimacy by total rejection of the Third Reich - the National Socialist regime. Simultaneously, however, much of the German political heritage was abandoned. The new beginning was conceived as a way to shed feelings of guilt with respect to the immediate past, and therefore led to great expectations.

It is thus understandable that elections were perceived in West Germany as a commitment to the status of citizenship. A second reason the electoral process was held in such high esteem is that the German electoral system combines majority rule and representation rule. Every German voter has two votes: one for a candidate (majority rule), the other for a party (rule of representation). The mechanism of the representation rule guarantees that each vote is counted at the state (*Länder*) level; if a party gains more representatives by majority vote than by the vote for the party, the total number of members in the Parliament increases by these additional representatives. The whole system is therefore perceived to rule out "unjust" results.

The turnout for federal elections has always been fairly high. With the exception of 1987, each federal election for the German parliament has drawn more than 85% of eligible voters. In Germany, elections at the federal level are conducted every four years – at least in principle. If the German parliament should for any reason be dissolved earlier than the end of the mandate by the president of the republic, an election is held before the four years is up. Since the Federal Republic of Germany was founded, the Bundestag has been dissolved prior to the end of its regular term three times: in 1972 because of problems in forming a party coalition, then in 1983 because the governing coalition had changed in 1982, and again in 1990 because of German reunification and a first federal election for the entire German people. Voter turnouts were highest in 1972 and 1976, because those elections were highly polarized between the conservative and the social democratic-liberal cleavages in German politics. Observation of general voting behaviour shows that the young, the very old, and women vote slightly less frequently than the average (see table 1). It is very likely that voter turnout will decrease in the future, because the very high expectations German voters have with respect to what a political system can achieve may deteriorate over the long term.

In addition, other elections give Germans the chance to comment, by means of their vote on the perceived achievements of the government and the parliamentary system at federal level. Between federal elections, there are, for example, elections for state parliaments (*Länderwahlen*), the term of which is also four years. In addition, there are elections at the local level, in communities and in counties (*Gemeinden*, *Städte* and *Kreise*). Local elections take place every five years, as do elections for the European parliament. Voter turnout for European elections is considerably lower in Germany – as it is in other European countries, with the exception of Belgium, where failure to vote is punishable by a fine – in comparison to federal elections (see table 2). Both the state-level elections and the European election serve as opportunities for criticism of the federal government. In these "mid-term" elections, individual interests and political affiliations come more into the foreground (see table 3). German workers also have the opportunity to elect representatives to supervise their pension funds; this electoral procedure is very little known and is used only by small portions of the work force.

It is not yet possible to publish data on a number of surveys that have been carried out. Oral information from various sources supports the assumption that the importance of surveys is increasing rapidly. This year, about 250 institutions are conducting market research, 121 of them maintaining a "full service" (service, data processing, and service analysis). The turnover for this is assessed at 1.009 billion DM for 1990. About 13% of the adult population have been interviewed in surveys, but this number also includes marketing interviews. In 1990, 5.4 million interviews were conducted (5.16 million on a quantitative basis, 242,000 on a qualitative basis). Of these interviews, 588,000 were conducted by mail, 1.67 million by phone, and 2.895 million in person. The proportion of political opinion polling amounts to about 2.3%, for a market share of 23 million DM (all data from Informationsdienst Kontext, Köln). According to all of the interviewed experts, the importance of this social phenomenon is increasing. Since 1977, the television program "Politbarometer" (Second German TV channel) has explored general attitudes toward political parties and politicians. Since January of 1986, the weekly magazine *Der Spiegel* has been regularly publishing surveys inquiring into attitudes about special political problems, and prevailing opinions about the popularity of parties and politicians. One explanation for the increased importance of surveys could be that people adhere increasingly to life styles instead of social classes, and that their behaviour is therefore more heavily influenced by new fashions in thinking and behaving. Another explanation (from Forschungsgruppe Wahlen, Mannheim), has to do with improved survey techniques, which make the instruments more reliable and therefore more attractive to potential users (businesses and political parties). In Germany, electoral behaviour, political interest and criticism, and participation in surveys seem to be perceived as cumulative opportunities for citizens to express their expectations. While political protest and surveys may increase, voter turnout at elections can increase no further, and will decrease. Whether participation in the European electoral process will increase after the advent of Europe 1992 will not be known until 1994, when the next election for a European parliament takes place.

Jakob Schissler

References

Niedermayer, Oskar
1989 "Die Europawahlen 1989: Eine international vergleichende Analyse." *Zeitschrift für Parlamentsfragen*, no. 4, 469-487.

Statistisches Bundesamt, ed.
1989a *Datenreport 1989*. Bonn: Bundeszentrale für politische Bildung.

–, ed.
1989b *Fachserie 1*. Wiesbaden.

–, ed.
1990 *Statistisches Jahrbuch 1990*. Stuttgart: Metzler-Poeschel.

Table 1
Federal elections - voter participation by men and women in federal parliamentary elections according to age groups and states since 1953 (West Germany excluding Berlin)
(voter participation in %)

Age in years	1953	1957	1961	1965	1969	1972	1976	1980	1983	1987
Total										
18-21	-	-	-	-	-	84.6	84.1	80.4	84.3	76.8
21-25	-	-	79.5	76.8	76.6	84.4	82.9	78.9	81.5	73.1
21-30	80.3	82.9	-	-	-	-	-	-	-	-
25-30	-	-	84.1	81.7	81.4	88.2	86.5	82.2	83.8	75.9
30-35	-	-	-	86.2	86.1	90.8	89.2	86.2	87.0	80.3
30-40	-	-	89.2	-	-	-	-	-	-	-
30-60	88.7	89.9	-	-	-	-	-	-	-	-
35-40	-	-	-	88.2	87.8	92.4	91.5	88.6	89.3	83.8
40-45	-	-	-	89.0	89.4	93.1	92.7	90.3	91.1	86.0
40-50	-	-	90.4	-	-	-	-	-	-	-
45-50	-	-	-	88.8	89.6	93.9	93.6	91.2	92.2	87.9
50-60	-	-	90.5	89.4	89.6	94.1	93.8	92.3	92.7	89.4
60-70	-	-	89.3	88.5	88.6	93.2	93.7	92.2	92.3	87.9
60 and older	84.8	86.1	-	-	-	-	-	-	-	-
70 and older	-	-	80.5	79.3	79.5	85.9	88.0	85.7	84.9	79.4
Total	86.3	87.8	87.4	85.9	86.1	90.8	90.4	87.6	88.4	83.1
Men										
18-21	-	-	-	-	-	85.0	84.9	81.6	85.4	78.9
21-25	-	-	78.9	76.1	76.3	83.9	83.0	79.8	82.2	74.4
21-30	80.5	83.3	-	-	-	-	-	-	-	-
25-30	-	-	84.5	81.6	80.4	87.6	86.3	81.9	83.9	76.6
30-35	-	-	-	86.6	86.2	90.4	88.8	85.8	86.6	80.2
30-40	-	-	90.1	-	-	-	-	-	-	-
30-60	89.7	91.3	-	-	-	-	-	-	-	-
35-40	-	-	-	89.2	88.5	92.4	91.0	88.1	89.0	83.7
40-45	-	-	-	90.3	90.4	93.4	92.8	90.3	90.8	85.8
40-50	-	-	91.6	-	-	-	-	-	-	-
45-50	-	-	-	90.8	91.3	94.5	93.9	91.6	92.3	88.0
50-60	-	-	92.0	91.3	91.6	95.2	94.8	93.1	93.2	90.0
60-70	-	-	91.8	91.2	91.1	94.5	94.8	93.5	93.6	91.5
60 and older	90.2	90.9	-	-	-	-	-	-	-	-
70 and older	-	-	87.1	86.4	85.9	90.2	91.2	89.6	88.5	85.1
Total	88.0	89.6	88.9	87.5	87.5	91.4	90.8	88.2	89.1	84.2
Women										
18-21	-	-	-	-	-	84.3	83.2	79.2	83.2	74.6
21-25	-	-	80.0	77.5	77.0	85.0	82.9	78.0	80.6	71.7
21-30	80.0	82.3	-	-	-	-	-	-	-	-
25-30	-	-	83.7	81.7	82.5	88.8	86.8	82.6	83.7	75.2
30-35	-	-	-	85.7	86.0	91.3	89.7	86.6	87.4	80.3
30-40	-	-	88.5	-	-	-	-	-	-	-
30-60	87.8	88.8	-	-	-	-	-	-	-	-
35-40	-	-	-	87.3	87.0	92.3	92.0	89.2	89.7	83.9
40-45	-	-	-	88.0	88.5	92.8	92.6	90.4	91.3	86.3
40-50	-	-	89.5	-	-	-	-	-	-	-
45-50	-	-	-	87.5	88.5	93.5	93.3	90.8	92.0	87.9
50-60	-	-	89.2	88.1	88.2	93.3	93.0	91.6	92.2	88.8
60-70	-	-	87.3	86.4	86.7	92.2	93.0	91.3	91.5	88.4
60 and older	80.6	82.5	-	-	-	-	-	-	-	-
70 and older	-	-	75.8	74.8	75.7	83.3	86.0	83.6	82.9	76.5
Total	84.9	86.2	86.2	84.6	84.9	90.2	90.0	87.1	87.8	82.1

Source: Statistisches Bundesamt, Fachserie 1, Wiesbaden 1989 b.

Table 2
European elections: voter participation (in %)

Item	1979/81	1984/87	1989
Belgium	91.4	92.1	90.7
Denmark	47.8	52.4	46.2
F.R.Germany	65.7	56.8	62.3
France	60.7	56.7	48.7
Greece	78.7	77.2	79.9
Ireland	63.6	47.6	68.3
Italy	84.9	83.4	81.0
Luxemburg	88.9	88.8	87.4
Netherlands	57.8	50.6	47.2
Portugal	-	72.6	51.2
Spain	-	68.9	54.6
United Kingdom	32.3	32.6	36.2

Source: Zeitschrift für Parlamentsfragen, Heft 4/1989, p.472.

Table 3
Political interest and personal evaluation of importance of political influence (in %)

Item	Very strong/strong political interest			Political influence personally very important		
	1978	1984	1988	1980	1984	1988
Total	27	29	31	26	36	46
Union members	36	41	41	34	45	62
Union non-members	24	26	30	25	34	43
Party members	-	69	70	53	65	68
Party non-members	-	26	29	26	34	45
Members of civic organizations	-	82	65	72	84	75
Non-members of civic organizations	-	23	31	26	35	45

Data basis: Wohlfahrtssurvey 1978, 1980, 1984, 1988.

Source: Statistisches Bundesamt, 1989a, p. 492.

8. State and Service Institutions

8.1 Educational System

While the education systems of many Western European countries underwent rapid transformation after World War II, the German education system changed more slowly. In the 1960s, a phase of education reform and expansion took place with the aim of relieving the "educational emergency" and actualizing equal opportunity. Though the reform stagnated in the mid-1970s, it has led to a stronger mobilization of educational reserves.

School System

Looking at the school and educational system of the Federal Republic from a long-term historical perspective, it is obvious that two fundamental structures have weathered all changes. These structures distinguish the West German educational system from those of most other industrial countries. The first is the existence of three separate school types: intermediate school, with its work-oriented curriculum; secondary school (high school up to the tenth school year); and the full academic high school. All three follow directly after grade school. The second is the great importance of professional apprenticeship, featuring on-the-job training, supplemented by mandatory part-time attendance at a public trade school or technical college (see figure 1).

The composition of the German educational system has its roots in the school policy of the Weimar Republic (1919–1933), which undertook the first reforms of a pedagogic system that had ensured the social separation of the upper and lower classes. A first step toward a democratic educational system was the establishment of a common elementary school and the elimination of the old pre-grammar schools with their three classes. Interrupted by National Socialist policy, which subjected the entire pedagogic system to selection criteria and the command-and-obey principle, the debate on pedagogic reform was revived after the defeat of Fascism. The problem of democratizing education played a main role in this debate, while the questions, for example, of taking religion out of the schools or of centralizing the system remained marginal.

Educational developments and policy in the 1950s took place in the shadow cast by the heritage of World War II: the primary goal in the immediate postwar period was the reorganization of political and economic life. The "conception that we should, first of all, start learning again after the confusion of the Third Reich" (Becker, 1983, p. 329) prevailed, leading to a re-establishment of the school system along the lines of the Weimar Republic, and not to reform. This phase is often called the "restoration era," as it was dominated by the desire for quiet, order, and re-establishment of the old ways (Becker, 1983). Nonetheless, there were some changes concerning authorization in education matters, taking religion out of schools, and – to a limited degree – democratization. These changes were later to influence the school system of the Federal Republic, as the power of decision of the central authority (the Federation) was curbed in favour of the states. The states' autonomy in educational planning did not, however, infer increased autonomy for the schools: "Generally speaking, pedagogics are decentralized on a collective societal level and centralized on the county level" (Arbeitsgruppe am Max-Planck-Institut, 1984, p. 14).

Matters of religion and secularization in the schools were settled largely in the 1950s. During this phase, religious schools became fewer, so that there now remain a very small number of mostly government-subsidized private schools catering to religiously oriented groups desiring church-associated schools. The overwhelming majority of students attend government-financed educational institutions. During this phase, democratization meant, among other things, the "denazification" of education. In a statement on the Three Powers Conference in Berlin, the Potsdam Conference of 1945 said the following regarding German education: "German pedagogy must be supervised, with the aim of seeing to the total elimination of Nazi and militarist teachings and to the successful actualization of democratic ideals" (cited in Becker, 1983, p. 329). The substance of the educational reform was dedicated to elimination of Nazism and militarism from school textbooks.

Education Reform

The West German pedagogical system experienced a strong push toward modernization during the 1960s and 1970s. As income rose in many parts of the population, so did the desire for better education of young people. Fewer and fewer parents were content with a mere primary-school education for their children, and more children entered secondary and high schools. The economic success of the Federal Republic led to the political question of how this success was to be ensured in a world of rapid technological and industrial change. The cry for more and better training for youth dovetailed with the popular trend toward higher education. In the course of this transformation of attitude, it became obvious that neither the extent nor the organization of the West German educational system could keep up with the new requirements. The three-part school system became the symbol for methodical exclusion of the lower classes from better education, and was considered to hamper mobilization of educational reserves. Talk of an "educational emergency" and an "educational catastrophe" was heard. Expansion and actualization of equal opportunity in the educational system were put in the agenda.

The subsequent efforts can be deduced from the development of the education budget: expenditures rose steeply between 1960 and 1975 (from 8,977 million DM to 60,052 million DM; see table 1). These expenditures not only increased in absolute figures, but were also responsible for a burgeoning part of the public budget – 8.6% in 1960 and 15.3% in 1975 (table 1) – thereby becoming the second-highest expense in the West German domestic budget.

These numbers indicate general pedagogical improvements which should be defined and treated as clearly separate from substantive or organizational reforms. The substantive reforms involved, among other things, updating curricula. The curriculum reform added interdisciplinary qualification to the old specialization-oriented curriculum. This revision was modelled on reforms in the United States, where examples were found for newly developed "general curricula" with detailed planning for entire school terms, even for whole school levels, in the form of fixed goals and subject matter, teaching approaches, and pedagogical media. The traditional textbook gave way to a profusion of teaching materials: the teacher's handbook, the textbook, the work plan for students, tests, photographic slides, tapes and films, and so on. This new orientation influenced teacher training: between 1966 and 1976, colleges expanded their teacher-training programs. This led to the subordination of teaching content to the criterion of an academic education, which occurred in all school branches. The basic duality between the practical training in the elementary and intermediate schools and the scholarly education in the high schools was eliminated. A "polytechnics" course and one foreign language were introduced at the intermediate level. Natural sciences have taken priority over cultural skills in the secondary schools. High schools have added subjects such as jurisprudence (*Rechtskunde*), psychology, computer sciences, and so on.

As regards organization, reform efforts concentrated on opening the system to groups previously more or less excluded from higher education (for example, the lower classes and rural populations) via pre-school programs, lengthening mandatory school attendance from nine to ten years, and also via the *Gesamtschule* (comprehensive secondary-level school) – a core item in the reform. The idea behind the comprehensive school, which was tested in several counties in so-called school experiments, was that the traditional three types of school – intermediate, secondary, and high – be eliminated in favour of a more flexible teaching arrangement within a single school. The purpose was to breach the predetermination characteristic of the old three-part school system.

College education was also extended to cover more ground, which in turn caused an expansion in college personnel (see table 2) and led to construction of new colleges. Simultaneously, the number of high-school graduates and college students was growing fast: the number of high-school graduates had doubled by 1970; the number of college students rose from 300,000 to approximately 500,000 (table 2).

Starting in the mid-1970s, however, the educational expansion was followed by a phase of stagnation: critical economic developments from the mid-1970s on, unemployment, and budget deficits put an end to the boom. The budget-consolidation policy has since led to, among other things, cuts in the social and educational sectors (table 1). Many programs ideas have been nipped in the bud – and there is talk of ending the reforms.

Results of the Reform

In retrospect, the changes in the West German educational system can be portrayed as follows. The attempt to integrate the three-part school system into one comprehensive secondary-school system has failed. Comprehensive schools were established in only a few counties; elsewhere, they either never gained a foothold or were revoked. In the relative balance between the three school types – intermediate, secondary, and high – there has been an enormous shift: up to the late 1960s, the great majority of 13-year-olds attended intermediate school, while a minority went to the academically oriented high schools. By early 1980s, well under 40% of 13-year-olds were at intermediate school and over 50% were at secondary or high school (see table 4).

The teacher-student ratio has substantially improved since the postwar years. The elementary schools of 1955 had 37 pupils per teacher, while in 1985 this ratio was only 16 to 1. The ratio in high schools went from 22 to 14 pupils per teacher (see table 3). However, class size is still relatively high (approximately 30 pupils per class).

In 1985, there were 10 times as many college students as there were in 1950. The proportion of those who qualified for college increased from 44 students per 10,000 in 1960 to 219 per 10,000 in 1985. The growing number of examinations passed also provides an indication of the achievement level (table 2). These numbers should not serve to hide the fact that new problems arose in the 1980s: the desire to study motivated so many students that attendance at some colleges is double their capacity. Student strikes at several colleges in 1989 directed attention to this problem. Another serious problem in the 1980s is unemployment, which has resulted in high-school graduates streaming into professional apprenticeships, presenting competition for the traditional applicants for such training, - those with intermediate and secondary-school diplomas.

The new problems in the educational sector are reflected in the fact that the desire for an academic education has gained a bad reputation: if the 1970s witnessed a big push toward "scientification" of education in all types of schools, this very movement is now denounced as "waterheadedness." Emphasis on traditional values, as opposed to scientifically oriented education, is again finding loud support.

Barbara Wörndl

References

Arbeitsgruppe am Max-Planck-Institut für Bildungsforschung

1984 *Das Bildungswesen in der Bundesrepublik Deutschland. Ein Überblick für Eltern, Lehrer, Schüler*. Hamburg.

Ballerstedt, Eike, and Wolfgang Glatzer

1979 *Soziologischer Almanach*. Frankfurt am Main/New York: Campus.

Becker, Hellmut

1983 "Bildungspolitik." In Wolfgang Benz, ed., *Die Bundesrepublik Deutschland*. Vol. 2: Gesellschaft. Frankfurt am Main: Fischer.

Claessens, Dieter, Arno Klönne, and Armin Tschoepe

1985 *Sozialkunde der Bundesrepublik Deutschland. Grundlagen, Strukturen, Trends in Wirtschaft und Gesellschaft*. Reinbek: Rowohlt.

Diewald, Martin

1984 *Das "SPES-Indikatorentableau 1976" (Fortschreibung bis zum Jahre 1982)*. Arbeitspapier Nr. 150 des Sonderforschungsbereich 3 der J.W. Goethe-Universität Frankfurt und Universität Mannheim. Frankfurt am Main/Mannheim.

Institut der Deutschen Wirtschaft, ed.

1986 *Zahlen zur wirtschaftlichen Entwicklung der Bundesrepublik Deutschland*. Köln: Deutscher Institutsverlag.

Konradt, Hans-Joachim

1982 "Aktuelle Probleme des Bildungswesens in den achtziger Jahren." *Aus Politik und Zeitgeschichte*, Beilage zur Wochenzeitung "Das Parlament", no. 47.

Meulemann, Heiner

1982 "Bildungsexpansion und Wandel der Bildungsvorstellungen zwischen 1958 und 1979. Eine Kohortenanalyse." *Zeitschrift für Soziologie*, 11, no. 3, 227-253.

Schneider, Reinhart

1982 "Die Bildungsentwicklung in den westeuropäischen Staaten 1970-1975." *Zeitschrift für Soziologie*, 11, no. 3, 207-226.

Statistisches Bundesamt, ed.

1974 *Bildung im Zahlenspiegel*. Ausgabe 1974. Wiesbaden.

–, ed.
1982 *Statistisches Jahrbuch für die Bundesrepublik Deutschland 1982*. Stuttgart/Mainz: Kohlhammer.

–, ed.
1986 *Statistisches Jahrbuch für die Bundesrepublik Deutschland 1986*. Stuttgart/Mainz: Kohlhammer.

–, ed.
1987a *Bildung im Zahlenspiegel*. Wiesbaden.

–, ed.
1987b *Datenreport 1987. Zahlen und Fakten über die Bundesrepublik Deutschland*. Bonn: Bundeszentrale für politische Bildung.

–, ed.
1987c *Von den zwanziger zu den achtziger Jahren. Ein Vergleich der Lebensverhältnisse der Menschen*. Wiesbaden: Kohlhammer.

Zapf, Wolfgang, ed.
1978 *Lebensbedingungen in der Bundesrepublik Deutschland. Sozialer Wandel und Wohlfahrtsentwicklung*. Frankfurt am Main/New York: Campus.

Table 1
Public expenditures for education

Year	Public expenditures for education + sciences, in million. DM[1]	Education expenditures in proportion to total public budget	Expenditures per capita in DM
1960	-	-	-
1961	8,977	8.6	159
1965	-	10.7	268
1970	28,072	13.5	460
1975	60,052	15.3	971
1976	-	15.0	-
1977	-	14.8	-
1978	-	14.4	-
1980	83,274	-	1,353
1984	89,066	-	1,456

1 New method after and including 1974.

Source: Bundesministerium für Bildung und Wissenschaft, 1974, p.161; Statistisches Bundesamt, 1987a, p. 123; Meulemann, 1982, p. 229; Bundesministerium für Bildung und Wissenschaft 1974, p. 161; Statistisches Bundesamt, 1987a, p. 123.

Table 2
Universities

Year	Students at technical universities (Germans, foreigners) in winter semester, in 1,000	Passed exams (Germans, foreigners)[1]	Academic personnel at technical universities in 1,000
1950	128.1	-	-
1960	291.1	33,475	16.9
1970	510.5	62,089	48.2
1980	1,273.2	123,680	69.4
1984	1,314.2	141,546	-
1985	-	146,920	-

1. Number of persons: in 1973 to 1981, numbers registering for first teacher's examination was used as departure point for calculations. Usually, each teaching graduate is certified for 2 subjects. As of 1982, this calculation basis was replaced by individual surveys).

Source: Institut der Deutschen Wirtschaft, 1986; Statistisches Bundesamt, 1987a, p. 107; Meulemann, 1982, p. 229.

Table 3
Supply of teachers

Item	Unit	1926/27[1]	1955[2]	1985
Sole-professional teachers				
- grade- and intermed. school	1,000	188	126	234
- secondary school	1,000	12	11	61
- academic high school	1,000	45	35	126
Pupil-teacher ratio (pupil per sole-prof. teacher)				
- grade- and intermed. school	1,000	36	37	16
- secondary school	1,000	21	29	17
- academic high school	1,000	19	22	14

1. German Imperial territory.
2. Federal Republic of Germany without Hamburg, Bremen, the Saarland and West Berlin.

Source: Statistisches Bundesamt, 1987c, p. 23.

Table 4
School attendance by 13-year-olds in %

Item	1960	1970	1980	1985
Intermediate school	70	55	39	37
Secondary school	11	19	25	26
Academic high school	15	20	27	28
Comprehensive high school	-	-	4	4

Source: Statistisches Bundesamt, 1987b, p. 57.

Figure 1
Structure of education system in West Germany 1980

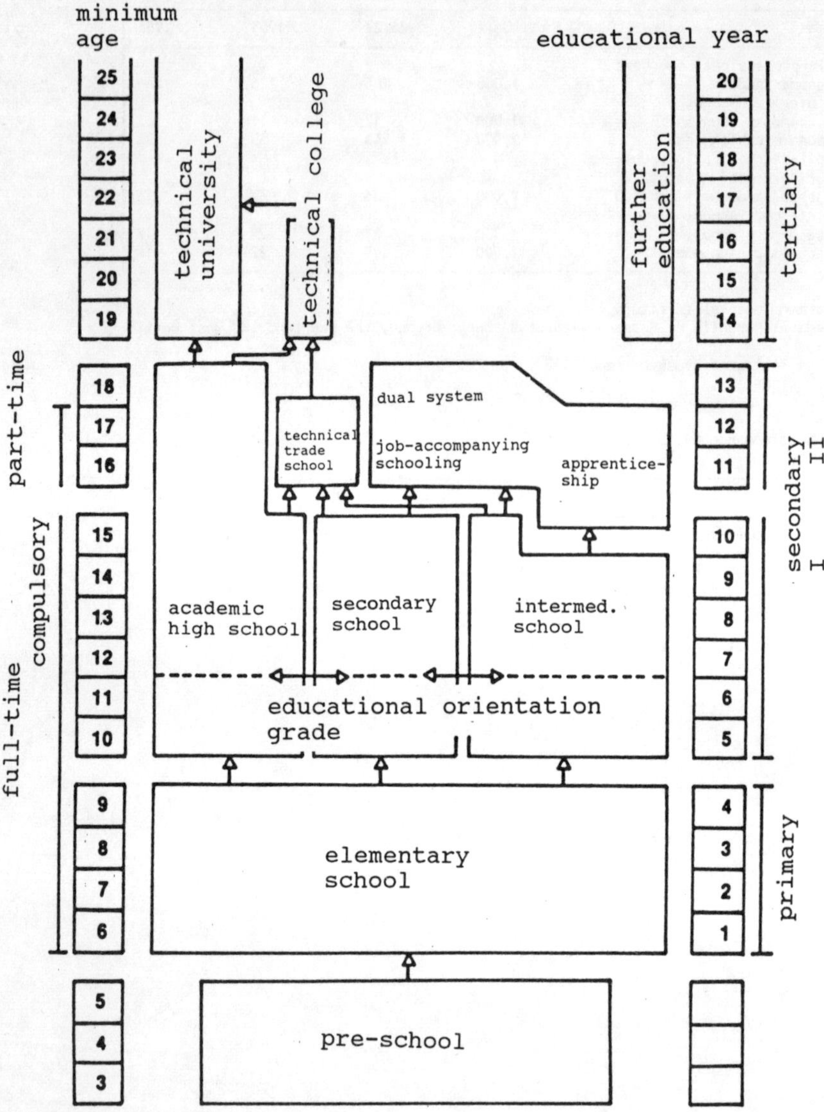

Source: AG am Max-Planck-Institut, 1984, p. 13.

8.2 Health System

Health care is characterized by two opposing tendencies: first, a growing number of (specialized and clinical) doctors and – in relation to this high number of doctors – a low number of nurses and their growing utilization by the population: second, government efforts of the past 15 years to reduce costs have kept the share of health care constant in the gross domestic product (after it had tripled between 1950 and 1975).

The number of patients going to a doctor or a hospital increased slightly between 1970 and 1987. In table 1, the numbers are given for subscribers to the largest health insurance organization (following the *Reichsversicherungsordnung* or RVO). The average subscriber went to the doctor for treatment 6.01 times in 1970; this number rose to 7.56 in 1987. There was also a slight increase in dental treatments per patient per year between 1970 and 1987.

The number of hospital patients per 10,000 persons rose nearly constantly. In 1970, there were 1,531 hospitalized patients per 10,000 persons. By 1987, the number of patients admitted had risen to 2,101 per 10,000.

Mortality rates, including infant mortality, have gradually declined, and life expectancy has increased. For women born between 1901 and 1910, life expectancy at birth was 48.33 years, and for men it was amounted to 44.82 years; between 1970 and 1972 it was 73.83 for women and 67.41 for men; between 1985 and 1987 it was 78.37 for women and 71.81 for men. Occupation-specific differences in life expectancy are still remarkably high.

We know more about the costs of the health-care system in the Federal Republic of Germany than we do about its efficiency and efficacy. The age structure of the population and the resulting morbidity shift will not, by themselves, lead to the widely expected increased expenditures for the health-care system. The increase in the number of doctors, the improvement and diffusion of treatment possibilities, and new technologies have convinced, and could continue to convince, the urbanized, more educated, and therefore medically knowledgeable society to take increasing advantage of medical services.

The total number of physicians has more than doubled since 1960. Since 1970, the number of physicians per 100,000 persons has sharply increased, especially the number of hospital doctors (see table 2). By 1970, the number of listed physicians per 100,000 persons was 171; 153 of them were actually working as doctors. By 1980, the number of physicians per 100,000 persons had risen to 267 (listed members of the Chamber) and 226 (working members), and by 1987 to 354 (listed) and 280 (working).

The representation of dentists in the population has also increased, though less notably (table 2). In 1970, there were 51 dentists per 100,000 persons, and this rate rose to 63 in 1987.

The number of nurses per 100,000 persons has increased steadily since 1970 (table 2). In 1987, there were 529 nurses per 100,000 persons. Even though the number of nurses is at its highest level ever, there continues to be a serious shortage. The demand for nurses in nursing homes and senior-citizens' centres has risen dramatically as the German population has aged. At present, it is difficult for health-care and nursing-care facilities to maintain a full nursing staff. The institutions of the Federal Republic are typically distinguished by a low number of nurses – in relation to the very high number of doctors – but also by a stringent differentiation between the family doctor's practice and the clinic.

Fewer beds, more patients, and higher occupancy rates mark the evolution of facilities within the health system. Between 1975 and 1988, the total stock of hospital beds declined by about 7%, and the number of beds per 10,000 persons fell steadily (see table 3), from 118.4 to 110. While the number of hospital beds per capita decreased, the occupancy rate of the available beds increased. In 1970, 89% of the available beds were occupied; by 1975 only 82.2% were, but, by 1987 86.6% were (table 3).

The number of hospital personnel has been on a steady rise, even as the numbers of hospital beds has declined (table 3). The number of hospital patients has also increased (table 3). In 1970, there were 5.86 hospital personnel per 100 patients; by 1987 this figure stood at 6.549. One explanation for this ratio may be intensification of treatment: more patients spend less time in hospital (table 3), so they need fewer beds but more personnel. Advances in the medical sciences have reduced the time needed for recovery from many surgical procedures.

Health-care costs have tripled in share of the GDP, going from barely 2% to 6%. Growth was most dynamic between 1965 and 1975, when expenditures rose by 3% (Alber, 1988). This rate has stabilized since 1975.

Johann Behrens

References

Alber, Jens

1988 "Die Gesundheitssysteme der OECD Länder im Vergleich." In Manfred G. Schmidt, ed., *Staatstätigkeit*, Politische Vierteljahresschrift. Sonderheft 19. Opladen: Westdeutscher Verlag.

–

1990 "Gesundheitspolitische Entwicklungen in OECD-Ländern: Zur Einordnung der bundesrepublikanischen Erfahrung." *Zeitschrift für Sozialreform*, 36.

Behrens, Johann
1989 "Schichtungsstruktur und Wettbewerb im System der gesetzlichen Krankenversicherung. Eine Gegenthese." *Zeitschrift für Sozialreform*. 35.

Bundesminister für Jugend, Familie, Frauen und Gesundheit
1989 *Daten des Gesundheitswesens - Ausgabe 1989*. Vol. 159. Stuttgart/Berlin/Köln: Kohlhammer.

OECD, ed.
1985 *Measuring Health Care 1960-1983. Expenditure, costs and performance*. Paris.

Sachverständigenrat für die Konzertierte Aktion im Gesundheitswesen (SVRKAIG)
1990 *Herausforderungen und Perspektiven der Gesundheitsversorgung. Vorschläge für die Konzertierte Aktion im Gesundheitswesen*. Baden-Baden: Nomos.

Table 1
Patients (per 10,000 residents)

Item	1970	1975	1980	1985	1987	1988
Treatment cases/health-insured persons[1]	6.01	6.80	7.06	7.20	7.36	7.56
Hospital patients[2]	1.53	1.69	1.88	1.99	2.10	-

1. Outpatient treatment cases per member of the RVO (Reichsverordnung) health insurances.
2. Patients admitted to hospital per 10,000 residents.

Source: Kassenärztliche Bundesvereinigung, SVRKAiG 90, tab. 201; Deutsche Krankenhaus Gesellschaft, SVRKAiG 90, tab. 528.

Table 2
Personnel (per 10,000 persons)

Item	1970	1975	1980	1985	1987	1988
Registered doctors[1]	17.1	-	26.7	-	35.4	-
Working doctors[2]	15.3	-	22.6	-	28.0	-
Dentists[3]	5.1	5.2	5.4	6.0	6.3	6.5
Nurses[4]	28.7	-	46.1	-	52.9	-

1. Registered doctors: members of Chamber (Ärztekammerangehörige) per 10,000 persons.
2. Working doctors: "Berufstätige Ärzte" per 10,000 persons.
3. Dentists: dentists and dental technicians active in health care per 10,000.
4. Nurses: health-care and obstetrics personnel in hospitals.

The population density calculated herein is nearly twice that published by the OECD (1985). Upon using the same data from the Statistisches Bundesamt, the difference is explicable solely by varying definitions of nurses: OECD counts as nurses only registered nurses and trained health care personnel and midwives, whereas we add pediatric nurses and health- care personnel, nurses' assistants, uncertified health- care personnel, and health-care and obstetrics personnel in training. The table allows for individual indicators for nursing- personnel density. The table also makes clear that the near-doubling of health- care personnel since 1970 is accompanied by a strong decrease in some categories, i.e. baby and pediatric nurses' assistants, uncertified health- care personnel, and midwives and some obstetrics personnel.

Source: Kassenärztliche Bundesvereinigung, SVRKAiG 90, tab. 17; author's calculations; Statistisches Bundesamt, SVRKAiG 90, tab. 521; author's calculations.

Table 3
Hospital Facilities

Item	1970	1975	1980	1985	1987
Hospital beds[1]	112.0	118.0	114.0	110.7	110.0
Occupancy rate in %	88.5	83.3	84.9	85.7	86.6
Average days of stay	24.9	22.2	19.7	18.0	17.1
Patients in hospitals[1]	1.53	1.69	1.88	1.99	2.1

1. Per 10,000 persons

Source: Deutsche Krankenhaus Gesellschaft, SVRKAiG 90, tables 528, 530, 529, 528.

8.3 Welfare System

The institutions of the German welfare state, some with a tradition of over a century, have experienced a remarkable expansion since the end of World War II: coverage has been extended to additional social groups, existing benefits and services have been considerably improved, and new benefit types have been introduced. Consequently, the social expenditure ratio has risen from about 20% of the gross national product in the early 1950s to more than 30% nowadays – that is, by about half. In a developmental perspective, the reform period of 1970–1975 stands out, whereas development since then is characterized by consolidation at the high level attained, or even by stagnation.

It is common knowledge that Germany was one of the pioneers of the welfare state. As early as 100 years ago, extensive social legislation was brought about (1881), in the course of which a health insurance scheme (1883), an industrial-accident scheme (1884), and an invalidity and old-age pension scheme for blue-collar workers (1889) were introduced, the latter being extended to white-collar workers in 1911. This social-insurance system was completed in 1927 by an unemployment-insurance scheme.

This legacy is one of the main reasons that the development of the welfare system in the Federal Republic is distinguished by a high degree of institutional continuity, without major structural breaks and reforms. The basic institutions of social security were already in existence, and the threads of the traditional structural principles (compulsory insurance, earnings replacement, financing by social-security contributions rather than taxes, semi-autonomous self-administration) could be taken up again. In addition to the extended coverage of established programs and the improvement of their benefit levels, some new social policy programs were introduced.

Among the most important social-security reforms of the postwar period are the pension reforms of 1957 (dynamization of old-age, survivors', and disability pensions) and 1972 (introduction of the flexible retirement age); the general introduction in 1969 of mandatory wage-continuation payments (*Lohnfortzahlung*) by the employer in case of illness (instead of sickness benefits through health insurance); the Job Promotion Act (*Arbeitsförderungsgesetz*, or AFG) of 1969, which marked the step to an active labour-market policy; the introduction (1954) and later reform (1975) of child benefits; thorough revisions of the Youth Welfare Act (*Jugendwohlfahrtsgesetz*, or JWG) in 1961, and of the Federal Social Assistance Act (*Bundessozialhilfegesetz*, or BSHG) in 1962; and the introduction of educational grants (for college and high-school students) in 1969 and 1971.

Perhaps most notable institutional innovations, however, are to be found in the field of industrial relations, going beyond social security proper: the

Betriebsverfassungsgesetz of 1952, instituting workers' councils at the company level, and its reform in 1972; and the *Montanmitbestimmung* (co-determination in the coal and steel industry) of 1951 and the general Co-determination Act of 1976.

Trends in Social Expenditures

An overall view of the developmental pattern of social expenditures is presented in table 1. Taken comprehensively (including education, which is usually not considered part of social policy in Germany), they rose from under 20% of the GNP in 1950 to over 30% in 1980. As the offical social budget is defined (excluding education, but including so-called indirect benefits; see below), the social expenditure ratio shows a steep rise in the decade of 1965 to 1975 and a slightly declining trend in the following decade, though it did not fall below the level of the early 1970s. Corresponding to this disproportionate growth, social expenditures also gained additional weight in the public sector budget. With the exception of housing, all social-policy sectors contributed to the growth of the social budget. Expenditures for health and education show the most dynamic trend: their shares in GNP have more than doubled since 1960. However, the bulk of social expenditures is still made for purposes of income maintenance in the stricter sense, that is, as cash and noncash benefits.

Periods of Welfare-State Development

With regard to the political determinants of welfare-state development in West Germany, the various governmental constellations since the foundation of the Federal Republic exhibit quite different profiles. It appears that more than half of the total increase in the social-expenditure ratio (see table 2) was achieved during the governing period of the social-democratic–liberal coalition (1969–1982). Viewed from this perspective, the governments led by Social Democrats seem to have been much stronger promoters of an expansionist welfare system than were the governments under Christian Democratic leadership. However, there was also a considerable increase during the period of conservative coalition governments, from 1950 to 1966, while a slight decrease can be observed under the conservative-liberal coalition that has been in power since 1983.

The picture changes, however, when one takes a closer look at real annual growth rates of social expenditures (see table 3), in which the early periods of Christian Democratic–liberal government appear to show the most marked growth tendencies. This seemingly contradictory result can be reconciled, however, by reference to the fact that during the CDU/CSU-led government in the 1950s and 1960s, economic growth rates were higher on the average, so that the resources for expansion of social-policy programs were available without necessitating substantial increases in proportion to GNP. The expansion of the welfare system under the social democratic-liberal governments, on the other hand, took place during a time of decreasing (and, on average, lower) economic growth rates, which led to a greater increase in their proportion to GNP.

Closer analysis shows, however, that the periods of development of the welfare state do not coincide with the respective "political" periods of the various governmental constellations in each case (see table 4). With this distinction, the early Christian-Democratic governmental periods can be broken up into a "take-off" phase of rapid expansion (1949 – 1957) and a phase of stabilization, with only moderate real growth rates (1958 – 1969). Likewise, the expansion phase under Social Democratic leadership occurred between 1970 and 1975, whereas from 1976 on there was a consolidation with noticeably reduced growth rates in all sectors, reflecting the effects of cut-back legislation.

Social Budget: Benefits and Revenue Structure

A more detailed account of the structure of (and the structural changes in) social expenditures can be derived from the official social budget (see tables 5, 6). This budget includes – in addition to the social expenditures borne at the federal, state, and community level and by the social-insurance institutions – tax allowances for social purposes (so-called indirect benefits) and certain benefits provided by public and private employers (for example, wage continuation, company pension plans). The necessity and rationale for distinguishing between "institutions" and "functions" lies in the fact that – particularly in the West German social security system – certain institutions perform functionally different tasks (for example, insurance for old age, survivors, and disability) while similar tasks (for example, providing retirement benefits) are carried out by different institutions for specific target groups.

In functional terms, approximately two-fifths of social expenditures go to the "old age and survivors" sector and approximately one-third to "health (including disability)." This corresponds to about 12% and 10% of GNP, respectively. The "employment" function absorbs an increasing proportion of expenditures, due to persistently high unemployment rates since the 1970s, while expenditures for "marriage and family" (especially for child-rearing and family-related tax relief) are clearly on the decline.

The traditional dominance of "classic" social-insurance institutions has been reinforced over time: they now account for about 60% of all social expenditures. The most rapid growth has taken place in health insurance (in the 1970s) and employment-related measures (since 1975); the latter field includes cash benefits for the unemployed as well as active labour-market policy measures. Likewise, expenditures for "social assistance and services" (especially welfare) are rising, though their quantitative importance within the total social-security system is usually overestimated.

The dominance of insurance-type social-transfer programs is also reflected in the revenue structure (see tables 7, 8): over half of all social expenditures have always been financed through employer and employee contributions. The strong emphasis placed on social-security contributions has been reinforced in the long run, while direct financing through general tax revenues has fallen to about one-third. Leaving aside indirect benefits, the tax-financed share of expenditures was further reduced, to only 26%, in 1985. Correspondingly, private households are increasingly involved in paying directly for social security. The corporate sector's share is stagnating at about one-third, and the public sector's share has fallen from approximately 45% to less than 40%. The latter figure also includes the (actual and imputed) employer contributions for civil servants and public employees. With regard to distribution by level of government, more than half of the tax-financed social expenditures is under the responsibility of the federal government, although with a declining trend.

Clienteles of the Welfare State

The expenditure developments sketched out above have arisen from many causes, varying in importance from sector to sector: changes in the demographic structure, legislative extensions of eligibility, improvements in benefit levels (per recipient).

Table 9 shows the evolution of the target groups of major social-security programs. Especially in the field of statutory pensions, there is a strong increase in the number of beneficiaries which exceeds by far the effect of demographic growth, but which indicates the inclusion of new social groups and the lowering of the average retirement age. The number of recipients of unemployment benefits has multiplied since the 1970s; at the same time, however, the share of all unemployed persons receiving benefits – which indicates the actual social protective effect of the program – has decreased. In sum, the various sector-specific developments have led to a consistently growing proportion of individuals and households depending on public social transfers to make their living. The fact that, in 1985, for approximately every third person with an income social transfers constituted the main source of that income is a meaningful indicator for the importance of income redistribution via government transfer programs.

Selected Benefit Levels

Trends in benefit levels for several important social security programs are shown in table 10. Since the pension reform of 1957, the standard pension – presuming average earnings and a contribution period of 40 years – amounts to 60% of the so-called general calculation base (*allgemeine Bemessungsgrundlage*). Because the general calculation base is lagging behind current earnings by about three to five years, this corresponds to a gross benefit level of only about 45% of current average earnings. However, due to the tax exemption of most retirement pensions, as opposed to the increasing tax burden on earnings from employment, the net benefit level is considerably higher and has tended to rise, stabilizing in the 1980s at a level of approximately 65%.

Empirical averages for retirement pensions remain, however, well below figures for the standard pension, and this is particularly so in the blue-collar workers' scheme. This can be attributed to the fact that in a large number of cases neither the earnings level nor the presumed period of contribution are reached, thus leading to proportional reductions of pension benefits. Nevertheless, an improvement of net benefit levels over time can also be ascertained, due to the general increase brought about by the pension reform in 1957 and to the above-mentioned effect of increased tax burdens on the active labour force.

As part of the pension reform of 1957, the principle of "dynamic adjustment" – indexation of pensions according to (gross) earnings – was introduced. This mode of adjustment was later extended to other earnings-replacement benefits (for example, accident insurance and war-victim benefits).

Since 1969, the employer has been obliged by law to grant full salary or wage payment during the first six weeks of an employee's sickness; these are followed by sickness benefits amounting to 80% of previous gross income, which as a rule suffices to maintain previous net income.

Unemployment pay, which is the social-insurance benefit in the case of unemployment, was raised to 68% of previous individual net earnings in 1969, but was reduced to 63% for single persons in the course of the cutback legislation in 1984. Compared to average net earnings, unemployment pay scarcely runs over 50%, which can be explained by the fact that unemployment is more widespread among below-average wage earners.

The standard scale rates of social assistance, which can be considered an operationalization of the subsistence minimum (for a single person), have consistently been below 20% of the average net earnings. For couples and families with children, the social assistance rates are, of course, graded according to the number of household members, but the levels are still comparatively low.

In summary, it can be said that the levels of the major income-substituting insurance programs, in relation to disposable net income, have been at least maintained and mostly improved. In contrast to this, the levels of a number of income-supplementing tax-financed programs (such as child benefits, social assistance, rent assistance, and educational grants) have been subject to creeping erosion, due to insufficient adjustment mechanisms.

Jürgen Kohl

References

Alber, Jens

1986 "Germany." In Peter Flora, ed., *Growth to Limits. The Western European Welfare States Since World War II.* Vol. 2, 1-154. Berlin/New York: de Gruyter.

–

1987 "Germany." In Peter Flora, ed., *Growth to Limits. The Western European Welfare States Since World War II.* Vol. 4, (Institutional Synopsis), 247-353. Berlin/New York: de Gruyter.

–

1989 *Der Sozialstaat in der Bundesrepublik 1950-1983.* Frankfurt am Main: Campus.

Bundesminister für Arbeit und Sozialordnung

1986 *Sozialbericht 1986.* Bonn.

–

1990 *Sozialbericht 1990.* Bonn.

Kohl, Jürgen

1987 "Was kostet, was leistet der Sozialstaat? Analyse und Kritik des Sozialbudgets." In Michael Opielka, and Ilona Ostner, eds., *Umbau des Sozialstaats*, 48-71. Essen: Klartext.

Zapf, Wolfgang

1986 "Die deutsche Version des Wohlfahrtsstaates." In Klaus Hanau, et al., eds., *Wirtschafts- und Sozialstatistik. Empirische Grundlagen politischer Entscheidungen*, 379-403. Göttingen: Vandenhoeck und Ruprecht.

Table 1
Evolution of social expenditures 1950 - 1985 (in % of the GNP)

Year	Total	Social expenditures acc. to Alber (1987)				Social expenditures acc. to Social Report (1990)	
		Social security	Health	Housing	Edu-cation	Total	Direct services
1950	19.2	13.5	1.8	1.7	2.1	-	-
1955	19.1	13.2	1.9	1.7	2.3	-	-
1960	22.2	15.7	2.4	1.7	2.4	22.7	19.3
1965	23.5	16.2	2.9	1.3	3.1	25.0	20.7
1970	24.7	16.8	3.6	0.7	3.7	26.7	23.0
1975	32.7	20.8	5.9	0.9	5.2	33.7	30.9
1980	31.0	19.6	5.7	0.8	4.9	32.2	29.4
1985	-	-	-	-	-	31.2	28.5
1989	-	-	-	-	30.0	27.4	

Source: Column 2-6: Alber, 1987, p. 325, tab. 4; column 7-8: Sozialbericht, 1990, p. 203, tab. I-1a.

Table 2
Growth of social expenditure ratio per government

Governments	Total social expenditures	Expenditures for			
		Social security	Health	Housing	Education
Conservative-liberal coalition (1950-1966)	4.4	2.1	1.4	-0.3	1.3
Conservative-socialdemocratic coalition (1966-1969)	0.4	0.3	0.3	-0.5	0.2
Socialdemocratic-liberal coalition (1969-1982)	7.5	3.5	2.5	0.2	1.5
Conservative-liberal coalition (1982-1983)	-0.6	-0.4	0.0	-0.1	-0.2
Total post-war period	11.7	5.5	4.2	-0.7	2.8

Source: Alber, 1989, p. 256, tab. 39.

Table 3
Real growth rates of social expenditures per governments

Governments	Total social expenditures	Expenditures for			
		Social security	Health	Housing	Education
Conservative-liberal coalition (1950-1966)	8.4	8.9	8.7	6.0	8.1
Conservative-socialdemocratic coalition (1966-1969)	4.9	5.6	6.0	-9.9	4.6
Socialdemocratic-liberal coalition (1969-1982)	4.4	4.4	5.3	4.3	4.0
Conservative-liberal coalition (1982-1983)	(-0.8)	(0.8)	(-0.8)	(-5.9)	(-2.1)
Total post-war period	6.3	6.5	6.9	3.5	5.9

Source: Alber, 1989, p. 257, tab. 40.

Table 4
Periods of social expenditure development

Item	Period	Total	Average real growth rate			
			Social security	Health	Housing	Education
Take-off	1949-57[1]	10.6	11.5	8.8	11.4	8.8
Stabilization	1958-69	6.3	6.6	7.9	-1.1	6.8
Expansion	1970-75	7.8	7.7	8.7	7.2	7.7
Consolidation	1976-83	1.3	1.3	2.3	0.9	0.4
Post-war average	1951-83	6.3	6.5	6.9	3.5	5.9

1. Data from 1951 to 1957.

Source: Alber, 1989: 233, tab. 31.

Table 5 (Part I)
Social expenditures by function (in % of GNP)

Item	1960	1965	1970	1975	1980	1985	1989	1989[1]
Social budget	22.75	25.01	26.66	33.67	32.22	31.20	30.02	678,465
Marriage and family	4.67	5.11	4.56	4.66	4.56	3.86	3.95	89,193
Children	2.28	2.59	2.21	2.44	2.62	2.05	2.37	53,656
Spouses	2.15	2.30	2.15	2.01	1.69	1.62	1.41	31,919
Motherhood	0.25	0.22	0.20	0.21	0.25	0.20	0.16	3,618
Health	6.13	6.74	7.86	10.44	10.62	10.37	9.87	223,102
Prevention	0.49	0.64	0.65	0.79	0.66	0.61	0.68	15,410
Sickness	3.97	4.34	5.38	7.49	7.61	7.37	6.98	157,820
Work injuries, occupational diseases	0.55	0.68	0.72	0.81	0.81	0.76	0.70	15,713
Invalidity (general)	1.12	1.08	1.10	1.36	1.54	1.64	1.51	34,159
Employment	0.60	0.52	0.86	2.15	1.92	2.47	2.45	55,413
Vocational training	0.17	0.14	0.35	0.68	0.55	0.48	0.52	11,704
Mobility (Promotion of..)	0.08	0.16	0.25	0.21	0.40	0.33	0.41	9,361
Unemployment	0.35	0.22	0.26	1.26	0.97	1.66	1.52	34,348
Old age and survivors	9.38	9.90	10.71	13.12	12.47	12.43	12.07	272,722
Old age	8.89	9.33	10.07	12.34	11.67	11.80	11.53	260,683
Survivors	0.49	0.57	0.64	0.78	0.80	0.63	0.53	12,039
Other functions	1.98	2.74	2.68	3.30	2.65	2.07	1.68	38,035
Consequences of political events	1.02	0.84	0.70	0.74	0.55	0.31	0.20	4,489
Housing	0.24	1.08	0.88	0.80	0.70	0.63	0.53	11,996
Promotion of savings and asset formation	0.37	0.58	0.89	1.56	1.25	0.93	0.78	17,638
General assistance	0.35	0.24	0.21	0.20	0.15	0.20	0.17	3,913

1. In million DM.

Table 5 (Part II): Social expenditures by function (in % of total)

Item	1960	1965	1970	1975	1980	1985	1989
Social budget	100.0	100.0	100.0	100.0	100.0	100.0	100.0
Marriage and family	20.5	20.4	17.1	13.8	14.2	12.4	13.1
Children	10.0	10.4	8.3	7.3	8.1	6.6	7.9
Spouses	9.4	9.2	8.1	6.0	5.3	5.2	4.7
Motherhood	1.1	0.9	0.8	0.6	0.8	0.6	0.5
Health	26.9	26.9	29.5	31.0	33.0	33.2	32.9
Prevention	2.1	2.5	2.5	2.3	2.0	1.9	2.3
Sickness	17.4	17.3	20.2	22.2	23.6	23.6	23.3
Work injuries, occupation diseases	2.4	2.7	2.7	2.4	2.5	2.4	2.3
Invalidity (general)	4.9	4.3	4.1	4.0	4.8	5.3	5.0
Employment	2.6	2.1	3.2	6.4	6.0	7.9	8.2
Vocational training	0.7	0.6	1.3	2.0	1.7	1.5	1.7
Mobility (Promotion of..)	0.4	0.6	0.9	0.6	1.2	1.0	1.4
Unemployment	1.6	0.9	1.0	3.8	3.0	5.3	5.1
Old age and survivors	41.2	39.6	40.2	39.0	38.7	39.8	40.2
Old age	39.1	37.2	37.8	36.6	36.2	37.8	38.4
Survivors	2.1	2.3	2.4	2.3	2.5	2.0	1.8
Other functions	8.7	10.9	10.1	9.8	8.2	6.6	5.6
Consequences of political events	4.5	3.4	2.6	2.2	1.7	1.0	0.7
Housing	1.0	4.3	3.3	2.4	2.2	2.0	1.8
Promotion of savings and asset formation	1.6	2.3	3.4	4.6	3.9	3.0	2.6
General assistance	1.6	1.0	0.8	0.6	0.5	0.6	0.6

Source: Sozialbericht, 1986, pp. 178, tab. I-3, for 1965, 1975; Sozialbericht, 1990, pp. 205, tab. I-3 for 1960, 1970, pp. 1980.

Table 6
Social expenditures by institutions (in %)

Item	1960	1965	1970	1975	1980	1985	1989	1989[1]
Social budget	100.0	100.0	100.0	100.0	100.0	100.0	100.0	678,465
General schemes	48.0	47.9	49.4	58.2	58.9	61.5	60.8	412,625
Pension insurance	28.4	27.5	29.0	29.2	29.8	30.4	30.2	204,937
Health insurance	14.0	14.0	14.5	17.6	18.8	19.9	19.2	130,362
Work injury insurance	2.5	2.8	2.4	2.1	2.1	2.0	1.9	12,917
Unemployment and labour market measures	1.7	1.4	2.2	5.2	4.8	6.8	7.0	47,742
Child benefits	1.3	2.5	1.6	4.2	3.7	2.5	2.1	13,986
Up-bringing benefits	-	-	-	-	-	-	0.6	4,048
Special schemes	0.3	0.5	0.6	0.7	0.8	0.8	0.9	6,112
Farmers' pensions	0.3	0.4	0.5	0.5	0.6	0.6	0.6	4,220
Pension institutions for professionals	0.1	0.1	0.1	0.2	0.2	0.2	0.3	1,892
Civil service schemes	13.9	14.1	13.3	10.7	9.7	9.1	8.9	60,521
Civil service pensions	9.8	9.3	8.8	7.5	6.9	6.4	6.1	41,358
Family supplements	3.2	3.8	3.5	2.0	1.6	1.4	1.4	9,576
(Sickness) allowances	0.9	1.0	1.1	1.1	1.2	1.3	1.4	9,587
Employers' benefits	7.2	7.1	10.4	8.6	9.4	8.9	9.2	62,575
Wage-continuation payments	4.4	3.9	6.9	5.3	5.8	4.5	4.7	31,620
Occupational (company) pension schemes	1.7	1.7	1.7	1.5	1.7	2.2	2.4	16,050
Supplementary pensions for public employees	0.5	0.6	1.0	1.0	1.2	1.5	1.5	9,960
Other employers' benefits	0.6	0.8	0.8	0.7	0.6	0.7	0.7	4,945
Compensations	11.9	8.8	6.4	4.6	3.7	3.0	2.5	16,755
Social compensations (war victims and dependents)	5.7	5.1	4.2	3.2	2.8	2.3	1.9	13,102
Equalization of burden fund (property compensations for refugees)	2.9	1.8	1.0	0.5	0.4	0.2	0.2	1,132
Indemnification for victims of political persecution	3.1	1.6	1.1	0.7	0.5	0.3	0.3	1,740
Other compensations	0.1	0.4	0.2	0.2	0.1	0.1	0.1	781
Social assistance and services	3.8	4.8	6.5	9.3	9.0	8.4	9.3	62,965
Social assistance	1.9	1.9	2.0	2.7	3.1	4.0	4.8	32,325
Youth assistance	0.6	0.9	0.9	1.2	1.7	1.7	1.9	13,140
Educational grants	0.1	0.1	0.3	0.7	0.7	0.1	0.1	520
Housing benefits	0.0	0.2	0.4	0.5	0.4	0.5	0.6	3,967
Public health service	0.4	0.5	0.4	0.4	0.3	0.3	0.3	2,150
Assets formation	0.6	1.2	2.5	3.9	2.7	1.9	1.6	10,863
Direct benefits	84.7	82.9	86.2	91.7	91.2	91.5	91.3	619,685
Indirect benefits	15.3	17.1	13.8	8.3	8.8	8.5	8.7	58,780
Tax expenditures	15.2	13.8	11.5	6.9	7.6	7.6	7.8	53,000
Housing allowances (tax relief)	0.1	3.3	2.2	1.3	1.2	1.0	0.9	5,780

1. In million DM.

Source: Sozialbericht, 1986, pp. 180, tab. I-4 for 1965, 1975; Sozialbericht, 1990, pp. 207, tab. I-4 for 1960, 1970, pp. 1980.

Table 7
Kinds of contributions to the social budget (in %)

Item	1960	1970	1975	1980	1985	1989	1989[1]
Contributions	51.5	56.9	58.5	61.9	64.3	64.4	457,844
of the insured	19.7	21.9	24.2	25.0	27.3	27.7	196,864
- employees	16.2	17.1	16.7	18.3	19.6	19.9	141,142
- self-employed	0.5	0.6	1.1	1.0	1.1	1.1	7,874
- other[2]	3.0	4.3	6.3	5.7	6.5	6.7	47,848
of the employers	31.8	35.0	34.3	36.9	37.0	36.7	260,980
- actual contributions	20.5	19.9	20.4	22.1	23.5	23.6	167,971
- imputed contributions	11.3	15.1	13.9	14.8	13.5	13.1	93,009
Subsidies	45.8	40.7	38.9	36.0	33.3	33.7	239,563
from public revenues	41.3	38.5	36.0	33.6	31.3	31.8	226,165
from subsidies	4.5	2.2	2.9	2.3	2.0	1.9	13,398
Other revenues (e.g. interest)	2.7	2.4	2.6	2.1	2.4	1.9	13,495
Total financing	100.0	100.0	100.0	100.0	100.0	100.0	710,902

1. In million DM.
2. For instance, pensioners, other social insurance institutions.

Source: Sozialbericht, 1986, p. 184, tab. I-5 for 1975; Sozialbericht, 1990, 211, tab. I-5, for 1960, 1970, pp. 1980.

Table 8
Sources of contributions to the social budget (in %)

Item	1960	1970	1975	1980	1985	1989	1989[1]
(Private) companies	31.7	30.9	30.4	32.0	31.8	31.1	221,067
Federal	25.4	24.9	24.4	22.4	20.5	19.9	141,324
State	14.1	13.9	12.1	11.5	10.9	11.2	79,569
Local	7.2	6.5	7.1	7.2	7.6	8.4	59,880
Social insurance institutions	0.1	0.3	0.3	0.2	0.2	0.3	1,879
Private (non-profit) organizations	0.7	0.7	0.7	0.6	0.6	0.6	4,079
Private households	20.7	22.8	24.9	26.0	28.4	28.5	202,841
Rest of the world	-	-	0.0	-	-	-	264
Total	100.0	100.0	100.0	100.0	100.0	100.0	710,902

1. In million DM.

Source: Sozialbericht, 1986, p. 185, tab. I-6 for 1975; Sozialbericht, 1990, p. 212, tab. I-6 for 1960, 1970, pp. 1980.

Table 9
Major groups of social benefit recipients 1950 - 1985

	1950	1955	1960	1965	1970	1975	1980	1983
Pension scheme: old age-, disability-, surviors'-, pensions								
in 1,000	5,333	6,946	7,976	8,837	10,211	11,839	13,107	13,623
in % of pop. over 60 years	81.1	93.4	90.0	83.6	87.5	95.5	110.2	111.1
Work injury insurance: pensioners								
in 1,000 636	830	916	1,011	1,018	1,018	1,005	982	
in % of the labour force	2,9	3,5	3,5	3,7	3,8	3,9	3,9	3,6
Health insurance: recipients of continued payment of wages resp. sickness benefit:								
in 1,000	(447)	(621)	(902)	(850)	(1,003)	(1,014)	(1,176)	(914)
in % of compulsorily insured	3.6	4.0	5.1	4.9	5.6	5.3	5.7	4.4
Unemployment insurance: recipients of unemployment benefit or assistance:								
in 1,000	1,455	890	226	109	113	817	576	1,500
in % of unemployed	77.8	82.9	83.4	74.1	75.8	76.1	64.8	66.4
Social assistance: recipients overall								
in 1,000	1,633	1,328	1,134	1,404	1,491	2,049	2,144	2,437
in % of pop.	3.4	2.6	2.0	2.4	2.5	3.3	3.5	4.0
Social assistance: recipients of supplementary assistance ('poverty line')								
in 1,000	-	-	-	760	749	1,190	1,322	1,726
in % of pop.	-	-	-	1.3	1.2	1.9	2.1	2.8
Persons with predominant coverage of living costs through social benefits								
in 1,000	-	-	7,200	7,799	9,087	10,538	11,195	11,910
in % of persons with own income			21.3	22.3	25.2	28.2	28.7	30.7

Source: Alber, 1989 , p.140f, tab. 11; last row, Alber, 1986, p. 46, tab. 6; for 1985 own calculation based on: Statistisches Bundesamt, 1987, p. 98, tab. 6.1.

Table 10
Standard rates and average benefits of social security programs

Item	1950	1955	1960	1965	1970	1975	1980	1983
Pension scheme: standard pension								
in constant prices (1976)	-	-	433	527	684	862	945	956
in % of gross income	-	-	47.3	43.7	44.0	43.2	44.6	44.6
in % of net income	-	-	56.2	52.7	56.8	59.0	63.2	64.5
Average insured pension (ArV)[1]:								
in constant prices (1976)	132	177	288	337	438	555	585	583
in % of net earnings	29	29	37	33	35	40	39	40
Average old age pension (ArV)[1]:								
in constant prices (1976)	-	-	302	350	494	618	615	569
in % of net earnings	-	-	39	35	39	44	41	39
Average widow's pension (ArV)[1]:								
in constant prices (1976)	78	114	198	238	348	456	501	494
in % of net earnings	17	18	25	24	28	33	33	34
Sickness benefit:								
earnings replacement ratio, first six weeks	50	50	90	100	100	100	100	100
sickness benefit, from 7 th week (in % of regular wage)	50	50	50	70	75	80	80	80
Unemployment insurance:								
earnings replacement ratio of unemployment benefit	(40)	(47)	(50)	55	62.5	68	68	68
average unemployment benefit in constant prices (1976)	190	276	367	527	655	756	762	721
in % of net earnings	41	45	47	52	52	54	50	50
Social assistance: standard scale rate								
in constant prices (1976)	-	-	151	185	217	263	266	259
in % of net earnings	-	-	19	18	17	19	18	18

1. ArV: Workers' scheme.

Source: Alber, 1989, p. 147f, tab. 12, 13; Sozialbericht 1986, p. 190, tab. IV-13.

8.4 The State

During the last 40 years, the number and extent of state activities (federal) in society increased, as did the state's share in distribution in a broader sense (from 37% in 1950 to 47% in 1985). This increase was caused mainly by the social-security system. While, after expenditures, the relationship between the federal, state, and local governments is relatively constant at 4:3:2, a centralization of decision-making authority at the federal level has taken place. Twenty percent of all employees are recruited by the federal government, which employed twice as many persons in 1985 as in 1950.

Federal Budget

With the exception of military service, citizens are no longer called upon for implementation of state activities. Therefore, public-sector revenues and expenditures are the most important indicators for activities and manipulation by the state in society. However, they are not the only expression of the presence of the state in society, since many private and public sectors have – mainly by means of legal devices – injunctions and precepts which guide citizens or limit their freedom of action.

Taxes are the most significant source of state revenue, bringing in between 80% and 85% of the total (see table 1). The state's "capital share" (income from economic activities of state and capital gains) in financing itself and its activities in the Federal Republic has never exceeded 8%.

The state's share in distribution – that is, its share of expenditures in the gross national product (GNP) – serves as a global measurement for its activities in a society. Expenditures by the public sector in the Federal Republic are displayed in two different ways: by the finance statistics and by the national-accounts statistics. Table 2 indicates the state's share in distribution in a broader and in a narrower sense: while the share of the state in distribution has remained at an astonishingly constant one-third for the last three decades, the state's share in distribution in the broader sense points to a steady increase, which brought state expenditures up to half of the GNP from the mid-1970s to the 1980s. The lion's share of this increase can be traced back to the rise in social expenditures financed by contributions (see 8.3, "Welfare System"). In these increases, the increase in the relative price of state activities (lower technical level at even wage level) and inflation processes (losses of the state) are also manifested.

The structure of state expenditures is of more interest than are general trends. If we look at the different levels of government, the share of the states and communities rises continually up to the beginning of the 1980s (see table 3). This depends mainly on the structure of expenditures according to the level of government. While the spending categories of defence and social disbursements (including expenses pertaining to the aftermath of World War II, such as military-occupation costs, the significance of which is diminishing) are borne by the federal government, expenditures on culture and health, which are paid by the state governments, are increasing rapidly. Personnel costs are also distributed very unequally: in 1989, 43% of the state governments' expenditures went toward personnel, while the federal government spent 14% and the communities 32% in this category (Statistisches Bundesamt, 1989a, p. 217).

In contrast to the trend toward maintaining federative principles shown in these expenditures, a degree of centralization can be noted regarding responsibility for decision making. Legislation clearly mainly in the federal government's jurisdiction, while implementation is mostly left to the lower levels (about 35 amendments to the federal constitution refer to this phenomenon) (Weidenfeld & Zimmermann, 1989).

Looking at state expenditures in respect to various functions (see table 4), two developments stand out: state activities concerning infrastructure, such as transportation, communication, and construction of housing, are decreasing, while expenditures for social protection have risen strongly. The first trend can be explained by the need to rebuild housing following World War II. In some areas, the discontinuation of state activities did, however, have negative consequences, such as the housing shortage in urban areas toward the end of the 1980s. The increase in spending on social protection can be traced back to the expansion of the social-security system (see 0.1, "Demographic Trends"; 8.1, "Educational System"; and 8.3, "Welfare System").

Federal Personnel

In 1986, about 4.6 million persons (excluding soldiers) were employed in the public service. This means that every fifth employee and every thirteenth citizen was working for West Germany's largest employer. The number of the employees in the civil service doubled between 1950 and 1985, the largest growth rates being for part-time employees, whose share went from 3% to 17% over this period (see table 5).

The proportion of civil servants and judges to all persons employed in the public sector rose from 44% in 1960 to 47% in 1983. The portion of female civil servants increased disproportionately. However, the growth in number of white-collar workers was equal for men and women: from 24.5% to 31.1%. This growth can be traced back to the expansion of public education and public health, where white-collar workers are employed – in the public-health sector predominantly women, in the academic sector predominantly men (Brandes et al., 1989). The share of personnel costs for the different functions is highest in the communities, not least because it is here that the most personnel-intensive activities are carried out (e.g., social welfare office).

Looking at personnel developments per function, the decline in the percentage of employees at the federal railway is the most striking, having fallen in 1985 to only half the number in 1950. An increase in personnel took place in different areas due to explicit political decisions – for instance, implementation of the defence administration in the 1960s and expansion of education and science since the end of the 1960s (see table 6).

Although increases in the areas of health care and sports have been considerable, they have not been high enough to prevent an emergency situation in the nursing service at the end of the 1980s. Similarly, growth rates in the areas of public security and jurisdiction could not prevent bottleneck situations concerning the number of personnel, which caused considerable prolongations in the duration of lawsuits.

Expansion of Federal Functions

Deregulation is found in only a few state management areas, including federal mail service and the media. The federal mail service previously included communication services (telephone, telegraph, etc.), the Postbank Service (offering standard banking services), and traditional postal service. It has now been divided into three departments, which will be turned into separate private companies. A transition has also taken place in television, which has evolved from a system organized "under public law" into a mixed system (see 9.5, "Mass Media").

Overall, the above-mentioned expansion of the state within society predominates, in particular as the state repeatedly takes on functions such as, for example, the introduction of (compulsory) nursing insurance. It would be wrong to deduce a growing public demand from this. On the contrary, Kaase (in Weidenfeld & Zimmermann, 1989) indicates that there is rather a desire for the state's public functions to decrease.

Mathias Bös

References

Alber, Jens

1987 "Germany." In Peter Flora, ed., *Growth to Limits*. Vol. 4. Berlin/New York: de Gruyter.

Albers, Willi, et al., eds.

1987, 1988 *Handwörterbuch der Wirtschaftswissenschaften*. Stuttgart/New York: Mohr.

Brandes, Wolfgang, et al., eds.

1990 *Der Staat als Arbeitgeber*. Frankfurt am Main/New York: Campus.

Statistisches Bundesamt, ed.

1989a *Datenreport 1989*. Bonn: Bundeszentrale für politische Bildung.

–, ed.

1989b *Statistisches Jahrbuch 1989*. Stuttgart: Metzler-Poeschel.

Weidenfeld, W., and Hartmut Zimmermann, eds.

1989 *Deutschland-Handbuch. Eine doppelte Bilanz 1949-1989*. Bonn: Bundeszentrale für politische Bildung.

Table 1
Calculated income of the public sectors (in %)

Year	Total (in billion)	From taxes	Fees	Business income	Capital income
1950	26.4	80	6	6	1
1960	65.5	82	6	5	3
1970	188.3	82	7	4	3
1975	460.7	86	6	2	2
1980	690.0	86	5	2	2
1985	870.1	84	6	4	2
1986	905.9	85	6	4	2

Source: Statistisches Bundesamt, 1989b, p. 429; author's calculations.

Table 2
Share of the state in distribution

Year	A GNP Market Value (in billion)	B State expenditure national accounts stat. (in billion)	C State expenditure finance stat. (in billion)	B/A (in %)	C/A (in %)
1950	98.1[1]	36.5[1]	28.1[2]	37	29
1955	182.0[1]	67.3[1]	50.4[2]	37	28
1960	302.8	114.0	63.3[3]	38	-
1965	459.3	179.8	139.1	39	30
1970	678.8	277.7	196.2	41	29
1975	1,034.0	519.7	359.9	50	35
1980	1,488.9	742.4	498.1	50	33
1985	1,844.3	875.5	588.8	47	32

1. Without Saarland and Berlin.
2. Without Saarland.
3. Incomplete statistical year, not comparable.

Source: Albers, 1987 (1,2); 1988, p. 177 (3); Statistisches Bundesamt 1989a, pp. 215 231; Statistisches Bundesamt 1989b, p. 558, author's calculations.

Table 3
State expenditures according level of government (in %)

Year	Federal government	State government	Communi-ties	Others	Total
1950	41	33	19	7	100
1955	44	30	21	5	100
1960	48	29	20	3	100
1965	46	32	20	2	100
1970	45	33	21	2	100
1975	39	36	25	-	100
1980	38	37	25	-	100
1986	44	36	20	-	100

Source: Alber 1987, Datenreport, 1989a, p. 216.

Table 4
Expenditures according level of government (in %)

Item	1950	1960	1970	1975	1980	1985	1986
Defense	17	13	10	6	6	6	6
Public security	4	4	4	3	3	3	3
Education	7	9	13	10	10	9	9
Science	0	1	1	1	1	1	1
Culture	1	1	1	1	1	1	1
Social security	27	24	21	47	46	47	47
Healthcare, Sports	4	4	5	4	4	4	4
Housing-construction	11	10	5	4	4	4	4
Promotion of the economy	7	7	7	3	4	4	4
Transportation, Communication	5	7	9	4	4	3	3

Source: Statistisches Bundesamt, 1989b, p 429.

Table 5
Employees in direct and indirect civil service

Year	Total	Increase (in %)	Full-time	Increase (in %)	Part-time	Increase (in %)	Total share
1950	2,259	-	2,192	-	67	-	3.0
1955	2,599	15.1	2,507	14.4	92	37.3	3.5
1960	3,002	15.5	2,808	12.0	194	110.9	6.5
1965	3,351	11.6	3,080	9.7	271	39.7	8.1
1978	3,644	8.7	3,266	6.0	378	39.5	10.4
1975	4,184	14.8	3,669	12.3	515	36.2	12.3
1980	4,420	5.6	3,802	3.6	618	20.0	14.0
1985	4,594	3.9	3,824	0.6	770	24.6	16.8

Source: Brandes et. al., 1990, p. 54; author's calculations.

Table 6
Development of the full-time personnel stock of single functions (in 1,000 and 1960=100)

Year	Total		Federal Railway		Federal Mail Service[1]		Community administration	
	1,000	Index	1,000	Index	1,000	Index	1,000	Index
1950	2,192	78	525	107	259	72	1,299	72
1955	2,508	89	499	102	334	93	1,548	86
1960	2,808	100	490	100	360	100	1,803	100
1965	3,080	110	458	93	387	108	2,068	115
1970	3,266	116	405	83	402	112	2,273	126
1975	3,669	131	418	85	419	116	2,612	145
1980	3,802	135	338	69	426	118	2,805	156
1985	3,824	136	295	60	440	122	2,837	157

Year	Total		Federal administration		Defense		Public security	
	1,000	Index	1,000	Index	1,000	Index	1,000	Index
1950	2,192	78	290	78	-	-	135	73
1955	2,508	89	346	93	-	-	173	94
1960	2,808	100	371	100	86	100	184	100
1965	3,080	110	400	108	155	180	208	113
1970	3,266	116	414	112	171	199	227	123
1975	3,669	131	457	123	178	207	259	141
1980	3,802	135	479	129	172	200	291	158
1985	3,824	136	480	129	172	200	299	163

Year	Total		Elementary education		Academic education		Healthcare, Sports	
	1,000	Index	1,000	Index	1,000	Index	1,000	Index
1950	2,192	78	218	80	30	54	113	65
1955	2,508	89	249	92	40	71	140	81
1960	2,808	100	272	100	56	100	173	100
1965	3,080	110	324	119	91	163	207	120
1970	3,266	116	401	147	130	232	241	139
1975	3,669	131	508	187	194	346	297	172
1980	3,802	135	575	211	210	375	333	192
1985	3,824	136	544	200	220	393	345	199

1. Incl. Communication service and Postbank.

Source: Brandes, 1990, p. 44.

9. Mobilizing Institutions

9.1 Labour Unions

The German labour unions have overcome their prewar splintering into single and occupational trade unions. After the World War II, they united under an umbrella organization in which the employed of all parties and denominations work together. The unions registered growing membership starting in the 1960s, though numbers have been decreasing slightly since the early 1980s. The union's influence in shaping the economy and politics gained markedly in the course of postwar development. This has meant, however, a certain institutionalization and Verrechtlichung *(tying up in rules and regulations) of the German union movement.*

Organization

Typical of the German labour-union movement before its destruction by National Socialism (1933) was its lack of a unified system of beliefs and world outlook (*Weltanschauung*) and its organizational division into different occupational splinter groups. The refounding of the unions after the collapse of the Third Reich (1945) was not a simple reconstruction of an organization dating from the days of the Weimar Republic. Benefiting from experience – the schisms in the workers' and union movements had facilitated the Fascist take-over – the goal of a confederated labour union was proposed in the stead of single and specialized unions. The German Federation of Trade Unions (DGB) was established in 1949 as an umbrella organization for 16 (later, 17) unions, with the aim of bringing salaried and wage workers from the entire religious and party spectrum into one organization. The union's organization, according to the industrial sector, corresponded to its political and religious neutrality, and put workers of all levels within one plant or business to a single union. The idea of a confederated labour union was not effectively realized: in addition to the unions belonging to the DGB, other large labour organizations were formed. The founding of the German Union of Salaried Workers (DAG, 1947), the German Federation of Civil Servants (DBB, 1950), and the Christian Federation of Trade Unions (CGB, 1959) brought occupational groupings back into play. Political neutrality is in fact limited: though the DGB is not an organizationally integral part of the idea of social democracy (as is the case, for instance with the English union), it does stand politically much closer to the Social Democratic Party (SPD) than it does to the Christian Democrats (the other major West German party). Similarly the CGB favours the conservative party.

Membership

A total of about 9.4 million salaried and wage workers were organized into unions by the end of 1986, 80% of them in the DGB. Union members comprise 40% of the total number of dependently employed (23.5 million as of June,1985), as compared to 37% in 1960. There has been a slight downward trend since the beginning of the 1980s, hitting the unions of the DGB, the CGB, and the DAG the hardest (Statistisches Bundesamt, 1987; for changes in gross degree of organization for each union since 1950, see table 1). This developmental pattern corresponds to an analogous trend in membership common to almost all of the unions. While the unions could boast of growing membership numbers since the 1950s, the four top organizations, the DGB, the DAG, the DBB (German Federation of Civil Servants), and the CGB had to accept losses - or, at best, minimal growth - in the 1980s (see table 2). Alemann (1987) has surmised that this downward trend is due to the economic crisis of the early 1980s.

The proportion of women union members has slowly increased over time. They made up just under 23% of DGB members in 1986 (versus 16% in 1950), 41% of DAG members (versus 32% in 1951), and 25% of DBB members (versus 16% in 1969) (author's statistics).

Activities

The German labour unions aim at being more than just an economic interest group representing the employed. As the largest mass organization in the Federal Republic, they have always striven to be "pillars of the democratic way," although they rethought this goal after the war.

In the basic program of 1949, in which the DGB formulated its social and economic policy concepts, the demands for political-economic planning, nationalization of key industries, and codetermination by organized labour were all given equal priority. The DGB soon withdrew its demands for planning and nationalization. Under the catchphrase "social partnership with business" (partnership between parties engaged in labour negotiations), the union's interest was directed toward job creation, increased production, and raising workers' standard of living. Against a background of economic stagnation, mass unemployment, and progressive rationalization, the DGB supplemented its 1981 program, an updating of the previous program, with demands for extension of codetermination at the plant level and for humanization of job conditions. This program contains, in fact, quite a comprehensive list of points touching on almost all societal areas with any influence on the interests of the employed – starting with the economic policy of recent years, going into matters of social security and education, and into media and cultural policies. The constructive function within society, which the West German union lays claim to – in contrast to the class-struggle unions of the last century or the unions of other European countries –, has thus taken on clear-cut features. The unions' requests were partially granted by the state: the unions were invested with public functions and responsibilities (in the social and educational sectors, via codetermination on plant level and – at times – a voice in government economic policy, known as "concerted action"). This, however, led to increasing institutionalization of the unions, which was strengthened by the *Verrechtlichung* of industrial relations. Since then, theoreticians have coined the term "corporatism of the German labour union" (Esser 1982; see also 10.1, "Dispute Settlement," and 10.2, "Institutionalization of Labour Unions").

In addition to political goals, which the union pursued on a macrosocial level, the union pursues goals on a daily basis at the plant level. To realize the former, the union uses the collective trade-agreement policy (*Tarifpolitik*); to realize the latter, it uses actualization of the right of codetermination. The matters mainly dealt with in collective-bargaining rounds (*Tarifrunden*, the annual fixing of salaries, wages, performance standards, and work hours) up to 1984 were wages and salaries and working conditions. Since 1984, the question of shortening the work week to 35 hours has become more prominent.

Contrary to other countries, collective bargaining in the Federal Republic is accompanied by few strikes. The years 1971 and 1978, when labour strife resulted in 4 million working days lost, respectively, and 1984 – the year the struggle over the 35-hour week began – with 5.6 million working days lost, were the exceptions. All other years had a far lower number of days lost. Employers reacted to the bigger strikes with lock-outs, which sometimes drew non-striking workers into the labour struggle (see figure 1; see also 7.1, "Conflict"). The regulations concerning the course of a labour conflicts are a leading cause of the low incidence of strikes. Before the union can call a strike, a neutral mediator must have tried to bring the stalled union-employer negotiations to a compromise solution. Should this mediation fail, 75% of the ballots cast in a strike vote (by involved union members) must favour strike action.

Codetermination at the plant level comprises the second pillar of union policy. It was introduced into the coal and steel industries in 1951, and the laws of 1972 and 1976 extended it to all large enterprises and made its content more comprehensive. This gave workers the opportunity to have more say in plant management and job structuring (see 7.2, "Negotiations", and 10.2, "Institutionalization of Labour Unions").

The workers' councils (*Betriebsräte*, elected by vote at plant level) have always been predominantly filled with union members. Only a negligible minority of those elected to the councils are not organized in a union. In correspondence with its large size, the councils formed or dominated by the DGB are firmly anchored at the plant level. The DGB took a slight loss in the workers'-council elections of 1975 and 1978, but recouped in 1981 and 1984, to the disadvantage of non-union candidates and of other unions (see table 3).

Barbara Wörndl

References

Adamy, Wilhelm, and Johannes Steffen
1985 *Handbuch der Arbeitsbeziehungen*. Bonn: Bundeszentrale für politische Bildung.

Alemann, Ulrich von
1987 *Organisierte Interessen in der Bundesrepublik*. Opladen: Leske und Budrich.

Armingeon, Klaus
1988 "Gewerkschaftliche Entwicklung und ökonomischer, beschäftigungsstruktureller und politischer Wandel. Das Beispiel der Gewerkschaften in der Bundesrepublik Deutschland." *Soziale Welt*, 39, no. 4.

Beyme, Klaus von
1977 *Gewerkschaften in Arbeitsbeziehungen in europäischen Ländern*. München/Zürich: Piper.

Breum, Walter, et al.
1981 *Die Gewerkschaften der Bundesrepublik. Mitglieder, Theorie, Politik*. Hamburg: VSA.

Esser, Josef
1982 *Gewerkschaften in der Krise. Die Anpassung der Gewerkschaft an die neuen Weltmarktbedingungen*. Frankfurt am Main: Suhrkamp.

Friedrich, Karl
1984 *Gewerkschaften in Zahlen*. Bonn.

Institut der Deutschen Wirtschaft, ed.
1986 *Zahlen zur Entwicklung der Bundesrepublik*. Köln: Deutscher Instituts-Verlag.

Niedenhoff, Horst-Udo, and Wolfgang Pege
1987 *Gewerkschafts-Handbuch. Daten, Fakten, Strukturen. Ausgabe 1987*. Köln: Deutscher Instituts-Verlag.

Nohlen, Dieter, ed.
1983 *Pipers Wörterbuch zur Politik*. München/Zürich: Piper.

Presse- und Informationsamt der Bundesregierung, ed.
1982 *Gesellschaftliche Daten*. Freiburg.

Schoenhoven, Klaus
1987 *Die deutschen Gewerkschaften*. Frankfurt am Main: Suhrkamp.

Statistisches Bundesamt, ed.
1987 *Datenreport 1987*. Bonn: Bundeszentrale für politische Bildung.

Table 1
Gross degree of worker organization of DGB, DAG, DBB, CGB[1]

Year	DGB	DAG	DBB	CGB
1950	33.0	7.9	-	-
1960	31.2	7.7	42.9	1.0
1970	30.9	6.0	37.9	-
1980	33.4	4.9	35.8	1.2
1981	33.4	4.9	35.5	1.2
1982	33.2	4.9	34.1	1.3
1983	33.2	5.2	32.5	1.4
1984	34.9	5.2	32.0	1.4
1985	32.9	4.8	32.5	1.3

1. DGB (German Federation of Trade Unions), DAG (German Union of Salaried Workers), DBB (German Federation of Civil Servants), and CGB (Christian Federation of Trade Unions).

Comments: The organizational degree is the percentage of actual union members among potential members (membership potential). The corresponding membership potentials are - for the DGB and CGB - all employed persons; for the DAG it is all employees, and for the DBB all civil servants. The gross organizational degree is spoken of because the membership numbers refer to all members, that is also unemployed or retired members. The net degree, which is about 12 to 25 percent under the gross degree, refers solely to employed members.

Source: Amingeon, 1988, p. 461.

Table 2
Members of some exemplary employed-person organizations (in 1,000)

Union	1951	1960	1970	1980	1986
DGB[1]	5,912	6,379	6,713	7,883	7,765
DAG	344	450	461	495	496
DBB	234	650	721	821	782

1. For names of unions, see table 1.

Source: Statistisches Bundesamt, 1987, p. 160.

Table 3
Results of plant-level elections (in %)

Workers' council	Election year	DGB[1]	DAG	CGB	ULA	Other	Non-organized
Members	1975[2]	67.9	10.4	2.6	-	1.6	17.5
Chair		78.8	2.6	0.0	-	0.0	1.5
Members	1978	58.6	14.6	0.7	-	2.8	23.3
Chair		71.8	14.4	0.1	-	0.7	13.1
Members	1981	63.2	8.5	3.7	0.4	0.9	23.3
Chair		79.9	5.2	0.5	0.5	3.4	10.5
Members	1984	63.9	8.9	0.8	0.3	0.7	25.4
Chair		75.1	6.8	0.1	0.0	0.8	17.0

1. For names of unions, see table 1.
2. In 1975, 17.1% gave no answer.

Source: Institut der Deutschen Wirtschaft, 1986.

Figure 1
Working days missed due to labour strike (days missed in million)

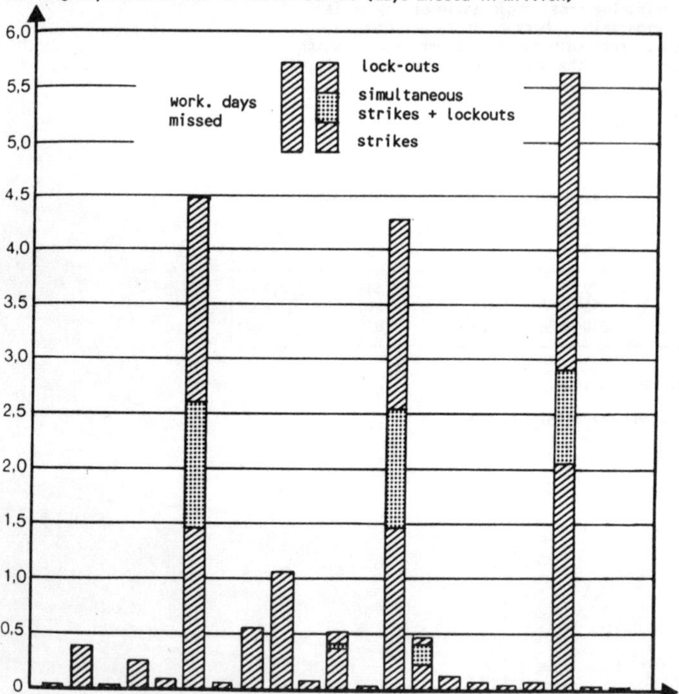

Source: Statistisches Bundesamt, 1987, p. 163.

9.2 Religious Institutions

The Catholic and Protestant churches have always enjoyed a strong institutional position in the Federal Republic, which they have been able to consolidate. They were, however, confronted in the late 1960s with West Germans' dwindling interest in religious life. This was accompanied by increasing personnel problems in both denominations. The churches reacted to the "de-churching" process in society by modernizing their religious practices.

Organization and Position of Christian Churches in West German Social Life

The Christian churches have always dominated religious life in the Federal Republic. Since 1945, aproximately 90% of the population have belonged to either the Catholic or the Protestant church, in about equal numbers, though the membership has tipped somewhat in favour of the Catholic church. Whereas there were slightly more Protestants during the entire postwar period, in 1987 there were, for the first time, more Catholics (42.7%) than Protestants (41.6%) in the Federal Republic. A small minority belong to other Christian communities, including Methodist, Baptist, and Old Catholic churches, the Society of Friends (Quakers) and the Salvation Army.

The growing immigration of foreign workers has caused a rise in religions that were previously nearly nonexistent in Germany – for example, the Greek Orthodox church and Islam, the latter which had about 1.6 million disciples in the Federal Republic in 1985. About 30,000 Jews live in the Federal Republic. In 1933, before their persecution under the National Socialist regime, there were approximately half a million living in the German Reich.

The Catholic and Protestant churches are institutionally well established in the Federal Republic. Their strong positions were secured at the time of the founding of the Federal Republic by government decrees concerning the relationship between church and state. The new constitution of 1949 (*Grundgesetz*), which adopted part of the legislation of the Weimar Republic constitution of 1919, guarantees freedom of religious assembly and assures churches the status of public corporations. They thus have the power of self-administration and can charge church taxes of their members (these taxes are not collected by the church, but by the state for the church). Moreover, the state's financial commitments to the churches are anchored in the law (for example, the state subsidizes the salaries of the clergy and takes on expenses for clerical and organizational matters), as is observation of Sundays and religious holidays. The churches also got the assurance that religion would be a standard school subject and that the churches would have a say in the nomination of professors of theology at the university level. The state's readiness to make such great concessions is grounded in the numerous tasks – above and beyond ministerial work – carried out by the church from the beginning of Federal Republic onward.

After World War II, the Catholic and Protestant churches were almost the only major organizations with a functioning institutional apparatus at their disposal. At this stage of internal and external collapse, the churches not only functioned as a source of moral support for large sections of the population, they also took over a profusion of tasks that would not normally fall into their field of responsibility: they provided material assistance to the needy and exercised political influence: only the church had any kind of international political clout, and it acted as a kind of advocate of the conquered. The churches succeeded in consolidating their position within the social structure of the Federal Republic, starting with their great influence in many societal sectors and extending into the field of social services. Church representatives are on the administrative boards of radio and television stations, the supervisory boards for self-censorship in publishing, educational commissions, and advisory committees for schools, teacher and adult education, and the army. They have also consolidated their activities in the fields of church associations (youth and labour organizations), foreign aid, and welfare.

The Catholic Caritas and the Protestant Diaconics are the leaders among the public-welfare leagues (founded in 1950). Many of the currently active church institutions in the fields of health, the handicapped, youth, family, and elder care are carrying on a centuries-old tradition. The charitable institutions' activities have taken on a new accent, moving from a straight charitable stance in the early years of the Republic to an attempt toward "helping to self-help." Institutionally, this is expressed in extensive walk-in services, which have been rapidly growing. There now exist hundreds of advisory and assistance authorities for the unemployed, refugees and other uprooted people, immigrants, foreign workers, asylum-seekers, addicts, the homeless, and convicts and ex-convicts. With their hospitals, services for the handicapped and disadvantaged groups, senior citizens' rest and care homes, and schools, the churches are an integral part of the welfare system.

Another main field of church activity is foreign aid, with its strong ties to official foreign-aid policy. In 1962, the church headquarters for foreign aid was founded; it has since then pursued its own policy with the help of government subsidies. In 1968, this sector of church activity also underwent a change: no longer strictly charitable and limited to easing suffering, it now concentrates on constructive aid. The self-help principle is also manifested in this area. Two percent of the church budget is taken up by foreign aid.

Membership and Church Activity

The strong institutional position of the Christian church in the Federal Republic and the high proportion of membership in both major churches was not always a sign of acceptance of the churches by their members, nor of steady interest within the postwar population. Though the church was *the* moral authority in the Federal Republic after the war, many people distanced themselves from it as life returned to normal. This can be seen in the exodus of church members and the dwindling interest in religious life toward the end of the 1960s.

This development is elucidated by tables 1 and 2 which summarize the reduction in members of both churches since the 1970s (Catholics from 27.192 million in 1970 to 26.308 million in 1985; Protestants from 28.480 million to 25.106 million over the same period). The conjunction of these figures with the trend toward leaving the church can be inferred from the fact that while the number of exits remained stable until 1967, there then followed a drastic increase for both churches. Not until 1982 was there a small decrease in exits (see table 3).

Participation in church services also markedly declined for Catholic churches over the above-mentioned period. From 11.895 million participants per Sunday Eucharist in 1960, attendance was down to 6.8 million in 1985. A long-term comparison shows that Sunday attendance at Protestant churches was quite stable until 1963, and declined between 1963 and 1970. Contrary to this trend, participation at evening services of Protestant churches decreased slightly between 1960 and 1970, then grew again after 1985 (tables 1 and 2). In 1985, about 26% of Catholics and 5% of Protestants went to church on Sundays. This trend away from the church has also had an influence on the church press – many periodicals have gone out of print (Mahrenholz, 1969; Von der Görnes Gesellschaft, 1986).

Clergy

The "de-churching" process has been accompanied by a crisis the priesthood (Daiber, 1983). This is reflected in the number of Catholic priests leaving the clergy and in the clear decline of the newly ordained: between 1970 and 1982, the number of priests decreased, then stabilized. The Catholic church's problems in finding "new blood" can also be expressed statistically between 1965 and 1977, when the number of newly ordained fell from 473 to a mere 165. There has since been a slight rise (see tables 4 and 5). Simultaneously, the Protestant church is going through a critical confrontation with the professional role of the ministry.

*Religious Practice and the Question of Church Creed (*Weltanschauung*)*

The cause of the above-mentioned situations has been examined in numerous studies. A discrepancy was discovered to have developed between the value systems of church members (especially among the young generation) and the official values of the church. The view of the church as backward and inflexible was widely shared. Particular points of criticism were traditional religious practice and the positions of the churches in political and *Weltanschauung* matters.

The stance of the church regarding its own past under the Nazi regime was perceived as an indication of its antiquation: the church only very reluctantly confronted its own role during the Third Reich (it played only a small role in the resistance against Hitler). A further indication of the church's stubbornness was seen in its position on current political themes: the Catholic church – more than the Protestant – usually took a conservative stand on questions of marriage, family, birth control (abortion), sexuality, homosexuality, and so on. Up to the early1960s, and again since 1972, the churches indirectly recommended voting for the Christian conservative parties (the CDU and the CSU). As well, the church debate on remilitarization of the Federal Republic began much later than did the public debate.

Nonetheless, the changes that commenced in the Federal Republic in the early 1960s have also had an influence on the church. "Grassroots parishes" have formed within the Protestant and the Catholic churches, presenting opposition to the official church line in all religious and political matters. The "grassroots parishes" are pressing for an active voice and for democratization of the hierarchical structure in the churches. In addition to critical discussion, this period saw new forms of church services (beat and jazz masses) being tried out. Mass went through a certain remodelling: it was no longer read in Latin but in the native language, and lay priests came to excercise influence on some aspects of the service.

The innovators were always faced with a strong pro-restoration front. Even if the internal debate has left its mark, it cannot be ignored that peace reigns in the Protestant and Catholic churches of the 1980s. Modern religious practices (new forms of the mass, etc.) have indeed been established, and critical opinions on current political matters expressed by church representatives are no longer the exception. The peace and conservationist movements and the debate on alternative forms of foreign aid have received strong input from the church. Yet it seems that many Christians see all this as an over-politicizing of the church. The "new piety," religious services, and prayer are regaining in popularity.

Barbara Wörndl

References

Amtsblatt der Evangelischen Kirche in Deutschland
1989 Statistische Beilage zum Amtsblatt der EKD, no. 6.

Daiber, Karl-Fritz
1983 *Religion in den Gegenwartsströmungen der deutschen Soziologie*. München: Kaiser.

Greschat, Martin
1983 "Die Evangelische Kirche." In Wolfgang Benz, *Die Bundesrepublik Deutschland*. Vol. 2: Gesellschaft. Frankfurt am Main: Fischer.

Groner, Franz, ed.
1969 *Kirchliches Handbuch 1962-1968*. Köln: Bachem.

Hanselmann, Johannes, ed.
1984 *Was wird aus der Kirche? Ergebnisse der 2. EKD-Umfrage über Kirchenmitgliedschaft*. Gütersloh: Mohn.

Hauschild, W.D, and E. Wilkens, eds.
1978 *Kirchliches Jahrbuch für die evangelische Kirche 1975*. Gütersloh: Mohn.

Hellwig, Gisela, and Detlev Urban
1987 *Kirchen und Gesellschaft in beiden deutschen Staaten*. Köln: Verlag Wissenschaft und Politik.

Hollenstein, Günther
1983 "Die katholische Kirche." In Wolfgang Benz, *Die Bundesrepublik Deutschland*. Vol. 2: Gesellschaft. Frankfurt am Main: Fischer.

Kuphal, Armin
1979 *Abschied von der Kirche: Traditionsbruch in der Volkskirche*. Gelnhausen/Berlin: Stein.

Mahrenholz, Ernst Gottfried
1969 *Die Kirchen in der Gesellschaft der Bundesrepublik*. Hildesheim: Verlag für Literatur und Zeitgeschehen.

Presse- und Informationsamt der Bundesregierung, ed.
1987 *Bonner Almanach*. Bonn.

Statistisches Bundesamt, ed.
1987 *Datenreport 1987*. Bonn: Bundeszentrale für politische Bildung.

–, ed.
1968 *Statistisches Jahrbuch für die Bundesrepublik Deutschland 1968*. Stuttgart/Mainz: Kohlhammer.

–, ed.
1972 *Statistisches Jahrbuch für die Bundesrepulik Deutschland 1972*. Stuttgart/Mainz: Kohlhammer.

–, ed.
1977 *Statistisches Jahrbuch für die Bundesrepublik Deutschland 1977*. Suttgart/Mainz: Kohlhammer.

–, ed.
1984 *Statistisches Jahrbuch für die Bundesrepublik Deutschland 1984*. Stuttgart/Mainz: Kohlhammer.

–, ed.
1988 *Statistisches Jahrbuch für die Bundesrepublik Deutschland 1988*. Stuttgart/Mainz: Kohlhammer.

Von der Görres Gesellschaft, ed.
1986 *Staatslexikon: Recht - Wirtschaft*. Vol. 2. Freiburg/Baal/Wien: Herder.

Zapf, Wolfgang, ed.
1977 *Lebensbedingungen in der Bundesrepublik*. Frankfurt am Main/New York: Campus.

Table 1
Catholic church (in thousands)

Year	Members	Christenings	Marriages	Participation in Sunday Eucharist
1960	24,710	473	214	11,895
1970	27,192	370	164	10,159
1980	26,720	258	125	7,769
1985	26,308	254	113	6,800

Source: Statistisches Bundesamt, 1987, p. 166.

Table 2
Protestant church (in thousands)

Year	Members	Christenings	Marriages	Holy Communion	Attendance at offices on Sundays
1963	28,796	476	204	7,727	1,705
1970	28,480	346	156	6,813	-
1980	26,104	222	94	9,056	1,146
1985	25,106	224	93	9,942	1,118

Source: Statistisches Bundesamt, 1987, p. 167; Amtsblatt der Evangelischen Kirche, 1989, p. 17.

Table 3
Curch-member exit (1956 = 100)

Year	Roman Catholic		Protestant	
1956	20,485	100	32,532	100
1960	23,889	117	32,077	99
1967	22,499	110	42,270	130
1970	69,455	339	189,134	581
1980[1]	66,438	-	119,814	-
1982	54,962	-	113,375	-
1984	-	-	127,002	-

1. From 1980 on: from Statistisches Bundesamt, 1982, pp. 88; 1986, pp. 93.

Source: Zapf, 1977, p. 910.

Table 4
Number of ministers

Year	Protestants	Catholics
1965	-	26,667
1970	-	26,286
1975	15,544	24,909
1980	15,614	23,842
1982	16,118	23,842
1984	16,696	23,842

Source: Statistisches Bundesamt 1968, p. 75; 1972, pp. 94; 1977, pp. 89; 1984, pp. 92; 1986, pp. 93.

Table 5
New ministers 1962 - 1986

Year	New ministers
1962	504
1965	473
1968	384
1971	242
1974	174
1977	165
1978	163
1980	201
1983	231
1986	240

Source: Sekretariat der Deutschen Bischofskonferenz - Referat Statistik, 1987.

9.3 Military Forces

The character and function of the armed forces in postwar Germany must be regarded against the background of the military defeat suffered by Germany in 1945, and in conjunction with the role that the Bundeswehr (military forces of the Federal Republic) plays as an allied army within NATO. When the military was reorganized after 1945, the priority of politics over the military was ensured. The internal command structure of the military forces was adapted to democratic principles. Numerically, the military forces achieved the strength prescribed by NATO toward the end of the 1960s, where it has since remained, at around the level of half a million soldiers. The West German armed forces now represent the largest conventional contingent of troops within NATO.

Organization

The Allies of World War II agreed, at the Potsdam Conference, that any German military potential should be crushed and that all precautions should be taken against German rearmament. This agreement was revised in the course of the escalating East-West conflict; the decision that the Western military alliance should be strengthened by building up a German armed force was made in 1950. In 1955, the year the Federal Republic joined NATO, the first soldiers to see the inside of a West German caserne were mustered. After about 10 years, the West German military had achieved the size prescribed by NATO.

Postwar reorganization of the German military took place along lines recommended to cause a break with the militaristic tradition of the preceding regimes. This meant, first, that the priority of politics be guarded against impingement from the military, and second, that the internal lines of command of the new *Bundeswehr* be structured according to democratic principles.

As opposed to the preceding *Reichswehr* (German armed forces up to 1945), which enjoyed partial freedom from control by constitutional law, legal measures passed in 1954 and 1956 assigned the armed forces a place within the executive branch. This amounted to the federal government taking sole directive responsibility for the West German military forces. Command during peacetime is under the (civilian) minister of defence; in wartime, command is passed to the chancellor. Parliament, via the domestic budget, the defence committee, and military experts, controls the organization and size of the West German military forces. Because of the West German military forces' subordination to NATO, operative directive responsibility lies, in the end, with the alliance.

A further step toward curbing the militarist tradition was the reformulation of West German soldiers' legal status. The concept of the soldier as a "citizen in uniform," possessing essentially the same rights as any other citizen, presents itself in outright opposition to the former "command and obey" principle of military life. The soldier's liberty is to be limited only insofar as is absolutely necessary to his function. There was opposition within the military against the new concept during the first decade of existence of the *Bundeswehr*; the principle of "inner leadership" – the official title for the new command structure – was too modernistic, too unmilitary, and too far removed from actual practice for some people. However, the reform was asserted against the wishes of the traditionalists. Organizationally, it has had the greatest influence on the training and education system in the military: the soldier's training is not supposed to separate him from society, but rather to further qualify him for civilian life. The West German military now runs technical colleges in which soldiers can obtain general or specialized diplomas. There are also two academic colleges run by the military.

Size of the Armed Forces

The recommended numerical strength of the West German armed forces was set at 500,000 troops by NATO as early as 1952. The West German military did not approach this number until 1967. It achieved a strength of nearly 500,000 in the early 1970s, but subsequently remained always somewhat short of this number (see tables 1 and 2). In 1987, there were 495,000 soldiers in the Federal Republic, of whom 467,000 were assigned to divisions of the armed forces (Presse- und Informationsamt der Bundesregierung, 1987). Recently, following the trend toward international disarmament, the minister of defence announced a reduction from 495,000 to 420,000 soldiers. The army has always recruited the lion's share: 340,000 were in this branch in 1986, versus 110,000 in the air force and 38,300 in the navy.

This size necessitated a draft from the very beginning. It started with a period of 12 months' service for all 18-year-old men (1956), which was later increased to 15 months. The military forces do not rely exclusively on the draft, but also recruit a large proportion of volunteers, who sign up for longer periods of service, as well as a smaller number of career soldiers. The ratio of draftees to long-termers and career soldiers has been about the same since 1969: the latter make up a total of 10% to 15% of all soldiers in the forces.

Armament

The arming of the West German military forces started with the taking over of American material of Korean War vintage and the appropriation of primarily American products, such as M47 and M48 tanks. West German weapon manufacturing started up with licensed-contract fabrication of American weapon systems such as the plane Starfighter; thereafter, a West German armaments industry sprang up. The armed forces' most important weapon, the Leopard armored tank, was a German product of the 1970s. Production of the Tornado fighter plane was begun in the same decade (von Schubert, 1983). Tables 3 to 5 show the armaments that the army, the air force, and the navy have at their disposal in the 1980s.

The German armed forces comprise the largest conventional troop contingent in NATO. As part of the NATO concept of nuclear deterrence in Europe, atomic weapons began to be stationed on German soil as of the early 1970s – the nuclear warheads remained in American hands, while the West German armed forces provided the carrier systems. In 1972, 75 Pershing 1A short-range missiles were stationed there; the stationing of mid-range atomic missiles (108 Pershing II, 96 slow-flying cruise missiles) commenced in 1983, and was completed in 1987. As a result of new armament treaty negotiations between the East and the West, the removal of mid-range missiles began in mid-1989.

The West German forces have neither made war nor undertaken any military expeditions since the end of World War II. Their role is confined to that of an allied army with the obligation of readiness to defend against the Warsaw Pact; they refrain from independent military actions. (For pacifism in the Federal Republic and popular attitudes toward the military, see 10.3, "Social Movements," and 11.2 "Confidence in Institutions").

Barbara Wörndl

References

Bielfeldt, Carola, and Peter Schlotter
1980 *Die militärische Sicherheitspolitik der Bundesrepublik Deutschland.* Frankfurt am Main/New York: Campus.

Brock, Lothar, et al.
1987 "Nationale Interessen und westeuropäische Kooperation in der Sicherheitspolitik." *HSFK-Report*, no. 8.

Bundesministerium der Verteidigung, ed.
1972 *Weißbuch 1971/72.* Bonn.

–, ed.
1974 *Weißbuch 1973/74.* Bonn.

–, ed.
1976 *Weißbuch 1976*. Bonn.

–, ed.
1977 *Die Bundeswehr 1977. Neue Waffen und Geräte der Bundeswehr 1977*. Bonn.

–, ed.
1979 *Weißbuch 1979*. Bonn.

–, ed.
1985 *Weißbuch 1985*. Bonn.

Hübner, Emil, and Horst-Hennek Rohlfs
1987 *Jahrbuch der Bundesrepublik Deutschland 1987/88*. München: Beck.

Presse- und Informationsamt der Bundesregierung, ed.
1987 *Bonner Almanach 1987/88*. Bonn.

Rattinger, Hans
1988 *Sicherheitspolitik der Bundesrepublik Deutschland*. Berlin: Colloquium.

Schubert, Klaus von
1983 "Sicherheitspolitik der Bundeswehr." In Wolfgang Benz, ed., *Die Bundesrepublik Deutschland*. Vol. 1: Politik. Frankfurt am Main: Fischer.

SIPRI, ed.
1980 *Rüstungsjahrbuch 1980/81*. Reinbek: Rowohlt.

Walitschek, Reinfried, ed.
1978 *Die Bundeswehr - Eine Gesamtdarstellung*. Vol. 9. Regensburg.

Table 1
Personnel in the Armed Forces

Year	Personnel[1]
1956	66,100
1960	270,400
1964	435,300
1968	439,700
1972	485,400
1976	484,300
1980	481,400
1984	480,700

1. Includes officers, non-commissioned officers, long-term service personnel, and draftees.

Source: Bundesministerium der Verteidigung, 1985, p. 241.

Table 2
Civilian personnel (including temporary and part-time workers)

Year	Personnel[1]
1972	181,017
1976	178,519
1980	180,161
1984	176,034

1. Includes civil servants, employees, and workers.

Source: Bundesministerium der Verteidigung, 1985, p. 243.

Table 3
Large machinery of the Army

Weapon system	Number of units
combat tanks Leopard 1 Leopard 2 M48	85 tank battalions 11 strategic tank battalions
armored tanks Marder	64 tank grenadier battalions
anti-missile tanks Jaguar 1 Jaguar 2	33 anti-tank companies
scouting tanks Luchs	11 strategic tank battalions
anti-tank helicopter PAH 1	7 echelons
anti-plane tank Gepard Roland	90 batteries
armored howitzer 155 mm howitzer 203 mm field howitzer 155 mm, 105 mm	201 gun artillery batteries
multiple rocket launcher 110 mm rocket launcher LANCE	34 rocket artillery batteries
strategic communication helicopter BO 105 Alouette transport helicopter UH 1 D CH 53 G	32 echelons
anti-tank rocket system MILAN TOW anti-artillery tank armored grenade projector mountain tank M 88 BP 2 transport tanks	large systems, distribution among various types of troops

Source: Bundesministerium der Verteidigung "Heer," Bonn, 1986 cited in Huebner & Rohlfs, 197, p. 155.

Table 4
Air Force weapon systems

Weapon system	Number of units
strategic vehicles RF-4E fighter planes/ bombers F-4 F	4 echelons 8 echelons
bomber F-104G bomber Tornado	9 echelons
bomber Alpha Jet	7 echelons
air vehicle Pershing 1 A	8 echelons
steered air vehicle Nike steered a. v. Patriot	24 batteries, plus duty by 12 US-batteries
steered a. v. Hawk	36 batteries
steered a. v. Roland	68 take-off units, plus duty by 27 US-units
major radar locations	13 direction locations
low-flyer register- and direction services	48 radar troop units
transport plane C-160	4 echelons
transport helicopter UH-1 D	5 echelons
flight alert BMVg	2 echelons

Source: Bundesministerium der Verteidigung "Luftwaffe," Bonn, 1986, cited in Huebner & Rohlfs, 1987, p. 156.

Table 5
Navy weapon systems

Weapon system	Number of units
destroyers Hamburg-class Lütgens-class	1 squadron 1 squadron
frigates Bremen-class Köln-class	1 squadron 1 squadron
speed-boats class 143 class 143 A class 148	1 squadron 1 squadron 2 squadrons
submarines class 205 class 206	2 squadrons
anti-mine vehicles	6 squadrons
supply units	2 squadrons
fighter submarine Thetis-class	1 squadron
strategic vehicle F-104 G	1 echelon
bombers F-104 G Tornado	1 echelon 2 echelons
telescopic strategic vehicle and fighter plane Breguet Atlantic	2 echelons
strategic helicopters and strategic communication planes	2 echelons

Source: Bundesministerium der Verteidigung "Marine," Bonn, 1986 cited in Huebner & Rohlfs, 1987, p. 158.

9.4 Political Parties

Since the Federal Republic of Germany was founded, in 1949, its political landscape has always stood under the influence of a few large parties: the Social Democratic Party (SPD), the Christian Democratic Union of Germany (CDU) and its sister party, the Christian Social Union (CSU), and the Free Democratic Party (FDP). These parties registered strong membership gains, particularly in the 1970s. In the early 1980s an ecological party, the Green Party, entered the German party system and established itself as a political force.

Evolution of Parties

Observation of the historical evolution of the German party system as a whole shows that a fundamental transformation from an unstable multi-party system to a relatively stable party landscape has taken place since the Weimar Republic (1918). The German parties were formed under a monarchy that allowed them only very limited say in political life. When the parliamentary system was introduced by the Weimar Republic, there existed numerous ideological and interest-oriented parties (*Weltanschauung*, or credo parties) incapable of making lasting compromises. National Socialism took advantage of this discord between the parties to aggravate a popular "party phobia." Based on the accusation that they were nothing but *Spalter der Nation* (dividers of the nation), all parties except the Fascist NSDAP (Nationalsozialistische Arbeiterpartei Deutschlands – the Nazi party) were outlawed. After the World War II, the freedom to form parties was constitutionally guaranteed in West Germany (the *Grundgesetz* of 1949). The constitution defined the contribution to the *politische Willensbildung des Volkes* (forming of political will of the people) as the responsibility of parties in a democratic system. The constitution also laid down the organizational principles to which parties must conform: the "inner order" of the parties must correspond to democratic principles; parties are obliged to account for their financial sources. These rules, along with the definition of "unconstitutional" parties – "Parties that . . . aim to hamper or eliminate the fundamental free democratic order or to endanger the existence of the Federal Republic of Germany" (Grundgesetz, Article 21) – were aimed at preventing developments similar to those of the Weimar and Fascist eras. This allowance for prohibiting parties has been applied twice in the course of postwar history: in 1952, against the neo-Nazi Sozialistische Reichspartei (SDP) and in 1956, against the Communist Party of Germany (KPD) (see 11.3, "Radical Parties").

The rapid distillation down to the present small number of parties represented in parliament is one of the most notable developments of the postwar years of the Federal Republic. In 1949 there were 11 parties in the federal parliament; this number fell to only three, the CDU, the SPD, and the FDP, and remained there from 1961 to 1983. One reason for this was the so-called 5% clause, which excluded parties with less than 5% of the electoral vote from entering state or federal parliaments. A fourth party, the Green Party, entered the federal parliament in 1983.

The character of the major parties has also changed, evolving from interest parties to people's parties. Upon its re-establishment after the war, the SPD built upon its tradition, dating back to the nineteenth century, as a leftist workers' party. In 1959, the SPD became a people's party and succeeded in appealing to almost all classes. The CDU, originally anchored in the Catholic social and political milieu, was able to gradually overcome denominational separation and become a reservoir for a large mass of voters, including farmers and sectors of Christian-oriented workers.

While the CDU and the SPD grew into regular people's parties, the FDP remained too small to operate as an actual people's party. It oriented itself toward the middle classes, particularly the upwardly mobile. As a third force in the party spectrum, its attractiveness was largely due to its status as a coalition partner to both big parties – it represented a corrective force to the Christian parties' orientation to the interests of the upper class, and the SPD's orientation to the lower classes. In contrast to these three traditional parties, a new type of political party appeared on the scene with the Green Party. Emerging from the social movements and grassroots citizens' initiatives that often opposed local or regional political measures considered environmentally damaging (for example, atomic power plants, highway construction), the Green Party was originally viewed as a typical "one-issue party" (a party with few program points; see 10.3, "Social Movements"). In the course of getting established in the West German political system, the Green Party has developed a political platform that goes above and beyond environmental protection. Recently, it formed state-level coalitions with the SPD. The success of the Green Party has often been perceived as a sign that the population has wearied of the large major parties and is losing its confidence in the established parties' ability to solve social problems.

Membership Statistics

In spite of obvious dissatisfaction with the large parties, membership in them continued to increase, especially in the 1970s.

Since the parties were refounded after World War II, the SPD has had the most members; it had 875,000 members in 1947, and – with temporary losses – raised membership to over 1 million by 1977. Membership has fallen slightly since then. The CDU and CSU combined mobilized approximately 482,000 members in the early years of the Republic. In the 1970s, both parties doubled their membership. The FDP registered its highest membership, 87,000, in 1981. Since then, it has lost almost 20,000 members. Given its political importance as a coalition partner in numerous state parliaments and in the federal parliament, the FDP possesses a rather narrow membership base.

The rise of the Green Party was continuous, from a little more than 25,000 members in 1982 to 39,000 members in 1985 (see table 1). It has the largest percentage of women members: 33% in 1987; the SPD registered 26% in late 1986, and the CDU and the CSU registered 22% and 14%, respectively.

Activities

The constitutionally stated mandate of the parties, that is, contributing to the formation of the popular political will, is traditionally carried out via their publicity for their platforms – mainly in electoral campaigns. In addition, they take care to be represented in as many of the influential societal and cultural organizations as possible. The strong position they have thereby gained is reflected in the fact that the most important positions in German radio and television broadcasting (public corporations), as well as in the education system and in bureaucracy, are as a rule occupied by party members. As it is also next to impossible in West Germany – with the exception of municipal elections – to enter into the state, federal or European parliaments without belonging to a political party, the parties' "monopoly" on the forming of the public will is often spoken of (Médunien, 1986; Sontheimer, 1985).

Voting participation by West Germans can be used as an indicator of the public will and the mobilizing power of the parties, as voting is not compulsory in the Federal Republic. It is notable that there has always been a sharp disparity between party membership and voter participation: since the end of World War II, the proportion of the voting public that actually belonged to one of the parties was well under 10% (2 million, or 4% of the voting public, in 1987), but the parties always drew many times this amount in ballots. This is expressed in a relatively high participation in elections. The political activity of citizens does, however, show marked differences depending on whether it is a federal, state, municipal, or European parliamentary election. Popular interest is greatest for federal elections. Voter turnout reached 78.5% in the first federal elections, in 1949. For subsequent elections from 1953 to 1987, turnout always was over 80%. The record turnout of 91.1% was for the federal elections of 1972 (which took place earlier than normal because of the chancellor's resignation). The lowering of the voting age from 21 to 18 had an effect at that time. The lowest turnout registered after 1949 was for the federal elections of 1987, when only 84.3% made use of their right to vote (see table 2).

Although the Green Party has enjoyed considerable success since the early 1980s (with 8.3% of the vote in the federal elections of 1987), the big parties continue to dominate, drawing approximately 90% of the vote (see figure 1; for more on electoral results see 10.1, "Political Differentiation").

Barbara Wörndl

References

Dettling, Warnfried
1983 *Deutsche Parteien im Wandel*. München: Olzog.

Grebing, Helga
1983 "Die Parteien." In Wolfgang Benz, ed., *Die Bundesrepublik Deutschland*. Vol. 1: Politik. Frankfurt am Main: Fischer.

Kaack, Heino, and Reinhold Roth, eds.
1980 *Handbuch des deutschen Parteiensystems. Struktur und Politik zu Beginn der achtziger Jahre*. Vol. 1: Parteienstrukturen und Legitimation des Parteiensystems. Opladen: Leske und Budrich.

Krockow, Christian Graf von, and Peter Lösche
1986 *Parteien in der Krise*. München: Beck.

Ménudier, Henri
1986 *Parteien und Wahlen im politischen System der Bundesrepublik Deutschland*. München: Indicium.

Olzog, Günther, and Hans J. Liese
1985 *Die politischen Parteien in der Bundesrepublik Deutschland - Geschichte, Programmatik, Organisation*. München/Wien: Olzog.

Sontheimer, Kurt
1985 *Grundzüge des politischen Systems der Bundesrepublik Deutschland*. München: Piper.

Statistisches Bundesamt, ed.
1987 *Datenreport 1987*. Bonn: Bundeszentrale für politische Bildung.

Tempel, Karl G.
1987 *Die Parteien in der Bundesrepublik Deutschland und die Rolle der Parteien in der Deutschen Demokratischen Republik*. Düsseldorf: Landeszentrale für politische Bildung Nordrhein-Westfalen.

Wolf, Werner
1985 *Wahlkampf und Demokratie*. Köln: Verlag Wissenschaft und Politik.

Zapf, Wolfgang, ed.
1977 *Lebensbedingungen in der Bundesrepublik Deutschland*. Frankfurt am Main/New York: Campus.

Table 1
Party membership[1]

Year	SPD	CDU	CSU	FDP	Greens
1947	875,000	400,000	82,000	-	-
1951	650,000	-	-	83,000	-
1954	585,000	215,000	-	-	-
1960	650,000	-	-	53,000	-
1964	678,000	280,000	-	70,000	-
1970	820,000	329,000	93,000	57,000	-
1973	974,000	457,000	112,000	63,000	-
1975	998,000	590,000	133,000	74,000	-
1977	1,006,000	664,000	160,000	80,000	-
1980	987,000	693,000	172,000	85,000	ca. 18,000
1981	956,000	705,000	175,000	87,000	-
1982	926,000	719,000	179,000	80,000	ca. 25,000
1983	926,000	735,000	185,000	72,000	ca. 30,000
1984	916,000	730,000	184,000	71,000	ca. 32,000
1985	919,000	719,000	183,000	67,000	ca. 39,000

1. Rounded off to thousands.

Source: Grebing, 1983, p. 177; Menudier, 1986, p. 82.

Table 2
Federal Parliamentary elections[1]

Year	Franchised voters (1,000)	Electoral participation (in %)
1949[2]	31,208	78.5
1953[2]	33,121	86.0
1957	35,401	87.8
1961	37,441	87.7
1965	38,510	86.8
1969	38,677	86.7
1972	41,446	91.1
1976	42,058	90.7
1980	43,232	88.6
1983	44,089	89.1
1987	45,328	84.3

1. Federal Republic excluding West Berlin.
2. Excluding the Saarland.

Source: Statistisches Bundesamt, 1987, p. 150.

Figure 1
Proportions of votes in federal elections[1]

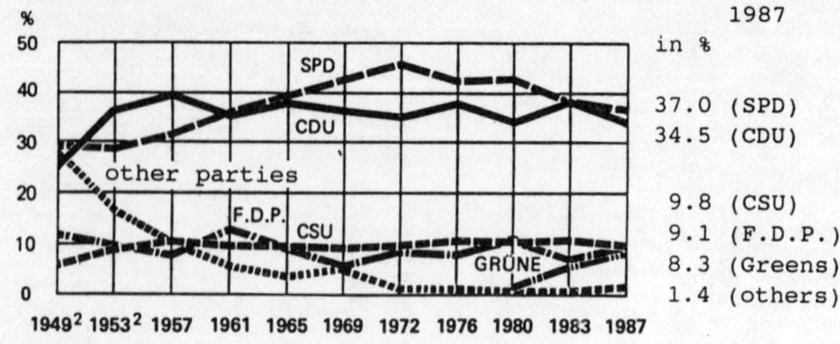

year of federal election

1. Second vote since 1953.
2. Excluding the Saarland.

Source: Statistisches Bundesamt, 1987, p. 152.

9.5 Mass Media

Electronic media are in a "dual market" – that is, there are both private and public broadcasting companies. In the print media there is a growing degree of monopolization.

Organization

The West German mass media after 1945 were shaped as follows: the press was in the form of private enterprise free of government influence, while in the electronic media, public corporations reigned exclusively up to the mid-1980s. A second characteristic of the electronic media in West Germany is the ties of public broadcasting corporations to government, or to the respective decentralized zonal administrations of the victorious Allied Forces of World War II.

Public broadcasting draws its legal status from contracts with the German states, in which rights and obligations, as well as the influence of political parties or socially relevant groups, are set forth and regulated. The obligations comprise – in simplified form – the presentation of well-balanced programming touching on the interests of all social groups and dedicated to democracy and the constitution. To this end, the radio-broadcasting companies have the right to finance themselves from fees charged or, in some cases, to draw a certain amount of income from advertising (while not permitting interruptive advertising, advertising after 8:00 p.m., or advertising on Sundays and holidays).

The first developmental phase of the electronic media was the creation of independent stations – that is, independent of licensing by the occupying forces. The nine state-run radio companies of the time united to form the Arbeitsgemeinschaft öffentlich # – rechtlicher Rundfunkanstalten in the Bundesrepublik Deutschland (ARD) in 1950. This cooperative has been broadcasting a common television schedule since 1954, to which the member companies contribute according to fees collected and to viewer population. In contrast, production and broadcasting of radio programs were largely decentralized.

In 1961, the Second German Television Company was founded as a federal institution. Between 1963 and 1968, the state broadcasting companies added – in partial cooperation – five more channels (called "third" channels), which were limited to their respective broadcasting areas. The program content of these channels was educational and cultural. Attempts to extend television programming via private-enterprise initiatives were quashed by decisions of the Constitutional Supreme Court, on the grounds of the potential threat of a concentration of power in this field.

A completely new situation emerged in the mid-1980s, when whole neighbourhoods were made accessible to cable television, thereby giving many stations the opportunity to offer television programs. The beginning of the so-called dual television market – that is, both public-corporation and private-enterprise channels – was initially limited to pilot cable projects. In addition to opening the market for potential commercial broadcasters, these projects were also meant to test the possibilities for local and special-interest television, as well as other forms ("open channel," "alternating communication," etc.).

The status and internal organization of commercial stations vary. Local "window" programs and broadcasting of programs not originally meant for the German market are quantitatively negligible. Currently, two channels dominate commercial television: SAT.1 and RTL+. RTL+ belongs to a world-wide media consortium (Bertelsmann); SAT.1 was originally conceived as a common initiative by newspaper publishers, as a means of entry into the electronic media. This concept, however, has since been eliminated by the factual power concentration which means that a few participants rule SAT.1. Since October 1989, pay television has also been available. The technical side of television and radio broadcasting is monopolized by the Federal Postal Administration.

The evolution in the field of printed media has been, after a postwar build-up phase, marked by strong concentration on economically sound publishers. The economic concentration among magazines provides a particularly good example: the four largest publishers had a 66.07% share of the market in 1986; among daily newspapers, one publisher had a 25% share of the market.

Activities

The current state of television broadcasting in the Federal Republic is as follows: The ARD provides nation-wide programming, Second German Television and at least one "third" channel can be received in any area, and cable television is expanding rapidly, especially in the metropolitan areas. By late 1989, more than every second household was hooked up to one or more cable network.

The programming offered by the public corporations has been continuously expanded; in 1989 it amounted to 10 hours on the 'first' channel and approximately 7 hours on the "third" channels; the "second" channel broadcasts an average of 10 hours daily. The broadcasting time of private stations varies widely, from a few hours (local channels) to 24 hours a day, especially when foreign shows, often "out of the can," are part of the programming (see figure 1).

Radio expanded quantitatively more and earlier than television. Besides mixed programming and "high-level cultural programming," the so-called wire service (with traffic information and music for a young audience) was introduced in the early 1970s. Almost all state-run radio companies have added "fourth" programming, tailored to a regional or a special-interest public. Private-enterprise radio is usually regional and directed at a young public.

New media in the strict sense – CD players, video, and television and computer games – play a negligible role in West Germany, though considerable growth rates can be observed. The field of data communication (for example, BTX) is of little quantitative importance for private households.

In the print media, the number of publications has increased notably since the early 1980s (see figure 2). This trend toward so-called special-interest magazines reflects the plurality of lifestyles. In the daily-newspaper field, however, the number of "journalistic units" (independent working unit) dropped from 225 in 1954 to 121 in 1976, and has remained constant since then. The regional newspaper markets are often dominated by one newspaper to the extent that one can speak of a monopoly.

Bernhard Engel

References

ARD
ann. pbl. *ARD Jahrbuch*. Eigenverlag.

Media Perspektiven
1987 *Daten zur Mediensituation in der Bundesrepublik*. Basisdaten. Eigenverlag.

ZDF
ann. pbl. *ZDF Jahrbuch*. Eigenverlag.

Figure 1
Daily television broadcast time

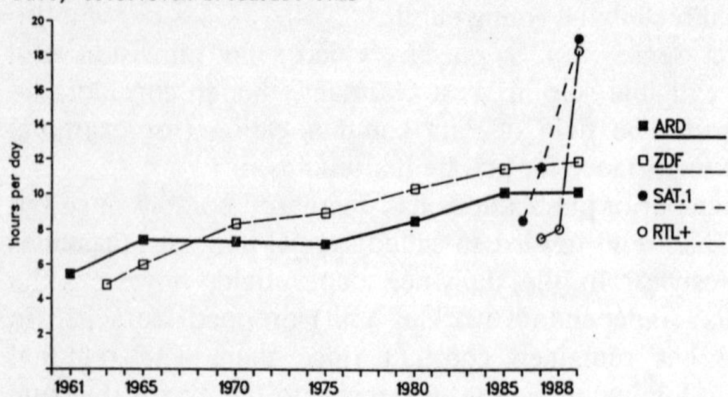

Source: Media Perspektiven. Daten zur Mediensituation in der Bundesrepublik. Basisdaten 1987. ARD-Jahrbuch, ZDF-Jahrbuch, annual publications.

Figure 2
Daily and weekly newspapers, general and special magazines
- paid circulation in million -

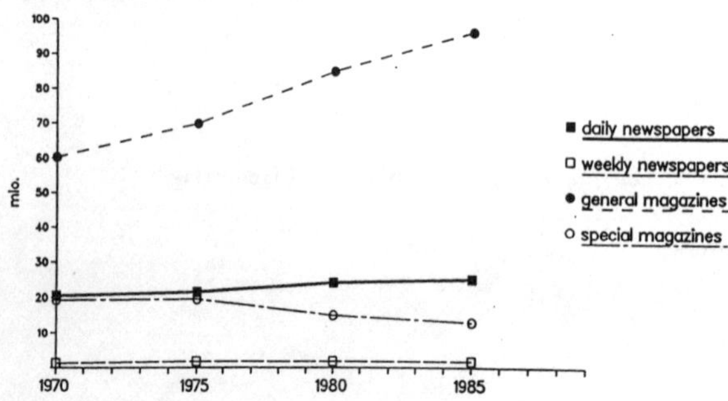

Source: ZAW-Jahrbücher und IVW-Auflagenlisten, cited in Media Perspektiven. Daten zur Mediensituation in der Bundesrepublik. Basisdaten 1987.

10. Institutionalization of Social Forces

10.1 Dispute Settlement

In the Federal Republic of Germany, the willingness to settle economic and private conflicts in court has increased since the end of World War II. The tendentially strengthened role of the courts as mediator should be viewed against a background of the increasing importance of legislative regulation in nearly all areas of life. In the past few years, however, forces have emerged which set a certain Entrechtlichung *(relaxation or increased flexibility of legislation) against the above-mentioned* Verrechtlichung *(tying up, restricting, or even defining fields of action by rules and regulations).*

Litigation

Jurisdiction in the Federal Republic includes, on the one hand, the "regular" courts, responsible for civil and criminal cases, and, on the other hand, special courts concerned with questions of labour, social, administrative, and financial law. Each of the judicial branches is divided into several stages of appeal, whereby it is usually possible to take the decision of the original court to the next-higher court for examination.

In 1985, the Federal Republic had a total of 684 courts (*Amtsgerichte*, or police courts, *Landgerichte*, or petty session courts, and *Oberlandesgerichte*, or courts of appeals) involved in civil and criminal cases. Their numbers were nearly three times as high 60 years ago (see table 1).

Personnel involved in regular jurisdiction has experienced a continuous increase since World War II: in 1957, there were 11,304 people – judges and district attorneys included – employed in regular courts; in 1985 there were 16,686 (see table 2). This clear increase becomes understandable when seen in conjunction with the business volume of most courts.

Police courts alone settled 1.6 million civil suits (including 370,000 family-court proceedings) and 1.5 million criminal cases in 1985. This was twice as many proceedings as in 1970 (see table 3). The rise is traceable in large part to the establishment of family courts in 1977. Since World War II, a change in the proportion of types of proceedings in civil jurisdiction is noticeable: since the late 1950s, the number of *Mahnverfahren* (default proceedings, or summary proceedings in order to settle debts) has been about four times that of actual trials. The latter, after cresting immediately following the war, have consistently declined, while the number of proceedings and default proceedings have remained about parallel to the population development (Wollschläger, 1985).

The decline in trials is therefore not the consequence of a dwindling of conflict settlement in courts, but rather of increased use of simpler and cheaper default proceedings. The growing business volume of civil courts points toward a rising tendency among people to defend themselves against alleged or actual cases of injustice. The cause of the growing business volume of criminal courts is most likely a growing number of punishable acts (see 16.2, "Crime and Punishment").

Arbitration and Mediation

An increased business volume has also been registered in the judicial field of industrial relations. Nowadays, only a small fraction of capital-labour conflicts are settled "on the spot" – that is, at the plant level. The majority of disputes are resolved in labour or industrial-relations courts. The industrial-relations jurisdiction is considered a classic example of the fact that the rise in court arbitration between social groups not only illustrates their increasing willingness to engage in conflict, but also binds them to government regulations concerning acceptable forms of conflict.

Industrial-relations courts were created as early as 1927 as a special section of the judiciary. The Industrial Relations Court Act of 1953 made industrial-relations jurisdiction completely independent of regular justice administration. It is responsible for private suits resulting from job contracts or collective-bargaining agreements, from work-constitutional disputes, and from election of workers' representatives into supervisory boards; in other words, for almost all legal conflicts in the working world.

The number of suits settled in labour courts nearly doubled between 1970 and 1985; proceedings concerning wages, salaries, and dismissals predominated (see table 3). The economic crises of 1974/1975 and the early 1980s can most likely be blamed for the steep increase in suits filed with the labour courts.

The *Verrechtlichung* of labour conflicts through their handling in the courts has been complemented since the end of the war by the spread of codetermination legislation (see 10.2, "Institutionalization of Labour Unions").

Regulation and Deregulation

The increasing readiness to resolve disputes in court comprises only a part of the global trend toward *Verrechtlichung* of nearly all areas of life in postwar Germany. The degree of *Verrechtlichung* can be deduced from the flood of regulatory standards, especially in the last 20 years: in 1963, 3,500 *Stammgesetze* (ordinary laws) with 75,000 individual regulations were on the books; by 1984, another 7,000 legislative acts, with around 70,000 individual regulations had been passed (Bundesministerium der Justiz, 1987).

In general, legislation has been influenced by a variety of purposes and goals. During the first years of the new Federal Republic, lawmakers were concerned with eliminating the shakiness of justice typical of the postwar period, and passed laws particularly related to the economy, finance, traffic, agriculture, and social matters. Legal developments in the next phase of reconstruction were largely dedicated to formation of the new order and adaptation of laws to the new constitution (*Grundgesetz*). Legislation concerning compensation for war participants was of great importance during this time. The social-insurance network was consolidated; at the same time, laws against unchecked business competition were passed, and the model of a social market economy gained in profile. However, legislation in this phase lagged, volume-wise, far behind what was to come. From the mid-1960s to the early 1980s was a period of legislative-policy reforms in which a spate of new laws and regulations were passed, on the premise that law should be used as an instrument of societal change. Outstanding areas of reform were the updating of criminal and criminal-trial law, the reform of marriage and family law, and legislation concerning protection of data privacy and the environment.

Though most of the laws passed during the reform era have not been disputed, the quantitative growth in regulatory standardization, or norms, also means that the government intervenes more, therefore threatening individual liberties:

> In the past decades, the liberty-restricting effects of *Verrechtlichung* have been clearly shown. It is, thus, the freedom-guaranteeing means of the state itself that pose a threat to the liberty of the citizen, in that it [the state] becomes more and more perfectionistic in administering, protecting, planning, and patronizing. In other words, there are so many major interventions in individuals' lives that the question arises of whether we have not already gone beyond the fork in the road to more freedom through too much legislation. (Bundesministerium der Justiz, 1987)

Deregulation of West German society on the other hand, is an offsetting trend to *Verrechtlichung*. At the level of government action, for example, Voigt (1983) notes that legally standardized directives are often not carried out by the authorities responsible for them, so that the set goals cannot be achieved. At the level of unofficial regulation of economic and private affairs by the people themselves, the heavy standardization of areas of life and the sometimes inneffective enforcement of the law (especially visible in long, wearisome court trials) is finding a response in alternative, non-judicial procedures. For example, large companies are more and more often presenting their disputes to *Schiedsgerichte* (arbitration courts or tribunals), in which they voluntarily subordinate themselves to a board of, usually, three persons. Disputes between West German companies are sometimes even mediated by foreign arbitration authorities. And, when it does come to court proceedings, many firms try for an out-of-court settlement. "Aside from the written law, a special law has arisen which is utilized by the tribunal of arbitration and in conciliatory or compromise proceedings" (Wirtschaftswoche, 1986).

Further examples of this trend are the growing "de-judicialization" of consumer disputes, indemnity practices regarding dismissals by employers, and the formation of "non-marriage cohabitation partnerships," which are increasingly accepted even by conformists as an alternative to government-regulated marriage and divorce law.

In the face of the "over-standardization" of society, the federal government began deregulation on its own in 1983. Simplification of laws and de-bureaucratization were declared to be main goals of this effort. A *Rechtsbereinigungsgesetz* (aiming to disentangle and reduce the number of legislative measures) was intended to eliminate 12 laws and to delete 155 individual regulations from 27 other acts (Waffenschmidt, 1987). The *Notwendigkeitsprüfung* (investigation of necessity) of pending legal rules and regulations was the subject of particular attention. There are, of course, critical observers of these deregulatory processes who warn against using the deconstruction of unclear and ineffective laws as a cover for cutting down laws that protect and guarantee the rights of the employed and the socially disadvantaged. These critics also posit that deregulation entails the risk of opening the door to unchecked entrepreneurial freedom.

Barbara Wörndl

References

Adamy, Wilhelm, and Johannes Steffen
1985 *Handbuch der Arbeitsbeziehungen*. Bonn: Bundeszentrale für politische Bildung.

Bundesministerium der Justiz, ed.
1987 "Mehr Recht durch weniger Gesetze?" *Bundesanzeiger*. Köln.

Hege, Hans
1983 "Recht und Justiz." In Wolfgang Benz, ed., *Die Bundesrepublik Deutschland*. Vol. 1: Politik. Frankfurt am Main: Fischer.

Kotzorek, Andreas
1985 "Zur Häufigkeit arbeitsrechtlicher Prozesse in der Bundesrepublik Deutschland. Eine ökonomische Analyse." *Zeitschrift für die gesamte Staatswissenschaft*, 141.

Statistisches Bundesamt, ed.
1987a *Datenreport 1987*. Bonn: Bundeszentrale für politische Bildung.

–, ed.
1987b *Von den zwanziger zu den achtziger Jahren. Ein Vergleich der Lebensverhältnisse der Menschen*. Wiesbaden: Kohlhammer.

Voigt, Rüdiger, ed.
1983 *Gegentendenzen zur Verrechtlichung*. Opladen: Westdeutscher Verlag.

Waffenschmidt, Horst
1987 "Rechts- und Verwaltungsvereinfachung aus der Sicht der Bundesregierung." In Bundesministerium der Justiz, ed., *Mehr Recht durch weniger Gesetze?* Wiesbaden.

Wirtschaftswoche
1986 no. 29.

Wollschläger, Christian
1985 "Das Wachstum der Ziviljustiz seit dem 19. Jahrhundert." In Hans-Werner Franz, ed., *Deutscher Soziologentag*, Dortmund 1984. Opladen: Westdeutscher Verlag.

Table 1
Number of courts in the FRG

Courts	1925[1]	1985
Police courts	1,750	551
Petty sessions courts	159	93
Courts of appeals	27	20
Total	1,936	684

1. German Imperial Kingdom.

Source: Statistisches Bundesamt, 1987b, p. 68.

Table 2
Personnel in official jurisdiction

Year	Judges	District attourneys	Total
1957	8,883	2,421	11,304
1967	10,299	2,715	13,014
1981	12,968	3,593	16,561
1985	13,040	3,646	16,686

Source: Statistisches Bundesamt, cited in Wirtschaftswoche, no. 29/1986.

Table 3
Cases settled in exemplary courts[1]

Courts/trials	1970	1985
Police courts (civil courts, since 1977 excluding family courts)		
- trials settled	863,472	1,243,172
Family courts[2]		
- trials settled	-	371,155
- divorce cases among the settled trials	-	160,179
Police courts (criminal courts)[3]		
- trials settled	734,656	1,472,538
Labor courts		
- cases settled	187,084	363,102

1. As only certain, exemplary courts are listed here, the total number of court trials settled considerably exceeds the sum of the above-given statistics.
2. Established in 1977.
3. 1971.

Source: Statistisches Bundesamt, 1987a, p. 206.

10.2 Institutionalization of Labour Unions

From their very inception, the German labour unions did not limit themselves to the struggle for material security for the employed, but rather wanted to play an active role in the forming of a democratic, economic, and societal order. With codetermination rights handed down from the Weimar Republic as their point of departure, as of 1945 they strove to extend their influence on the economy and politics, and have in fact become an important factor in West German society. Codetermination at the plant level, as well as union representation on boards and committees in the political-administrative sector, have developed into crucial pillars of union participation in the economy and politics. The extension of both plant-level and industry-wide rights of influence means increasing institutionalization of union interest politics, whereby conflicts between the employed, on one side, and employers and government, on the other, has lost some of its explosive potential.

Codetermination at the Plant Level

In the Federal Republic, there are various forms of plant-level codetermination, depending on the size, type, and sector of the business involved. Plant-level codetermination had its precedent in the Workers' Councils Act of 1920, which for the first time allowed for establishing elected workers' representatives in all businesses. It was on this law that the Allied Forces based their general rules on formation and responsibilities of workers' councils after the collapse of National Socialism. The workers' councils were obliged to carry out their functions in cooperation with the officially recognized unions (Control Council Act No. 22, 1946).

The current form of codetermination is based on the *Montan-Mitbestimmungsgesetz* (an act concerning codetermination by employees within the supervisory and management boards in the iron and steel industries) of 1951, the Works Constitution Act of 1972, and the general Codetermination Act of 1976.

In 1951, the federal government, faced with a massive strike threat by the two unions in the metal and mining industries, granted the unions a legislative guarantee of *Montanmitbestimmung*. This law, affecting large iron- and steel-producing enterprises employing over 1,000 people, stipulates that the supervisory board of the company be made up in equal parts of representatives of the capital or employers' side and of the workers' and employees' side; both sides agree upon one further neutral member. This law, the first to allow for "parity codetermination" by those employed in an enterprise, was seen as a victory for the unions. However, the unions gave a concession in return: tacit support for the federal government in important parts of its economic, foreign, and defence policies (including rearmament in the Federal Republic; see also 10.3, "Institutionalization of Social Movements").

Large companies employing over 2,000 people in other industrial sectors are subject to the general Codetermination Act of 1976. This law also prescribes that the supervisory board be composed in equal parts of representatives of the employers and of the workers. However, one member of the workers' group is a "upper-echelon employee," who cannot unconditionally be counted on to represent the interests of the employed; the chair of the supervisory board, who cannot be nominated without consent of the employer, casts the deciding vote in the case of a draw.

In small and medium-sized companies and corporations (joint stock companies employing up to 2,000 persons and companies of other types employing between 500 and 2,000), codetermination is based on the Works Constitution Act. The proportion of workers' representatives on supervisory boards in these enterprises is only one-third.

In other firms, workers' representatives have no legally grounded right of codetermination with management. According to the Works Constitution Act of 1972, workers do have the right to elect a workers council (this applies to all firms employing over five persons) with a say in social and personnel matters. Similar regulations exist for large public enterprises. The Works Constitution Act commits the workers' councils to cooperate with the company and explicitly forbids putting pressure on the company. Since the workers' council is conceived as a representative organ of unionized and non-unionized workers, the Works Constitution Act has often been considered a means of preventing what might be called a "union lobby" at the plant level. In fact, a higher proportion of workers' councils are non-union than was the case during the Weimar Republic. Still, unionized councils do predominate. After slight losses in the 1970s, the DGB (German Federation of Trade Unions) could boast a membership of nearly 80% in key industrial sectors in 1984 (see table 1).

Industry-Wide Codetermination

In constrast to their forerunners, which were caught up in the struggle for legalization, the unions of today have become a recognized institution in the political framework of the Federal Republic. In addition to representation of interests at the plant level, they also perform public functions and are represented in almost all areas of political decision making. This is often referred to as the "corporatism problem."

> In the modern state, the working class exists as little as does capitalism. There are metal workers, postal civil servants, and railway employees, just as there are steel and textile businesspersons. And the modern state is used to negotiating with, and comparing itself with, these interest groups and segments of the major social classes. (Breum, 1981)

A particularly striking example of corporatist relations between unions, business, and politics was the so-called concerted action, a discussion circle that lasted from 1967 to 1976 and was made up of representatives of business and organized labour under the auspices of the Ministry of the Economy. During this time, when the Federal Republic was experiencing symptons of economic crisis for the first time since the war, employers and government tried, in cooperation with the unions, to regulate wages and salaries in a way that was favourable to the economy. In return for its conflict-resolving role, organized labour counted on obtaining further plant-level and industry-wide codetermination rights. It withdrew from the committee in 1977, when this hope proved to be unfounded. Unofficial meetings have since taken place between the unions, the employers, and the Minister of the Economy.

As table 2 shows, the unions are currently represented on numerous committees, especially in the areas of the job market, working conditions, and social security. Almost one-third of all corporatist committees with union participation are to be found in these political areas. The Self-administration Act of 1952 granted the unions extensive influence on health, accident, and retirement insurance. The social-insurance authorities are made up of an equal number of employers and employees (usually union members).

Through members of parliament who are also union members – most of them belonging to the German Social-Democratic Party (SPD) – in federal, county, and municipal parliaments, the unions have gained entry into numerous legislative committees. Union members also participate in federal and county governments and in the executive branches of regional and local governments (see table 3). Table 4 shows the close collaboration between union members and parliamentarians. West Germany's federal parliament exhibited an increasing proportion of union members among its members from the first to the eighth legislative period (from 28.0% to 63.1%). In the 1980s, however, the proportion of union members declined slightly.

Barbara Wörndl

References

Adamy, Wilhelm, and Johannes Steffen
1985 *Handbuch der Arbeitsbeziehungen*. Bonn: Bundeszentrale für politische Bildung.

Breum, Walter, et al.
1981 *Die Gewerkschaften der Bundesrepublik Deutschland*. Hamburg: VSA.

Deppe, Frank, Georg Füllberth, and Jürgen Harrer, eds.
1977 *Geschichte der deutschen Gewerkschaftsbewegung*. Köln: Pahl Rugenstein.

Friedrich, Karl
1984 *Gewerkschaften in Zahlen*. Bonn.

Milke, Siegfried, and Fritz Vilmar
1983 "Die Gewerkschaften." In Wolfgang Benz, ed., *Die Bundesrepublik Deutschland*. Vol. 1: Politik. Frankfurt am Main: Fischer.

Müller-Jentsch, Walther
1986 *Soziologie der industriellen Beziehungen*. Frankfurt am Main/New York: Campus.

Niedenhoff, Horst Udo, and Wolfgang Pege
1987 *Gewerkschaftshandbuch. Daten, Fakten, Strukturen. Ausgabe 1987*. Köln: Deutscher Instituts-Verlag.

Schlaffke, Winfried, ed.
1982 *Gewerkschaften und Gesellschaft*. Köln.

Schuster, Dieter
1973 *Die deutsche Gewerkschaft seit 1945*. Stuttgart: Kohlhammer.

Statistisches Bundesamt, ed.
1987 *Datenreport 1987*. Bonn: Bundeszentrale für politische Bildung.

Süllow, Bernd
1982 *Korporative Repräsentation der Gewerkschaften. Zur institutionellen Verbandsbeteiligung in öffentlichen Gremien*. Frankfurt am Main/New York: Campus.

Table 1
Results of worker'-council elections 1965 to 1984 (according to DGB[1] data, absolute numbers of workers'-council members) (in %)

Year	DGB	DAG	Other organized	Non-organized
1984	147,184 (77.4%)	5,703 (3.0%)	1,068 (0.6%)	36,238 (19.0%)
1981	154,282 (77.5%)	6,728 (3.4%)	1,098 (0.5%)	37,017 (18.6%)
1978	151,807 (78.1%)	6,364 (3.3%)	1,039 (0.5%)	35,245 (18.1%)
1975	148,102 (77.7%)	5,872 (3.1%)	959 (0.4%)	36,082 (18.8%)
1972	134,697 (77.6%)	5,266 (3.0%)	935 (0.5%)	32,772 (18.9%)
1968	118,351 (83.1%)	4,260 (3.0%)	701 (0.5%)	19,100 (13.4%)
1965	117,924 (82.6%)	4,899 (3.4%)	1,058 (0.9%)	18,791 (13.1%)

1. DGB=German Federation of Trade Unions; DAG=German Union of Salaried Workers; other organizations: mainly CGB=Christian Federation of Trade Unions.

Source: DGB - Deutscher Gewerkschaftsbund, in Niedenhoft & Pege, 1987.

Table 2
Labour unions' participation in cooperative boards or committees

Theme	Number of boards/ committees total	Union participation	
		Absolute	In %
Job market and working conditions	39	34	87.2
Income, savings	6	3	50.0
Education/training	15	7	46.7
Social security	14	10	71.4
Economic policy	12	5	41.7
Research, technology	24	2	9.1
Environment protection	14	5	35.7
Energy policy	9	2	22.2
Health policy	27	5	18.5
Housing construction and planning	6	4	66.7
Agriculture	23	7	30.4
Social problem groups	11	5	45.5
Statistical and technical institutions	18	11	61.1
Culture	32	22	68.8
Traffic and public transport	18	5	27.8
Other	33	6	18.2

Source: Süllow, 1982, p. 48.

Table 3
Unions in the legislative, jurisdictional and self-administrative fields

Legislative	Executive	Jurisdictional	Self-administrativ
- Fed. Parliament - State parliaments - Community council	- Fed. government - State governments - Regional and municipal executive authorities - Econom. and social committees of the EC (advises EC Commission)	- Labour/industrial relations courts - Social jurisdiction	- Ssocial security insurance - Hhealth insurance - Aaccident insurance - Job administration - Employment chambers (Bremen and the Saarland)

Source: Friedrich, 1987, p. 84.

Table 4
Members of Federal Parliament also belonging to a labour union (since 1949)

Federal Parliament	1949	1953	1957	1961	1965[1]	1969	1972	1976	1980[1]	1983
Representatives including Berlin	410	509	519	521	518	518	518	518	519	520
Union-member representatives	115	194	202	222	265	286	318	327	322	307
In percent	28.0	38.1	38.9	42.6	51.2	55.2	61.4	63.1	62.1	59.0

1. Including DBB (German Federation of Civil Servants) since 1965, and ULA (smaller labor union organization) since 1980.

Source: Müller, E.-P., Gewerkschaftsreport 4/83, cited in Friedrich, 1987, p. 85.

10.3 Social Movements

Among the many protest groups, citizens' initiatives, and self-help groups that arose in the wake of the students' movement, the following movements have made the most lasting impression on West German political culture: the peace movement, the women's movement, and the anti-nuclear movement, which became increasingly ecologically oriented. These movements have – to varying degrees – obtained recognition and institutionalization in the political system in the 1980s. The themes of "women," "environment," and "peace" are still the object of much attention and official political interest . This has, however, also meant a certain channelling of the protest movement.

Definition

"Social movements" in the Federal Republic of Germany refers to the protest movements which started at the end of the 1960s, inspired primarily by the problems of social reproduction. Destruction of natural and social territory due to ruthless industrialization, the danger of atomic war, and discrimination against women, on the one hand, and the attempt to develop a context for living oriented toward individual needs and the effort to expand the basis for political participation, on the other hand, were the catalysts of the West German social movements. The so-called new social movements differ dramatically from the workers' struggle, which was the prototype of social movements for a long time. The term "new social movement" serves to emphasize their difference from the Fascist mass movements of the Third Reich.

The genesis and development of the new protest culture took place in the following phases: after World War II, the workers' movement, dominated by the Social Democrats and the unions, lost impetus. The Social Democratic Party was transformed from a workers' party to a people's party; the trade union was integrated, via codetermination, into the market-economy system. A new kind of movement first arose in the late 1950s with the protest against rearmament in the Federal Republic, and in the 1960s with the student movement. The disintegrating student movement gave issue to the new social movements of the 1970s and 1980s.

While the protest against rearmament had strong ties to the established political oppositional front of the SPD and the trade unions, and only got around to developing its own forms of resistance in later phases (see below for details), the student movement very soon moved to extra-parliamentary ground. The main goal of this movement was the democratizion of all social sectors. This involved the assumption that the capitalistic economic structures and the political system, which are affected by the preceding Fascist state, lack the institutions necessary to effect the desired changes. An extra-parliamentary movement, independent of established politics, would offer the means to democratize all social sectors – schools and colleges, the church, the family, and so on. In the course of the debate on alternative ways of life (*Lebenspraxis*) and of trying to put experience into practice in an "other society" (in the sense of a protest or anti-society, or a subculture), the student movement founded an alternative culture of political circles, bookstores, publishing businesses, local and alternative periodicals, communes, and communication centres. In spite of dwindling mobilization toward the end of the 1960s, the student movement left the inheritance of a kind of infrastructure of political opposition on which the new social movements of the 1970s and 1980s could build.

Pacifism and Anti-militarism

In the Potsdam Agreements of 1945, the Allies decided to disarm and demilitarize Germany entirely. This decision was revised as early as 1950, and a protest against rearmament arose in the same year with the so-called *Ohne-mich* (literally "without me") movement. Between 1951 and 1953, the protest evolved into a movement demanding a popular referendum on the question of the Federal Republic's neutrality, only to fade out after the signing of the Paris Agreements of 1955.

With the Federal Republic's admission to NATO in 1956 and the reintroduction of the draft, a new protest cycle began, directed against atomic armament as spelled out in NATO military doctrine. Supported by prominent nuclear scientists and theologists, and with Social Democrats and trade unionists as spokespersons, the "Fight Atomic Death" campaign of 1957 – 1958 was highly politicized. The campaign mobilized approximately 150,000 demonstrators, and about two-thirds of the population condoned the movement, but it lost strength after the Social Democrats and the union withdrew their support.

Two years later, the "Easter March movement" (anti-nuclear and anti-rearmament protest marches) organized protests relatively independently of large political organizations. Twenty-three thousand demonstrators were mobilized in 1961, 100,000 in 1964 and 150,000 in 1967. In spite of the high degree of participation, popular reaction remained indifferent, media coverage was sparse, and the movement flagged.

Not until the early 1980s did a new peace movement arise, this time to protest against the stationing of mid-range missiles in Europe. The initiative for this movement began with celebrities and small church-related and pacifist groups, and protest eventually spread. In 1981, 300,000 people attended a mass demonstration in Bonn. It became obvious that the movement could count on a wide spectrum of parliamentary and extra-parliamentary opposition. At its peak, in the autumn of

1983, the peace movement mobilized 600,000 demonstrators, a record for the Federal Republic; the occasion was the federal parliament's decision to station the mid-range missiles. The movement so noticeably lost ground in the following two years that there was talk of the death of the peace movement. Though the movement's efforts were crowned with another surprising success with a major demonstration in 1986, it has subsided as an autonomous movement ever since. Reasons for this may be the current disarmament talks between the NATO and the Warsaw Pact, which have led to a reduction in atomic weapons. The majority of the West German population sees official, institutionalized politics as so strongly supportive of the "politics of peace" that a pro-peace protest movement seems increasingly superfluous.

Anti-nuclear and Ecological Movements

One cannot speak of an ecological movement as an entity separate from other social movements. Only the protest against nuclear power plants has achieved a sufficiently high degree of organization and mobilization to actually qualify as a single movement. Through its gradual conversion to the cause of ecology it banded together some very ideologically different protest movements, alternative projects, and initiatives, which formed the programmatic basis of the environmental protection and protest entity called the Green Party.

The theme of ecology began in the parliamentary arena. In the early 1970s, several environmental-protection laws were passed. Numerous suggestions for environmental-protection programs were formulated by political parties and other organizations (the trade union, among others). As zeal for furthering these programs waned during the economic crisis of the mid-1970s – costs for environmental conservation were considered to retard economic activity (*Konjunkturbremsen*, or economic brakes) – citizens' initiatives and groups formed which were dedicated solely to environmental protection as a political issue.

Protest against atomic power plants began organizing in the early 1970s. In the second half of the decade, locations for atomic power plants (Brokdorf, Grohnde, Kalkar, and Gorleben) became targets of mass demonstrations which mobilized more people than ever before in postwar West German history. The anti-nuclear movement found support among experts (scientists) opposing atomic power, various groups in the leftist and subcultural milieu, and local populations. The fact that this opposition developed into a huge mass movement is most definitely due to official declarations that atomic power was an absolute necessity for a modern national economy. A major debate on the future prospects of a policy for economic growth based on modern technology was thus set in motion for the first time.

Protest against nuclear power comprised the vanguard of the environmental-protection movement. For example, protest against destruction of the environment was organized into citizens' initiatives. Many of these initiatives then joined together in a national organization (*Bundesverband der Bürgerinitiativen* – BBU), which has since spoken for the initiatives and the environmental-protection movement. The disintegration and subsequent reorientation of the traditional West German traditional left was advantageous to the movement; this turn of events has often been referred to as the ecological turning point of the left (Roth, 1985). The most visible expression of this reorientation was the founding of the environmental-conservation Green Party in 1979 – 1980. Through this party, the environmental issue gained a foothold in parliament, which in turn has led to a certain co-opting of protest activity. The result was an internal conflict in the Green Party between the "fundamentalists," who wanted to retain the character of a social movement with radical goals, and the realists, who were striving toward political institutionalization. Although ecological problems have indeed worsened in the past few years, a major protest movement is lacking. The ideological bloc softened in the early 1980s. The large parties have once again incorporated the environmental issue into their programs: all parties are "wearing green." There has been a minister of the environment since 1986. Environmental-conservation organizations, politicized during the 1970s, have influenced public awareness. Publicity-grabbing actions of exemplary character are now carried out by small, well-organized groups.

Feminism

The so-called new women's movement originated in the student movement of the 1960s. Criticism by women was first directed against the disparity between an official promise of equality in Article 3 of the Consitution (*Grundgesetz*) and the factual discrimination against women in all social sectors. Women saw their struggle against discrimination in the context of the fight for overall political change. In the course of the next few years, women increasingly emphasized their independence from the rest of the student protest movement and started to focus mainly on "suppression by a male-dominated environment."

The women's movement crystallized around the *Kinderfrage* (refusal to see the upbringing of children as solely the woman's concern), which led to the *Kinderladenbewegung* (a new form of kindergarten in which a group of parents take joint responsibility for the care and raising of their children); while this phase of protest was characterized by women's issues being imbedded in general criticism of the system by the student movement, feminist protest consolidated into an autonomous women's movement during the fight against Bill 218 (a law criminalizing abortion) in the late 1960s and early 1970s. Radical groups and initiatives (lesbian groups, radical feminists) organized within the movement.

In the mid-1970s, the women's movement underwent a new stage of development influenced by consciousness-raising groups and a feminist protest culture. The so-called women's project movement, instead of turning to official political organizations or institutions for reform, concentrated on building up a decentralized, locally and regionally coordinated "women's infrastructure." Women's pubs, women's bookshops and presses, houses for abused women, women's health centres, and so on, were founded. They have since become part of a women's subculture which explicitly rejects official recognition and institutionalization.

The feminist movement has not been without consequences for the political culture of the Federal Republic. Following media coverage of the abortion issue, the Year of the Woman (declared by the United Nations in 1973) brought about extensive journalistic treatment of women's subjects. Traditional women's groups gained membership and became more political. Adult education (public institutions such as the *Volkshochschulen*, and church and union-related institutes) discovered women's issues. The Social Democrats and the trade unions have set up "women's bureaus." The Green Party was the first to introduce a quota and insist on parity of women and men in all public offices; the Social Democrats advocate a quota of 40% women. More than 150 communities have "women's-equal-opportunity offices," and the number is growing.

Today there is a "women's house" in nearly every large town, often financed by public welfare organizations or the municipality. Women are seeking alternatives for reproduction in a variety of social sectors, in keeping with their feminist perspectives.

This development has produced two tendencies within the women's movement: while the movement comprehends itself as autonomous, the above-mentioned specialization, professionalization, and institutionalization of women's issues and political demands has dulled their protest. This specialization leads to involvement in other social movements, or at least to multiple commitments. Thus the women's movement is losing its profile.

There is occasional talk of the end of the women's movement. The turning point in domestic politics in 1982 (the switch from a social-democratic line to a more conservative one) certainly strengthens this impression. Although cuts in the social network affect many women and endanger projects dependent upon government funds, there has been no massive protest against them.

Barbara Wörndl

References

Bernardoni, Claudia, and Vera Werner, eds.
1983 *Der vergeudete Reichtum*. Bonn.

Bredow, Wilfried von
"Sozialer Protest und Friedensbewegung in Westeuropa." *Beiträge zur Konfliktforschung*, 15, no. 4, 35-50.

Brand, Karl-Werner, ed.
1985 *Neue soziale Bewegungen in Westeuropa und den USA. Ein internationaler Vergleich*. Frankfurt am Main/New York: Campus.

Bundesminister für Jugend, Familie und Gesundheit, ed.
1984 *Frauen in der Bundesrepublik*. Pfaffenhofen.

Doormann, Lottemi
1979 *Keiner schiebt uns weg. Zwischenbilanz der Frauenbewegung in der Bundesrepublik*. Weinheim/Basel: Beltz.

Horné, Florence, ed.
1983 *Geschichte der Frauenbewegung*. Köln.

Kress, Karl-Heinz, and Klaus Günther Nikolai
1985 *Bürgerinitiativen*. Bonn: Bouvier.

Raschke, Joachim
1986 *Soziale Bewegungen. Ein historisch-systematischer Grundriß*. New York: Campus.

Rolke, Lothar
1987 *Protestbewegungen in der Bundesrepublik*. Opladen: Westdeutscher Verlag.

Roth, Roland
1985 "Neue soziale Bewegungen in der politischen Kultur der Bundesrepublik. Eine vorläufige Skizze." In Karl-Werner Brand, ed., *Neue soziale Bewegungnen in Westeuropa und den USA. Ein internationaler Vergleich*. Frankfurt am Main/New York: Campus.

Schmitt, Rüdiger
1987 *From "Old Politics" to "New Politics": Three Decades of Peace Protest in West Germany*. Amsterdam.

Vogel, Angela
1983 "Frauen und Frauenbewegung." In Wolfgang Benz, ed., *Die Bundesrepublik Deutschland*. Vol. 2: Gesellschaft. Frankfurt am Main: Fischer.

10.4 Interest Groups

There exists in the Federal Republic a pronounced network of organized interests. Most of these associations are relatively nonpolitical organizations, such as professional or occupational groups, or clubs for the express purpose of engaging in leisure or hobby interests or for upholding traditions; only rarely do these groups attempt to exert political pressure. Constant observation of, and influence on, politics is the reserve of a few large associations with relatively high positions within the power structure in the Federal Republic – in particular, employers' associations and trade unions, farmers' and war victims' organizations, and the churches. A notable trend has been observed over the past two decades; the classic interest organizations are getting competition from new forms of interest politics. New social movements – citizens' initiatives, women's groups, peace and conservation movements – have taken it upon themselves to articulate previously uncontroversial interests which had not been taken into account by the classic associations.

Large Organizations

"Organized-interest politics" in the Federal Republic is almost exclusively dominated by large organizations in the economic, labour and socio-political fields. The large organizations possess a widely ramified network of channels for influencing political leaders. Although some of the current national interest organizations were not formed until after the founding of the Federal Republic, the basis for their structure had long been present within German society.

After destruction of the National Socialist regime, the employers' associations were reconstituted. These associations did not manage to reconsolidate their position of power until the postwar economic boom took place. There are presently several hundred employers' associations in the Federal Republic – some related to specific industries, some regional – which are grouped in three umbrella organizations. The employers' level of membership in these associations is extremely high. The Bundesvereinigung Deutscher Arbeitgeberverbände (BDA, Confederation of German Employers' Associations) acts as the "opponent" to, or negotiating partner of, the unions in matters concerning collective bargaining. The Bundesverband der Deutschen Industrie (BDI, Federation of German Industries) concentrates on influencing government economic policy, as does the Deutsche Industrie und Handelstag (DIHT, German Industrial and Trade Conference). All important governmental measures in the economic and tax fields have been either influenced or initiated by these associations.

Among the affiliations of independent businesspersons (Handwerksverband, or Skilled Crafts Fraternity, Bundesverband der freien Berufe, or Federation of Independent Professions, etc.), the Deutsche Bauernverband (DBV, German Farmers' Association) is one of the most influential. It was established after 1945 as an umbrella organization for diverse agricultural trade associations, and represents nearly all farmers. Though agriculture, as a typical "old" mid-level economic sector, has undergone a thorough structural transformation in the Federal Republic and is losing in macro-economic importance, the DBV has managed to keep its privileged power position. It has consistently lobbied governments robustly and has, by exerting massive pressure, succeeded in keeping even unprofitable agricultural enterprises alive via government subsidies.

In general, no transformation tendencies in organizational behaviour among enterpreneurs and independent businesspersons can be discerned. The organizational degree of these groups remains at a constant level, and they stick to exerting influence on government and administration as their classic means of interest representation.

The most important organization of the employed is the Deutsche Gewerkschaftsbund (DGB, German Federation of Trade Unions), founded in 1949. It comprises of 17 individual unions and is, with its approximately 7.8 million members, the numerically strongest union. The DGB has always laid a claim to having a say in the shaping of society. Codetermination at the plant level, and union representation on boards of experts in the politico-administrative field have become the pillars of union participation in politics and the economy. Overall, the unions have not been able – especially under the Christian Democrats regime – to push or secure their interests to the degree that the employers' associations have. Their actual codetermination rights almost always fall short of their goals (see also 9.1, "Labour Unions," and 10.2, "Institutionalization of Labour Forces").

The civil servants' organization, the Deutsche Beamtenbund (DBB, German Federation of Civil Servants), is the second largest union in the Federal Republic. Its membership increased from about 200,000 in 1951 to 800,000 in the 1980s. More than any other association, it has the means of direct influence: DBB functionaries work in government administration and ministries and participate personally "qua office" in civil-service-related decision making.

Another successful policy for ensuring material interests is pursued by organizations in which victims of World War II have banded together. The largest are the Reichsbund der Kriegsopfer, Behinderten, Sozialrentner und Hinterbliebenen (Imperial Affiliation of War Victims, Handicapped, Pensioners, Widows, Widowers, and Orphans, with 760,000 members in 1984) and the Verband der Kriegs- und Wehrdienstopfer, Behinderter und Sozialrentner Deutschlands e.V. (Association of War and Military Victims, Handicapped, and

Pensioners of Germany – VdK for short – with 1.1 million members in 1985). Both associations were constituted as self-help groups for war victims in the first months following the war. The Imperial Affiliation was able to gather over 200,000 new members over the past ten years, while the overall numbers in this field decreased and other associations experienced membership losses (VdK lost about 10,000). The associations of war victims have – via constant pressure on the government and parliament – achieved extensive social security for war victims.

Organizations of displaced persons and refugees follow a social policy of furthering integration of the groups they represent into postwar society, and in the political arena they demand restitution of their *Heimatrecht* (home-country claim) in Soviet-bloc countries. Naturally, the position of the displaced-persons' associations was stronger in the immediate postwar period than in the late 1960s, by which time integration of refugees had been pretty well completed. As well, their political clout to veto reconciliation with Eastern Europe was scaled down in the course of the Social Democratic government's détente policy of the early 1970s.

Among voluntary interest affiliations in the social field, six independent private associations for public welfare rank highest in importance (Arbeiterwohlfahrt, a labour-oriented welfare service; Caritasverband, of the Catholic church; Deutscher Paritätischer Wohlfahrtsverband; the German Red Cross; Diakonisches Werk, of the Protestant church; and Zentralwohlfahrtsstelle der Juden in Deutschland, a public-welfare authority of the Jewish community). In accordance with the principle of subsidiarization (versus federal centralism or collectivism, meaning here that assistance by private associations is given priority over assistance by public institutions), they are active in important socio-political fields. Their importance and their monopoly position become obvious when their accomplishments are examined: private associations run 71% of the kindergartens and children's homes, 70% of *Jugendbildungsstätten*, 60% of senior citizens' homes and nursing homes, and so on. Private welfare organizations employ a total of over 550,000 people, supported by at least three times as many volunteer workers. For this reason, they are highly respected and are closely involved with federal institutions.

In contrast to the established welfare organizations, the past few years have seen the formation of more and more social self-help groups as a new type of loosely organized interests (drug addicts, the homeless, etc.).

The Catholic and Protestant churches are omnipresent in the societal system of the Federal Republic. Since they were the only institutions still functioning immediately after the war, they occupied very strong positions due to the social and political functions that they took on in addition to their own mission of *Weltanschauung* (beliefs and creed). To this day, the churches still fulfill subsidiary social functions. Although the West German churches reject the label of "interest groups," they do exercise strong influence on relevant policy decisions, particularly concerning moral questions (see 9.2, "Religious Institutions").

Korporatistische Konsensbildung *(Corporatist Formation of Public Consensus) and New Forms of Organizational Behaviour*

The institutionalization of interests in affiliations has become a major influential factor in federal decision making in postwar Germany. This means, on the one hand, that the leading organizations influence the legislative process. They present their ideas to ministries which have a standing mandate to grant them consideration. Representatives of interest groups make up about one-third of the parliament. In certain committees of the federal parliament, such as the Agricultural Committee and the Committee for Socio-political Affairs, interest-group representatives make up half of the members. On the other hand, the major groups' influence on political decision making has led the federal government to impose responsibility for economic and social developments on them. A good example for this was the *Konzertierte Aktion* (concerted action, lasting from 1967 to 1977), a debate between organized capital and labour under the auspices of the Minister of the Economy, which aimed at wage and salary regulations favourable to the economy. Another example is the concerted action in the health-care field, in which all groups having to do with health-care participate. Its purpose is cost reduction in the health-care field.

In contrast to the Weimar Republic, organized interest groups are no longer an undermining element in the political system; instead, they have become a stabilizing factor. The symbiosis between established interest groups and federal authorities has led modern political scientists to coin the term *Korporatismus* (corporatism): "the inclusion of associations in politics as formally institutionalized boards (advisory bodies, committees, etc.), as well as in informal discussions, which often go against strict parliamentary procedure, change ... the intended impulse of the associations. They then become more easily an instrument for federal regulatory functions" (Heinze, 1981, p. 139).

The new social movements (citizens' initiatives, women's groups, the peace and conservation movements) are often comprehended as protests against the centralized forms of interest representation by the large organizations. Recent surveys show that youth particularly favours new, unconventional forms of articulation of interests, as opposed to the old, conventional organizations. About 10% of the young people polled in 1982 acknowledged involvement in the peace, anti-nuclear, and environmental movements or in church youth organizations, while the proportion involved in the youth organizations of the political parties had fallen to between 1.6% and 0.6%. A survey on personal attitudes toward various organizations lends emphasis to the picture: more than 50% were in favour of conservation, citizens' intiatives, self-help groups, the peace movement, and so on (see table 1). The number of new independent organizations vacillated between 3,000 and 50,000 during the 1970s. In the mid-1980s, it was estimated that there were between 15,000 and 35,000 groups (Alemann, 1987).

Despite their great popularity among youth, and the public attention they have attracted, the impact of the new social movements still lags behind that of the traditional organizations. A loosening up of organizational forms has indeed been brought about by the new social movements, but an undermining of traditional interest politics cannot be distinguished.

Barbara Wörndl

References

Alemann, Ulrich von

1985 "Der Wandel organisierter Interessen in der Bundesrepublik Deutschland." *Aus Politik und Zeitgeschichte*, no. 49, 3-21.

–

1987 *Organisierte Interessen in der Bundesrepublik*. Opladen: Leske und Budrich.

Hartmann, Jürgen

1985 *Verbände in der westlichen Industriegesellschaft*. Frankfurt am Main.

Heinze, Rolf G.

1981 "Neokorporatistische Strategien in Politikarenen und die Herausforderung durch neue Konfliktpotentiale." In Ulrich von Alemann, ed., *Neokorporatismus*. Frankfurt am Main: Campus.

Müller-Jentsch, Walter

1986 *Soziologie der industriellen Beziehungen*. Frankfurt am Main/New York: Campus.

Nohlen, Dieter, ed.

1983 *Pipers Wörterbuch zur Politik*. München: Piper.

Rudzio, Wolfgang

1982 *Die organisierte Demokratie. Parteien und Vebände in der Bundesrepublik Deutschland*. Stuttgart: Metzler.

Sontheimer, Kurt

1985 *Grundzüge des politischen Systems der Bundesrepublik Deutschland*. München/Zürich: Piper.

Statistisches Bundesamt, ed.

1986 *Statistisches Jahrbuch 1986*. Mainz/Stuttgart: Kohlhammer.

Steinberg, Rudolf, ed.

1985 *Staat und Verbände. Zur Theorie der Interessenverbände in der Industriegesellschaft*. Darmstadt.

Ullmann, Hans-Peter
1988 *Interessenverbände in Deutschland*. Frankfurt am Main: Suhrkamp.

Varain, Heinz J.
1973 *Interessenverbände in Deutschland*. Gütersloh.

Weber, Jürgen
1976 *Interessengruppen im politischen System der Bundesrepublik Deutschland*. München.

Table 1
Behaviour and attitudes of West German youth aged from 15 to 30 years toward groups and organizations (year 1982) (in %)

(N=2,012)	Environm. protection	Citizens' initiatives	Amnesty International	Self-help groups	Peace movemt.	Youth-center initiatives	Anti-nuclear movemt.
I'll join (or have joined)	9.7	4.0	2.1	2.9	11.2	4.3	8.0
Don't belong, but approve	73.8	66.5	66.3	65.8	63.9	52.5	37.0
Don't approve	1.4	3.6	4.6	3.7	5.0	4.1	22.0
They're my enemies	0.3	0.2	0.7	0.7	0.4	0.6	5.0

(N=2,012)	Pupil/ student goverment	Church youth	Labour union youth	Farmers' League youth	CDU[1] youth	SPD youth	FDP youth
I'll join (or have joined)	5.1	8.6	3.5	2.7	1.6	0.8	0.6
Don't belong, but approve	55.8	35.1	33.9	31.4	18.6	17.8	16.4
Don't approve	3.1	8.2	7.9	5.7	19.8	17.2	16.1
They're my enemies	0.6	1.0	1.0	0.4	5.2	2.7	2.2

Comment: The percentages do not add up to 100, as the answers "no interest/never heard of it/no reply" were left out. The question was: "Here is a list of groups and organizations concerned with certain goals. What do you think of each group?"

1. CDU - Christian-democratic Union; SPD - Social-democratic Party; FDP - Liberals.

Source: Sinus-Institut 1985, pp. 230, cited in Alemann, 1987, p. 66.

11. Ideologies

11.1 Political Differentiation

Since the founding of the Federal Republic of Germany in 1949, a process of distillation down to four civil political parties has taken place. These four parties, confront each other – as in a two-party system – as governing and opposition parties. Ideologically, the dominant Christian Democratic parties and the Social Democrats have come to resemble each other. Radical parties have never played more than a subordinate role in the postwar Republic. The electoral success of an ecological party in the 1980s has yet to pose any threat to the major parties.

Election Results

The multi-party system of the Weimar Republic (1918) was not revived in postwar Germany. Immediately after World War II, a four-party system was created in the occupied zones, comprising Christian Democratic, Liberal, Social Democratic, and Communist parties.

In the elections for the first German federal parliament (Deutscher Bundestag) in 1949, as many as eleven parties ran candidates for parliament. Only six did so, however, in the next election (1953). As of 1961, only four parties (the Christian Democratic Union – CDU – and its sister party, the Christian Social Union – CSU, the Free Democratic Party – FDP, and the Social Democratic Party – SPD) were represented. Not until 1983 did an additional party, the Green Party, gain a foothold in parliament (see table 1).

These few parties became predominant during the 1950s, rather one-sidedly weighted in favour of the conservative parties (CDU and CSU). With 31% of the vote and 139 seats in the federal parliament, they had only a slight edge over the SPD (with 29.2% of the vote and 131 seats) in the first elections. As early as 1953, however, they obtained a share of 45%, and have had no considerable drop from this level since then. Up to 1966, the Christian Democrats, in coalition with the

Liberals (FDP), formed the government. The fact that the Christian Democrats succeeded in overcoming old political and denominational divisions among the citizenry relatively early on may be the reason for their stable position. As the first people's party of postwar West Germany, the CDU formed a reservoir for the large majority of the middle classes, the farmers, and parts of the Christian-oriented working classes.

The SPD was the representative of the interests of the German working class until it opened itself to new segments of the population for the first time with its Godesberger Programm (1959), thereby losing the character of a definite left-wing party. The SPD thus could appeal to a new electorate in the 1960s, though its appeal was not strong enough to provide an alternative to the governing CDU/CSU coalition. Its increased electoral strength in the fifth parliamentary elections, in 1965 (the SPD got 39.3% of the vote, the CDU 47.6%) led to the *Große Koalition* (Big Coalition) of 1966, a joint government of the CDU, and the CSU, and the SPD. Only after the SPD had managed to integrate parts of the extra-parliamentary opposition (which had formed, among other reasons, in protest against the Big Coalition), students, and those involved in the academic and social professions, was the party strong enough to govern without the Christian Democrats. It first gained an edge over the CDU in the parliamentary elections of 1969 and formed, with the FDP, the "Social-liberal Coalition." This put the SPD and FDP on one side of the scale and the CDU and the CSU on the other, with nearly even weight. West Germany thus had its two-party system.

The SPD was forced out of office when the FDP dissolved its partnership with the SPD and formed a new coalition with the CDU and the CSU. The parliamentary elections of 1983 brought the CDU its best result (48.8%) since 1957 and gave it a 10% lead over the SPD. At the same time, the Green Party became the first new party to enter the federal parliament since 1961 (see tables 1 and 2).

The increasing concentration of the vote in the CDU and the SPD, which started in the 1950s and reached a peak in 1976 with a total of 91%, may have been disrupted by the formation of the Green Party, but the two major parties' proportion of the vote remains extremely high.

In addition to postwar prosperity, social and ideological changes were also possible causes of the particular structure of the West Germany's political scene: the *Wirtschaftswunder* (economic boom) created affluence, which reduced the social distance between the various classes and furthered the formation of a new middle class. Simultaneously, a secularization of the political culture took place (Tempel, 1987). The evolution of the CDU, the CSU, and the SPD into people's parties is also of great importance for this process of convergence. An important factor in the nearly competition-free positions of the major parties is the so-called five-percent clause, which excludes parties with less than 5% of the vote from entering into federal or state parliaments (a measure intended to prevent the parliamentary confusion of the Weimar Republic).

Extremist and Marginal Parties

Among the small parties, the FDP and the Green Party are the only ones that have proven capable of gaining any notable political influence. The FDP is the only small party that has cleared the 5% hurdle in all federal-parliament elections; with a proportion of around 10% of the vote, it was able to establish itself among the big parties. Compared with its actual size, its power, as a coalition partner for the CDU, the CSU, and the SPD, is disproportionate. As a party that sees its identity alternately as a guarantee against the overly conservative politics of the CDU and against the socialistic experiments of the SPD, the FDP had difficulty finding a political profile of its own. The two coalition switches since 1966 (in 1969 the switch from the CDU to the SPD, and in 1982 the switch back again) brought about massive membership and electoral losses. The FDP was often called a "toppler party" and accused of betraying its respective coalition partners. In 1982, disappointed FDP members founded a new party, the Liberal Democrats, which never succeeded in establishing itself.

The Green Party, which managed to consolidate its position after its initial success in national elections (from 5.6% in 1983 to 8.3% in 1987), is a result of the new social movements (citizens' initiatives, and the conservation, women's, and peace movements) of the 1970s. Parts of the "new left," such as ex-members of Communist groups, extra-parliamentary activists, and various other leftists, are also in the Green Party. Its success in "straight" politics has aggravated internal contention: "realists" and "fundamentalists" (no relation to religiously oriented fundamentalists in other countries) continue to fight over adaptation to and reform of the system versus radical change of the system. This contention has more than once brought the party to the edge of obliteration; the realists have finally won out – for the time being.

Extremist parties have played a negligible role in West Germany since 1969. "Extreme right-wing parties are discredited by the memory of National Socialism, and Communist parties by the present examples of real socialism" (Tempel, 1987, p. 93). On the extreme right, the German National Democratic Party (NPD) was the only party that proved capable, after it was formed in 1964 as a compilation of various nationalistic and neo-Nazi groups, of attracting more than 1% of the vote. In 1969, the NPD, with 4.3% of the vote, fell just short of entering the federal parliament (due to the 5% clause). Its share of the vote subsequently fell to less than 1%. The NPD had more success on state level. During the "Big Coalition" (1966–1969), and again in the most recent state-parliament elections, it cleared the 5% hurdle and entered various state parliaments.

Radical leftist parties were never nearly as strong as was the NPD in the second half of the 1960s. The radical left was initially represented by the Communist Party of Germany (KPD), which was outlawed in 1956. A new Communist party, the German Communist Party (DKP), was founded in 1968. The DKP views, as did the KPD, the countries under "real socialism" (i.e., in which socialism is the official ideology) as its political models. At the federal parliament level, it has consistently drawn under 1% of the vote. The DKP has had to accept heavy membership losses over the past few years. Since the advent of Gorbachev's politics of reform, an internal argument pitting the organizational principle of democratization of the party against retention of a Leninist structure has plunged the party into the biggest crisis since its founding.

Other small communist parties emerged from the student movement; these parties tended to be – as opposed to the DKP – Maoist-oriented (Communist Party of Germany, Communist Party of Germany/Marxists, Leninists, Communist League of West Germany). The proportion of the vote drawn to these so-called K groups is even smaller than that drawn to the DKP (for all election results, see table 1). In the course of the emergence of an alternative culture in the 1970's, these groups suffered badly from disintegration, and some were disbanded.

Self-location on the Right-Left Axis

The fact that "radical" standpoints are in the minority in the Federal Republic is confirmed by surveys on basic attitudes regarding society which have been carried out by the European Commission since 1970. Responses to a question about a "revolutionary" or "reformist" standpoint and about a desire for "energetic defence of existing society against subversive forces" indicate that a middle-of-the-road reformist position clearly reigns. Numerically, it declined somewhat in the 1970s (from over 70% of those polled to about 50%), and stabilized at nearly 60% in the early 1980s. Among attitudes deviating from the middle, the strongly conservative standpoints were clearly more widespread than were the revolutionary ones. From a proportion of about 20% in 1970, the "energetic defenders of the system" increased vigorously during the 1970s, and remained at 40% in the 1980s.

The advocates of a revolutionary remodelling of the Federal Republic grew in numbers in the 1980s, but always remained at under 10% (see table 3). These general trends were confirmed for the 1980s by polls concerning self-location on a "left-to-right scale." This ten-point scale made clear that very few people defined themselves as holding extreme positions on a left-to-right spectrum (see table 4).

The stronger identification with "leftist" positions in the 1980s is generally considered to be a clear expression of how many young people view the nearly competition-free positions of the established parties: as a hindrance to active participation in and identification with society. This slight shift, however, is not synonymous with a loss in importance for the established parties (see also 9.4, "Political Parties").

Barbara Wörndl

References

Ballerstedt, Eike, and Wolfgang Glatzer
1979 *Soziologischer Almanach*. Frankfurt am Main/New York: Campus.

Bundesminister des Inneren, ed.
1988 *Verfassungsschutzbericht 1987*. Bonn.

Grebing, Helga
1983 "Die Parteien." In Wolfgang Benz, ed., *Die Bundesrepublik Deutschland*. Vol. 1: Politik. Frankfurt am Main: Fischer.

Kaack, Heino, and Reinhold Roth, eds.
1983/84 *Handbuch des Parteiensystems der Bundesrepublik. Struktur und Politik zu Beginn der 80er Jahre*. 2 vols. Opladen: Leske und Budrich.

Kaltefleiter, Werner
1984 *Parteien im Umbruch. Ein Beitrag zur politischen Geschichte der Bundesrepublik Deutschland*. Düsseldorf: Econ.

Kommission der Europäischen Gemeinschaft, ed.
1984 *Eurobarometer. Die öffentliche Meinung in der Europäischen Gemeinschaft*. Brüssel.

Langguth, Gerd
1984 *Der grüne Faktor. Von der Bewegung zur Partei*. Osnabrück: Fromm.

Ménudier, Henri
1986 *Parteien und Wahlen im politischen System der Bundesrepublik Deutschland*. München: Iudicium.

Sontheimer, Kurt
1984 *Grundzüge des politischen Systems der Bundesrepublik Deutschland*. München: Piper.

Statistisches Bundesamt, ed.
1987 *Datenreport 1987*. Bonn: Bundeszentrale für politische Bildung.

Tempel, Karl G.
1987 *Die Parteien in der Bundesrepublik Deutschland und die Rolle der Parteien in der DDR*. Düsseldorf: Landeszentrale für politische Bildung Nordrhein-Westfalen.

Table 1
Results of federal parliamentary elections 1949 - 1987

Party	1949	1953	1957	1961	1965	1969	1972	1976	1980	1983	1987
CDU/CSU[1]	31.0	45.2	50.2	45.3	47.6	46.1	44.9	48.6	44.5	48.8	44.3
SPD	29.2	28.8	31.8	36.2	39.3	42.7	45.8	42.6	42.9	38.2	37.0
FDP/DVP	11.9	9.5	7.7	12.8	9.5	5.8	8.4	7.9	10.6	6.9	9.1
Green Party	-	-	-	-	-	-	-	-	1.5	5.6	8.3
DP	4.0	3.3	3.4	-	-	-	-	-	-	-	-
GDP	-	-	-	2.8	-	0.1	-	-	-	-	-
GB/BHE	-	5.9	4.6	-	-	-	-	-	-	-	-
ZP	3.1	0.8	0.3	-	-	-	-	-	-	-	0.1
BP	4.2	1.7	0.5	-	-	0.2	-	-	-	-	0.1
DRP; NPD	1.8	1.1	1.0	0.8	2.0	4.3	0.6	0.3	0.2	0.2	0.6
KPD; DFU; DKP	5.7	2.2	-	1.9	1.3	0.6	0.3	0.3	0.2	0.2	-
Others	9.1	1.5	0.5	0.2	0.3	0.2	0.1	0.3	0.1	0.1	0.7
Numbers of seats in federal parliament											
CDU/CSU[1]	139	243	270	242	245	242	225	243	226	244	223
SPD	131	151	169	190	202	224	230	214	218	193	186
FDP/DVP	52	48	41	67	49	30	41	39	53	34	46
Green Party	-	-	-	-	-	-	-	-	-	27	42
DP	17	15	17	-	-	-	-	-	-	-	-
GDP	-	-	-	-	-	-	-	-	-	-	-
GB/BHE	-	27	-	-	-	-	-	-	-	-	-
ZP	10	3	-	-	-	-	-	-	-	-	-
BP	17	-	-	-	-	-	-	-	-	-	-
DRP	5	-	-	-	-	-	-	-	-	-	-
KPD	15	-	-	-	-	-	-	-	-	-	-
Others	16	-	-	-	-	-	-	-	-	-	-
Total	402	487	497	499	496	496	496	496	497	498	497
West Berlin	19	22	22	22	22	22	22	22	22	22	22

1. Names of parties: CDU/CSU=Christian Demodratic/Christian Social Union; SPD=Social Democratic Party; FDP/DVP=the Liberals; DP=German Party; GB/BHE=Pan-German Bloc/League of Displaced Persons; ZP=Center Party; BP=Bavaria Party; DRP=German Imperial Party; DFU=German Peace Union.

Source: Tempel, 1987, p. 78.

Table 2
Parties in the federal government

Cabinet	Cabinet seats and coalitions					
Adenauer (CDU) first cabinet (1949-1953)	6 CDU	3 CSU	3 FDP	2 DP		
Adenauer (CDU) second cabinet (1953-1957)	8 CDU	2 CSU	4 FDP	2 BHE	2 DP	1 independent
	after cabinet re-foarmation of Oct. 16, 1956:					
	10 CDU	3 CSU	2 FVP	2 DP		
Adenauer (CDU) third cabinet (1957-1961)	12 CDU	4 CSU	2 DP			
Adenauer (CDU) fourth cabinet (1961-1962)	12 CDU	4 CSU	5 FDP			
Adenauer (CDU) fifth cabinet (1962-1963)	12 CDU	4 CSU	5 FDP			
Erhard (CDU) first cabinet (1963-1965)	13 CDU	4 CSU	5 FDP			
Erhard (CDU) second cabinet (1965/1966)	13 CDU	5 CSU	4 FDP	(on Oct. 27,1966, FDP ministers resign)		
Kiesinger (CDU) (1966-1969)	8 CDU	3 CSU	9 SPD			
Brandt (SPD) first cabinet (1969-1972)	12 SPD	3 FDP	1 independent			
Brandt (SPD) second cabinet (1972-1974)	13 SPD	5 FDP				
Schmidt (SPD) first cabinet (1974-1976)	12 SPD	4 FDP				
Schmidt (SPD) second cabinet (1976-1980)	12 SPD	4 FDP				
Schmidt (SPD) third cabinet (1980-1982	13 SPD	4 FDP	(after resignation of FDP ministers Sept. 17.1982: 13 SPD)			
Kohl (CDU) first cabinet (1982-1983)	9 CDU	4 CSU	4 FDP			
Kohl (CDU) second cabinet (1983-1987)	9 CDU	5 CSU	3 FDP			
Kohl (CDU) third cabinet (1987-)	9 CDU	5 CSU	4 FDP			

Source: Datenhandbuch zur Geschichte des Deutschen Bundestages 1949 bis 1982, 1983, pp. 304-321. Der Tagesspiegel, 12.3.1987, cited in Tempel, 1987, p. 77.

Table 3
Fundamental attitude toward society[1]
(per 100 persons answering)

Item	in %
Feb.-March 1970[2]:	
revolution	2
reforms	76
defense against subversive forces	22
November 1976:	
revolution	2
reforms	56
defense against subversive forces	42
Oct.-Nov. 1981:	
revolution	5
reforms	55
defense against subversive forces	40
October 1983:	
revolution	3
reforms	53
defense against subversive forces	44
March-April 1984:	
revolution	3
reforms	56
defense against subversive forces	41
Oct.-Nov. 1984:	
revolution	3
reforms	62
defense against subversive forces	35
March-April 1985:	
revolution	3
reforms	62
defense against subversive forces	35
Oct.-Nov. 1985:	
revolution	4
reforms	56
defense against subversive forces	40

1. For each category, the percentages total 100.
2. 1970 wording: "through 'intelligent reforms'."

Source: Kommission der Europäischen Gemeinschaft, 1985, p. 40.

Table 4
Answers on a "left-to-right" scale (in %)[1]

"left-to-right" scale		1980	1982	1986
Left	1	1.9	0.7	2.1
	2	2.4	2.0	2.7
	3	6.6	5.7	9.3
	4	10.8	8.8	9.6
	5	17.4	16.4	19.9
	6	26.9	30.7	25.2
	7	15.0	14.1	12.8
	8	9.8	11.9	10.4
	9	5.2	5.5	4.7
Right	10	4.1	4.3	3.3
Average[2]		5.89	5.97	5.72

1. Wording of question: "Many people use the terms 'left' and 'right' when characterizing various political attitudes. We have here a scale going from left to right. Where would you place your own political views on this scale? Please draw an 'x' in one of the boxes." The questionee is presented with a ten-point scale. In the evaluation, the middle values 5 and 6 were both taken together as the "center," and the respective extreme values 1 to 4 as "left" and 7 to 10 as "right."

2. Value on the "left-to-right" scale.

Data basis: ALLBUS 1980 (N=2,955), 1982 (N=2,991), 1986 (N=3,095).

Source: Statistisches Bundesamt, 1987, p. 487.

11.2 Confidence in Institutions

In the Federal Republic of Germany, public approval of the political and economic order has experienced long-term growth and has stabilized at a high level. Although institutions such as schools and the army were subject to public criticism in the postwar period, with its background of domestic- and foreign-policy developments, these institutions were never seriously questioned.

General Developments

The early postwar years were characterized mainly by concentration on reconstruction. The population's dominant interest was elimination of economic need and ensuring basic individual living conditions. As the new order became successful in satisfying its citizens' most urgent material needs, West Germans increasingly identified with the economic and social order. Twenty years after the end of World War II, the Republic and its central institutions had gained high public esteem. This positive identification went into some decline in the 1960s. Economic growth was exposed as not only creating a higher standard of living, but also creating new dangers: West Germans became aware of the problems of protecting the environment and a humane way of life against uncontrolled growth. A new interest in reform and change of the existing system arose. The climate of reform was decisive for the political environment in the Federal Republic up to the mid-1970s, and generally shifted political consciousness to the left.

Enthusiasm for reform and for criticism retreated once again into the background as of the mid-1970s. It became evident that the protest, carried mostly by the educated classes, had not seriously damaged confidence in public institutions. A heritage of the reform and protest phase is an alternative culture which has established itself beside the "straight" political culture. Advocates of the "critical distance" from institutions have remained in the minority.

Political System

Growing public approval of the social order in postwar Germany is illustrated by the visibly deteriorating election results for radical political groups. A running survey (since 1973), examining satisfaction with the way democracy functions, shows that the share of those "very satisfied" and "quite satisfied" has increased considerably since the mid-1970s (from 44% to around 70%; see table 1), which puts the Germans, compared with citizens of other Common Market countries, among those with the most confidence in the functioning of democracy. These numbers mirror the picture of public opinion presented by official political representatives: "The majority of West Germans consider their government to be democratic, just, tolerant, and reliable. Governmental organization is neither too strong nor too weak for them, but is just right. The majority give this governmental organization good reference" (Koch, 1972). Theories of the past few years, which have predicted a "legitimacy deficit" of the state under "late-capitalistic conditions" have not been borne out.

Army

Confidence in the *Bundeswehr* (West German military forces) was initially shaken by the total defeat in World War II; in the first few years after the refounding of the military forces, in 1950, the *Bundeswehr* was a target of protest. Its opponents were, however, able to mobilize only a relatively small part of the population. The majority took a stance toward the military forces ranging from benevolent indifference and passive agreement to explicit welcome. A poll on general opinions toward the military forces shows a vigorous upswing since the 1960s in the approval rating of the military. Compared to approving and indifferent attitudes, those with an explicitly low opinion remained in the minority (see table 2). The internal security policy, in contrast to the military, suffers from a lack of legitimacy. This is manifested in the many new peace initiatives, which are particularly concerned with the question of atomic armament of the West German military forces as prescribed in NATO strategy. Demonstrations climaxed in the 1950s, around rearmament of the military forces, and West Germany's entry into NATO, and in the early 1980s, when the decision was made to station atomic mid-range missiles in Europe. The fact that the internal-security policy of the West German military related to NATO was rejected by more than just adherents to the peace movement is shown in table 3. In 1958, 67.1% of those polled (including adherents to and opponents of the peace movement) were against atomic armament of the West German military. In 1982, 55.1% of those polled wanted no atomic weapons, "regardless of what the East bloc does." Since Gorbachev has repeatedly been making new disarmament offers to the West, the public has regarded the internal-security concept of the West German military as increasingly dubious.

Churches

While the churches (Protestant and Catholic) were the incontestable moral authorities for the majority of people during the immediate postwar period, this changed in the course of normalization of life in the Republic. Waning confidence in the church was manifested in an exodus of members in the late 1960s and the 1970s. Many Germans saw the church's *Weltanschauung* (creed) as outdated and rigid. A poll concerning religious questions and attitudes toward the official churches confirms the "de-churching" tendency: in the early 1970s, 49% of Catholics and 37% of Protestants still considered themselves "pious members of a church, and following the doctrine" (see table 4, answer 1), but these figures fell to 38% among Catholics by 1982, and to a very low 14% among Protestants. More and more members of both groups view themselves as believers, who practise their "own belief, their own life philosophy, completely independent of the church" (table 4, answer 4).

Schools

The evaluation of educational opportunity can be taken as an indicator of popular confidence in the schools. Development of talent and ability and equal opportunity were declared to be of central importance for educational institutions during the period of mobilization of educational reserves in the 1960s.

Up to the early 1960s, 70% of the population saw in the German school system the possibility of education according to talent and ability; in the late 1970s and the 1980s, barely 50% did so. The biggest decrease was between 1963 and 1979, in the acute phase of education expansion, whereas after the expansion phase had ended, in 1979, educational opportunities were once again judged more favourably (see table 5). It should be noted that those who have benefited from the education expansion – the younger and the better educated – have a more negative opinion of education opportunity than do the older and the less well educated. Before the education expansion – in 1958 and 1963 – a positive view of education opportunities among older people was only slightly more widespread than among younger people, while after the education expansion – in 1979 and 1986 – the difference of opinion was more pronounced. Evaluation of educational opportunity according to various educational levels offers a similar picture. The better educated had more trust in equal opportunity before the education expansion, and less after the expansion, than did the less well educated (Statistisches Bundesamt, 1987).

The education expansion made an objective improvement in families' chances to send their children to higher-level secondary schools. Popular confidence in the ability of schools to guarantee education opportunity has, however, dropped. This disparity can be explained by increased awareness of problems regarding equal opportunity – awareness that has risen in conjunction with the expansion. School as an institution has once again been experiencing an upswing in public confidence since 1982.

Barbara Wörndl

References

EMNID
1986 *EMNID-Informationen*, no. 10.

Koch, Manfred
1982 *Die Deutschen und ihr Staat*. Hamburg.

Kommission der Europäischen Gemeinschaft, ed.
1985 *Eurobarometer. Die öffentliche Meinung in der Europäischen Gemeinschaft*. Brüssel.

Noelle-Neumann, Elisabeth, and Erich Peter, eds.
1974 *Jahrbuch der öffentlichen Meinung*. Allensbach/Bonn: Verlag für Demoskopie.

Noelle-Neumann, Elisabeth, ed.
1983 *Allensbacher Jahrbuch der Demoskopie, 1978-1983*. München/New York/London/Paris: Saur.

–, ed.
1981 *The Germans. Public Opinion Pools, 1967-1980*. Westport, Conn./London: Greenwood.

Schmitt, Rüdiger
1987 *From "Old Politics" to "New Politics": Three Decades of Peace Protest in West Germany*. Amsterdam.

Sontheimer, Kurz
1985 *Grundzüge des politischen Systems der Bundesrepublik Deutschland*. München: Piper.

Statistisches Bundesamt, ed.
1987 *Datenreport 1987*. Bonn: Bundeszentrale für politische Bildung.

Vogt, Wolfgang R., ed.
1983 *Sicherheitspolitik und Streitkräfte in der Legitimitätskrise. Analysen zum Prozeß der Delegitimierung des Militärs im Kernwaffenzeitalter*. Baden-Baden: Nomos.

Table 1
Satisfaction with how West German democracy functions[1]

Item	1973 Sept.	1983 Oct.	1984 Oct.-Nov.	1985 Oct.-Nov.
Very satisfied	5	7	11	10
Fairly satisfied	39	59	61	59
Not very satisfied	44	21	21	22
Not at all satisfied	11	3	5	4
No reply	1	10	2	5
Index[2]	2.38	2.78	2.78	2.78

1. Percentages totalling 100.
2. "Very satisfied"=4; "not at all satisfied"=1. Non-replies do not count.

Source: Kommission der Europäischen Gemeinschaft, 1985, pp. 35.

Table 2
Opinions regarding the Army (in %)

Wording of question: "Do you generally speaking have a good opinion of the Federal Armed Forces?"

Item	1964 Jan.	1969 June	1971 April	1980 Dec.
Good opinion	36	33	35	47
Yes and no	26	30	25	27
Lesser opinion	22	24	27	16
No opinion	16	13	13	10
Total	100	100	100	100

2,000 personed aged 16 years and over in Federal Republic and West Berlin.

Source: Noelle-Neumann, 1980, p. 142.

Table 3
Attitudes toward security policy planning in the 1950s and the 1980s

Wording of question: "In general are you for or against a West Germany's participation in the military defense of western Europe?"

	Very much for	Somewhat for	Somewhat against	Very much against	No opinion	Total	N
Jan. 1955	17.6	27.0	14.1	22.9	18.3	100.0	1,867

Wording of question: "As you know, there is much discussion at present about questions of nuclear energy. In your opinion, should our military be equipped with nuclear weapons?"

	Yes	No	No opinion	Total	N
April 1958	20.4	67.1	12.5	100.0	927

Wording of question: "Here is a list of political demands. Please tell us if you are more for or against... - no new missiles in West German regardless of what the East bloc does."

	Against new missiles	For new missiles	No opinion	Total	N
Nov. 1982	55.1	42.9	2.0	100.0	1,622

Source: Schmitt, 1987, p. 41.

Table 4
Opinions regarding the Church (in %)

Wording of question put to Protestants and Catholics: "Where would you place yourself on this list - which statement would apply?"

Item	70/71 Cath.	1972 Prot.	1979 Cath.	1979 Prot.	1982 Cath.	1982 Prot.
1. I am a believing member of my church and follow its doctrine	49[1]	37	42	14	38	14
2. I consider myself a Christian, but the Church doesn't mean much to me	24	31	28	34	25	28
3. I would like to believe but I am uncertain about so many things	7	-	6	6	9	7
4. I have my own beliefs, my own philosophy of life, completely independent of the Church	9	16	10	20	10	19
5. I live and work. Everything else takes care of itself - I don't need any beliefs	3	7	4	8	5	9
6. Belief means nothing to me. Instead, I concentrate on the problems of this world and the problems of my fellow human beings	2	5	2	4	2	5
7. I don't know what I should believe in. That's why I'd rather leave such questions open	4	8	6	12	7	11
8. No answer	5	4	2	2	4	7
Total	103	108[2]	100	100	100	100

Item	Winter 70/71 Catholics	Summer 1972 Protestants	
I am a believing member of my church and follow its doctrine	49	24	37
I am loyal to the church, but it must change	-	14	

2,000 interviewed persons, not younger than 16

1. Key to first statement to be found in survey of 1970/71 or, respectively, 1972.
2. Comment: in the Catholic-synod survey, the question was appended with: "If possible, only one answer!"

Source: Noelle-Neumann, 1983, p. 127; 1974, p. 100; 1980, p. 229.

Table 5
Evaluation of educational opportunity, 1958 to 1986 (in %)

Wording of question: "What is your opinion: Does everyone have the chance nowadays to get an education suited to his talent and abilities?"

Item	1958	1963	1979	1986
Yes	66	73	50	52
No	32	27	39	41
No opinion, no reply	2	-	11	6

Data basis: 1958: Strzelewicz, W.,1973 et al., Bildung und gesellschaftliches Bewußtsein, Stuttgart, Enke Verlag, p. 73 (N=1,850); 1963: Zentralarchiv-Studie no. 0021 (N=1,819); 1979: ZUMABUS (N=2,007); 1983: ALLBUS (N=3,095).

Source: Statistisches Bundesamt, 1987, p. 473.

11.3 Economic Orientations

The swift reconstruction of Germany after 1945 and the great economic growth of the following period were accompanied by the firm confidence in the free-market economy, and by a predominantly positive opinion of private enterprise and of performance as a value per se. As the West German economy experienced crises in the 1970s and 1980s, the optimistic standpoint lost some of its bounce and criticism of unchecked growth spread.

Attitude Toward the Economy

In the first two decades of existence of the Republic, public confidence in the performance capability of the *Marktwirtschaft* (free-market economy) was unusually high. The economic growth rate was called a *Wirtschaftswunder* (economic miracle), which shows that the blossoming economy was considered to be the prerequisite for public and private affluence. This high esteem should be seen against the background of the rising share of private consumption in the GNP, and also of a rapid reduction in unemployment. As economic crises hit the economy – in 1967, 1975 and 1981 – 1982 the GNP stagnated, and unemployment increased starting in the mid-1970s, reaching approximately 9% in the 1980s – the *Wachstumseuphorie* (boom euphoria) was dampened somewhat. At this point, the problematic sides of economic growth also came to light.

The fact that the state of the economy is reflected in the public mood is illustrated by a polling of the populace's prognoses for growth since the late 1950s, which showed that those polled "often predicted the growth rate for the coming year more precisely than clever economic assessments" (Klipstein, 1985, p. 131). Another survey, gauging prognoses for the 1970s and 1980s shows how modest popular expectations were during that phase of economic development: while 47% still thought that the economy was going "uphill" in 1976, versus a mere 14% claiming it was going "downhill," this ratio had completely reversed by 1981: only 9% expected an upturn, 56% a downturn. Not until the 1980s did the optimistic view regain predominance: in 1983, positive and negative opinions had returned to nearly the proportions of 1976 (41% and 17%, respectively; see table 4). The upward trend of the 1980s can be explained by the fact that after the economic crisis of 1981 – 1982, the German economy was strong in comparison to those of other nations.

A poll taken every two years since 1982 to examine the evaluations of general and personal economic situations, confirms the trend for the 1980s. While negative assessments of the general economic situation still outweighed positive ones in 1982 (by approximately 30% to 10%), opinion had reversed by 1986 (10% to approximately 35%). Remarkably, the personal economic situation was judged more positively during this time than was the general situation: positive ratings started at the high level of 50% (1982) and continued to rise, while negative ratings were at 10% in 1982 and remained about constant. Overall, the gap between evaluation of the personal and the general economic situation has closed since 1984 (see figure 1).

A notable development of the past two decades is the shift in evaluation of economic growth. If growth of the GNP was once an unchallenged dogma, burgeoning environmental problems have induced the population to judge it more critically. Poll results of the past 15 years show that a stable majority of those questioned favour giving priority to environmental protection, even at the cost of slowed economic growth and rising prices. Economic growth, however, is more highly valued when those polled are asked to decide between environmental protection and the guarantee of jobs (Klipstein, 1985; see also 17.4, "Values").

Image of Private Enterprise and Profit

The rapid reconstruction of Germany and its subsequent economic success have often been traced to the "German work ethic" and the willingness to sacrifice. This point of view is reflected in Germans' interpretations of their own performance motives, showing an almost fervent conception of work, with virtues such as industriousness, willingness to work, and willingness to perform being relatively highly rated, and a luxury-oriented attitude tendentially rejected. A long-term comparison of "ascetic" and "hedonistic" stances (Meulemann, 1982) showed that the former had a consistent majority over the latter. The number of those willing to sacrifice had, however, decreased in comparison to 40 years before. The greatest change was registered between the mid-1960s and the mid-1970s. A clear decrease in the ascetic standpoint became visible at this time, while those aspiring to enjoyment of life increased (see 17.4, "Values").

The readiness to engage in business was analogous to the statements concerning personal-performance and work motives: the proportion of those favouring independent business activity decreased simultaneously with reduced willingness to see work as an end in itself. Neither pattern took an upturn until 1980 (see table 1).

This was also the period of the most marked transformation in the image of the businessperson. While the proportion of people judging businesspersons to be "hard-working" grew between 1952 and 1965 (from 42% to 50%), the number of those viewing entrepreneurs as profiting from the work of others rose only slightly (22% to 23%). The generally high esteem accorded to businesspersons had, however, been badly depleted by 1970. Positive opinions then took an upturn, and by 1980 had exceeded even the evaluations of the immediate postwar period (see table 2).

The proportion of those considering businesspersons "socially conscious" rose between 1950 and 1980 (from 16% to 40%). The number of those viewing businesspersons as "pure egoists" was on a clear downswing during this period (see table 3). This can be seen in conjunction with the many voluntary social benefits granted by employers, which were gradually consolidated in the course of collective bargaining between labour and employers.

Barbara Wörndl

References

Hondrich, Karl Otto
1989 "Value Changes in Western Societies. The Last Thirty Years." In Burkhard Strümpel, ed., *Industrial Societies after the Stagnation of the 1970's - Taking Stock from an Interdisciplinary Perspective*. Berlin/New York: de Gruyter.

Institut für Demoskopie Allensbach, ed.
1981 *The Germans. Public Opinion Polls 1967-1980*. Westport, Conn./London: Greenwood.

Klipstein, Michael von
1984 *Der Überdruß am Überfluß. Die Deutschen nach dem Wirtschaftswunder*. München: Olzog.

Klipstein, Michael von, and Burkhard Strümpel
1985 *Gewandelte Werte - Erstarrte Strukturen. Wie die Bürger Wirtschaft und Arbeit erleben*. Bonn: Verlag Neue Gesellschaft.

Marissen, Norbert
1986 *Leistungsorientierung in the Bundesrepublik Deutschland: Einstellungsveränderungen als Folge der sich wandelnden Berufsstruktur*. Frankfurt am Main/Bern/New York: Lang.

Meulemann, Heiner
1982 *Value Change in West Germany, 1950-1980: Integrating the empirical evidence*. Vortrag auf dem 10. Weltkongress für Soziologie in Mexico City. Köln.

Noelle-Neumann, Elisabeth, and Edgar Piel, eds.
1983 *Allensbacher Jahrbuch für Demoskopie 1978-1983*. München/New York/London/Paris: Saur.

Rythlewski, Ralf, and Manfred Opp den Hint
1987 *Die Bundesrepublik in Zahlen 1945/49-1980. Ein sozialgeschichtliches Arbeitsbuch*. München: Beck.

Scholz, Joachim
1987 *Wertewandel und Wirtschaftskultur*. München.

Statistisches Bundesamt, ed.
1987 *Datenreport 1987*. Bonn: Bundeszentrale für politische Bildung.

Zeitmagazin
1989 *Zeitmagazin*, no. 22.

Table 1
Opinions regarding self-employment (in %)

Wording of question to currently employed wage and salaried workers: "Would you be principally interested in going into "business for yourself?"

Item	Total of 1962	Employed 1976	Persons 1980
Yes, definitely	17	7	13
Maybe	20	21	25
No	63	72	62
Total	100	100	100

2,000 persons 16 years and over in Federal Republic of Germany.

Source: Noelle-Neumann, 1983, p. 390.

Table 2
Opinions regarding workethic of industrialists (in %)

Wording of question: "When you hear about industrialists - do you think of hard-working people, or of people who only profit from the work of others?"

Item	1952 Oct.	1965 May	1970 Sept.	1976 June	1980 Jan.
Hard-working people	42	50	44	48	55
Profit from work of others only	22	23	27	22	18
Undecided	36	27	29	30	27
Total	100	100	100	100	100

1,000 persons 16 years and older in Federal Republic of Germany and West Berlin.

Source: Institut für Demoskopie Allensbach, 1981, p. 292.

Table 3
Opinions regarding social consciousness of industrialists (in %)

Wording of question: "Do you think the majority of industrialists think only of their personal gain today or are they also social - minded?"

Item	1950 May	1965 July	1973 Aug.	1980 Jan.
Think only of gain	60	40	34	39
Also social-minded	16	34	35	40
Undecided	24	26	31	21
Total	100	100	100	100

1,000 persons 16 years and older in Federal Republic of Germany and West Berlin.

Source: Institut für Demoskopie Allensbach, 1981, p. 292.

Table 4
Presumed economic development

Wording of question: "Do you think our economy will tend upward or downward in the next six months?"

Year	Tendency upwards	Tendency downwards
1976 (May)	47	14
1977 (Feb.)	32	27
1977 (May)	26	24
1978 (March)	19	28
1978 (Oct.)	28	19
1979 (Oct.)	26	18
1980 (March)	17	30
1980 (Oct.)	10	45
1981 (May)	13	44
1981 (Nov.)	9	56
1982 (May)	22	36
1982 (Oct.)	18	41
1983 (April)	41	17

Source: Noelle-Neumann & Piel, 1983, p. 373.

Figure 1
Evaluation of economic situation 1982, 1984, 1986

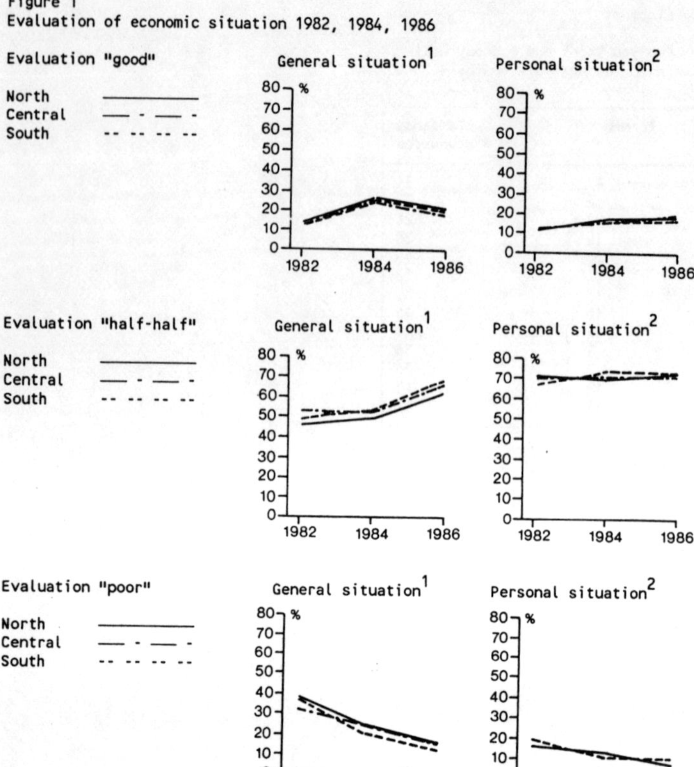

Results of representative popular polling in % of respondents

1. Wording of question: "How would you judge in general the current economic situation in West Germany?"
2. Wording of question: "How would you judge your own current economic situation?"

Data basis: Allbus, 1982, 1984, 1986.

Source: Statistisches Bundesamt, 1987, p. 447.

11.4 Radicalism

As opposed to the situation in the Weimar Republic, groups on the extreme right and left had great difficulty gaining a foothold in postwar Germany. In the first three decades after the war, the influence of the radical right dwindled sharply. Not until the 1980s did right-wing organizations again register any success. Radical leftist groups have had the support of a steadily shrinking constituency since the end of World War II. It was only during the 1970s that the descent in popularity of the radical left was slowed.

Manifestations on the Extreme Right

A rough overall sketch of the development of right-wing radicalism in postwar Germany shows the following tendencies: membership in extreme right-wing organizations – from parties and youth groups, publishers, and clubs which spread radical right-wing ideas to militant, and even violent, neo-Nazi groups – followed a downward curve from 1954 to 1979, falling from 76,000 to 17,300, then gradually increased. The *Verfassungsschutzbericht* (Report on Unconstitutional Activities) of 1980 put the number of members at 19,800, the report of 1987 as high as 25,200 (see table 1). This development disproved the assumption that right-wing radicalism in West Germany was mainly a generational problem that would die out with the ex-Hitlerians.

Observation of the various groupings, however, presents a more subtly differentiated picture: during a period when the number of organizations decreased (between 1966 and 1969), a radical right-wing party (National Democratic Party of Germany – NPD) succeeded in gathering together the radical rightist forces. Formed in 1964 as a catch-all for various nationalist, neo-Nazi, racist, and radical anti-communist groups, the NPD enjoyed healthy membership gains, and was able to enter some state parliaments. In the elections of 1969, the party, with 4.3% of the vote, just missed entry into the federal parliament. Economic difficulties among the traditional middle class and the rural population, as well as the revival of the *Deutsche Frage* (the question of the West German claim to the former German regions in eastern Europe) served in large part to explain the NPD's successes (for election results, see 11.1, "Political Differentation"). Following 1970, the party's influence dwindled, while the number of rightist organizations gradually increased (see table 2).

Since the mid-1970s, neo-Nazi groups have consolidated their position within the extreme-right bloc. Membership in such groups more than tripled between 1975 and 1981, while the influence of the extreme right stagnated. The influence of these groups within the extreme right was on the rise up to 1986. In contrast to radical right-wing parties that envision coming to power via the democratic procedure (elections) and emphasize their conformity with the order of democratic freedom, neo-Nazis usually openly acknowledge their loyalty to Adolf Hitler and the Third Reich. A certain propensity for violence reigns among these groups. Since the late 1970s, the Report on Unconstitutional Activities has registered a definite rise in all officially recognized categories of violence ("National Socialist and anti-Semitic incidents," "transgressions with extreme-right background," "legal offenses by German right-wing extremists").

The growing influence of extreme-right parties and groups in the 1980s can presumably be traced to a spreading hostility toward foreigners, which worked to the advantage of the radical right. A glance at the publications of the extreme right makes it obvious that the right is riding this wave: while the *Kriegsschuldfrage* (question of blame for World War II), the war experience, and denials or downplaying of the genocide of Jews during the Third Reich were formerly the main themes in agitation, propaganda has since been shifting to "dilution of the German people through foreigners." Using this motto, a new right-wing party, the Republikaner, recently got enough votes in municipal elections to enter local parliaments.

Manifestations on the Extreme Left

In the postwar Federal Republic, groups on the radical left wing of the political spectrum have had to rely upon a dwindling potential number of advocates of revolutionary upheaval. The radical left enjoyed a short upswing in popularity in the 1970s, but has since been less and less capable of attracting and keeping alive the potential for protest. Nowadays, those espousing socially critical positions have been integrated into the parliamentary spectrum via an alternative party, the Green Party.

In the immediate postwar period, the Moscow-oriented Communist Party of Germany (KPD) was the only leftist organization that could boast a noteworthy membership, 70,000 members, in 1956. When the party was banned that same year, the radical left in West Germany was deprived of its only means of gathering people with revolutionary convictions. The ban met with widespread approval, as polls of the 1950s show. In 1952, 43% of those polled were for and 35% were against the bans; in 1954, the proportion was 55% to 30%. In 1967, about 10 years after the KPD was banned and shortly before the founding of a new communist party (the equally Moscow-oriented German Communist Party – DKP), 61% of the population expressed its rejection of a Communist party in West Germany, while only 23% would have welcomed the founding of such a party. In 1973, the proportion of those advocating the banning of the DKP (which was five years old at the time) was well below previous results (39% – see tables 3, 4, 5, and 6), but the party's actual influence was extremely minor. The DKP managed to attract members up to the mid-1970s (peaking at 40,000), but subsequently lost popularity. Its share of the vote at the federal level stayed below under 1% (see 11.1, "Political Differentation").

The temporary upswing in popularity of the DKP took place in conjunction with a leftist protest culture that originated in the student movement of the late 1960s and early 1970s. Student criticism of undemocratic social structures and of imperialism and capitalism brought a new influx of adherents to orthodox communism, represented by the DKP. The protest also flowed into new circles, organizations, and parties of the radical left. This "new left" confronted the Moscow-oriented orthodox communists with alternative concepts for communist politics (with, for example, China and Albania as models). At the same time, the new left also produced "spontaneistic" (spontaneous, i.e., un- and anti-dogmatic leftist) and anarchistic groups.

The phase of leftist protest was characterized by intense examination and discussion of classic Marxist theory. This "theory movement," which produced a batch of literature, remained limited to the intelligentsia, and the radical leftist organizations generally drew their members from these educated circles. None of these groups managed to become the classic communist party that "grips the proletarian masses."

This relative lack of success eventually led to a debate within the left as to whether one could still speak of the working class as the revolutionary subject, or whether other movements and segments of the population should be taken into consideration as potential for social change. This self-criticism finally led to a downturn in membership and a rapid decimation of these organizations. Many of the previously "dogmatic" parties underwent an "ecological turn" and were later absorbed by the Green Party.

The rise of anarchist groups in the early 1970s can be seen as a consequence of meagre popular support for the left. As opposed to the other above-mentioned groups, which rejected violence under any conditions, the anarchist groups justified violence against persons or objects with the claim that "revolutionary violence" forms a beacon for the masses. Ulrike Meinhof, co-founder of the best-known anarchist group (*Rote Armee Fraktion*) justified the group's attacks on representatives of state and economy as "revolutionary intervention by a small force of people, setting free the triumph of the people." These attacks were carried out by a tiny circle of people in the underground. In the 1970s, the *Verfassungsschutz* (West German Secret Service for detection of and protection against unconstitutional activities) registered a growing incidence of acts of violence by anarchist groups, though they decreased late in the decade. This is presumably due to the government's fight against terrorism, which destroyed the logistics of the anarchist groups. Not until the 1980s did new assassinations and assassination attempts take place which were alleged to come from terrorist circles.

Observation of the entire radical-left spectrum shows that up to the mid-1970s, left-extremist endeavours increased their membership, reaching a peak of 102,000 in 1974 (versus 78,000 in 1972). Membership has decreased markedly since then (62,000 in 1987; see table 7).

Barbara Wörndl

References

Bundesminister des Innern, ed.
1970 *Verfassungsschutz 1969-1970*. Bonn.

–, ed.
1974 *Verfassungsschutz 1974*. Bonn.

–, ed.
1978 *Verfassungsschutz 1978*. Bonn.

–, ed.
1980 *Verfassungsschutz 1980*. Bonn.

–, ed.
1981 *Verfassungsschutz 1981*. Bonn.

–, ed.
1987 *Verfassungsschutz 1987*. Bonn.

Der Spiegel
1982 *Der Spiegel*, no. 18.

Duve, Freimut
1986 *Aufbrüche. Die Chronik der Republik 1961 bis 1986*. Reinbek: Rowohlt.

Gress, Franz, and Hans Gerd Jaschke
1982 *Rechtsextremismus in der Bundesrepublik nach 1960*. München: Pressedienst Demokratische Initiative.

Institut für Demoskopie Allensbach, ed.
1956 *Jahrbuch der öffentlichen Meinung 1947-1955*. Allensbach/Bonn: Verlag für Demoskopie.

–, ed.
1974 *Jahrbuch der öffentlichen Meinung 1968-1973*. Allensbach/Bonn: Verlag für Demoskopie

–, ed.
1981 *The Germans. Public Opinion Polls 1967-1980*. Westport, Conn./London: Greenwood.

Presse- und Informationsdienst der Bundesregierung, ed.
1987 *Bonner Almanach 1987/88*. Bonn.

Table 1
Membership in organized right-wing extremism

Year	Sum total[1]
1954	76,000
1959	56,200
1965	26,300
1970	29,700
1975	20,400
1979	17,300
1980	19,800
1986	22,100
1987	25,600

1. Includes parties, youth groups or organizations, groups of the "new right," neo-Nazi groups, those working with affiliated publishing houses, and other groups; Sum total= sum after subtraction of all double memberships. Reports of the authority on unconstitutional activities dated before 1966 consider double membership to be small.

Source: Gress & Jaschke, 1982, pp. 9; Bundesminister des Innern, 1987.

Table 2
Members in the "New right," neo-Nazis

Year	"New right"	Neo-Nazis
1975	800	400
1976	600	600
1977	200	900
1978	-	1,000[1]
1979	-	1,400
1980	-	1,200
1981	-	1,250
1986	-	1,380

1. Starting in 1978, members of "new right" groups are counted among "other groups."

Source: Gress & Jaschke, 1982, pp. 11; Bundesminister des Innern, 1987.

Table 3
Opinions regarding the Communist Party (in %)

Wording of question: "The West-German government wants to outlaw the Communist Party. Are you for or against this prohibition?"

Item	January 1952		
	Total	Male	Female
Outlaw	43	36	48
Don't outlaw	35	49	25
Undecided	22	15	27
Total	100	100	100

1,000 persons 18 years and older in Federal Republic and West Berlin.

Source: Institut für Demoskopie, 1956, p. 272.

Table 4
Opinions regarding the Communist Party (in %)

Wording of question: "Should the Communist Party of West Germany be outlawed or not?"

Item	June 1954		
	Total	Male	Female
Outlaw	55	47	62
Don't outlaw	30	42	18
Undecided	15	11	20
Total	100	100	100

1,000 persons 18 years and older in Federal Republic and West Berlin.

Source: Institut für Demoskopie, 1956, p. 272.

Table 5
Approval of the DKP (German Communist Party) (in%)

Wording of question: "Would you approve of a Communist party being permitted once again in West Germany?"

Item	Dec. 1967
Approve	23
Disapprove	61
Other answer, undecided	16
Total	100

1,000 persons 16 years and older in Federal Republic and West Berlin.

Source: Institut für Demoskopie, 1974, p. 318.

Table 6
Opinions regarding the Communist Party (in %)

Wording of question: "There is a Communist Party, here in West Germany. Did you know this?" (Yes, I knew = 88%) "In your opinion, should the DKP be banned or should it not be banned?"

	September 1973			
	Should not	Should	undecided	Total
Total population	43	39	18	100

1,000 persons 16 years and older in Federal Republic and West Berlin.

Source: Institut für Demoskopie, 1981, p. 204.

Table 7
Membership in left-extremist groups

Year	Orthodox Communism	"New left"[1]	Total	Total minus multiple members
1972	88,500	14,600 (300)[2]	103,100	78,000
1974	117,000	19,200 (500)	136,200	102,000
1976	71,600	19,300	90,900	68,000
1978	78,100	17,930	96,030	72,000
1980	74,300	10,000	84,300	63,700
1985	72,000	9,200	81,200	61,500
1986	74,000	9,700	83,700	63,000
1987	70,500	10,900	81,400	62,000

1. "New left" = Maoist, Trotskyist, "spontaneistic," anarchist left, as opposed to the Moscow-oriented orthodox left.
2. Numbers in parentheses: anarchist groups within the "new left."

Source: Bundesminister des Inneren, 1974, 1978, 1980, 1987.

11.5 Religious Beliefs

In the Federal Republic of Germany, the Protestant and Catholic denominations are predominant. Relatively few people are Jewish or Moslems. The influence of religious sects has never been very high in the Federal Republic. Although "youth religions" were able to achieve a certain amount of success in the 1970s, they have remained a peripheral phenomenon. Religious life continues to be decisively influenced by the large churches, even though – as of the 1970s – more Christians see their own beliefs as not conforming with the line of the official churches.

Mainline and Sectarian Practices

Religious life in the Federal Republic is traditionally determined by the Christian religions. The great majority of the population subscribes to Catholicism or Protestantism, a small minority to other Christian beliefs. Other religions did not gain any degree of importance until foreign workers entered the Federal Republic, in which context Islam is uppermost on the list. Islam has remained confined to the foreign population. In 1985, there were 1.6 million Moslems in the Federal Republic, with fewer Shiites than Sunnis. The influence of the Judaism is also very small: about 300,000 Jews are estimated to live in West Germany.

Sects have managed to attract only negligible membership in the Federal Republic. The Evangelische Zentralstelle für Weltanschauungsfragen (Protestant central authority for belief and creed systems) differentiates between traditional Christian sects, so-called Christian special parishes, and the non-Christian sects or so-called new youth religions. The Christian special parishes see themselves as representing true Christianity and take a critical stance against the major churches. It is quite another case with the youth religions, which promise a "new absolution." Their religious practices are usually characterized by cults (Zentrale für Weltanschauungsfragen, 1984). While the influence of the Christian sects has stagnated, the non-Christian sects have had an increase in members and adherents since the 1970s.

Among the Christian special parishes, with their tiny constituencies, are the Johanneische Kirche (Weissbergianer, or St. John's Church), the Gralsbewegung (Holy Grail movement), the Apostelamt Jesu Christi (Church of Jesus Christ the Apostle), the Christliche Wissenschaft (Christian Scientists), the Kirche Gottes (Church of God, founded by Armstrong, Ambassador College), and the Unitarier (Unitarians) (Hach, 1980). Only six Christian sects can currently claim a large membership and constituency in the Federal Republic: the Neuapostolische Kirche (New Apostles, with 327,000 members in 1978), the Zeugen Jehovas

(Jehovah's Witnesses, with 106,000 members in 1982), the Pfingstbewegung (Pentecostals), the Mormonen, the Adventisten (Seventh-Day Adventists), the Christengemeinschaft (Church of Christ), and the Apostolic parishes (see table 1). Except for the Mormons, which registered a good membership growth (from 20,000 in 1978 to 26,000 in 1982), all of the sects experienced either constant membership numbers or, at best, minimal growth from 1978 to 1982. The sects have a total of approximately half a million members in the Federal Republic. An additional estimated 150,000 sympathize with a sect.

Over the past decade, non-Christian sects (such as Bhagwan, Transcendental Meditation, Scientology, etc.) have been the subject of critical attention in the Federal Republic. Most of these groups did not begin their missionary activity until the 1970s. Only widely divergent estimates exist concerning their members and adherents. The Evangelische Zentralstelle für Weltanschauungsfragen estimates that these sects had approximately 2,000 members in 1979, and as many as 6,000 in 1982 (see table 2). However, these sects may be much more influential: it is thought, for example, that Bhagwan, Transcendental Meditation, and the Scientology Church of Germany have a total of 220,000 adherents.

The new youth religions may be, numerically, a peripheral phenomenon, but their tight organization and the continued efficacy of their recruitment methods indicates that they have been able to take advantage of a malaise with established society that is especially widespread among youth. Motivations for entering a youth sect, include "a desire to drop out of this complicated, socially tense and performance-obsessed society, general fear about the future, disillusionment about social injustice, personal problems with one's family, school, or job, as well as yearning for a secure, fulfilled life in a community of people sharing the same belief. It can also be a form of protest by young people for whom the present society provides too little fulfillment and purpose in life" (Hach, 1980, p. 128). Another interpretation of the attraction to cults sees it as an expression of deep religiosity among youth which the established churches cannot satisfy: "It is the old-type religion that creates new forms, corresponding to today's needs and possibilities for experience. The religious revolt signals the fact that religion has, at least partially, abandoned the outmoded and institutionalized system" (Mildenberger, 1979, p. 283).

Anti-religious Manifestations

The latter interpretation seems plausible when seen against the background of a tendency which has arisen since the 1970s: the established churches experienced an exodus of members and were faced with waning church activity by their parishioners (see 9.2, "Religious Institutions"). However, as surveys of religious content, piety, and church orientation show, this development is not analogous to a general reduction in religiosity. A poll among Catholics and Protestants shows, in a 10-year comparison, a growing rejection of the official churches by both groups (see also 11.2, "Confidence in Institutions"). In general matters of belief, however, only a slight drift toward real doubt or explicitly atheistic attitudes can be distinguished (see table 3). These developments are in no way significant enough to indicate an overall decline in religious belief among Germans.

Innovations in Practices

Declining acceptance of the established churches, starting in the early 1960s, incited the churches to think up new forms of religious expression (see also 9.2, "Religious Institutions"). An example of this is the new forms of church services in both churches and the *Kirchentag* (national meetings with mass participation) of the Protestant church.

Among the new forms of church services, aimed primarily at young and politically active Christians, the beat, jazz and youth services are best known. The family service is also popular. The explicitly political church service met with less favour, while the *Fürbittgottesdienst* (prayer meeting) – for peace, for the Third World, and so on – fared somewhat better.

The *Kirchentag* is indubitably the occasion on which the Protestant church portrays itself at its "newest" and most modern. It is attended mainly by young and politically active Christians. The *Kirchentag* has become a symbol of the strengthening of Christian solidarity, intensive community experience, exchange of Christian opinions and attitudes, and spiritual contemplation and action.

Combination of Religious and Secular Activity

The combination of religious and secular activities has a long tradition in the social work carried out by the West German churches since the end of the war (public welfare, foreign aid, etc.; see also 9.2, "Religious Institutions"). While Christian contributions in this field used to be limited to donations, many Christians have, with the rise of the new social movements (conservation and peace movements, solidarity with the Third World), come to regard participation in these movements as an expression of true piety. The social movements have received strong support from church circles.

Barbara Wörndl

References

Eggenberger, Oswald
1984 *Die Kirchen, Sondergruppen und religiöse Vereinigungen*. Zürich: Theologischer Verlag.

Hach, Jürgen
1980 *Gesellschaft und Religion in der Bundesrepublik Deutschland*. Heidelberg: Quelle und Meyer.

Hanselmann, Johannes, ed.
1984 *Was wird aus der Kirche?* Gütersloh: Mohn.

Hauschild, W. D., and E. Wilkens, eds.
1978 *Kirchliches Jahrbuch für die evangelische Kirche*. Gütersloh: Mohn.

Klages, Helmut
1985 *Wertorientierungen im Wandel*. Frankfurt am Main/New York: Campus.

Mildenberger, M.
1979 *Die religiöse Revolte*. Frankfurt am Main: Fischer.

Noelle-Neumann, Elisabeth, ed.
1983 *Allensbacher Jahrbuch der Demoskopie 1978-1983*. München/New York/London/Paris: Saur.

–, ed.
1981 *The Germans. Public Opinion Poll 1967-1980*. Westport, Conn./London: Greenwood.

Noelle-Neumann, Elisabeth, and Peter Erich, eds.
1974 *Jahrbuch der öffentlichen Meinung 1968-1973*. Allensbach/Bonn: Verlag für Demoskopie.

Reimer, Hans-Diether, and Reinhart Hummel
1984 "Jugendreligionen in den 80er Jahren. Eine Bestandsaufnahme." *Materialdienst - Evangelische Zentralstelle für Weltanschauungsfragen*, no. 4. Sonderdruck.

Zapf, Wolfgang, ed.
1977 *Lebensbedingungen in der Bundesrepublik Deutschland*. Frankfurt am Main/New York: Campus.

Table 1
Christian special parishes

Group	Members (in strict sense) 1978	Members (in strict sense) 1982
Church of the New Apostle	327,000=	-
Jehovah's Witnesses	105,000=	106,000
Pentecostals	(36,000)	36,000
Adventists	26,000=	25,000
Mormons	20,000+	26,000
Catholic-apost. parishes	(10,000)	-
Free Apostolic parishes	10,000=	-
The Christ parishes	(10,000)	13,000
Free Circle of Brothers		Groups with membership numbers of under 10,000
Christian Congregations		
Free Christian People's Church		
"Ecclesia"		
Christian Scientists		
Friends of Man		
Church of God		
Holy Grail Movement		
Church of John the Baptist		
Church of Christ		
Free Bible Parish		
Nazarenes		
Templars		

Key: consistent tendency =; increasing tendency +; decreasing tendency -; estimated ().

Source: Evangelische Zentralstelle für Weltanschauungsfragen.

Table 2
"Youth religions" in West Germany

Groups	Members 1979	Members 1982
Bhagwan	-	9,000
Transc. Meditation	1,000-15,000	1,000
Vereinigungskirche (Mun)	300-600	800
Scientology	250-800	300-400
Mission of Godly Love	200-2,000	500
Krishna	80-100	200
Children of God	50-100	200

All numbers are estimates.

Source: Evangelische Zentralstelle für Weltanschauungsfragen.

Table 3
Religions beliefs and the Church (in %)

Wording of question put to Protestants and Catholics: "Where would you place yourself on this list - which statement would apply?"

Item	70/71 Cath.	1972 Prot.	1979 Cath.	1979 Prot.	1982 Cath.	1982 Prot.
1. I am a believing member of my church and follow its doctrine	49[1]	37	42	14	38	14
2. I consider myself a Christian, but the Church doesn't mean much to me	24	31	28	34	25	28
3. I would like to believe but I am uncertain about so many things	7	-	6	6	9	7
4. I have my own beliefs, my own philosophy of life, completely independent of the Church	9	16	10	20	10	19
5. I live and work. Everything else takes care of itself - I don't need any beliefs	3	7	4	8	5	9
6. Belief means nothing to me. Instead, I concentrate on the problems of this world and the problems of my fellow human beings	2	5	2	4	2	5
7. I don't know what I should believe in. That's why I'd rather leave such questions open	4	8	6	12	7	11
8. No answer	5	4	2	2	4	7
Total	103	108[2]	100	100	100	100

Item	Winter 70/71 Catholics	Summer 1972 Protestants	
I am a believing member of my church and follow its doctrine	49	24	37
I am loyal to the church, but it must change	-	14	

2,000 interviewed persons, not younger than 16

1. Key to first statement to be found in survey of 1970/71 or, respectively, 1972.
2. Comment: in the Catholic-synod survey, the question was appended with: "If possible, only one answer!"

Source: Noelle-Neumann, 1983, p. 127; 1974, p. 100; 1980, p. 229.

12. Household Resources

12.1 Personal and Family Income

National income per inhabitant had, as a secular trend, about tripled between 1850 and 1950. This was not a continual increase, but rather a series of "fever curves." After World War II, there was a burgeoning of average incomes. Various sources of income – wages and salaries, income from self-employment and capital, old-age pensions, and social benefits – had different growth rates and changed in significance within the overall composition of household incomes. It is estimated that the degree of inequality of household incomes has not changed significantly in the postwar period.

Evaluation of Income Level

Income in the Federal Republic of Germany shows extraordinary growth rates in comparison to earlier times. From the beginning of the eighteenth century to 1950, real per-capita income little more than tripled. The increases were not continuous; rather, against a background of collapses and interruptions due to wars and economic crises, the term "fever curve" is very appropriate. Only after World War II did a new development start – an "underestimated revolution" (Miegel, 1983) – including a burgeoning of household incomes. In the 1950s alone, real per-capita income increased twice as much as it had the previous 150 years. A long-term historical comparison supports the claim of an explosive multiplication of income. It is true that the income growth-rate was lower in the 1960s and 1970s, and stagnated in the first half of the 1980s, but this did not present a severe difficulty because of the high level it had by then achieved.

Growth rates were different for the various kinds of income, as is illustrated by selected indicators for income development. In table 1, global development is represented by national income (per inhabitant). Selected sources of income are shown: average take-home pay per employee, capital gains of private households, and average pensions paid out by the National Insurances to blue- and white-collar workers. During the last two decades, growth of wages and salaries was lower than that of the average national income; retirement pensions kept pace with the latter, and sometimes rose faster than take-home wages and salaries. Even though capital incomes show the most growth, they have not yet reached the level of employees' and transfer incomes in absolute terms.

Inequality of Household Incomes

Indicators of the overall inequality of income distribution in West Germany are available in a model calculation of the Deutsche Institut für Wirtschaftsforschung (German Institute for Economic Research) (see table 2). This deals with a reconstruction of the distribution of household incomes correcting the incomplete data situation by plausible estimations. Indicators of inequality of income distribution, such as the Gini coefficient or the share of different income quintiles of the total available income, tend to stay rather constant, with insignificant fluctuations. From 1950 to 1980, there had been a slight trend away from inequality of household income. Then the model was revised, and the new ratio changed very little from 1981 to 1985. With some caution, we can assume a far-reaching structural stability of the inequality of household incomes.

Despite the very clear differences between average household incomes according to occupational level, the large areas in which the groups overlap should not be ignored. In middle-income groups, a good number of households comprise gainfully employed persons at all occupational levels. The current problem with income distribution involves income groups threatened with or hit by poverty (see 16.4, "Poverty").

Growing Cross-Distribution of Household Income

A household can have several income recipients as well as different sources of income. This has been an increasingly common situation in recent decades, and has led to an increasing cross-distribution of incomes (see table 3). The composition of household income, with the exception of one household category (households without gainfully employed members), is marked by a loss of significance of the main source of income over the long run. More income has been received from capital, as has more transfer income from the welfare state. Both are indicators of rising prosperity and the partially successful redistribution of wealth in the welfare state. However, as important as the long-term increase in distribution may be, the main income is still predominant, especially in households of employees.

Gender Differences

A growing number of women contribute to household income as new gainfully employed persons. At all occupation levels, however, women primarily earn lower incomes, while very high incomes are (still) reserved for men (see table 4).

Class Differences

Cross-distribution has not been accompanied by a reduction in income gaps between occupation levels (see table 5). Self-employed households have consistently had the highest average income, and blue-collar workers the lowest. Over time, the gap has widened somewhat. Self-employed persons and blue-collar workers as groups are shrinking in size, while the number of households of civil servants and white-collar workers, whose average incomes are situated in the middle ranks, is increasing. Households of pensioners (which are usually smaller), have the lowest average income; the numbers of these households have been increasing rapidly. Income distribution has changed because the size of the most important population groups has changed, but this does not seem to influence the degree of concentration on the whole.

Wolfgang Glatzer

References

Bedau, Klaus-Dietrich
1988 "Einkommensverteilung." In Hans-Jürgen Krupp, and Jürgen Schupp, eds., *Lebenslagen im Wandel. Daten 1987*. Frankfurt am Main/New York: Campus.

Bretschneider, Joachim, et al.
1990 *Handbuch einkommens-, vermögens- und sozialpolitischer Daten*. Köln: Bachem.

Deutsches Institut für Wirtschaftsforschung
ann. pbl. *Wochenberichte*.

Hauser, Richard, and Wolfgang Glatzer
1989 "Von der Überwindung der Not zur Wohlstandsgesellschaft." In Norbert Blüm, and Hans F. Zacher, eds., *40 Jahre Sozialstaat Bundesrepublik Deutschland*. Baden-Baden: Nomos.

Krupp, Hans-Jürgen, and Wolfgang Glatzer, eds.
1978 *Umverteilung im Sozialstaat - empirische Einkommensanalysen für die Bundesrepublik Deutschland*. Frankfurt am Main/New York: Campus.

Miegel, Meinhard
1983 *Die verkannte Revolution*. Stuttgart: Bonn-Aktuell.

Table 1
Selected income categories, 1950 - 1990

Item		1950	1955	1960	1965	1970	1975	1980
National income per inhabitant	DM/year	1,674	2,889	4,353	6,115	8,745	12,997	18,656
Net wages/salaries per employee	DM/month	213	315	431	645	894	1,345	1,764
Capital gains of private households	DM/year	-	-	-	-	1,030	1,820	2,910
Average pensions of blue-collar workers (retirement age 65)	DM/month	-	-	168	242	353	592	713
Average pensions of white-collar workers (retirement age 65)	DM/month	-	274	422	606	634	963	1122
Net pension level	in %	-	-	56.3	52.7	57.0	59.5	63.8

Item		1981	1982	1983	1984	1985	1986	1987
National income per inhabitant	DM/year	19,248	19,850	20,941	22,197	23,270	24,718	25,626
Net wages/salaries per employee	DM/month	1,843	1,897	1,940	1,974	2,006	2,090	2,128
Capital gains of private households	DM/year	3,440	3,820	3,600	3,860	4,020	-	-
Average pensions of blue-collar workers (retirement age 65)	DM/month	717	745	757	-	-	-	-
Average pensions of white-collar workers (retirement age 65)	DM/month	1,116	1,153	1,180	-	-	-	-
Net pension level	in %	63.4	-	-	-	-	-	-

Sources: Bretschneider et. al., 1990.

Table 2
Inequality of available income of private households in the Federal Republic of Germany, 1950 - 1985

Item	Dimension	1950	1960	1970	1980	1981	1985
Median	DM/month	357	838	1,581	3,158	3,279	3,705
Gini Coefficient		0.396	0.380	0.392	-	0.347	0.344
Share of total available income (in %)							
lowest 20% of households		5.4	6.0	5.9	6.9	7.2	7.4
medium 60% of households		49.4	50.1	48.5	49.9	50.4	49.6
highest 20% of households		45.2	43.9	45.6	43.3	42.4	43.0
Total		100	100	100	100	100	100

Source: DIW-Wochenberichte no. 25/1973, no. 30,31/1976, no. 4/1982, no. 30/1983, no. 51, 52/1986.

Table 3
Composition of gross household income according to social status of head of household (in %)

Occupational level	Share of gross household income from											
	Employed work			Self-employed work			Capital			Pensions, transfers		
	1963	1973	1983	1963	1973	1983	1963	1973	1983	1963	1973	1983
Self-employed person	5.2	8.4	19.7	86.5	78.4	59.8	4.8	10.0	14.2	3.5	3.2	4.9
Farmer	7.0	10.3	17.2	77.9	69.6	56.5	8.9	12.7	16.2	6.2	7.4	9.6
Civil servant	90.4	86.5	82.8	1.6	1.7	1.4	3.5	6.0	8.3	4.5	5.8	3.7
White-collar worker	89.6	87.0	85.6	1.5	1.4	1.4	3.1	5.9	7.3	5.8	5.7	3.9
Blue-collar worker	87.2	86.0	83.0	0.8	1.5	1.6	3.3	5.8	7.3	8.7	6.7	6.5
Unemployed person	21.7	14.1	9.2	2.4	2.1	1.8	7.5	11.6	13.5	68.4	72.2	67.7
Total	55.3	59.7	58.1	22.4	13.5	9.1	4.7	7.7	9.7	17.6	19.1	19.8

Note: The results are based on the documents of nearly 50,000 households in which during the survey years, all income and expenses were recorded. Parts of the gross household income are income from employed work (excluding employers' contributions to social security and additional social disbursements toward pensions by employers), income from business activities and capital gains, pensions, other current transfers, as well as single transfers of less than DM 1,000. The income from business activities was generally calculated as the difference between total expenditures and income not stemming from business activities.

Sources: Wirtschaft und Statistik 2/1967, 4/1977, 7/1987.

Table 4 (Part I)
Employed men and women according to occupational level and net wage group (according to the micro census)

Occupational level	Year	Employed persons (in 1,000)		Belonging to income group from DM ... to DM ...			
				under 600		600 to 1,200	
	(March)	Men	Women	Men	Women	Men	Women
Self-employed persons[1]	1965	1,471	418	17.6	53.8	47.4	34.2
	1970	1,381	377	7.3	36.4	35.4	38.2
	1980	1,277	379	1.6	18.1	7.5	27.9
	1987	1,308	468	3.1	15.4	7.6	23.3
Ccivil servants	1965	1,145	181	2.9	20.5	50.9	67.6
	1970	1,205	225	2.9	6.4	50.9	51.5
	1980	1,705	391	12.0	-	6.1	14.4
	1987	1,810	472	11.4	1.3	2.8	10.6
White-collar workers[2]	1965	3,436	3,330	22.6	77.5	61.6	21.9
	1970	3,950	3,700	9.6	48.4	51.7	47.9
	1980	4,628	5,070	4.6	17.3	5.1	36.4
	1987	4,604	5,137	1.4	7.9	3.1	28.3
Blue-collar workers[2]	1965	9,136	3,571	54.6	97.3	45.1	2.7
	1970	8,850	3,428	17.8	81.4	78.4	18.6
	1980	8,032	3,088	8.8	28.0	10.8	52.7
	1987	6,696	2,611	1.6	17.3	5.0	38.6
Total	1965	15,188	7,499	40.8	84.2	50.5	14.6
	1970	15,385	7,731	13.6	61.2	65.6	34.5
	1980	15,641	8,929	7.3	20.3	8.3	40.7
	1987	15,285	9,406	7.1	15.8	5.4	30.0

1. Excluding self-employed persons in agriculture and helping family members in all economic branches, as well as employed persons who either did not make statements on their income situation or did not have any income.
2. Including apprentices.
3. In the years 1965 and 1970: income groups of DM 1,200 to DM 1,800 and more.

Table 4 (Part II)
Employed men and women according to occupational level and net wage group (according to the micro census)

Occupational level	Year	Belonging to income group from DM ... to DM ...					
		1,200 - 2,200[3]		2,200 to 4,000		4,000 and more	
	(March)	Men	Women	Men	Women	Men	Women
Self-employed persons[1]	1965	35.1	11.9	-	-	-	-
	1970	57.2	25.5	-	-	-	-
	1980	31.1	31.6	36.6	14.9	23.2	7.4
	1987	25.5	33.5	33.6	18.4	30.2	9.6
Civil servants	1965	45.9	11.8	-	-	-	-
	1970	45.9	41.3	-	-	-	-
	1980	38.2	58.4	38.5	35.7	5.3	-
	1987	28.1	42.1	43.3	42.4	14.3	3.6
White-collar workers[2]	1965	15.7	0.6	-	-	-	-
	1970	38.7	3.7	-	-	-	-
	1980	46.2	41.9	25.5	13.5	6.5	0.2
	1987	30.9	52.4	30.6	22.3	16.3	1.0
Blue-collar workers[2]	1965	0.2	0.0	-	-	-	-
	1970	3.7	1.0	-	-	-	-
	1980	73.8	19.1	6.0	0.6	0.1	-
	1987	70.3	41.1	20.0	2.6	0.4	-
Total	1965	8.6	1.3	-	-	-	-
	1970	20.9	4.2	-	-	-	-
	1980	58.3	33.8	15.7	8.0	4.4	0.5
	1987	45.7	43.9	24.4	13.4	9.4	1.2

1. Excluding self-employed persons in agriculture and helping family members in all economic branches, as well as employed persons who either did not make statements on their income situation or did not have any income.
2. Including apprentices.
3. In the years 1965 and 1970: income groups of DM 1,200 to DM 1,800 and more.

Source: Statistisches Bundesamt; Wirtschaft und Statistik; Fachserie 1; Reihe 4.1.1.

Table 5 (Part I)
Income of private households[1] according to social status of head of household

Item	Year	Total households	Self-employed persons in agriculture and forestry	Self-employed persons in other sectors	White-collar workers
Number of households in 1,000	1950[2+3]	15,250	-	2,820[5]	2,885[6]
	1960[3]	18,905	-	2,945[5]	4,020[6]
	1970	21,190	665	1,625	4,360
	1980	23,890	460	1,615	4,980
	1983	24,760	408	1,466	5,561
			In DM per month		
Gross wages and capital income	1970	1,785	2,555	4,890	2,375
	1980	3,756	4,474	12,249	5,503
	1983	4,066	4,267	13,090	6,263
Transfers effected	1970	570	315	1,350	800
	1980	1,425	835	3,454	2,391
	1983	1,746	1,583	4,353	2,837
Transfers received	1970	335	90	85	120
	1980	832	330	205	370
	1983	1,113	927	1,039	457
Available income	1950[2+4]	-	-	567[5]	425[6]
	1960[4]	-	-	1,423[5]	972[6]
	1970[4]	-	-	3,267[5]	1,842[6]
	1970	1,550	2,330	3,625	1,695
	1980	3,163	3,969	9,000	3,482
	1981	3,278	4,017	9,204	3,635
	1983	3,432	3,611	9,776	3,883

1. Excluding persons living in institutions.
2. Excluding Saarland and West Berlin.
3. Including households in institutions.
4. Including income of households in institutions and nonmarket organizations.
5. Including households of self-employed persons in agriculture and forestry.
6. Including civil servants and judges.
7. Including recipients of payments from the public domain.

Table 5 (Part II)
Income of private households[1] according to social status of head of household

Item	Year	Civil servants	Blue-collar workers	Pensioneers	Recipients of ocial security other payments rom the public domain
Number of households in 1,000	1950[2+3]	-	5,285	4,260[7]	-
	1960[3]	-	6,285	5,655[7]	-
	1970	1,325	6,870	6,055	1,000
	1980	1,510	6,410	7,900	1,015
	1983	1,552	5,949	8,799	1,025
			in DM per month		
Gross wages and capital income	1970	2,185	2,065	300	225
	1980	4,862	4,455	499	632
	1983	5,613	4,809	747	989
Transfers effected	1970	465	755	100	185
	1980	1,198	1,978	160	406
	1983	1,842	2,284	320	1,142
Transfers received	1970	80	160	685	1,210
	1980	248	471	1,491	2,338
	1983	550	514	1,804	3,246
Available income	1950[2+4]	-	331	203[7]	-
	1960[4]	-	781	504[7]	-
	1970[4]	-	1,519	911[7]	-
	1970	1,800	1,470	885	1,250
	1980	3,912	2,947	1,829	2,564
	1981	4,015	3,091	1,931	2,899
	1983	4,321	3,038	2,231	3,093

1. Excluding persons living in institutions.
2. Excluding Saarland and West Berlin.
3. Including households in institutions.
4. Including income of households in institutions and nonmarket organizations.
5. Including households of self-employed persons in agriculture and forestry.
6. Including civil servants and judges.
7. Including recipients of payments from the public domain.

Source: Deutsches Institut für Wirtschaftsforschung, Berlin, Wochenbericht 34/1973, 4/1982, 30/1983 und 14/1985.

12.2 Informal Economy

The informal economy, as opposed to the formal economy documented in the national accounts, is a broad field of unrecorded economic activities. One major aspect not represented in the national accounts – though it should be, according to existing concepts – is the hidden or shadow economy. Though it is not measurable directly, some indirect measurement approaches hint at an increase of this "unobservable" economy since the late 1970s.

Terminology

In dealing with the informal economy, many terminologies are used. "Informal economy" is a comprehensive term for economic activities which, on the one hand, the concept of national accounts tries to include but cannot record (variously called the hidden, shadow, underground, subterranean, or black economy), or which, on the other hand, the concept of national accounts does not include, but which nevertheless can be regarded as production activities (for example, household production; see 13.4, "Time Use"). Whereas household production is a legal activity, the underground economy is by and large not legal: it involves tax evasion, *Schwarzarbeit* (illegal and/or unregistered labour), pay in kind, prostitution, drug abuse, bank robbery, and so on.

Measurement Approaches

It is a characteristic of the shadow economy that it cannot be observed or directly measured. However, it leaves its traces in the observable economy (in, for example, the demand for money), and some approaches try to use this as a means of indirect measurement. Various concepts have been used: the national-account approach uses the difference between national tax income and national expenditures for goods and services. A negative difference indicates hidden income and hints at the volume of the shadow economy. The currency-demand approach analyzes the relationship between cash and deposits, with the understanding that the shadow economy creates a demand for cash. The transaction approach looks at the relationship of economic transactions to national income, and builds upon the insight that the shadow economy reduces transaction costs. The labour-market approach assumes that there is a normal employment ratio which remains constant in the long term. Deviations indicate developments in the shadow economy. A theoretical model of the determinants of the shadow economy makes it possible to estimate its volume.

Developments in the Shadow Economy

In general, the estimated empirical results show increases and discontinuity in the size of the hidden economy (see table 1). An exception is the national-account approach, covering the period from 1961 to 1974, during which the hidden economy receded; this approach shows a declining trend. Other approaches rely more on the present or the recent past. Two studies using the currency-demand approach discern, respectively, an increase from 1965 to 1980 and small changes in the short period from 1976 to 1980. The transaction approach shows a very large increase of the hidden economy from 1970 to 1980. The labour-market approach, whose main indicator is the ratio of illegal or shadow labour supply to official labour supply, records a strong upward trend between 1970 and 1978, and a small downward trend from 1978 to 1980.

One of the most reliable investigative methods, using two different currency-demand approaches (Kirchgässner, 1983) yields basically identical results (see figure 1). Both approaches show an increasing trend starting with a low level in the 1950s, then developing in waves up to a first peak in 1967. In the second half of the 1960s, the hidden economy seems to have suffered a setback before accelerating in the second half of the 1970s, reaching about 12% of the GNP. Measurement of the hidden economy stops in the 1980s. It is assumed that the change in economic policy was once again accompanied by a reduction in hidden activities. A cross-sectional analysis for 1984 shows that informal economic activities still have substantial significance as working-time input and source of income (Merz & Wolf 1989).

Social scientists agree that the shadow economy has expanded during recent decades, though measurement is indirect and depends to a large extent on the plausibility of the methods used. One researcher summarizes, "Though precise information about the size and evolution of the shadow economy are not yet available, it is certain that, in the shadow of the official economy, a statistically unmeasurable secondary economy has spread" (Langfeldt, 1984).

Wolfgang Glatzer

References

Gretschmann, Klaus, and Bernd Mettelsiefen
1984 "Die Schattenwirtschaftsdebatte - Eine Retrospektive." In K. Gretschmann, et al., eds., *Schattenwirtschaft - Wirtschafts- und sozialwissenschaftliche Aspekte, internationale Erfahrungen*. Göttingen: Vandenhoeck und Ruprecht.

Langfeldt, Ernst
1984 "Konsequenzen einer wachsenden Schattenwirtschaft für die geldpolitische Steuerung in der Bundesrepublik Deutschland." In Wolf Schäfer, ed., *Schattenökonomie - Theoretische Grundlage und wirtschaftspolitische Konsequenzen*. Göttingen: Vandenhoeck und Ruprecht.

Merz, Joachim, and Klaus Wolff
1989 "Schwarzarbeit und Eigenarbeit - Informelle familiale Versorgungsstrategien." In G. Wagner, et al., eds., *Familienbildung und Erwerbsbeteiligung im demographischen Wandel*. Berlin: Springer.

Schrage, Horst
1984 "Schattenwirtschaft - Abgrenzung, Definition, Methoden der quantitative Erfassung." In Wolf Schäfer, ed., *Schattenökonomie - Theoretische Grundlage und wirtschaftspolitische Konsequenzen*. Göttingen: Vandenhoeck und Ruprecht.

Table 1
Methods and results for quantification of the shadow economy in the FRG

Method	Year	Size of shadow economy in % of GNP	Source
National-accounting approach	1961	16.7	
	1968	12.6	Petersen (1982)
	1971	6.5	
	1974	4.8	
	1968	8.9	Albers (1974)
Currency-demand approach	1965	4.3	
	1970	3.1	Kirchgässner (1982)
	1975	6.0	
	1980	10.3	
	1976	12.1	
	1978	11.8	Langfeldt (1982)
	1980	12.6	
Transaction approach	1970	16.0	
	1976	17.5	Langfeldt (1982)
	1978	24.0	
	1980	27.5	
Labour-market approach	1970	22.0[1]	
	1976	39.5[1]	Langfeldt (1982)
	1978	37.5[1]	
	1980	35.0[1]	
Determinant-indicators approach[2]	1978	8.3	Weck (1982)

1. Langfeldt calculates the potential labour supply in the shadow economy as a percentage of the official labour supply.
2. The results of the determinant-indicators approach is based on estimates done by Klovlands.

Source: Schrage, 1984.

Figure 1
Evolution of the shadow economy in the FRG. Measured in % of the official national product

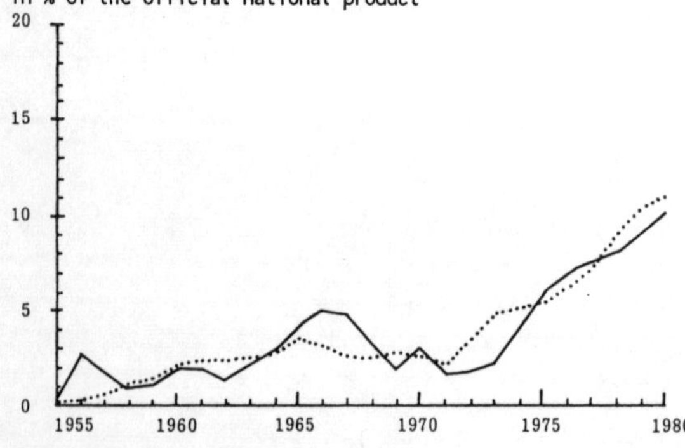

Source: Langfeldt, 1984.

12.3 Personal and Family Wealth

Wealth in conventional terms shows a long-term evolution similar to that of income. In 1950, wealth per household was not much greater than it was in 1800, and had barely doubled per capita . Since 1950, however, the speed of increase in wealth has accelerated and the amount of wealth has multiplied. Various kinds of wealth have spread to different degrees in the population, and are more or less concentrated. Control of the means of production,in particular, is highly concentrated.

Components of Wealth

The term "wealth" is highly variables, and therefore it may be advisable to start by defining how the term is used in official statistics. The following kinds of wealth are designated: savings-account deposits, life and other insurance, securities (e.g., savings bonds, collateral bonds, shares), deposits in building and loan associations, other monetary assets such as fixed deposits, assets in real estate, and ownership of or stock in companies. Deposits in chequing accounts and cash, which represent an essential part of financial assets, are not recorded in the income and consumption samples because of the difficulty of recording them.

From the gross property accruing from shares deducted credit obligations (debts) in order to arrive at net property. To base the calculation on a comprehensive concept of property, it would be necessary to include a much broader range of assets – for example, durable consumer goods owned by private households. Some even consider pension annuities to be property. There could also taken into account the "working capacities" of private households, their "human capital," and even the most basic aspects of life – the availability of clean air, clean water, intact woods, natural resources, and favourable climate. Taken together, these represent "the people's wealth" in a broad sense.

Distribution and Redistribution of Wealth

The starting point for the present distribution of wealth was set with the currency reform (*Währungsreform*) of 1948. It included a differentiated treatment of financial assets, which were devalued, and remaining tangible assets, which were left untouched.

With the Law for the Compensation of Burdens of 1952 (in the aftermath of the postwar occupation and division of Germany, and of massive shifts in population), a capital tax for indemnification of the loss of property by displaced persons was instituted. The tax for compensation for this war burden was put on the available properties, amounting to 50% of their "rateable value" (a statutory term; the rateable value lay far beneath the properties' market value). This reform has been called the "largest capital redistribution in history"; it did not, however, lead to a distinct redistribution of wealth, nor to a change in the social structure. It did lead to the social integration of an uprooted part of the population (Klessmann, 1984).

Regarding the distribution of types of wealth, one can determine a spreading in all occupational groups, being in the upper groups on the highest level. Savings accounts are as common to households as are such basics as washing machines and televisions, and no group lags behind in this respect (see table 1). Life insurance is also seen as "standard equipment," as it has been purchased by more than half of all private households. Real estate is owned by a little fewer than half of households in the Federal Republic. Among these households, 18% inherited the property, while 78% have purchased it themselves. Shares in building and loan associations are also extensively distributed, with 40% of the population owning such shares. Securities are the least well distributed, especially among blue-collar workers and farmers.

Different kinds of wealth are concentrated in different ways in the population. Ownership of the means of production (participation in trade and industry – without shares) shows the greatest concentration, while deposits in building and loan associations are more equally distributed. In between are, in order of decreasing concentration, security deposits, real estate, life insurance, and cash and demand deposits (Hornung-Draus, 1989).

From the foundation of the Federal Republic of Germany, a gap between the wealth of the self-employed and that of the employed has developed. It must be taken into account that self-employed persons have to finance their old age from their own savings, while pension annuities of employed persons are not counted in their wealth. The relative gap in distribution positions between these groups changed insignificantly in the first decades of the Federal Republic (Engels, 1974). According to the 1983 official statistics, the average net monetary wealth of a self-employed household (i.e., without real estate and productive wealth) is 36,200 DM, and that of a blue-collar household is 14,800 DM (see table 2). Estimates (Mierheim & Wicke, 1978) show that real estate amounts to approximately two-thirds of the gross wealth of private households. For the net value of durable consumer goods, an amount of 26,700 DM per household at replacement value was estimated (Schäfer, 1985).

There is little reason to suppose that the inequality of wealth distribution will decrease significantly over time. Comparison of the wealth analyses available for the Federal Republic does not allow for a reliable estimate. A study for the period 1969 – 1973 shows a slight recession in concentration of net wealth; on the other hand, later comparisons of monetary wealth, from 1973 through 1978 to 1983, point to a slightly increase in concentration (Hornung-Draus, 1989).

Debt

Along with the increase in wealth, there was a parallel increase in debt. Although the average debt per household was only 1,800 DM in 1983, it is becoming a problem, since debt is extremely concentrated. In 1983, 17% (versus 16% in 1973) of households had credit obligations connected with the purchase of durable consumer goods and the financing of installment purchases (not including acquisition of real estate), creating an average residual debt of 10,200 DM. In 1983, there were 116,000 households in the Federal Republic with more than 30,000 DM in net debts (again, not including credit obligations for the purchase of real estate). Sixty percent of households owning real estate had to pay interest and amortization costs and were encumbered with an average residual debt of 81,000 DM (see table 3). In 1983, 5.3% of households had no wealth, and 8.1% of housholds had so-called negative net monetary wealth. Therefore, there is a certain plausibility to the claim that a wealthy society is at the same time a highly indebted society. Public debt-counselling centres have been set up to deal with this problem. The gap between highly indebted and very wealthy households is widening; this gap, to all appearances, is preserving social precarious inequality.

Wolfgang Glatzer

References

Bretschneider, Joachim, et al.
1990 *Handbuch einkommens-, vermögens- und sozialpolitischer Daten*. Köln: Bachem.

Engels, Wolfram, et al.
1974 *Das Volksvermögen. Seine verteilungs- und wohlstandspolitische Bedeutung*. Frankfurt am Main/New York: Herder.

Hornung-Draus, Renate
1989 "Das Vermögen der privaten Haushalte in der Bundesrepublik Deutschland: Bestand, Entwicklung und Verteilung." In *Jahrbücher für Nationalökonomie und Statistik*, 206/1, 18-47.

Klessmann, Christoph
1984 *Die doppelte Staatsgründung. Deutsche Geschichte 1945-1955*. Göttingen: Vandenhoeck und Ruprecht.

Miegel, Meinhard
1983 *Die verkannte Revolution - Einkommen und Vermögen der privaten Haushalte*. Stuttgart: Bonn-Aktuell.

Miehrheim, Horst, and Lutz Wicke
1978 *Die personelle Vermögensverteilung in der Bundesrepublik Deutschland*. Tübingen: Mohr.

Schäfer, Dieter
1985 "Wert des Gebrauchsvermögens der privaten Haushalte." *Wirtschaft und Statistik*, no. 2.

Table 1
Type of wealth according to social status of head of household in the Federal Republic of Germany 1963 - 1983

Per 100 households owned	At year end	Social status of head of household						
		Blue-collar worker	White-collar worker	Civil servant	Farmer	Self-employed	Unemployed	Total
Savings accounts	1963	57	73	72	63	65	54	60
	1973	94	96	96	89	91	84	91
	1983	93	94	96	93	88	87	90
Contracts with building and loan associations	1963	9	17	23	11	29	5	12
	1973	37	49	62	47	58	16	35
	1983	54	54	68	60	56	18	40
Life insurance	1963	47	49	53	37	64	22	41
	1973	84	81	80	68	88	64	76
	1983	81	75	77	77	84	51	67
Stocks/shares	1963	3	17	15	5	20	10	10
	1973	15	35	30	14	37	22	24
	1983	24	37	34	28	41	27	30
Real estate	1969	37	35	39	96	66	30	39
	1973	41	37	41	92	67	30	40
	1983	50	48	54	93	72	36	46

Note: This table shows results for households with some exceptions. Not covered were the households of foreigners, private households in institutions, households with a monthly net income of DM 10,000 (1969), DM 15,000 (1973), DM 20,000 (1978), and DM 25,000 or more (1983).

Source: Income and Expenditure Surveys from 1963, 1969, 1973, 1983.

Table 2
Private households according to the social status of heads of households and average stock of selected types of wealth and average residual debt from credit obligations (in DM)

Social status of head of household	Year	Average stock of wealth per household				Average residual debt from credit obligations per household	Average stock of wealth less residual debts per household
		In savings accounts	At building and loan associations	In stocks and shares	Total		
Farmer	1973	11,640	4,608	1,260	17,508	1,294	16,214
	1978	15,141	4,830	3,629	23,600	1,242	22,358
	1983	16,200	6,450	7,010	29,648	1,516	28,132
Self-employed	1973	10,700	7,201	7,056	24,957	1,973	22,984
	1978	14,396	8,348	16,034	38,778	2,181	36,597
	1983	13,500	9,490	18,440	41,427	5,238	36,189
Civil servant	1973	7,766	7,110	2,786	17,662	1,063	16,599
	1978	10,153	9,205	4,294	23,651	1,730	21,921
	1983	9,680	11,300	6,220	27,211	2,096	25,115
White-collar	1973	7,583	4,979	3,177	15,739	1,166	14,573
	1978	10,139	6,365	5,436	21,940	1,557	20,383
	1983	9,010	7,020	7,070	23,099	2,458	20,641
Blue-collar	1973	6,311	2,910	731	9,952	868	9,084
	1978	8,814	4,130	1,594	14,538	1,375	13,164
	1983	8,790	5,300	2,900	16,985	2,156	14,829
Unemployed	1973	6,603	1,310	2,555	10,468	258	10,210
	1978	9,265	1,290	4,727	15,282	312	14,969
	1983	9,830	1,640	8,010	19,485	673	18,812
Total households	1973	7,227	3,389	2,454	13,070	817	12,253
	1978	9,842	4,015	4,761	18,618	1,044	17,574
	1983	9,740	4,770	7,180	21,697	1,756	19,941

Source: Income and expenditure surveys 1973, 1978, 1983.

Table 3
Private households[1] owning real estate[2] according to the social status of heads of households and share and level of indebtedness

Social status of head of household	Year	Households owning real estate		Residual debts[3] from DM.. to DM.. per 100 households paying interest and amortization rates					Average residual debt[3] per househ. paying interest and amortization rates
		Total	Those paying interest and amortization rates	under 10,000	10,000 to 20,000	20,000 to 40,000	40,000 to 60,000	60,000 and more	
		1,000	%	%	%	%	%	%	DM
Farmer	1973	572	27.8	25.7	16.4	20.8	10.7	26.4	50,103
	1983	364	43.0	(14.9)	(12.3)	(17.2)	(16.0)	(39.6)	75,444
Self-employed	1973	995	62.4	17.1	15.6	19.0	14.0	34.1	70,443
	1983	990	71.1	(11.0)	(7.5)	16.4	(8.7)	56.3	136,251
Civil servant	1973	560	78.6	15.0	13.4	21.4	16.4	34.1	56,664
	1983	825	84.2	8.1	8.2	13.2	11.9	58.6	101,509
White-collar	1973	1,588	74.7	19.4	14.0	21.4	15.3	29.8	53,294
	1983	2,471	80.0	10.7	9.7	13.7	11.8	54.2	96,669
Blue-collar	1973	2,422	60.2	31.0	18.8	23.3	13.1	13.7	31,463
	1983	2,505	64.7	20.2	13.6	18.3	12.5	35.3	59,854
Unemployed	1973	2,214	40.1	40.8	21.5	20.6	9.0	8.1	24,501
	1983	3,347	34.4	39.8	19.6	18.2	8.6	(13.7)	58,742
Total	1973	8,351	56.9	26.5	17.1	21.5	13.2	21.6	43,663
	1978	9,609	59.6	23.0	15.3	19.7	11.7	30.3	55,140
	1983	10,667	60.0	18.3	12.2	16.2	11.2	42.2	81,218

Note: The table shows results from the income- and expenditure surveys of 1973, 1978, and 1983 regarding private households owning real estate according to the social status of heads of households as well as the share and level of indebtedness. Not covered were households of foreigners, private households in institutions, and households with higher income (see 1). The households whose real estate was still encumbered by debt were questioned about the level of the residual debt.

1. Excluding households of foreigns, private households in institutions and households with a monthly net income of DM 15,000 or more in 1973, DM 20,000 or more in 1978, and DM 25,000 or more in 1983.
2. Excluding industrial real estate used by the owner.
3. Amortization rates and interest still to be payed.

Source: Wirtschaft und Statistik, 1975, 1981, 1985.

13. Life Style

13.1 Market Goods and Services

An increasing command of goods and services by private households represents a fundamental trend which, since its beginning with the advent of industrialization, underwent major ups and downs before the Federal Republic of Germany was founded. It has shown continual growth during the more than four decades since then. Significant differences between richer and poorer groups of the population have persisted due to the inequality of income distribution. With respect to the composition and division of household expenditures, the old hypothesis ("Engels' law") about a dwindling fraction being spent on nutrition has been confirmed, whereas expenditures for housing have taken up an increasing percentage. Changes in the composition of household expenditures are partly a result of developing needs and demands, and partly a result of price changes.

Household expenditures

Expenditures by private households are useful indicators of the level of material living conditions, since there are spending structures typical to levels of income. In 1907, low-income four-person households spent most of their income, the scarcity of income leaving no room for savings. The burden of taxes and social-security dues was still low, since the welfare state was at an early stage of development. By far the largest proportion of expenditures was restitutive, and had to be spent for immediate subsistence; disposable income was very low. The spending structure of employees' households in 1950 strongly resembled that at the beginning of the century. Not until later did important changes take place.

For a middle-income four-person employee household, the evolution from 1950 to 1985 can be summarized as follows (see table 1): the tax burden on gross income increased continuously, from 2.6% to 9.6%; however, there was a more or less equivalent rise in the increasing supply of public goods. There was also a rise, though lower than that in the tax burden, in social-security dues; in 1950 they were at a much higher level than were tax levies (8.5%), while in 1985 they were at only a slightly higher level (13.9%). Together, rising taxes and social-security levies comprise the increasing burden on citizens of public contributions. Increasing income offers the opportunity for absolutely and proportionally growing savings; the savings rate exhibits considerable inconsistency, however, and reacts flexibly to changing economic conditions.

The proportions of special-expenditure categories have changed radically. The share of nutrition, beverages, and tobacco in total expenditures decreased in conformity with Engels' law: from more than half of private consumption, it dwindled to less than a quarter. Even though the combination of foodstuffs purchased was earmarked less by basic goods and more by luxury items (including alcohol and cigarettes), this spending category lost in overall significance. Contrary to other basic needs and to Schwabe's law, the share of expenditures for housing grew with the rising income level, going from 10% to 20% of the total. The context was a continuing housing shortage, along with more sophisticated demands regarding size and fittings; thus, disproportionate rent hikes could be effected on the housing market.

The expenditure items that increased the most were travel, transportation, and communication services (from 2.1% to 15.5%). In this category in particular, obvious new needs – expressions of a mobile society – emerged. A growing portion of these expenditures went toward the purchase and maintenance of automobiles.

In comparison with a middle-income four-person household, a two-person household composed of pensioners and/or recipients of social-security benefits conforms to the typical picture of a low prosperity level. A higher share is spent on nutrition and on housing, and less is saved; there is no tax burden, though social-security dues must be paid. The typical spending structure of a well-to-do household is exemplified in a four-person household of civil servants and/or white-collar workers with higher incomes. The smallest portion goes for nutrition and rent, while the greater part is spent on hygiene and health care, clothing and shoes, transportation and communication, and education and entertainment; material wealth is expressed by disproportionate increases in these spending categories. Well-to-do households also have the highest savings rate (13.7% in 1985) and the highest tax rate (15.1% in 1985). They do, however have, lower social-security dues, because of ceilings on these dues and on tax payments.

One spending category which partially intersects with the others should be mentioned because of its high rate of growth: travel and recreation. The largest items in this category are vacation, leisure-time automobile use, and entertainment electronics. Well-to-do households of civil servants and of higher-income white-collar workers increased the proportion of total income they spent on vacations and recreation from 14.9% to 20.2% between 1965 and 1987. Even two-person households comprising pensioners and recipients of social security increased their expenditures in this category, from 5.5% to 14.2%. In 1962, only 26% of West Germans travelled, and among them a minority (two-fifths) went abroad, while in 1982 50% made trips of five or more days, with almost two-thirds going abroad (Gesellschaftliche Daten, 1983).

Consumer-Price Indices

The changing composition of expenditures is partly due to growing and differing needs, and partly to specific price increases. Prices in general have nearly doubled since 1970 (see table 2). This inflation rate (which keeps the quality of goods constant) seems modest. The strongest increases are in prices for heating and electricity, followed by housing, education, entertainment, and recreation. The smallest price increases have been in household durables and nutrition.

Changes in the spending structures of West German households can be characterized as follows: purchasing power is shifting from basic needs to higher-value luxury items. Hence, the share of income devoted to basic needs is decreasing. There are a number of specific developments, however, such as proportionally higher expenditures for clothing in well-to-do households and, for all household types, housing costs that increase with rising incomes.

Wolfgang Glatzer

References

Biervert, Bernd, et al.
1974 *Konsum und Qualität des Lebens*. Opladen: Westdeutscher Verlag.

Reinhold, Gerd, ed.
1988 *Wirtschaftssoziologie*. München/Wien: Oldenbourg.

Schmucker, Helga, ed.
1980 *Studien zur empirischen Haushalts- und Verbrauchsforschung*. Berlin: Duncker und Humblot.

Statistisches Bundesamt
ann. pbl. *Einkommens- und Verbrauchsstichproben*. Fachserien. Wiesbaden.

Wiegand, Erich
1982 "Die Entwicklung der Einnahmen- und Ausgabenstrukturen privater Haushalte seit der Jahrhundertwende." In Erich Wiegand, and Wolfgang Zapf, eds., *Wandel der Lebensbedingungen in Deutschland*, 155-236. Frankfurt am Main/New York: Campus.

Table 1 (Part I)
Expenditure of household income by three different types of households according to main categories of goods

Item		Two-person household of pensioners and recipients of social security				
		1955	1960	1970	1980	1989
Gross household income	DM	196	285	558	1,330	2,099
Income/property tax	%	0.0	0.0	0.0	0.0	0.0
Social-security dues	%	0.0	0.0	0.2	0.0	5.0
Available income (net)	DM	189	285	564	1,348	2,027
Savings rate	%	3.6	3.0	4.8	7.6	7.9
Expenditures for private use	DM	189	267	518	1,171	1,673
Nutrition, beverages, and tobacco	%	53.0	52.7	43	33.5	28.4
Clothing and shoes	%	8.0	7.4	7.2	6.8	5.7
Rents	%	13.4	13.9	20.5	22.4	26.9
Energy (electricity, fuel, etc.)	%	-	8.3	7.7	8.8	8.1
Goods for transportation and communication	%	1.7	2.0	3.9	7.2	9.4
Goods for health-care and hygiene	%	2.7	5.2	3.6	4.9	4.6
Goods for education, entertainment, and recreation	%	3.2	4.0	4.4	4.6	6.5
Number of households	N	-	-	154	163	165

Note: The data are not fully comparable, since the way the surveys are conducted has changed over time. In 1980 the savings rate was calculated as the residual difference between available income and expenditures for private use, while as of 1989 the yearly wealth increase is considered.

Table 1 (Part II)
Expenditure of household income by three different types of households according to main categories of goods

Item		Four-person -employees' household with medium income				
		1950	1960	1970	1980	1989
Gross household income	DM	343	759	1,507	3,697	5,244
Income/property tax	%	2.6	2.0	8.6	10.8	9.6
Social-security dues	%	8.5	9.7	10.4	12.3	13.9
Available income (net)	DM	305	670	1,256	2,993	4,246
Savings rate	%	3.6	4.3	7.7	12.8	11.3
Expenditures for private use	DM	285	621	1,089	2,443	3,325
Nutrition, beverages, and tobacco	%	52.2	45.0	35.3	28.1	23.8
Clothing and shoes	%	13.6	13.5	10.8	9.3	8.0
Rents	%	10.5	10.3	15.5	16.4	20.9
Energy (electricity, fuel, etc.)	%	5.4	4.6	4.7	6.5	5.4
Goods for transportation and communication	%	2.1	4.8	10.9	14.0	15.5
Goods for health-care and hygiene	%	4.3	5.0	3.6	3.0	3.3
Goods for education, entertainment, and recreation	%	5.5	7.1	7.3	8.6	10.7
Number of households	N	-	-	342	381	384

Note: The data are not fully comparable, since the way the surveys are conducted has changed over time. In 1980 the savings rate was calculated as the residual difference between available income and expenditures for private use, while as of 1989 the yearly wealth increase is considered.

Table 1 (Part III)
Expenditure of household income by three different types of households according to main categories of goods

Item		Four-person-household of white-collar workers and civil servants with higher income			
		1965	1970	1980	1989
Gross household income	DM	2,106	2,654	5,839	8,313
Income/property tax	%	10.4	12.4	15.9	15.1
Social-security dues	%	0.8	2.7	4.8	6.2
Available income (net)	DM	1,957	2,375	4,991	7,058
Savings rate	%	11.6	13.1	15.4	13.7
Expenditures for private use	DM	1,572	1,867	3,799	4,953
Nutrition, beverages, and tobacco	%	28.5	26.1	22.0	20.4
Clothing and shoes	%	11.0	10.7	9.3	8.4
Rents	%	12.1	14.0	15.5	19.8
Energy (electricity, fuel, etc.)	%	3.8	3.8	5.4	4.5
Goods for transportation and communication	%	16.2	15.1	15.3	15.9
Goods for health-care and hygiene	%	5.3	6.5	6.1	6.1
Goods for education, entertainment, and recreation	%	8.0	8.4	9.9	11.7
Number of households	N	367	393	428	401

Note: The data are not fully comparable, since the way the surveys are conducted has changed over time. In 1980 the savings rate was calculated as the residual difference between available income and expenditures for private use, while as of 1989 the yearly wealth increase is considered.

Sources: Statistisches Jahrbuch, 1957 p. 545; 1962, p. 543-545; 1972, p. 490-493, 1982, p. 450-453; 1990, p. 482-485.

Table 2
Consumer-price indices by selected categories of goods (four-person-employees' household with middle income) (1970 = 100)

Year	Total consumption	Nutrition	Beverages and tabacco	Dwelling	Heating, lighting
1950	64.5	64.6	103.5	41.4	56.0
1960	77.8	81.9	87.3	54.4	80.7
1965	89.3	95.2	89.7	72.6	88.6
1970	100.0	100.0	100.0	100.0	100.0
1975	134.0	132.9	121.8	135.8	154.0
1980	162.1	155.3	147.0	165.1	215.5
1985	196.0	178.9	177.9	205.1	289.8
1986	195.6	178.6	182.3	209.2	257.7
1987	195.7	178.1	179.9	212.8	230.2

Year	Consumer durables	Clothing	Hygiene	Education, entertainment recreation	Transportation
1950	84.2	76.4	65.2	55.2	61.2
1960	91.0	80.8	75.1	69.1	80.9
1965	97.2	90.9	85.9	83.3	89.6
1970	100.0	100.0	100.0	100.0	100.0
1975	125.7	136.6	130.2	135.5	140.9
1980	146.5	71.9	52.1	63.0	73.3
1985	168.3	204.8	188.3	203.4	210.4
1986	170.3	208.9	191.6	208.7	202.9
1987	171.9	211.7	194.5	212.6	204.3

Note: For the spending structure of the price index in the base-year 1980 the consumption groups have the following weight:

- nutrition	215.07
- beverages and tobacco	66.48
- dwelling	157.18
- heating and lighting	63.86
- consumers' durables	100.60
- clothing	90.63
- hygiene	45.63
- education, entertainment and recreation	109.91
- travel (transportation)	150.64
total cost of living	1,000

Source: Statistisches Bundesamt, Fachserie 17, Reihe 7.

13.2 Mass Information

Radio and television are used by all persons; circulation of daily newspapers has stagnated, and that of journalistic magazines has grown. New media are still not widespread, but their use is rapidly increasing.

The availability of mass-communication media in West German households is characterized by a saturation of radios since the early 1960s, a saturation of television sets since the early 1970s, a rapid increase in the number of video-cassette recorders since the early 1980s, and a stagnation of subscriptions to or regular purchase of daily newspapers (see figure 1), coinciding with a growth in popularity of news magazines. Book publishing is on the rise (in 1970, 47,096 titles; in 1986, 63,679 titles), though there have been decreases in some individual years.

In addition to the saturation of television sets and radios, there is a continuously growing density of apparatuses. In 1972, 324 out of 1,000 persons had a radio, and 283 per 1,000 had a television set; in 1987 these figures were 424 and 376, respectively. The electronic-media sector exhibits continuous adaptation to technical innovations (colour television, videotex, remote control, stereo).

Among types of recordings purchased, record albums and singles experienced strong growth up to 1980 (78.5 million albums and singles in 1970; peaking at 158.4 million in 1981) and then a slight drop (132.7 million in 1986), while the purchase of music cassettes continued to rise (2.1 million in 1970; 47.6 million in 1981; 61.9 million in 1986). Extremely high growth has been registered for compact discs, which have been available since 1983 (0.9 million in 1983; 13.4 million in 1986).

There is no common standard for measuring use in West Germany. Data provided by the suppliers (for example, movie theatres), data from time-budget surveys (comparing the different media), and registration of apparatuses (televisions) are sources that often lead to very different results.

According to the data gleaned from time-budget surveys, the daily published and daily broadcast media (television, radio) reached well over 90% of the population between 1964 and 1985. The use of several media per day has strongly increased. Time budgeted for media use on an average work day climbed from 3.08 hours in 1964 to 4.55 hours in 1985 (Berg & Kiefer 1987). The largest gains were registered by radio (+1.05 hours) and television (+1.21 hours). Time devoted to reading the newspaper remained constant at about a half-hour (see figure 2). Listening to the radio outside of leisure time is responsible for about two-thirds of the use of this medium; the growth in television-watching is largely explained by the spread of this medium. This corresponds with a major change in the chronological allocation of radio use: in 1964, use peaked in the evening hours, but the number of listeners at this time of day has since been falling continuously. There is a greater tendency to watch television late in the evening. Households with access to cable and satellite broadcasts watch television approximately ten more minutes per day.

The average use of videocassette recorders has been measured only since 1985. In households equipped with videocassette recorders, about 20% of members use the apparatus, and this group's viewing time is about 1.5 hours, with a slight upward tendency. The strong rise within the total population is mainly explained by the increasing supply of videocassette recorders in households.

Movie attendance reached a per-capita peak in the 1950s, with 15.7 trips to the movies per person in 1954. Subsequently, these visits declined continuously up until 1976 (1.9); after a slight increase (to 2.3 in 1980), a decline set in once again (to 1.7 in 1986).

Bernhard Engel

References

Berg, Klaus, and Marie Luise Kiefer
1987 *Massenkommunikation III. Eine Langzeitstudie zur Mediennutzung und Medienbewertung 1964-1985*. Schriftenreihe Media Perspektiven 9. Frankfurt am Main/Berlin: Alfred Metzner.

Media Micro Census GmbH, ed.
ann. pbl. *Media Analyse*. Datensatz Grundzählung.

Media Perspektiven
1987 *Daten zur Mediensituation in der Bundesrepublik*. Basisdaten.

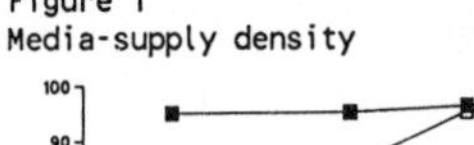

Figure 1
Media-supply density

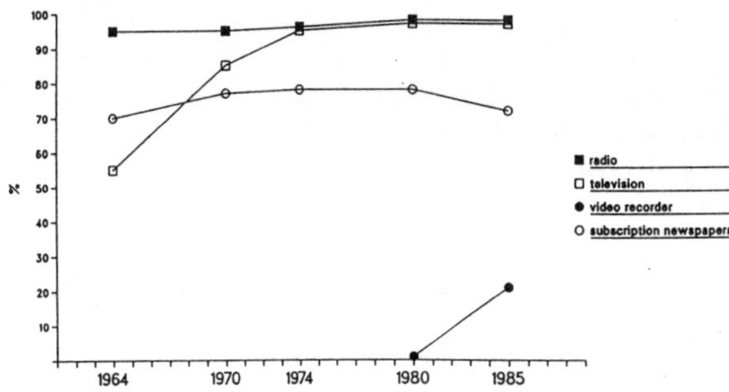

Source: Massenkommunikation 1964, 1970, 1974, 1980, 1985, cited in Berg, Klaus and Marie-Luise Kiefer 1988, p. 21.

Figure 2
Time use of daily published and daily broadcasted media
- Monday to Sunday -

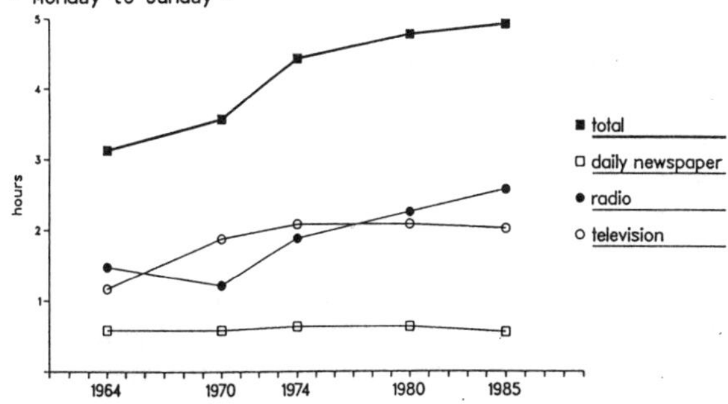

Source: Massenkommunikation 1964, 1970, 1974, 1980, 1985, cited in Berg, Klaus and Marie-Luise Kiefer 1988, p. 30.

13.3 Personal-health and Beauty Practices

The few available data on the use of medical services do not allow for clear conclusions concerning changes within time series. A transformation of attitude toward body and health can, however, be observed to have taken place within the framework of growing sensitivity toward the environment.

Use of Health-care Institutions

In comparison with other industrial nations – for example, Great Britain, France, the Scandinavian countries, the United States, Canada, and Japan – Germany has an unusual paucity of information concerning the use of health-care services.

The proportion of people who visit a doctor, undergo hospital stays, and report that they are sick at least once a year is not known. Random samples concern persons who were sick during one particular month of the survey year. Seasonal deviations in sickness rates are not taken into consideration in these surveys. Equally little is known about how many people take medicine, visit a dentist or non-physician medical personnel, or undergo a preventive examination within a defined period of time (Schach, 1985). Developments can thus only be approximated, based on institutional data.

The national cost of health care rose from 69.9 billion DM in 1970 to 241.5 billion DM in 1985 – an increase of 346%. There was a disproportionate increase in expenditures on public health insurance (459%); the inflationary growth rate of these expenses for private households (349%) corresponds to the general rate. Similarly, the "body- and health-care" sector experienced only slight deviations in the consumer structure of private households in time series. Pharmaceutical wholesale sales quadrupled between 1970 and 1986 (from approximately 3.7 billion DM to 15.2 billion DM). The number of inpatients per 1,000 persons rose from 132 to 199 between 1960 and 1985. At the same time, the average length of hospitalization dropped from 29 to 18 days.

Whether the rising costs of health care and the increase in inpatient treatment – with a simultaneous drop in period of hospitalization – was caused by the change in the population's age-cohort structure, by changes in the disease spectrum, by new treatment methods, or by other factors cannot by judged based on available statistics (Bundesverband des Pharmazeutischen Industrie, 1988).

Homeopathic/Natural Healing Methods, Care of Self

Aside from the above-mentioned developments, the past several years have exhibited a marked transformation in health beliefs.

The discussion in Germany concerning body and health goes back to the *Lebensreformbewegung* of the nineteenth century, a movement that attempted to check the advance of civilized ailments by means of vegetarianism, sports and exercise, nudism, tee-totalling, physiatry, and homeopathic medicine. After the racist practices of National Socialism, which applied euthenasia and genocide to further a *gesunder Volkskörper* (health of a nation, in which the concept of "nation" is nationalistically and race-ideologically defined), were eliminated, this theme was played down. In the student movement, it "was indeed [often] considered ideal to live unhealthily, that is, free from the constraints of a society fixated on cleanliness, fitness, and orderliness" (Bopp, 1987, p. 51). A central point of the new social movements' criticism, on the other hand, was the physical threat to individuals posed by atomic and chemical environmental destruction, most visible in poisoned or radioactive food, and in polluted air and earth.

In 1982, around 300 *Naturkostläden* (natural-food stores) existed in West Germany; since then, their numbers have been rising by 200 to 300 annually. Established businesses have also discovered this new market and now offer *Vollwertkost* (whole-grain, natural foods) and *Lebensmittel aus kontrolliertem Anbau* (produce from organic farming); production of household articles is gradually switching over to low-pollution methods.

As physical well-being is increasingly perceived as being maintained and furthered by a "health-conscious life style," readiness to choose unconventional healing methods in the case of illness is also on the rise. Associations of physiatrists and physicians practising natural healing methods have ascertained an increasing demand for natural remedies, including those whose efficacy has not been scientifically proven – for instance, homeopathy and cell therapy – due to spreading uncertainty about the side effects of chemical treatment. The number of qualified physiatrists increased from between 4,000 and 4,500 in 1975 to approximately 9,000 in 1987. Exact data are not available about physicians who apply natural methods when their patients wish it, but do so discreetly in order to avoid any scientific controversy. In 1987, about 15,000 of them (physiatrists and doctors using homeopathic methods) banded together in a national association.

Illness is becoming a calculated risk, to be dealt with preventively, whether through abstinence (see 13.8, "Mood-altering Substances") or through physical training. Over three-fourths of West Germans claimed never to engage in sports in 1950, while fewer than one-half did so in 1982 (Noelle-Neumann & Piel, 1983). Increasing numbers of people participate in *Volkswandern* (organized hikes) and organized bicycle tours, or go skiing and swimming (see 14.3, "Athletics and Sports"). American-style "parasports" such as jogging, walking, and aerobics, have gained numerous fans; there is much talk of "wellness," a concept involving harmony of body and soul. Health has once again become a key theme in the public discourse.

> Perfection of medicine, idealization of youthfulness in advertising, private enterprise's greed for profit, the American fitness craze, alternative criticism of civilization, reactionary crusaderism, sexual puritanism, technocratic omnipotence fantasies, religious missionary zeal, the struggle of the workers' movement for acceptable working conditions – it is a contradictory as well as scintillating mish-mash of groups that have concerned themselves with the matter of health. (Bopp, 1987, p. 49)

Karin Stiehr

References

Bopp, Jörg
1987 "Die Tyrannei des Körpers." In *Kursbuch 88. Gesundheit*. Berlin.

Bundesverband der Pharmazeutischen Industrie e. V., ed.
1988 *Basisdaten des Gesundheitswesens 1987/88*. Frankfurt am Main.

Noelle-Neumann, Elisabeth, and Edgar Piel, eds.
1983 *Allensbacher Jahrbuch der Demoskopie 1978-1983*. München/New York/London/Paris: Saur.

Roll, Evelyn
1987 "Der schöne, neue Markt." In *Kursbuch 88. Gesundheit*. Berlin.

Schach, Elisabeth, ed.
1985 *Von Gesundheitsstatistiken zu Gesundheitsinformation*. Berlin/Heidelberg/New York/Tokio: Thieme.

Statistisches Bundesamt, ed.
1988 *Statistisches Jahrbuch für die Bundesrepublik Deutschland*. Stuttgart/Mainz: Kohlhammer.

13.4 Time Use

The total time available to individuals is their lifetime, and this shows, on average, an increasing secular trend. A growing portion of life is spent in educational institutions and, at the end of the life cycle, in the "third age" following retirement. The change in time use through the decades of industrialization is characterized by a reduced number of hours spent on the job. The work week was reduced from the six-day, 68-hour week of around 1850 to the five-day, 38-hour week of today. Vacation time per day increased steadily in recent decades, but various kinds of work at home demanded a growing share of time. Transformation of time use is tending toward less structure and more pluralization.

The frames of reference for time as a social category are lifetime, years, weeks, and days. The relevant issue is the division between working and free-time activities, aside from sleep and restitution.

Per Lifetime

The length of time individuals in Germany live is increasing over the long run (see table 1). Average life expectancy for women increased from 38 years in 1871/1880 to 72 years in 1960/1962, then to 79 years in 1986/1988. Of course, this is partly due to a reduction in infant mortality, but the lengthening of life expectancy also holds for individuals aged one year or older. Women's average life expectancy at 60 years of age grew from a further 13 years (1871/80) to 22 years (1986/88) years, and this points to the growing importance of the "third age." Men have always had a lower life expectancy than women, and the difference grew over time from three years (1871/88) to six-and-a-half years (1986/88).

Lifetime is roughly structured, by societal arrangements, into the educational stage, labour-force participation, and the retirement stage. Participation in the educational system extends from three years of age (kindergarten) to 23 years of age (university). More and more people spend increasing amounts of time in educational institutions, and many attend them beyond the age of 23.

From various levels of the educational system, people enter the labour force, in which they participate for a number of decades. Exit from the labour force used to occur at 65 years of age for men (60 for women), and is now officially between 60 and 65, but may be below or above this age in special cases. The trend for moving into retirement is roughly toward a dispersal of years around 60, plus or minus 7 years. The "years gained" after retirement are thus becoming a more significant portion of the life span.

Per Year

The composition of the year in respect to work and non-work days has greatly changed, though some major parts of the year remain quantitatively the same: the number of work-free Sundays (52) and legally declared holidays (around 10). Saturdays became more and more work-free, and the number of vacation days multiplied up to 32 days on average (before 1933, for example there were only three basic vacation days in the metal industries). The number of vacation days varies considerably among employed people, and this inequality has widened with the addition of more and more days of leave (see table 2). On the whole, the work year is dwindling; this is sometimes referred to as the beginning of a vacation society.

Per Week

In the middle of the last century, the week consisted of one Sunday and six work days comprising 68 hours. In 1900, the unions were successful in obtaining a six-day work week with a 10-hour day. The five-day week was introduced in 1956. Up to the end of the 1980s, a normal work week consisted of 40 work hours and a two-day work-free weekend (Glaubrecht et al., 1985). In 1989, the 38-hour work week was introduced, and this is seen as leading to the 35-hour week.

There are many exceptions to the normal working week (see table 3). Women in particular work fewer than 40 hours weekly, and men tend to work 41 or more hours. A wide variety of types of time use is becoming the new picture. There is a widespread societal debate about the acceptability of industrial work on the weekend, and about the acceptable amount of additional working hours.

Per Day

Days are structured by many institutional regulations: for example, many shops and public facilities open between eight and nine o'clock; 6:30 p.m. is closing time for nearly all shops, with the exception of Thursdays, when, in recent times, longer opening hours have been allowed. An increase in use of days for vacation time is documented by self-reports (see table 4). Calculation of averages shows that free time exceeds working time (see table 5). It is also to be noted that there is increasing flexibility in working time, with the consequence that fewer people adopt a standard pattern of use of the day.

Time budgets

Time-budget research is concerned with the question of how people spend their time. Available empirical results are not representative of the whole population, and the time series are not built on strict replications. Thus, any conclusions must be drawn carefully. In respect to time used for housework and caring for children, a reduction in total household time input can be assumed due to figures which show 64.2 hours per week devoted to these activities in 1953, 61.7 hours in 1968, and 52.6 hours in 1977 (Lakemann, 1984). Because the size of households changes, it is worthwhile to look at households of different sizes. It is summarized that the time women dedicated to housework and child care was significantly reduced between the beginning of the 1950s and the end of the 1970s. A general conclusion is "that as well as for the interests which people articulate in interviews, there is also a general trend to more activities outside of formal employment" (Lakemann, 1984).

Wolfgang Glatzer

References

Glaubrecht, Helmut, Dieter Wagner, and Ernst Zander
1985 *Arbeitszeit im Wandel - Neue Formen der Arbeitszeitgestaltung*. Freiburg: Rudolf Haufe Verlag.

Lakemann, Ulrich
1984 *Das Aktivitätspektrum privater Haushalte in der Bundesrepublik Deutschland 1950 - 1980: Zeitliche und inhaltliche Veränderungen Erwerbstätigkeiten, unbezahlten Arbeiten und Freizeitaktivitäten*. Wissenschaftszentrum Berlin, discussion paper 84-19.

Müller-Wichmann, Christiane
1987 *Von wegen Freizeit - Argumente pro und contra 7-Stunden-Tag*. Frankfurt am Main: Union.

Rinderspacher, Jürgen P.
1987 *Am Ende der Woche. Die soziale und kulturelle Bedeutung des Wochenendes*. Bonn: Verlag Neue Gesellschaft.

Table 1
Life expectancy at birth and at sixty years for men and women

	1901/10	1924/26	1932/34	1949/51	1960/72	1970/72	1978/80	1986/88
At birth								
Men	44.82	55.97	59.86	64.56	66.86	67.41	69.60	72.13
Women	48.33	58.82	62.81	68.48	72.39	73.83	76.36	78.65
60 years								
Men	13.14	14.60	15.11	16.20	15.49	15.31	16.30	17.47
Women	14.17	15.51	16.07	17.46	18.48	19.12	20.60	21.92

Up to 1932/34: German Empire; 1949/51: Federal Republic of Germany without Saarland and West Berlin.

Source: Statistisches Jahrbuch, 1982, 1990.

Table 2
Entitlement to paid leave by wage and salary earners
(of 100 wage-/salary earners, ...% had paid leave of... work days)

Year	Work days						
	15-17	18-20	21-22	23-24	25	26	27
1973	5.9	21.9	53.3	14.2	0.2	1.5	0.4
1980	-	4.0	8.9	7.3	10.6	6.5	6.5
1986	-	0.3	2.3	1.9	1.7	1.3	6.4
Year	Work days						Average days of leave
	28	29	30	31-32	33-34	35-36	
1973	2.5	-	0.1	-	-	-	21.0
1980	23.7	-	2.5	25.5	4.5	-	27.3
1986	4.3	0.2	9.3	21.5	2.5	48.3	32.5

Source: Bundesminister für Arbeit und Sozialordnung, Bundesarbeitsblatt no. 3/1979ff.

Table 3
Weekly working hours of employed persons, according to occupation and gender

Item	Total in 1,000		Actual working hours in %							
	Men	Women	Men				Women			
			0-20	21-39	40	41 and older	0-20	21-39	40	41 and older
1970										
-self employed	2,237	574	5.1	3.6	7.6	83.8	17.2	10.3	3.7	68.8
-wage and salary earners	14,227	7,496	2.9	1.9	25.9	69.3	17.4	14.9	24.1	43.6
-total	16,741	9,602	3.5	2.3	22.0	72,2	14.3	14.7	19.8	51.2
1975										
-self employed	1,902	496	5.0	3.6	9.9	81.4	16.1	10.1	11.9	61.9
-wage and salary earners	14,228	8,036	4.4	4.1	65.1	26.4	19.6	15.8	51.8	12.8
-total	16,321	9,639	4.7	4.1	58.0	33.2	19.9	15.6	45.0	19.5
1980										
-self employed	1,834	482	4.5	3.0	13.5	79.0	17.8	10.4	17.4	54.4
-wage and salary earners	14,822	8,813	3.8	2.5	72.0	1.7	18.6	15.9	56.4	9.1
-total	16,782	10,092	4.1	2.6	65.1	28.2	19.1	15.7	50.9	14.2
1985										
-self employed	1,862	562	5.9	4.1	14.9	75.2	20.1	11.2	18.0	50.5
-wage and salary earners	14,429	9,062	5.8	13.9	61.8	18.6	21.2	20.8	49.6	8.4
-total	16,402	10,225	5.9	12.8	56.1	25.2	21.4	20.1	45.6	13.0

Source: Statistisches Bundesamt, Fachserie 1, Reihe 4.1.1.

Table 4
Amount of leisure time

Year	hours:min.	Year	hours:min.
Aug. 1952	2:33	May 1967	3:16
May 1957	2:43	April 1972	3:27
May 1970	2:54	July 1973	3:40
Oct. 1961	2:56	Feb. 1976	3:54
Nov. 1963	3:10	July 1979	3:54
April 1964	3:18	Sept./Oct. 1981	4:18
Sept. 1965	3:14		

Subjective information about average leisure time per day.
Population 16 years and over.

Source: Allensbacher Jahrbuch der Demoskopie, 1974-76; Allensbacher Archiv; Gesellschaftliche Daten, 1982.

Table 5
Amount of free time
("Objective" measurement by "key day" surveys - time budget for average work days (Monday-Saturday), general types of activity in hours and minutes)

Population 14 years and older	Work	Timerelated to work-activities incl.travel	Housework incl. shopping	Leisure time	Leisure time at home	Leisure time away from home	Other[1] (sleeping, eating)
Gainfully employed and non-employed:							
spring 1964	7:53	4:48	3:05	5:41	3:38	2:02	10:26
fall 1970	7:40	4:45	2:55	6:15	4:31	1:45	10:05
Nov. 1974	6:48	4:12	2:36	6:53	5:01	1:52	10:18
Nov. 1980	6:26	3:54	2:32	7:29	5:10	2:19	10:05
Thereof:							
fully employed	8:15	7:08	1:08	6:22	4:17	2:05	9:22
part-time employed and trainees	6:41	4:37	2:04	7:28	4:20	3:08	9:51
non-employed housewives	6:08	0:48	5:20	7:25	5:43	1:42	10:27
pensionees, unemployed	3:07	0:25	2:42	9:40	7:09	2:31	11:13

1. Surveys on everyday activities were limited to the time between 5:30 and 24:00. The night time of 0:00 to 5:30 is relegated entirely to the "other" category (sleep).

Source: Allensbacher Jahrbuch der Demoskopie, 1974-1976; Allensbacher Archiv; Gesellschaftliche Daten, 1982.

13.5 Daily Mobility

The number of persons using private transportation and transportation volume, measured in passenger-kilometres, have multiplied several times since the 1960s. This cannot be explained solely by a heightened trend toward individual mobility, but is also a necessary consequence of suburbanization.

After World War II, the area that became the Federal Republic of Germany had at its disposal a road network extending over a total of about 350,000 kilometres, as well as a railroad network totalling just under 37,000 kilometres. The local and regional road systems jumped from 368,300 to 432,300 kilometres between 1960 and 1970, and reached a total of 491,200 kilometres by 1985. Construction during this period more than tripled the amount of highways, while railroads were gradually reduced from 36,000 to 30,600 kilometres (see table 1). Even more drastic was the increase in personal transportation in automobiles, from 25 billion to over 480 billion passenger-kilometres between 1950 and 1985, with a simultaneous decline in importance of public transit (see figure 1).

Local Transportation

Automobiles have become the dominant element of daily mobility. Whereas just 11 private automobiles per 1,000 persons were registered in 1950, this figure was up to 422 in 1985. According to estimates made for 1980 by the Bundesministerium für Städtebau, Raumordnung und Bauwesen (Federal Ministry for Urban, Regional, and Housing Development), 96% of all automobile traffic density was in local travel within a distance of under 50 kilometres, and 55% of all trips took place within a three-kilometre area, of which 40% were by car (Wolf, 1986).

The causes of these developments in local travel lie with suburbanization. In the 1960s, there was a move out of inner cities and into urban peripheries, first to high-rise "satellite cities," but then increasingly to surrounding communities in which large one- and two-family housing areas – often with insufficient or no public-transit connections – were erected. Inner-city housing came to be increasingly used for commercial purposes, and the distance between place of residence and place of work grew (see also 2.3, "Community and Neighbourhood Types"). Use of private commuter transport rose from 15 billion to 101 billion passenger-kilometres between 1960 and 1982 (see table 2). Travelling time went up: in 1961, 20.7% of employees needed less than 15 minutes to get to work, while a mere 2% did so in 1979/1980. The proportion of those needing 15–30 minutes, on the other hand, rose from 25.1% to 40%, those needing 30–45 minutes rose from 14.7% to 40%, and those needing 40–60 minutes rose from 6.1% to 11% (Lakemann, 1984).

In the 1960s, construction of shopping centres began, as did, later, construction of specialized stores with large parking lots just outside of towns. Between 1960 and 1982, the volume of shopping traffic rose from 23 billion to 45 billion passenger kilometres (table 2), although a simultaneous trend to large-volume shopping was observed.

Moreover, suburbanization and increased construction of industrial and service enterprises in urban ambit areas were responsible for the destruction of numerous local recreational areas; longer distances became necessary for trips *ins Grüne* (to natural, wooded areas). In 1960, 76 billion passenger-kilometres were registered for leisure traffic, and as many as 196 billion were in 1982 (table 2; Wolf, 1986).

Developments and Differences in Mobility

Expenditures for transport and transmission of news were responsible for a steadily increasing share of total private consumption. While these expenses amounted to only 2.8% for low-income households (retirees and welfare recipients) in 1965, they amounted to 9.4% in 1985. Another clear increase for this period, of 9.7% to 14.8%, was recorded for middle-income households. Households with high incomes were the only ones to maintain a relatively constant level of about 16% (Statistisches Bundesamt, 1987).

Freedom of movement is decisively determined by the possession or non-possession of an automobile nowadays. In a society oriented toward "auto-mobility" and decentralization of institutions, children, youths, old people, and housewives increasingly find themselves at a disadvantage. In spite of a considerable upward trend since 1973, fewer than one-third of retiree and welfare households possessed a car in 1985. In contrast, middle- and high-income households can boast of near-saturation (see table 3). At the end of the 1970s, 76% of men, but only 34% of women, had a driver's license. The statistics concerning newly issued driver's permits seem to show a hardening of this gender-specific difference: while the proportion of driver's licenses issued to women was about 34% in 1971, it had sunk to around 30% in 1983. "The hypothesis is not at all unthinkable, that only one-fourth of all women have access to a car in daily life, whereas over three-fourths of men do. Male dominance is even more distinctly expressed in the automobile society than in the wage and salary disparity that discriminates against women" (Wolf, 1986, p. 224).

It is generally agreed that frequency and length of trips have increased considerably. Gaps exist, however, in research on travel and trips by bicycle and by foot. It is also unclear to what degree the increase of kilometres travelled is an expression of increased individual mobility, and to what degree it is simply a logical result of socio-structural changes that have allowed the automobile to become the means of transportation for routes that used to be travelled by foot. These ruminations form the basis for the hypothesis that the mobility of those with little or no access to a car has actually declined (Wolf, 1986).

Karin Stiehr

References

Franz, Peter
1984 *Soziologie der räumlichen Mobilität*. Frankfurt am Main/New York: Campus.

Lakemann, Ulrich
1984 *Das Aktivitätsspektrum privater Haushalte in der Bundesrepublik Deutschland 1950 bis 1980: Zeitliche und inhaltliche Veränderungen von Erwerbstätigkeiten, unbezahlten Arbeiten und Freizeitaktivitäten*. Berlin: Wissenschaftszentrum Berlin.

Müller-Wichmann, Christiane
1987 *Von wegen Freiheit*. Gutachten für die IG Metall. Frankfurt am Main: Union.

Statistisches Bundesamt, ed.
1987 *Datenreport 1987*. Bonn: Bundeszentrale für politische Bildung.

Wolf, Winfried
1986 *Eisenbahn und Autowahn. Personen- und Gütertransport auf Schiene und Straße. Geschichte, Bilanz, Perspektiven*. Hamburg/Zürich: Rasch und Röhrig.

Table 1
Tansportation infrastructure,1960 to 1985 (in kilometers)

Standard used	1960	1970	1980	1985
Street network (federal, state and district roads)	135,300	162,300	171,521	173,240
Incl. highways	2,551	4,110	7,292	8,350
Municipal roads	233,000	270,000	308,000	318,000
Railway network	36,109	33,010	31,497	30,568
Waterways in use	-	4,383	4,395	4,429

Source: Statistisches Bundesamt, 1987, p. 311.

Table 2
Traffic frequency and traffic density in private personal transportation, categorized by purpose

Purpose of trip	Traffic density Persons transport in million			Traffic frequency Billion passengers km		
	1960	1965	1982	1960	1965	1982
Work	2,130	4,080	7,840	15	33	101
Shopping	4,340	4,820	5,690	23	37	45
School, etc.	150	340	1,045	1	3	13
Sum 1	6,620	9,230	14,575	39	73	159
Sum 1 in proportion to total motorized traffic	43%	47%	52%	24%	27%	35%
Leisure-time traffic	6,000	6,780	9,905	76	122	196
Sum 2	12,620	16,010	24,480	115	195	355
Sum 2 in proportion to total motor. traffic	83%	82%	87%	71%	73%	77%
Business trips and job-related travel	2,665	3,550	3,750	40	57	58
Vacation traffic	15	40	60	7	15	47
Sum total of motor. traffic	15,300	19,600	28,300	162	267	460

Calculated according to Verkehr in Zahlen, 1985, pp. 164, 174.

Source: Wolf, 1986, p. 556.

Table 3
Equipment (in 1973 and 1985) according to exemplary household types (in %)

Object	Household type					
	Retiree or welfare recipient		Middle-income		High-income	
	1973	1985	1973	1985	1973	1985
Automobile	5.3	31.3	69.4	92.7	89.6	96.3
Telephone	20.5	89.4	36.6	93.7	87.9	97.9

Source: Statistisches Bundesamt, 1987, p. 114.

Figure 1
Personal transportation 1950-1980

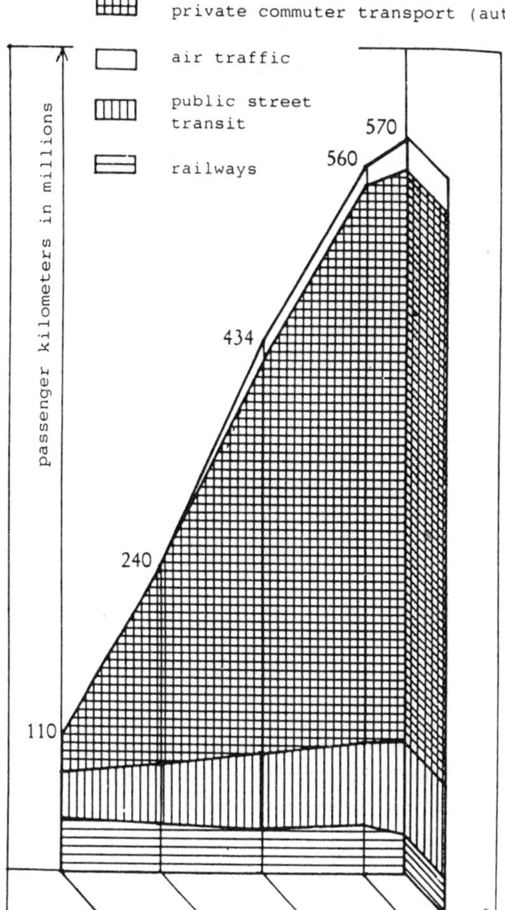

Source: Wolf, 1986, p. 150.

13.6 Household Production

There is controversy over the overall trend of household production, and it is nearly impossible empirically to prove the various theses. Some economic estimates of the relationship of the volume of household production to GNP show an increase, others a decrease, in recent decades. In respect to the various activities in household production, as well as to some indirect indicators (consumer durables, people's interests and competencies), there are many indications that some kinds of household production are spreading and gaining significance.

Household production is often negatively defined, by saying what it is not: it is neither market production nor collective or state production. A positive definition hints at activities and outcomes in the private household. Among the activities involved in household production, one can distinguish between manufacturing goods, on the one hand, and caring for persons, on the other. In the first category are activities as varied as preparing meals and housing construction; in the second are activities such as child care and nursing the elderly. These activities are performed by household members to produce outputs that are mainly exclusively for their own household, and, for the households belonging to their informal social network of relatives, neighbours, and friends.

Evolution of Household Production

The traditional hypothesis about the trend of household production is that it decreased in the context of secular industrialization and an accompanying expansion of the welfare state, with industrial enterprises and welfare institutions taking over tasks which, in the pre-industrial era, were performed by families and households. However, it is now posited that this trend was overestimated, and that household production will not continue to decline. First, there were warnings from a few social scientists not to overlook the many tasks that continued to be performed in private households. Later, hypotheses emerged that household production is growing again and that private households are gaining significance in the process of welfare production (Glatzer & Berger-Schmitt, 1986).

Relationship of Household Production to GNP

In absolute terms, the amount of household production per se is not informative; it is preferable to look at its relation to GNP. There are models showing that household production is a legitimate but neglected part of the national accounts.

Several reasonable ways to define and evaluate household production exist. Central to evaluating household working hours are the relationship between input-oriented (working time) and output-oriented (goods produced) measures and the relationship between market prices and opportunity costs (Schettkat, 1985). Therefore, there are different empirical estimates of the amount of household production in the FRG, and some authors give both a low and a high estimate (see table 1). For example, in table 1 the highest figure is 68% of GNP (1982), and the lowest is 23% of GNP (1953). This is indeed a wide discrepancy, which is due to real changes, different definitions, different measurement procedures,and different evaluations. There is no consensus, either, about a trend in time series: using the market-price evaluation of working hours in the household, one study shows an increase in the proportion of household production, while the other demonstrates no change for similar periods. Using the opportunity-cost method gives results showing a small relative decrease in household production (Schäfer, 1988). Thus, estimates of the volume of household production provide no convincing information about the overall trend of household production.

Interests

There are indirect approaches for measuring the development of household production; one is to ask people about their main areas of interest (see table 2). These have changed in a typical way for the German population. Significantly more persons report sociability activities, child care, garden work, and do-it-yourself as main interests in 1977 than in 1950. "It is remarkable that interest has strongly risen for nearly all listed areas. One reason is a general trend toward the growth and versatility of activities, presumably based on the expansion of available time outside of work" (Lakemann, 1984, p. 54). There seems to be a trend on the cultural level toward enforcing household production.

Consumer Durables as Means of Production

Households are "investing" their income in an growing range of electrical appliances (see table 3), which are used for household production. The 1950s can be seen as an early phase in the introduction of electrical appliances into households. In 1955, only 39% of FRG citizens owned a vacuum cleaner, 10% a refrigerator, and 6% a car. In 1969, three large appliances were deemed to be standard equipment (defined as 50% distribution) in private households: the vacuum cleaner, the refrigerator, and the television set. The greatest increase in electrical equipment in private households took place in the 1970s. By 1983, eight appliances were standard equipment in private households: the three above-mentioned appliances, a car, a washing machine, a telephone, a deep freezer, and an electric sewing machine. Other appliances had reached or crossed the 10% horizon for marginal goods; dishwashers, clothes dryers, and irons. A minority also owned luxury goods such as a mobile home or a motor boat. In 1983, 24% of households owned a second television set and 11% a second car. In this respect, the households have grown to the level of small firms with a quantitatively and qualitatively high means of production (Glatzer et al., 1991).

Competency Patterns

Household production affords competencies which are part of the social capital of society. Each generation acquires certain competencies, resulting in an age-specific competency distribution (see table 4). The younger and middle generations possess much more technical competency than do the older generations, whereas traditional housework skills are distributed in the opposite way. Gender is also associated with different technical skills. The difference between the age groups can in this case be interpreted as a trend toward enlargement of technical competencies for household production (Glatzer et al., 1991).

Activity Patterns

More direct information about household production concerns activities in households. Table 5 shows available data about weekend activities for the years 1955, 1964, and 1977. In the latter year, more people worked in the garden, tinkered and did needlework, and were concerned with children and vocational training. "In respect to the main fields of interest, as well as in respect to time use, a general trend toward increasing activities outside the working sphere can be observed" (Lakemann 1984, p. 55). The change in activity patterns is a clear hint at an increase in household production. Two dimensions for explaining the success of household production are of relevance: satisfaction from output (goods produced) and benefits from process (activities performed).

Wolfgang Glatzer

References:

Glatzer, Wolfgang, and Regina Berger-Schmitt, eds.
1986 *Haushaltsproduktion und Netzwerkhilfe*. Frankfurt am Main/New York: Campus.

Glatzer, Wolfgang, et al.
1991 *Haushaltstechnisierung und gesellschaftliche Arbeitsteilung*. Frankfurt am Main/New York: Campus.

Institut für Demoskopie, ed.
1957 *Jahrbuch der öffentlichen Meinung*. Allensbach: Verlag für Demoskopie.

–, ed.
1977 *Allenbacher Jahrbuch der Demoskopie*. Wien/München/ Zürich: Fritz Molden.

Koch, Achim, and Martina Wasmer
1990 "Allgemeine Kulturfertigkeiten." In Statistisches Bundesamt, ed., *Datenreport*. Bonn: Bundeszentrale für politische Bildung.

Lakemann, Ulrich
1984 *Das Aktivitätsspektrum privater Haushalte in der Bundesrepublik Deutschland 1950 bis 1980*. Wissenschaftszentrum Berlin, discussion paper 84-19.

Schäfer, Dieter
1988 "Haushaltsproduktion in gesamtwirtschaftlicher Betrachtung." *Wirtschaft und Statistik*, 5, 309-318.

Schettkat, Ronald
1985 "The Size of Household Production: Methodological Problems and Estimates for the Federal Republic of Germany in the Period 1964 to 1980." *The Review of Income and Wealth*, 3, 309-321.

Table 1
Estimates of amount of household production in the Federal Republic of Germany

Study	Year	Value of household production	
		In bill. DM	In % of GNP
Market price method			
Fürst	1953	35-42	23-28
Schmucker	1958	9-12	33-45
Langfeld/Adatia	1961	122	37
	1971	324	43
	1977	562	47
Langfeld	1965	229	50
Schettkat	1964	112-158	27-38
	1970	168-254	25-38
	1974	224-370	23-38
	1980	325-552	22-37
Hilzenbecher	1982	862-1,090	54-68
Opportunity cost method			
Schettkat	1964	156-220	37-53
	1970	230-347	34-51
	1974	296-490	30-50
	1980	425-722	29-49

Note: The figures do not allow exact comparison due to differences in concept of household production, quality of reported working time, and methods of evaluation.

Source: Schrage, 1984.

Table 2
Main fields of interest of German population (in %)

Wording of question: "Please tell me which of the items on this list are your main fields of interest, or what interests you especially?"
(Further comment: "Even if you are professionally involved in it.")

Main interests	1950	1966	1972	1975	1977
Needlework, sewing	18[1]	24	26	24	33
Gardening, agricult. work	8	-	35	38	33
Do-it-yourself	2	17	19	22	23
Child care	1	26	26	24	28
Political involvement	5	18	19	23	-
Cooking	-	31	26	32	-
Adult education	-	-	-	22	25
Interior Decorating	-	43	24	36	-
Social life	5	20	24	31	33

1. Inclusive domestic sciences.

Source: Institut für Demoskopie Allensbach, various volumes.

Table 3
Diffusion of durable consumer goods in private households since 1962 (in %)

Item	1962/63	1969	1973	1978	1983	1988
Vacuum cleaner	65	84	91	94	96	-
Refrigerator	52	87	93	84	79	78
Television	34	73	87	93	94	95
Automobile	27	44	55	62	65	68
Washing machine	9	39	59	70	83	86
Telephone	14	31	51	70	89	93
Deep freezer, or combination	3	14	28	58	69	70
Electric sewing machine	10	26	37	46	52	53
Dishwasher	0.2	2	7	15	24	29
Iron	1	6	10	14	15	14
Clothes dryer	-	-	-	-	10	17

Source: Statisches Bundesamt, Fachserie 15, Wirtschaftsrechnungen, Einkommens- und Verbrauchsstichprobe. No 1: Outfitting of private households with selected consumer durables, 1962/63, 1969, 1973, 1978, 1983, 1988.

Table 4
Competence in handicraft and housework activites and in using technical equipment (in %)

Competence	Total	Gender		Age group			
		Male	Female	18-34	35-49	50-64	Over 64
Hanging lamp	54	88	23	60	57	54	37
Wallpapering	57	70	45	61	65	54	38
Change spark plug	45	81	13	53	49	42	27
Patch bicycle tire	62	92	36	72	64	60	44
Knitting	48	4	86	46	45	50	55
Cooking	71	45	94	70	71	69	77
Sewing on buttons	89	78	99	88	87	91	90
Hemming pant leg	63	26	94	63	60	64	67
Set quartz watch	57	75	41	73	59	46	34
Computer operation	20	27	14	30	25	13	2
Use pocket calculator	76	85	68	92	84	65	42
Video recording	40	53	28	66	42	23	8
Taping radio programms	64	78	52	88	71	49	24

Data basis: ALLBUS 1986 (N=3,095).

Source: Koch & Wasmer, 1987.

Table 5
Weekend activities of German population (in %)

Wording of question: What do you generally do on the weekend, that is, saturday and sunday, in your free time?"

Item	Juni 1955	July 1964[1]	July 1964[2]	Feb. 1977
Television	-	32	31	69
Broadcasting	56	27	27	33
Reading books	23	8	11	29
Reading newspaper	39	27	22	43
Home repairs	26	-	-	30
To work in the garden	15	25	5	26
Do it yourself	13	-	-	25
House work and needle work	-	34	22	-
To visit friends and relatives	33	14	23	45
To visit a restaurant	18	8	11	21
To invite guests	16	8	14	32
Being with the children	22	-	-	27
To write letters	16	9	7	15
To have a walk	50	-	-	50
To sleep careful	37	21	42	29
To sleep/rest in the afternoon	31	-	-	23
To spend the day pleasant at home	35	22	28	45
Professional education	5	4	3	8
To visit a lecture/meeting	3	-	-	4
Going to cinema	31	5	3	11

Note: The question was in 1955 and 1977: "What are you doing general during the weekend, that is saturday and sunday in your freetime?" In 1964 there was an explicit distinction between saturday and sunday and the question was focused on a certain (the last saturday/sunday) day.

1. Saturday.
2. Sunday.

Source: Institut für Demoskopie, 1957, p. 31; 1977 p. 44.

13.7 Forms of Erotic Expression

Sexual mores in the Federal Republic of Germany were, until the reform of sexual criminal law in the late 1960s, subject to strict legislation dating from National Socialist times. External influences contributed to a liberalization following World War II, which became clearly visible in the early 1960s with the "sex wave." Positive attitudes toward sexuality have steadily increased ever since then, but reservations about taking sexual freedom for granted have increased, particularly since the emergence of AIDS.

Trends in Forms of Erotic Expression

In the Federal Republic, public nudity and open discussion of sex emerged around the mid-1960s. This phenomenon was called the *Sexwelle* (sex wave). The expression played upon two previous postwar trends: the *Fresswelle* (eating wave) and *Reisewelle* (travel wave). As was the case with both other waves, the expression "sex wave" implies making up for lost time. Some scandals of the 1950s preceded the wave. One involved the film "Die Sünderin," in which the actress Hildegard Knef appeared naked for several seconds. In the early 1960s, the Swedish director Ingmar Bergman's film "Das Schweigen" ("The Silence"), in which coitus was shown (though it was difficult to recognize), caused an uproar. Up to the late 1960s, the Federal Republic had rigid sexual legislation – for example, the so-called *Kuppeleiparagraph*, which forbade landlords, acquaintances, and family members (even parents!) to provide unmarried couples with accommodations in which they could indulge in "lasciviousness." Anyone, including neighbours, could report them. "Lasciviousness" meant all sexual contact between unmarried people. This made it nearly impossible to live together outside of marriage. A reform of the "lasciviousness" paragraph was unsuccessfully attempted in the 1920s, during the Weimar government. The law was tightened up under the Nazi regime, for example in the form of radical persecution of sexual minorities. These laws remained on the books of the Federal Republic until the sexual-rights reform at the end of the 1960s. The sex wave should therefore be seen in the context of political democratization and the overcoming of the old Nazi values. The conceptual change clearly reflects a socio-cultural value transformation. Whereas "crime and offence against sexual self-determination" was spoken of up until the sexual-rights reform, the post-liberalization wording was "punishable deeds against sexual self-determination." The "enlightenment wave" ran parallel to the sex wave. One of its protagonists was the journalist Oswalt Kolle, who wrote a sex-enlightenment series in popular-science style for the magazine *Neue Illustrierte-Revue* in the mid-1960s. At this time, "enlightenment films" emerged, such as

"Helga," in which genitals and sexual intercourse were plainly shown, though in a clinically sterile and non-eroticized manner. More marriage- and personal-counselling offices were established. The demand for enlightenment and advice was caused in part by the high number of "early marriages," in which one or both partners were under 21 years of age, the age of majority at the time. Unwanted pregnancies were often the reason for early marriage.

The transformation of attitudes toward sexuality is illustrated by a comparison of evaluations of the sex wave from two polls (in 1970 and in 1986). One-half of respondents (54%) claimed that the sex wave had made people more free in 1970, while nearly three-fourths did so (72%) in 1986. Also in 1986, 50% were of the opinion that sex makes life more enjoyable, while only 20% held this opinion in 1970. However, negative responses have increased along with positive ones. The view that the sex wave has contributed to a brutalization of romantic relations between people was held by as many as 39% in 1986, as opposed to only 26% in 1970. The answers to questions regarding a positive attitude toward sexuality makes the influence of age generally noticeable, in that the percentages rose more distinctly among older people (see table 1). The very positive overall attitude toward sexuality following the sex wave – it has liberated people, young people can get to know each other better before marriage, sex makes life nicer – has been to some degree qualified through the debate about AIDS. In 1987, 73% of those questioned in a representative poll believed that sexual freedom leads to the spread of dangerous diseases. There is also a growing skepticism about the explicit portrayal of sex, particularly in its quality as a threat to youth (Institut für Demoskopie Allensbach, 1988). More recent polls dealing with changes in sexual behaviour, particularly in conjunction with AIDS, show that sexuality is largely partner-oriented. In other words, the sex wave has not unleashed a sexual revolution, but is rather to be understood as a liberal sexual reform.

Pornography

Pornography is defined as writing in which "sexual excitation is the dominant purpose, a substantive representation of anything other than the sexual purpose is not intended, or the sexual contents are obtrusively brutalized, contorted, or sensationalized" (Creifelds & Meyer-Gossner, 1988, p. 871). Under paragraph 184 of the Criminal Law Book are included "hard" erotica, in which sexuality is portrayed in connection with representations of violence, abuse of children, or abuse of animals. Paragraph 184 was liberalized in 1975 and now concentrates on proffering, public exhibition of, or showing of pornographic material to minors. There are no statistics or exact turnover figures available for West Germany. Estimates put the number of pornography cinemas at about 350, in addition to mini-cinemas or one-person cinema booths (video peep-shows) in sex shops.

According to another estimate, 40% of all videos sold or rented are pornofilms. The sharp realism achievable by photo-technical representation makes pornography appear harder and more candid. Pornography as an economic factor is a modern development. The company Beate Uhse AG leads the West German market. With its 30 sex shops and 25 cinemas, it has an annual turnover of approximately 100 million DM. About 10 million customers per year patronize the shops and cinemas. It is assumed that only about one in six actually buys; the majority just looks. The proportion of women entering sex shops is estimated at a maximum of 1%. The over 250,000 female and male prostitutes in West Germany are also included in the commercial field of pornography, as are their approximately 5 million customers and numerous night bars, strip-tease clubs, and sauna clubs (Grimme, 1986).

Very few pornographic magazines are openly sold on the West German market. The best known are the German versions of *Lui*, *Penthouse*, and *Playboy*. The German version of *Playboy* is fully equivalent to the American magazine. The German version of *Penthouse* is, however, quite mild in comparison to its American counterpart. The spectrum of readers remained fairly constant between 1982 and 1988; as might be expected, they were mainly male. These magazines are, however, very different from the magazines, films, and representations in which portrayal goes beyond pornography to include violence. The feminist journal *Emma* and its publisher, Alice Schwarzer, have brought this state of affairs into the public discourse. A "PorNo" campaign was launched for a legislative initiative to change the law, so that every woman who feels that her human dignity is degraded by a pornographic portrayal can bring a lawsuit. In one poll, 59% felt that pornography is a private matter which the government has no business interfering in. The difference between women's and men's opinions in this matter is considerable. Whereas only 16% of the men notice misogyny in pornography, 41% of the women do. Just under one-half of women (49%) favour government censorship. Women's attitudes are highly dependent upon age: young women tend to want less censorship, while older women tend to want more (see table 2).

Innovation in Forms of Sexual Practices

The great majority of today's youths have had sexual experience by the age of 18 – that is before marriage (75% of the men, 73% of the women). In the majority of cases (91% among both men and women), the first sexual partner was of the opposite sex (Noelle-Neumann, 1981). A romantic relationship remains the most frequent reason for first coitus. Over time, however, men and women differ greatly in this. While this motive remained nearly constant for men, at about 40% between 1966 and 1981, it declined among women, from 71% in 1966 to only 52% in 1981. The "curiosity" motive doubled over this period for women (see table 3). The cause is undoubtedly the more liberal sexual attitudes and, especially, the introduction of the contraceptive pill. Young women have less occasion to fear for their "good reputation" and can protect themselves more reliably against unwanted pregnancy. More liberal sexual attitudes can be concluded from the widespread acceptance of premarital sexual intercourse: while only about one-third of those polled in 1966 found it acceptable, 80% of men and 87% of the women did so in 1981 (Clement, 1986). Extramarital sexual relations are also less frowned on today than they once were. Acceptance was even higher shortly before the end of World War II, then fell sharply during the years of postwar consolidation and up to the time immediately preceding the sex wave. The proportion of those permitting extramarital sexual relations has undergone an overall increase over the past four decades (see table 4). Earlier coital experience takes place among both sexes. In 1966, approximately 30% of women and approximately 35% of men had had their first experience by the age of 20. In 1981, as many as 80% of women and 70% of men had had their first encounter by the age of 20. Both sexes began coital experience at a younger age in 1981 than in 1966 (Clement, 1986).

Vicarious Sexual Involvement

The masturbatory experience of young women between 14 and 20 years of age increased considerably between 1966 and 1981. Approximately 40% of the women had cumulative experience with masturbation in 1966, and this proportion had reached nearly 70% in 1981. Whether these data are expressive of more enlightenment and, therefore, better knowledge of one's own body, the more liberal attitude toward sexuality, or a more honest response behaviour by women cannot be concluded. The proportion of men who mastubate rose only slightly, from 85% in 1966 to around 90% in 1981. A poll on student sexuality, carried out at twelve West German universities in 1966 (Sigusch et al., 1968), showed that at that time approximately one-third of 18-year-olds and one-half of 20-year-olds, both male and female, had petting experience. More recent surveys are not available, but it can be assumed that, here too, experience takes place at an earlier age.

Sex in Public

Whereas public nudity was next to unthinkable twenty years ago, nude bathing and suntanning are now taken for granted. The advertising and newspaper industries use nudity for purposes of visual publicity. The often unmistakable equation of women with sex objects has repeatedly resulted in complaints being filed with the Deutsche Werberat (public authority responsible for controlling publicity and advertising), so that advertisers have made their sexual signals more subtle. As a side effect - perhaps contradictory at first glance - of the more liberal attitudes toward nudity and sexuality, an increased sensitivity to the commercialization and objectivization of woman as sex object can be noted. The portrayal of pornographic scenes on television is forbidden by the pornography law, and also by self-censorship among German TV stations, but this is being undermined by the so-called soft pornos broadcast by private cable stations. The tough competition between public and private TV stations has led to increased use of erotica. The private TV station RTL+ in particular offers a late-evening so-called *Männermagazin* ("Men's Magazine") of unmistakable erotic content, and also special sexual-advice shows. Youth magazines carry erotic photo-stories and sexual-enlightenment columns. As well, novelettes (penny novels), with their large-volume printings, are quite at ease with sexual themes nowadays.

Karin Seibel

References

Allensbacher Archiv
1988 *IfD-Umfrage*, March, April.

Clement, Ulrich
1986 *Sexualität im sozialen Wandel*. Stuttgart: Enke.

Creifelds, Carl, and Lutz Meyer-Gossner, eds.
1988 *Rechtswörterbuch*. 9. neubearb. Aufl. München: Beck.

Giese, Hans, and Gunter Schmidt
1968 *Studentensexualität. Verhalten und Einstellung*. Reinbek: Rowohlt.

Grimme, Matthias T.J., ed.
1986 *Käufliche Träume. Erfahrungen mit Pornografie*. Reinbek: Rowohlt.

Institut für Demoskopic Allensbach
1988 *Allensbacher Berichte*, no. 14.

Noelle-Neumann, Elisabeth, ed.
1981 *The Germans. Public Opinion Polls 1967-1980*. Westport, Conn./London: Greenwood.

Noelle-Neumann, Elisabeth, and Edgar Piel, eds.
1983 *Allensbacher Jahrbuch der Demoskopie 1978-1983*. München/New York/London/Paris: Saur.

Piel, Edgar
1987 *Im Geflecht der kleinen Netze. Vom deutschen Rückzug ins Private*. Zürich: Edition Interfrom.

Table 1 (Part I)
Opinions on the "sex wave" 1970 - 1986

Wording of question: "One hears and reads a lot about the sex wave nowadays. We've written down a few opinions: which ones do you agree with? Would you pick out the corresponding card?" (cards, multiple answers)

Item	Total population		Age groups							
			16-29 years		30-44 years		45-49 years		60 yr.- older	
	Sept. 1970	March 1986	Sept. 1970	March 1986	Sept. 1970	March 1986	Sept. 1970	March 1986	Sept. 1970	March 1986
Positive statements:										
The sex wave has made people freer: they're no longer afraid to talk about things that should be discussed.	54	72	80	84	59	81	44	71	28	52
It lets young people get to know each other better before marriage.	38	63	63	79	37	69	29	59	18	44
It makes life better.	20	50	39	67	21	63	10	45	6	24
It helps parents to tell their children about sex.	34	45	45	54	40	51	26	44	20	30
Sexual freedom leads to a decrease in sexual crimes.	20	19	35	22	21	24	14	17	10	12
Total	166	249	262	306	178	288	123	236	82	162

Table 1 (Part II)
Opinions on the "sex wave" 1970 - 1986

Wording of question: "One hears and reads a lot about the sex wave nowadays. We've written down a few opinions: which ones do you agree with? Would you pick out the corresponding card?" (cards, multiple answers)

Item	Total population		Age groups							
			16-29 years		30-44 years		45-49 years		60 yr.- older	
	Sept. 1970	March 1986	Sept. 1970	March 1986	Sept. 1970	March 1986	Sept. 1970	March 1986	Sept. 1970	March 1986
Negative statements:										
Sex openly shown in films and magazines is a threat to youth.	48	46	26	26	44	39	59	53	69	69
If the sex wave goes on like this, people will value only the physical, not the spiritual things.	39	39	20	27	43	30	49	47	47	55
It leads to a brutalization of romantic relationships.	26	39	12	24	20	33	39	44	38	55
Open portrayal of sex acts necessarily leads to an increase in sex crimes.	32	38	16	24	28	31	39	44	47	56
The sex wave is a threat to marriage and family.	31	29	13	12	28	22	37	33	48	50
It leads to a degeneration of youth.	35	26	12	10	27	16	47	30	59	50
Total	211	217	99	123	190	171	270	251	308	335
No opinion	1	1	1	1	1	1	1	1	2	2

Source: Allensbacher Archiv, IfD-Umfrage 5003, 1988.

Table 2
Opinions on pornography (in %)

Wording of question: "In West Germany, pornography, in other words the portrayal of the sexual act in special magazines and films, permitted. Here are two people talking about it. Which of the two do you agree with?"

Total population			Age groups							
Total	Men	Women	16-29 years Men	16-29 years Women	30-44 years Men	30-44 years Women	45-59 years Men	45-59 years Women	60 yr.- older Men	60 yr.- older Women
"I think it should be left up to the individual whether he looks at pornography. It's a personal decision. The state should not censor, and should keep out of it."										
59	71	49	77	61	78	60	71	46	53	32
"I see it differently. Pornography discriminates against women and therefore should be outlawed. The state should take steps, and protect human dignity."										
29	16	41	11	28	11	31	17	44	28	57
Undecided										
12	13	10	12	11	11	9	12	10	19	11
100	100	100	100	100	100	100	100	100	100	100

Source: Allensbacher Archiv, IfD-Umfrage 5003, 1988, cited in Allensbacher Berichte 1988, p. 3.

Table 3
Motives for first coitus (coitally experienced, in %)

Motives for first coitus	1966		1981	
	Men	Women	Men	Women
Enjoyment	26	3	18	4
Seduction	4	8	7	5
Situation	10	4	13	9
Love relationship	42	71	44	52
Prestige	3	1	2	3
Curiosity	16	13	16	26
(N)	(1,822)	(456)	(945)	(737)

Source: Clement, 1986, p. 114.

Table 4
Extramarital Relationships (in %)

Wording of question: "Do you condone or condemn it if married persons have extramrital relationships?"
If "condemn": "Would you admit certain exceptions, e.g. if the marriage partner suffers from an incurable illness?"

Item	1949		1963		1978	
	Men	Women	Men	Women	Men	Women
Condemn it	51	68	76	79	45	48
- admitting no exceptions	17	30	34	36	23	21
- admitting certain exceptions	24	23	26	23	13	14
- undecided	10	15	16	20	9	13
- total	51	68	76	79	45	48
Condone it	7	3	2	4	25	14
That depends, undecided	42	29	22	17	30	38
Total	100	100	100	100	100	100

Question put to persons between 20 and 30 years of age.

Source: Noelle-Neumann, 1981, p. 253.

13.8 Mood-altering Substances

Consumption of classic luxury and intoxicating substances (coffee, tobacco, and alcohol) registered high growth rates in the years following World War II; tobacco and alcohol consumption is currently exhibiting signs of moderation. In contrast to this, the use of mood-changing pills is on the rise and recorded drug-caused deaths are once again increasing.

The taste for luxury and intoxicating substances such as coffee, tobacco, and alcohol has been cultivated in Western countries for hundreds of years: "Pleasures which were once exciting in their novelty have become part of common everyday life" (Schivelbusch, 1983, p. 235). Drugs such as opium, heroin, and hashish were excluded from mass consumption; even today, their use is limited to subcultures. In contrast, consumption of tranquillizers is widespread, although they are usually considered to be medications. The above-mentioned items, different as they may be, have in common their intoxicating qualities and their potentially harmful effects on health. Both congruent and disparate developmental tendencies regarding consumption of these substances have been registered during the last few decades.

About 400 years ago, coffee was imported from Arabia as a luxury product. Consumption remained a privilege for a long time, due to high prices and official restrictions; these barriers eventually disappeared. Table 1 shows a nearly continuous increase in consumption of coffee starting in 1850, with peaks in the years 1900–1910 and 1930–1938. During the latter period 40 to 50 litres per capita were being drunk annually.

In the immediate postwar period, coffee was almost prohibitively expensive, so many took to coffee substitutes. During the economic boom, this reason for doing without coffee faded. Coffee consumption in 1979 was more than 10 times that of 1950. The amount being imported confirms an unbroken upward trend: 4.7 million tons of coffee were imported in 1980, and 6.3 million tons in 1987 (Statistisches Bundesamt, 1981, 1988).

Coffee has joined beer as Germany's national drink (a consistency of preference which seems to be at least 200 years old; even then the tendency toward excessive beer and coffee consumption was subject of caricatures). Of the 628 litres of liquid drunk per capita in the Federal Republic in 1986, 170 litres were coffee and 146 litres beer. Other drinks – for example, tea (26 litres) and wine (19 litres) – ran far behind (IFO-Schnelldienst, 1988).

In the area of tobacco consumption, cigarettes, with their more-then-century-old tradition, were no more popular in the 1920s and 1930s than were pipes or cigars. Their share in total tobacco consumption now amounts to over 90%, which is why polls and surveys concentrate mainly on cigarette consumption.

Between 1950 and 1976, the number of cigarettes consumed per "potential smoker" (i.e., those over 15 years old) had quadrupled, and has remained about level since then. A notable slump in 1982 is traced back to those smokers who – following a drastic tobacco-tax hike – started rolling their own cigarettes (see table 2) (Kirchgässler, 1987). Long-term variation in the total population of smokers was slight: 18.9 million in 1960, as opposed to 18.4 million in 1979. This leads to the conclusion that the number of intensive, or addictive, users increased (see table 3). The proportion of female smokers rose from 29% in 1960 to 44% in 1979, while the proportion of male smokers fell from 71% to 56%. The consistent total population of smokers is therefore traceable to the increase in women smokers. Reasons for this development are seen in changing living and working conditions: "In advanced countries, smoking . . . is no longer associated with certain situations of male life, nor with social institutions reserved mainly for men; women are more or less subject to the same career-caused demands and burdens and turn to the same forms of compensation, stimulation, and relaxation as men do" (Hess, 1987, pp. 136).

Developments in youthful smoking habits took a turn between 1971 and 1982 toward an increase in "real non-smokers" and a decrease in "occasional smokers" (see table 6). Projections of future consumption patterns from current youthful smoking behaviour point toward an evening of the gender proportions among smokers, as well as an increase of consumption per smoker and a higher proportion of smokers in the lower classes than in the higher ones (Hess, 1987). A drastic slump in consumption as a result of medical warnings is not to be expected, even if pertinent publications make an impact on awareness. Nowadays, smokers choose light brands, and non-smokers have begun to defend themselves against the annoyance of tobacco smoke.

Similar developmental patterns can be ascertained for alcohol. In the immediate postwar period consumption was highly restricted due to the food shortage. Liquor distilling was outlawed up to 1956, but was performed illegally, as liquor fetched record prices on the black market and was considered, along with cigarettes, the hardest form of currency. Consumption of alcoholic drinks quadrupled between 1950 and 1976. Since then, a slight decrease can be distinguished, affecting not only beer, but also hard liquors and wine (table 2) (Statistisches Bundesamt, 1987).

National data do not regularly cover alcohol consumption in different age brackets or social groups, nor does comparison of field and representative surveys easily lend itself to conclusions. The number of tee-totallers or near-tee-totallers seems to have grown a little over the past 15 years, and the number of heavy drinkers seems to have somewhat decreased (see table 4). These tendencies hold true for men and women equally, despite repeated reference to the disproportionate increase in alcohol abuse by women. This development has also been observed among youths (Welz, 1983). It is quite possible that enlightenment campaigns on the dangers of alcohol, along with drunk-driving legislation (enacted in 1973), have contributed to moderation in alcohol consumption.

Over the past 30 years, tranquillizers have taken their place beside alcohol, which is "by far the oldest sedative" (Langbein et al., 1983). The word "tranquillizer" was first used by the West German media in 1956, the year of their introduction onto the German market. The term refers to a medication "which is supposed to provide the stressed, nervous participant in the German economic boom with inner peace and comfort" (*Der Spiegel*, Aug. 29, 1956). In the short period between 1965 and 1970, sales of Valium increased fourfold and total sales of mood-changing pills doubled. Between 1970 and 1980, consumption of medications of the benzodiazepine group, which comprise fear and tension reducers, muscle relaxants, and consciousness clouders, doubled (Langbein et al., 1983; Wolffersdorff-Ehlert, 1985).

Changing tendencies in the consumer structure cannot be discerned from available data. Particular target groups for treatment with mood-altering medication are children, women, and old people. According to recent surveys, anti-depressants are prescribed less often for girls up to 12 years of age than for boys, while young women in the 12–20 age bracket receive 17% more tranquillizers and neuroleptics than do young men of the same age. Seventy percent of all sedatives are prescribed for female patients, and 48% of all sleeping pills and sedatives for old people (i.e., mostly for old women) (Russland & Plogstedt, 1987). While men tend to take tranquillizers to relieve job-related stress, women use them as an inconspicuous drug which corresponds to their more dependent way of life.

Consumption of intoxicating drugs experienced an upswing in the protest culture of the 1960s. Experiments with hashish, marijuana, and LSD were linked with individual conceptions of liberation and with system-changing theories. As early as the beginning of the 1970s, the political scene began to put more distance between itself and the drug scene, which gradually began to associate with the criminal milieu. The switch from "soft" drugs (hashish and marijuana) to "hard" drugs (especially heroin, but also cocaine and opium), was first observed in the United States, and took place in the Federal Republic during the mid-1970s, leading to a jump in drug-caused deaths (see table 5). After years out of the public eye, drug deaths reached a recorded peak of 662 in 1988 (Frankfurter Rundschau, Jan. 4, 1989). The question remains whether they were caused by an increase in hard-drug consumption, by an increase in new users, or by lapsed ex-addicts.

In general, it can be claimed heightened health-consciousness has led to more moderate use of luxury and intoxicating substances. On the other hand, opposing trends can be found among groups with difficult life situations.

Karin Stiehr

References

Hess, Henner
1987 *Rauchen*. Frankfurt/New York: Campus.

IFO-Institut München, ed.
1988 *IFO-Schnelldienst*, no. 2.

Kirchgässler, K.-U.
1987 *Social Class Differences and Health Status in the Federal Republic of Germany: A Time-Serial Analysis*. Paper prepared for a WHO Conference on Social Equity and Health, Lisbon, 28-30 September 1987.

Kommission der Europäischen Gemeinschaften, ed.
1982 *Daten und Fakten zur Entwicklung des Rauchens in Mitgliedsländern der Europäischen Gemeinschaften*. Brüssel/Luxemburg.

Langbein, Kurt, et al.
1983 *Bittere Pillen*. Köln: Kiepenheuer und Witsch.

Noelle-Neumann, Elisabeth, and Edgar Piel, eds.
1983 *Allensbacher Jahrbuch der Demoskopie 1978-1983*. München/New York/London/Paris: Saur.

Rußland, Rita, and Sibylle Plogstedt
1986 *Sucht - Alkohol und Medikamente in der Arbeitswelt*. Frankfurt/Main: Fischer.

Schivelbusch, Wolfgang
1983 *Das Paradies, der Geschmack und die Vernunft. Eine Geschichte der Genußmittel*. Frankfurt/Berlin/Wien: Ullstein.

Statistisches Bundesamt, ed.
1981 *Statistisches Jahrbuch 1981 für die Bundesrepublik Deutschland*. Stuttgart/Mainz: Kohlhammer.

–, ed.
1984 *Zur Situation der Jugend in der Bundesrepublik Deutschland*. Stuttgart/Mainz: Kohlhammer.

–, ed.
1987 *Datenreport 1987*. Bonn: Bundeszentrale für politische Bildung.

–, ed.
1988 *Statistisches Jahrbuch 1988 für die Bundesrepublik Deutschland*. Stuttgart/Mainz: Kohlhammer.

Teuteberg, Hans J.
1980 "Kaffeetrinken sozialgeschichtlich betrachtet." *Scripta Maercaturae. Zeitschrift für Wirtschafts- und Sozialgeschichte*, no. 1.

Welz, Rainer
1983 *Drogen, Alkohol und Suizid. Strukturelle und individuelle Aspekte abweichenden Verhaltens*. Stuttgart: Enke.

Wolffersdorf-Ehlert, Christian von
1985 "Drogen - Neugier, Krankheit und Geschäft." In Deutsches Jugendinstitut, ed., *Immer diese Jugend! Ein zeitgeschichtliches Mosaik*. München: Deutsches Jugendinstitut.

Table 1
Coffee consumption per capita and year 1850 - 1979

Year	Kilogram	Liter	Year	Kilogram	Liter
1850	0.692	17.3	1925	0.958	24.0
1860	1.158	29.0	1930	1.575	39.4
1870	1.608	40.2	1938	1.917	47.9
1880	1.392	34.8	1950	0.508	12.7
1890	1.600	40.0	1960	2.864	71.6
1900	1.917	47.9	1970	4.057	101.4
1910	1.758	44.0	1979	5.607	140.2

Source: Teuteberg, 1980, p. 49.

Table 2
Alcohol and tobacco consumption in the Federal Republic of Germany 1950 - 1984

Year	Number of cigarettes per potential consumer (age > 15)	Liters of beer per potential consumer	Liters of hard liquor per potential consumer
1950	622	48	1.4
1960	1,619	120	2.4
1970	2,529	184	3.9
1975	2,566	188	3.9
1976	2,659	191	4.2
1977	2,363	187	3.7
1978	2,490	181	3.7
1979	2,501	179	4.2
1980	2,549	178	3.8
1981	2,538	178	3.4
1982	2,185	178	3.0
1983	2,303	177	2.9
1984	2,312	171	2.8

Source: Kirchgässler, 1987.

Table 3
Changes in smoking habits, according to gender

Year	Cigarette smokers (in million)		Proportion in potential smoker population (in %)		Proportions among cigarette smokers (in %)	
	Men	Women	Men	Women	Men	Women
1960	11.5	4.7	58	20	71.0	29.0
1965	12.1	4.9	58	20	71.2	28.8
1970	11.6	5.6	53	22	67.6	32.4
1975	9.8	7.5	44	29	56.6	43.4
1979	9.6	7.7	41	29	55.5	44.5

Source: Based on Merzdorf et. al., 1982, pp. 71, 203, cited in Hess, 1987, p. 137.

Table 4
Proportion of intensive users of mood-altering substances

According to own statement, drink (nearly) daily or fairly often	Total		Men		Women	
	1973	1981	1973	1981	1973	1981
Beer, wine, plus schnaps, liqueurs or other alcohol	26	20	31	23	22	16
Beer plus schnaps, liqueurs or other alcohol, but no wine	17	15	27	24	8	6
Wine and other alcoholic beverages, but no beer	14	11	6	5	21	16
Beer and wine, but no other alcoholic beverages	9	10	11	15	7	9
Only beer	8	10	10	15	6	6
Only wine	5	7	2	4	8	10
Schnaps or liqueurs, sometimes other alcohol, but never beer or wine	4	3	3	1	5	4
Only other alcohol	2	3	1	2	3	4
Never or only occasionally drink alcohol	15	21	9	11	20	29
Total	100	100	100	100	100	100

Source: Noelle-Neumann & Piel, 1983, p. 53.

Table 5
Drug-related deaths

Year	Drug-related deaths
1970	29
1971	67
1972	104
1973	126
1974	147
1975	242
1976	386
1977	406
1978	456
1979	625
1980	494
1981	360

Source: Wetz, 1983, p. 81.

Table 6
Spread of smoking habit among the 14- to 25-year-olds: 1971-1982

Item	1971	1973	1976	1979	1982
Never smoke	16	14	16	23	26
Triers, non-smokers	27	28	31	25	27
Occasional smokers	22	23	21	15	11
Steady smokers	35	35	32	37	36

Source: Hess, 1987, p. 139.

14. Leisure

14.1 Amount and Use of Free Time

In the course of postwar development in the Federal Republic of Germany, "leisure time" has gained importance: not only have working hours decreased and net free time increased, but popular attitudes also exhibit a trend away from a work orientation and toward leisure time.

Increase in Net Leisure Time

There has been a clear increase in average net leisure time in West Germany over the past 40 years. Net leisure time is defined as that segment of time dedicated neither to paid work, nor to personal care (sleep and other physical necessities), nor to so-called semi-leisure time, determined by family and social duties (housework, child care) (Ballerstedt & Glatzer, 1979). Table 1 illustrates the trend toward more and more leisure time: daily free time amounted to an average of 5 hours and 41 minutes in 1964, rising to 6 hours and 53 minutes ten years later, and to 7 hours 29 minutes in 1980.

Decreased Working Time

Important factors for this expansion of free time are the reduction in time per day devoted to paid work and housework, and the fact that a smaller proportion of the population participates in the working world.

As opposed to the "housework" factor, which is difficult to measure accurately (because, for example, of overlapping of housework and leisure time), the "paid work" factor can be examined by means of clear-cut, measurable evidence. It can thereby be ascertained that the average time devoted to paid work in the Federal Republic has been on a constant decline over the past 40 years. The average work week, as set forth in collective labour agreements, went from 44 hours in 1960 to

39.8 hours in 1985. The net working week of German workers (wage or salaried workers), however, has always remained shorter than working hours as regulated in the collective agreements. In 1960, a worker worked 38.8 hours per week. By 1985, the weekly working time had been reduced by 7.2 hours, to 31.6 hours (see table 2). It should be kept in mind that working time can be very unevenly distributed among workers: in 1985, 4.3 million workers (16.1%) still normally spent 42 hours or more per week at their place of work. On the other hand, 7.5% had a work week of less than 21 hours (Statistisches Bundesamt, 1987).

Per-capita annual work time dropped by a total of 400 hours between 1960 and 1985, declining by approximately one-fifth (from about 2,000 to 1,600; see table 2).

A notable role in the reduction in annual work time and the increase of free time is played by the annual paid vacation. According to the *Bundesurlaubsgesetz* (Federal Vacation Act), each worker has the right to a minimum vacation of 18 working days (three weeks). In fact, much more vacation time is negotiated in collective labour agreements. Between 1960 and 1985, the length of agreement-regulated vacations for all workers rose from an average of 17 to an average of 30 working days (table 2).

Evaluation of Working and Leisure Time

The growing importance of leisure time is illustrated by, for example, the fact that West Germans spend increasing amounts of money on leisure activities. Expenditures for leisure goods and vacations came to 94 DM monthly for a middle-income four-person worker's household in 1965, rising to as much as 465 DM in 1985, an increase of 394%. In comparison, total expenditures for private consumption rose by only 225% between 1965 and 1985. Thus, the proportion of the total private consumer goods consumed by a middle-income four-person workers' household on leisure goods and vacations rose from 10.7% in 1965 to 16.2% in 1985 (Statistisches Bundesamt, 1987). This places the leisure business among the faster-growing sectors in the Federal Republic.

This behaviour reflects a transformation of attitude toward work and leisure: "Work loses its value compared with its counterpart, leisure" (Meulemann, 1982, p. 6). This change is confirmed by surveys which show that an increasing proportion of the population agree with the statement "It would be best to live without having to work" (from 13% in 1952 to 20% in 1981). In response to a question comparing "the hours you work with the hours you do not work," the proportion of those who prefer non-working time rose from 33% to 47% between 1962 and 1980 (Meulemann, 1982). The heightened value accorded to leisure time cannot simply be identified with a slackening commitment to the work ethic:

The demand for more leisure time and free time for the family thus does not mean that people are turning away from work but that their attraction to the professional work system is greater than ever before. The higher value of leisure results from the higher value of work. Similarly, the higher value of reduced working time results from the higher and expanding value of participation in work. Values that initially seem to be contradictory are really complementary. (Hondrich, 1989, p.143; see also 17.4, "Values"; for use of free time, see 13.4, "Time Use")

Barbara Wörndl

References

Ballerstedt, Eike, and Wolfgang Glatzer
1979 *Soziologischer Almanach*. Frankfurt am Main/New York: Campus.

Hondrich, Karl-Otto
1989 "Values in Western Societies. The Last Thirty Years." In Burkhard Strümpel, *Industrial Societies after the Stagnating of the 1970's. Taking Stock from an Interdisciplinary Perspective*. Berlin/New York: de Gruyter.

Institut der Deutschen Wirtschaft, ed.
1986 *Zahlen zur wirtschaftlichen Entwicklung der Bundesrepublik Deutschland*. Köln: Deutscher Instituts-Verlag.

Lakemann, Ulrich
1984 *Das Aktivitätsspektrum privater Haushalte in der Bundesrepublik 1950 bis 1980: Zeitliche und inhaltliche Veränderungen von Erwerbstätigkeiten, unbezahlte Arbeiten und Freizeitaktivitäten*. Wissenschaftszentrum Berlin.

Meulemann, Heiner
1982 *Value Change in West Germany, 1950-1980: Integrating the Empirical Evidence*. Paper presented at the 10th World Congress of Sociology, August 16-21, 1982, Mexico City.

Myrell, Günter, ed.
1985 *Arbeit, Arbeit über alles? Arbeit und Freizeit im Umbruch*. Köln: VGS.

Opaschowski, Horst W.
1982 *Freizeit im Wertewandel*. Hamburg.

–
n.d. "Probleme im Umgang mit der Freizeit." In B.A.T.-Freizeitforschungsinstitut, ed., *Schriftenreihe zur Freizeitforschung*. Vol. 1. Hamburg.

Presse- und Informationsamt der Bundesregierung, ed.
1982 *Gesellschaftliche Daten*. Freiburg.

Statistisches Bundesamt, ed.
1987 *Datenreport 1987*. Bonn: Bundeszentrale für politische Bildung.

Table 1
"Objective" measurement, supported by Stichday surveys - time budget for average work day (Monday-Saturday), general task types in hours and minutes

Population 14 years and older	Work time	Of that		Leisure time	Of that		Remainder[1] (eating and sleep)
		job-related work + way to work	housework incl. shopping		at home	away from home	
Employed and non-employed:							
1964 (spring)	7:53	4:48	3:05	5:41	3:38	2:02	10:26
1970 (fall)	7:40	4:45	2:55	6:15	4:31	1:45	10:05
1974 (Nov.)	6:48	4:12	2:36	6:53	5:01	1:52	10:18
1980 (Nov.)	6:26	3:54	2:32	7:29	5:10	2:19	10:05

1. Day-schedule surveys were chronologically limited to time between 5:30 and midnight. Nighttime, from midnight to 5:30, is to be found in the "remainder" category (sleep).

Source: Institut Infratest, cited in Presse- und Informationsamt der Bundesregierung, 1982, p. 157.

Table 2
Working time (in %)

Year	Negotiated terms		Effective annual working time	Effective work week
	Yearly vacation	Working week		
1960-64	16.7	44.0	2,020.1	38.8
1965-69	19.5	42.3	1,932.0	37.2
1970	21.2	41.5	1,885.0	36.3
1972	22.3	41.0	1,831.7	35.2
1973	23.0	40.9	1,804.4	34.7
1974	23.7	40.7	1,776.4	34.2
1975	24.3	40.3	1,736.5	33.4
1976	24.7	40.3	1,770.2	34.0
1977	25.2	40.2	1,741.0	33.5
1978	25.9	40.2	1,717.0	33.0
1979	26.7	40.2	1,699.0	32.7
1980	27.3	40.1	1,688.3	32.5
1981	28.0	40.1	1,672.1	32.2
1982	28.8	40.0	1,677.5	32.3
1983	29.6	40.0	1,671.3	32.1
1984[1]	29.9	40.0	1,662.7	32.0
1985[1]	30.1	39.8	1,641.6	31.6

Components of annual work time per employed person in total economy.

1. Provisional results.

Source: Institut für Arbeitsmarkt- und Berufsforschung: IW-Berechnungen cited in, Institut der Deutschen Wirtschaft, 1986.

14.2 Vacation Patterns

Vacation is of particular importance as leisure time. An increasing proportion of the West German population spend their vacation travelling. The predominant tendency is toward several trips per year, including trips to foreign countries. Rest-cure vacations and visits to relatives have lost popularity as vacation types, whereas beachside and recreational vacations, as well as educational, health, and sport vacations, are becoming increasingly attractive.

Travel Intensity, Frequency, and Expenditures, Length of Vacation

Statistics on travel intensity illustrate the growing importance of travel for Germans. The proportion of travelling vacationers among the population rose continuously, from 24% in 1954 to 57.7% in 1980, and then remained level, after a slight, economically caused decline (see table 1).

The growing importance of travel for West Germans is also reflected in the development of travel expenditures. Between 1960 and 1986, the number of those spending between 1,000 and 1,500 DM annually for travel rose notably, while the number of those spending under 600 DM fell (see table 2).

Vacation length has also been extended over the last 20 years. The proportion of those travelling for up to eight days has decreased by half since 1960 (from 22% to 11% in 1986). Those travelling for 9 to 15 days increased by nearly 10% (from 35% to 44%). The frequency of vacation trips lasting 16 days or more, on the other hand, hardly changed (see table 3). Furthermore, a tendency toward taking not just one, but several vacation trips per year was distinguishable.

In many cases, annual vacation trips are also supplemented by weekend and short vacation trips (under six days). The ability to take short trips is, however, more highly dependent upon economic situation and income than is the case with longer vacation trips. Although the short trips were viewed by the tourism industry as a good prospect in the early 1980s, the last few years have been characterized by stagnation at best, and the number of these trips is on the decline. In the 1984 – 1986 period, weekend and short trips suffered an average decrease of 21% (see table 4).

Foreign and Domestic Trips

Germans' wanderlust stands in conjunction with a shift in the relationship between foreign and domestic travelling. In 1954, most travellers (85%) remained within Germany. As early as 1968, the number of foreign and domestic trips was equal. By 1986, foreign trips made up two-thirds of all travel (see table 5). Germans' favourite vacation spots have long been Austria and Italy, followed by Spain, Yugoslavia, France, and Switzerland. Only a negligible portion of trips are to beyond Europe.

Vacation Types and Planning

Rest cures and recreational and beachside vacations have been the favourite types for the past 15 years, and are responsible for two-thirds of all trips. The popularity of rest cures has, however, decreased in favour of recreational and beachside vacations. Interest in educational and cultural-study trips, as well as in health and sport vacations, has increased, while visits to relatives and acquaintances have declined (see table 6).

Among types of accommodation, the "classic" hostelry (hotel, guest houses, and boarding rooms) has retained its strong position since 1954. Staying at the homes of acquaintances and relatives declined (from 43% in 1954 to 9% in 1986). On the other hand, lodgings such as holiday apartments, bungalows, and so on enjoyed burgeoning popularity. This could be due to the fact that these types of accommodations not only offer more individual freedom, but are less expensive (see table 7).

The preferred means of travel are the automobile and the airplane (in 1986, 62% and 19% respectively). These two forms of transportation have taken the place of the bus and the train, which were used 73% of the time in 1954, and are used only 19% of the time nowadays (see table 8).

Barbara Wörndl

References

Axel Springer Verlag AG, Marketing Anzeigen, Märkte
1987 *Urlaubsreisen. Information für die Werbeplanung*. Hamburg.

Ballerstedt, Eike, and Wolfgang Glatzer
1979 *Soziologischer Almanach*. Frankfurt am Main/New York: Campus.

Dudler, Franz
1987 "Urlaubsreisen 1954-1986. 33 Jahre Erfassung des touristischen Verhaltens der Deutschen durch soziologische Stichprobenerhebung." Studienkreis für Tourismus e.V. Starnberg, ed., Starnberg.

Institut für Demoskopie Allensbach, ed.
1986 "Reisen macht süchtig." *Allensbacher Berichte*, no. 7.

Presse- und Informationsamt der Bundesregierung, ed.
1982 *Gesellschaftliche Daten 1982*. Freiburg.

Statistisches Bundesamt, ed.
1985 *Datenreport 1985*. Bonn: Bundeszentrale für politische Bildung.

Table 1
Travel intensity 1954 - 1986 (in %)

Year	Proportion of travellers
1954*	24.0
1960*	28.0
1970	41.6
1980	57.7
1982	55.0
1984	55.3
1985	57.1
1986	57.0

Source: * Urlaubsreisen 1968, DIVO - Institut; Reiseanalysen des Studien - kreises für Tourismus, durchgeführt von Infratest, Marplan, GfK Marktb - forschung, cited in Dundler, 1987.

Table 2
Total travel expenses (preparation, transportation, lodgings, food, and side expenses) per person for the main vacation trip 1960 -1986 (in %)

Travel expenses	1960*	1970	1980	1982	1984	1986
Under DM 600	57	72	22	27	21	23
DM 600-1,000	26	20	26	19	24	24
DM 1,000-1,500	11	8	25	17	21	22
DM 1,500 and more	-	-	24	19	27	28
No data	6	-	3	18	7	3
Total	100	100	100	100	100	100

Source: * Urlaubsreisen 1968, DIVO-Institut; Reiseanalysen des Studienkreises für Tourismus, durchgeführt von Infratest, Marplan, GfK Marktforschung, cited in Dundler, 1987.

Table 3
Length of annual (i.e., main) vacation trips 1960 - 1986 (in %)

Length of trips	1960*	1970	1980	1982	1984	1986
Up to 8 days	22	8	8	11	10	11
9-15 days	35	35	40	40	42	44
16-22 days	27	39	35	34	34	30
23 days or more	16	18	17	15	14	15
Total	100	100	100	100	100	100

Source: * Urlaubsreisen 1968, DIVO-Institut; Reiseanalysen des Studienkreises für Tourismus, durchgeführt von Infratest, Marplan, GfK Marktforschung, cited in Dundler, 1987.

Table 4
Weekend or short trips (under 6 days)

Weekend/short trips in last 12 months, total	1980	1981	1983	1984	1985	1986
In million	23.5	26.1	27.0	27.6	24.1	21.6
In percent	49.0	54.0	55.0	56.0	49.0	44.0

Source: AWA, cited in Märkte, Information für die Marktplanung, 1987, p. 24.

Table 5
Domestic versus foreign vacations (main vacation trips) 1954 - 1986

Year	Domestic		Foreign	
	%	Million	%	Million
1954*	85	7.9	15	1.4
1955*	69	8.1	31	3.7
1958*	49	8.2	51	8.6
1970	46	8.5	54	10.0
1980	38	10.2	62	16.8
1982	39	10.2	61	16.2
1984	34	9.2	66	17.5
1986	34	9.3	66	18.3

Source: * Urlaubsreisen 1968, DIVO-Institut; Reiseanalysen des Studienkreises für Tourismus, durchgeführt von Infratest, Marplan, GfK Marktforschung, cited in Dundler, 1987.

Table 6
Main vacation types 1974 - 1986 (in %)

Vacation types	1974	1980	1982	1983	1984	1985	1986
Recreational	12	15	19	28	28	23	21
Rest or restcure	67	67	20	21	22	28	25
Beachside	*	*	22	19	22	19	24
Visiting relatives/friends	12	9	15	10	9	9	8
Health-oriented	2	2	7	7	6	6	6
Educational	4	4	6	7	6	7	9
Sport-oriented	3	3	4	4	5	5	6
No data	*	*	6	2	-	2	-

* Statement change.

Source: Reiseanalysen des Studienkreises für Tourismus, durchgeführt von Infratest, Marplan, GfK Marktforschung, cited in Dundler, 1987.

Table 7
Lodging types during main annual vacation 1954 - 1986 (in %)

Lodging	1954*	1979	1980	1982	1984	1986
Hotel	14	21	25	24	29	27
Guest house	15	21	23	22	19	18
Private room	17	20	11	10	8	9
Staying with relatives	43	17	12	13	10	9
Camping holiday	5	9	10	11	12	11
apts./bungalows						
- rented	-	7	10	10	14	17
- owned	-	-	1	4	4	4
Other	6	5	9	10	4	5
Total	100	100	100	100	100	100

Source: * Urlaubsreisen 1968, DIVO-Institut; Reiseanalysen des Studienkreises für Tourismus, durchgeführt von Infratest, Marplan, GfK Marktforschung, cited in Dundler, 1987.

Table 8
Travel means on main annual vacation trips 1954 - 1986 (in %)

Travel means	1954*	1960*	1970	1980	1982	1984	1986
Car	19	38	61	59	59	60	62
Train	56	42	24	16	14	11	9
Bus	17	16	7	8	9	8	10
Airplane	0	1	8	16	16	18	19
Other	8	3	0	1	2	3	0
Total	100	100	100	100	100	100	100

Source: * Urlaubsreisen 1968, DIVO-Institut; Reiseanalysen des Studienkreises für Tourismus, durchgeführt von Infratest, Marplan, GfK Marktforschung, cited in Dundler, 1987.

14.3 Athletics and Sports

Over the past 40 years, sports have developed into one of the most important leisure activities for West Germans. Up to the 1960s, sport activities were almost exclusively limited to clubs. Since then, there has been a strong tendency to engage in sports independently of clubs. New kinds of sport activity, such as jogging, windsurfing, and so on, have become popular; some sports that used to be considered élite have evolved into mass sport activities.

Participatory Sports

After World War II, a certain disdain for sports reigned in the Federal Republic, a consequence of National Socialism's abuse of sports for political purposes. It did not take long for this negative attitude to fade. Active and passive participation in sport activities increased. The proportion of people regularly or occasionally engaging in sports has risen markedly (from 23% in 1950 to 52% in 1982; see table 1), as have the number of members of sport clubs. The Deutsche Sportbund (DSB, German Sport Affiliation) – an umbrella organization for the various sport clubs – has had a strong membership influx since the 1950s. While approximately 3 million Germans belonged to the DSB in 1950, nearly 18 million did so by 1987 (see table 2). This means that about 30% of the population are in organized sport associations. The number of clubs has nearly doubled over the last 20 years (from just under 30,000 to around 60,000). At the same time, the internal structure of the clubs has changed. While sports used to be the domain of men, women have increasingly become members: in 1950, the ratio of women to men was one to eight; in 1987, one-third of members were women. Nor is sport activity a privilege of the young any longer; more and more older people are members of sport clubs.

Judging by membership statistics, soccer and gymnastics have maintained their top positions and are considered the classic fields of *Breitensport* (popular mass sports, practised by, or at least an object of interest among, young and old). It is notable that in the last 25 years, some sports which had had a certain aura of exclusivity now comprise some of the largest associations: after soccer and gymnastics, the third-largest club in the DSB is devoted to tennis; shooting places fourth, and horseback riding tenth. The number of tennis players in clubs has multiplied eightfold since the 1960s (1.8 million in 1986), shooting hobbyists tenfold (1.2 million in 1986), and, equestrians six fold (510,000 in 1986). The so-called élite sports have, in other words, evolved into mass sports.

It can generally be assumed that the sport clubs owe their strong influx of members to growing health-consciousness in the population, induced in part by the government's fitness campaign ("*Trimm-Dich*" – "slim-down"). Sports are no longer limited to the high-performance sports, but rather have increasingly become health activities. This is evidenced by the fact that swimming has developed from a purely summertime activity into a year-round pursuit, and that sport clubs' events such as "people's hikes," bicycle rides, skiing, and swimming enjoy burgeoning popularity (see table 3).

No exact statements can be made about the number of passive participants in sport events – attendance at events and TV-watchers who follow the events in their home. It is, however, certain that Germans' growing enthusiasm for sport has also encouraged these forms of participation.

Parasporting Activities

The increasing importance of athletic activities among Germans has contributed to the development of new types of sports. Jogging, aerobics, windsurfing, fitness training, and body-building are increasing in popularity, especially among youth. These types of activity also indicate a certain tendency toward individualization. While in the 1960s, sports was mainly limited to clubs, these new types of sports are usually pursued independent of clubs. The new types of acitivities, characterized by a low degree of obligation to an organization, are now leading once-sedentary groups to engage in sports.

Barbara Wörndl

References

Deutscher Sportbund, ed.
1984 *3. Memorandum zum Goldenen Plan*. Frankfurt am Main.

Mrazek, Joachim
1987 "Sportangebote und ihre Organisation in der Wahrnehmung Aktiver." In Jürgen Friedrichs, ed., *23. Deutscher Soziologentag 1986. Sections- und Ad-hoc-Gruppen*. Opladen: Westdeutscher Verlag.

Noelle-Neumann, Elisabeth, ed.
1983 *Allensbacher Jahrbuch der Demoskopie, 1978-1983*. München/New York/London/Paris: Saur.

–, ed.
1981 *The Germans. Public Opinion Polls, 1967-1980*. Westport, Conn./London: Greenwood.

Presse- und Informationsamt der Bundesregierung, ed.
1982 *Gesellschaftliche Daten 1982*. Freiburg.

Rythlewski, Ralf, and Manfred Opp de Hipt
1987 *Die Bundesrepublik Deutschland in Zahlen 1945/49-1980*. München: Beck.

Statistisches Bundesamt, ed.
1987 *Datenreport 1987*. Bonn: Bundeszentrale für politische Bildung.

–, ed.
1988 *Statistisches Jahrbuch 1988*. Stuttgart/Mainz: Kohlhammer.

Table 1
Sport participants (in %)

Year	Regularly	Occasionally	Never
1950	9	14	77
1957	7	19	74
1973	18	26	56
1975	21	29	50
1976	23	27	50
1982	20	32	48

2,000 persons 16 years and older in West Germany and West Berlin.

Source: Noelle-Neumann, 1983, p. 71.

Table 2
Members of German Sport League (in %)

Year	Members	
	Total	Female
1950	3,204,005	-
1960	4,895,311	20
1970	8,266,955	27
1980	14,441,218	34
1987	17,520,409	36

Source: Rytlewski & Opp de Hipt, 1987, p. 169;
Statistisches Bundesamt, 1987, p. 383.

Table 3
German Sport League: people's hikes, bicycling, skiing and swimming

Year	Clubs	Events[1]	Participants[2]
1970	365	365	1,078,000
1975	1,463	1,361	7,011,000
1980	1,870	1,843	9,214,277
1982	1,866	1,932	9,383,167
1983	1,877	1,951	9,582,573
1984	1,883	1,942	9,723,464
1985	1,854	1,925	9,734,455

1. People's hikes, bicycling, skiing and swimming.
2. Multiple census of persons taking part in several events.

Source: Deutscher Volkssportverband e.V., Altötting, cited in
Statistisches Bundesamt, 1986, p. 381.

14.4 Cultural Activities

The expansion of leisure time has contributed – though less so than for sports – to intensified cultural activity by Germans. One of the most striking developments of the postwar period is the fact that so-called mass-communications media have edged out the classic cultural institutions. In other words, the spread of television is most likely responsible for the dwindling interest in the cinema and the theatre. Traditional cultural institutions such as museums, as well as conventional types of education and entertainment such as book-reading, have retained and even heightened their popularity.

Theatre

Theatre attendance has been on an overall decline for the past 30 years in West Germany. In 1954, there were nearly 18 million theatre-goers, and this number continued to grow into the mid-1960s, but it fell to only 16 million in 1986. Opera and ballet performances were constantly at the top of the popularity scale, with about 40% of the audience, followed by plays, operettas, and musicals. Only a very small group was interested in concerts.

Between 1954 and 1986, the cultural program in the theatrical sector was vigorously expanded. The number of theatre buildings grew year by year, increasing by over one-half since 1954 (see table 1). The number of stage personnel have increased heavily over the past 20 years. The proportion of expenses compensated for by ticket sales has shrunk, so that theatrical enterprises are dependent on municipal and state subsidies to cover operating costs.

Cinema

The number of movie-goers has also declined. In contrast to the theatrical sector, this has led to a real "cinema extinction." Up to the late 1950s, movies enjoyed great popularity among West Germans. The highest number of movie-goers was registered between 1954 and 1958 (more than 700 million yearly). During this time, Germans went to the movies an average of 14–15 times yearly. Since the 1960s, however, the cinema sector has been on a continuous downhill slide. Attendance was down to 167 million by 1970. With the exception of the years 1976–1980, during which time attendance rose, these numbers have continued to drop (table 1). Simultaneously, the number of movie theatres fell dramatically between 1958 and 1986 (from approximately 7,000 to about 3,000).

Museums

The number of museums has increased nearly sixfold since 1954 (from 306 in 1954 to 1,763 in 1986), and the number of visitors has multiplied by ten (6 million in 1954, 62 million in 1986; table 1). Interest in private collections has also undergone a marked increase over the past 20 years. Recently, *Heimatmuseen* (museums dedicated to national customs, costumes, etc.) have been the most popular with an attendance of 13 million, followed by art museums with 12 million.

Television and Radio

The drastic collapse of cinemas could be the result of the rapid spread of radio and, especially, television. There is now scarcely a home without one or the other. Radio was already fairly widespread in the 1950s (79 out of 100 households in 1956) and quickly approached the 100% mark. Television was still very rare in 1956 – only four of 100 households had one. In the 1960s, TV began its march of triumph, reaching nearly 100% saturation by the 1980s (see table 2). Music always dominated radio programming. TV programming in 1986 featured movies, TV movies, and documentaries (about 20%); entertainment (shows, etc.), theatre, and music (10.8%); and current-events programs (10.3%).

Singing, Reading

Cultural interests which – in contrast to movies and the theatre – require more active participation were not affected by television. Membership in singing clubs will be used here as one example among many. The Deutscher Sängerbund (German Singers' League) has registered an overall increase in members since the 1960s (see table 3).

Despite changes in ways and habits of acquiring information, books have retained their importance as a source of knowledge and entertainment, as the high number (though the early 1980s saw a drop) of book titles published shows. In 1986, there were 63,679 first and subsequent title printings in West Germany, versus 22,524 in 1960; production of first printings alone has increased by 155% over this period (see table 4). Divided by subject, fiction is the most popular.

Though reading for entertainment enjoys priority among Germans, there has been a growing interest in educational (or informative) reading since the mid-1970s (see table 5).

Barbara Wörndl

References

Noelle-Neumann, Elisabeth, ed.
1983 *Allensbacher Jahrbuch der Demoskopie, 1978-1983*. München/New York/London: Saur.

Presse- und Informationsamt der Bundesregierung, ed.
1982 *Gesellschaftliche Daten 1982*. Freiburg.

Statistisches Bundesamt, ed.
1987 *Datenreport 1987*. Bonn: Bundeszentrale für politische Bildung.

–, ed.
1961 *Statistisches Jahrbuch 1961*. Stuttgart/Mainz: Kohlhammer.

–, ed.
1973 *Statistisches Jahrbuch 1973*. Stuttgart/Mainz: Kohlhammer.

–, ed.
1988 *Statistisches Jahrbuch 1988*. Stuttgart/Mainz: Kohlhammer.

Table 1
Theaters, movie-theaters, museums,and visitors (in million)

Year	Theaters a)		Movie-theaters b)		Museums c)	
	Number	Visitors	Number	Visitors	Number	Visitors d)
1954	114	17.964	-	736 e)	306 e)	6.078 f)
1955	121 e)	18.388 e)	-	766 e)	-	-
1958	129	19.723	6,956	750 e)	346	7.905
1963	156	19.755	5,964	377	431	10.303
1966	175	19.781	4,784	280	484	12.171
1970	194	17.655	3,446	167	501	13.926
1976	211	17.487	3,092	115	658	25.700
1980	243	17.272	3.354	144	805	35.300
1986	280	16.009	3,262	105	1,763	62.432

a) Sites of public theatrical presentations incl. concert halls and outdoor theaters. The years given refer to theatrical seasons (for example 1960=season 1960/61). There also exist institutionalized private theaters which in 1963 registered 5.136 mill. spectators in 77 theaters, and in 1970 4.238 mill. spectators in 71 theaters.
b) Number of movie houses does not include travelling movie shows or drive-in movie theaters, but number of visitors includes visitors to travelling movie shows and drive-in movies.
c) Only museums in communities with over 20,000 residents.
d) Not all museums count their visitors, therefore, the numbers given here are below actual attendance numbers.
e) Excluding the Saarland.
f) Excluding Baden-Württemberg, Bavaria and the Saarland.

Sources: Presse- und Informationsamt der Bundesregierung, Gesellschaftliche Daten 1979, pp. 298; 1982, pp. 324; Deutscher Städtetag, Statistisches Jahrbuch Deutscher Gemeinden 1956, pp. 118, 120; Stat. Jb. BRD, 1960, tab. IV.19, tab. IV.20, tab.IV.21; 1965, tab.IV.18, tab. IV.19; 1968, tab. IV.17, tab.IV.18, tab.IV.19; 1972, tab. IV.5, tab. IV.6; 1982, tab. 16.22; Stat. Jahrbuch BRD, 1988, pp. 378-379, p. 381, cited in Rytlewski; Opp de Hipt, 1987, p. 228; Statistisches Bundesamt, 1988.

Table 2
Permits for possession of radios and televisions[1]

Year	Radios		Televisions	
	Number in 1,000	Saturation[2] in percent	Number in 1,000	Saturation[2] in percent
1946	5,442	-	-	-
1950	9,018	54	-	-
1954	12,800	-	84	-
1956	13,811	79	682	4
1970	19,622	91	16,675	77
1980	23,323	96	21,190	87
1987	26,391	-	23,378	-

1. As of 31 Dec. From 1976 to 1979, the registered radios were counted instead of the registered listeners.
2. Number of permits per 100 households.

Sources: Bundesminister für das Post- und Fernmeldewesen, Geschäftsbericht der Deutschen Bundespost 1975, pp. 8-9; Mitteilungen des Bundesministeriums; Stat. Jb. BRD, 1977, tab. 16.16; 1979, tab. 16.19; 1981, tab. 16.18; see also first chapter, tab. 3d); Stat. Jb. BRD, 1988, p. 376 cited in Rytlewski; Opp de Hipt, 1987, p. 227; Statistisches Bundesamt, 1988.

Table 3
Members in German Singers' League

Year	1,000	In %	
	Total members	Singing members	Auxiliary members
July 1960	1,346	41.2	58.8
July 1964	1,435	38.4	61.6
June 1968	1,489	37.1	62.9
July 1972	1,488	36.3	63.7
July 1974	1,510	36.3	63.7
July 1976	1,563	37.3	62.7
July 1978	1,618	38.1	61.9
July 1980	1,658	38.1	61.9
July 1987	1,755	37.6	62.4

Source: Statistisches Bundesamt, cited in Presse- und Informationsamt der Bundesregierung, 1982, p. 325; Statistisches Bundesamt, 1988, p. 382.

Table 4
Book production (first and reprintings)

Year	Titles
1960	22,524
1970	47,096
1984	51,733
1985	57,733
1986	63,679

Source: Statistisches Bundesamt, 1961; 1973, p. 105; 1988, p. 381.

Table 5
Books read (in %)

Item	At least once weekly in leisure time as:							
	entertainment				education, self-education			
	1967	1973	1978	1981	1967	1973	1978	1981
Total population	44	44	43	41	23	26	27	28
Men	40	38	36	35	29	31	33	31
Women	47	48	50	47	18	21	23	26

2,000 persons aged 16 years and older in Federal Republic of Germany and West Berlin.

Source: Noelle-Neumann, 1983, p. 571.

15. Educational Attainment

15.1 General Education

In the Federal Republic of Germany there is a clear and distinct trend toward extending the period of learning and acquiring higher certificates of education. This trend manifests itself in increasing numbers of students in schools of higher education, as well as in drastically increasing numbers of students. Educational inequalities have been reduced as far as sex-specific, regional, and religious differences are concerned, whereas class-specific inequalities have remained more or less unchanged.

The expansion of the educational system and a growing rate of enrollment in institutions of higher education reflects a long-term process of modernization of society as a whole. Ascription as a mechanism of status distribution is increasingly replaced by achievement. Since the beginning of the 1960s, there has been a general trend toward acquisition of degrees of higher education. The distribution of 13-year-old students in different types of schools (see table 1) is one indication of this development. Between 1960 and 1987, the proportion of 13-year-olds who attended lower secondary school (*Hauptschule*) decreased from 70% to 34%, while the proportion of those attending intermediate secondary school (*Realschule*) increased from 11% to 27% and the proportion of those attending upper secondary school (*Gymnasium*) increased from 15% to 30%.

The structure of school-leavers has also changed (see table 2). Whereas in 1970 only 11% of all school-leavers had acquired some kind of higher-education matriculation certificate, the proportion reached 30% in 1987. At present only 35% of all students leave the school system having completed the compulsory school years, compared to 78% in 1962.

This dramatic change in educational behaviour is also obvious in the distribution of the entire population according to different degrees of education (see table 3). The total number of university students grew strongly between 1960 and 1989 (see table 4) from 247,000 to 1,510,000, and the number of students entering university each year rose from 51,000 to 253,000.

In 1987, about 50% of all university students were enrolled in the humanities, law, economics, and the social sciences, 30% in natural sciences or engineering, and 10% in medicine or dentistry (see table 5). Within the last 10 years there was an above-average increase in the number of students in medicine, law, economics, and the social sciences.

The increase in the overall number of students was accompanied by changes in the structure of their social origin. The proportion of children of blue-collar workers and white-collar employees increased, while the proportion of children of civil servants and self-employed fathers decreased. Interestingly, the proportion of children of blue-collar workers increased from 10% to 19% between 1966 and 1976, but fell again slightly in the following years, to 13% in 1986. This decrease is a consequence of increasing restrictions on state assistance schemes, and a manifestation of a shrinking working-class population.

Looking from a different angle, we find class-specific differences in university attendance more or less unchanged. The proportion of children of blue-collar workers taking a university course is still much smaller than that of other social classes (see table 6). In 1988, only 8% of the children of blue-collar workers entered university, compared to 36% of the children of self-employed fathers and 49% of the children of civil servants. In this respect, equality of educational opportunity seems far from being reached, although there is no doubt that sex-specific, regional, and religious differences, which used to be significant, have been considerably reduced.

Heinz-Herbert Noll

References:

Bundesministerium für Bildung und Wissenschaft
1989 *Grund- und Strukturdaten 1989/90*. Bonn.

Bundesministerium für Bildung und Wissenschaft, ed.
1989 *Das Soziale Bild der Studentenschaft in der Bundesrepublik Deutschland: 12. Sozialerhebung des Deutschen Studentenwerks*. Bonn.

Information Bildung und Wissenschaft
1990 no. 2.

Institut der Deutschen Wirtschaft, ed.
1988 *Zahlen zur wirtschaftlichen Entwicklung der Bundesrepublik Deutschland*. Köln: Deutscher Instituts-Verlag.

Schnitzer, Klaus, Wolfgang Isserstedt, and Michael
1988 Lezcensky. *Die soziale Lage der Studierenden in der Bundesrepublik Deutschland im Jahre 1988.* Zusammenfassung der Ergebnisse der 12. Sozialerhebung des DSW. Hochschul-Informations-System, Kurzinformation A7/89, September 1989, p.6.

Statistisches Bundesamt, ed.
1987 *Datenreport 1987. Zahlen und Fakten über die Bundesrepublik Deutschland.* Bonn: Bundeszentrale für politische Bildung.

–, ed.
1989 *Datenreport 1989. Zahlen und Fakten über die Bundesrepublik Deutschland.* Bonn: Bundeszentrale für politische Bildung.

–, ed.
ann. pbl. *Bildung im Zahlenspiegel.* Wiesbaden.

–, ed.
ann. pbl. *Statistisches Jahrbuch.* Stuttgart/Mainz: Kohlhammer.

Weishaupt, Horst, et al.
1988 *Perspektiven des Bildungswesens der Bundesrepublik Deutschland.* Baden-Baden: Nomos.

Table 1
13 year-olds by type of school attended (in %)

Item	1960	1970	1980	1985	1987
Lower secondary school	70	55	39	37	34
Intermediate secondary school	11	19	25	26	27
Upper secondary school	15	20	27	28	30
Comprehensive school	-	-	4	4	5

Source: Statistisches Bundesamt, Datenreport, 1987 and 1989.

Table 2
School leavers by educational attainment

Year	Number of school leavers (in 1,000)	Completion of compulsory full-time education (in %)	Intermediate school leaving certificate or equivalent certificate (in %)	General or subject-specific certificate of aptitude for higher education (in %)
1962	685,4	77.6	13.4	9.0
1965	757,0	74.4	18.9	6.7
1970	764,3	63.0	26.1	10.9
1975	921,4	50.0	31.6	18.4
1980	1.105,0	45.7	34.5	19.8
1981	1.112,3	41.0	35.8	23.2
1982	1.176,0	39.1	36.6	24.3
1983	1.194,1	37.7	36.7	25.6
1984	1.167,2	36.7	37.2	26.1
1985	1.106,5	35.5	37.6	26.9
1986	1.031,6	33.9	37.9	28.2
1987	957,7	33.2	37.0	29.8

Source: Statistisches Bundesamt, Statistisches Jahrbuch, various volumes.

Table 3
Population aged 15 years and older by educational achievement (in %)

Year	Still at school			Lower secondary school leaving certificate			Intermediate secondary school leaving certificate or equivalent certificate			General or subjectspecific certificate of aptitude for higher education		
	Total	Male	Female	Total	Male	Female	Total	Male	Female	Total	Male	Female
1976	4.1	4.5	3.8	74.0	72.0	75.8	14.2	13.0	15.3	7.7	10.5	5.1
1978	5.0	5.4	4.7	72.6	70.6	74.3	14.3	13.1	15.5	8.0	10.9	5.5
1982	5.2	5.7	4.8	68.9	67.1	70.5	15.9	14.3	17.3	10.0	12.9	7.3
1985	5.1	5.1	5.0	65.2	63.6	66.5	17.7	15.6	19.5	12.1	15.6	8.9
1987	5.1	5.1	5.1	63.7	62.4	64.8	18.3	16.1	20.3	12.9	16.4	9.8

Source: Statistisches Bundesamt, Bildung im Zahlenspiegel, various volumes.

Table 4
Enrollments in university-type education (in 1,000)

Item	1960	1970	1980	1987	1989
Universities[1]	239	412	749	966	-
Comprehensive Universities	-	-	69	93	-
Colleges of art	7	10	18	22	-
Colleges[2]	-	-	200	327	-
Total	247	422	1,036	1,049	1,510
Of which: beginners	51	87	176	211	253

1. Including students at colleges of education and colleges of theology.
2. Not including students at former academies of engineering.

Source: Statistisches Bundesamt, Datenreport, 1989; Information Bildung Wissenschaft, 1990.

Table 5
Students at universities and colleges by subject of study[1] (in %)

Subject group	1975	1980	1985	1986	1987
Theology, languages literature and cultural studies	33	30	28	27	26
Law, economics, and social sciences	21	22	24	25	25
Natural sciences and mathematics	20	18	18	19	19
Engineering	12	11	12	12	12
Medicine	7	8	8	8	9
Dentistry	1	1	1	1	1
Agriculture, dietetics, and veterinary science	3	3	3	3	3
Art	5	5	5	5	5
Total 1,000	696	842	1,036	1,055	1,094

1. German and foreign students at universities, colleges of education, and colleges of art: date of reference: Wintersemester.

Source: Institut der Deutschen Wirtschaft, 1988; author's computations.

Table 6
University/college enrollment of 19-24-year-olds by social origin (in %)

Year	Children of ...			
	Self-employed fathers	Civil servants	White-collar workers	Blue-collar workers
1982	28.5	46.4	32.3	8.7
1983	27.3	43.9	33.4	8.8
1984	26.3	40.8	30.5	7.9
1985	25.4	42.1	27.8	6.9
1986	25.9	44.5	27.7	8.9
1987	31.9	45.3	30.1	6.9
1988	35.9	49.2	31.8	8.3

Source: Klaus Schnitzer, et. al., 1988, p. 6.

15.2 Professional and Vocational Education

Professional and vocational education constitutes a central part of the educational system. There is a clear and linear trend toward more and more people completing some kind of a formalized professional or vocational education at the beginning of their occupational career. Apprenticeship is still by far the most important type of vocational training, and has gained rather than lost popularity. Despite the labour-market crisis and the large birth cohorts of the baby-boom generation, the dual system of vocational training has proved to be successful.

In the Federal Republic of Germany, professional and vocational education is highly formalized and institutionalized. Within the last 30 years, vocational-training leaving certificates have gained considerable importance as requirements for access to employment and prerequisites for occupational careers, and they are now as significant as the level of attainment in general education. Thus, educational policy gives high priority to providing all graduates with the opportunity to take qualified vocational training, a goal that is supported by all relevant political forces.

Statistics indicate that the expansion of general education has been accompanied by an expansion of professional education. The fact that the proportion of economically active persons who have not completed vocational training decreased from 34% to 26% between 1978 and 1987 can be attributed to this development (see table 1). In 1987, only 17% of all economically active persons aged 25–40 years had no vocational-training leaving certificate (see table 2); 6% were university graduates, 4% had a college degree, 7% had attained a foreman or technician certificate, and 57% had completed an apprenticeship or some kind of comparable training. The level of attainment in professional education is lower for women than for men, but the gap has closed considerably over the last years.

In the Federal Republic, which has rightly been called a "high-skill" country, apprenticeship is by far the most important institution of vocational training. An apprenticeship is a two- to three-year course organized according to the so-called dual system: the central part of the course, practical vocational in-company training, is complemented by theoretical vocational training at a part-time vocational school. The outstanding importance of this kind of training is reflected in the fact that in 1987 about 60% of a birth cohort of 16- to 18-year-olds entered an apprenticeship and that almost 80% of all economically active persons who are vocationally qualified have completed this kind of training.

While in the past apprenticeship was usually taken up by young people who were not entitled to higher education, in-company vocational training is now gaining popularity among graduates qualified for college or university. An increasing number of young people choose to complete an apprenticeship before taking up an academic course: 12% of those entitled to university or college entrance in 1986 had commenced some form of vocational training by December of that year and intended to go on to higher education subsequently. In contrast, only 5% of those so entitled in 1976 expressed their intention to acquire both vocational and academic qualifications (Lewin, 1988). This development proves that apprenticeship training as a specific kind of vocational training has gained rather than lost popularity.

In the 1970s and 1980s, large birth cohorts not only created special problems for universities, they also put severe strains on the dual system of vocational training. Despite an enormous expansion, the supply of in-company training places, which is more or less market regulated, did not match the demand for quite a long time (see table 3). This situation resulted in intensified competition for the limited number of training places. The number of apprenticeships taken each year rose from 496,000 to 706,000 between 1976 and 1984. Nevertheless, in 1984, for example, almost 60,000 young people were not able to find a training place. Young people with educational deficits, girls, and children of migrant workers had particular difficulties. Furthermore, there were significant regional disparities. Special compensatory programs and school-based qualifying courses did not solve these market-induced problems, but they did help to mitigate them.

The apprenticeship market began to relax in the middle of the 1980s, when birth cohorts became smaller. Today, the number of training places offered exceeds the number of applicants, and in some crafts there even seems to be a shortage of junior staff members.

All in all, the German dual system of vocational training proved to be successful even in a time when conditions were less favourable due to a labour-market crisis and large birth cohorts. It significantly contributed to the fact that unemployment among young people and other problems of transition into working life have been less severe in the Federal Republic than in many other countries.

Unemployment rates broken down by qualification level indicate the labour-market opportunities provided by different educational certificates. The higher the level of vocational or professional education, the lower, on average, the general risk of unemployment (see table 3). There are, of course, considerable differences in job prospects according to type of training and occupation. Due to the specific system of vocational education in the Federal Republic, the impact of general education on job prospects is less direct than in other countries. However, general education does influence a graduate's opportunities to obtain access to different kinds and levels of vocational or professional training. When there was a severe shortage of training places, employers preferred applicants with higher certificates of general education to applicants without. The outcome of this situation has been described as a displacement competition. Moreover, the inflationary consequences of the expansion of higher education have become obvious.

As far as the academic professions are concerned, the chances of obtaining access to the labour market are quite diverse, depending on the area of study. An analysis of the relations between the numbers of job applicants and the numbers of respective vacancies registered at employment offices shows that in 1986, electrical engineers had the best prospect for finding a job, with about 3 vacancies per applicant, whereas sociologists had the worst prospects of all university graduates, with 187 applicants for each vacancy in 1986. It should be noticed, however, that vacancies registered at employment offices represent only some of the total number of jobs available and that the percentage of job placements obtained through public employment services differs among occupations. Compared to the beginning of the 1980s, the labour-market prospects have improved slightly for most of the academic professions. According to a recent forecast (Rothkirch & Tessaring, 1986), the future prospects for university graduates are quite promising.

Heinz-Herbert Noll

References:

Bundesministerium für Bildung und Wissenschaft
1989 *Berufsbildungsbericht 1989.* Bonn.

Lewin, Karl
1989 "Immer später ins Studium, Studien- und Berufswahl der Studienberechtigten 86." HIS-Kurzinformation A4/88. Hannover 1988.

Rothkirch, Christoph von, and Manfred Tessaring
1986 "Projektion des Arbeitskräftebedarfs nach Qualifikationsebenen bis zum Jahr 2000." *Mitteilungen aus der Arbeitsmarkt- und Berufsforschung*, 19, 105-118.

Schwab, Walter, and Hermann Voit
1989 "Vom Bildungsnotstand zur Akadamikerschwemme - Bildung für alle." In E. Hölder, ed., *Im Zug der Zeit*. Stuttgart: Metzler-Pöschel.

Statistisches Bundesamt
var.vol. *Bildung im Zahlenspiegel 1989*. Wiesbaden.

Table 1
Labour force by vocational and professional education 1978-1987 (in %)

Persons in the labour force	1978 Total	1978 Male	1978 Female	1982 Total	1982 Male	1982 Female
Completion of apprenticeship training	53	56	48	55	57	52
Master craftsman or technician diploma	6	8	3	6	9	3
College degree	2	3	1	3	4	1
University degree	5	6	5	6	6	5
No professional training certificate	34	27	43	30	24	39

Persons in the labour force	1985 Total	1985 Male	1985 Female	1987 Total	1987 Male	1987 Female
Completion of apprenticeship training	55	56	54	57	57	56
Master craftsman or technician diploma	7	10	4	7	9	3
College degree	3	4	2	4	5	1
University degree	6	7	5	6	7	5
No professional training certificate	29	23	36	26	22	35

Source: Statistisches Bundesamt, Bildung im Zahlenspiegel, various volumes.

Table 2
Labour force by vocational and professional qualification and age groups (in %)

Age groups	Completion of apprenticeship training		Master craftsman or technician diploma		College degree		University degree		No professional training certificate	
	1978	1987	1978	1987	1978	1987	1978	1987	1978	1987
20 - 24	64	69	3	2	1	1	2	1	28	27
25 - 29	61	66	6	6	3	4	8	6	23	18
30 - 39	56	58	8	9	3	5	8	11	25	17
40 - 49	52	57	8	9	2	4	5	8	34	22
50 - 59	51	53	7	9	2	3	5	5	35	30
60 - 64	47	48	9	10	3	5	7	9	34	28

Source: Statistisches Bundesamt, Bildung im Zahlenspiegel, various volumes.

Table 3
Apprenticeship places for young people 1976 - 1988[1] (in 1,000)

Year	Apprenticeschip contracts signed	Training places not occupied	Applicants not provided with a training place	Supply of training places	Demand for training places
	1	2	3	4=1+2	5=1+3
1976	495,800	18,100	27,000	513,900	523,500
1977	558,400	25,500	27,000	583,900	585,400
1978	601,700	22,300	23,800	624,000	625,500
1979	640,300	36,900	19,700	677,200	660,000
1980	650,000	44,600	17,300	694,600	667,300
1981	605,636	37,348	22,140	642,984	627,776
1982	630,990	19,995	34,180	650,985	665,170
1983	676,734	19,641	47,408	696,375	724,142
1984	705,652	21,134	58,426	726,786	764,078
1985	697,089	22,021	58,905	719,110	755,994
1986	684,710	31,170	46,270	715,880	730,980
1987	645,746	44,541	33,880	690,287	679,626
1988	604,002	61,962	24,791	665,964	628,793

1. Date of reference: September.

Source: Bundesministerium für Bildung und Wissenschaft, 1989.

15.3 Continuing Education

Continuing education is a growing sector of the educational system, and has been gaining importance for several years. At present, it is primarily used as a means to improve the qualifications of the labour force. While the numbers of participants in further training have increased considerably during the last decade, differences in participation rates between labour-force groups have not diminished.

In the Federal Republic of Germany, continuing education is considered the "fourth sector" of the educational system, and is a subject of growing interest and attention. There is increasing agreement that organized learning can no longer be limited to only one period of education in the early years of life. Growing and changing societal demands call for the supply of more and better opportunities to continue education throughout life.

During the 1960s and early 1970s, promotion of continuing education was guided primarily by reformative goals such as self-fulfillment, general personality development, and provision of opportunities to compensate for lost chances to aquire general certificates of education. Nowadays, continuing education is considered above all a means to accommodate qualifications of the work force to new requirements brought on by changes in technology and economic structure.

The common distinction between general, political, and professional continuing education is becoming obsolete, and there is a trend toward convergence. On the one hand, skills such as knowledge of foreign languages and other communicative competences are of growing importance as professional skills; on the other hand, technical qualifications such as the ability to use computers are gaining importance in everyday life.

Empirical data provided by the Continuing Education Reporting System (*Berichtssystem Weiterbildungsverhalten*) of the federal government show an increase in participation in continuing training between 1979 and 1988. The overall participation rate including general, political, and professional training rose from 23% to 35% (see table 1). Between 1982 and 1985, there was slight decrease in participation in general continuing education, while participation in professional training remained unchanged. After 1985, the trend toward growing participation continued. The trend is particularly strong in professional continuing education, where the participation rate reached 18% in 1988, compared to 10% in 1979.

Differences in participation rates between various groups of the working population are considerable, and are growing over time (see table 2). Whereas the difference between men and women is comparably small, there are fairly large differences between groups of different educational levels and occupational status: the higher the level of education and the higher the status, the higher the rate of participation in continuing training. These correlations explain why continuing education does not level out existing differences in qualification and status but, on the contrary, widens them.

The considerable differences in participation rate by size of establishment can be explained by the fact that in the FRG professional continuing training is to a large extent organized and offered within business enterprises, and small establishments do much less in this regard than large. About half of all professional continuing education takes place within firms. Other important providers of classes in continuing education are the unions, employer associations, and, most important, local adult-education centres. Compared to regular vocational training, continuing education is much more heterogeneously organized and less institutionalized.

From recent employment trends and trends in activity rates, we estimate a further increase in participation in continuing education in the foreseeable future. Continuing education will also gain importance compared to vocational training at the beginning of a person's career. Since participation in continuing education can be seen as a "positional good," we expect, however, that the more people participate the less it will pay off in terms of higher incomes and improved career opportunities.

Heinz-Herbert Noll

References:

Kuwan, Helmut

1989 *Berichtssystem Weiterbildungsverhalten 1988. Repräsentative Untersuchung zur Entwicklung der Weiterbildungsbeteiligung 1979 - 1988.* Reihe Bildung-Wissenschaft-Aktuell 5/89. Hrsg. vom Bundesminister für Bildung und Wissenschaft. Bonn.

Noll, Heinz-Herbert

1987 "Weiterbildung, Beschäftigungsstruktur und Statusdistribution." In A. Weymann, ed., *Bildung und Beschäftigung.* Sonderband der Sozialen Welt, 141 - 170. Göttingen.

Table 1
Participation in further education 1979 to 1988[1] (participation rate in %)

Item	1979	1982	1985	1988
Vocational further education	10	12	12	18
Non-vocational further education (general, political and other)	16	21	18	22
Total	23	29	25	35

1. Data source: representative sample survey of 8,000 persons (1979), 3,500 persons (1982, 1985) and 7,000 persons (1988); German citizens only, aged 19 to 64 years.

Source: Kuwan, 1989.

Table 2
Participation in further education 1979 to 1988[1] (participation rate in %)

	1979	1982	1985	1988
Total	10	12	12	18
Employment				
- employed persons	15	17	17	25
- not employed persons	1	2	2	6
Employed persons by sex				
- employed men	17	20	18	27
- employed women	12	14	15	21
Employed persons by qualification				
- no vocational training	8	3	3	9
- apprenticeship/training college	14	14	15	21
- master craftsmen's college, other technical college	23	22	26	37
- university, college	24	33	31	41
Employed persons by occupational status				
- blue-collar workers	8	8	5	12
- white-collar workers	1	19	21	29
- civil servants	27	32	28	40
- self-employed persons	12	20	16	25
Employed persons by size of establishment				
1 - 99 employees	11	13	13	17
100 - 999 employees	12	10	14	20
1,000 employees and more	17	19	22	31

1. Data source: representative sample survey of 8,000 persons (1979), 3,500 persons (1982, 1985) and 7,000 persons (1988); German citizens only, aged 19 to 64 years.

Source: Kuwan, 1989.

16. Integration and Marginalization

16.1 Immigrants and Ethnic Minorities

Although the Federal Republic of Germany does not see itself explicitly as a country of immigrants, demographic tendencies – age structure, gender proportion, and employment quotas – of ethnic minorities are approaching those of the domestic population, and markedly longer residence periods point toward a net immigration process. In spite of clear progress in certain segments, integration problems remain which manifest themselves in residential and educational segregation, with particularly serious consequences for future generations.

The immigration of foreign workers as a consequence of progressive industrialization and massive recruitment began in Germany in the late nineteenth century. At that time, the largest segment of immigrant workers were Polish, employed for the most part in the metal and coal industries of the *Ruhrgebiet* and in the Prussian agricultural sector; that is – as is the case in other industrial sectors nowadays – in the least safety-oriented sectors involving hard manual labour, with few required qualifications, in positions not attractive to Germans.

Employment of foreign workers lost importance between 1918 and 1933. The substitute and buffer functions which immigrant workers fulfilled in the German economy were expressed in the *Inländerprimat* (natives' primacy), according to which a foreigner could be hired only when no German could be found for the particular job. This primacy was based on a legal definition from the early 1920s; during the depression of the 1930s, it led to a nearly total suspension of recruitment of foreign workers.

In the 1930s, the migrant–worker issue was increasingly influenced by political and race-ideological aspects. During the economic boom from 1934 to 1938, the number of foreign workers rose from about 100,000 to just under 400,000. During World War II, the need for workers exceeded the number of voluntary immigrants (mainly from Austria and Italy). Pertinent laws were passed allowing for forced recruitment of men and women from the German-occupied zones. In 1945, about 8 million foreigners – 6 million indentured workers and about 2 million prisoners of war – were working in Germany.

> The situation of these *Fremdarbeiter* [a word emphasizing the non-belongingness of the worker] was characterized by an officially declared intention of greatest possible exploitation and suppression, especially of Poles and Russians, to the point of physical destruction. Private enterprise and the large concerns – just as in World War I – were far from the last to profit from the situation. The fact that production and supply collapsed only *after* the end of the war is primarily due to the fact that, with the liberation of indentured labourers and prisoners of war, production was robbed of one of its main pillars. (Esser, 1983, p. 130)

After the end of the war, chaotic conditions reigned in the labour market. Some sectors suffered a lack of workers, while others had a surplus. About 9 million people arrived from the eastern German sectors, and 3 million refugees left the German Democratic Republic before the building of the Berlin Wall in 1961. Their integration made recruitment of foreign workers superfluous up to the 1950s. In 1955, the first tight spots in labour supply, mainly in agriculture, arose; the first recruitment agreement between West Germany and Italy was made in December, 1955.

Place of Birth, Ethnic Origin, and Language

The number of foreign workers, however, remained small and therefore of little importance. In 1959, approximately 167,000 foreigners with work permits were working in the Federal Republic of Germany, and non-self-employed foreigners comprised 0.8% of the working population. Around 280,000 foreigners were working in the Federal Republic in mid-1960, about 44% of them from Italy. The first Greeks, Spaniards, Yugoslavs, and Turks arrived in the late 1950s, and from around 1960 on the major flow of what was long considered "typical" guest-worker nationalities began.

A series of further recruitment agreements were signed in the 1960s: with Spain in 1960, with Portugal in 1964, with Yugoslavia in 1968. As early as 1966, however, the steady upward climb of the number of foreigners had been interrupted by the beginning of an economic recession in West Germany. Fewer foreigners came in 1966 and 1967, and more returned to their native countries. The number of foreign workers reached a nadir of 903,600 in January, 1968, after having been at 1.3 million in mid-1966. In 1968, immediately after the end of the recession, there was the sharpest increase yet in the number of foreigners, continuing until the enforcement of a recruitment ceiling in November, 1973, then evening out and taking a downward turn as of 1975. Although immigration for reasons of employment from non-Common Market countries was entirely prohibited after 1973, the foreign residential population once again – as early as 1978 – began to grow due to family members joining those already in West Germany (see figure 1).

As a result of these family reunions, but also due to a strong influx of asylum-seekers (see table 1) and of work immigration from Common Market countries, the number of foreigners reached a peak of 4.7 million in 1982. In the course of the *Rückkehrhilfegesetz* (Assistance Act for Returning Foreigners), offering foreigners financial incentives for returning to their native countries, and also following the economic downswing of 1981–1982, their numbers declined slightly at first, only to increase again to 4.6 million, in 1987 (see figure 2). Currently, 7.6% of the population of the Federal Republic of Germany are of foreign nationality. These official data do not take illegally employed foreigners into consideration; a 1982 estimate places their numbers at over a million (*Der Spiegel*, 1982).

In conjunction with the long-term increase of foreigners in West Germany, there have been notable shifts in the composition of nationalities. Italians were the numerically dominant foreign nationality from the mid-1950s until well into the 1960s (among guest workers as well as in the foreign residential population in toto); Italians, Yugoslavs, and Turks formed groups of about equal size from this point until the late 1960s. Starting in the early 1970s, the proportion of Turks rose steadily and more steeply than that of other nationalities (figure 2).

After the step from a policy of straight rotation to one of integration was been taken in the mid-1970s, a conservative federal government brought about a shift in the three "pillars" of foreign-resident policy as of 1982. "Integration" was demoted to third priority, and "encouragement to return home" and "limits on family reunions" were given preference. This policy corresponds less and less with actual developments. The proportion of Italians with residency of under six years amounted to 62.8% in 1973, but it was down to 19.5% in 1985. For Turks, the last of the major recruitment nationalities, the proportion sank from 82.8% to 22.6% over this period (Nauck, 1988). In 1973, 16% of all foreigners had spent 10 years or more in the Federal Republic; in 1981 this proportion had risen to 42.8%, and in 1987 to 59.7%. Almost 14% have been here for 20 years or longer. The trend toward permanent residence is also exhibited in the number of family reunions. The fertility rate among foreign women, long exceeding that of German women, is now showing increasing conformity to German norms. Every eleventh child currently born in West Germany is of a foreign nationality, compared to every sixth child in 1974, the year with the highest registered number of foreign-nationality births (Statistisches Bundesamt, 1987). The unemployment quota for foreigners, well above average for some time, can be seen as indicative of their decision to remain in spite of economic difficulties (see figure 3).

Residential and Educational Segregation and the Second Generation

The places of residence of foreign workers are concentrated in industrial agglomeration areas, for example, around the Rhine and Ruhr rivers as well as in the Rhein-Main area; their proportion of the population in the less structured rural areas lies well under the national average. In 1986, 51% of foreigners lived in towns of more than 100,000 residents, as compared to only 44% in 1971 (though the urban proportion of the total population, about one-third, remained almost unchanged during this period). High concentrations of foreigners are more frequently observed in particular streets, city blocks, or apartment buildings than in large residential areas or city sections. Survey data from 1982 show certain parallels between national origin and degree of residential segregation: Turkish people lived more often in discrete coummunities, while Greeks were the most integrated (see table 2). As the majority of the foreigners are prepared to forgo consumption to save for a return to their native country, there has been a concentration of the foreign population in neighbourhoods with poor-quality housing – and, consequently, lower rents. The German population in these areas is often characterized by a high proportion of persons in difficult social situations.

This sharply restricts the integration chances for foreign children; in residential areas with a high concentration of foreigners, foreign children often make up the majority of students in school classes. Furthermore, their school situation presents additional problems: "It is characterized by insufficient school attendance, an extremely low achievement quota as early as the *Hauptschulabschluß*, (intermediate school diploma) and a considerable underrepresentation of foreign children in the higher-level schools" (Esser, 1983, p. 144). Yet the situation of foreign children and adolescents in regard to school education has not simply stagnated. Recent data on educational participation, school attendance, and school achievement by foreigners show that, very gradually and from a relatively low point of departure, they are catching up with Germans.

Data on the educational situation of young foreigners in Hessen (Hessia) show that the percentages of foreign pupils in higher-level schools have tendentially risen. For example, the proportion of foreigners among *Realschüler* (secondary-school students) increased from 3.6% in the mid-1970s to 8.5% in the school year 1984–1985, and among high-school students from 7.5% to 9.6% during this period. A specific evaluation of separate age groups confirms this slow evolution away from extreme underrepresentation of foreigners in secondary and high schools. The proportion of foreign secondary-school students of 14 years of age was 10.7% in 1979–1980, 12.3% in 1980–1981 and as high as 16.8% in 1983–1984. School achievement has developed similarly, according to the number of school diplomas awarded. Foreign students may still lag well behind Germans, but they are undeniably advancing; while only 37.2% of foreigners leaving intermediate school in 1974–1975 had diplomas, 48.1% did in 1976–1977, 51.4% in 1979–1980 and 62% in 1982–1983 (Der Hessische Minister für Wirtschaft und Technik, 1985). In job training and employment opportunities, the situation of young foreigners is still quite a bit worse than that of German youth. While 23% of 16- to 18-year-old foreigners underwent apprenticeship training in 1985, the comparative quota for Germans was about 66% (Statistisches Bundesamt, 1987). In the 1985–1986 school year, 90% of the German students, but only 60% of foreigners, at technical colleges in Hessia had an apprenticeship or job-training contract. Unemployment among foreign youth also increased much more steeply between 1980 and 1985 than it did among German youth (HLT-Gesellschaft, 1986).

The convergence of several factors – residential and educational segregation, differences in life style, religion, and mentality, and the strong influx of asylum-seekers and *Aussiedler* (foreigners of German descent arriving from eastern Europe) – has contributed to a renewed spread of hostility toward foreigners. On the other hand, public debate has produced the idea of a multi-cultural society as something worth aspiring to. Two surveys, from 1980 and 1984, point to a dropping tendency to discriminate in various sectors. Only 42% of those polled in 1984, as opposed to 52% in 1980, were of the opinion that foreigners should be sent back to their home country when jobs became scarce (see table 3). This result was surprising in the face of the increased unemployment at the time. In both years, however, there was widespread agreement that foreigners should adapt their life styles better to that of Germans. A time-series comparison of the proportions of Germans demanding in general the return of foreigners to their native countries presents a much less favourable picture: in 1978, 39% wanted foreigners to leave 68% did in 1982 and 80% did in 1983 (see figure 4). In 1989 polls, 55% of Germans said that it was "okay" that foreigners lived in West Germany, but 75% were also of the opinion that there were too many foreigners here. In February of 1989, 64% of Germans opposed local suffrage for foreigners; in another poll, in May 1989, 72% of those questioned held this view (*Der Spiegel*, No. 16, 1989; Forschungsgruppe Wahlen, 1989).

The numbers given here, as well as other recent surveys on the objective situation of foreigners and Germans' attitudes toward them, show that integration has progressed. But the particularistic liberal attitudes of the Germans obviously do not provide a reliable social basis for further steps toward integration, as events over the past few years have often touched off changes in these attitudes.

Claudia Koch-Arzberger and Karin Stiehr

References

Bade, Klaus
1983 *Vom Auswanderungsland zum Einwanderungsland? Deutschland 1880-1980*. Berlin: Colloquium.

Beauftragte der Bundesregierung für die Integration der ausländischen Arbeitnehmer und ihrer Familienangehörigen, ed.
1986 *Bericht zur Ausländerbeschäftigung*. Bonn.

Bendit, René, and Andrea Steinmayr
1985 "Ausländische Jugendliche - integriert oder ausgegrenzt." In Deutsches Jugendinstitut, ed., *Immer diese Jugend! Ein zeitgeschichtliches Mosaik. 1945 bis heute*. München: Deutsches Jugendinstitut.

Bundesminister für Arbeit und Sozialordnung, ed.
1986 *Situation der ausländischen Arbeitnehmer und ihrer Familienangehörigen in der Bundesrepublik Deutschland. Repräsentativuntersuchung '85*. Bonn.

Claessens, Dieter, et al.
1985 *Sozialkunde der Bundesrepublik Deutschland. Grundlagen, Strukturen, Trends in Wirtschaft und Gesellschaft*. Reinbek: Rowohlt.

Dohse, Knut
1981 *Ausländische Arbeiter und bürgerlicher Staat. Genese und Funktion von staatlicher Ausländerpolitik und Ausländerrecht. Vom Kaiserreich bis zur Bundesrepublik Deutschland*. Königstein i. Ts.: Hain.

Esser, Hartmut
1983 "Gastarbeiter." In Wolfgang Benz, ed., *Die Bundesrepublik Deutschland*. Vol. 2: Gesellschaft. Frankfurt/Main: Fischer.

Forschungsgruppe Wahlen
1989 *Politbarometer Februar 1989*. Mannheim.

Hagstotz, Werner
1986 "Determinanten der Diskriminierung von Gastarbeitern. Eine vergleichende Analyse mit Daten der "Allgemeinen Bevölkerungsumfrage der Sozialwissenschaften" (ALLBUS) 1980 und 1984." In Jürgen Hoffmeyer-Zlotnik, ed., *Segregation und Integration. Die Situation von Arbeitsemigranten im Aufnahmeland*. Mannheim: FRG.

Hessischer Minister für Wirtschaft und Technik
1985 *Ausländer in Hessen 1985*. Wiesbaden.

HLT-Gesellschaft für Forschung, Planung, Entwicklung
1986 *Ausländerreport Hessen '86*. Wiesbaden.

Koch-Arzberger, Claudia
1985 *Die schwierige Integration. Die bundesrepublikanische Gesellschaft und ihre 5 Millionen Ausländer*. Opladen: Westdeutscher Verlag.

Löwisch, Peter-Christian
1986 "'Sie wollen uns hier raushaben.'" In *Im Schatten der Krise. Rechtsextremismus, Neofaschismus und Ausländerfeindlichkeit in der Bundesrepublik*. Köln: Pahl-Rugenstein.

Mehrländer, Ursula
1978 "Bundesrepublik Deutschland." In E. Gehmacher, et al., eds., *Ausländerpolitik im Konflikt. Arbeitskräfte oder Einwanderer? Konzepte der Aufnahme- und Entsendeländer.* Bonn: Verlag Neue Gesellschaft.

Nauck, Bernhard
1988 "Zwanzig Jahre Migrantenfamilien in der Bundesrepublik. Familiärer Wandel zwischen Situationsanpassung, Akkulturation und Segregation." In Rosemarie Nave-Herz, ed., *Wandel und Kontinuität der Familie in der Bundesrepublik Deutschland*. Stuttgart: Enke.

Schäfer, Hermann
1986 "Zwischen Germanisierung und Verdrängung - Zur Lage der Arbeitsemigranten in der Bundesrepublik." In Hans-Günter Thien, and Hanns Wienold, eds., *Herrschaft, Krise, Überleben, Gesellschaft der Bundesrepublik in den achtziger Jahren*. Münster: Westfälisches Dampfboot.

Statistisches Bundesamt, ed.
1982 *Statistisches Jahrbuch 1982 für die Bundesrepublik Deutschland*. Stuttgart/Mainz: Kohlhammer.

–, ed.
1983 *Strukturdaten über Ausländer in der BRD*. Mainz: Kohlhammer.

–, ed.
1987 *Datenreport 1987*. Bonn: Bundeszentrale für politische Bildung.

–, ed.
1988 *Statistisches Jahrbuch 1988 für die Bundesrepublik Deutschland*. Stuttgart/Mainz: Kohlhammer.

Table 1
Asylum-seekers by exemplary nationalities

Nationality	1980	1983	1985	1987
Europe	65,809	6,589	18,174	36,629
Poland	2,090	1,949	6,672	15,194
Rumania	777	587	887	1,964
Czechoslovakia	2,385	1,400	1,411	1,516
Turkey	57,913	1,548	7,528	11,426
Hungary	1,466	587	736	1,585
Africa	8,339	3,484	8,093	3,568
Ethiopia	3,614	906	2,625	800
Ghana	2,768	1,611	3,994	783
America and Australia	217	114	97	206
Asia	31,998	8,152	44,298	15,961
Afghanistan	5,466	687	2,632	1,586
India	6,693	1,548	4,471	1,073
Iran	749	1,190	8,840	6,538
Lebanon	1,457	691	4,576	1,448
Pakistan	6,824	763	3,240	1,592
Sri Lanka	2,673	2,645	17,380	2,285
Stateless persons	1,455	1,398	3,170	1,015
Total	107,818	19,737	73,832	57,379

Source: Bundesamt für die Anerkennung ausländische Flüchtlinge, Zirndorf; Statistisches Bundesamt, 1988, p. 69.

Table 2
Nationalities of immediate neighbors (in %)

Item	Greeks	Italians	Turks	Total
Only Germans	26	32	24	27
Germans and foreigners	68	54	57	60
Only foreigners	6	14	19	13
Total	100	100	100	100

Source: Koch-Arzberger, 1985, p. 121.

Table 3
Discrimination against foreign workers

Item	Rejection		Indifference		Agreement	
	1980	1984	1980	1984	1980	1984
Foreigners should adapt their life styles to the German life style.	21	24	14	15	65	61
When work gets scarce, foreign workers should be sent back to their native country.	34	42	14	16	52	42
All political involvement within Germany should be refused to foreign workers.	36	41	13	12	51	47
Foreign workers should choose their spouses from among their own nationality.	42	53	14	13	44	34

Note: rejection=code 1-3, indifference=code 4, agreement=code 5-7 on the scale.

Source: Hagstotz, 1986, p. 145.

Figure 1
Immigration and emigration by foreigners

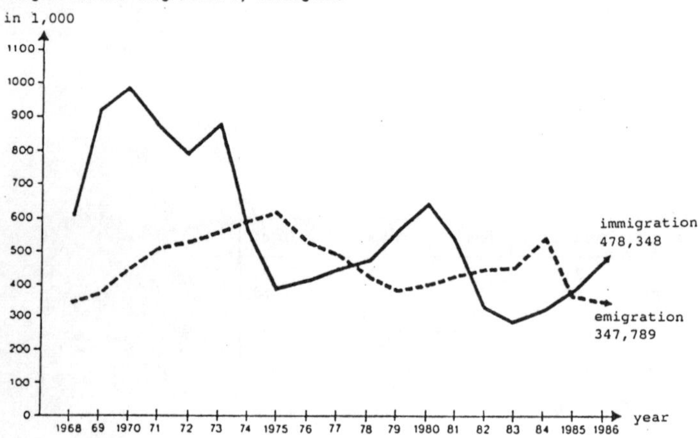

Source: Statistisches Bundesamt, 1987, p. 50.

Figure 2
Foreigners in the Federal Republic of Germany 1950 - 1987

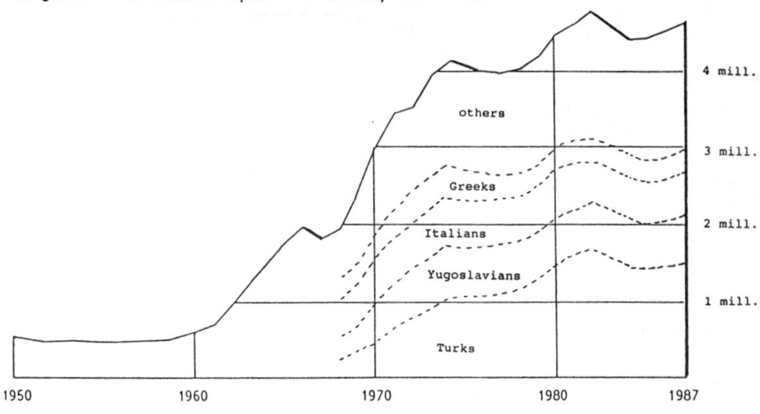

Source: Statistisches Jahrbuch, various volumes, author's figure.

Figure 3
Unemployment quotas of so-called problem groups

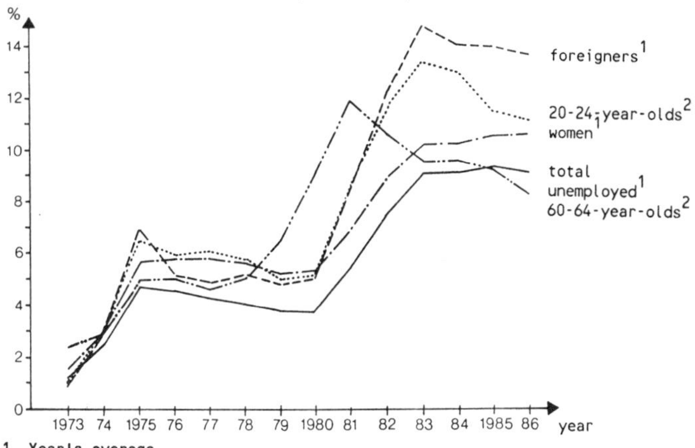

1. Year's average.
2. End of September.

Source: Bundesanstalt für Arbeit; Statistisches Bundesamt, 1987, p. 95.

Figure 4
People advocating return of foreigners to their native countries (in %)

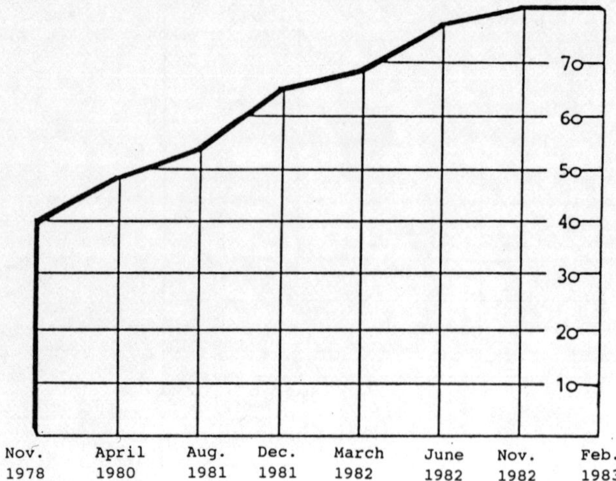

The questions were not always identical, but similar, author's figure.

Source: INFRATEST, INFAS, EMNID and IPOS.

16.2 Crime and Punishment

The general crime rate is rising over the long run, though data are subject to doubt due to a large "unreported" percentage. Embezzlement and crimes related to assets have taken a big jump in the past few decades, with a continued upward tendency. Violent crimes have, after a notable climb, stabilized at a high level over the past few years, though declines have been registered in some sectors. Correspondingly, there was an increase in the number of criminal trials, but with a higher incidence of fines and of prison sentences being converted to parole.

Violations of the law are recorded in two sets of official statistics in the Federal Republic. The Police Criminal Statistics contain information on crimes recorded and on suspects sought. The criminal-prosecution statistics count the accused who have been acquitted or declared guilty, the number of which is usually way below that of suspects. Official statistics go back to the 1950s; reliable information on criminality during the immediate postwar period is not available.

Long-term comparison of incidence of recorded punishable acts shows a nearly continuous increase, from 29 per 1,000 persons in 1954 to 69 per 1,000 in 1985 – in spite of traffic violations being dropped from police crime statistics as of 1963. The proportion of crimes solved dropped from 73.4% to 47.2% during this period (see table 1).

Statements concerning trends in criminality, based on police or court statistics, continue to have an inherent uncertainty factor. In addition to the fact that modes of registering crime have changed over time, many violations remain undetected. Particularly in cases of petty crime, but also in offences such as rape, the victim sometimes forgoes reporting the crime. Studies on "undetected" juvenile delinquency have shown that punishable acts are committed by a large majority of adolescents, and that violations of the law can be considered "normal" at this age. On the other hand, a survey of more than 20,000 young offenders who had come to the attention of the law between 1971 and 1980 has shown that those juveniles actually caught generally come from socially disadvantaged backgrounds (Kersten, 1985).

The overall number of youthful offenders has climbed steadily. Among 14- to 18-year-olds, 2.7% were registered as delinquents in 1965, 5.6% in 1982; in the 18- to 21-year age group, the proportion rose from 3.7% to 7.1% over this period (Helwig, 1985).

Most punishable acts are committed by men, though women's share in crime statistics is increasing: from 13.3% of all detected crimes in 1958, it rose to 23.7% in 1986.

Among the different forms of crime, there has been particular growth in offences concerning property or assets. The number of reported thefts increased fivefold between 1955 and 1987, and there was an above-average increase in major burglaries and of robberies in or out of houses. Fraud declined up to 1970, but then reached and exceeded its 1953 level; the incidence of embezzlement also declined temporarily, but has become more frequent again since the early 1970s. Reported document forgery increased strongly up to 1982, but the number has remained stable since then (Bundeskriminalamt, 1988).

Crime statistics include murder, manslaughter (including attempts), infanticide, rape, robbery, blackmail, and attacks on motorists with intent to rob under violent crime. In 1963, the definition of violent crime was extended to bodily injury with fatal consequences, dangerous and serious injury, and poisoning; in 1973 the definition was once again extended to include kidnapping for ransom, taking hostages, and attacks on air traffic (hijacking).

These adjustments affect the increase in reported cases, but cannot be considered the sole reason for the tripling of cases between 1955 and 1982. Clearly declining tendencies can be observed in the past few years. Reports of cases of attempted or successful murder and manslaughter more than doubled between 1953 and 1970, but have increased little since. A slightly decreasing trend in reported rapes has been registered since the mid-1970s; the number had been rising up to that point. Fewer cases of sexual abuse of children have been reported since the mid-1960s. In contrast, the number of reported cases of robbery and blackmail increased eightfold between 1953 and 1987. The equally drastic jump in cases of dangerous and serious bodily injury up to the early 1980s is exceeded by that of moderate bodily injury, which continues to trend upward (Bundeskriminalamt, 1988; for the number of accused being sentenced, divided according to offence, see table 2).

The definition and prosecution of white-collar crime did not come to theoretical and practical attention until after World War II. In order to compensate for the lack of reliable criminological knowledge in this field, the National Register of White-Collar Offences According to Standardized Aspects (BWE) was introduced in 1974.

The number of recorded trials per year increased between 1974 and 1983 from 2,888 to 3,747, and the number of accused from 5,058 to 6,423. Losses through crime, according to the BWE, rose from 1,380.6 million DM in 1974 to 5,477.4 million in 1978, and then decreased. By 1983, however, the sum of losses had reached 6,928.3 million DM. Though the BWE records only some offences – serious white-collar crime – it is obvious that losses incurred through white-collar crime far exceed those caused by "normal" crimes against property and assets (Liebl, 1985).

Crime legislation is enforced by the criminal-justice administration. The courts responsible for criminal cases are divided into four stages of appeal: *Amtsgericht* (police court), *Landgericht* (petty-session or county court), *Oberlandesgericht* (court of appeals), and *Bundesgerichtshof* (supreme or superior court). Thus, persons objecting to the decision at the first level of appeal may apply for revision by a higher court.

The number of criminal proceedings in the first stage of appeal taking place in the police courts rose from a little over half a million in 1960 to nearly one-and-a-half million in 1986; the number in petty-session courts remained about level at almost 13,000; the courts of appeals had a decrease from 320 to 47. Only slight increases can be observed during this period for proceedings resulting from appeals for revision to higher courts.

Statistics on convictions during the last few decades (see figure 1) show an increase among male juveniles and young men starting in 1954, with distinct peaks around 1960, in the early 1970s, and in the early 1980s. While only a slight increase in convicted women can be observed, more male adults were convicted in the 1950s and starting in the early 1980s than between 1960 and 1980. Robbery, blackmail, theft, and embezzlement led to more sentencings in 1985 than in 1960 (table 2). In an opposing trend, the number of convictions for acts against the right of sexual self-determination, endangerment of the public, offences against the government, and causing a public nuisance have fallen (Statistisches Bundesamt, 1987).

> The total number of prison sentences given out under adult criminal law rose from 88,000 to about 112,000 between 1970 and 1985, though it stayed well below the 1960 level of nearly 150,000 (Statistisches Bundesamt, 1962; see table 3). A long-term trend can be distinguished in which the ratio of fines to prison sentences has undergone a reversal: "If fines were the exception in 1900, with 33% of all convictions, they are the rule today. Fines are the legal consequence in more than 80%. Prison sentences are the exception: in 1986, 18% of trials resulted in imprisonment, which was usually converted to parole. Only 5.2% of those sentenced had to go to jail" (Schumann, 1988, p. 17).

Since parole was introduced for adults, in 1954, the proportion of suspended sentences has increased from 30% to 65%. The number of parole officers has quadrupled since 1964, and that of parolees has multiplied by five. At the same time, the proportion of suspended sentences converted to prison terms has decreased, though more serious offences are becoming liable to suspended sentences with parole (Schumann, 1988).

New tendencies have begun to prevail, especially in juvenile delinquency. Up to the 1960s, "therapeutic imprisonment" was considered a proven remedy against rising juvenile criminality; nowadays, an emphasis is placed on crime prevention.

Since the end of the 1970s, projects modelled after American precedents have been established in the Federal Republic which aim to avoid stigmatization by the justice administration. For example, they organize opportunities for serving out work injunctions in cooperation with juvenile courts, and efforts are made to offer a varied spectrum of jobs with which adolescents can identify. Other projects operate on the principle of "offender-victim-settlement." This not only has to do with actualization of official criminal punishment, but also attempts a form of compensation (within the framework of the trial itself) suitable to both wrongdoer and victim (Helwig, 1986).

Practical considerations are doubtless important in these reform endeavours: the courts are overloaded with criminal proceedings, and the prisons are crowded. But court verdicts also bear witness to a gradual rejection of the idea of atonement in favour of emphasizing chances of rehabilitation.

Karin Stiehr

References

Bundeskriminalamt, ed.
1986 *Gewalt und Kriminalität*. BKA-Vortragsreihe, vol. 31, Arbeitstagung des Bundeskriminalamtes Wiesbaden vom 17.-20. September 1985. Wiesbaden.

–, ed.
1988 *Polizeiliche Kriminalstatistik 1987*. Wiesbaden.

Helwig, Gisela
1985 "Jugendkriminalität und jugendstrafrechtliche Sozialkontrolle in der Bundesrepublik Deutschland." In Gisela Helwig, ed., *Jugendkriminalität in beiden deutschen Staaten*. Köln.

Kersten, Joachim
1985 "Jugendkriminalität - vom Tunichtgut zum Täter." In Deutsches Jugendinstitut, ed., *Immer diese Jugend! Ein zeitgeschichtliches Mosaik. 1945 bis heute*. München: Deutsches Jugendinstitut.

Liebl, Karlhans
1985 "Entwicklung und Strafverfolgung der Wirtschaftskriminalität im Zehnjahreszeitraum von 1974 bis 1983." In Hans-Werner Franz, ed., *22. Deutscher Soziologentag 1984. Sektions- und Ad-hoc-Gruppen*. Opladen: Westdeutscher Verlag.

Schumann, Karl F.
1988 "Eine Gesellschaft ohne Gefängnis." In Karl F. Schumann, Heinz Steinert, and Michael Voß, eds., *Vom Ende des Strafvollzugs. Ein Leitfaden für Abolitionisten*. Bielefeld.

Statistisches Bundesamt, ed.
1962 *Statistisches Jahrbuch 1962 für die Bundesrepublik Deutschland*. Stuttgart/Mainz: Kohlhammer.

–, ed.
1972 *Statistisches Jahrbuch 1972 für die Bundesrepublik Deutschland*. Stuttgart/Mainz: Kohlhammer.

–, ed.
1982 *Statistisches Jahrbuch 1982 für the Bundesrepublik Deutschland*. Stuttgart/Mainz: Kohlhammer.

–, ed.
1988 *Statistisches Jahrbuch 1988 für the Bundesrepublik Deutschland*. Stuttgart/Mainz: Kohlhammer.

–, ed.
1987 *Datenreport 1987*. Bonn: Bundeszentrale für politische Bildung.

Table 1
Punishable offenses and solved-cases

Year	Known offenses		Solved cases
	Total	Per 1,000 persons	In %
1954	150,467	29	73.4
1960	2,034,239	37	65.6
1970	2,413,586	40	48.3
1980	3,815,774	62	44.9
1986	4,367,124	72	45.8

Source: Statistisches Bundesamt, 1987, p. 207; 1988, p. 337; 1979, p. 412.

Table 2
Convictions per 100,000 persons

Item	1958	1960	1970	1980	1983	1986
Theft and embezzlement	240.0	223.1	290.0	317.9	382.7	323.6
Robbery, blackmail, attack on motorist with intent to rob[1]	4.5	4.5	6.5	10.4	13.9	12.2
Other robbery of assets	176.5	163.3	112.1	136.0	179.6	196.7
Offenses against sexual self-determination[2]	34.1	34.5	16.6	11.2	11.2	9.6
Other (non-traffic) offenses against persons[3]	141.0	139.8	103.5	109.6	115.3	102.4

1. Before 1980: only robbery and blackmail.
2. Before 1980: "against propriety."
3. Among others: murder, manslaughter, pregnancy termination and bodily injury, and also slander and verbal injury.

Source: Statistisches Bundesamt, 1962, 1972, 1982, 1985, 1988.

Table 3
Punishment 1970 and 1985 according to criminal law and official sentencing

Type of punishment	1970	1985
Prison sentences:	88,248	111,876
- up to 1 year	79,110	94,283
- over 1 year, up to 5 years	8,676	16,232
- over 5 years, up to 15 years	402	1,275
- life	70	86
Arrest	626	508
Fine (only)	464,818	488,414
Total	553,692	600,798

Source: Statistisches Bundesamt, 1987, p. 208.

Figure 1
Convictions for crimes and offenses[1] per 100,000 persons in same cohort

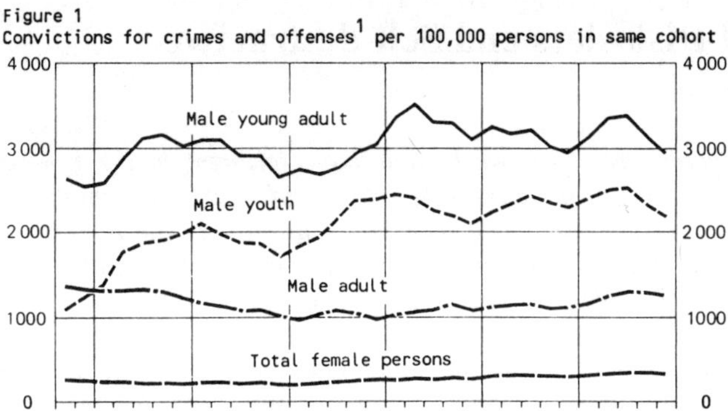

1. Not including road-tråffic offenses.
2. Until 1960: excluding the Saarland and Berlin.

Source: Statistisches Bundesamt, 1987, p. 210.

16.3 Emotional Disorders and Self-destructive Behaviour

Symptoms of anomie seem to have become more recurrent in the Federal Republic. Various forms of expression of behavioural and emotional disorder – that is, mental illness and addiction – are rising. The number of successful suicides, the only long-term statistic existing in this field, has been on the decline since 1977, while attempted suicides are on the rise.

Signs of anomie in the form of behavioural and emotional disorders can be comprehended as reactions to sudden changes in social stratification. According to Durkheim, social stability is hampered or prevented in times of economic crisis or fast-paced economic growth. Such conditions and other decisive changes were characteristic of the postwar period in the Federal Republic. According to the theory, rises in mental illness, suicide, and addiction are to be expected.

The definition of mental illness is influenced by its conceptualization by pertinent institutions. One hundred years ago, strictly scientific neurology (*Nervenheilkunde*) concerned itself with "insanity"; psychoanalysis was developed around the turn of the century, and the psychotherapeutic movements started after World War I. Psychosomatic medicine originated in the 1920s, and applied psychological therapy was first developed during and after World War II. In the 1960s, medicine and psychiatry were criticized, while, simultaneously, new clinical pictures were discovered in the field of neurology, as were new diagnostic possibilities and forms of therapy and care. Neurology developed into an individual medical branch; psychoanalysis, psychotherapy, and psychosomatics were grouped together, and child and adolescent psychiatry were added later. Presently, geriatric psychiatry is making strides toward establishing its own medical branch (Will, 1985).

Results of the microcensuses of 1974 and 1982 show a rise in mental and emotional disturbances, retardation, and disturbances of the nervous system from 65 to 74 persons in 10,000 (Statistisches Bundesamt, 1977, 1984). This increase has various causes, which can be exemplified by different expressions of mental illness.

Organic brain disorders, particularly among old people, have become more frequent, though it must be taken into account that the number of people over 65 grew from 4.8 million to 9.5 million between 1950 and 1980. Present estimates assume approximately 1 million cases of psychological disease among senior citizens in the Federal Republic.

The outpatient therapy system for endogenic psychoses has expanded dramatically, but an actual increase in morbidity is questionable. The validity of the hypothesis that risk of schizophrenia has stayed about the same in developed countries for the past 150 years is taken for granted. Still, the course of schizophrenic disease is closely linked with socio-economic factors. Therapy is more successful in rural areas than in metropolitan ones; the connection between high unemployement and increased inpatient admission of schizophrenic patients (with correspondingly lower possibility of reintegration) has been proven.

Psychoanalytic practice treats severe character neuroses associated with social deficiencies, including structural deprivation, narcissistic disturbances, and acute addiction. Diffuse suffering, directionless and somaticized fears, and inability to perform are core symptoms. In addition to explanations based on the constantly changing and speeding up of the work, living and consumption environments, there are relatively simple ones: ever since health insurance took over the costs of analysis, more lower-class patients with chronic and very serious disorders are being recommended for treatment that cannot easily be categorized as classic analytic technique.

Incidence of auto-aggressive, self-destructive diseases – inner restlessness, insomnia, functional physical complaints – is undoubtedly on the rise. This is explained by increasing isolation of many people on the one hand, and by the availabilitiy of antidepressive medication on the other; since the introduction of these medications, in 1957, there has been a marked upswing in diagnosis of depression (Will, 1985).

According to epidemiological studies, about 20% of the population suffer from emotional or mental disorders, including alcoholism, necessitating treatment. Neurotic and psychotic illnesses are more prevalent than the world average; the lower classes are hardest hit (Schmiedhofer, 1987). The middle class (and especially women) are overrepresented in the corresponding rehabilitation measures, which have more than doubled in the last 10 years, but the proportion of blue-collar workers remains on the rise (see table 1).

Suicidal acts are expressions of extreme psychic stress. The number of successful suicides are recorded in official statistics, providing comparative data for the past four decades. The suicide rate per 100,000 citizens moved in a gradual upward curvilinear pattern, from 17.7 in 1946 to a peak of 22.7 in 1977, thereafter trending downward to 20.7 in 1985 (Statistisches Bundesamt, 1987) (see table 2).

The suicide ratio of two men per woman has remained nearly unchanged. A somewhat lower proportion of women is noted up to 1955, and once again as of 1981: the standardized numbers (based on age structure in the population of 1970) project a male suicide quota of 23.4 per 100,000 and a female quota of only 10.8 per 100,000 (table 2; Statistisches Bundesamt, 1988).

The rate of attempted suicides lies well above that of successful suicides. Approximations of the ratio of suicides to attempted suicides vary between 1:2 and 1:10. It is considered an established fact that there exists a trend toward increases in suicide attempts. All age groups, with the exception of the over-65 bracket, are affected. While suicide is more often successfully committed by men than by women, the proportion of female suicide attempts outweighs male attempts. A similar picture presents itself in the relation between life-age and suicidal acts. More suicides are committed with increasing age – the highest rate being among men in the fifth decade of life – but the incidence of attempted suicide is higher among the young (Welz, 1983).

Dependence on addictive substances can be understood as a latent form of self-injury. The number of intensive, or addicted, smokers has strongly increased over the past few decades (see 13.8, "Mood-altering substances"), especially among groups with difficult living and working conditions; tendencies toward moderate cigarette consumption are notable in the middle classes, but not in the lower classes. The rising proportion of women smokers is the most important reason for the constant total number of smokers over the past decades; women living apart from their spouses and women with children are often excessive smokers (Infratest, 1989).

Current estimates of alcohol addiction vacillate between 1.5 and 2 million persons in need of treatment. In 1975, the federal government cited the figure 1 million. While a moderate downward trend in alcohol addiction is expected over the long run (Deutscher Bundestag, 1986), women are considered a special problem group in this context; they comprised 8% of those treated for alcoholism in 1950, and now comprise 30% (Russland & Plogstedt, 1987). A tendency toward increased alcoholism among young people has also been observed.

Data on addiction to medication which would allow for a time-series comparison are not available. Estimates put the figure at between 300,000 and 800,000 pill addicts, an assumed 70%–75% of this number being women. It is unanimously agreed that all signs point to a further upward trend (Deutscher Bundestag, 1986).

Consumption of hard drugs reached a peak in the 1970s; for unknown reasons, the number of drug-caused deaths has, after a slump in the early 1980s, begun to climb again. The number of rehabilitation measures for alcohol and drug addicts quadrupled between 1975 and 1985. In these groups of diseases, social-class differences are extreme compared with other diseases. The proportion of affected blue-collar workers remains disproportionately higher than that of white-collar workers (Kirchgässler, 1987) (see table 3).

In the recent past, new forms of addiction have come to the attention of the authorities, especially anorexia and bulimia among girls and women; as well, compulsive gambling among youths and adults is on the rise. A tendential development is recognizable "toward an addiction structure which is no longer fixed upon a specific addictive substance, but which is equally divided between sedatives, alcohol, and illicit substances. Numerous 'normal' medications are suited to addiction structures: laxatives, appetite and cough suppressants, and cerebral stimulants" (Schmiedhofer, 1987, p. 74).

All in all, mental and emotional disorders seem to be occurring more frequently in West German society; however, this high incidence must be regarded in the light of more refined diagnosis and a wider spectrum of therapy: "The sharp increase in the total [rehabilitation] measures perhaps does not indicate increased actual incidence but increased awareness of psychological problems and an increasing supply of psychiatric services" (Kirchgässler, 1987, p. 24). Nor does the incidence of successful suicides lead to the conclusion of increasing pathological tendencies toward disintegration and anomie in the Federal Republic; rather, these tendencies can be inferred from the increase of suicide attempts. Overall consensus exists regarding the assumption of addictive behaviour which expresses itself in a variety of forms instead of being fixed upon a certain addictive substance.

Karin Stiehr

References

Deutscher Bundestag, ed.
1986 *Bericht der Bundesregierung über die gegenwärtige Situation des Mißbrauchs von Alkohol, illegalen Drogen und Medikamenten in der Bundesrepublik Deutschland und die Ausführung des Aktionsprogramms des Bundes und der Länder zur Eindämmung und Verhütung des Alkoholmißbrauchs*. Drucksache 10/5856. Bonn.

Durkheim, Emile
1973 *Der Selbstmord.* Neuwied/Berlin: Luchterhand.

Hess, Henner
1987 *Rauchen. Geschichte, Geschäfte, Gefahren*. Frankfurt am Main/New York: Campus.

Infratest Gesundheitsforschung, ed.
1989 *Alleinstehende Frauen*. München.

Kirchgässler, K. U.
1987 *Social Class Differences and Health Status in the Federal Republic of Germany: A Time-Serial Analysis*. Paper Prepared for a WHO Conference on Social Equity and Health, Lisbon, 28-30 September 1987.

Russland, Rita, and Sibylle Plogstedt
1986 *Sucht - Alkohol und Medikamente in der Arbeitswelt*. Frankfurt am Main: Fischer.

Schmiedhofer, Martina
1987 *Gesundheitsideal, Morbiditätsstruktur. Grenzen politisch-administrativer Gesundheitspolitik*. Frankfurt am Main: Verlag für Interkulturelle Kommunikation.

Statistisches Bundesamt, ed.
1977 *Die Lebensverhältnisse älterer Menschen 1977*. Stuttgart/Mainz: Kohlhammer.

–, ed.
1984 *Wirtschaft und Statistik*, no. 4.

–, ed.
1987 *Von den zwanziger zu den achtziger Jahren. Ein Vergleich der Lebensverhältnisse der Menschen*. Wiesbaden/Mainz: Kohlhammer.

–, ed.
1988 *Statistisches Jahrbuch 1988 für die Bundesrepublik Deutschland*. Wiesbaden/Mainz: Kohlhammer.

Welz, Rainer
1983 *Drogen, Alkohol und Suizid. Strukturelle und individuelle Aspekte abweichenden Verhaltens*. Stuttgart: Enke.

Will, Herbert
1985 "Selige Gesundheit. Systeme der Therapiegesellschaft." In *Kursbuch 82*. Berlin.

Table 1
Rehabilitation measures for psychiatric disorders in the Federal Republic of Germany 1975 - 1985

Year	Absolute number of rehab. measures	Blue-collar workers (in %)			Percentage of white-collar workers	Percentage of blue-collar workers in work populace	Percentage of white-collar workers in work populace
		Unskilled workers	Skilled workers	Foremen			
1975	7,981	18.9	26.9	0.0	40.0	42.7	42.6
1976	9,945	16.8	22.0	0.0	50.3	42.3	43.4
1977	12,136	19.2	11.9	0.7	54.1	42.8	43.9
1978	13,555	23.3	10.2	0.9	54.3	42.3	44.9
1979	13,873	27.3	11.3	0.7	55.9	42.3	45.3
1980	16,835	27.6	12.6	1.0	49.1	42.3	45.6
1981	11,913	25.7	11.2	0.9	51.9	42.2	46.1
1982	12,856	24.6	10.7	1.5	55.0	41.3	47.0
1983	12,717	23.8	9.3	1.0	57.6	39.9	47.3
1984	15,835	26.0	10.9	1.0	52.1	39.5	47.6
1985	18,211	27.0	11.4	0.9	50.9	39.4	47.7

Source: Kirchgässler, 1987.

Table 2
Suicides in West Germany (per 100,000 persons)

Year	Total	Male	Female
1946	17.7	24.9	11.7
1950	19.2	27.4	11.9
1955	19.2	26.0	13.0
1960	19.4	26.3	13.3
1965	20.0	26.8	13.8
1970	21.5	28.5	15.2
1975	20.8	27.7	14.6
1980	20.8	28.2	14.1
1986	19.0	26.6	12.0

Source: Welz, 1983, p. 90; Statistisches Bundesamt, 1988; author's calculations.

Table 3
Rehabilitation measures for alcohol and drug dependency in the Federal Republic of Germany

Year	Absolute number of rehab. measures	Percentage of blue-collar workers	Percentage of white-collar workers	% Blue-collar workers in work populace	% White-collar workers in work populace
1975	5,998	66.0	13.5	42.7	42.6
1976	7,495	71.4	9.2	42.3	43.4
1977	9,931	72.2	12.1	42.8	43.9
1978	13,709	86.0	9.6	42.3	44.9
1979	13,342	79.0	15.1	42.3	45.3
1980	13,664	78.0	17.7	42.3	45.6
1981	19,729	76.8	18.5	42.2	46.1
1982	19,541	75.4	14.9	41.3	47.0
1983	19,437	75.4	19.0	39.9	47.3
1984	22,826	69.2	25.1	39.5	47.6
1985	26,665	61.1	20.8	39.4	47.7

Source: Kirchgässler, 1987.

16.4 Poverty

Poverty, in terms of an insufficient income, seemed to become a marginal problem in the Federal Republic of Germany, because it significantly declined in the two decades after World War II. This development was interrupted at the beginning of the 1970s and began to increase in the 1980s. A so-called new poverty arose, which is to a large extent the consequence of an unsolved unemployment problem.

Number of Poor

The number of poor people depends on the poverty standard used. In Germany, one officially defined poverty level was given by the social maintenance assistance standard (*Sozialhilfe-Regelsatz*), which was based on a market basket of the goods necessary for a decent life differentiated according to the age of the members of a household. In recent decades, financial support given on the basis of this standard grew less than average wages and pensions but more than the inflation index (see figure 1). The statistically monitored number of people getting a "continual cost-of-living allowance" gives a first hint of the volume of poverty. Continual assistance is nowadays the bigger part of financial support beside occasional aid, which is granted in needy situations. The number of people receiving continual assistance decreased constantly from 1950 to 1962. A new social-aid system was introduced in 1963; there after, the proportion of continual welfare recipients in the population was nearly stable until the early 1970s, reaching a low point in 1969 – 1970 at about 925,000 people, or 1.2%. It climbed to 5.5%, or 2.3 million people in 1987. This figure is called the "reduced poverty" (*Bekämpfte Armut*). Some observers argue that about half of the people below the official poverty line are, for various reasons, not applying for social assistance; they constitute the "hidden poor," and their numbers could be equal to those of the fought poor.

If a relative poverty standard in relationship to average income is used (see table 2), the results are the following: 7.0% of all inhabitants were below a 50%line and 2.1% were below a 40%line in 1983. This is more than in 1973 and less than in 1963 – the same sequence of downward and upward trends as are shown in the official statistics from social-assistance authorities.

The most conservative estimators of poverty in the Federal Republic of Germany say that the poor are only those people who have a claim to social assistance but don't use it. The broadest conceptions of poverty have it that one-third of the population is affected by some degree of poverty.

Composition of the Poor Population

As new poverty evolved, the composition of the poor population changed significantly: there is a strong shift from elderly people to younger ones. In 1963, 31.2% of assistance recipients were 65 years and over; they comprised only 8.2% of recipients in 1986.

A second shift is – contrary to many assumptions – a lessening of female dominance among the poor (table 1). On average, the relative share of men receiving social aid increased from 33.9% to 44.6% between 1963 and 1986. This amounts to a certain defeminization of poverty, but women are still the overwhelming majority among those receiving social assistance.

A third shift is a growing percentage of foreigners among recipients of social assistance. Their proportion was for a long time far below their proportion in the population as a whole, but now has grown 8% above it.

The Risk of Falling into Poverty

The question of who is at risk to fall into poverty is not identical with the question of who is already poor, though there are similarities. The chance of becoming poor in terms of social-maintenance assistance is, in line with expectations, higher for women than for men, but this tendency has declined in recent decades. In 1986, 53 out of 1,000 females and 45 out of 1,000 males were receiving continual social-maintenance assistance. In 1966 these figures were 29 and 20, respectively. The most important change occurred in respect to age groups; elderly people are the only group whose poverty risk has fallen in recent decades, while poverty risk increased for all age groups below 65, and especially for children below the age of 18. The percentage of children at risk for poverty strongly increased though the total number of children decreased.

These results are supported by data from the income and expenditure survey (table 2), which also show strong differences in poverty risk according to type of household. An exceptionally high poverty risk exists for single parents. Married couples with two or more children and male one-person households have a somewhat lower risk, though it is still above average. Poverty has become a new threat for population groups that were not at great risk previously. On average, the poverty risk decreased somewhat from 1963 to 1973, and then increased up to 1983.

Causative Factors

Poverty is caused by a lack of income which may have various sources; the first is no or insufficient income from employment. The lack of income from employment, due to structural unemployment, was the most important cause of poverty in the 1980s. In 1978, 16% of recipients were recceiving social assistance due to unemployment; in 1986 the percentage was twice as high. Also important is insufficient income from employment; this problem could grow due to the increase in part-time employment. Second, poverty may arise from a lack of social benefits which can be claimed in the case of need, for example, in the case of retirement or illness. In terms of a percentage of all recipients, illness and insufficient subsistence were a much less significant cause of poverty in 1988 than they were in 1978. Third, a lack of assistance from family or relatives can lead to poverty. This kind of assistance has lost its pre-industrial dominance, but it is still important because much redistribution occurs within families and among kin. This is indicated by the fact that, since 1978, the lack of a provider due to divorce, disappearance, or death has been a cause of poverty for 13% of recipients. All in all, structural unemployment has to be perceived as the main cause of increasing poverty. It must be stated, however, that the social system does not fulfill its function of preventing people from falling below the poverty line as well as it did two decades ago.

Fighting Poverty

Poverty levels react not only to specific social-policy programs, but also to the development of socio-economic conditions on the whole. The fight against poverty had, against a background of good economic growth, some success in the 1950s and 1960s. It stalled in the 1970s and suffered a setback in the 1980s, as growth rates in the economy declined. The main factor in the increase of poverty is structural unemployment. A large number of unemployed are less and less helped by unemployment insurance (entitlement is restricted to special conditions) but a growing number received *Arbeitslosenhilfe* (reduced unemployment aid) and welfare. The costs of unemployment are, by means of this mechanism, transferred from the Bundesanstalt für Arbeit (Federal Office for Employment) to the federal government (which is responsible for unemployment aid) and local authorities (which pay for social-maintenance assistance). Given this situation, some restrictions to and cuts in social aid were introduced. On the other hand, new solutions for the problem of decoupling income and work, such as a guaranteed minimum income, are being discussed.

The problem of fighting poverty is much more complex if poverty is understood in a multidimensional sense. Using special standards, poverty can be found, for example, in the areas of housing, education, health, and social relations. Most people fall below a social poverty standard in at least one area.

Wolfgang Glatzer

References

Altmeyer-Baumann, Sabine
1987 *"Alte Armut" - "Neue Armut"*. Weinheim: Deutscher Studien Verlag.

Armutsbericht des Paritätischen Wohlfahrtsverbandes
1989 *Blätter der Wohllfahrtspflege*, no. 11+12.

Döring, Diether, Walter Hanesch, and Ernst-Ulrich Huster, eds.
1990 *Armut*. Frankfurt am Main: Suhrkamp.

Hauser, Richard, Helga Cremer-Schäfer, and Udo Nouvertné, eds.
1981 *Armut, Niedrigeinkommen und Unterversorgung in der Bundesrepublik Deutschland*. Frankfurt am Main/New York: Campus.

Hauser, Richard, and Peter Semrau
1990 *Poverty in the Federal Republic of Germany*. Report for the Commission of the European Community. Sonderforschungsbereich 3. Frankfurt am Main.

Informationszentrum Sozialwissenschaften, ed.
1988 *Armut in einem Reichen Land. Literatur- und Forschungsdokumentation 1984-1987*. Bonn.

Klein, Thomas
1987 *Sozialer Abstieg und Verarmung durch Arbeitslosigkeit*. Frankfurt am Main/New York: Campus.

Leibfried, Stephan, and F. Tennstedt, eds.
1985 *Politik der Armut und die Spaltung des Sozialstaats*. Frankfurt am Main: Suhrkamp.

Table 1
Welfare recipients according to gender and type of assistance, and welfare expenditures

Year	Recipients								Gross expenditure		
	Total	Total[1]	Current assistance- to-living costs		Male[1]	Female[1]	Occasional				
	1,000	Per 1,000 resid.	1,000	Per 1,000 resid.	Per 1,000 resid.	Per 1,000 resid.	1,000	Per 1,000 resid.	DM mill.	Change from previous year	DM per resid.
1963	1,849[2]	32	1,311[2]	23	26	38	814	14	1,860	-	32
1964	1,418	24	816	14	20	29	832	14	1,943	+4.4	33
1965	1,404	24	760	13	19	28	862	15	2,106	+8.4	36
1966	1,445	24	773	13	19	29	895	15	2,318	+10.0	39
1967	1,531	26	835	14	21	30	925	15	2,550	+10.0	43
1968	1,503	25	795	13	20	30	942	16	2,671	+4.7	44
1969	1,479	25	759	12	20	29	946	16	2,859	+7.0	47
1970	1,491	25	749	12	19	29	965	16	3,335	+16.6	55
1971	1,548	25	803	13	20	31	979	16	4,017	+20.4	66
1972	1,645	27	867	14	20	32	1,025	17	4,817	+19.9	78
1973	1,730	28	918	15	21	34	1,064	17	5,656	+17.4	91
1974	1,916	31	1,057	17	24	37	1,126	18	7,136	+26.2	115
1975	2,049	33	1,190	19	26	39	1,147	19	8,405	+17.8	136
1976	2,109	34	1,276	21	28	40	1,123	18	9,597	+14.2	156
1977	2,164	35	1,362	22	29	41	1,098	18	10,452	+8.9	170
1978	2,120	35	1,335	22	28	40	1,079	18	11,349	+8.6	185
1979	2,095	34	1,311	21	28	40	1,080	18	12,129	+6.9	198
1980	2,144	35	1,322	21	29	40	1,125	18	13,266	+9.4	215
1981[3]	2,083	34	1,291	21	28	39	1,080	18	14,783	+11.4	240
1982	2,320	38	1,560	25	33	42	1,061	17	16,329	+10.5	265
1983[3]	2,437	40	1,726	28	35	44	1,016	17	17,569	+7.6	286
1984	2,570	42	1,837	30	37	46	1,047	17	18,784	+6.9	307
1985[3]	2,814	46	2,063	34	42	50	1,108	18	20,846	+11.0	342
1986	3,020	49	2,239	37	45	53	1,196	20	23,197	+11.3	380
1987	3,136	51	2,332	38	47	55	1,256	21	25,199	+8.6	412

1. Excluding those repeatedly registered.
2. Incl. recipients of on-time assistance-toward-living costs.
3. Results based in part on random surveys.

Sources: Wirtschaft und Statistik, 1988, no. 4, p. 268; 1989, no. 8, p. 537; Statistisches Bundesamt, Fachserie 13: Sozialleistungen, Reihe 2: Sozialhilfe 1987, p. 20; Statistisches Jahrbuch, 1987, p. 52.

Table 2
Poverty ratios of persons living in selected household[1] types and by individual gender and age

Item	40% line			50% line		
	1973	1978	1983	1973	1978	1983
All	1.4	1.6	2.1	5.5	6.2	7.0
Females	1.5	1.7	2.0	5.6	6.5	7.0
- 17	1.6	2.2	3.0	7.1	8.7	9.8
18-24	(0.6)	1.3	3.3	3.2	5.1	9.3
25-49	0.9	1.2	2.0	4.1	5.0	6.3
50-64	1.3	1.2	1.0	4.3	4.3	4.3
65 or over	3.2	2.9	1.7	9.2	9.3	7.2
Males	1.4	1.5	2.1	5.4	5.9	7.0
- 17	1.8	2.1	3.6	7.7	8.7	10.4
18-24	1.2	1.4	2.5	3.8	4.7	7.8
25-49	0.7	1.0	1.6	3.6	4.4	5.7
50-64	1.0	0.7	1.2	3.1	3.1	3.9
65 or over	2.8	2.8	1.9	8.6	8.5	7.8
One-person household	2.2	1.9	1.8	6.3	6.9	6.8
Female	2.2	2.0	1.4	6.7	7.3	6.1
Male	(2.1)	(1.9)	2.7	4.8	5.5	8.5
Married couples	1.1	1.4	1.6	5.0	5.7	6.1
Without children	1.5	1.6	1.1	4.5	4.9	4.5
1 child	0.2	0.5	1.1	1.3	2.2	3.5
2+ children	1.7	1.6	2.3	6.8	7.7	8.89
Single parents	2.9	6.7	10.9	7.7	16.3	22.1
1 child	(1.8)	(2.8)	4.1	6.7	7.1	11.0
2+ children	4.9	10.5	19.0	9.5	25.1	35.3
Others	2.9	1.6	2.4	8.3	6.2	7.7

1. Only persons in households with German head, excluding institutionalized population, exluding households with high income, exluding households with 7 and more members; ( ) = 20 to 29 unweighted cases (figures above are weighted)

Source: Author's computations based upon Income and Expenditure Surveys 1969, 1973, 1978, and 1983.

Figure 1
Development of the Regular Social Assistance Rate (Index) in comparison to the standard benefits through Statutory Pension Scheme to the net wage per worker (Index) and the Cost of Living Price Index for a two-person household of pension and social-assistance recipients

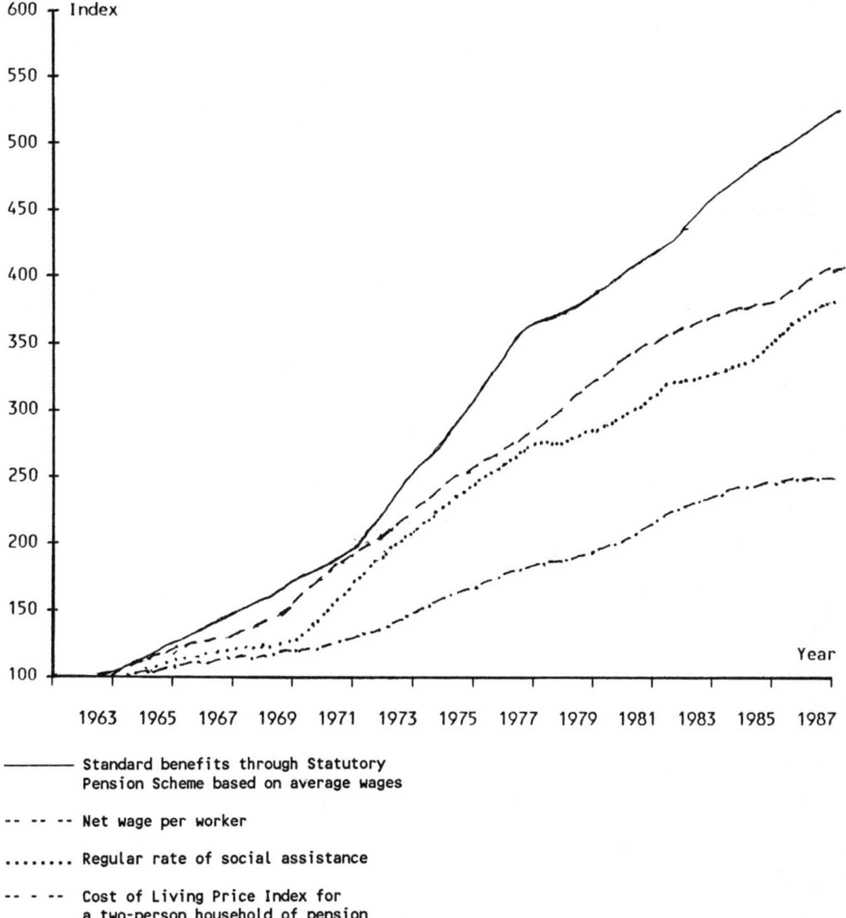

Source: Bundesminister für Arbeit und Sozialordnung, in Statistisches Taschenbuch, 1988. tables 1.14, 6.11, 6.12, 7.11, 8.16.

17. Attitudes and Values

17.1 Satisfaction

Satisfaction levels among the German population are very differentiated: there is a relatively high level of general satisfaction and of satisfaction with most specific areas of life. At the same time – and this is somewhat ambivalent – there are a lot of worries and personal problems. Satisfaction varies significantly depending on the area of life; there is in general higher satisfaction with personal areas and less satisfaction with public areas.
The societal level of satisfaction seems to be fairly stable in the middle range, with the exception of satisfaction with the environment, which has changed the most. In some cases a U-curve can be detected showing a somewhat higher satisfaction in 1978, less satisfaction in 1980 and 1984, and a higher level of satisfaction again in 1988. Though there is far-reaching structural stability, there is nevertheless individual fluctuation. In the long run, there appears to be a slight increase of satisfaction and happiness in Germany.

Global Satisfaction

Satisfaction studies based on representative data usually surprise with their high satisfaction scores. But when negative aspects of good feelings are explicitly looked for, they show a severe burden of ill feelings despite a high reported satisfaction. This is called the ambivalence of well-being.

In the aggregate, satisfaction seems to be fairly high and stable. The continuity of structures is demonstrated by the near-total stability of satisfaction with life from 1978 to 1988 (see table 1); this is next to no change in the average figure – with a range from 7.7 to 7.9 – having only marginal changes in the dispersion profile. There is also a striking dominance of feelings of happiness in contrast to feelings of unhappiness (see table 2). Happiness showed a slight tendency to decrease from 1978 through 1980 to 1984, and then to increase again, but in terms of the entire decade it has been quite stable. In contrast, on the side of negative aspects of well-being there exists a fairly broad diffusion of symptoms of anxiety (stress, fears, nervousness, depression) (see table 3) and of alienation (work alienation, meaninglessness, loneliness) (see 17.2, "Perception of Social Problems"). Again, the continual impact of those negative aspects of well-being is remarkable: in response to questions about worries and personal problems, Germans report many severe burdens. These burdens have led to a certain degree of resignation, as some people think that they cannot overcome their problems.

The development of global satisfaction with life has been monitored for many years in different surveys. They are not comparable in the strict sense because they do not use the same scales and are not conducted at the same points of time. For example, the *Eurobarometer* monitors overall satisfaction with life since 1973 (see table 4). The measurement results are available for two points in each year. Between 13% and 25% of the German population have remained very happy with their life over the years. Around two-thirds (56%–68%) are fairly satisfied, 10% to 17% are not very satisfied, and 1% to 3% are not at all satisfied. The result for 1988 shows the strongest polarization: a relatively large proportion of people are either very satisfied or not at all satisfied, whereas the percentage of fairly satisfied is low. All in all, there are many small shifts but no trend or regular development.

The data going furthest back (to 1958) are available from the Allensbacher Institute, which asked, "Are you generally satisfied with your present life, or do you wish some things were different?" According to these data, satisfaction with life was quite low in 1958, then rose to a first peak in the mid-1960s and to a second peak in the late 1970s. It then dropped, experiencing a comeback in 1988 (see figure 1). The picture given is that satisfaction with life is growing and the wish to change things is diminishing in the long run. Somewhat different are the answers to the "happiness" question for the same time span (see figure 2). The question is, "If someone said about you that you are very happy, would he be right or not?" The results seem to indicate a slight trend: people saying "right" are stable at around 30%, people saying "not right" are decreasing somewhat, and people saying "partly right" are increasing somewhat.

Overall, well-being shows a complex differentiation, indicating that many individuals have ambivalent feelings of satisfaction and deprivation simultaneously. In individual cases, well-being is changing to some degree; in structural terms many aspects of well-being and the lack thereof seem to remain the same.

Satisfaction with Private and Public Life

In studies which treat private and public life and public matters, a discrepancy seems to emerge in satisfaction levels. The areas of marriage and partnership range at the top of the hierarchy of satisfaction levels, and public security and environmental protection are found at the bottom (see table 5). Individuals are not likely to gloss over their private life, which falls under their own responsibility; they do not avoid talking about their personal and family worries and conflicts. The assumption is that primary social relationships are the most important source of subjective satisfaction, and that positive contributions in this area outweigh negative restrictions in the private sphere. This would lead to the conclusion that the relationship between contributions and restrictions is quite different within the public sphere.

The highest specific satisfaction is found in the area of marriage/partnership. This result is fully consistent with the fact that the increased annual number of divorces is much lower than the small number of dissatisfied couples. In addition, of course, divorces contribute to a high average satisfaction of the remaining couples. Changes here between 1978 and 1988 are very small.

Environmental protection is the only area where the number of "rather dissatisfied" exceeds the number of "rather satisfied." The changes that occurred between 1978 and 1988 serve to document that satisfaction scales do not always produce stable results. Real danger and diffuse fears are closely associated in the public areas that garner the highest dissatisfaction. Environmental protection and public safety are topics of strong opinions in the mass media, as well as in everyday life. The correlation between dissatisfaction with environmental protection and public safety is quite moderate, however, and shows that there is no general negative stereotyping of areas of public responsibility. As well, it must be mentioned that public areas such as social security garner a higher level of satisfaction than do the two subjects mentioned above. The standard-of-life related to material areas (housing, leisure, income) are positioned in the middle of the hierarchy of satisfaction levels. It seems that the thesis of private wealth and public poverty finds a certain degree of expression in this assessment of the German population.

Two particular areas often earn special attention: job satisfaction and satisfaction with the way democracy works. Job satisfaction is high and remains quite stable. Satisfaction with the way democracy works is a question that has been included since 1973 in the *Eurobarometer* (see table 6). Starting from a relatively low level in 1973, satisfaction increased somewhat, showing an important deviation only in 1988, when there was the largest proportion of "not very satisfied" since 1973, as well as the highest number of the "very satisfied" ever.

The same holds true for many of the areas measured in 1978, 1984, and 1988 (table 5); only minor changes are recorded in most cases, and these are mostly aligned along a U-curve. They are somewhat higher in 1978, somewhat lower in 1980, even lower in 1984, and then somewhat higher in 1988. A striking change happened only in one area: that of satisfaction with environmental protection.

In the area of individual well-being, structural stability is accompanied by extensive individual fluctuation. The positive and the negative changes in the population must sum up to an equal amount if the mean is to remain the same. How satisfaction is guided by attraction and rejection, by push and pull, by constraints and decisions is, however, an open question.

Wolfgang Glatzer

References

Europäische Gemeinschaften, ed.
1989 *Eurobarometer Nr. 31. Die öffentliche Meinung in der europäischen Gemeinschaft.* Brüssel.

Glatzer, Wolfgang, and Wolfgang Zapf, eds.
1984 *Lebensqualität in der Bundesrepublik. Objektive Lebensbedingungen und subjektives Wohlbefinden.* Frankfurt am Main/New York: Campus.

Greiffenhagen, M. and S.
1988 *Das Glück. Realitäten eines Traumes.* München: Piper.

Hofstätter, P.R.
1986 *Bedingungen der Zufriedenheit.* Zürich: Edition Interfrom.

Noelle-Neumann, Elisabeth, ed.
1981 *The Germans. Public Opinion Polls, 1967 - 1980.* London: Greenwood.

Siara, Ch.
1980 *Komponenten der Wohlfahrt. Materialien zu Lebensbedingungen und Lebensqualität.* Frankfurt am Main/New York: Campus.

Statistisches Bundesamt, ed., in Zusammenarbeit mit dem Sonderforschungsbereich 3 der
1989 Universitäten Frankfurt und Mannheim, *Datenreport 1989 - Zahlen und Fakten über die Bundesrepublik Deutschland.* Stuttgart: Verlag Bonn-Aktuell.

Zapf, Wolfgang, ed.
1987 "German Social Report. Living Conditions and Subjective Well-Being 1978 - 1984." *Social Indicators Research*, 19, no. 1, 170.

Table 1
Satisfaction with life 1978 - 1988[1] (in %)

Year	Completely dissatisfied 0-4	5	6	7	8	9	Completely satisfied 10	Total	Mean
1978	4.2	5.6	7.3	15.4	31.5	18.0	17.9	100	7.8
1980	4.2	8.4	8.3	17.7	29.8	13.0	18.4	100	7.7
1984	6.0	6.6	6.2	14.4	32.0	17.3	17.4	100	7.7
1988	3.4	4.6	7.3	15.2	33.8	18.8	16.8	100	7.9

1. Wording of question: "All things considered, how satisfied are you with your life as a whole these days?" (satisfaction scale "0" to "10")

Source: Wohlfahrtssurvey, 1978, 1980, 1984, 1988.

Table 2
Emotional well-being: Happiness 1978 - 1988[1] (in %)

Year	Very happy	Quite happy	Quite unhappy	Very unhappy	Total
1978	21.5	74.0	3.8	0.7	100
1980	25.6	68.7	5.1	0.6	100
1984	19.8	71.2	7.9	1.1	100
1988	23.0	72.4	4.0	0.6	100

1. Wording of question: "Do you feel that your life at the present is very happy, quite happy, quite unhappy or very unhappy?"

Source: Wohlfahrtssurvey, 1978, 1980, 1984, 1988.

Table 3
Anxiety and life satisfaction (in %)

Item	Total			Rather dissatisfied[1]			Completely satisfied[2]		
	1978	1984	1988	1978	1984	1988	1978	1984	1988
Anxiety symptoms[3]									
Often spells of complete exhaustion or fatigue	54	47	44	82	69	75	46	37	37
Recurring frightening thoughts	19	21	19	69	55	56	11	9	14
Constantly keyed up and jittery	16	16	12	51	33	22	9	10	9
Usually unhappy or depressed	14	15	10	64	55	55	7	6	5
Often shake or tremble	9	8	6	31	23	23	7	6	4
No symptoms	41	43	47	8	19	15	51	58	56

1. Range 0 to 4 on satisfaction scale from 1 to 10.
2. Point 10 on satisfaction scale.
3. Items of the anxiety scale. See E. Allardt, "About dimensions of Welfare", Research Report, Vol. 1, Research Group for Comparative Sociology, University of Helsinki, 1973.

Source: Wohlfahrtssurvey, 1978, 1984, 1988.

Table 4
The feeling of overall life satisfaction (in %)

Wording of question: "All in all, to what extent would you say you are satisfied with the life you lead at this time? Please use this scale (10 points) to decide on your reply. "10" means you are completely satisfied and "1" means you are completely dissatisfied."

Item	1973 IX	1975 X-XI	1976 X-XI	1977 X-XI	1978 X-XI	1979 IV	1980 IV	1981 IV
Very satisfied	17	14	22	24	20	24	17	16
Fairly satisfied	65	65	60	61	65	62	68	61
Not very satisfied	15	17	15	12	12	10	11	16
Not at all satisfied	2	2	2	2	1	2	2	3
No reply	1	2	1	1	2	2	2	4
Total	100	100	100	100	100	100	100	100
N	1,957	1,002	1,007	999	1,006	1,003	1,009	1,004

Item	1982 X	1983 X	1984 X-XI	1985 X-XI	1986 X-XI	1987 X-XI	1988 X-XI
Very satisfied	19	12	13	14	18	15	25
Fairly satisfied	65	66	71	64	65	68	56
Not very satisfied	12	15	13	17	14	14	17
Not at all satisfied	2	2	2	3	2	2	1
No reply	2	5	1	2	1	1	1
Total	100	100	100	100	100	100	100
N	1,012	1,058	1,053	1,028	1,084	957	1,051

Recoding on this table is as follows: Point 1 and 2 of the scale=not at all satisfied; points 3, 4, 5=not very satisfied; points 6, 7, 8=fairly satisfied; points 9 and 10=very satisfied.

Source: Eurobarometer, 1989.

Table 5
Satisfaction with major life domains 1978 - 1988

Life domains	Year	Rather satisfied[1]	Completely satisfied in percent	Rather dissatisfied	Mean
Marriage/ partnership[2]	1978	97.4	48.4	0.8	9.0
	1984	95.1	43.7	2.4	8.8
	1988	96.1	47.2	1.5	8.9
Family life[3]	1978	95.7	38.6	2.0	8.7
	1984	93.4	29.6	1.8	8.4
	1988	96.6	37.9	1.9	8.7
Division of household tasks[2]	1978	85.6	28.4	6.9	7.9
	1984	85.4	29.6	8.4	7.9
	1988	88.4	40.9	6.5	8.2
Housing	1978	83.2	29.2	6.8	7.8
	1984	85.4	35.8	5.6	8.0
	1988	88.8	37.4	4.7	8.2
Being a housewife[5]	1978	86.9	24.9	5.1	7.9
	1984	85.1	27.0	7.6	7.8
	1988	86.3	29.1	5.6	7.9
Job[4]	1978	89.0	11.5	5.2	7.6
	1984	90.3	21.2	5.7	7.9
	1988	92.3	15.3	3.7	7.8
Leisure	1978	82.7	25.8	10.4	7.6
	1984	81.5	26.9	9.6	7.7
	1988	85.2	28.6	8.1	7.8
Living standard	1978	84.6	14.5	6.6	7.4
	1984	80.8	16.2	9.5	7.4
	1988	83.1	16.3	7.3	7.5
Health	1978	79.0	16.3	11.6	7.3
	1984	74.1	18.5	14.9	7.1
	1988	78.1	19.7	12.6	7.3
Education[6]	1978	70.9	14.7	17.1	6.7
	1984	72.2	19.0	15.5	7.0
	1988	76.7	22.6	13.1	7.2
Household income	1978	82.2	13.3	10.0	7.2
	1984	74.1	14.0	14.5	6.9
	1988	77.7	14.3	10.8	7.1
Social security system	1978	76.6	9.7	13.6	6.9
	1984	74.2	11.2	13.7	6.8
	1988	77.1	11.2	10.1	7.0
Public safety	1978	43.7	1.9	40.0	5.0
	1984	46.5	2.3	31.4	5.2
	1988	58.2	4.4	23.4	5.8
Church[7]	1978	56.8	8.6	24.6	5.9
	1984	54.8	9.2	25.1	5.8
	1988	49.5	7.1	30.3	5.5
Environmental protection	1978	40.4	1.6	38.7	5.0
	1984	22.2	0.9	58.3	3.8
	1988	30.3	1.8	46.1	4.5

1. Satisfaction scale 0-10; "rather satisfied"=6-10; "completely satisfied"=10; "rather dissatisfied"=0-4.
2. Only respondents with spouse or partner.
3. Only respondents with spouse and children under 18 years.
4. Full- and part-time employed persons.
5. Non-employed housewives only.
6. Students and pupils only.
7. Only members of Protestant or Catholic churches.

Source: Wohlfahrtssurvey, 1978, 1980, 1984, 1988.

Table 6
The feeling of satisfaction with the way democracy works (in %)

Wording of question: "On the whole, to what extent would you say you are satisfied with the way democracy works (in our country). Answer on this scale (10 points)."

Item	1973 IX	1976 XI	1977 X-XI	1978 X-XI	1979 X	1980 X-XI	1981 X-XI
Very satisfied	5	13	9	9	12	9	11
Fairly satisfied	39	66	69	68	68	64	59
Not very satisfied	44	16	16	15	12	17	18
Not at all satisfied	11	3	2	2	2	4	5
No reply	1	2	4	6	6	6	7
Total	100	100	100	100	100	100	100
N	1,957	1,007	999	1,006	1,005	1,008	962

Item	1982	1983 X	1984 X-XI	1985 X-XI	1986 X-XI	1987 X-XI	1988 X-XI
Very satisfied	8	7	11	10	12	6	18
Fairly satisfied	59	59	62	59	59	62	50
Not very satisfied	22	21	21	22	22	25	28
Not at all satisfied	4	3	5	4	4	4	2
No reply	7	10	1	5	3	3	2
Total	100	100	100	100	100	100	100
N	1,012	1,058	1,053	1,028	1,084	957	1,051

Recoding on this table is as follows: Point 1 and 2 of the scale=not at all satisfied; points 3, 4, 5=not very satisfied; points 6, 7, 8=fairly satisfied; points 9 and 10=very satisfied.

Source: Eurobarometer, 1989.

Figure 1
Satisfaction with life and wishes for change 1958 - 1988 (in %)

Wording of question: "Are you generally satisfied with your present life, or do you wish some things were different?"

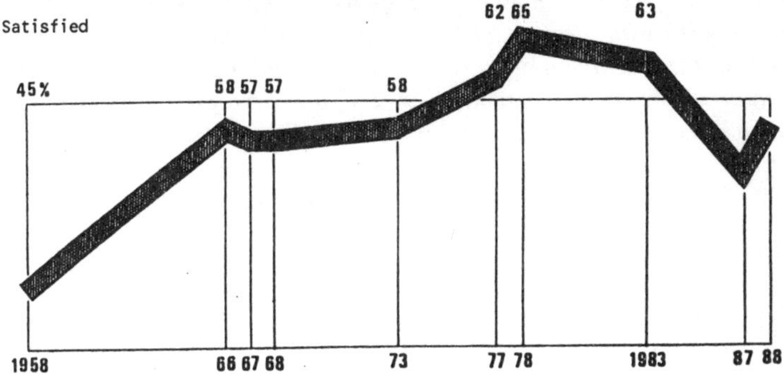

Source: Allenbacher Archiv, IfD-Umfrage.

Figure 2
Estimations of individual happiness 1954 - 1987 (in %)

Wording of question: "If somebody said about you that you are were very happy, would he be right or not?"

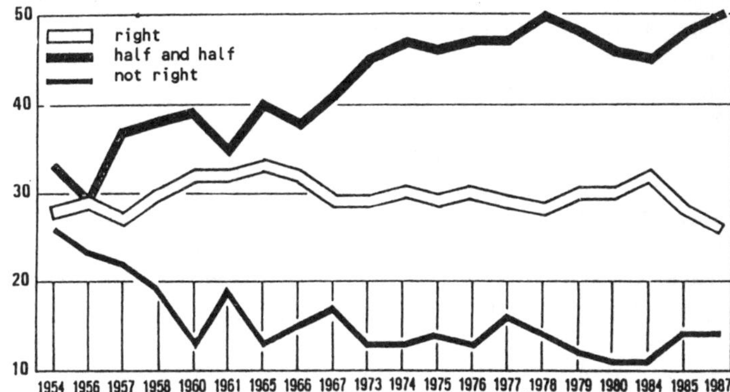

Source: Allensbacher Archiv, Ifd-Umfrage.

17.2 Perception of Social Problems

Social problems can be defined in different ways. People perceive that the most important concerns for their nation are preservation of peace and economic prosperity. Concern with these issues is shifting over time; in the 1980s, worries about war and unemployment declined. Poverty has re-ermerged as a perceived problem, and environmental pollution is the big new problem. Everyday problems such as alienation and anxiety seem to be constantly present to a certain degree.

Most Important Concerns

Social problems are not defined consistently; one of many definitions involves relatively large numbers of people who are aware of a undesired social condition (Glatzer, 1982). These social problems can be seen in two perspectives: the problems that people think are important for the nation, the society, or the population, and the problems that large numbers of people feel they personally have. The actual problems may be identical, but public awareness of them may differ from individual exposure to them.

The significant social problems or issues perceived by the majority of the population are similar in many nations; economic problems and the preservation of peace are of prime concern, though their importance varies over time. When the question was asked "What in your opinion is the most important question we in West Germany should at present concern ourselves with?" (see figure 1), the answer "economic problems" was relatively rare from the mid-1950s to the mid-1960s, and reached its highest level in 1975, during the oil crisis. Unemployment is the most important problem among the different economic issues. Public awareness of unemployment bears some relationship to unemployment statistics. "Preservation of peace" has less often been a concern than "economic problems." Worries in this respect peaked at the beginning of the 1950s and the beginning of the 1980s.

Aside from these general problems, there are special national issues such as the reunification of Germany. This topic was high in the public awareness up to the middle of the 1960s and then fell rapidly. By the time reunification of Germany came close to reality, at the end of the 1980s, it was no longer a public concern. As well, it should be mentioned that European integration never became a very "important question" in the public mind.

Domestic affairs is another category of social problems that do worry many people. In surveys in the 1980s, environmental protection is among the most important political tasks and goals defined by the people, just behind the goal of fighting unemployment (Daten zur Umwelt 1988/1989).

Perception of Individual and Collective Conditions

In the economic area, as in other areas, there is an important difference between assessment of the country's economic situation and of individuals' household economic situation (see tables 1 and 2). For example, in 1982, 62% of the population thought that the country's economic situation had worsened over the past twelve months, but only 24% said the same thing about their household's financial situation. Opinion was reversed in 1986: 13% believed that their individual situation had worsened, but 11% thought that this was true for the country. There is a gap between public and individual moods, and the collective climate is not at all the sum of individuals' self-perceptions (Noelle-Neumann, 1988). In the second half of the 1980s, the gap between definitions of the individual and the collective situations was much smaller than previously.

Perception of Poverty and Inequality

Poverty has been one of the most persistent and increasing social problems in recent years (see 16.4, "Poverty"). Rating their own standard of living, 4% to 6% of the German population perceived themselves as poor or near poor between 1983 and 1989 (see table 3). The changes are too small to ascertain a trend in the subjective perception of poverty. The perception of the poor by the entire population is shifting as well: the reasons "because there is much injustice in our society" and "it is an inevitable part of modern progress" were given more often from 1976 to 1989 than were the reasons "because they have been unlucky" and "because of laziness and lack of willpower" (European Community, 1990). The poverty problem is an inequality issue in modern society; acceptance of the existing socio-economic inequality is quite precarious (ISI, 1990).

Perception of Environmental Pollution

One of the main problems that arose in public awareness, especially after 1978 with the start-up of the ecological movement, is environmental pollution. This problem is split into many concerns – for example, quality of drinking water, noise, air pollution, garbage disposal, missing green and natural areas, loss of arable land, deterioration of the landscape. Air pollution and noise are defined by the population as the most serious problems (European Community, 1986). In the second half of the 1980s, some environmental aspects – for example, noise – were perceived as improved by the German population.

Personal Problems and Worries

As many studies point out, subjective well-being is ambivalent: many people and the entire population have feelings of both well-being and anomie. Studies concerned with negative aspects of well-being show that people in the Federal Republic have many personal problems and worries.

Feelings of loneliness, meaninglessness, and alienation at work are indicators of insufficient social integration (see table 4). For example, in 1988 14% of the population often felt lonely. Overall, these problems seem to be stable; however, loneliness decreased between 1978 and 1988. Surveys using a panel-design show that many individuals change mental state rapidly; extreme states, in particular, do not last long. Therefore, the relative stability of aggregate negative well-being is astonishing.

Wolfgang Glatzer

References

Europäische Gemeinschaften
1986 *Die Europäer und ihre Umwelt*. Brüssel.

European Communities
1990 *The Perception of Poverty in Europe*. Eurobarometer, Poverty 3. Brüssel.

Glatzer, Wolfgang
1982 "Soziale Probleme und Zufriedenheit." In H.J. Hoffmann-Nowotny, ed., *Unbeabsichtigte Folgen sozialen Handelns*, 51 - 86. Frankfurt am Main/New York: Campus.

Glatzer, Wolfgang, and Wolfgang Zapf, eds.
1984 *Lebensqualität in der Bundesrepublik Deutschland*. Frankfurt am Main/New York: Campus.

ISI (Informationsdienst Soziale Indikatoren)
1990 *ISI*, no. 3.

Noelle-Neumann, Elisabeth, ed.
1981 *The Germans, Public Opinion Polls, 1967 - 1980.* London: Greenwood.

–
1988 *Soziale Indikatoren - Die deutsche Erfahrung.* Manuskript. Allensbach.

Umweltbundesamt
Daten zur Umwelt 1988/89. Berlin.

Table 1
Assessment of the changes in the country's economic situation over the past twelve months[1] (in %)

Item	1982 X	1983 X	1984 X-XI	1985 X-XI	1986 X-XI	1987 X-XI	1988 X-XI
A lot better	-	1	3	3	7	2	3
A little better	3	23	25	30	42	18	27
A little worse	43	29	20	19	9	23	12
A lot worse	19	7	5	3	2	2	2
Index[2]	1.76	2.29	2.47	2.59	2.89	2.44	2.71

1. "Don't knows" included in calculation of percentages.
2. Index calculated by applying coefficients 4, 3, 2, and 1, respectively, to the replies "a lot better," "a little better," "a little worse," and "a lot worse". Replies that the situation remained the same are excluded, as are "don't know." The mid-point is 2.5. Below this level, the negative answers predominate and above, the positive ones.

Source: Eurobarometer, 1989.

Table 2
Assessment of the changes in the financial situation of individual over the past twelve months[1] (in %)

Item	1982 X	1983 X	1984 X-XI	1985 X-XI	1986 X-XI	1987 X-XI	1988 X-XI
A lot better	1	3	4	3	5	3	3
A little better	13	14	17	18	23	20	21
A little worse	21	20	15	12	9	13	9
A lot worse	3	2	2	2	4	3	1
Index	2.32	2.43	2.57	2.61	2.71	2.01	2.73

1. "Don't knows" included in calculation of percentages.

Source: Eurobarometer, 1989.

Table 3
Self-positioning on the poverty scale (in %)

Wording of question: "Taking everything into account, at what level is your family as far as its standard of living is concerned? You may answer by giving a figure between 1 and 7. Number 1 means a poor family and number 7 a rich one. The other numbers are for positions in between."

Item	1976	1983	1989	1976	1983	1989	1976	1983	1989
	Values on the poverty scale								
	1	1	1	2	2	2	1+2	1+2	1+2
EC	2.0	2.9	2.3	5.6	7.8	6.3	7.6	10.7	8.6
Germany	1.1	1.0	0.9	3.3	4.9	3.8	4.4	5.9	4.7

Source: Eurobarometer, 1989.

Table 4
Indicators of alienation[1] 1978 - 1988 (in %)

Item	Year	True	Rather true	Rather untrue	Untrue	Total
Social isolation						
"I often feel lonely."	1978	9.0	10.8	24.6	55.7	100
	1980	8.2	12.9	24.7	54.3	100
	1984	7.1	10.1	27.4	55.5	100
	1988	4.6	9.3	29.7	56.4	100
Meaninglessness						
"Things have become so complicated	1980	4.1	11.1	28.5	56.2	100
in the world today that I don't	1984	4.0	9.7	27.5	58.8	100
understand just what is going on."	1988	3.0	8.0	28.6	60.3	100
Work alienation						
"I don't really enjoy most	1980	5.1	10.1	28.5	56.3	100
of the work I do."	1984	6.2	8.5	29.3	56.0	100
	1988	4.2	9.3	29.7	56.4	100

1. Items of the "Middleton Scale"; see R. Middleton: Alienation, Race and Education, in AJS 28, 1963, pp. 973-977.

Source: Wohlfahrtssurvey, 1978, 1980, 1984, 1988.

Figure 1
Most important concerns

Wording of question: "Which, in your opinion, is the most important question we in West Germany should at present concern ourselves with?"

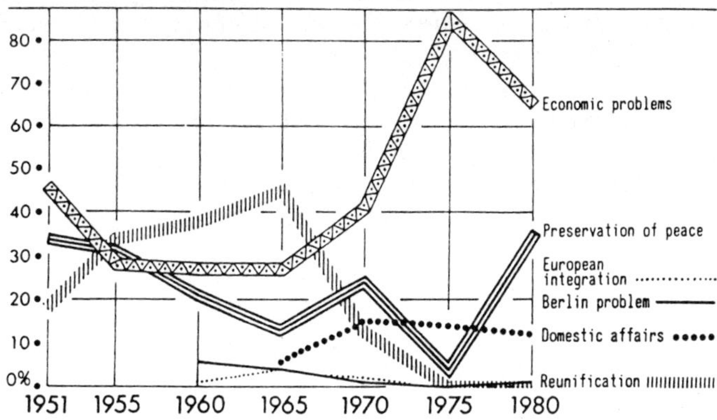

Source: Noelle-Neumann, 1981.

17.3 Orientations toward the Future

How people see their future, for themselves and for their nation, is part of their quality of life. Optimism and pessimism, the general criteria characterizing orientations toward the future, are shifting a great deal. In the second half of the 1980s, people believed more than before that the next year would be better, and that it would be peaceful. In contrast, optimism regarding an easy life in the future and trust in a better future declined. Expectations in respect to personal satisfaction with life in the future followed a U-curve over the last ten years.

Hopes and Fears

What people are expecting for their future – in the short and in the long run – is an additional element for characterizing individual well-being and social atmosphere. People with similar evaluations of their present situation may have very different expectations for their future. Furthermore, expectations for individuals' personal future may differ from their expectations for the collective future of the nation.

Orientations toward the future are often described in terms of hopes and fears. One of the most frequent survey questions, which is also posed in everyday life, concerns the next year – for instance, "As far as you are concerned, do you think that next year will be better or worse than this year?" (see table 1). In response to this question, which was asked in representative surveys in the 1980s (Europäische Gemeinschaften, 1989), a majority of Germans (in all years) expected no change. Nevertheless, the ratio of optimists to pessimists changed quite a bit. In the early 1980s, there was a very low proportion of optimists (8%) and a high proportion of pessimists (37%). By 1984, the situation had changed radically, and from then on the ratio of optimists to pessimists remained stable, with a overwhelming number of optimists (28% to 13% in 1988). This reflects the partial easing of the economic crisis in the second half of the 1980s.

The question "Do you have hopes or fears for the coming year?" has garnered similar results since 1949 (see table 2), with the same evolution for the 1980s as for optimism and pessimism. In previous decades, with the exception of the year 1950, when the Korean war began, more people were hopeful than fearful. Expression of fears also peaked in 1961, when the Berlin Wall was built, and in 1973, the year of the oil shock. As well, it is concluded that "hopes before the beginning of a new year forerun the economic developments (of the respective year)" (Noelle-Neumann, 1987, p. 52).

Peace and War

More specific orientations toward the future are particularly concerned with the question of living in peace. Fear of international conflict and war seems to be a widespread burden. Asked, "Looking ahead to the next year, do you think it will be a peaceful year more or less free of international disputes, a troubled year with much international discord, or remain the same?" (see table 3), a majority of people in 1980 feared a troubled year; in 1988 this pessimistic expectation was held by a minority. In 1988, five times as many as in 1980 believed that the coming year would be peaceful. Trust in peace has become a major trait of orientation toward the future. New developments in international relations seem to have resulted in increased optimism. No doubt, the Gulf War – at the time of the survey still in the future – will change this attitude.

When directly asked how they assess the chance of a world war breaking out in the next 10 years, people's tendency to be optimistic during the 1980s was confirmed (see table 4). Again, 1988 was the year in which German people saw the lowest risk of world war; 1981 was the year in which they perceived the highest risk. Both time series about concern with peace and war in the 1980s move in the same direction as do increasing expectations for a peaceful future.

Quality of Life

Another specific aspect of expectations for the future is dealt with in the question "When you think of the future, do you think life will become easier or increasingly difficult for people?" (see table 5). From 1952 to the present, a plurality of the population believed that life would become more difficult, though the proportion varied between 39% and 63%. The beginning of the 1950s and the beginning of the 1980s were characterized by disproportionate pessimism.

Similar results are garnered from the question "Do you believe in progress – I mean, that mankind will have a better future – or don't you believe in it" (see table 6). There was an overwhelming belief in progress from 1967 up to 1977, but from 1978 on, a majority of the population no longer believed in a better future for mankind. This runs somewhat contrary to the increasing optimism in respect to peace and war. The long-term trend in future orientations toward everyday life can be called "sinking optimism."

Expectations for Personal Satisfaction

People differentiate between their general expectations and their expectations for their personal situation (Zapf, 1987; see also 17.2, "Perception of Social

Problems"). For the most part, people expect no change in their personal life (see table 7). This can be observed by combining rates in life satisfaction for different points in time: present satisfaction, satisfaction five years ago, and expected satisfaction five years hence. Though it does not measure real changes in life satisfaction, it indicates perceptions of personal satisfaction over time, from the worst outlook of feeling bad and foreseeing a hopeless future to the best outlook of feeling good and viewing the future optimistically.

In 1978, on average, optimism ruled (see figure 1). The level of life satisfaction of five years ago ranked below present satisfaction, while future satisfaction ranked above. This situation changed drastically in 1980. Although satisfaction with the past life continued to be lower than present satisfaction, expected future life satisfaction now also lay below the level of present satisfaction. One reason for this shift is that 1978 marked the end of an economic boom; 1980 was a crisis year in which the recession spread and unemployment increased. By 1984, people had adapted to the continuing crisis; the levels of satisfaction for the past, the present, and the future were almost even. In 1988, the crisis seemed to have somewhat abated. Positive expectations for the future grew, but they did not exceed present life satisfaction.

In addition, most people perceive a consistency in their life satisfaction over the respective past five years, somewhat fewer see an increase, and even fewer a decrease (see table 7). The overwhelming majority expects the same life satisfaction in the future as in the present. The ratio of optimistic to pessimistic people changes according to the particular circumstances. In 1978 and 1988, there were more optimists, in 1980 and 1984 more pessimists, but at all times those who expected a constant satisfaction with life constituted the large majority.

Future orientations are characterized by a varying mixture of optimism and pessimism in respect to people and areas; they show ups and downs and seem to react in a complex way according to real events and cultural changes. There are no differentiated and thorough investigations of this question in Germany.

Wolfgang Glatzer

References

Europäische Gemeinschaften, ed.
1989 *Eurobarometer Nr. 31. Die öffentliche Meinung in der europäischen Gemeinschaft*. Brüssel.

Glatzer, Wolfgang, and Wolfgang Zapf, eds.
1984 *Lebensqualität in der Bundesrepublik. Objektive Lebensbedingungen und subjektives Wohlbefinden*. Frankfurt am Main/New York: Campus.

Noelle-Neumann, Elisabeth, ed.
1981 *The Germans, Public Opinion Polls, 1967 - 1980*. London: Greenwood.

–
1988 *Soziale Indikatoren - Die deutsche Erfahrung.* Manuskript. Allensbach.

Zapf, Wolfgang, ed.
1987 "German Social Report. Living Conditions and Subjective Well-Being 1978 - 1984." *Social Indicators Research*, 19, no. 1, 170.

Table 1
Expectations for the next year (in %)

Wording of question: "As far as you are concerned, do you think that the next year (...) will be better or worse than the year which is ending?"

Item	1980 X-XI	1981 X-XI	1982 X	1983 X	1984 X-XI	1985 X-XI	1986 X-XI	1987 X-XI	1988 X-XI
Better	8	13	13	20	25	27	29	26	28
Worse	37	28	22	17	12	11	10	11	13
Same	48	50	53	51	58	56	52	56	56
No reply	7	9	12	12	5	6	9	7	3
Total	100	100	100	100	100	100	100	100	100
N	1,008	962	1,012	1,058	1,053	1,028	1,084	957	1,051

Source: Eurobarometer, 1989.

Table 2 Part 1
Hopes and fears in the coming year (in %)

Wording of question: "Is it with hopes or with fears that you enter the coming year?"

Item	1949	1950	1951	1952	1953	1954	1955
With hope	48	27	45	48	60	54	61
With misgivings	23	43	26	21	14	18	11
With skepticism	17	17	14	16	12	13	12
Undecided	12	13	15	15	14	15	16
Total	100	100	100	100	100	100	100

Item	1956	1957	1958	1959	1960	1961	1962
With hope	53	58	53	65	58	44	61
With misgivings	20	15	18	8	13	25	13
With skepticism	14	14	14	12	14	18	14
Undecided	13	13	15	15	15	13	12
Total	100	100	100	100	100	100	100

Item	1963	1964	1965	1966	1967	1968	1969
With hope	62	65	49	52	56	65	63
With misgivings	11	10	18	19	14	10	13
With skepticism	13	13	19	19	19	14	14
Undecided	14	12	14	10	11	11	10
Total	100	100	100	100	100	100	100

Item	1970	1971	1972	1973	1974	1975	1976
With hope	54	44	60	30	44	52	54
With misgivings	18	24	13	34	25	15	15
With skepticism	17	20	17	24	21	24	21
Undecided	11	12	10	12	10	9	10
Total	100	100	100	100	100	100	100

Table 2 Part 2
Hopes and fears in the coming year (in %)

Wording of question: "Is it with hopes or with fears that you enter the coming year?"

Item	1977	1978	1979	1980	1981	1982	1983
With hope	55	60	51	34	32	34	45
With misgivings	14	10	16	27	32	32	22
With skepticism	19	17	21	29	28	27	24
Undecided	12	13	12	10	8	7	9
Total	100	100	100	100	100	100	100

Item	1984	1985	1986	1987	1988	1989
With hope	55	61	59	57	59	68
With misgivings	14	11	12	15	13	10
With skepticism	22	19	19	18	19	14
Undecided	9	9	10	10	9	8
Total	100	100	100	100	100	100

Source: Allensbacher Datenarchiv.

Table 3
Expectations for the next year (in %)

Wording of question: "Looking ahead to (next year), do you think it will be a peaceful year more or less free of international disputes, a troubled year with much international discord, or remain the same?"

Item	1980 X-XI	1981 X-XI	1982 X	1983 X	1984 X-XI	1985 X-XI	1986 X-XI	1987 X-XI	1988 X-XI
Peaceful	6	10	5	8	18	17	18	15	31
Troubled	55	54	51	48	26	29	27	36	16
The same	31	26	32	36	49	45	46	44	48
No reply	8	10	12	8	7	9	9	5	5
Total	100	100	100	100	100	100	100	100	100
N	1,008	962	1,012	1,058	1,053	1,028	1,084	957	1,051

Source: Eurobarometer, 1989.

Table 4
Risk of a new world war in the next ten years (in %)

Wording of question: "Here is a sort of scale. Would you tell me how you assess the chance of a world war breaking out in the next 10 years?"

Item	1971 VII	1977 X-XI	1980 IV	1981 X-XI	1982 X	1983 X
World war within the next 10 years:						
60 to 100	10.3	12.2	21.9	29.0	16.1	16.4
10 to 50	51.3	58.8	50.7	47.3	46.5	47.8
No danger of war 0	30.4	21.0	13.8	12.7	20.7	25.2
No reply	8.0	8.0	13.6	11.0	16.7	10.6
Total	100.0	100.0	100.0	100.0	100.0	100.0
Mean score	2.44	2.72	3.75	4.11	3.21	2.99
N	2,000	999	1,009	962	1,012	1,058

Item	1984 X-XI	1985 X-XI	1986 X-XI	1987 X-XI	1988 X-XI
World war within the next 10 years:					
60 to 100	12.7	10.9	10.4	8.6	4.1
10 to 50	46.8	50.3	41.6	50.4	38.7
No danger of war 0	31.0	28.9	33.8	30.3	49.5
No reply	9.5	9.9	14.2	10.7	7.7
Total	100.0	100.0	100.0	100.0	100.0
Mean score	2.50	2.48	2.20	2.21	1.29
N	1,053	1,028	1,084	957	1,051

Source: Eurobarometer, 1988.

Table 5
Expectations for the future (in %)

Wording of question: "When you think of the future, do you think life will become easier or increasingly difficult for people?"

Item	1952	1957	1960	1963	1966	1973	1980
Don't know	10	7	10	12	15	5	4
Will remain the same	19	19	21	20	18	19	19
Easier	15	19	27	22	28	27	14
Increasingly difficult	56	55	42	46	39	49	63
Total	100	100	100	100	100	100	100

Source: Allensbacher Archiv.

Table 6
Belief in progress in the long run (in %)

Wording of question: "Do you believe in progress - I mean that mankind has a better future - or don't you believe in it?"

Item	1967	1972	1975	1977	1978	1980	1981
Believe in progress	56	60	48	39	34	28	32
Don't believe	26	19	30	35	40	35	48
Undecided, no opinion	18	21	22	26	26	37	20
Total	100	100	100	100	100	100	100

Item	1982	1983	1983	1984	1985	1986	1987
Believe in progress	27	34	35	39	39	33	37
Don't believe	46	47	44	41	38	37	39
Undecided, no opinion	27	19	21	20	23	30	24
Total	100	100	100	100	100	100	100

Source: Allensbacher Archiv.

Table 7
Comparative evaluation of past, present and future overall life satisfaction (in %)

Item	1978	1980	1984	1988
Comparison past-present 5 years ago - now				
Increase	41	34	31	35
Constant	44	48	46	47
Decrease	14	18	23	18
Comparison future-present now - 5 years' time				
Increase	24	21	19	22
Constant	64	54	56	60
Decrease	12	25	25	18

Source: Wohlfahrtssurvey, 1978, 1980, 1984, 1988.

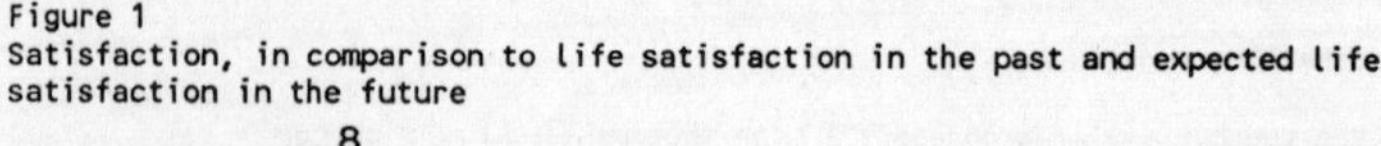
Figure 1
Satisfaction, in comparison to life satisfaction in the past and expected life satisfaction in the future

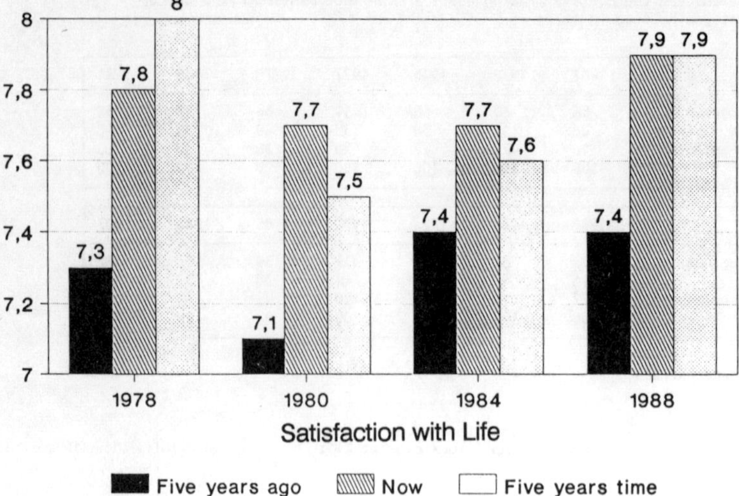

Source: Wohlfahrtssurvey, 1978, 1980, 1984, 1988.

17.4 Values

Out of the broad field of "values," only those pertinent to integration into society will be treated here (Meulemann, 1989): equality, achievement, codetermination, and acceptance. With the exception of the value "equality," the time series of the values exhibit extensive concurrence of development. The levels remain constant into the 1960s. In the late 1960s and early 1970s there was a definite change, followed by renewed constancy. Achievement and acceptance fell, while codetermination gained ground; these value changes can be interpreted as secularization. The reduction in acceptance means that the sense and orientation of people's lives were derived less and less from religion and tradition, but instead were constructed more and more by the individual. This is not to be found in the field of achievement, but rather in the field of codetermination. Codetermination has replaced acceptance; activity and involvement have taken over from obedience and submission; and belief in things traditionally taken for granted has given way to the demand to know why.

Equality

Two time series pertain to the value "equality." Assessment of realization of equality in the macrosocial order can be concluded from the question in which social structure is characterized either by opportunity for upward mobility ("Everyone is responsible for his own destiny") or by its hindrance ("Some are at the top of the ladder, the others down below") (see table 1, column 1). The statistics vary without exhibiting a trend; evaluation of equality in the macrosocial order has not changed. The assessment of realization of educational opportunity (table 1, column 2) has, however, lost about 20% since 1973. This drop can be explained by the simultaneous rise in participation in education, which heightened competition and reduced available opportunities within the education system. While assessment of actualized equality within the given social order has stayed level, assessment of equality in the education system has worsened due to simultaneous expansion of the system.

Achievement

Three time series, with increasing concretization, pertain to the value "achievement." "Life as work" (table 1, column 3) concerns overall life attitude, "life without work" (table 1, column 4) compares work with other life spheres, and "intrinsic work motivation" (table 1, column 5) contrasts work as self-realization with work as a means to an end. All three time series exhibit a decline for the value "achievement" between the late 1960s and early 1970s, preceded and followed by phases of relative constancy. In other words, the status of achievement in everyday life has fallen; this, however, does not mean less work being done.

Codetermination

The value "codetermination" refers to the balancing out of power differentials, and to the control of people in power positions by those who are not in such positions. It can therefore be seen as a value in politics and in upbringing. Three time series relate to codetermination in politics, dealing with increasingly higher forms of political involvement. Political interest (table 1, column 6) rose by about 10% between 1960 and 1969, with previous and subsequent constancy. The incidence of political discussion (table 1, column 7) rose steeply between 1965 and 1969, while it had increased only gradually before then, and remained fairly constant afterward. The feeling of political ineffectiveness (table 1, column 8) clearly declined during the second half of the 1960s, and was constant before and after this period. Thus, all three time series exhibit a corresponding upswing of codetermination in politics in the late 1960s, framed by before-and-after phases of relative constancy. Two time series relate to codetermination in upbringing, by polling people on the choice between the pedagogical goals of autonomy versus conventionality in the family or, respectively, in school. The family-upbringing goal of "independence" (table 1, column 9) gained 15% between 1965 and 1972, with consistency before and after. The educational goal of "orderliness" (table 1, column 10) lost about 20% by 1973, and then remained level, while school-educational goal values such as personal independence and self-confidence increased. Both time series show corresponding growth for the value of codetermination in upbringing during the late 1960s, framed by phases of relative consistency. Thus, in politics as in upbringing, codetermination gained in importance in the second half of the 1960s.

Acceptance

"Acceptance" refers to self-evident and tradition-supported acquiescence to the conditions of life. Church-defined religion may well be the most important tradition supporting this particular value; degree of acceptance can be concluded from church attendance (table 1, column 11), which dropped dramatically in the late 1960s: between 1963 and 1972, the proportion of those never going to church rose by about 20%, then remained constant. Attendance, however, is only indirectly symptomatic of the everyday importance of an institution that inspires acceptance. Acceptance can be directly measured by the feeling of obligation to personal-life planning and to the institutions involved therein; one example is marriage. The desire to simplify divorce increased strongly between 1953 and 1976. A decisive transformation in this case – as a slightly modified question shows, the answers to which are given in parentheses in the table – took place between 1966 and 1969. After 1976, these values could no longer be interpreted in the same way, as alienation instead of guilt was introduced as grounds for divorce in 1977, a genuine simplification of divorce. By means of the indirect indicator "church attendance" and the exemplary indicator "divorce," a decline in acceptance can be concluded for the second half of the 1960s, again framed by phases of relative consistency.

Heiner Meulemann

References

Meulemann, Heiner

1983 "Value Change in West Germany, 1950–1980: Integrating the Empirical Evidence." *Social Science Information,* no. 22, 777-800.

–

1989 *Wertwandel und kulturelle Teilhabe.* Fernuniversität-Gesamthochschule Hagen, Fachbereich Erziehungs-, Sozial- und Geisteswissenschaften. Lehreinheit.

Table 1 Part 1
Changes in values 1949-1988[1]

Year	Equality		Achievement			Co-determination					Acceptance	
						Politics			Upbringing			
	Own destiny	Educational opportunity	Life as work	Life without work	Intrin. work motives	Interest yes	Discuss. average	Ineffectivity rejected	Goal independence	School goal orderl.	Never attend church	Should simplify divorce
	(1)	(2)	(3)	(4)	(5)	(6)	(7)	(8)	(9)	(10)	(11)	(12)
1949	-	-	-	-	51	-	-	-	-	-	-	-
1950	-	-	-	-	-	-	-	-	-	-	-	-
1951	-	-	-	-	47	-	-	-	28	-	-	-
1952	-	-	-	13	50	27	-	-	-	59	-	-
1953	-	-	-	-	46	-	1.17	-	-	-	13	13
1954	-	-	-	-	51	-	-	-	27	-	-	-
1955	53	-	-	13	46	-	-	-	-	-	-	-
1956	-	-	59	-	52	-	-	-	-	-	15	-
1957	-	-	-	11	50	-	-	-	28	-	-	-
1958	-	66	-	12	-	-	-	-	-	-	-	-
1959	-	-	-	14	49	29	1.71	25	-	-	16	-
1960	-	-	61	13	-	27	-	-	-	-	-	-
1961	-	-	-	-	-	31	1.70	-	-	-	17	(8)
1962	65	-	52	13	60	37	-	-	-	-	-	-
1963	62	73	58	13	-	-	-	-	-	-	19	-
1964	-	-	60	-	-	-	-	-	29	-	24	-
1965	-	-	-	-	52	35	1.85	-	29	-	32	-
1966	-	-	-	-	-	-	-	-	-	(38)	-	(18)
1967	-	-	-	-	49	39	-	-	32	-	32	-
1968	-	-	58	-	-	-	-	35	-	-	30	-
1969	-	-	-	-	47	41	2.10	31	39	-	35	(42)

1. Indicators for equality, achievement, co-determination and acceptance. All time series include results from the 1950s and 1970s as well as at least one result dating from between these years.

Source: Meulemann, 1989.

Table 1 Part 2
Changes in values 1949-1988[1]

Year	Equality		Achievement			Co-determination					Acceptance	
						Politics			Upbringing			
	Own destiny	Educational opportunity	Life as work	Life without work	Intrin. work motives	Interest yes	Discuss. average	Ineffectivity rejected	Goal independence	School goal orderl.	Never should attend church	simplify divorce
	(1)	(2)	(3)	(4)	(5)	(6)	(7)	(8)	(9)	(10)	(11)	(12)
1970	-	-	-	-	-	-	-	-	-	-	-	-
1971	-	-	-	-	-	43	-	-	-	-	-	-
1972	-	-	53	18	-	46	2.34	35	45	-	39	-
1973	-	-	48	20	-	49	-	-	-	28	-	(43,4)
1974	-	-	-	17	42	47	-	26	45	-	-	-
1975	62	-	50	18	-	41	-	-	-	-	-	-
1976	55	-	-	16	-	46	2.23	39	51	-	39	31
1977	59	-	48	13	-	-	-	-	-	-	43	-
1978	63	-	51	18	-	-	-	-	45	-	-	-
1979	-	50	-	-	40	43	-	-	44	30	42	28
1980	61	-	48	21	-	49	-	40	-	-	41	26
1981	-	-	49	17	46	48	-	-	52	-	-	-
1982	-	-	43	-	-	47	-	-	-	-	42	-
1983	-	-	-	-	-	-	-	-	49	-	-	-
1984	-	45	-	-	52	-	-	-	-	-	-	-
1985	-	-	-	-	-	-	-	-	-	32	41	-
1986	-	52	-	-	-	-	-	-	56	-	-	-
1987	-	-	-	-	39	-	-	39	-	-	44	-
1988	-	-	-	-	-	-	-	-	-	-	-	-

1. Indicators for equality, achievement, co-determination and acceptance. All time series include results from the 1950s and 1970s as well as at least one result dating from between these years.

Source: Meulemann, 1989.

Questions in Table 1:

Column 1: "Two men are talking about life. One says: Everyone is responsible for his own happiness. Whoever really makes the effort can achieve something. The other says: It's a fact that some areon top and others are down below and there's no way they can get up top no matter how they try. What is your personal opinion: who is right- the first or the second man?"

Col. 2:"In this country, does everyone have the possibility of educating himself according to talent and ability?"

Col. 3: "Two men/women are talking. The first one says: I see my life as a job of work to which I invest all my energy. I want to achieve something in life, even if it's often difficult. The second one says: I want to enjoy my life and not make any more effort than necessary. You only live once, and the main thing is to have something of it. Which of these two people are right?"

Col. 4: "Do you think it would be nicest to live without having to work?"

Col. 5: "Do you see your work as a heavy burden, necessary evil, way to make money, something satisfying, or as carrying out a duty?"

Col. 6: "Are you interested in politics?"

Col. 7: various wordings of question. Average results from various answers, high results = frequent discussion.

Col. 8: "People like me don't have any influence on what the government does anyway." Percentage rejecting. The disparity in 1974 is probably explained by the fact that it was not an election year, as opposed to other years.

Col. 9: "What characteristics should children's upbringing aim towards: obedience and meekness, orderliness and hard-workingness, or self-reliance and free will?" Percentage self-reliance and free will.

Col. 10: "In your opinion, what is most important that children learn at school? Please choose from this card the three points that seem most important to you."

Col. 11: "seldom" was integrated with "never", and replaced "once a year" or several times a year". Those without a religious denomination were counted as non-churchgoers.

Col. 12: "Should divorce be simplified as much as possible, or should marriages be indivisible?" (question asked 1953, 1976, 1979, 1980); Are you for easing divorce or for making it more difficult, or do you consider it to be right in its present form?" (question 1961, 1966, 1969, 1973, in 1961 slightly modified) The second wording gives "as is" as possible answer, the first does not. - Two measurements in 1973.

17.5 National Identity

The national identity of Germans is historically characterized by breaks and torment. In the approximately 40 years of postwar history, the body politic of the Federal Republic of Germany has been accepted by its citizens. For about the past 10 years, efforts toward a new national self-concept expounded on Germans' economic and political achievements after World War II. Following the fall of the East German regime, in 1989, the reunification question, which up to then had been continuously dwindling in importance, became the dominant political issue.

The history of the Federal Republic of Germany begins with the *Stunde Null* (zero hour, the end of World War II and of Germany as it was). The unconditional surrender of the German armed forces on May 8, 1945, was followed by military occupation and the take-over of governmental powers by the Allied Forces, and by the prohibition of German governmental sovereignty. Due to the incipient East-West conflict, Germany was divided into two separate states, the Federal Republic of Germany and the German Democratic Republic, in 1949. Some German-settled eastern regions had already been ceded to Poland.

Exogenous factors formed the basis for the bodies politic of the Federal Republic and the German Democratic Republic, both of which perceived themselves, according to their constitutions, as temporary. The preamble of the Federal Republic constitution states that "the whole of the German people [are] called upon to carry out the unity and freedom of Germany in an act of free will." The German Democratic Republic also long subscribed to the proposition that both German states were only temporary, but changed the corresponding text in its constitution in 1974, after mutual recognition of both states as subjects in the sense of international law. The original formulation, "responsibility to show the whole German nation the way into a future of peace and socialism," was replaced by the statement "the people of the German Democratic Republic [has] realized its right to socio-economic, governmental, and national self-determination."

In contrast to other countries, the political identities of the Federal Republic of Germany and the German Democratic Republic were not based upon cultural borders or public will. The division of Germany, made unavoidable by world political constellations, into two states with different political systems had not been the intention of any German before 1945 (Conze, 1983).

The division of Germany is to be perceived as another result of a series of occurrences in which German ideals were often crushed beyond repair: in 1848–1849, the first civil-liberation movement with hopes of introducing national unity suffered military defeat. Not until 1871, late by Western European standards, was an empire founded under the leadership of German princes, led by Prussia.

World War I ended with military defeat and the conditions, perceived as humiliating, dictated in the Treaty of Versailles. The failure of the democratic Weimar Republic led to the totalitarian system of National Socialism. The attempt of the Third Reich to re-establish national greatness via the ideal of one German people was permeated by racial hatred and technically and methodically precise genocide, and ended in another military defeat. This discontinuity made for an uneasy mixture of aggressivity and resignation, and German identity is to this day "less a reliable point of reference than a constant challenge. One is tempted to say that it exhausts itself in identity loss, identity deficit, damaged identity, and identity crises" (Hoffmann & Even, 1984, p. 55).

Confrontation of the Nazi Past in Postwar West Germany

The accusation of responsibility for the atrocities of the Third Reich forced a people to realize that it had produced not only poets and thinkers, but also Auschwitz. Withdrawal from this knowledge took place via sublimation. In spite of "denazification," a poll in the American-occupied zone in November of 1945 showed that 50% of those questioned considered National Socialism a good idea that had been poorly carried out; only 20% accepted German responsibility for the war, while 70% denied any guilt (Sommer, 1986). In a 1949 survey, 53% cited the characteristics of the Jewish people as the cause for Nazi anti-Semitism, and 12% cited the Jewish religion as the cause. Fewer than one-third of those polled traced anti-Semitic attitudes to propaganda (Maier, 1980).

The psychoanalyst Margarete Mitscherlich sees the political culture of the postwar period as being influenced by avoidance of inner confrontation with the past. Instead, all energy was devoted to cranking up the economy. The reward for this "national occupational therapy by reconstruction" (Mitscherlich, 1987) was, indeed, economic prosperity that raced along at a dizzying pace and harvested international admiration. Pride in this proven ability played a key role in West Germans' identification process, as it replaced the missing historically rooted national consciousness (Mommsen, cited in Hoffmann & Even, 1984). In 1985, three-fourths of West Germans believed that they could be proud of the "reconstruction after the war" and of "the personal freedom that we have here" (see table 1).

Aside from the reigning apolitical, pragmatic attitudes typical of the postwar period, there are isolated ideas of new social concepts as well as attempts to formulate a sort of ahistorical new beginning. There was enthusiasm, mainly among younger generations, for the idea of a united Europe, and an idealization of American culture and politics. Both attitudes were laced with resentment of socialist systems – especially that of the Soviet Union, but also that of the German Democratic Republic. Western-oriented values led West German students and youths to join – originally with a sense of cultural identification, but then exhibiting autonomous development – the American wave of protest against the Vietnam war.

The student movement was the first to return to the theme of collective guilt for Nazi war crimes: the children of the guilty had an account to settle with their Fascist parents. Any kind of real confrontation with or overcoming of the past has yet to make real progress, but the process of facing Nazi war crimes had been set in motion.

This was expressed in a certain transformation of attitude: in a 1964 poll, only 54% of those questioned were willing to call the Nazi state an *Unrechtsstaat* (i.e., not based on constitutionally guaranteed rights), but 71% were ready to do so in 1979 (Noelle-Neumann & Piel, 1983). According to a media analysis (Bodemann, 1988) the storm of violent actions taken against Jews and their synagogues, their businesses, and their residences (which took place throughout Germany in November, 1938) were mentioned not at all in magazines and newspapers in 1948, and only casually in 1958 and 1968. In 1978, however, numerous well-researched articles were published. In 1988, the fiftieth anniversary of the *Reichspogromnacht*, the event not only merited discussion in all media, there were also thousands of exhibitions, shows, and so on, all over West Germany, including eye-witness reports presented at educational institutions, exhibitions in local museums, and Philip Jenninger's controversial speech in the federal parliament.

National Identity, National Pride

Parallel to this development, tendencies toward a new search for identity have been discernable since the mid-1970s – West Germans express the least national pride of all Common Market countries (Herdegen, 1987). The proportion of those who were "unconditionally" proud to be German dropped from 42% in October of 1971 to 35% in December of 1986, while the proportion of those who were "for the most part" proud of their nationality rose from 34% to 46%. The percentage of the "less" or "not at all" proud minority deviated only marginally (see table 2).

The question arises as to what West Germans in times before the reunification associated with feelings of national identity. Did they relate to the state of the Federal Republic of Germany – relatively tradition-poor for purposes of identification – or with German-speaking countries in general? Was it the cultural heritage of German history, which also lacks continuity, or was it the German countryside and symbols of the homeland, which have the least suspicious political reputation?

Poll data from 1981 and 1986 show that, in response to a question regarding a "German nation of tomorrow," the idea of a "united Germany" had lost profile (see table 3). The tendency toward increased acceptance of two German nations is confirmed by other empirical findings. In 1974, the Federal Republic and the Democratic Republic formed one national unit in the minds of 70% of both West Germans and East Germans, but only 42% held this view in 1984; among this group, the older generations were more highly represented than the younger ones (Kühnl, 1986).

The reasons given for national pride are, as mentioned above, "performance during the reconstruction" and "personal freedom," with three-fourths of the responses in the top part of the scale, closely followed by cultural heroes – that is, German poets and composers. Two-thirds of those polled are proud of economic achievements (German science and research, high-technology achievements of German industry), medieval towns, cathedrals, and the beautiful countryside. In the socio-political field, social security, the political system, the constitution, and 40 years of peace inspired pride in over half of the West German citizens. At the bottom of the scale are politically controversial themes such as the bravery of German soldiers, German-American friendship, the German national anthem, and performance of athletes from the German Democratic Republic (table 1).

These data lend support to the hypothesis that social consciousness was oriented more toward the Federal Republic, and that the idea of a "unified Germany" was of subordinate importance (Korte, 1987). It is also true that the German search for identity is not spurred on by nationalism, though groups propagating a new national consciousness in the search for national identity have increased over the past few years. Distrust of U.S. military policy has engendered a desire for national sovereignty, especially regarding West Germany's membership in NATO.

Conservatives criticize the persistent feelings of guilt for the Nazi past. One of their arguments is that people should have an opportunity to relate normally to their own history. The Deutschlandrat, a group of conservative intellectuals, states in its proclamation, "We want to be a normal nation again. This necessitates the decriminalization of our history" (Klönne, 1986, p. 23). The "historians' debate" should not be ignored in this context. This heated discussion started in 1986 by Ernst Nolte's hypothesis that the Nazi-organized genocide had had comparable forerunners – especially in the U.S.S.R. Since this hypothesis – contradicted by Nolte's academic colleagues – is not supported by any new historical findings, the claim that Hitler acted in self-defence can only be interpreted as a re-evaluation of well-known facts (Schneider, 1987).

The politically effective change of mood has met with an increasing positive response. Particularly among youths in the industrial centres, who are threatened with mass unemployment and social disintegration, the attraction to nationalist symbols and the tendency to discriminate against ethnic or religious "differentness" are growing (Kühnl, 1986). Though the data on development of organized right-wing extremism exhibited sharply declining tendencies from 1954 until the end of the 1970s, there has been a reverse trend since 1980 (see 11.4, "Radicalism").

A controversy, not yet full-blown, concerns the question of how desirable it is for West Germany to consider itself multicultural. Advocates of multiculuralism, mostly from the left of the political spectrum, demand more integration of foreign citizens, including investing them with political rights. Opponents point out that the Federal Republic is not an immigration country, and that ethnic homogeneity is desirable. German *Aussiedler* (people of German descent from non-German Eastern European countries who move to West Germany) play an ambivalent role in this context: they claim to belong to the German nation, while West Germans view them, due to their different cultural backgrounds, as foreigners.

After the opening of the Berlin Wall, on November 9, 1989, there was national euphoria on both sides. In the course of the reunification negotiations and consideration of the costs involved in modernizing the GDR's economy, however, increasing reservations have become noticeable among the West German population. It is to be expected that reunification will not lead to a break in the national identity of the West German population. In fact, it is more likely that radical rejection of socialist society and extensive acceptance of West German models in the course of modernization in East Germany will cause any critical distance from societal conditions in West Germany to retreat into the background.

Karin Stiehr

References

Bodemann, Y. Michal
1988 "Was hat der Gedenktag überhaupt mit den Juden zu tun?" *Frankfurter Rundschau* vom 29.11.88.

Conze, Werner
1983 "Staats- und Nationalpolitik. Kontinuitätsbruch und Neubeginn." In Werner Conze, and M. Rainer Lepsius, eds., *Sozialgeschichte der Bundesrepublik Deutschland*. Stuttgart: Klett-Cotta.

Fetscher, Iring
1985 "'Und das liebste mag's uns scheinen ...'" In Marielouise Janssen-Jureit, *Lieben Sie Deutschland? Gefühle zur Lage der Nation*. München/Zürich: Piper.

Greß, Franz, and Hans Gerd Jaschke
1982 *Rechtsextremismus in der Bundesrepublik nach 1960*. Sonderheft 18 des Pressedienstes demokratische Initiative. München.

Grün-Alternative Basis-Liste im 26. Studentenparlament der
1986 J-L-U-Giessen, ed., *Vergangenheit, die nicht vergehen will. Ein notwendiger Pressespiegel*. Giessen.

Herdegen, Gerhard
1987 "Einstellungen der Deutschen (West) zur nationalen Identität." *Politische Vierteljahresschrift*, Sonderheft 18.

Hoffmann, Lutz, and Herbert Even
1984 *Soziologie der Ausländerfeindlichkeit. Zwischen nationaler Identität und multikultureller Gesellschaft*. Weinheim/Basel: Beltz.

Klönne, Arno
1986 "Rechtsextreme Tendenzen in der politischen Kultur der Bundesrepublik." In Matthias v. Hellfeld, ed., *Im Schatten der Krise*. Köln: Pahl-Rugenstein.

Kommission der Europäischen Gemeinschaften, ed.
1985 *Euro-Barometer*, no. 24. Brüssel.

Korte, Karl-Rudolf
1987 "Nationale Identifikation und europäische Bindung." *Politische Vierteljahresschrift*, Sonderheft 18.

Kühnl, Reinhard
1986 *Nation - Nationalismus - Nationale Frage. Was ist das und was soll das?* Köln: Pahl-Rugenstein.

Lepsius, M. Rainer
1982 "Bundesrepublik." In Kolloquien des Instituts für Zeitgeschichte, *Nachkriegsgesellschaften im historischen Vergleich. Großbritannien - Frankreich - Bundesrepublik*. München/Wien: Oldenbourg.

Maier, Hans
1980 "Demoskopie und Geschichte." In Elisabeth Noelle-Neumann, ed., *Wahlentscheidung in der Fernsehdemokratie*. Würzburg: Ploetz.

Mampel, Siegfried
1982 *Die sozialistische Verfassung der Deutschen Demokratischen Republik*. Kommentar. Frankfurt am Main: Metzner.

Mitscherlich, Margarete
1987 *Erinnerungsarbeit. Zur Psychoanalyse der Unfähigkeit zu trauern*. Frankfurt am Main: Fischer.

Noelle-Neumann, Elisabeth, and Edgar Piel, eds.
1983 *Allensbacher Jahrbuch der Demoskopie 1978-1983*. München/New York/London/Paris: Saur.

Schneider, Peter
1987 "Im Todeskreis der Schuld." *Die Zeit*, March 3, 1987. Hamburg.

Sommer, Karl-Ludwig
1986 "Von Hauptschuldigen, Mitläufern und Persilscheinen - Vergangenheitsbewältigung im Nachkriegsdeutschland." In *Heiß und kalt. Die Jahre 1945-69*. Berlin: Elefanten Press.

Table 1
Sources of national pride

Wording of question: "We would like to know what one can be proud of as a German. Here are some things written on this card: could you look through them and distribute them according to what you think Germans can be proud of or not proud of. Please lay the cards you cannot decide about aside." (set of cards and list)

Item	Germans can be:			Total
	proud	not proud	undecided	
Reconstruction after WWII	75	4	21	= 100
Our individual liberties	75	4	21	= 100
Goethe, Schiller and other great poets	72	4	24	= 100
Beethoven, Bach and other classical composers	71	4	25	= 100
German science and research	66	6	28	= 100
Medieval cities and churches	66	5	29	= 100
Beautiful countryside	65	7	28	= 100
Technical achievements of German industry	64	7	29	= 100
Performance of the German economy	62	8	30	= 100
Our socieal security and welfare	61	12	27	= 100
Quality of German products: made in Germany	58	9	33	= 100
Political system, the Constitution	57	9	34	= 100
German philosophers	57	6	37	= 100
The fact that we have not had a war in 40 years	56	11	33	= 100
Performance of West German athletes	54	12	34	= 100
West German cars	54	11	35	= 100
international prestige of Germany	49	0	35	= 100
Working spirit and hard-workingness of Germans	48	15	37	= 100
Frederick the Great, Bismarck and other statesmen	43	14	43	= 100
German resistance during the Third Reich	38	20	42	= 100
Loyalty and dependability of Germans	38	16	46	= 100
Courage of German soldiers	38	24	38	= 100
German-American friendship	36	17	47	= 100
German national anthem	30	19	51	= 100
Rebellion in East Germany of June 17	26	23	51	= 100
Performance of East German athletes	24	27	49	= 100

Allensbacher Archiv, IfD Umfrage.

Source: Herdegen 1987, p. 213 et.

Table 2
Degree of national pride (in %)

Wording of question: "Are you proud to be a German?"

Item	Absolutely	Mostly	Not very	Not at all	Undecided	Total
Oct. 1971	42	34	7	4	13	100
Oct./Nov. 1975	36	40	6	6	12	100
Aug./Sept.1982	29	45	10	5	11	100
Dec. 1986	35	46	9	3	7	100

Allensbacher Archiv, IfD Umfragen.

Source: Herdegen 1987, p. 209.

Table 3
Boarders of the German nation (in %)

Wording of question: "Let us assume that a TV-program is shown called "The German Nation Today" (in representative parallel groups: "The German Nation Tomorrow/The German Nation Yesterday). Can you tell us according to what is on this list, what is meant by the German nation in this case?"

Item	November 1981 German nation			July 1986 German nation		
	Today	Tomorrow	Yesterday	Today	Tomorrow	Yesterday
It means...						
- West Germany	43	38	6	37	41	10
- West and East Germany	32	30	20	35	31	25
- West and East Germany and the former German eastern regions (lost after WWII)	12	12	52	12	13	42
- All German-language areas	7	11	14	11	7	14
- Impossible to say	6	9	8	5	8	9

Allensbacher Archiv, IfD-Umfragen 4002, 4075.

Source: Herdegen 1987, p. 208.

Comparative Charting of Social Change

Editor: Simon Langlois
Laval University and IQRC, Canada

Recent Social Trends in the United States 1960-1990
Theodore Caplow, Howard M. Bahr, John Modell,
Bruce A. Chadwick

Recent Social Trends in Québec 1960-1990
Simon Langlois, Jean-Paul Baillargeon, Gary Caldwell, Guy Fréchet,
Madeleine Gauthier, Jean-Pierre Simard

Recent Social Trends in the Federal Republic of Germany 1960-1990
Wolfgang Glatzer, Karl-Otto Hondrich, Heinz Herbert Noll,
Karin Stiehr, Barbara Wörndl

In preparation:

Recent Social Trends in France 1960-1990
Louis Dirn, Michel Forsé, Jean Pierre Jaslin, Yannick Lemel, Henri Mendras,
Denis Stoclet, Jean-Hugues Déchaux

Recent Social Trends in Greece 1960-1990
Constantin Tsoucalas, Laura Alipranti, Andromaque Hadjiyannis,
Roy Panagiotopoulo, Ersi Zacopoulou

Recent Social Trends in Spain 1960-1990
Salustiano Del Campo et al.